Debbies Book®

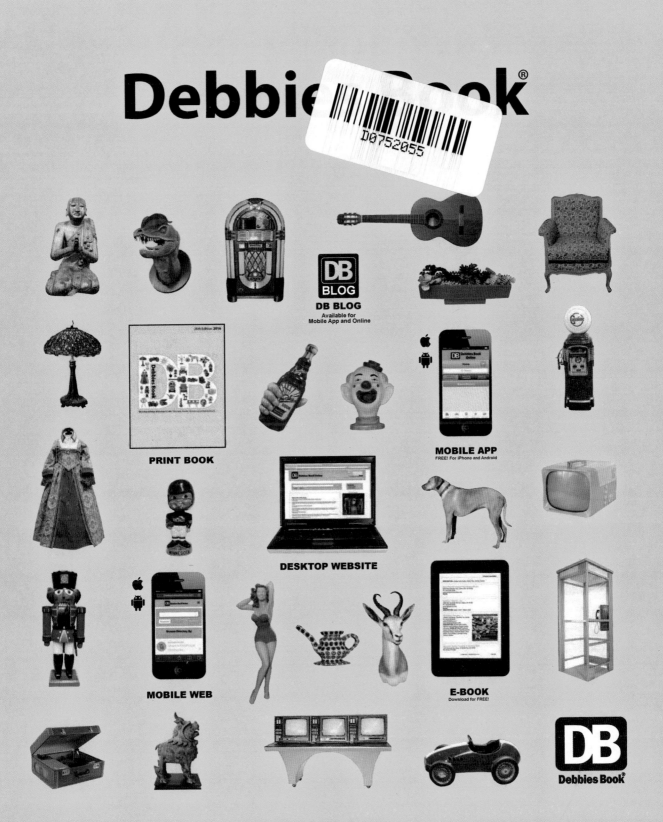

DB BLOG
Available for
Mobile App and Online

PRINT BOOK

MOBILE APP
FREE! For iPhone and Android

DESKTOP WEBSITE

MOBILE WEB

E-BOOK
Download for FREE!

Debbies Book®

28th Edition 2016

Debbies Book®

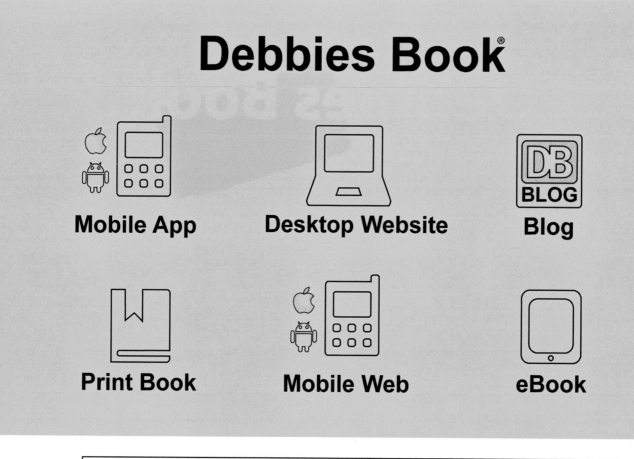

Mobile App

Desktop Website

Blog

Print Book

Mobile Web

eBook

A REMINDER: In print book, **Prop House & Costume Rental House**
All listings are shortened to 1-2 lines to save space. Full contact
information/addresses located within their respective categories.

ACKNOWLEDGEMENTS Thank you Faux Library, RC Vintage, History for Hire, Ob-jects, LA Circus,
The Costume House and Modern Props for the use of photographs used in the cover of this book.

Thank you Bryce Nicholson, Laura Bradley, Leah Tadena, and of course, Ruby.
And, as always, Earl Carlson, Jim Newton and Don Roberts.

Debbies Book®, Inc.
P.O. Box 6378
Altadena, CA 91003-6378

Phone (626) 797-7699
www.debbiesbook.com
email: info@debbiesbook.com

Accessories

See: Decorative Accessories* Leather (Clothing, Accessories, Materials)* Wardrobe, Accessories

Acrylics

See: Plastics, Materials & Fabrication

Adding Machines

See: Business Machines

Adhesives, Glues & Tapes

See: Expendables

Adirondack Chairs

See: Furniture, Outdoor/Patio

Adult Toys & Novelties

See: Goth/Punk/Bondage/Fetish/Erotica Etc.

Advisors

See: Art, Artists For Hire* Research, Advisors, Consulting & Clearances* Search Tools, Directories, Libraries

Aerobic Equipment

See: Exercise & Fitness Equipment

Aerospace

See Also: Aircraft, Charters & Aerial Services* Airport Dressing & Hangars* Space Shuttle/Space Hardware* Space Suits

Air Hollywood - Prop House & Standing Sets   **(818) 890-0444**
Gulfstream, Pan Am, airport terminal, jet interior, private jets, 737s to 767s, lear jet, airplane sets, airport seating

LCW Props   **(818) 243-0707**
Jet Parts, Exterior Lighting of Planes, Wind Tunnel, Test Planes, Titanium & Inconel Parts, Turbines, Exhaust, Cones

6439 San Fernando Rd. Glendale, CA 91201
Phone: 818-243-0707 - www.lcwprops.com

N.S. Aerospace Props   **(818) 765-1087**
7429 Laurel Canyon Blvd, North Hollywood, CA 91605
Rocket Engines, Rocket Components, Hardware, Fittings and Industrial parts for various time periods, consultations too.
nortonsalesm@aol.com * www.nortonsalesinc.com

Afghans

See: Linens, Household

African Themed Parties

See: Costume Rental Houses* Events, Decorations, Supplies & Services* Events, Design/Planning/Production* Prop Houses* Themed Environment Construction* Travel (City/Country) Themed Events

African/Oceanic Decorative Items

See Also: Furniture, Moroccan

Badia Design, Inc.   **(818) 762-0130**
5420 Vineland Ave, N. Hollywood, CA, 91601
Moroccan handmade furniture, home decor, tribal rugs, brass chandeliers, mosaic tables, tiles, themed event rentals
info@badiadesign.com * www.badiadesign.com

Benson's Tropical Sea Imports   **(714) 841-3399**
7442 Vincent Cir, Huntington Beach, CA 92648
seashells, leis, tikis, masks, bamboo/thatching/tropical plants, Easter Island Heads
sales@bensonsimport.com * www.bensonsimport.com

Bob Gail Special Events   **(310) 202-5200**
Take your guests on an African Safari to see zebras, lions, elephants, etc. with our Exotic Animal Props.

The Hand Prop Room LP.   **(323) 931-1534**

History For Hire, Inc.   **(818) 765-7767**
masks, tools, weapons

Hollywood Studio Gallery   **(323) 462-1116**
masks & shields

Oceanic Arts   **(562) 698-6960**
thatching & hut roofing, bamboo, shields, masks, dugout canoe

Omega/Cinema Props   **(323) 466-8201**
African/oceanic items of various types from masks and religious items to artwork and vases.

Prop Services West   **(818) 503-2790**

Sony Pictures Studios-Prop House (Off Lot)   **(310) 244-5999**
wall dressing

Susanne Hollis, Inc.   **(626) 441-0346**
230 Pasadena Ave, South Pasadena, CA, 91030
20th - 17th century Antiques, Accessories, and Fine Art from around the world in our 19,000sqft. warehouse and showrooms
sales@susannehollis.com * www.susannehollis.com

Universal Studios Property & Hardware Dept   **(818) 777-2784**
African masks, African spears, African sculptures, African busts, African wood carvings and much more.

Warner Bros. Studios Property Department   **(818) 954-2181**
Masks, spears, shells, driftwood, coastal accessories and decorative items

Air Cannons

See: Special Effects, Equipment & Supplies

Air Cargo & Freight

See: Transportation, Trucking and/or Storage* Aircraft, Charters & Aerial Services

Air Conditioning & Heating, Production/Event

See Also: Plumbing Fixtures, Heating/Cooling Appliances

Aggreko Event Services   **(818) 767-7288**
13230 Cambridge St, Santa Fe Springs, CA 90670
big, quiet power, heating & HVAC systems, over 130 locations globally for filming, tours, events

Castex Rentals   **(323) 462-1468**
1044 N. Cole Ave, Hollywood, CA, 90038
portable air conditioning units, misters, floor fans, propane heaters, electric heaters
service@castexrentals.com * www.castexrentals.com

Air Conditioning Vents

See: Plumbing Fixtures, Heating/Cooling Appliances

Air Hockey Game

See: Game Tables & Equipment

Air Tools

See: Tools

Air Tubulars

See: Balloons & Balloon Sculptures

Aircraft, Charters & Aerial Services

See Also: Airport Dressing & Hangars

Aerial Focus (805) 455-3142
Call for Appt
extreme sports cinematography, base jumping, wing walking, skydiving, hang gliding

Aerial Stunt Service (310) 543-2222
3128 Via La Selva, Palos Verdes, CA, 90274
aerial cinematography & coordination, skydivers/stunts, extreme sports & stock footage

Aero Jet Services (800) 582-3641
15100 N. 78th Way, Scottsdale, AZ, 85260
Jet charters, maintenance, management & purchasing

AirCharter World (925) 602-5330
395 Taylor Blvd, Ste 100, Pleasant Hill, CA, 94523
Air & charter worldwide, Biz Jets & transport aircraft available
larry@acworld.com

Airnet Private Charters (877) 293-8463
7250 Star Check Dr, Colombus, OH, 43217
Jet services, charter, express, bank, medical, government, private, cargo, sales

Airpower Aviation Resources (805) 499-0307
702 Paseo Vista, Thousand Oaks, CA, 91320
Aircraft-airplanes & helicopters: civilian, military,commercial, vintage & antique. Full aerial coordination services.
airpowerinc@earthlink.net * www.airpower-aviation.com

Camera Copters (888) 463-7953
copters & planes, camera mounts & systems, SAG pilots, aerial coord. for stunts, location scouting & pre-prod.

Celebrity Helicopters (877) 999-2099
961 W. Alondra Blvd, Compton, CA, 90220
wide variety of helicopters, with camera mounts, FAA approved "Movie Manual" for special camera positions

Goodyear Blimp (310) 327-6565
19200 S. Main St, Gardena, CA, 90248
"Spirit of America" follows a line of Goodyear blimps that have appeared in dozens of movies.

Jet Productions (818) 781-4742
13351 Riverside Dr #530, Sherman Oaks, CA, 91423
jet charters including private & production transportation, & photo shoot

Orbic Helicopters, Inc. (805) 389-1070
777 Aviation Dr, Camarillo, CA, 93010
helicopter tours/charters, aerial filming

Rock-It Air Charter (215) 947-5400
Web Based Business
executive jet charters, 24X7, 95 offices worldwide
www.rockitair.com

Rotor Aviation (562) 595-6867
3200 Airflite Way, Long Beach, CA, 90807
helicopter charters/tours, aerial photography support

Sun Quest (800) 529-7595
7415 Hayvenhurst Pl, Van Nuys, CA, 91406
executive air charters

Airplane & Aircraft Mockups

See Also: Airport Dressing & Hangars Locations, Insert Stages & Small Theatres*

Aero Mock-Ups (888) 662-5877
Aviation prop house. Complete airplane interiors & airport dressing, service area gallery model airplanes. No hangars.

Aviation mockups and prop rentals for film & television production set dressing, wardrobe, cockpits aviation interior mock-ups airline cabin interiors

Air Hollywood - Prop House & Standing Sets (818) 890-0444
Gulfstream, Pan Am, airport terminal, jet interior, private jets, 737s to 767s, lear jet, airplane sets, airport seating

Airpower Aviation Resources (805) 499-0307
702 Paseo Vista, Thousand Oaks, CA, 91320
Aircraft-airplanes & helicopters: civilian, military,commercial, vintage & antique. Full aerial coordination services.
airpowerinc@earthlink.net * www.airpower-aviation.com

Art, Models & Props, Inc. (951) 206-9156
1725 Marengo Ave, Pasadena, CA, 91103
Custom design/fabr. cockpit interiors. See ad in "Prop Design & Manufacturing"
modelsandprops@msn.com * www.artmodeltech.com

RJR Props (404) 349-7600
Large commercial airline interior; navy helicopter

Airport Dressing & Hangars

See Also: Model Ships/Planes/Trains/Autos Etc. Security Walk-Through & Baggage Alarms* Aerospace*

Air Hollywood - Prop House & Standing Sets (818) 890-0444
Studio, gulfstream, learjet, airport terminal, jet interior, private jets, 737, 747, 757, airplane sets, airport seating

C. P. Valley (323) 466-8201

E.C. Prop Rentals (818) 764-2008
Int. Hangar, Ext. Ramp, Terminal Seats, Runway Lights, Stanchions, Rolling Ladders

LCW Props (818) 243-0707
Terminal Seating, Baggage X-Ray Machines, Security Wands & Walk Through Metal Detectors, Kiosks, Stewardess Carts

Modern Props (323) 934-3000
x-ray, walk-thru detectors, hand held metal detectors, seating, counters, Airport Bench units, hand held metal detectors

RC Vintage, Inc. (818) 765-7107
Airport Seating, airport seats, modern airport seats, vintage airport seats.

RJR Props (404) 349-7600
Airport dressing including x-ray baggage scanners, metal detector wands, walkthrough metal detectors and more.

Airstream Trailers

See: RV Vehicles & Travel Trailers, Equip & Parts

Aladdin Lamps

See Also: Arabian Decorations
Badia Design, Inc. (818) 762-0130
5420 Vineland Ave, N. Hollywood, CA, 91601
info@badiadesign.com * www.badiadesign.com
The Hand Prop Room LP. (323) 931-1534
Brass lamps, Aladdin lamps, oil lamps, eastern lamps
History For Hire, Inc. (818) 765-7767
good selection

Alarms

See Also: Security Devices or Services* Security Walk-Through & Baggage Alarms
Alley Cats Studio Rentals (818) 982-9178
burglar, fire, modern, period
E.C. Prop Rentals (818) 764-2008
burglar, fire, modern to period, multiples
LCW Props (818) 243-0707
Bells, Fire Alarms, Fire Pulls, Electronic, Emergency Lights
Mike Green Fire Equipment Co. (818) 989-3322
11916 Valerio St, N Hollywood, CA, 91605
Fire Alarms, Fire Alarm Strobes, Fire Alarm Bells, Fire Bells. Vintage to New.
info@mgfire.com * www.Mgfire.com
Modern Props (323) 934-3000
contemporary alarms, futuristic alarms, electronic alarms, radio alarm clocks, oversized alarms, contemporary and vintage alarm clocks, security alarms
RJR Props (404) 349-7600
Security alarms, alarm panels, fire alarm pulls and more for rent.
Sony Pictures Studios-Prop House (Off Lot) (310) 244-5999
horn alarms, fire lights, fire bells, fire alarm, police alarms, smoke alarms, and more

Aliens

See Also: Futuristic Furniture, Props, Decorations
Art, Models & Props, Inc. (951) 206-9156
1725 Marengo Ave, Pasadena, CA, 91103
Custom design/fabr. See ad in "Prop Design & Manufacturing"
modelsandprops@msn.com * www.artmodeltech.com
Dapper Cadaver/Creatures & Cultures (818) 771-0818
Alien bodies & monsters. Alien skulls & enlongated human skulls. Autopsy tables & instruments. Oddities & specimen jars.
LCW Props (818) 243-0707
Alien Body Parts, Alien Corpses, Men In Black Dressing
Modern Props (323) 934-3000
Prints, sculptures, skulls, monster mounted heads, pinball machine, futuristic weapons and futuristic equipment.

Alley Dressing

AIR Designs (818) 768-6639
Trash cans, barrels, pallets, signage, dumpsters, crates & boxes, lighting & more.
Alley Cats Studio Rentals (818) 982-9178
clean metal rolling dumpsters, pallets, crates, fence. New York Street Dressing. street lamps, platform construction
C. P. Two (323) 466-8201
Fire hydrants and other pieces of alley dressing.

E.C. Prop Rentals (818) 764-2008
Clean Dumpsters, Pallets, Crates, Trash Cans, Clutter, Shopping Carts

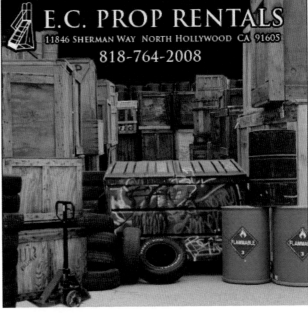

The Hand Prop Room LP. (323) 931-1534
barricades, drums, crates, trash cans
History For Hire, Inc. (818) 765-7767
LCW Props (818) 243-0707
Our Specialty, We Own Our Own Recycling Center Next Door, Quantity And Quality Cannot Be Beat

Sony Pictures Studios-Prop House (Off Lot) (310) 244-5999
dumpsters, trash cans & bins, fire escape, exterior stairs, exterior stair lights
Universal Studios Property & Hardware Dept (818) 777-2784
Alley dressing; trash dumpsters, trash bins, trash cans, traffic barricades, recycling bins more

Ambulance/Paramedic

See Also: Hospital Equipment* Medical Equip/Furniture,
Graphics/Supplies* Stretchers* Vehicles

A-1 Medical Integration (818) 753-0319
Medical devices for Set Decoration & Property, from minor procedures to
detailed hospital units.

Alpha Companies - Spellman Desk Co. (818) 504-9090
complete interior ambulance dressing from the #1 source for medical in the
industry.

The Earl Hays Press (818) 765-0700
services the Industry only. paper & plastic signage

The Hand Prop Room LP. (323) 931-1534

History For Hire, Inc. (818) 765-7767
period & contemporary

LCW Props (818) 243-0707
Heart Defibrillators, Medical Bags, Gurneys, Crash Unit, First Aid

American Folk Art

See: Antiques & Antique Decorations* Carved Figures* Furniture,
Early American/Colonial* Paintings/Prints

American Indian

See: Native American* Rugs

Americana

See: Antiques & Antique Decorations* Furniture, Early
American/Colonial* Furniture, Rustic* Paintings/Prints

Ammunition & Blanks

See: Firearms, Gunsmith, Firearm Choreography

Amusement Park

See: Animal Costumes & Walk Around Characters* Arcade
Equipment, Games & Rides* Carnival Dressing/Supplies*
Flags/Banners* Kiosks* Ticket Booths

Anatomical Charts & Models

See Also: Body Parts* Bones, Skulls & Skeletons

Dapper Cadaver/Creatures & Cultures (818) 771-0818
Anatomical models and scientific models. No charts.

LCW Props (818) 243-0707
Skeletons, Heart, Lungs, Reproductive Models, Brain, Prosthetics

Anchors

See: Nautical Dressing & Props

Anesthesia Equipment

A-1 Medical Integration (818) 753-0319
Anesthesia Machines, Ventilators, Vitals Monitors, IV Pumps, Endotracheal
Tubes, Oxygen Masks & Tubing, Anesthetic Drugs.

LCW Props (818) 243-0707
Full Hospital Setup, Hospital Equipment, Syringes, Sharps Containers

Angels & Cherubs

See: Christmas

Animal Cages

E.C. Prop Rentals (818) 764-2008
lrg castered stainless & heavy metal, small animal type

LCW Props (818) 243-0707
Large Selection Of Different Sizes, Single Cages or Banks, Rolling

Sony Pictures Studios-Prop House (Off Lot) (310) 244-5999
lab testing cages, pet habitats, litter boxes, bird feeders, cat posts, fish bowls,
pet dishes, bird cages, birdhouse

Universal Studios Property & Hardware Dept (818) 777-2784
Lots of birdcages, hamster cages, large animal cages and more.

Animal Costumes & Walk Around Characters

See Also: Costumes* Prop Design & Manufacturing

The Costume House (818) 508-9933
rabbit walk around, bunny walk around, eagle walk around, chicken walk
around, roach walk around

Geppetto Studios (718) 398-9792
201 46th Street, 2nd Floor, Brooklyn, NY, 11220
full body puppet costumes, puppet displays, walkarounds

International Costume, Inc. (310) 320-6392
mascots, body, oversized heads

Marylen Costume Design & Mfg Inc (800) 628-6417
5 Corning Court, Medford, OR, 97504
over 2,500 animal, character & mascot costumes
online@marylen.com * www.marylen.com

Sony Pictures Studios-Wardrobe (310) 244-5995
alterations, call (310) 244-7260

Stagecraft Inc. (513) 541-7150
3950 Spring Grove Ave, Cincinatti, OH, 45223
walkaround cartoons, animals, & illusion walkarounds

Tech Works FX Studios (504) 722-1504
13405 Seymour Meyers Blvd. #5, Covington, LA, 70433
Specializes in Costume Design, Creature Suits, Make Up FX, Monsters and
Custom Characters.
info@techworksstudios.com * www.techworksstudios.com

Ursula's Costumes, Inc. (310) 582-8230
2516 Wilshire Blvd, Santa Monica, CA, 90403

Animal Glue

See: Expendables

Animal Hides & Mounted Heads

See: Costume/Wardrobe/Sewing Supplies* Prop Houses* Rugs*
Taxidermy, Hides/Heads/Skeletons

Animal Mock-ups

See: Fiberglass Products/Fabrication* Puppets, Marionettes,
Automata, Animatronics* Taxidermy, Hides/Heads/Skeletons

Animal Skulls & Skeletons

See: Bones, Skulls & Skeletons* Jungle Dressing* Taxidermy,
Hides/Heads/Skeletons

Animals (Live), Services, Trainers & Wranglers

See Also: Aquariums & Tropical Fish* Horses, Horse Equipment,
Livestock

All Creatures Great & Small (914) 232-3623
3 Little Lane, White Plains, NY, 10605
professional trainers & handlers, all animal talent incl. cats & dogs, farm, exotic,
birds, reptiles, insects

All Star Animals (516) 569-5014
Call for Appt
dogs & cats, farm animals, exotics, also animal locator, live promotional events
in NY area

American Humane Association (818) 501-0123
11530 Ventura Blvd, Studio City, CA 91604
National HQ in Denver, CO - guidelines for production; protects all animals in
film & media

Animal Actors of Hollywood, Inc. (805) 495-2122
860 W. Carlisle Rd, Thousand Oaks, CA, 91361
hoofstock, domestic animals, reptiles, small exotics

Bee & Insect People Unltd. (800) 924-3097
Claremont, CA, 91711
bees, insects, spiders & wasps, stunt people

Benay's Bird & Animal Source (818) 881-0053
By Appointment Only
Birds, dogs & cats, farm animals, forest animals, primates, exotics, hoofstock,
insects, rodents, reptiles, sea lions
benays@aol.com * www.benaysanimals.com

Birds & Animals Unlimited (877) 542-1355
animal & trainer talent, offices in S. Cal., Florida, NY, & London

Bob Dunn's Animal Services (818) 896-0394
16001 Yarnell St, Sylmar, CA, 91342
birds, dogs, cats, apes, exotics, insects, hoofstock, monkeys, reptiles, rodents

Boone's Animals for Hollywood (661) 257-0630
32727 Merritt Rd, Acton, CA 93510
dogs, cats, birds, rodents

Bow Wow Productions (800) 926-9969
domestic & exotic animals & wranglers for film/TV, special events

Brockett's Film Fauna, Inc. (805) 379-3141
reptiles, insects, domestic animals

Critters of the Cinema (661) 724-1929
PO Box 378, Lake Hughes, CA, 93532
dogs & cats, big cats, aquatic mammals, birds, primates, hoofed small/large mammals, insects, kangaroos, reptiles
Rob@crittersofthecinema.com * www.crittersofthecinema.com

Exotic Life Fish & Reptiles (818) 341-1007
9919 Topanga Canyon Blvd, Chatsworth, CA, 91311
fresh/salt water fish, wide variety reptiles, tortoises, tanks, equip., service

Gentle Jungle (661) 248-6195
801 Lebec Rd., P.O. Box 832, Lebec, CA, 93243
animals/trainers, domestic dogs/cats, small animals, livestock/horses, big cats, wolves & exotics

Hollywood Animals (661) 299-9000
PO Box 2088, Santa Clarita, CA 91386
Lions, working pride, tigers, bears, elephants, leopards, panthers & animal stunts for film, TV & print ads

Jules Sylvester's Reptile Rentals Inc. (818) 621-4101
Thousand Oaks, CA
Reptiles, Snakes, Spiders, Scorpions, Frogs, Turtles, Tortoises, Alligators, bugs and more!
reptilerentals@gmail.com * www.reptilerentals.com

Jules Sylvester's
REPTILE
RENTALS, Inc.

(818) 621-4101
reptilerentals@gmail.com
www.reptilerentals.com

Jungle Exotics (909) 887-3500
16215 Cajon Blvd, San Bernardino, CA, 92407
cats & dogs, lions, wolves, wide variety of birds & reptiles

Living Art Aquatic Design, Inc. (310) 822-7484
2301 South Sepulveda Blvd, Los Angeles, CA, 90064
30 yrs exp. fish wrangler, custom aquarium setups, saltwater/freshwater
ron@aquatic2000.com * www.aquatic2000.com

Paws For Effect (877) 729-7439
P.O. Box 650, Lake Hughes, CA, 93532
dogs & cats, birds, exotics (lions, tigers) reptiles, insects, offices in CA, NY, CT, MI, IL

Phil's Animal Rentals (805) 521-1100
P.O. Box 309, Piru, CA, 93040
Domestic/exotic. Horses, dogs, birds, cows, yak, water buffalo, flamingos, huge variety wagons & carriages, vintage prop
www.philsanimalrentals.com

Randy Miller's Predators in Action (909) 499-9064
P.O. Box 1691, Big Bear City, CA, 92314
exotic large cats, wolves, black & grizzly bears, controlled wrestling & attacks, snarls & roars on cue

Silver Screen Animals (661) 269-0231
34540 Brock Lane, Acton, CA, 93510
dogs & cats, farm animals, forest animals, some insects, birds, exotic animals, barnyard animals, rodents.

Studio Animal Services (661) 257-4798
28230 San Martinez Grande Canyon Rd, Castaic, CA, 91384
small/med/large dogs, cats, hoofstock, birds, & exotics (bears, wolves, monkeys, etc.)

Talented Animals (310) 858-8722
1033 N Carol Dr Ste 401, W Hollywood, CA, 90069
birds, cats & dogs, exotics, hoofstock, primates, reptiles, rodents, wild animals incl. wolves

Worldwide Movie Animals, LLC (661) 252-2000
Call for Appt
dogs/cats, birds, primates, reptiles, insects, camels, kangaroos, porcupines, beavers

Animation Control Systems

See: Puppets, Marionettes, Automata, Animatronics Special Effects, Electronic*

Animatronics

See: Prop Design & Manufacturing Puppets, Marionettes, Automata, Animatronics* Special Effects, Electronic* Special Effects, Make-up/Prosthetics*

Antenna

E.C. Prop Rentals (818) 764-2008
rooftop TV, satellite, antenna towers

LCW Props (818) 243-0707
Large Selection, TV, Satellite, Radio, High Frequency, Wifi, Dual Band, Large & Small

Antiques & Antique Decorations

See Also: Asian Antiques, Furniture, Art & Artifacts Linens, Household* Salvage, Architectural*

Angel Appliances (877) 262-6435
8545 Sepulveda Blvd, Sepulveda, CA, 91343
practical, stoves, fridges, washers, dryers, wringer-washers, ironer, etc.
props@angelappliances.com * www.angelappliances.com/rentals.php

Angelus Medical & Optical Co., Inc. (310) 769-6060
13007 S Western Ave, Gardena, CA, 90249
Antique Medical Furniture & Antique Medical Equipment
www.angelusmedical.com

Antiquarian Traders (310) 247-3900
4851 S. Alameda Street, Los Angeles, CA 90048
Large collection of antique furniture and lighting, architectural pieces
antiques@antiquariantraders.com * www.antiquariantraders.com

ANTIQUARIAN TRADERS
Victorian • Art Deco • Art Nouveau
Architectural • Lighting

(310) 247-3900 • (310) 345-9419
antiquariantraders.com

DISPLAY ADS AND LISTINGS FOR THIS CATEGORY
CONTINUE ON THE FOLLOWING PAGE

Bountiful (310) 450-3620
1335 Abbot Kinney Blvd, Venice, CA, 90291
furniture & accessories

Castle Antiques & Design (855) 765-5800
11924 Vose St, N Hollywood, CA, 91605
American, Art Deco, Art Nouveau, Chippendale, Brutton, European, George I -
George IV, Louis XIII - Louis XVI, Greek
info@castleantiques.net * www.castleprophouse.com

35,000 sq.ft. Showroom
Antique Furniture,
Lighting and Accessories
CASTLE
ANTIQUES & DESIGN
www.castleantiques.net

Design Mix Furniture (323) 939-7500
442 S La Brea Ave, Los Angeles, CA, 90036
Global imports of Indian, Indonesian, Chinese, African, Moroccan art, acc.,
antiques, reprod. & Industrial Furniture
www.mixfurniture.com

Eric's Architectural Salvage, Wells Antique Tile (213) 413-6800
2110 W Sunset Blvd, Los Angeles, CA, 90026
The new Architectural Salvage store in Los Angeles that you haven't been to
yet.
ericstiques@aol.com * www.ericsarchitecturalsalvage.com

Galerie Sommerlath - French 50s 60s (310) 838-0102
9608 Venice Blvd, Culver City, CA, 90232
10,000 sq ft Mid-Century - 80s furniture, lighting & accessories
info@french50s60s.com * http://www.galeriesommerlath.com

The Hand Prop Room LP. (323) 931-1534

History For Hire, Inc. (818) 765-7767

International Printing Museum (714) 529-1832
315 Torrance Blvd, Carson, CA, 90745
antique printing/office equipment 1450-1980. old presses, machines, related
furniture, period artwork
www.printmuseum.org

Jas. Townsend & Son, Inc. (574) 594-5852
133 N 1st St, P.O. Box 415, Pierceton, IN, 46562
catalog sales; American Colonial period inspired reprod. of wardrobe &
household items, books/patterns of Colonial perio

Ob-jects (818) 351-4200
Antique chairs, Antique furniture, antique upholstery, folk furniture, antique
objects

Omega/Cinema Props (323) 466-8201
Antique furniture, items and tools.

Pasadena Antique Warehouse (626) 404-2422
1609 East Washington Blvd., Pasadena, CA, 91104
Furniture, jewelry, decorative, radios, cameras, typewriters, art, candelabras,
chandeliers, paintings, ceramics, silver
pasadenaantiquewarehouse@gmail.com *
www.pasadenaantiquewarehouse.com

Pasadena Antiques & Design (626) 389-3938
330 S. Fair Oaks Avenue, Pasadena, CA 91105
Antiques of all ages and descriptions. 17th. through 20th. century
roy@antiquesofpasadena.com * www.antiquesofpasadena.com

The Rational Past (310) 476-6277
By Appointment, West Los Angeles, CA
Authentic science, industrial, technical antiques & collectibles. Many
professions & eras represented. See web site.
info@therationalpast.com * www.therationalpast.com

The Rug Warehouse (310) 838-0450
3270 Helms Ave, Los Angeles, CA, 90034
Antique rugs, antique carpets, antique recreations, area rugs, runners,
traditional, tribal
www.therugwarehouse.com

Scavenger's Paradise (818) 843-5257
3425 W. Magnolia Blvd, Burbank, CA 91505
18th C to 1940s antique furniture, chandeliers, lamps & sconces, display cases
+ more
gilliamgreyson@sbcglobal.net * www.scavengersparadise.com

The Seraph (740) 369-1817
5606 State Route 37 E, Delaware, OH, 43015
Mfg. authentic reprod. 17th/18th C. furnishings & case goods, etc. 1000s of
items, hrs Th-Sun, 10-5 Eastern, call for ca

Sony Pictures Studios-Prop House (Off Lot) (310) 244-5999

Susanne Hollis, Inc. (626) 441-0346
230 Pasadena Ave, South Pasadena, CA, 91030
20th - 17th century Antiques, Accessories, and Fine Art from around the world
in our 19,000sqft. warehouse and showrooms
sales@susannehollis.com * www.susannehollis.com

Unique Antiques & Collectibles　　　　(805) 499-2222
2357 Michael Drive, Newbury Park, CA, 91320
We carry paintings, statues, dolls, tankards, china, other housewares, furniture, jewelry, and much, much, more.
diamond-m-enterprises@live.com * www.uniqueantiquesandcollectibles.com

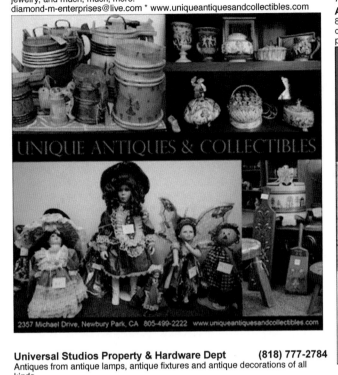

Universal Studios Property & Hardware Dept　(818) 777-2784
Antiques from antique lamps, antique fixtures and antique decorations of all kinds.

Used Church Items, Religious Rentals　　(239) 992-5737
216 Cumer Road, McDonald, PA, 15057
1000's of Vintage Antique Religious items for large cathedrals, churches, and home chapels.
warehouse@religiousrentals.com * www.religiousrentals.com

Warner Bros. Studios Property Department　(818) 954-2181
Large collection period and antique furniture, hand props, fixtures and accessories

Warner Bros. Studios Property Dept. - Atlanta, GA　(404) 878-0002
3645 Southside Industrial Pkwy., Atlanta, GA 30354
Large selection of antiques and antique decorations at our Atlanta Prop House location.
nikki.giovacchini@warnerbros.com * www.WBPropertyAtlanta.com

Apothecary

See: Drugstore/Apothecary Lab Equipment*

Apple Boxes

See: Expendables

Appliances

See Also: Refrigerators Stoves* Vacuum Cleaners* Washing Machines/Dryers*

Angel Appliances　　　　　　　(877) 262-6435
8545 Sepulveda Blvd, Sepulveda, CA, 91343
customized, mockups, practical, classic-current, kitchen-laundry;kitchenette
props@angelappliances.com * www.angelappliances.com/rentals.php

C. P. Valley　　　　　　　　　　　(323) 466-8201
The Hand Prop Room LP.　　　　　　(323) 931-1534
sm. household
Kimos Appliance LLC　　　　　　　(818) 787-8995
15430 Cabrito Road #1, Van Nuys, CA, 91406
We rent and/or sell all major home appliances. Most makes, models, styles, sizes, and colors available. Call today!!
kimosappliances@yahoo.com * www.kimosappliances.com
LCW Props　　　　　　　　　　　(818) 243-0707
Commercial, Disabled For Debris, Non-Working, Old, Rusty
Modern Props　　　　　　　　　　(323) 934-3000
contemporary, household, backs cut out, vintage, refrigerators, stoves, freezers, countertop appliances, toy appliances.
NEST Studio Rentals, Inc.　　　　　(818) 942-0339
small household
Omega/Cinema Props　　　　　　　(323) 466-8201
Residential appliances and commercial appliances from period to contemporary.
RC Vintage, Inc.　　　　　　　　　(818) 765-7107
40s, 50s & 60s selection Fridges, Toasters, Blenders, Large selection of Vintage Stoves, Refrigerators, and more
Sony Pictures Studios-Prop House (Off Lot)　(310) 244-5999
Air conditioner, coffee maker, compacter, dishwasher, dryer, fountains, freezers, furnaces, hair dryers, ironing boards and more.
Universal Studios Property & Hardware Dept　(818) 777-2784
Appliances from coffee makers and refrigerators to stoves and toasters, commercial appliances and residential appliances.
Warner Bros. Studios Property Department　(818) 954-2181
Refrigerators, stoves, washing machines, dryers, microwaves, household appliances
ZG04 DECOR　　　　　　　　　　(818) 853-8040
Kitchen appliances

Aprons

See: Protective Apparel* Uniforms, Trades/Professional/Sports* Wardrobe

Aquariums & Tropical Fish

See Also: Plastics, Materials & Fabrication

Living Art Aquatic Design, Inc. (310) 822-7484
2301 South Sepulveda Blvd, Los Angeles, CA, 90064
30 yrs exp. fish wrangler, custom aquarium setups, saltwater/freshwater
ron@aquatic2000.com * www.aquatic2000.com

RC Vintage, Inc. (818) 765-7107
Full Selection of Shapes and sizes Saltwater and Freshwater Available,
Aquarium with matching stand, tropical fish!

Arabian Decorations

Badia Design, Inc. (818) 762-0130
5420 Vineland Ave, N. Hollywood, CA, 91601
brass arabian decorations, hanging lanterns, metal moroccan furniture,
moroccan pillow
info@badiadesign.com * www.badiadesign.com

Bob Gail Special Events (310) 202-5200
Create the perfect Arabian event with Genie Lamps, Moroccan Furniture,
Persian Rugs and more!

History For Hire, Inc. (818) 765-7767
brass, fabrics

Arcade Equipment, Games & Rides

See Also: Pinball Machines* Scales* Vendor Carts & Concession
Counters* Video Games

AIR Designs (818) 768-6639
Video, skill, claw, pinball, rides, dart, pool & more.

Arcade Amusements (866) 576-8878
802 West Washington Ave Ste E, Escondido, CA, 92025-1644
Planning a Party? How about having some games there? How about 10? How
about 20? How about... Well, you get the idea.
phil@arcadeamusements.com * www.arcadeamusements.com

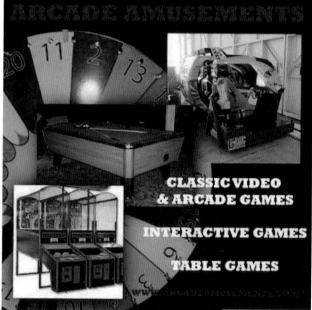

Dynamic Amusement (213) 239-3645
10600 Victory Blvd, N Hollywood, CA, 91606
All coin operated equipment you need in pristine/working condition. Kiddie
rides, gumball machines, toy cranes and more.
dynamicamusement@yahoo.com

L. A. Party Works (888) 527-2789
9712 Alpaca St, S El Monte, CA, 91733
in Vancouver tel. 604-589-4101 photo booth, kiddie rides, carnival games, dunk tank, Mocap Boxing Arcade
partyworks@aol.com * www.partyworksusa.com

LCW Props (818) 243-0707
Arcade Games, Gaming Systems, Joysticks, Coin Operated, Money Changers

Lennie Marvin Enterprises, Inc. (Prop Heaven) (818) 841-5882
pinball, video games, kiddie rides & more

RC Vintage, Inc. (818) 765-7107
30s-90s free standing games/rides, mutoscope, fortune teller....Pinballs and Video Games..Funhouse Mirrors. Clown Heads!

Archery Equipment, Training

See Also: Sporting Goods & Services Weaponry, Historical* Weaponry, Medieval*

C. P. Valley (323) 466-8201
Archery targets, bows and arrows, bow carriers, archery racks, and more.

The Hand Prop Room LP. (323) 931-1534
real, mfg., stunts, crossbows, sport, medieval, Native American

History For Hire, Inc. (818) 765-7767
ethnic & period bows & arrows

Sony Pictures Studios-Prop House (Off Lot) (310) 244-5999

Sword & Stone (818) 562-6548
longbows, crossbows, arrows, bolts, quivers

Universal Studios Property & Hardware Dept (818) 777-2784
Archery equipment such as bows and arrows, arrow quivers, archery trophy and more.

Architectural Lighting

See: Searchlights/Skytrackers, Architectural Lights

Architectural Pieces & Artifacts

See Also: Columns Doors* Fiberglass Products/Fabrication* Pedestals* Salvage, Rubble, Clutter & Trash (Prop)* Scenery/Set Construction* Scenery/Set Rentals* Staff Shops*

Antiquarian Traders (310) 247-3900
4851 S. Alameda Street, Los Angeles, CA 90048
Grand scale bronze and iron doors, entryways, gates, fireplaces, statuary, stained glass
antiques@antiquariantraders.com * www.antiquariantraders.com

Castle Antiques & Design (855) 765-5800
11924 Vose St, N Hollywood, CA, 91605
American, Art Deco, Art Nouveau, Chippendale, Brutton, European, George I - George IV, Louis XIII - Louis XVI, Greek
info@castleantiques.net * www.castleprophouse.com

Charisma Design Studio, Inc. (818) 252-6611
8414 San Fernando Road, Sun Valley, CA, 91352
high-end 1-off large scale metal/glass/wood art
info@charismadesign.com * www.charismadesign.com

Dapper Cadaver/Creatures & Cultures (818) 771-0818
Gargoyles and angel statues, Gothic and other. Obelisks and monuments. cemetery angels, maiden busts, Greek busts

Eric's Architectural Salvage, Wells Antique Tile (213) 413-6800
2110 W Sunset Blvd, Los Angeles, CA, 90026
The new Architectural Salvage store in Los Angeles that you haven't been to yet.
ericstiques@aol.com * www.ericsarchitecturalsalvage.com

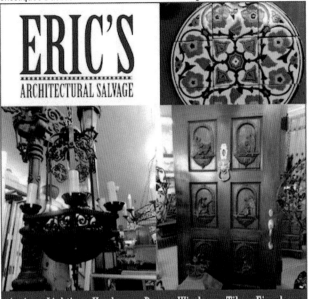

ERIC'S ARCHITECTURAL SALVAGE

Antique Lighting · Hardware · Doors · Windows · Tiles · Fireplaces

Freeway Building Materials & Supply (323) 261-8904
1124 S. Boyle Ave, Los Angeles, CA, 90023
bricks, steel windows

The Hand Prop Room LP. (323) 931-1534

Monument Sign Mfg. LLC (800) 711-3626
401 N Warren St, Orwigsburg, PA, 17961
catalog sales; custom made foam, wide variety arch. applications

Pasadena Architectural Salvage (626) 535-9655
2600 E Foothill Blvd, Pasadena, CA 91107-3408
circa 1880s-1930s entry doors, s/g windows, iron gates, columns, mantels, footed tubs, spec. Arts & Crafts period
pasarcsalvage@aol.com * www.pasadenaarchitecturalsalvage.com

Scavenger's Paradise (818) 843-5257
3425 W. Magnolia Blvd, Burbank, CA 91505
vintage doors, windows, leaded & stained glass, columns, fireplace surround
gilliamgreyson@sbcglobal.net * www.scavengersparadise.com

Sword & Stone (818) 562-6548
gargoyles, stone work, custom design-wrought iron & sheet metal

Universal Studios Property & Hardware Dept (818) 777-2784
Architectural pieces and architectural artifacts.

Warner Bros. Studios Hardware Rentals (818) 954-1335
4000 Warner Blvd., Bldg. 44 Burbank, CA 91522
Door Knobs & Door Plates, Door Hinges, Window Fixtures, Elevator Panels, Train Accessories & Boat Accessories
wbsfconstructionservices@warnerbros.com * www.wbsf.com

Warner Bros. Studios Staff Shop (818) 954-2269
Manufacturer of exterior & interior details used for the creation of sets in all architectural styles & eras.

Architectural Research

See: Research, Advisors, Consulting & Clearances

Archiving Media/Records Management

Bonded Services   **(818) 848-9766**
3205 Burton Ave, Burbank, CA, 91504
media storage archives/vaults, climate control, physical distribution, studio services

Iron Mountain   **(800) 899-IRON**
1 Federal St, Boston, MA 02110
locs. in Hollywood, NY, PA, & International; climate controlled vaults, media storage, records mgmnt, film preservation

Kiss Media Vaults   **(818) 769-5477**
4444 Vineland Ave, Toluca Lake, CA, 91602
All media, film-tape, self-storage, climate control, 24 hr access, electronic security; + more loc. in S. Cal.

Pacific Title Archives   **(818) 760-4223**
10717 Vanowen St, N Hollywood, CA, 91605
film & video storage, high security, p/u & delivery, database mgmnt, film/video inspection/preservation

Producers Film Center   **(323) 851-1122**
948 N Sycamore Ave, Hollywood, CA, 90038
film/videotape storage, climate control, 24 hr guards, computerized inventory, immediate access

Arenas

See: Stages/Studios, Film/TV/Theatre/Events

Armoires

See: Antiques & Antique Decorations

Armor, Chainmail, Suits of Armor

See Also: Weaponry, Historical* Weaponry, Medieval

Costume Armour Inc.   **(845) 534-9120**
2 Mill Street, Building 1 Suite 101, Cornwall, NY 12518
theatrical armor

The Costume House   **(818) 508-9933**
bathing suits, vintage beach wear, mens bathing suit, women bathing suit, children bathing suits

Omega/Cinema Props   **(323) 466-8201**
Suits of armor, coat of arms, shields, samurai armor, and armor display stands.

Sony Pictures Studios-Wardrobe   **(310) 244-5995**
alterations, call (310) 244-7260

Sword & Stone   **(818) 562-6548**
alum, bronze, chainmail, mesh, human-horse, shields, historic & future

Universal Studios Property & Hardware Dept   **(818) 777-2784**
Suit of armor; helmets, shields, breastplates and more from different time periods and countries.

Warner Bros. Studios Costume Dept   **(818) 954-1297**
Gothic, Medieval, European, English, Japanese, Hoods, Suits, Hats, Boots

Army-Navy Equipment

See: Military Props & Equipment* Military Surplus/Combat Clothes, Field Gear* Walkie-Talkies* Weapons

Art & Picture Framing Services

See Also: Easels

Aaron Bros.   **(818) 243-7661**
320 N. Glendale Ave, Glendale, CA, 91206

Clearedart.com/El Studio Granados   **(818) 240-4421**
958 Verdugo Circle Dr, Glendale, CA, 91206
Complete one-stop custom-framing services, over 4000 mouldings, plexi boxes, museum mounting.
fineart@elstudiogranados.com * www.clearedart.com

The Hand Prop Room LP.   **(323) 931-1534**

Hollywood Cinema Arts, Inc.   **(818) 504-7333**
Certified museum grade framers that can make any artwork look like a masterpiece.

Hollywood Studio Gallery   **(323) 462-1116**
classical to posters, fast turnaround-mounting services

Omega/Cinema Props   **(323) 466-8201**
Photography frames, art frames, old picture frames, contemporary picture frames, wood frames, antique frames, ornate frames.

U-Frame It Gallery   **(818) 781-4500**
6203 Lankershim Blvd, N Hollywood, CA, 91606
Over 1,000 frames in stock, 1-hr. turnaround. We also do frame repairs.
uframit@aol.com * www.uframeitgallery.com

Art Deco Carpet & Rugs

Antiquarian Traders   **(310) 247-3900**
4851 S. Alameda Street, Los Angeles, CA 90048
Lovely and unusual collection of high Art Deco rugs
antiques@antiquariantraders.com * www.antiquariantraders.com

Modern Props   **(323) 934-3000**
modern rugs, contemporary rugs, many patterns, many colors, wool rugs, silk rugs, and more.

RC Vintage, Inc.   **(818) 765-7107**
large patterned rugs, multiple designs, hand woven looks, water colored, house hold rugs, shag rugs, vintage carpet

The Rug Warehouse   **(310) 838-0450**
3270 Helms Ave, Los Angeles, CA, 90034
High quality area rugs & carpet. Contemporary, traditional, antique, modern, art deco, custom options & more
www.therugwarehouse.com

Unique Antiques & Collectibles   **(805) 499-2222**
2357 Michael Drive, Newbury Park, CA, 91320
Authentic antique furniture from Italy, France, & England. Furniture & accessories from 1700's, 1800's & early 1900's.
diamond-m-enterprises@live.com * www.uniqueantiquesandcollectibles.com

Universal Studios Property & Hardware Dept   **(818) 777-2784**
Art deco carpets and art deco rugs

Art Deco Dressing/Accessories

Antiquarian Traders   **(310) 247-3900**
4851 S. Alameda Street, Los Angeles, CA 90048
Great collection of parlor suites, club chairs, dining suites, bedroom suites and lighting
antiques@antiquariantraders.com * www.antiquariantraders.com

History For Hire, Inc.   **(818) 765-7767**
smalls

Susanne Hollis, Inc.   **(626) 441-0346**
230 Pasadena Ave, South Pasadena, CA, 91030
20th - 17th century Antiques, Accessories, and Fine Art from around the world in our 19,000sqft. warehouse and showrooms
sales@susannehollis.com * www.susannehollis.com

Universal Studios Property & Hardware Dept   **(818) 777-2784**
Art deco dressing; art deco trays, art deco sconces, art deco chairs, art deco vases, art deco plateware and more.

Art Deco Furniture & Rugs

See: Art Deco Carpet & Rugs* Art Deco Dressing/Accessories* Furniture, Art Deco

Art For Rent

See Also: Art, Artists For Hire Carved Figures* Glass & Mirrors,
Art/Finishing/Etching/Etc.* Paintings/Prints* Photographs* Posters,
Art/Movie/Travel/Wanted Etc.* Sculpture*

Alpha Companies - Spellman Desk Co.   **(818) 504-9090**
cleared art, abstract, landscapes, oil paintings, photographs

Art By Kidz   **(818) 240-6650**
Call for Appt, Glendale, CA, 91207
100s of ORIGINAL CHILDRENS 2D & 3D ARTWORKS for rent at low flat rates
based on size. Cleared copyright, located in Glendale.
www.artbykidz.com

Art Dimensions Inc.   **(310) 433-8934**
Web Based Business
Cleared contemporary art for lease including paintings, prints, sculptures and
photography by more than 80 artists.
info@artdimensionsonline.com * www.artdimensionsonline.com

ART PIC   **(818) 503-5999**
6826 Troost Ave, N Hollywood, CA, 91605
contemporary art, all mediums sculpture; photos, paint. all art cleared
artpicla@mac.com * www.artpic2000.com

ARTagogo.net   **(310) 753-9991**
2041 Glencoe Ave, Venice, CA, 90291
Cleared art & photography; custom art & graphics, delivery available. Call
Cynthia Hill for unlisted items not on web.
cynthiahill@mac.com * www.artagogo.net

Artery Props   **(877) 732-7733**
7684 Clybourn Ave 2nd Floor Unit C, Sun Valley, CA, 91352
100% cleared artwork & owned artwork: posters, stickers, flyers, gold records,
signs, CDs, DVDs, albums, mic flags, more
info@arteryprops.com * www.arteryprops.com

Artspace Warehouse   **(323) 936-7020**
7358 Beverly Boulevard, Los Angeles, CA, 90036
Huge selection of cleared original art in stock for same day rent or sale at
affordable prices.
info@artspacewarehouse.com * www.artspacewarehouse.com

DISPLAY ADS AND LISTINGS FOR THIS CATEGORY
CONTINUE ON THE FOLLOWING PAGE

Bassman-Blaine   (213) 748-5909
1933 S. Broadway, #1005, Los Angeles, CA 90007
Most images cleared for studio use. We stock a large variety of images, styles,
subject matter & sizes from Leftbank Art
lashowroom@bassman-blaine.com * www.bassmanblainelamart.com

Breen/Graham   (323) 663-3426
Unusual art made from recycled materials
www.claregraham.com

Bridge Furniture & Props Los Angeles   (818) 433-7100
We carry modern & traditional furniture, lighting, accessories, cleared art,&
rugs. Items are online for easy shopping.

BRIDGE LA
FURNITURE & PROPS

3210 Vanowen St.   BridgeProps.com
Burbank, CA 91505   Tel: 818.433.7100

Chris's Art Resource (C.A.R.)   (323) 669-1604
1035 N Myra Ave, Los Angeles, CA, 90029
Hundreds of CLEARED paintings, All Sizes and Styles-Sleek to Cozy, All Art on
Premises
w99lulu@yahoo.com * www.chrisartresource.com

Beautiful cleared paintings for rent
C.A.R.
Chris's Art Resource
323.669.1604
ChrisArtResource.com

Clearedart.com/El Studio Granados   (818) 240-4421
958 Verdugo Circle Dr, Glendale, CA, 91206
Galleries full of eclectic fine art in a variety of mediums and techniques for
gallery installations, & corporate decor.
fineart@elstudiogranados.com * www.clearedart.com

clearedart.com

Fine Arts for Film
and Television Production

ClearedINK   (310) 463-6544
ClearedINK is an online platform, providing direct access to contemporary
cleared artwork around the clock.
art@clearedink.com * www.clearedink.com

CLEAREDINK

Cope Studios: The Haven   (818) 913-7187
926 Western Ave Ste A & B, Glendale, CA, 91201
Our studio ranges from creating high end realistic figurative sculpture and drawings to a vast range of painting styles.
figurativesculptor@hotmail.com * www.copestudios.com

Daylight Dreams Editions   (323) 205-0719
Website and by Appt. Only
Highly unique cleared art in styles from Modern to Historical as unframed or framed Fine Art Prints for sale or rent.
mark@ddeditions.com * www.ddeditions.com

Dina Art Co.   (323) 469-4073
6433 W Sunset Blvd, Los Angeles, CA, 90028
Cleared art, art posters, custom framing, hand colored prints & more. Over 3,000 images in 22 categories available.
dina@dinaart.com * www.dinaart.com

Faux Library Studio Props, Inc.   (818) 765-0096
Cleared Art, cleared photographs, book artwork and more including presidential portraits!

FILM ART LA   (323) 461-4900
Culver City Warehouse at Jefferson & Hauser. Call for address.
Period+Contemporary Art. Cleared art rentals available for immediate pick up.
13000 high rez images, print to all sizes.
filmartla@gmail.com * www.artimagela.com

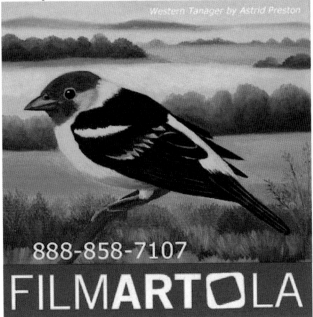

FormDecor, Inc.   (310) 558-2582
America's largest event rental supplier of 20th Century furniture and accessories for Modern and Mid-Century styles.

The Hand Prop Room LP.   (323) 931-1534
lrg sel. cleared pieces

Hollywood Cinema Arts, Inc.   (818) 504-7333
Artwork for every type of set. Paintings, Prints, Sculptures and Photography.

Hollywood Studio Gallery   (323) 462-1116
60,000 items on display in our art rental gallery. Cleared art rentals and sales

LCW Props   **(818) 243-0707**
Paintings, Sketches, Photos, Cuustom Graphics, Art Supplies, Kiln, Pottery Wheel

Little Bohemia Rentals   **(818) 853-7506**
11940 Sherman Rd, N Hollywood, CA, 91605
cleared modern photography, cleared original artworks, wall hangings, tapestries, fiber art, framed and unframed
sales@wearelittlebohemia.com * www.wearelittlebohemia.com

Modern Props   **(323) 934-3000**
modern art for rent, contemporary prints, originals, wall art, sculptures & more cleared art

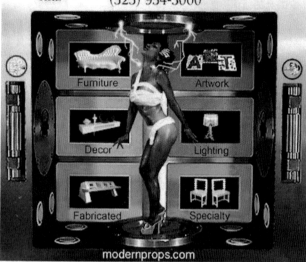

"WHERE **MODERN PROPS** OUR *THINGS* BRING YOUR CREATIVE IMAGINATION TO LIFE ARE" (323) 934-3000
Furniture · Artwork · Decor · Lighting · Fabricated · Specialty
modernprops.com

Modernica Props   **(323) 664-2322**

NEST Studio Rentals, Inc.   **(818) 942-0339**
cleared paintings, prints, photographs, family photos, kid's artwork in stock

Ob-jects   **(818) 351-4200**

Omega/Cinema Props   **(323) 466-8201**
Paintings, sculptures, photographs, prints, tribal artifacts, portraits, needlepoint, presidential artwork and prints

Pasadena Antique Warehouse   **(626) 404-2422**
1609 East Washington Blvd., Pasadena, CA, 91104
Paintings and prints for rent or sale in Antique frames. Original artwork.
pasadenaantiquewarehouse@gmail.com * www.pasadenaantiquewarehouse.com

Prop Services West   **(818) 503-2790**

RC Vintage, Inc.   **(818) 765-7107**
Cleared Art, many framed pictures, framed paintings, paintings of ships, flowers, vases, people, instruments, you name it!

Robert James Company   **(415) 420-4011**
2110 West 20th St, Los Angeles, CA, 90018
Specializing in large-scale steel sculpture and creative steel works. Turn key projects available at a moments notice.
rob@robertjamesstudio.com * www.robertjamesstudio.com

Sculpture by Bruce Gray   **(323) 223-4059**
688 South Avenue 21, Los Angeles, CA, 90031
modern sculptures, abstract paintings, mobiles, unique furniture, giant objects, kinetic art, custom metal work, metal a
bruce@brucegray.com * www.brucegray.com

Sony Pictures Studios-Prop House (Off Lot)   **(310) 244-5999**
acrylic artwork, glass artwork, metal artwork, wood artwork

Susanne Hollis, Inc.   **(626) 441-0346**
230 Pasadena Ave, South Pasadena, CA, 91030
20th - 17th century Antiques, Accessories, and Fine Art from around the world in our 19,000sqft. warehouse and showrooms
sales@susannehollis.com * www.susannehollis.com

Sword & Stone   **(818) 562-6548**

Temporary Contemporary Art   **(562) 900-6115**
7815 Gazette Ave, Winnetka, CA 91306
Kids Art, Tiki, Lowbrow, Abstract Expressionism, Contemporary Art, Neo Surrealism, Gallery Art, Modern Art, Toys
temporarycontemporaryart@gmail.com * www.temporarycontemporaryart.com

Temporary Contemporary
www.TemporaryContemporaryArt.com

U-Frame It Gallery   **(818) 781-4500**
6203 Lankershim Blvd, N Hollywood, CA, 91606
Cleared photographs, wide variety, custom framing
uframit@aol.com * www.uframeitgallery.com

Wallspace   **(323) 930-0471**
607 N La Brea, Los Angeles, CA 90036
Contemporary abstract art gallery and photography. Available for rent and sale with permission to use on tv film & print
art@wallspacela.com * www.wallspacela.com

wallspace contemporary abstract gallery
tel: 323 930 0471 wallspacela.com
607 Nth La Brea, Los Angeles, CA 90036

ZG04 DECOR   **(818) 853-8040**
Cleared Art, Paintings, Drawings, Photography

Art Glass, Hand Blown/Leaded Etc.

See: Glass & Mirrors, Art/Finishing/Etching/Etc.

Art, Artists For Hire

Art, Models & Props, Inc. **(951) 206-9156**
1725 Marengo Ave, Pasadena, CA, 91103
custom objets d'art of arbitrary complexity. See ad in "Prop Design & Manufacturing"
modelsandprops@msn.com * www.artmodeltech.com

Charisma Design Studio, Inc. **(818) 252-6611**
8414 San Fernando Road, Sun Valley, CA, 91352
custom metal/glass/wood/stone mixed media functional art
info@charismadesign.com * www.charismadesign.com

Clearedart.com/El Studio Granados **(818) 240-4421**
958 Verdugo Circle Dr, Glendale, CA, 91206
Commissions considered for original paintings, drawings, sculptures, installations, murals, maps, masks, and miniatures.
fineart@elstudiogranados.com * www.clearedart.com

Cope Studios: The Haven **(818) 913-7187**
926 Western Ave Ste A & B, Glendale, CA, 91201
Our studio ranges from creating high end realistic figurative sculpture and drawings to a vast range of painting styles.
figurativesculptor@hotmail.com * www.copestudios.com

Famous Frames **(310) 642-2721**
5839 Green Valley Circle, Ste 104, Culver City, CA, 90230
In NY call (212) 980-7979: Artist reps for storyboards, comps, illustrations & animatics

FILM ART LA **(323) 461-4900**
Culver City Warehouse at Jefferson & Hauser. Call for address.
Painted & Digital Commissions Art, Murals, Portraits. Cleared art rentals We clear and print famous artists and artwork.
filmartla@gmail.com * www.artimagela.com

HPR Graphics **(323) 556-2694**
5674 Venice Blvd, Los Angeles, CA, 90019
Graphic design, photo retouching, photo compositing, custom graphics, and more.
hprcan@earthlink.net * www.hprgraphics.net

Kathleen Swaydan **(626) 798-7637**
Fine reproductions & art historical research specializing in Italian Renaissance. Call for appt.

PropArt **(323) 461-5842**
6142 Rockcliff Dr, Los Angeles, CA, 90068
Script specific art, props & set dressing. Commissioned fine art paintings & sculpture, also student & character driven
wright-douglas@sbcglobal.net * www.douglaswrightfineart.com

Robert James Company **(415) 420-4011**
2110 West 20th St, Los Angeles, CA, 90018
Artist studio proficient in architectural and structural steel, mosaics, glass, and complicated logistics and timeframes
rob@robertjamesstudio.com * www.robertjamesstudio.com

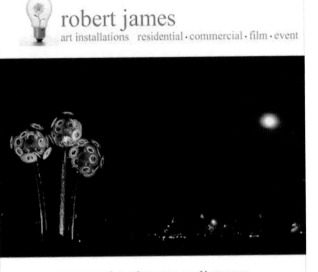

www.robertjamesstudio.com

Temporary Contemporary Art **(562) 900-6115**
7815 Gazette Ave, Winnetka, CA 91306
Custom Art, Script Specific Art, Curation/ Gallery Experience; MFA Degree; Mural Painting; Murals
temporarycontemporaryart@gmail.com * www.temporarycontemporaryart.com

Wallspace **(323) 930-0471**
607 N La Brea, Los Angeles, CA 90036
Contemporary abstract art gallery and photography. Available for rent and sale with permission to use on tv film & print
art@wallspacela.com * www.wallspacela.com

Art, On The Floor

See: Carpet & Flooring

search by
Keyword

Find it fast **DB** Debbies Book®

Art, Supplies & Stationery

See Also: Certificates* Desk Dressing* Easels* Hobby & Craft
Supplies* Pens, Fountain* Art & Picture Framing Services

Aaron Bros. (818) 243-7661
320 N. Glendale Ave, Glendale, CA, 91206

Blick Art Materials (323) 933-9284
7301 W. Beverly Blvd, Los Angeles, CA, 90036

Carter Sexton Fine Art Materials (818) 763-5050
5308 Laurel Canyon Blvd, N. Hollywood, CA, 91607
wide selection of artist supplies

Cheap Joe's (800) 227-2788
374 Industrial Park Dr, Boone, NC, 28607
Catalog: extensive selection of artist supplies

Continental Art Supplies (818) 345-1044
7041 Reseda Blvd, Reseda, CA, 91335
artist supplies & drafting materials

Francis-Orr Fine Stationery (310) 271-6106
320 N. Camden Dr, Beverly Hills, CA, 90210
huge sel. of fine papers: in-stock & custom, unique desk access. & gifts,
calligraphy services, no art supplies

LCW Props (818) 243-0707
Easels, School Art & Science Projects, Paperwork

Lee's Art Shop (212) 247-0110
220 West 57th Street, New York City, NY, 10019
paints & fine arts supplies

Michael's (818) 260-0527
1551 N Victory Pl, Burbank, CA, 91502

Mittel's Art Center (310) 399-9500
2499 Lincoln Boulevard, Venice, CA, 90291

New York Central Art Supply (212) 473-7705
62 3rd Ave, New York City, NY, 10003
primed/unprimed linen canvas, fine art supplies, handmade paper 100 years in
business

Sony Pictures Studios-Prop House (Off Lot) (310) 244-5999
Art & Craft supplies, artist paint box, artist drawing box, art set, canvas, clay,
paints, tracing light box, acorn, animal art

Sticker Planet (Original Farmers Market) (323) 939-6933
6333 W. 3rd Street, Los Angeles, CA, 90036
Creative, artistic stickers for decorating, crafting & collecting. Thousands of
stickers in many themes and sizes.
www.stickerplanetLA.com

Swain's (818) 243-3129
537 N Glendale Ave, Glendale, CA, 91206

Art, Tribal & Folk

See Also: Asian Antiques, Furniture, Art & Artifacts* Baskets*
Mexican Decorations

Badia Design, Inc. (818) 762-0130
5420 Vineland Ave, N. Hollywood, CA, 91601
Moroccan Decorations, Moroccan Art, traditional African art, Moroccan
ornaments
info@badiadesign.com * www.badiadesign.com

Clearedart.com/El Studio Granados (818) 240-4421
958 Verdugo Circle Dr, Glendale, CA, 91206
Cleared multi-media fine art; paintings, folk art carvings and sculptures, masks,
miniatures, and hero items.
fineart@elstudiogranados.com * www.clearedart.com

Dapper Cadaver/Creatures & Cultures (818) 771-0818
Tribal props & tribal decor. Tribal masks, Tiki masks & shrunken heads.

The Hand Prop Room LP. (323) 931-1534
masks, totems, figures, Native American

History For Hire, Inc. (818) 765-7767

Prop Services West (818) 503-2790

Sony Pictures Studios-Prop House (Off Lot) (310) 244-5999
masks & drums

Artificial Food

See: Food, Artificial Food

Artificial Plants & Trees

See: Flowers, Silk & Plastic* Greens

Arts & Crafts

See: Furniture, Arts & Crafts

Ash Trays

See: Decorative Accessories* Office Equipment & Dressing

Asian Antiques, Furniture, Art & Artifacts

See Also: Pottery* Shoji Screens

Castle Antiques & Design　　　　　　　　**(855) 765-5800**
11924 Vose St, N Hollywood, CA, 91605
Asian antiques and Asian furniture for rent and purchase.
info@castleantiques.net * www.castleprophouse.com

Design Mix Furniture　　　　　　　　　　**(323) 939-7500**
442 S La Brea Ave, Los Angeles, CA, 90036
Global imports of Indian, Indonesian, Chinese, African, Moroccan art, acc.,
antiques, reprod. & Industrial Furniture
www.mixfurniture.com

WWW.MIXFURNITURE.COM
442 SOUTH LABREA AVE. LA 90036

F. Suie One Company　　　　　　　　　　　**(626) 795-1335**
1335 E Colorado Blvd, Pasadena, CA, 91106
Open 11-5 Wed-Sat or by Appt. Our specialty
fsuieone@earthlink.net

Established 1888. Specializing in fine Asian
antiques and furniture for over 100 years.

Faux Library Studio Props, Inc.　　　　　**(818) 765-0096**

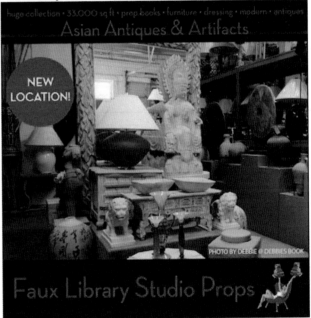

Asian Antiques & Artifacts

NEW LOCATION!

PHOTO BY DEBBIE @ DEBBIES BOOK

Faux Library Studio Props

The Hand Prop Room LP.　　　　　　　　　**(323) 931-1534**
History For Hire, Inc.　　　　　　　　　　**(818) 765-7767**
smalls, lots of Japanese
Hollywood Studio Gallery　　　　　　　　**(323) 462-1116**
panels, prints, paintings

**DISPLAY ADS AND LISTINGS FOR THIS CATEGORY
CONTINUE ON THE FOLLOWING PAGE**

J.F. Chen Antiques   **(323) 463-4603**
By Appt, Los Angeles, CA, 90038
antique & reproduction Continental, Asian and vintage furniture & accessories
Modern Props   **(323) 934-3000**
contemporary asian antiques, futuristic asian art, asian sculptures to asian prints
Ob-jects   **(818) 351-4200**
furniture, wall pieces, museum mounted
Omega/Cinema Props   **(323) 466-8201**
Samurai armor, asian portraits, persian rugs, asian themed furniture, asian trunks, and more.
Sony Pictures Studios-Prop House (Off Lot)   **(310) 244-5999**
Susanne Hollis, Inc.   **(626) 441-0346**
230 Pasadena Ave, South Pasadena, CA, 91030
20th - 17th century Antiques, Accessories, and Fine Art from around the world in our 19,000sqft. warehouse and showrooms
sales@susannehollis.com * www.susannehollis.com
Tara Design   **(310) 559-8272**
3223 S La Cienega Boulevard, Los Angeles, CA, 90016
Furniture and home decor importer from India, Indonesia, China, Morocco, Tibet and Turkey. Rental packages available
info@tara-design.com * www.tara-design.com

Tara DESIGN — Hand Crafted, Exotic & One of a Kind Pieces.

Universal Studios Property & Hardware Dept   **(818) 777-2784**
Antique asian carts, antique asian jars, antique asian trays and more.

Asian Themed Parties

See: Costume Rental Houses* Events, Decorations, Supplies & Services* Events, Design/Planning/Production* Travel (City/Country) Themed Events

Associations

See: Guilds, Unions, Societies, Associations

Astrological

The Hand Prop Room LP.   **(323) 931-1534**
crystal balls, charts
History For Hire, Inc.   **(818) 765-7767**
Modern Props   **(323) 934-3000**
crystal balls, globe statues, desk globes with maps spinning and solid mount, oversized ribbed globes

Athletic Equipment

See: Boxing, Wrestling, Mixed Martial Arts (MMA)* Exercise & Fitness Equipment* Sporting Goods & Services* Sportswear* Track & Field Equipment* Uniforms, Trades/Professional/Sports

Athletic Themed Parties

See: Events, Decorations, Supplies & Services* Events, Design/Planning/Production* Events, Entertainment* Sports & Games Themed Events

Atmospheric Effects

See: Expendables* Fog Machines* Snow, Artificial & Real* Special Effects, Equipment & Supplies

ATMs (Automated Teller Machines)

See: Bank Dressing

Audience Cutouts & Stand-Ups

Sony Pictures Studios-Prop House (Off Lot)   **(310) 244-5999**
actual present day people
Universal Studios Graphic Design & Sign Shop   **(818) 777-2350**
Standees
Universal Studios Property & Hardware Dept   **(818) 777-2784**
Audience cutouts for rent

Audience Response Systems

See: Game Show Electronics & Equipment

Audience Seating

See Also: Bleachers & Grandstand Seating* Folding Chairs/Tables* Stages, Portable & Steel Deck* Theater Seating
Bill Ferrell Co.   **(818) 767-1900**
10556 Keswick St, Sun Valley, CA, 91352
Stages, risers, steps, handrails, casters and ramps for audience seating and handicap lifts. Set construction.
www.billferrell.com
C. P. Valley   **(323) 466-8201**
Theatre seating and other various seating options; theater seating, stadium seating, auditorium seating
Mike Brown Grandstands   **(800) 266-2659**
2300 Pomona Blvd, Pomona, CA, 91768
chair to grandstand risers, audience seating
RC Vintage, Inc.   **(818) 765-7107**
stadium seats Baseball and Football and Soccer!
Sony Pictures Studios-Prop House (Off Lot)   **(310) 244-5999**
audience seats, theater seats
Universal Studios Property & Hardware Dept   **(818) 777-2784**
Various audience seating
Upstage Parallels   **(818) 247-1149**
4000 Chevy Chase Dr, Los Angeles, CA, 90039
www.upstagerentals.com

Audio Equipment

See Also: Control Boards* Editing Equipment & Services* Lighting & Sound, Concert/Theatrical/DJ/VJ* Microphones* Phonographs* Radio/TV Station* Recording Studio (Prop)* Stereo Equipment* Tape Recorders* Victrolas/Gramophones
Ametron Audio & Video   **(323) 464-1144**
1546 N. Argyle Ave, Hollywood, CA, 90028
Parking available in the back
Astro Audio Video Lighting, Inc.   **(818) 549-9915**
6615 San Fernando Rd, Glendale, CA, 91201
PA system small/large concert, DJ system, soundboards, mics
www.astroavl.com
Coast Recording Audio Props   **(818) 755-4692**
10715 Magnolia Blvd, N Hollywood, CA, 91601
Professional Audio Equipment, Radio Station, Recording Studio, DJ Setup. 1950s - Present. Audio equipment props, practical audio parts
props@coastrecording.com * www.coastrecordingprops.com
E.C. Prop Rentals   **(818) 764-2008**
speakers; lg/sm, indoor/outdoor, wall/pole mounts
EFX- Event Special Effects   **(626) 888-2239**
125 Railroad Ave, Monrovia, CA, 91016
PA- Stage- Concert- Sound
info@efxla.com * www.efxla.com
The Hand Prop Room LP.   **(323) 931-1534**
History For Hire, Inc.   **(818) 765-7767**
microphones, mixers, etc., very complete
LCW Props   **(818) 243-0707**
DJ, Mixing Boards, Headphones, Stage Lighting, On Air, Recording Studio, Microphones, Reel To Reel
Modern Props   **(323) 934-3000**
contemporary audio equipment, futuristic audio equipment, home audio equipment & commercial audio equipment

RJR Props (404) 349-7600
Audio mixers, microphones, and more audio props for rent.
Sony Pictures Studios-Prop House (Off Lot) (310) 244-5999
radios, mics, microphone, mic stand, speakers, tape recorder player, walkie talkie, walkman, turntables
Warner Bros. Studios Production Sound & (818) 954-2511
Video
4000 Warner Blvd, Burbank, CA, 91522
A/V Equipment Rental, Design, Presentations, Install & Support; Visual Display Creation; Communication.
wbsfproductionsound@warnerbros.com * www.wbsoundandvideo.com
Woody's Electrical Props (818) 503-1940
period to futuristic consoles, panels & electrical equipment

Audio/Visual Film Equipment

See Also: Audio Equipment* Motion Picture Projectors* Themed Environment Construction* Video Camera Equipment & Services
Astro Audio Video Lighting, Inc. (818) 549-9915
6615 San Fernando Rd, Glendale, CA, 91201
We can design & install integrated, intelligent AVL systems
www.astroavl.com
Edwards Technologies, Inc. (310) 536-7070
139 Maryland St, El Segundo, CA, 90245
designs multisensory media & technology systems, for themed environments
Electrosonic, Inc (818) 333-3600
3320 N. San Fernando Blvd, Burbank, CA, 91504
Design, mfg & install specialized systems; projection, audio, interactives, show control & event scheduling
Harkness Hall (540) 370-1590
10 Harkness Blvd, Fredericksburg, VA, 22401
Design & mfg. custom front & rear projection screen systems, for indoor/outdoor themed environments
LCW Props (818) 243-0707
Plasma, LCD, Monitors, Stage Lighting, AV Server Racks, Media Centers, Consoles, Presentation, Projectors & Screens
Mad Systems, Inc. (714) 259-9000
733 N Main St, Orange, CA, 92868
Specialize in innovative multimedia solutions, interactives, & exhibits, systems design & integration
Personal Creations, Inc. (310) 391-8300
12336 Marshall St Studio Ste 1A, Culver City, CA, 90230
design/produce large scale multi-media shows; lighting, slide/digital projection, show control
RJR Props (404) 349-7600
Video mixers, studio monitors and more audio/visual equipment for rent.
TechnoMedia Solutions (407) 351-0909
4545 36th St, Orlando, FL, 32811
media-based concept, production & development, NY office: (212) 452-1100
Thorburn Associates, Inc. (818) 569-0234
1317 N San Fernando Blvd #212, Burbank, CA, 91504
Acoustics, audio visual, themed entertainment, presentation lighting, & technology systems design

Automata

See: Robots

Automobiles

See: Police Car, Police Motorcycle* RV Vehicles & Travel Trailers, Equip & Parts* Vehicle Preparation Services* Vehicles

Automotive/Garage Equip. & Parts

See Also: Chain Hoists* Emissions Analyzers* Gas Pumps/Islands, Gas Station* License Plates* Ramps, Automobile* RV Vehicles & Travel Trailers, Equip & Parts* Tires* Tools
AIR Designs (818) 768-6639
Nascar, gas station, junk & wrecking yard, chop shop, diagnostic, mechanic, home, racing, period & modern.
Alley Cats Studio Rentals (818) 982-9178
gas station/garage/mechanic dressing, motorcycle parts
C. P. Valley (323) 466-8201
Autopart shelves, auto mechanic tool chests, automobile creepers, engine repair stands, engine hoists and much more.

E.C. Prop Rentals (818) 764-2008
commercial & residential, diagnostic equip., tool boxes/chests

E.C. PROP RENTALS
11846 SHERMAN WAY NORTH HOLLYWOOD CA 91605
818-764-2008

The Hand Prop Room LP. (323) 931-1534
History For Hire, Inc. (818) 765-7767
period
LCW Props (818) 243-0707
Tools, Shelving, Hoses, Presses, Cleared Paint Cans
Sony Pictures Studios-Prop House (Off Lot) (310) 244-5999
car battery charger, car alarm control, automotive parts, bike parts, buckets, pales, car club, air compressors, more

Autopsy Equipment

See: Morgue

Awards

See: Calligraphy* Certificates* Engraving* Prop Houses* Trophies/Trophy Cases

Awnings

See Also: Canopies, Tents, Gazebos, Cabanas* Canvas* Sewing Services, Industrial* Window Treatments
American Awning (323) 222-7500
1901 N San Fernando Rd, Los Angeles, CA 90065
Canvas Specialty (323) 722-1156
PO Box 22268, Los Angeles, CA 90022-0268
LCW Props (818) 243-0707
store awnings
Sarris Interiors & Marine (562) 531-8612
8225 Alondra Blvd, Paramount, CA, 90723
mfg. & fabrication, will ship anywhere, for semi trailers, dressing room trailers, household
Warner Bros. Drapery, Upholstery & Flooring (818) 954-1831
4000 Warner Blvd, Burbank, CA, 91522
Soft pipe awnings with & without wings: custom manufacturing; many colors & fabrics
wbsfdrapery@warnerbros.com * www.wbdrapery.com

Baby Doubles, Realistic Babies

See: Puppets, Marionettes, Automata, Animatronics

Baby Items

See: Children's & Baby Clothing* Children/Baby Accessories & Bedroom

Back Packs

See: Camping Equipment* Prop Houses* Sporting Goods & Services

Backdrops

See: Backings Scenery/Set Construction*

Backings

See Also: Events, Backings & Scenery Graphics, Digital & Large Format Printing* Scenery/Set Rentals*

AAA Flag & Banner Mfg Co　(310) 836-3341
8937 National Blvd, Los Angeles, Los Angeles, CA 90034
Large Format Printing - Backdrops, Step & Repeat Press Walls, Prop Signage, Vehicle Wraps, Custom Graphics Solutions.
fred@aaaflag.com * www.aaaflag.com

Apollo Design Technology　(260) 497-9191
4130 Fourier Dr, Ft. Wayne, IN, 46818
Gobos, largest mfg. of custom glass & steel patterns; plus accessories, adhesives, filters & motion effects

iWeiss Theatrical Solutions　(888) 325-7192
815 Fairview Ave #10, Fairview, NJ 07022
digitally printed day & night drops

Modern Props　(323) 934-3000
carnival backings, amusement drops, many colored block-glass divider walls, wood dividers

Schmidli Backdrops LA　(323) 938-2098
5830 W Adams Blvd, Culver City, CA, 90232
High end texture & scenic backdrops for Film/TV & photography. Full installation service & custom paintings.
backdrops@schmidli.com * www.schmidli.com

Julianne Moore　Photo: Peter Lindberg

Schmidli Backdrops NY　(800) 724-0171
601 West 26th St, 10th floor, New York, NY, 10001
High end texture & scenic backdrops for Film/TV & photography. Full installation service & custom paintings.
backdrops@schmidli.com * www.schmidli.com

Studio Dynamics　(800) 595-4273
7703 Alondra Blvd, Paramount, CA, 90723
canvas & muslin, textures, chromakey, scenic, custom motorized lifts

UV/FX Scenic Productions　(310) 821-2657
171 Pier Ave Suite 355, Santa Monica, CA, 90405
leader in day to night, dual image, completely invisible, & 3D scenic effects & scenery

Warner Bros. Design Studio Scenic Art & Sign Shop　(818) 954-1815
4000 Warner Blvd, Burbank, CA, 91522
hand-painted art to grand-format digital printing for backings, billboards, murals and portraits
wbsigns@warnerbros.com * www.wbsignandscenic.com

Backlots/Standing Sets

See: Locations, Insert Stages & Small Theatres

Badges, Patches & Buttons

See Also: Engraving Memorabilia & Novelties* Name Plates* Promotional Items & Materials*

The Earl Hays Press　(818) 765-0700
services the Industry only. name pins to engraving

G-Man Emblem　(727) 862-7419
11832 Aranda Ct, Hudson, FL 34667
Embroidered patches, lapel pins, challenge coins, direct garment embroidery & silk screening for law enforcement, milita

The Hand Prop Room LP.　(323) 931-1534
U.S., custom, foreign, federal, police, fire, name pins

History For Hire, Inc.　(818) 765-7767
Police, paramedic, security guard, props

Hollywood Studio Gallery　(323) 462-1116
framed patches only

Pasadena Antique Warehouse　(626) 404-2422
1609 East Washington Blvd., Pasadena, CA, 91104
Russian, German, and American military and security badges, patches, and medals.
pasadenaantiquewarehouse@gmail.com *
www.pasadenaantiquewarehouse.com

RHS Enterprises　(714) 840-4388
P.O. Box 5779, Garden Grove, CA, 92846-0779
Police & Federal law enforcement badges, patches, credentials, history, consulting, books. We answer Federal questions
rhsenterprises@earthlink.net * www.raymondsherrard.com

Sony Pictures Studios-Prop House (Off Lot)　(310) 244-5999
Federal Badges, Fire Department Badges, Security Badges, Sheriff Badges, Marshall Badges, dog tags, employee IDs and more

Sony Pictures Studios-Wardrobe　(310) 244-5995
alterations, call (310) 244-7260

Sword & Stone　(818) 562-6548

Universal Studios Property & Hardware Dept　(818) 777-2784
Various badges, patches and buttons.

Western Costume Co.　(818) 760-0900

Badminton Equipment

See: Prop Houses Sporting Goods & Services*

Bag Lady Carts

E.C. Prop Rentals　(818) 764-2008
shopping carts only

The Hand Prop Room LP.　(323) 931-1534
fully outfitted

LCW Props　(818) 243-0707
Carts, Recyclables, Dressed, Large Quantity

Universal Studios Property & Hardware Dept　(818) 777-2784
Shopping carts, commercial shopping carts, and grocery shopping carts.

Bags & Sacks

See: Boxes Expendables* Packing/Packaging Supplies, Services* Promotional Items & Materials* Shopping Bags (Silent)*

Bakery

See Also: Delicatessen Equipment Display Cases, Racks & Fixtures (Store)* Food, Artificial Food*

AIR Designs　(818) 768-6639
Glass cases, racks, ovens, pie cases, trays, counters, signage, display items, faux food & more.

C. P. Valley　(323) 466-8201
Residential bakery items including a bread makers; bread display cases, bakery racks, bread racks and more.

The Hand Prop Room LP.　(323) 931-1534
fake cakes, breads, rolls, rolling pins

LCW Props　(818) 243-0707
Racks, Misc. Equipment, Display Cabinets

Lennie Marvin Enterprises, Inc. (Prop Heaven)　(818) 841-5882
rolling racks, glass cases, fake cakes/bread, pastry

Modern Props　(323) 934-3000
stainless steel racks, display shelves and display cases,

Sony Pictures Studios-Prop House (Off Lot)　(310) 244-5999

Balance Beam

See: Gymnasium & Gymnastic Equipment

Ball Park Concessions

See: Carnival Dressing/Supplies

Ballet Barres & Dance Mirrors

See Also: Dance Floors

C. P. Valley　(323) 466-8201
Ballet barres, metal ballet bars, wooden ballet barres, adjustable ballet bars, wall mounted ballet bars, and more.

Dance Equipment International　(800) 626-9258
2103 Lincoln Ave, Ste C, San Jose, CA, 95125
glassless mirrors, adjustable portable/wallmount barres

E.C. Prop Rentals　(818) 764-2008
free standing dance castered mirrors

Balloon (Hot Air) Gondolas

See Also: Aircraft, Charters & Aerial Services
History For Hire, Inc. (818) 765-7767
wicker

Balloons & Balloon Sculptures

See Also: Inflatables, Custom
Aah-Inspiring Balloons (562) 494-7605
Call for an Appointment.
After 14 years in the TV and Film Industry, Aah-Inspiring Balloon Decor has been seen in over 200 TV shows and Films.
aahinspiring1@aol.com * www.aahinspiringballoons.com

Amazing Balloons By Gee (310) 676-1524
4516 W. Broadway Ave, Hawthorne, CA 90250
Since 1994, Arches, bouquets, columns, drops and theme decor for the "right look".
claudiagee@socal.rr.com * www.amazingballoonsbygee.com

Balloon Haven (888) 591-8449
Call for appointment.
26 year balloon pros, diverse, timely & professional. Rush service, on location. Helium rentals.
www.balloonhaven.com

Bill Ferrell Co. (818) 767-1900
10556 Keswick St, Sun Valley, CA, 91352
Balloon drops for conventions and special events.
www.billferrell.com
L. A. Party Works (888) 527-2789
9712 Alpaca St, S El Monte, CA, 91733
in Vancouver tel. 604-589-4101
partyworks@aol.com * www.partyworksusa.com

Bamboo

See: Greens* Tikis & Tropical Dressing

Bank Dressing

See Also: Metal Detectors* Money (Prop)* Security Walk-Through & Baggage Alarms* Surveillance Equipment

Advanced Liquidators Office Furniture　　　**(818) 763-3470**
Bank dressing including bank teller stations, bank deposit stations, and lighting.

AIR Designs　　　**(818) 768-6639**
Exterior ATM Machines, Signage, Stanchions

Alley Cats Studio Rentals　　　**(818) 982-9178**
ATM machines

ATM Cash Connect/Financial Product, Inc.　　　**(818) 848-1025**
624 S San Fernando Blvd, Burbank, CA, 91502
ATMs: all models, full function, custom paint/enclosures/screens manipulate cash dispensing, other bank machines
www.financialproductinc.com

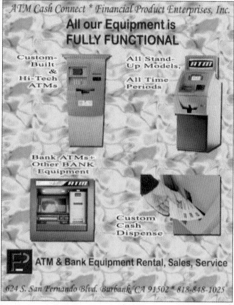

C. P. Valley　　　**(323) 466-8201**
Bank teller counters, bank dressing, bank counters, bank name plates, mortgage rate chart, floor displays and more.

The Earl Hays Press　　　**(818) 765-0700**
services the Industry only. interior graphics & signage

History For Hire, Inc.　　　**(818) 765-7767**
safe deposit boxes, tables etc.

Hollywood Studio Gallery　　　**(323) 462-1116**
signage only

LCW Props　　　**(818) 243-0707**
ATM's, Bank Printer, Card Sliders, Money Counters, Check Encoders, Fake Money / Coins

6439 San Fernando Rd. Glendale, CA 91201
Phone: 818-243-0707 - www.lcwprops.com

Modern Props　　　**(323) 934-3000**
ATMs, bank counters, bank stanchions, bank kiosks

RJR Props　　　**(404) 349-7600**
Bank dressing/bank props including teller terminals, money counters, cash drawers, check scanners and more for rent.

Universal Studios Property & Hardware Dept　　　**(818) 777-2784**
Bank dressing from banker's lamps, banker signs, bundled money and more.

Banners

See: Flags/Banners* Sign Painters* Signs

Banquets/Booths (Seating)

AIR Designs　　　**(818) 768-6639**
Restaurant, Diner, Bar, Cafeteria, Fast Food, Booths & Modular Seating

C. P. Two　　　**(323) 466-8201**
Various restaurant booths, restaurant settees, cafe tables, porcelain coffee cups, table tops, formica tables & more.

FormDecor, Inc.　　　**(310) 558-2582**
America's largest event rental supplier of 20th Century furniture and accessories for Modern and Mid-Century styles.

Lux Lounge EFR　　　**(888) 247-4411**
106 1/2 Judge John Aiso St #318, Los Angeles, CA, 90012
Banquet Seating: Curved Banquettes, High Back Banquette, Straight Banquette
info@luxloungeefr.com * www.luxloungeefr.com

RC Vintage, Inc.　　　**(818) 765-7107**
diner restaurant booths Tables ...Chairs etc

Universal Studios Property & Hardware Dept　　　**(818) 777-2784**
Banquettes and restaurant booths.

Bar Stools

See: Bars, Nightclubs, Barware & Dressing* Chairs* Stools

Barbecues

Alley Cats Studio Rentals　　　**(818) 982-9178**
large & small, gas grills vintage to contemporary, grill smokers

C. P. Two　　　**(323) 466-8201**
Charcoal barbecues, gas barbecues, personal barbecues, barrel barbecues, barbecue accessories, portable barbecues

The Hand Prop Room LP.　　　**(323) 931-1534**
Weber, large, charcoal, gas, stainless steel, open pit, barbecue utensils

History For Hire, Inc.　　　**(818) 765-7767**
Weber, 55-gallon drum style

RC Vintage, Inc.　　　**(818) 765-7107**
BBQ's, barbecue carts, bbq pig sign

Sony Pictures Studios-Prop House (Off Lot)　　　**(310) 244-5999**
BBQs, barbeques, barbeque tools, barbecue tools

Universal Studios Property & Hardware Dept　　　**(818) 777-2784**
Barbecue tools, hibachi barbecues and barbecues including a 55-gallon one.

Barbells

See: Exercise & Fitness Equipment* Weightlifting Equipment

Barber Shop

See Also: Beauty Salon* Make-up & Hair, Supplies & Services* Salon & Spa Equipment* Shaving, Old Fashion, Non-Electric

C. P. Valley (323) 466-8201
Barber shop signs, barber shop chairs, period barber chairs to contemporary barber chairs, salon chairs and more.

The Hand Prop Room LP. (323) 931-1534
barber shop dressing

History For Hire, Inc. (818) 765-7767
chairs, signs, products, accessories

Lennie Marvin Enterprises, Inc. (Prop Heaven) (818) 841-5882
chairs,poles,coat racks,towels,steamers,signage,period-modern

RC Vintage, Inc. (818) 765-7107
40s-60s, poles to chairs, general supplies & products Full Barber Shop

Sony Pictures Studios-Prop House (Off Lot) (310) 244-5999
barber cloth, salon brush, salon comb, salon clippers, salon comb jar, salon equipment holder, finer soaker, manicure set

Universal Studios Property & Hardware Dept (818) 777-2784
Barber shop dressing; barber shop chairs, barber shop aprons, barber shop accessories, barber shop poles & more.

Barns

See: Western Americana

Barrels & Drums, Wood/Metal/Plastic

See Also: Crates/ Vaults* Oil Cans & Drums* Wine Kegs

Absolute Packaging (800) 567-9190
11940 Sherman Road, N. Hollywood, CA 91605
www.absolutepackagingsupply.com

AIR Designs (818) 768-6639
5-55 Gallon Drums, Wine Barrels & Racks, Plastic Drums

Alley Cats Studio Rentals (818) 982-9178
many sizes and styles & drums, also cardboard

C. P. Valley (323) 466-8201
Hollywood's largest selection! All shapes, all sizes, all types.

E.C. Prop Rentals (818) 764-2008
multiples of sizes & styles

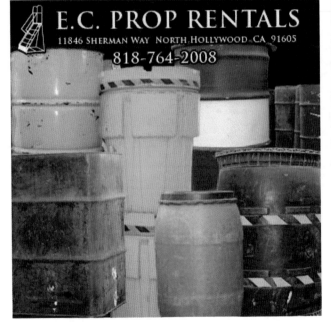

Evans Family Barrels (818) 523-8174
7918 Fairchild Ave, Canoga Park, CA, 91306
59 gal oak wine barrels and 55 gal oak whiskey barrels, whole and half sizes, and products made from barrels
evansbarrels@gmail.com * www.EvansFamilyBarrels.com

The Hand Prop Room LP. (323) 931-1534
wood, metal

History For Hire, Inc. (818) 765-7767

LCW Props (818) 243-0707
Wood, Metal, Plastic, Colored. Large Quantities

Sony Pictures Studios-Prop House (Off Lot) (310) 244-5999

Universal Studios Property & Hardware Dept (818) 777-2784
All kinds of barrels; whiskey barrels, wine barrels, wooden barrels, metal barrels, cask barrels and more.

Barricades

See Also: Crowd Control: Barricades, Turnstiles Etc.* Fences* Stanchions & Rope* Traffic/Road Signs, Lights, Safety Items

AIR Designs (818) 768-6639
Police barricades, Construction, Cones, Bollards, Parking Blocks, Cafe Railing, Pedestrian

Alley Cats Studio Rentals (818) 982-9178
wood, plastic w/flashing lights, guard gate arm, short metal stand up barricade units, Stand up chain link fences.

Castex Rentals (323) 462-1468
1044 N. Cole Ave, Hollywood, CA, 90038
traffic signs, cones, barricades, stanchions, caution tape, aisle dividers
service@castexrentals.com * www.castexrentals.com

E.C. Prop Rentals (818) 764-2008
construction, crowd control, police, traffic, military checkpoint

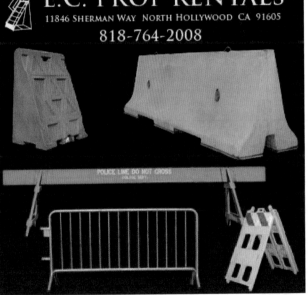

The Hand Prop Room LP. (323) 931-1534
police, parade, road cones, construction, working signs

History For Hire, Inc. (818) 765-7767
old style wood

LCW Props (818) 243-0707
Police, Crowd Control, Concert

Statewide Traffic Safety & Sign (714) 468-1919
13261 Garden Grove Blvd, Garden Grove, CA, 92840
signage, barricades, equipment, traffic control personnel many credits

**DISPLAY ADS AND LISTINGS FOR THIS CATEGORY
CONTINUE ON THE FOLLOWING PAGE**

Sterndahl Enterprises, Inc. (818) 834-8199
11861 Branford St, Sun Valley, CA, 91352
traffic control equipment, signage, barricades, striping, trucks & bobcats
www.sterndahl.com

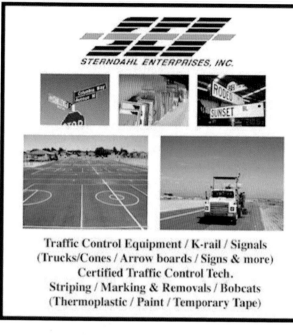

Traffic Control Equipment / K-rail / Signals
(Trucks/Cones / Arrow boards / Signs & more)
Certified Traffic Control Tech.
Striping / Marking & Removals / Bobcats
(Thermoplastic / Paint / Temporary Tape)

Universal Studios Property & Hardware Dept (818) 777-2784
many barricades; traffic barricades, road barricades, street barricades, &
orange cones of various styles and sizes.

Bars, Nightclubs, Barware & Dressing

See Also: Banquets/Booths (Seating)* Beer Equipment, Taps &
Coolers* Chairs* Dance Floors* Darts & Dartboards* Irish, All Things
Irish* Liquor Bottles* Pool/Billiard Tables & Accessories* Pub Signs*
Sports Bar Dressing* Tables

AIR Designs (818) 768-6639
Neon, Bar Smalls, Bottles, Taps, Bars (Front & Back), Tables, Chairs, Stools,
Glassware, Complete Set Ups

Astro Audio Video Lighting, Inc. (818) 549-9915
6615 San Fernando Rd, Glendale, CA, 91201
Nightclub lighting, nightclub sound systems, and nightclub video for rent or
purchase.
www.astroavl.com

C. P. Two (323) 466-8201
Bar dressing, portable bars, commercial bars, modular bar setup, bar stools,
bar chairs, saloon to contemporary

The Hand Prop Room LP. (323) 931-1534
signs, bottles, glasses, labels

History For Hire, Inc. (818) 765-7767
bottles, glasses, cash registers

LCW Props (818) 243-0707
Seating, Bars, Glassware, Taps, Neons, Sporting Memorabilia, Display Cases

Lennie Marvin Enterprises, Inc. (Prop Heaven) (818) 841-5882
complete

LM Treasures (626) 252-7354
10557 Juniper Ave Unit A, Fontana, CA 92337
Car inspired Sofas, Clocks, shelves, & Bars all allow for more uniqueness &
personality in any type of restaurant.
lmtreasures.ll@gmail.com * www.lifesizestatues.net

Lux Lounge EFR (888) 247-4411
106 1/2 Judge John Aiso St #318, Los Angeles, CA, 90012
Event Bar Rentals: Tufted Bars, Illuminated Bars, Circle Bar
info@luxloungeefr.com * www.luxloungeefr.com

Modern Props (323) 934-3000
contemporary bar dressing, futuristic bar dressing, bar glassware, bar lighting,
bar seating

RC Vintage, Inc. (818) 765-7107
40s, 50s & 60s large selection, high tables Stools and Many Bar Counter
tops....Many Bar Lamps

Sony Pictures Studios-Prop House (Off Lot) (310) 244-5999
bar organizer, beer taps, bottle openers, bottle trays, liquor caddy, bar tables,
equipment, glassware, dishes and more

Universal Studios Property & Hardware Dept (818) 777-2784
Bar dressing including; bar stools, bar lighting, bar glasses, and more.

Baseball Equipment

See: Baseball Pitching Machine* Scoreboards & Scoring Systems*
Sporting Goods & Services* Sports/Athletic Field Lining/Graphics

Baseball Pitching Machine

The Hand Prop Room LP. (323) 931-1534
baseballs, pitching machine, vintage pitching machine, softballs

L. A. Party Works (888) 527-2789
9712 Alpaca St, S El Monte, CA, 91733
Variety of different baseball pitching machines available, direct
source.%u200B
partyworks@aol.com * www.partyworksusa.com

Basketball Court & Backboards

See Also: Carpet & Flooring* Sporting Goods & Services

Alley Cats Studio Rentals (818) 982-9178
outdoor rim, chain & cloth net, metal backboard, fixed park basketball rims and
stand up home basketball hoops

The Hand Prop Room LP. (323) 931-1534
wall-mounted, portable

L. A. Party Works (888) 527-2789
9712 Alpaca St, S El Monte, CA, 91733
Portable basketball courts/basketball flooring and basketball baskets. Panel system flooring
partyworks@aol.com * www.partyworksusa.com

FULL & HALF COURT FLOORING / BRANDING / PRO GOALS / SHOT CLOCKS / BALL RACKS

PARTYWORKS
I N T E R A C T I V E

Universal Studios Property & Hardware Dept (818) 777-2784
Basketball backboards; garage mounted basketball backboards, portable basketball backboards and freestanding basketball backboards

Baskets

C. P. Valley (323) 466-8201
Baskets: American Indian baskets, fishing baskets and much more.
The Hand Prop Room LP. (323) 931-1534
History For Hire, Inc. (818) 765-7767
many types
Prop Services West (818) 503-2790
Sony Pictures Studios-Prop House (Off Lot) (310) 244-5999
large selection
Universal Studios Property & Hardware Dept (818) 777-2784
All kinds of baskets; woven baskets, decorative baskets, picnic baskets, bread baskets, laundry baskets and more.

Bath Tubs

See: Bathroom Fixtures* Plumbing Fixtures, Heating/Cooling Appliances* Prop Houses

Bathing Suits, Swim & Beach Wear

The Costume House (818) 508-9933
20s to 60s, M/W/children
Sony Pictures Studios-Wardrobe (310) 244-5995
alterations, call (310) 244-7260
TYR Sport, Inc. (714) 897-0799
15391 Springdale St, Huntington Beach, CA, 92649
product placement: M/W/ children's swimwear, multi-sport / triathlon apparel, contact PR Dept.
www.tyr.com
Universal Studios Costume Dept (818) 777-2722
Rental, mfg., & alterations
Warner Bros. Studios Costume Dept (818) 954-1297
One-Piece, Two-Piece, Bikini, Mallet, Tankini, Halter, Bandeau, Caftans, Cover-Ups, Shorts, Hats

Bathroom Decorations

C. P. Two (323) 466-8201
Soap dishes, towel rings, toilet paper holders, bathroom sinks, bathroom storage baskets, wall mounted cabinets and more.
History For Hire, Inc. (818) 765-7767
everything but the plumbing

Modern Props (323) 934-3000
contemporary bathroom decorations, futuristic bathroom decorations, hardware & accessories, bathroom sinks, bathtubs
NEST Studio Rentals, Inc. (818) 942-0339
small furnishings, decorative accessories, linen
Ob-jects (818) 351-4200
furniture
Prop Services West (818) 503-2790
Sony Pictures Studios-Prop House (Off Lot) (310) 244-5999
aftershave, cologne, bath set, shower brush, shower loofah, combs, commode, cosmetics, toothbrushes, makeup brushes
Universal Studios Property & Hardware Dept (818) 777-2784
Bathroom dressing, bathroom fixtures, bathroom toiletries, bathroom vanity, bathroom scales and more.

Bathroom Fixtures

See Also: Plumbing Fixtures, Heating/Cooling Appliances* Prop Houses* Sinks
E.C. Prop Rentals (818) 764-2008
hand dryers, soap dispenser, towel dispenser, mirrors, signage
Eric's Architectural Salvage, Wells Antique Tile (213) 413-6800
2110 W Sunset Blvd, Los Angeles, CA, 90026
The new Architectural Salvage store in Los Angeles that you haven't been to yet.
ericstiques@aol.com * www.ericsarchitecturalsalvage.com
LCW Props (818) 243-0707
Stalls, Sinks, Toilets, Lighting
Omega/Cinema Props (323) 466-8201
Bathroom light fixtures: Urinals, bathroom sinks, bathroom counters, public paper towel dispensers, hand dryers & more.
RC Vintage, Inc. (818) 765-7107
40s, 50s & 60s, sconces, outlet lights, sink units and more
Sony Pictures Studios-Fixtures (310) 244-5996
5933 W Slauson Ave, Culver City, CA, 90230
period to present day, fixtures, hardware, cloth towel dispenser, condom dispenser, commercial hand dryer
www.sonypicturesstudios.com
Sony Pictures Studios-Prop House (Off Lot) (310) 244-5999
Restroom grab bars, hand dryers, liquid soap dispensers, liquid dispensers, paper towel dispenser, toilet seat cover dispenser

Batteries & Battery Chargers

See: Automotive/Garage Equip. & Parts* Electrical/Electronic Supplies & Services* Expendables

Beach Props

See Also: Sporting Goods & Services* Surfboard, Wakeboard* Volleyball Setup
Bob Gail Special Events (310) 202-5200
Who says you can't go to the beach year round? With an array of beach props and surfboards, it can be summer all year!
E.C. Prop Rentals (818) 764-2008
set of volleyball poles, signage, trash cans, bike racks
The Hand Prop Room LP. (323) 931-1534
beach, nautical props, cruiser bikes, kayaks
History For Hire, Inc. (818) 765-7767
umbrellas, cabanas, folding chairs etc.
LCW Props (818) 243-0707
Chairs, Umbrellas, Surf Boards, BBQ's, Kayaks, Towables
Sony Pictures Studios-Prop House (Off Lot) (310) 244-5999
Universal Studios Property & Hardware Dept (818) 777-2784
Beach props, beach chairs, beach umbrellas, beach towels, beach lounge chairs, Polynesian torches and more.

Beach Theme Events

See: Events, Backings & Scenery* Events, Decorations, Supplies & Services* Events, Design/Planning/Production* Events, Entertainment

Beaded Curtains

See: Events, Backings & Scenery* Theatrical Draperies, Hardware & Rigging

Beads & Beading

See: Costume/Wardrobe/Sewing Supplies* Embroidery, Screen Printing, Etc.* Jewelry, Costume* Jewelry, Fine/Reproduction

Bean Bag Chairs

See: Bedroom Furniture & Decorations* Futons & Bean Bag Chairs

Beatles Musical Instruments

History For Hire, Inc. (818) 765-7767
exactly right!

Beauty & Grooming Supplies

See: Make-up & Hair, Supplies & Services* Shaving, Old Fashion, Non-Electric

Beauty Salon

See Also: Barber Shop* Make-up & Hair, Supplies & Services* Salon & Spa Equipment

C. P. Valley (323) 466-8201
Salon chairs, salon shampoo sinks, salon cabinets, manicures table, beauty salon stools

Galaxy Enterprises, Inc. (323) 728-3980
5411 Sheila St, Los Angeles, CA, 90040
Mfg. of complete line of beauty & barber salon equipment. stylish, modern, wide variety, antique items too!
sales@galaxymfg.com * www.galaxymfg.com

History For Hire, Inc. (818) 765-7767
lots. period products too.

RC Vintage, Inc. (818) 765-7107
period hair dryers and chairs, 40s-60s supplies/products, more

Sony Pictures Studios-Prop House (Off Lot) (310) 244-5999
furniture, dressing, supplies

Universal Studios Property & Hardware Dept (818) 777-2784
Beauty shop chairs, hair cutting accessories, blow driers, curling irons, cosmetics, and more.

Bedding

See: Linens, Household

Bedroom Furniture & Decorations

See Also: Children/Baby Accessories & Bedroom* Prop Houses

Antiquarian Traders (310) 247-3900
4851 S. Alameda Street, Los Angeles, CA 90048
Variety of American Victorian, European, French, Art Deco, Art Nouveau bedroom suites, King, Queen and Full sizes
antiques@antiquariantraders.com * www.antiquariantraders.com

Blueprint Furniture (310) 657-4315
8600 Pico Blvd. Los Angeles, CA 90035
Modern furniture lighting accessories early classic bauhaus mid-century contemporary design. Good studio rental history.
www.blueprintfurniture.com

Bridge Furniture & Props Los Angeles (818) 433-7100
We carry modern & traditional furniture, lighting, accessories, cleared art,& rugs. Items are online for easy shopping.

Castle Antiques & Design (855) 765-5800
11924 Vose St, N Hollywood, CA, 91605
beds, clocks, candelabras, head boards, bookcases, mirrors, side tables, end tables, credenzas, chests, dressing screens
info@castleantiques.net * www.castleprophouse.com

LCW Props (818) 243-0707
Armoires, Head Boards, Dressers, Tables, Chairs, Lighting

Little Bohemia Rentals (818) 853-7506
11940 Sherman Rd, N Hollywood, CA, 91605
headboards, dressers, nightstands, vanities, benches, shelving
sales@wearelittlebohemia.com * www.wearelittlebohemia.com

Modern Props (323) 934-3000
contemporary bedroom, futuristic bedroom furniture, bedroom accessories & beds, end tables, many head boards

NEST Studio Rentals, Inc. (818) 942-0339
contemporary, queen sets, juvenile

Ob-jects (818) 351-4200
Biedermeier, vanity mirrors, chaises, daybeds, chest of drawers, bedroom cabinets

Omega/Cinema Props (323) 466-8201
Bedroom dressers, bedroom mirrors, cheval mirrors, furniture & accessories, contemporary to period.

P. J.s Sleep Company Inc. (323) 782-9767
415 N Fairfax Ave, Los Angeles, CA, 90036
mattresses, bedroom furniture, a unique bedroom store for less

Prop Services West (818) 503-2790

Rapport International Furniture (323) 930-1500
435 N La Brea Ave, Los Angeles, CA, 90036
Over 60 bedroom sets to choose from! We carry designer contemporary and modern furniture.
rapport@rapportusa.com * www.rapportfurniture.com

Sony Pictures Studios-Prop House (Off Lot) (310) 244-5999
clothes brush, coat hangers, headrest, jewelry holder, shoe dryer, tie rack, bed warmers

Susanne Hollis, Inc. (626) 441-0346
230 Pasadena Ave, South Pasadena, CA, 91030
20th - 17th century Antiques, Accessories, and Fine Art from around the world in our 19,000sqft. warehouse and showrooms
sales@susannehollis.com * www.susannehollis.com

Universal Studios Property & Hardware Dept (818) 777-2784
Bedroom furniture; dressers, nightstands, wardrobe cabinets, chest of drawers, bedroom lamps & more.

ZG04 DECOR (818) 853-8040
Beds, Dressers, Bed frames, Headboards, Highboys, Nightstands, Upholstered Headboards, Vanitys, Mattresses

Beds

See: Bedroom Furniture & Decorations* Children/Baby Accessories & Bedroom

Beer Equipment, Taps & Coolers

See Also: Bars, Nightclubs, Barware & Dressing

AIR Designs (818) 768-6639
Beer Taps, Towers, Coolers, Kegs, CO2 Canisters, Glassware & More

C. P. Two (323) 466-8201
Beer glasses, taps, coolers, pitchers, cleared beer taps, beer kegs, corked kegs, wooden kegs, metal beer kegs and more.

California Beverage (818) 997-3831
PO Box 44366, Panorama City, CA, 91412-0366
beer - soda, practical - prop; I make it work for you, since 1971
bruhozer@yahoo.com * www.californiabev.com

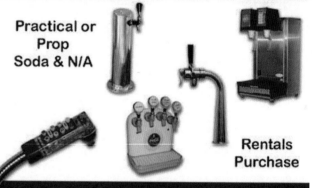

The Hand Prop Room LP. (323) 931-1534
kegs, coolers, beer taps, beer much, beer signs, beer neon signs

History For Hire, Inc. (818) 765-7767
huge supply of vintage cans

LCW Props (818) 243-0707
Kegs, Taps, Vendor Signs, Jockey Boxes

RC Vintage, Inc. (818) 765-7107
period, 40s, 50s & 60s European Vintage Bar Taps, and American Stainless Modern

Sony Pictures Studios-Prop House (Off Lot) (310) 244-5999
taps & coolers, beer kegs, beer bottles, liquor bottles

Universal Studios Property & Hardware Dept (818) 777-2784
Beer coolers, beer taps, beer glassware

Bees & Beekeeping

See: Animals (Live), Services, Trainers & Wranglers

Bells

See: Chimes & Bells

Belt Massagers

See: Exercise & Fitness Equipment

Belts

See: Military Surplus/Combat Clothes, Field Gear* Uniforms, Military* Uniforms, Trades/Professional/Sports* Wardrobe, Accessories

Benches

See Also: Audience Seating* Courtroom Furniture & Dressing* Theater Seating

AIR Designs (818) 768-6639
Bus Benches, Park Benches, Airport Seating, Interior & Exterior Restaurant & Bar

Alley Cats Studio Rentals (818) 982-9178
wood, metal work benches, fiberglass park tables w/benches, bleachers

C. P. Two (323) 466-8201
Various benches of various styles

C. P. Valley (323) 466-8201
Various benches of various styles

E.C. Prop Rentals (818) 764-2008
bus stop, ext. fiberglass/aluminum/aluminum w/ back, int. locker room, park, metal w/ handcuff bars

FormDecor, Inc. (310) 558-2582
America's largest event rental supplier of 20th Century furniture and accessories for Modern and Mid-Century styles.

The Hand Prop Room LP. (323) 931-1534
park benches, bus stop benches, playground benches, antique benches, vintage benches, wooden benches, sports, signage

History For Hire, Inc. (818) 765-7767
sports, bus, park

Jackson Shrub Supply, Inc. (818) 982-0100
park benches, bus benches, garden benches in lightweight reinforced foam/fiberglass

LCW Props (818) 243-0707
Locker Room, Court Room, Bus, Prison, Library, Park

Lennie Marvin Enterprises, Inc. (Prop Heaven) (818) 841-5882
all styles, shapes, sizes of bus, park,comp,metal,wood

Modern Props (323) 934-3000
outdoor benches, modern benches, metal benches, aluminum benches

Omega/Cinema Props (323) 466-8201
Various benches of various styles

Prop Services West (818) 503-2790

RC Vintage, Inc. (818) 765-7107
business, parks and court.

Sony Pictures Studios-Prop House (Off Lot) (310) 244-5999
general, park benches, bus benches; wood benches & metal benches

Universal Studios Property & Hardware Dept (818) 777-2784
Period to modern benches; courtroom benches, park benches, bus benches, church benches, workout benches and more.

Warner Bros. Studios Property Department (818) 954-2181
Park, picnic, church, weight, outdoor, bus, children's, wicker, rattan, rustic, piano/organ

Beverages

See: Beer Equipment, Taps & Coolers* Food, Artificial Food

Bibles

See: Books, Real/Hollow & Faux Books* Religious Articles

Bicycles & Bicycling Supplies

See Also: Prop Houses* Sporting Goods & Services

Alley Cats Studio Rentals (818) 982-9178
bicycles & racks

Beverly Hills Bike Shop (310) 275-2453
10546 W. Pico Blvd. Los Angeles, CA 90064
any contemporary bicycle need

The Bicycle Kitchen (323) 662-2776
4429 Fountain Ave, Los Angeles, CA 90029
bicycle repairs, Sat-Sun 12-6, M 12-5, T-TH 6:30-9:30PM

Big City Props (818) 394-9724
8217 Lankershim Blvd #42, Los Angeles, CA, 91605
Contemporary & vintage bicycles w/ large selection of bicycles in many styles & sizes; generic, road, & mountain bikes.
BigCityLA@gmail.com * www.bigcityprops.com

C. P. Two (323) 466-8201
Kids bikes, mountain bikes, street bikes, highwheeler bikes, tricycles, bike racks, and more.

E.C. Prop Rentals (818) 764-2008
racks & some distressed frames

The Hand Prop Room LP. (323) 931-1534
period-present, mountain, amazing restored collection

History For Hire, Inc. (818) 765-7767
contemp & period, men, women, children

I. Martin Imports (323) 653-6900
8330 Beverly Blvd, Los Angeles, CA, 90048

Lennie Marvin Enterprises, Inc. (Prop Heaven) (818) 841-5882
mens, ladies, childrens, tandem, from high wheeler to contemp.

Little Bohemia Rentals (818) 853-7506
11940 Sherman Rd, N Hollywood, CA, 91605
Dutch, Holland, China, Flying Pigeon, European, Fixies, City, Step-Through; Bicycles & bicycle accessories.
sales@wearelittlebohemia.com * www.wearelittlebohemia.com

DISPLAY ADS AND LISTINGS FOR THIS CATEGORY
CONTINUE ON THE FOLLOWING PAGE

Palms Cycle Shop　　　　　　　　　(310) 838-9644
3770 Motor Ave, Los Angeles, CA, 90034
Rentals & sales of new, used and classic bikes & accessories
palmscycle@yahoo.com * www.palmscycle.com

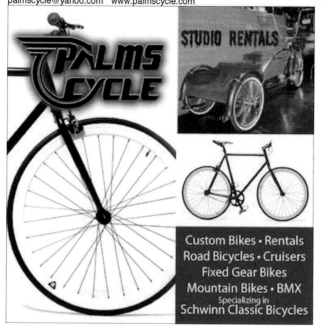

**Custom Bikes • Rentals
Road Bicycles • Cruisers
Fixed Gear Bikes
Mountain Bikes • BMX**
Specializing in
Schwinn Classic Bicycles

Prop Services West　　　　　　　　　(818) 503-2790
contemp & period, children's
Sony Pictures Studios-Prop House (Off Lot)　(310) 244-5999
period & contemp., adult & child
Universal Studios Property & Hardware Dept　(818) 777-2784
men & women, period to present

Billboards & Billboard Lights

See Also: Street Dressing, Exterior Signs
Alley Cats Studio Rentals　　　　　　(818) 982-9178
lights-working, on goosenecks/poles
E.C. Prop Rentals　　　　　　　　　(818) 764-2008
high multiples in many styles, w/goosenecks & straight pipe

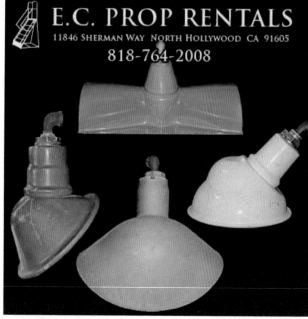

E.C. PROP RENTALS
11846 SHERMAN WAY NORTH HOLLYWOOD CA 91605
818-764-2008

LCW Props　　　　　　　　　　　　(818) 243-0707
Neon Signs, Custom Graphics

Billiards

See: Bowling Equipment Game Tables & Equipment* Pool/Billiard Tables & Accessories*

Bingo

See: Gambling Equipment

Binoculars, Scopes & Telescopes

Alley Cats Studio Rentals　　　　　　(818) 982-9178
pier binoculars
The Hand Prop Room LP.　　　　　　(323) 931-1534
personal/military binoculars, night vision scopes, telescopes
History For Hire, Inc.　　　　　　　(818) 765-7767
large selection
Jadis　　　　　　　　　　　　　　(310) 396-3477
2701 Main St, Santa Monica, CA, 90405
Antique & replica binoculars & telescopes. Period microscopes.
jadis1@gmail.com * www.jadisprops.com
LCW Props　　　　　　　　　　　　(818) 243-0707
Star Gazing, Bird Watching, Hunting, Rifle Scopes, Period - Present
Omega/Cinema Props　　　　　　　(323) 466-8201
New binoculars and vintage binoculars with carrying cases.
Orion Telescopes & Binoculars　　　(800) 447-1001
89 Hangar Way, Watsonville, CA, 95076
catalog sales; telescopes, binoculars, spotting scopes night vision equipment
The Rational Past　　　　　　　　　(310) 476-6277
By Appointment, West Los Angeles, CA
Authentic science, industrial, technical antiques & collectibles. Many professions & eras represented. See web site.
info@therationalpast.com * www.therationalpast.com
Sony Pictures Studios-Prop House (Off Lot)　(310) 244-5999

Bird Baths

See: Fountains, Decorative & Garden Garden/Patio*

Bird Cages/Houses

Badia Design, Inc.　　　　　　　　(818) 762-0130
5420 Vineland Ave, N. Hollywood, CA, 91601
info@badiadesign.com * www.badiadesign.com
Dapper Cadaver/Creatures & Cultures　(818) 771-0818
Decorative birdcages and ornate birdcages.
The Hand Prop Room LP.　　　　　　(323) 931-1534
History For Hire, Inc.　　　　　　　(818) 765-7767
cages
LCW Props　　　　　　　　　　　　(818) 243-0707
large & small
Omega/Cinema Props　　　　　　　(323) 466-8201
Decorative bird cages; vintage bird cages, antique bird cages, wooden bird cages, classic bird cages, steel bird cages
Prop Services West　　　　　　　　(818) 503-2790
RC Vintage, Inc.　　　　　　　　　(818) 765-7107
bird cages Brass Vintage, swivel bird cages, hanging bird cages, cages on stands
Sony Pictures Studios-Prop House (Off Lot)　(310) 244-5999
bird cages, cricket cages
Universal Studios Property & Hardware Dept　(818) 777-2784
Many bird cages/birdcages and bird houses/birdhouses

Birds

See: Animal Cages Animals (Live), Services, Trainers & Wranglers* Bird Cages/Houses* Feathers*

Birthing Room

See Also: Hospital Equipment* Medical Equip/Furniture, Graphics/Supplies* Intensive Care Unit / NICU (Natal Intensive Care Unit)

A-1 Medical Integration   **(818) 753-0319**
Medical devices for Set Decoration & Property, from minor procedures to detailed hospital units.

Alpha Companies - Spellman Desk Co.   **(818) 504-9090**
The #1 source for medical equipment in the Industry.

Blackboards

See: Chalk Boards* Office Equipment & Dressing* School Supplies, Desks & Dressing

Blacklights

See: Lighting & Sound, Concert/Theatrical/DJ/VJ

Blacks

See: Theatrical Draperies, Hardware & Rigging

Blacksmith Shop/Foundry

C. P. Valley   **(323) 466-8201**
forges, anvils, bellows, smelting equipment, all blacksmith tools

The Hand Prop Room LP.   **(323) 931-1534**
hammers, anvil, bellows, tongs

Harry Patton Horseshoeing Supplies   **(626) 359-8018**
223 W. Maple Ave, Monrovia, CA, 91016
blacksmith shop avail. as location; horseshoeing supplies, can locate farriers

History For Hire, Inc.   **(818) 765-7767**

LCW Props   **(818) 243-0707**
Tools, molds, Equipment

Sword & Stone   **(818) 562-6548**
anvil, bellows, tongs, hammers, medieval also

Blankets

See: Linens, Household* Native American

Blanks

See: Firearms, Gunsmith, Firearm Choreography

Bleachers & Grandstand Seating

See Also: Audience Cutouts & Stand-Ups* Audience Seating* Crowd Control: Barricades, Turnstiles Etc.* Rigging, Equipment or Services* Stages, Portable & Steel Deck

Alley Cats Studio Rentals   **(818) 982-9178**
9' four row bleacher and 4' three row bleacher available for rent.

Alley Cats Props

www.alleycatsprops.com

Brown-United Grandstands & Staging   **(800) 442-7696**
PO Box 1700, Monrovia, CA, 91017
info@brownunited.com * www.brownunited.com

E.C. Prop Rentals   **(818) 764-2008**
15' long aluminum 4-tier bleachers, castered

E.C. PROP RENTALS
11846 SHERMAN WAY NORTH HOLLYWOOD CA 91605
818-764-2008

Merrill Carson Entertainment   **(818) 780-1735**
7905 Lloyd Ave, N Hollywood, CA, 91605
carsonentertainment@gmail.com * www.merrillcarson.com

Blinds

See: Window Treatments

Bling

10 Karat Rentals   **(818) 635-4124**
7100 Tujunga (At R.C. Vintage), N. Hollywood, CA 91605
10karatrentals@gmail.com

AIR Designs   **(818) 768-6639**
20"/22"/24"/26" Chrome Wheels for Pimped Out Rides

The Hand Prop Room LP.   **(323) 931-1534**
rapper jewerly in stock & will mfg

JARED JAMIN - jewelry & accessories   **(310) 248-0537**
8917 Cynthia St. #3, Los Angeles, CA 90069
Rental/Made-to-Order: We create gemstone jewelry and accessories inspired by or made from rescued & vintage pieces.
info@jaredjamin.com * www.JaredJamin.com

LCW Props   **(818) 243-0707**
Jewelry, Gold, Silver, Gaudy, Rings, Watches, Over The Top

Rhinestone Guy   **(888) 594-7999**
We Ship To You.
rhinestones & other jewelry making supplies
http://rhinestoneguy.com

ShopWildThings   **(928) 855-6075**
2880 Sweetwater Ave, Lake Havasu City, AZ, 86406
Event Decor, Beaded Curtains, Chain Curtains, String Curtains & Columns, Crystal Columns. Reliable service & delivery.
help@shopwildthings.com * www.shopwildthings.com

Block And Tackle Sets

See: Automotive/Garage Equip. & Parts* Chain Hoists* Construction Site Equipment* Factory/Industrial* Nautical Dressing & Props* Rigging, Equipment or Services

Blood

See Also: Special Effects, Make-up/Prosthetics

A-1 Medical Integration (818) 753-0319
Medical devices for Set Decoration & Property, from minor procedures to detailed hospital units.

Dapper Cadaver/Creatures & Cultures (818) 771-0818
Original edible, easy clean and animal-safe fake blood. Resin blood pools and vials. Blood paint, makeup and moulage.

The Hand Prop Room LP. (323) 931-1534
fake blood, prop blood, lab test tubes, capsules

Blu-Ray Rentals/Sales Store

See: Video Store Dressing* Video Rental/Sales Store

Blue Screens

See: Green Screens, Blue Screens

Blueprint Equipment & Supplies

LCW Props (818) 243-0707
Tons Of Blueprints, Buildings, Offices, Residential

Repro-Graphic Supply (818) 771-9066
9838 Glenoaks Blvd, Sun Valley, CA, 91352
drafting & engineering supplies, equipment & service, all Ind.'s. large format xerographics printing
info@reprographicsupply.com * www.reprographicsupply.com

Steven Enterprises (800) 491-8785
17952 Skypark Circle Unit E, Irvine, CA, 92614
Wide Format Printers. Rent/Buy. Authorized Dealer: HP, KIP, Canon, Oce, Epson. We service & supply everything we install
sales@plotters.com * www.plotters.com

Board Games

See: Sporting Goods & Services

Boats & Water Sport Vehicles

See Also: Nautical Dressing & Props* Nautical/Marine Services & Charters* Sporting Goods & Services

Alley Cats Studio Rentals (818) 982-9178
8' dinghies, 8' lap strakes, 12 ' rowboat with oars

Gondola Adventures®, Inc. (949) 646-2067
3101 West Coast Highway, Suite 110, Newport Beach, CA 92663 **x801**
Authentic Venetian gondolas, both in and out of water, piloted by professional gondoliers. Expert staff. Since 1993
cruises@gondola.com * www.gondola.com

The Hand Prop Room LP. (323) 931-1534
antique canoes, rowboats/kayaks, past-present

LCW Props (818) 243-0707
Kayak, Boat Parts, Outboard Engines, Dock Buoys, Large Outdoor Kitchen BBQ

Sony Pictures Studios-Prop House (Off Lot) (310) 244-5999
shipwrecked row boats, canoes, dinghy

Tally Ho Marine Salvage & Decor (310) 548-5273
406 22nd St, San Pedro, CA, 90731
If we don't have it & can't find it, we can build it. rowboats

Universal Studios Property & Hardware Dept (818) 777-2784
Inflatable boats, rowboats, kayaks, canoes

West Marine (800) 262-8464
2450 17th Ave, Santa Cruz, CA, 95062
catalog sales; 400+ stores, compl. line boating access., inflatable boats, dinghies, kayaks, motor/sail boats & clothing

Bobbinettes

See: Theatrical Draperies, Hardware & Rigging

Bobble Heads

See: Nodders

Bobcats

See: Construction Site Equipment

Body & Face Painting

See: Tattoos (Temporary) Body/Face Painting

Body Parts

See Also: Anatomical Charts & Models Bones, Skulls & Skeletons* Mannequins* Special Effects, Equipment & Supplies*

Dapper Cadaver/Creatures & Cultures   **(818) 771-0818**
Lifelike fake body parts, bodies & dummies. Severed heads, fake arms & legs, hearts & organs. Wound, burn & custom FX.

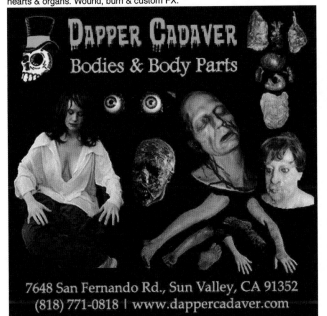

Bones, Skulls & Skeletons

See Also: Dinosaurs Fossils* Taxidermy, Hides/Heads/Skeletons*

Dapper Cadaver/Creatures & Cultures   **(818) 771-0818**
Human skeletons with hidden bolts. Lifecast, antique, forensic skull & bone replicas. Animal & dinosaur. T-rex skeleton.

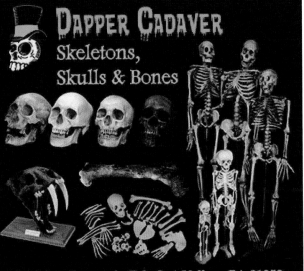

The Hand Prop Room LP.   **(323) 931-1534**
History For Hire, Inc.   **(818) 765-7767**
LCW Props   **(818) 243-0707**
Misc. Limbs, Skeletons, Anatomical Models

Body Piercing

See: Goth/Punk/Bondage/Fetish/Erotica Etc. Tattoo & Body Piercing Equipment & Supplies*

Boiler Room

See: Plumbing Fixtures, Heating/Cooling Appliances

Bondage

See: Goth/Punk/Bondage/Fetish/Erotica Etc. Leather (Clothing, Accessories, Materials)*

The Hand Prop Room LP.   **(323) 931-1534**
human, animal, sealife, human bones, loose bones, skeletons, skulls, animal skulls, steer head, taxidermy animals
History For Hire, Inc.   **(818) 765-7767**
complete skeletons,parts,human & animal
LCW Props   **(818) 243-0707**
Skeletons, Heart, Lungs, Reproductive Models, Brain, Prosthetics
Sony Pictures Studios-Prop House (Off Lot)   **(310) 244-5999**
Sword & Stone   **(818) 562-6548**
Universal Studios Property & Hardware Dept   **(818) 777-2784**
Various bones from human bones to animal bones

Boneyard (Junk)

See: Architectural Pieces & Artifacts Salvage, Rubble, Clutter & Trash (Prop)*

Bonnets

See: Headwear - Hats, Bonnets, Caps, Helmets Etc.

Book Covers & Bookbinding

The Earl Hays Press   (818) 765-0700
services the Industry only. Custom and pre-made prints, many styles.
Faux Library Studio Props, Inc.   (818) 765-0096
Book coverings, book art, faux book covers, book casing, experts at creating a
real looking fake library
Gibbs Bookbinding   (214) 673-0329
140 S Mariposa, Los Angeles, CA, 90004
Custom books and boxes of all sizes. Leather, cloth, and paper, in current or
historic/aged styles. Fast turnaround.
stephaniegibbs@gmail.com * www.GibbsBookbinding.com

GIBBS BOOKBINDING

scrapbooks | presentation copies | faux books
editions | historic bindings | repair

www.GibbsBookbinding.com
stephaniegibbs@gmail.com
214-673-0329

site visits and
consultations by
appointment

H & H Book Services   (818) 242-2665
236 N. Glendale Ave, Glendale, CA, 91206
repair & restorations, fine bindings, book bindery, book binding
Kater-Crafts Bookbinders   (562) 692-0665
4860 Gregg Rd, Pico Rivera, CA, 90660
Custom work, any size. Fine hand binding. Industry credits. Museum quality
restoration.
sales@katercrafts.com * www.katercrafts.com

Books, Real/Hollow & Faux Books

See Also: Paperwork, Documents & Letters, Office Scrapbooks*
Abbotoir Books   (818) 506-7380
Call for Appt, Valley Village, CA, 91607
Art books, coffee table, novels, classics, psychology, magic, and more.
dfsaalexander@roadrunner.com * www.abbotoirbooks.com
Alpha Companies - Spellman Desk Co.   (818) 504-9090
hollow books, law books, school books, medical books, novels, journals
Bassman-Blaine   (213) 748-5909
1933 S. Broadway, #1005, Los Angeles, CA 90007
Reclaimed books in many styles; canvas, faux leather, stenciled hide,
marbleized paper, metallics & faux patent leathers
lashowroom@bassman-blaine.com * www.bassmanblainelamart.com
Books For Libraries, Inc.   (800) 321-5596
28064 Ave Standford Unit L, Santa Clarita, CA, 91355
Compl. real book academic libraries up to 50,000, by type, subject or mixed
JStitz@pacbell.net * www.booksforlibraries.com
E.C. Prop Rentals   (818) 764-2008
manuals, binders, printouts

Faux Library Studio Props, Inc.   (818) 765-0096
1000s of feet of hollow books, medical to classics, library shelving, real books,
hollow books, faux books.

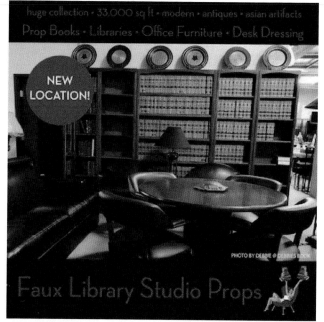

Gibbs Bookbinding   (214) 673-0329
140 S Mariposa, Los Angeles, CA, 90004
Custom books and boxes of all sizes. Leather, cloth, and paper, in current or
historic/aged styles. Fast turnaround.
stephaniegibbs@gmail.com * www.GibbsBookbinding.com
The Hand Prop Room LP.   (323) 931-1534
period-present wide sel.
History For Hire, Inc.   (818) 765-7767
specialty book mfg
LCW Props   (818) 243-0707
Large Selection, Legal, Fiction, Non-Fiction, Reference, Leather Bound
Ob-jects   (818) 351-4200
leather sets, coffee table, cook, garden
Omega/Cinema Props   (323) 466-8201
Cookbooks, recipe books, leather bound books, king james replica bible, faux
books and more.
Prop Services West   (818) 503-2790
law books, paper backs, children, novels
Sony Pictures Studios-Prop House (Off Lot)   (310) 244-5999
paperbacks to law, autographed books, binders, bookends, bookmaker, comic
books, composition books, cookbooks, diary, dictionary
Universal Studios Property & Hardware Dept   (818) 777-2784
All manner of books available.
Warner Bros. Studios Property Department   (818) 954-2181
Faux, hardcover, soft cover, research, cookbooks, antique, travel, law, faux
ZG04 DECOR   (818) 853-8040
Books, Magazines, Comics

Bookstores

See Also: Search Tools, Directories, Libraries
Psychic Eye Book Shops, Inc.   (818) 784-3797
13435 Ventura Blvd, Sherman Oaks, CA, 91423
new age, metaphysical, self help, occult, astrology, also several other stores in
LA area
Alexandria II New Age Bookstore   (626) 792-7885
170 S. Lake Ave, Pasadena, Ca 91101
Metaphysical books, DVDs, music, incense, gifts, Tarot cards, altar items, yoga
supplies & more
Book Castle, Inc.   (818) 845-1563
212 N. San Fernando Blvd, Burbank, CA, 91502
used books, period books, memorabilia books. Industry experience for over 30
years
www.bookcastlesmovieworld.com

Book Soup (310) 659-3110
8818 Sunset Blvd, W.Hollywood, CA, 90069
open 7 days, 9AM to 9PM
Cook Books by Janet Jarvits (626) 296-1638
1353 N. Hill, Pasadena, CA, 91104
over 15,000 used & rare cookbooks
Distant Lands (800) 310-3220
20 S. Raymond Ave, Pasadena, CA, 91105
traveler's bookstore & outfitter, international maps
Drama Book Shop (212) 944-0595
250 W. 40th St, New York, NY, 10018
Faux Library Studio Props, Inc. (818) 765-0096
Complete bookstore dressing, books & bookcases, book shelving, book
shelves.
Hennessey & Ingalls, Inc. (310) 458-9074
214 Wilshire Blvd, Santa Monica, CA, 90401
books on the visual arts, and architecture.
International Fashion Publications (213) 622-5663
110 E 9th St Ste AL19 (Lobby), Los Angeles, CA, 90079
Fashion, trend, costume books/mags & new Digital Project Cafe
Larry Edmunds Bookshop (323) 463-3273
6644 Hollywood Blvd, Hollywood, CA, 90028
Also we carry posters, memorabilia, photos & novelties
Samuel French, Inc. (866) 598-8449
7623 Sunset Blvd, Hollywood, CA, 90046
Strand Bookstore, Inc. (212) 473-1452
828 Broadway (at 12th St), New York, NY, 10003-4805
world's largest used book store, see Jenny McKibben X150
U.S. Government Bookstore (866) 512-1800
732 N Capitol St NW, Washington, DC, 20401
Online sales for all government publications
Vroman's Bookstore (626) 449-5320
695 E Colorado Blvd, Pasadena, CA, 91101

Boom Lifts

See: Construction Site Equipment

Booths

See: Banquets/Booths (Seating) Carnival Dressing/Supplies* Game
Booths* Telephone Booths & Pay Telephones* Ticket Booths*

Boots

See: Shoes, Boots & Footwear Western Wear*

Bottles

See Also: Bars, Nightclubs, Barware & Dressing Glassware/Dishes*
Liquor Bottles* Milk Bottles & Cans*
AIR Designs (818) 768-6639
Liquor, Wine, Beer, Display Bottles, Crates, Boxes, Multiples & Generic
E.C. Prop Rentals (818) 764-2008
5 Gallon Water Coolers, Glass Bottles, Plastic Bottles
The Hand Prop Room LP. (323) 931-1534
period-present personal, medical, liquor, household, soda, beer
History For Hire, Inc. (818) 765-7767
soda, liquor, other
LCW Props (818) 243-0707
Jars, Lab Glassware, We Own The Recycling Center Next Door
Modern Props (323) 934-3000
contemporary bottles, futuristic bottles, household bottles & commercial bottles
Omega/Cinema Props (323) 466-8201
All kinds of bottles: Classic and period bottles, clay bottles, tonic bottles, glass
bottles, apothecary bottles & more.
Prop Services West (818) 503-2790
Sony Pictures Studios-Prop House (Off Lot) (310) 244-5999
champagne bottles, liquor bottles, decorative bottles, milk bottles, oil bottles,
vinegar bottles, spice bottles, sports bottles
Universal Studios Property & Hardware Dept (818) 777-2784
All manner of bottles.

Bounce Houses

See: Inflatables, Custom

Bouquets

See: Balloons & Balloon Sculptures Florists/Floral Design*

Bourns & Pouffes

See: Hotel, Motel, Inn, Lodge

Bowling Equipment

See Also: Sporting Goods & Services
C. P. Valley (323) 466-8201
Bowling lanes, bowling balls, bowling bags, bowling pins, bowling trophies and
more.
The Hand Prop Room LP. (323) 931-1534
bowling shoes, bowling bags, vintage bowling, bowling pins, bowling trophies,
rubber bowling pins, bowling balls
History For Hire, Inc. (818) 765-7767
pins, bags & shoes, trophies
Murrey International (310) 532-6091
14150 S. Figueroa St, Los Angeles, CA 90061
Ball returns, seating, tables, ball racks, lanes, custom graphics
www.murreybowling.com
Universal Studios Property & Hardware Dept (818) 777-2784
Bowling balls, bowling ball bags, bowling gloves, bowling pins

Bows & Arrows

See: Archery Equipment, Training Native American* Sporting Goods
& Services* Weapons*

Boxes

See Also: Crates/ Vaults Gift Wrapping* Packing/Packaging
Supplies, Services*
Absolute Packaging (800) 567-9190
11940 Sherman Road, N. Hollywood, CA 91605
std/custom, boxes, wardrobe, custom foam, bubble wrap, tape, shipping boxes
www.absolutepackagingsupply.com

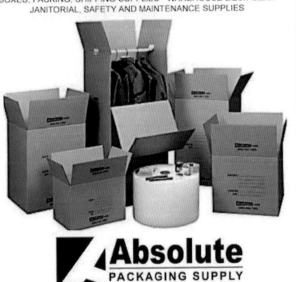

Acme Display Fixture & Packaging (888) 411-1870
3829 S Broadway St., Los Angeles, CA 90037
Complete store setups: garment racks, displays/display cases, counters,
packaging, shelving, hangers, mannequins
sales@acmedisplay.com * www.acmedisplay.com
Basaw Manufacturing, Inc. (818) 765-6650
7300 Varna, N Hollywood, CA, 91605
Basaw builds crates to order, large inventory in stock. wooden, corrugated,
specialized packs
fredy@basaw.com * www.basaw.com
E.C. Prop Rentals (818) 764-2008
wood, metal, fiberglass, cardboard
History For Hire, Inc. (818) 765-7767
wood, hat, shoe

**DISPLAY ADS AND LISTINGS FOR THIS CATEGORY
CONTINUE ON THE FOLLOWING PAGE**

Imperial Paper Co.　　　　　　　　　**(818) 769-4400**
5733-37 Cahuenga Blvd, N Hollywood, CA, 91601
Wardrobe, tape, cushioning, foam, bubblewrap, custom & stock shipping
boxes. Mailing tubes, void fill
www.imperialpaper.com

Kater-Crafts Bookbinders　　　　　　**(562) 692-0665**
4860 Gregg Rd, Pico Rivera, CA, 90660
Custom work. Clamshell boxes, slipcases, portfolio/photo boxes. Museum
quality.
sales@katercrafts.com * www.katercrafts.com

LCW Props　　　　　　　　　　　　　**(818) 243-0707**
Wood Crates, Molded Plastic, Cardboard, Large & Small, New & Old

Sony Pictures Studios-Prop House (Off Lot)　　**(310) 244-5999**
apothecary boxes, candy boxes, cheese box, cigar boxes, cigarette boxes,
decorative boxes, display boxes, wrapped gift

Boxing, Wrestling, Mixed Martial Arts (MMA)

See Also: Exercise & Fitness Equipment Gymnasium & Gymnastic
Equipment*

American Hapkido Karate / Fight Factory MMA　**(818) 998-2441**
20928-B Osborne St, Canoga Park, CA
12,000sq.ft MMA Studio & Equipment for Rent: classic meets modern,high
ceilings,octagon cage,rings,punching bags,offices
mastersayed@msn.com * www.americanfightfactory.com

American Hapkido Karate / Fight Factory MMA

LARGEST MARTIAL ARTS ACADEMY IN THE VALLEY. 12,000 sq.ft. FULLY LOADED!

MMA Studio for Rent　*www.americanfightfactory.com*　*Equipment for Rent*

History For Hire, Inc.　　　　　　　　**(818) 765-7767**
boxing gloves, bells

L. A. Party Works　　　　　　　　　　**(888) 527-2789**
9712 Alpaca St, S El Monte, CA, 91733
Boxing rings available. Our print shop can customize the graphics and branding
too!
partyworks@aol.com * www.partyworksusa.com

Pro Boxing Supplies　　　　　　　　　**(818) 760-9500**
4405 Laurel Canyon Blvd, Studio City, CA, 91607
Boxing rings, Wrestling rings, MMA cages, punching bags, boxing gloves,
heavy bags, weapons, dummies, and much more...
proboxingsupplies@yahoo.com * www.proboxingsupplies.com

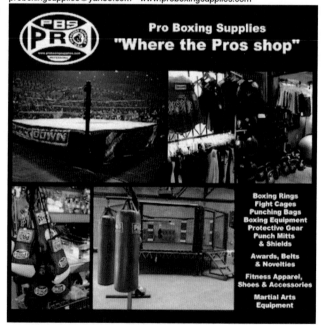

Pro Fight Shop   **(323) 460-4600**
1062 Vine Street, Hollywood, CA, 90038
Boxing rings, Wrestling rings, Punching bags, Boxing gloves, Heavy bag stands, MMA cages, MMA Rings, Fight Rings, Mats
profightshop@yahoo.com * www.profightshop.com

Sony Pictures Studios-Prop House (Off Lot)   **(310) 244-5999**
boxing equipment, punching balls, speed bags
Whittier Fight Shop   **(562) 695-1155**
11555 Whittier Blvd. Whittier, CA 90601
We sell all kinds of equipment including uniforms, weapons, and rings for boxing, wrestling, Mixed Martial Arts & more.
whittierfightclub@gmail.com * www.WhittierFightShop.com

Brass Accessories

See: Decorative Accessories Prop Houses*

Brass Lamps

See: Light Fixtures

Break Room

AIR Designs   **(818) 768-6639**
Vending Machines; Soda & Snack, Coffee Machines, Counters, Seating, Refrigerators
E.C. Prop Rentals   **(818) 764-2008**
employee break room dressing

Breakaways (Glass, Props, Scenery)

See Also: Expendables Special Effects, Equipment & Supplies*
Alfonso's Breakaway Glass, Inc.   **(818) 768-7402**
8070 San Fernando Rd, Sun Valley, CA, 91352
largest mfg; 1000 breakaway glass,props & scenery, windshield to test tube, & custom
info@alfonsosbreakawayglass.com * www.alfonsosbreakawayglass.com
General Veneer Manufacturing Co.   **(323) 564-2661**
8652 Otis St, South Gate, CA, 90280
Breakaway balsa wood sheets & boards
balsasales@generalveneer.com * www.generalveneer.com
The Hand Prop Room LP.   **(323) 931-1534**
designed to your needs, glasses, vases, plates, etc.
HPR Custom   **(323) 931-1534**
5700 Venice Blvd, Los Angeles, CA, 90019
Breakaway chairs, breakaway tables, breakaway guitars, breakaway branches, breakaway clubs, breakaway pool cues and more
www.hprcustom.com
J & M Special Effects, Inc.   **(718) 875-0140**
524 Sackett St, Brooklyn, NY 11217
Formerly Jauchem & Meeh. bottles, glasses,breakaway bottles,breakaway vases, breakaway wine bottles
info@jmfx.net * www.jmfx.net
New Rule FX   **(818) 387-6450**
7751 Densmore Ave, Van Nuys, CA 91406
Breakaway props-all types & categories. Balsa furniture, Fake food. Foam Weapons. Tools, custom props, molding & casting
ryan@newrulefx.com * www.NewRuleFX.com

Peter Geyer Action Props, Inc   **(818) 768-0070**
8235 Lankershim Blvd Ste G, N Hollywood, CA, 91605
balsa furniture
Rohan Glass Company, Inc   **(818) 984-1000**
12442 Oxnard St, N Hollywood, CA, 91606
breakaway sheet glass, 2-way mirrors, regular glass windows etc
Universal Studios Property & Hardware Dept   **(818) 777-2784**
Breakaways and breakaway fabrication

Breaker Boxes

See Also: Control Boards* Control Panels/Boxes*
Electrical/Electronic Supplies & Services* Electronic Equipment
(Dressing)* Gas & Electric Meters

AIR Designs (818) 768-6639
Home Breaker Boxes & Industrial Breaker Boxes
Alley Cats Studio Rentals (818) 982-9178
period, modern
E.C. Prop Rentals (818) 764-2008
extensive sel., period-contemp.
LCW Props (818) 243-0707
Tons of Different Styles & Sizes, Rigged, With Conduit, Can Make Custom

Brick

See: Concrete Block, Brick, Gravel, Sand, Rocks, Etc.

Bridal Dress

See: Wedding Attire

Briefcases

See Also: Luggage
The Hand Prop Room LP. (323) 931-1534
period-present, great selection, rigged, custum design
History For Hire, Inc. (818) 765-7767
huge sel, all periods
LCW Props (818) 243-0707
Haliburton, Rigged With Electronics, Spy Kits, Surveillance Style, Bomb
Detonators
Modern Props (323) 934-3000
contemporary briefcases, futuristic briefcases, espionage briefcases
Sony Pictures Studios-Prop House (Off Lot) (310) 244-5999
Universal Studios Property & Hardware Dept (818) 777-2784
Leather briefcases, lockable briefcases, aluminum briefcases, worn briefcases,
computer briefcases, and more.

Broadcast Studio

See: Radio/TV Station* Video Camera Equipment & Services

Bronzes

See: Sculpture

Brush Hauling

See: Transportation, Trucking and/or Storage

Bubble Gum Machines

See: Vending Machines

Bubble Machines

Astro Audio Video Lighting, Inc. (818) 549-9915
6615 San Fernando Rd, Glendale, CA, 91201
Bubble machines and bubble machine fluid available.
www.astroavl.com
EFX- Event Special Effects (626) 888-2239
125 Railroad Ave, Monrovia, CA, 91016
Bubble Machies- Bubble Master- Fluid
info@efxla.com * www.efxla.com
L. A. Party Works (888) 527-2789
9712 Alpaca St, S El Monte, CA, 91733
Bubble machines for rent
partyworks@aol.com * www.partyworksusa.com
LCW Props (818) 243-0707
Working Machines
Universal Studios Special Effects Equip. (818) 777-3333

Bubble Wrap

See: Expendables* Packing/Packaging Supplies, Services

Buckboard

See: Carriages, Horse Drawn

Buckets

See Also: Barrels & Drums, Wood/Metal/Plastic* Western Dressing
E.C. Prop Rentals (818) 764-2008
new/used, metal/plastic
The Hand Prop Room LP. (323) 931-1534
wood, metal
History For Hire, Inc. (818) 765-7767
metal, wood, tin, enamel
LCW Props (818) 243-0707
Large & Small, Stainless Steel, Plastic, Metal, Ice
Sony Pictures Studios-Prop House (Off Lot) (310) 244-5999
Universal Studios Property & Hardware Dept (818) 777-2784
Many kinds of buckets from mop to coal, many periods.

Buggies

See: Carriages, Horse Drawn

Bugs

See: Animals (Live), Services, Trainers & Wranglers* Insects,
Artificial

Building Supply, Lumber, Hardware, Etc.

See Also: Architectural Pieces & Artifacts* Concrete Block, Brick,
Gravel, Sand, Rocks, Etc.* Glass & Mirrors* Hardware, Decorative*
Paneling, Veneers & Laminates* Tile, Marble, Granite, Etc.
A & A Building Materials (626) 447-3595
310 N. Santa Anita Ave, Arcadia, CA 91006
drywall, lath, plaster; limited lumber, plywood, sand
A & G Lumber (310) 838-6222
5942 W. Washington Blvd, Culver City, CA, 90232
Anawalt Lumber (323) 464-1600
1001 N. Highland, Hollywood, CA, 90038
multiple locations in north L.A.
Anderson International Trading (714) 666-8183
1171 N. Tustin Ave, Anaheim, CA, 92807
1/64" to 1" plywood & veneers, curves & cylinders, musical drums, bendable
substrates
Anderson Plywood Sales (310) 397-8229
4020 Sepulveda Blvd, Culver City, CA, 90230
Arrow Fence & Lumber (818) 686-3553
10865 Sutter Ave, Pacoima, CA, 91331
lumber/plywood, beams, peeler poles
Arroyo Building Materials (818) 365-6170
890 Arroyo St, San Fernando, CA, 91340
stone, steel products, lumber, drywall, doors/windows etc.
Austin Hardwoods & Hardware (714) 953-4000
610 N. Santiago St, Santa Ana, CA, 92701
Exotic/domestic hardwoods, sheet goods, hardware, woodworking tools
B & B Hardware (310) 390-9413
12450 W. Washington Blvd, Los Angeles, CA, 90066
Bear Forest Products, Inc (951) 727-1767
4685 Brookhollow Circle, Riverside, CA, 92509
Wood construction materials, Plywood- Softwood and Hardwood. MDF, PB,
etc. Lumber 1x3, 1x4, 2x4, etc.
matto@bearfp.com * www.bearfp.com
Bourget Bros. Building Materials (310) 450-6556
1636 11th St, Santa Monica, CA, 90404
C & E Lumber Co. (909) 626-3591
2692 N. Towne Ave, Pomona, CA, 91767
lumber/plywood, peeler poles, rail fencing
California Do-It Center (818) 845-8301
3221 W. Magnolia Blvd, Burbank, CA, 91505
multiple loc. in L.A.
Dykes Lumber (212) 246-6480
124 East 124th St, New York, NY, 10035
8 loc. in NYC area, lumber, mouldings, const. products
E.C. Prop Rentals (818) 764-2008
construction dressing, shelving, fencing, power & hand tools
Far West Plywood (818) 885-1511
18450 Parthenia Pl, Northridge, CA, 91325
Feldman Lumber (973) 910-2600
100 Dale Ave, Paterson, NJ, 07501

Forest Plywood (714) 523-1721
14711 Artesia Blvd, La Mirada, CA 90638
lumber, plywood, melamine, etc.
Goldenwest Plywood & Lumber (562) 867-3386
17326 Woodruff Ave, Bellflower, CA, 90706
lumber/plywood
Home Depot (323) 461-3303
5600 W. Sunset Blvd, Hollywood, CA, 90028
mult. loc. in LA/NYC: website has store locator function
Jansen Ornamental Supply Co., Inc. (800) 423-4494
10926 Schmidt Rd, El Monte, CA, 91733
architectural ornamental hardware, stair railings, wholesale only
Jones Lumber (323) 564-6656
10711 S. Alameda St, Lynwood, CA, 90262
extensive
Lenoble Lumber (718) 784-5230
38-20 Review Ave, Long Island City, NY, 11101
no hardware
Neiman Reed Lumber Co. (818) 781-3466
7875 Willis Ave, Panorama City, CA, 91402
lumber/plywood, wholesaler
North Hollywood Hardware, Inc. (818) 980-2453
11847 Ventura Blvd, Studio City, CA, 91604
Full service hardware store with hard to find items.
nohohardware@gmail.com * www.ehardware2go.com
Northridge Lumber (818) 349-6701
18537 Parthenia St, Northridge, CA, 91324
Orchard Supply Hardware (818) 779-7292
5960 Sepulveda Blvd, Van Nuys, CA, 91411
multiple loc. in L.A., call (888) 746-7674 for store nearest you
Pasadena Lumber (626) 797-2220
1464 Lincoln Ave, Pasadena, CA, 91103
Quixote (504) 266-2297
10289 Airline Hwy, St. Rose LA 70087
Set Building Supplies, Set Construction, Power Tools, lumber, glues, delivery
nola@quixote.com * www.quixote.com
The ReUse People (818) 244-5635
3015 Dolores St, Los Angeles, CA, 90065
Thousands of board feet of reused lumber and used building materials. All
denailed and ready for use.
JefCockerell@TheReUsePeople.org * www.TheReUsePeople.org

The ReUse People reduces the solid waste stream and changes the way the built environment is renewed by salvaging building materials and distributing them for reuse.

Building Supply Lumber Hardware Plumbing
www.thereusepeople.org

Roadside Lumber (818) 991-1880
29112 Roadside Dr, Agoura Hills, CA, 91301
Rosenzweig Lumber (718) 585-8050
801 East 135th St, Bronx, NY, 10454
building supplies but no hardware
Royal Plywood (562) 404-2989
14171 E Park Place, Cerritos, CA, 90703
lumber/plywood & veneers, wholesaler
Stock Building Supply (818) 982-6046
7151 Lankershim Blvd, N Hollywood, CA, 91605
multiple locations in L.A.

Virgil's Hardware (818) 242-1104
520 N Glendale Ave, Glendale, CA, 91207
Warner Bros. Studios Mill Store (818) 954-4444
4000 Warner Blvd, Burbank, CA, 91522
Production expendables & supplies to the entertainment community at great
prices
wbsfmillstore@warnerbros.com * www.wbmillstore.com

Bulkhead Lights

See Also: Caged Vapor Proof Lights Nautical Dressing & Props*
E.C. Prop Rentals (818) 764-2008
multiple sizes & styles
LCW Props (818) 243-0707
Ship, Submarine, Train, Dock Lights

Bull Horns

See: Megaphones

Bullet Proof Vests

See: Military Props & Equipment Police Equipment*

Bulletin Boards

C. P. Valley (323) 466-8201
Wooden framed bulletin boards, aluminum framed bulletin boards, cork bulletin
boards and others in many sizes available.
E.C. Prop Rentals (818) 764-2008
many sizes & styles, wood & metal, int. wall-mount, ext. free standing
The Hand Prop Room LP. (323) 931-1534
wall, floor, office, academic, wooden, metal
History For Hire, Inc. (818) 765-7767
wall-mount
Hollywood Studio Gallery (323) 462-1116
pre-dressed
LCW Props (818) 243-0707
Large & Small, Behind Glass, Many Styles
Linoleum City, Inc. (323) 469-0063
4849 Santa Monica Blvd, Hollywood, CA, 90029
Bulletin board cork, decorative wall cork, insulation cork, underlayment cork,
cork floors, floating cork floors.
sales@linocity.com * www.linoleumcity.com
On Set Graphics (661) 233-6786
Web Based Business
100% Cleared Printable Flyers, Bulletin Board Dressing, Posters, Office Notes,
Signage, and so much more.
info@onsetgraphics.com * www.onsetgraphics.com

Sony Pictures Studios-Prop House (Off Lot) (310) 244-5999
all sizes, wall & free-standing
Universal Studios Property & Hardware Dept (818) 777-2784
Bulletin boards including; rolling bulletin boards, hanging bulletin boards, two
sided bulletin boards and more.

Buoys

See: Nautical Dressing & Props

Bus Benches

See: Benches

Bus Depot Lockers

See: Lockers

Bus Rentals

See: Vehicles

Bus Shelter

See Also: Benches* Street Dressing

AIR Designs (818) 768-6639
Shelters & Enclosures, Benches, Trash Cans, Signage, Poster Displays
Alley Cats Studio Rentals (818) 982-9178
complete shelters
E.C. Prop Rentals (818) 764-2008
contemp. & bus stop ad benches, multiples

E.C. PROP RENTALS
11846 SHERMAN WAY NORTH HOLLYWOOD CA 91605
818-764-2008

Lennie Marvin Enterprises, Inc. (Prop Heaven) (818) 841-5882
various styles, quantity avail.

Business Machines

See Also: Bank Dressing* Cash Registers* Computers* Copy
Machines* Office Equipment & Dressing* Typewriters
Advanced Liquidators Office Furniture (818) 763-3470
used adding machines, typewriters, vintage typewriters, vintage tape
dispensers, shredders, and more
C. P. Valley (323) 466-8201
Period to modern business machines of various kinds.
History For Hire, Inc. (818) 765-7767
period typewriters, adding machines, etc.
LCW Props (818) 243-0707
Copiers, Faxes, Printers, Large Selection Of New & Old
Modern Props (323) 934-3000
contemporary business machines, futuristic business machines, electronic
business machines
Sony Pictures Studios-Prop House (Off Lot) (310) 244-5999
Adding machines, abacus, appointment books
Universal Studios Property & Hardware Dept (818) 777-2784
Prop business machines for all of your office dressing rentals.

Busts

See: Sculpture

Buttons

See: Badges, Patches & Buttons* Costume/Wardrobe/Sewing
Supplies* Memorabilia & Novelties

Cabinets

See: Kitchen Counters & Cabinets* Staff Shops

Cable Covers

See: Electrical/Electronic Supplies & Services* Events, Decorations,
Supplies & Services* Floor, Ground & Surface Protection

Cactus, Live & Artificial

See Also: Greens

California Cactus Center (626) 795-2788
216 S. Rosemead Blvd, Pasadena, CA, 91107
California Nursery "Cactus Ranch" (818) 894-5694
19420 Saticoy St, Reseda, CA, 91335
Over 100,000 cacti & succulent plants - by appt only
Green Set, Inc. (818) 764-1231
Cactus, succulents and other desert plants, both live and artificial, many many
types and styles of cacti
Jackson Shrub Supply, Inc. (818) 982-0100
Saguaro 5' to 18', beaver tail, succulents, live cactus, artificial cactus, fire
retardant brush, plus more

Cafe Tables/Chairs/Umbrellas

See Also: Coffee House* Delicatessen Equipment* Restaurant
Furniture & Dressing
AIR Designs (818) 768-6639
Round and Square, Period/Modern Diner, Cafe, Coffee Shop, Bistro,
Umbrellas
C. P. Two (323) 466-8201
Cafe tables, cafe chairs, cafe lamps and more.
FormDecor, Inc. (310) 558-2582
America's largest event rental supplier of 20th Century furniture and
accessories for Modern and Mid-Century styles.
LCW Props (818) 243-0707
Tables, Chairs, Patio Dressing
Lennie Marvin Enterprises, Inc. (Prop Heaven) (818) 841-5882
wrought iron, marble, tile top, bistro
Modern Props (323) 934-3000
contemporary cafe furniture, futuristic cafe furniture, various heights, cafe
furniture multiples
Sony Pictures Studios-Prop House (Off Lot) (310) 244-5999
Taylor Creative Inc. (888) 245-4044
At Taylor Creative Inc. we offer a large selection of cafe, dining, and
conference tables.
Universal Studios Property & Hardware Dept (818) 777-2784
Prop cafe tables, cafe chairs, cafe umbrellas and more for rent.

Cafeteria Counter/Line

See Also: Counters* Vendor Carts & Concession Counters
AIR Designs (818) 768-6639
Complete Cafeteria Setups, Food Prep, Heat Lamps, Trays, Dishwasher,
Tables, Modular Seating, Trash Cans
C. P. Valley (323) 466-8201
Cafeteria trays and cafeteria tray holders

Caged Vapor Proof Lights

See Also: Bulkhead Lights* Lanterns* Light Fixtures* Nautical Dressing & Props

Alley Cats Studio Rentals   (818) 982-9178
working, w/cages
E.C. Prop Rentals   (818) 764-2008
high multiples & mounting styles, w/all globe colors

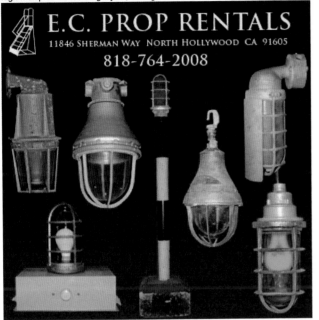

E.C. PROP RENTALS
11846 SHERMAN WAY NORTH HOLLYWOOD CA 91605
818-764-2008

Modern Props   (323) 934-3000
RC Vintage, Inc.   (818) 765-7107
Large Selection
Sony Pictures Studios-Fixtures   (310) 244-5996
5933 W Slauson Ave, Culver City, CA, 90230
period to present day
www.sonypicturesstudios.com
Universal Studios Property & Hardware Dept   (818) 777-2784
Caged vapor proof lights/vapor lights for rent.

Cages

See: Animal Cages* Bird Cages/Houses

Cakes

See: Food, Artificial Food* Food, Food Stylists

Calculators

See: Business Machines* Computers* Science Equipment

Calendars

See: Art, Supplies & Stationery* Office Equipment & Dressing

Calligraphy

Anne Robin Calligraphy   (917) 863-0899
Call for Appointment - Los Angeles & New York
Lettering and calligraphy for props, credits, titles, logos and for events (invitations, place cards, envelopes, etc.)
anne@annerobin.com * www.annerobin.com
Designing Letters   (310) 702-4042
4032 Marcasel Ave, West Los Angeles, CA, 90066
custom lettering props, ancient/modern, manuscript & letters, logo lettering, titles

Calliopes

Enchanted Melodies Music Machine Co.   (818) 894-5694
Call for Appt.
Circus Organ/Carousel Band Organ/Calliope on wheels Must see & hear to believe! Create a festive atmosphere!

Camera Equipment

See Also: Motion Picture Camera Equipment* Motion Picture Production Equip., Period* Motion Picture Projectors* Press Equipment* Surveillance Equipment* Video Camera Equipment & Services

C. P. Valley   (323) 466-8201
Polaroid cameras, kodak cameras, instamatic cameras, and much more from period to modern.
Castex Rentals   (323) 462-1468
1044 N. Cole Ave, Hollywood, CA, 90038
Profoto, lighting, soft boxes, tripods, tripod heads.
service@castexrentals.com * www.castexrentals.com

Hollywood CASTEX California

Serving the Motion Picture & Photography Industries Since 1955

Production, Grip, Lighting Expendables & More...

1044 Cole Avenue, Hollywood, CA 90038
Tel: 323.462.1468 • Fax: 323.462.3719

www.castexrentals.com

The Hand Prop Room LP.   (323) 931-1534
Cameras and Camera Equipment
History For Hire, Inc.   (818) 765-7767
period,motion picture,still; full line period dollies, darkroom
Kitsch N Sync Props   (323) 343-1190
Specializing in 70's and 80's props. Large collection of cameras, electronics, phones, art, games, stereos, & much more.
LCW Props   (818) 243-0707
Point & Shoot, Digital SLR, Tripods, Period - Present, News, ID & Passport, 35mm
Motion Picture Marine   (310) 951-1110
578 W Washington Blvd Ste 866, Marina Del Rey, CA, 90292
marine production company, camera & boats, camera stabilization mounts including the Perfect Horizon
RJR Props   (404) 349-7600
Security cameras, movie cameras, personal cameras, news cameras and more for rent.
Samy's Cameras   (323) 938-2420
431 S Fairfax Ave, Los Angeles, CA, 90036
everything photographic
Sony Pictures Studios-Prop House (Off Lot)   (310) 244-5999
Albums, camera bags, film cans, film reels, projector screens, slide viewers, photographic supplies, tripods, more
Universal Studios Property & Hardware Dept   (818) 777-2784
All kinds of camera equipment rentals available.

Camouflage Nets

See Also: Cargo Nets* Military Props & Equipment

Alley Cats Studio Rentals   **(818) 982-9178**
different sizes, shapes
E.C. Prop Rentals   **(818) 764-2008**
assorted desert color
Green Set, Inc.   **(818) 764-1231**
Nets & Skins, Camouflage nets including: camo brown nets, camo green nets, even erosion cloths
The Hand Prop Room LP.   **(323) 931-1534**
different sizes & shapes, military nets, large camouflage nets, army nets, fishing nets, large nets
History For Hire, Inc.   **(818) 765-7767**
lots
Jackson Shrub Supply, Inc.   **(818) 982-0100**
erosion cloth, dirt skins, camouflage netting, camo nets
LCW Props   **(818) 243-0707**
Different Sizes & Shapes, Brown, Green
RDD U.S.A. Inc.   **(213) 742-0666**
4638 E Washington Blvd., Commerce, CA 90040
various sizes & styles, woodland & desert
www.rddusa.com
Supply Sergeant   **(323) 849-3744**
503 N. Victory Blvd, Burbank, CA 91502
military nets, army nets, navy nets, camping nets, camp nets
david@jacksgt.com * www.supplysergeantshop.com
Universal Studios Property & Hardware Dept   **(818) 777-2784**
Camouflage nets of various sizes for rent.

Campers

See: RV Vehicles & Travel Trailers, Equip & Parts

Camping Equipment

See Also: Binoculars, Scopes & Telescopes* Camouflage Nets* Canopies, Tents, Gazebos, Cabanas* Fishing Equipment & Tackle* Lanterns* Sporting Goods & Services* Walkie-Talkies

The Hand Prop Room LP.   **(323) 931-1534**
stoves, ice chest, lanterns, sleeping bags, adult
History For Hire, Inc.   **(818) 765-7767**
period, contemporary, great coolers
LCW Props   **(818) 243-0707**
Tents, Cots, Outdoor Kitchen BBQ, Pots & pans, Backpacks, Military Surplus
Sony Pictures Studios-Prop House (Off Lot)   **(310) 244-5999**
hiking backpacks, backpacking backpacks, bedrolls, sleeping bags, canteens, fanny packs, canes, walking sticks, more
Sport Chalet   **(310) 235-2847**
11801 W Olympic Blvd, Los Angeles, CA, 90025
Website has store locator. sleeping bags to cookware
Universal Studios Property & Hardware Dept   **(818) 777-2784**
Prop camping equipment for rent.

Candelabras

See Also: Lanterns

Castle Antiques & Design   **(855) 765-5800**
11924 Vose St, N Hollywood, CA, 91605
Candelabras and chandeliers for rent or purchase.
info@castleantiques.net * www.castleprophouse.com
Dapper Cadaver/Creatures & Cultures   **(818) 771-0818**
Wrought iron candelabras. Tabletop candelabras and floor candelabras.
The Hand Prop Room LP.   **(323) 931-1534**
period-present
History For Hire, Inc.   **(818) 765-7767**
table top, Gothic, iron, brass
LCW Props   **(818) 243-0707**
Brass, Religious, Silver Plated, Many
Modern Props   **(323) 934-3000**
contemporary candlebras, futuristic candelabras
Prop Services West   **(818) 503-2790**

ShopWildThings   **(928) 855-6075**
2880 Sweetwater Ave, Lake Havasu City, AZ, 86406
Event Decor, Beaded Curtains, Chain Curtains, String Curtains & Columns, Crystal Columns. Reliable service & delivery.
help@shopwildthings.com * www.shopwildthings.com
Sony Pictures Studios-Fixtures   **(310) 244-5996**
5933 W Slauson Ave, Culver City, CA, 90230
period to present day, large sel
www.sonypicturesstudios.com
Universal Studios Property & Hardware Dept   **(818) 777-2784**
Candelabras of all kinds; period to present; fancy to plain; electric to candle all for rent.
Used Church Items, Religious Rentals   **(239) 992-5737**
216 Cumer Road, McDonald, PA, 15057
Candelabras - 3-lite, 7-lite, floor, tabletop, wrought iron, large, small, catholic, votive stands, sanctuary.
warehouse@religiousrentals.com * www.religiousrentals.com
Warner Bros. Studios Property Department   **(818) 954-2181**
Period, hanging, silver, ornate, metal, floor standing, candelabra shades, brass, decorative

Candles

See Also: Candelabras* Hobby & Craft Supplies

Antonino Ajello & Bros. House of Candles   **(310) 204-4724**
10315 Washington Blvd, Culver City, CA, 90232
Double Wick Candles and Triple Wick Candles all sizes/dimensions. Cater to industry schedules. Events/home design.
www.houseofcandlesculvercity.com
General Wax & Candle Company   **(818) 765-6357**
6863 Beck Ave, N. Hollywood, CA, 91605
Open Tues-Sat
ShopWildThings   **(928) 855-6075**
2880 Sweetwater Ave, Lake Havasu City, AZ, 86406
Event Decor, Beaded Curtains, Chain Curtains, String Curtains & Columns, Crystal Columns. Reliable service & delivery.
help@shopwildthings.com * www.shopwildthings.com
Sony Pictures Studios-Prop House (Off Lot)   **(310) 244-5999**
battery operated candles, bar candles, candelabras, tapers, glass candels, candle holders, candle lamps, candle lanterns
Universal Studios Property & Hardware Dept   **(818) 777-2784**
Scented candles, religious candles, prayer candles, tea candles and more.
Used Church Items, Religious Rentals   **(239) 992-5737**
216 Cumer Road, McDonald, PA, 15057
Beeswax Candles, Candle Holders, Candlesticks, Processional Candles, Votive Candles, Altar Candles
warehouse@religiousrentals.com * www.religiousrentals.com

Candy Counters

See: Candy Jars* Candy Racks* Display Cases, Racks & Fixtures (Store)

Candy Jars

See Also: Candy Racks

C. P. Valley   **(323) 466-8201**
Glass candy jars, ceramic candy jars, apothecary candy jars, plastic candy jars.
The Hand Prop Room LP.   **(323) 931-1534**
period-present
History For Hire, Inc.   **(818) 765-7767**
large inventory, filled
RC Vintage, Inc.   **(818) 765-7107**
40s, 50s & 60s Glass, jars to entire display cases and racks for candy specifically, including faux candy and gumball machines
Universal Studios Property & Hardware Dept   **(818) 777-2784**
Glass jars and plastic jars for candy or with candy all for rent.

Candy Machines

See: Vending Machines

Candy Racks

AIR Designs (818) 768-6639
Displays, Convenience Store, Countertop & Free Standing
C. P. Valley (323) 466-8201
Candy racks, candy jars, candy dispensers, candy vending displays
The Hand Prop Room LP. (323) 931-1534
vintage candy racks, antique candy rack, metal candy rack, steel candy rack, 3 level candy rack
History For Hire, Inc. (818) 765-7767
filled
Sony Pictures Studios-Prop House (Off Lot) (310) 244-5999

Canes

The Costume House (818) 508-9933
DutchGuard (800) 821-5157
412 W. 10th Street, Kansas City, MO, 64105
customer service (816) 221-3581. canes, staffs, sword canes & walking sticks, a novel selection
The Hand Prop Room LP. (323) 931-1534
period-present
History For Hire, Inc. (818) 765-7767
plain & fancy
LCW Props (818) 243-0707
Plain & Fancy
Omega/Cinema Props (323) 466-8201
Walking canes & walking sticks; wooden canes, metal canes, bamboo canes
Prop Services West (818) 503-2790
Universal Studios Property & Hardware Dept (818) 777-2784
Walking sticks and canes of many time periods and taste all for rent.

Canoes

See: Boats & Water Sport Vehicles

Canopies, Tents, Gazebos, Cabanas

See Also: Audience Seating* Carnival Dressing/Supplies* Military Props & Equipment* Sewing Services, Industrial

American Awning (323) 222-7500
1901 N San Fernando Rd, Los Angeles, CA 90065
canopies
Badia Design, Inc. (818) 762-0130
5420 Vineland Ave, N. Hollywood, CA, 91601
Badia Design Inc. has tents for your Moroccan themed party, wedding or special event.
info@badiadesign.com * www.badiadesign.com
Castex Rentals (323) 462-1468
1044 N. Cole Ave, Hollywood, CA, 90038
Caravan and EZ up dealer (all sizes), sales and rentals, custom canopies and canopy parts
service@castexrentals.com * www.castexrentals.com
Chattanooga Tent Co. (800) 843-8514
1110 Oak St, Chattanooga, TN, 37403
event & production tents & awnings
Fall Creek Corporation (765) 482-1861
PO Box 92, Whitestown, IN, 46075
Civil War era, military & civilian. historical to custom
tents ajfulks@fcsutler.com * www.fcsutler.com
History For Hire, Inc. (818) 765-7767
pup tents, also cabanas

L. A. Circus (323) 751-3486
Call for Appt, Los Angeles, CA, 90047
circus tents, vintage circus tents, largest circus trailers, ticket booths, circus trailers, circus linens
circusinc@aol.com * www.lacircus.com

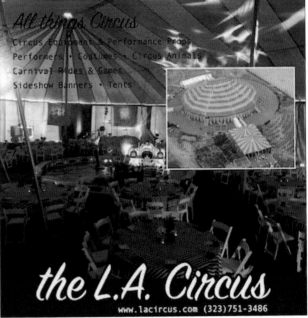

L. A. Party Works (888) 527-2789
9712 Alpaca St, S El Monte, CA, 91733
Canopies and cabanas, EZ UPs and tents for rent.
partyworks@aol.com * www.partyworksusa.com

LCW Props (818) 243-0707
Tents, Inflatable Domes, EZ-Ups
RDD U.S.A. Inc. (213) 742-0666
4638 E Washington Blvd., Commerce, CA 90040
largest supplier of many styles of tents & tarps
www.rddusa.com
Supply Sergeant (323) 849-3744
503 N. Victory Blvd, Burbank, CA 91502
military tents, camping tents, army tents, heavy duty tents, weather tents, military tarps, army tarps
david@jacksgt.com * www.supplysergeantshop.com
Sword & Stone (818) 562-6548
Yurts of America (317) 377-9878
4375 Sellers St, Lawrence, IN, 46226
14'-30' yurt kits

Canvas

See Also: Fabrics* Nautical Dressing & Props
Damian Canvas Works　　　　　　　　**(310) 822-2343**
322 Culver Blvd #261, Playa Del Rey, CA 90293
Mainly for boats & props. Canvas, paintings, furniture, clothing, jewelry
Sony Pictures Studios-Prop House (Off Lot)　　**(310) 244-5999**
Canopy, canopies, 6x9 canvas'
Universal Studios Property & Hardware Dept　　**(818) 777-2784**
Painting canvases, canvas tents, canvas supplies and more.

Caps

See: Headwear - Hats, Bonnets, Caps, Helmets Etc.

Car Hoists

See: Automotive/Garage Equip. & Parts

Car Parts

See: Automotive/Garage Equip. & Parts

Car Seat, Child

See: Children/Baby Accessories & Bedroom

Cargo Nets

See Also: Chain & Rope* Nautical Dressing & Props* Warehouse
Dressing
LCW Props　　　　　　　　　　　　**(818) 243-0707**
Fishing nets, fishing webb net, crate of nets, and more nautical equipment
Pacific Fibre & Rope Co.　　　　　　　**(800) 825-7673**
903 Flint Ave, Wilmington, CA, 90748
moreinfo@pacificfibre.com * www.pacificfibre.com

Carhop Trays

AIR Designs　　　　　　　　　　　　**(818) 768-6639**
Door & Steering Wheel Mount
The Hand Prop Room LP.　　　　　　　**(323) 931-1534**
vintage carhop trays, aluminum carhop trays, metal carhop trays, plastic carhop
trays
History For Hire, Inc.　　　　　　　　**(818) 765-7767**
and the stuff that goes on them
RC Vintage, Inc.　　　　　　　　　　**(818) 765-7107**
40s, 50s & 60s, large and small trays
Sony Pictures Studios-Prop House (Off Lot)　　**(310) 244-5999**

Caribbean Dressing

See: Jungle Dressing* Tikis & Tropical Dressing

Caricature Drawings

See: Art For Rent

Carnival Dressing/Supplies

See Also: Balloons & Balloon Sculptures* Calliopes* Carnival Games
& Rides* Carousel Horses* Circus Equipment/Dressing/Costumes*
Clowns* Fun House Mirrors* Memorabilia & Novelties* Ticket Booths*
Vendor Carts & Concession Counters
Amusement Svcs/Candyland Amusements　　**(818) 266-4056**
18653 Ventura Blvd Ste 235, Tarzana, CA, 91356
Games, rides, food stands, ticket booths. We are the owner, no middleman.
Straight from the Carnival itself
www.candylandamusements.com
Artistic Carnival & Circus Design　　　　**(323) 751-3486**
Circus & carnival dressing, costumes, consulting services

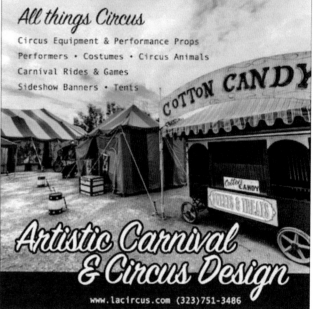

All things Circus
Circus Equipment & Performance Props
Performers • Costumes • Circus Animals
Carnival Rides & Games
Sideshow Banners • Tents

Artistic Carnival & Circus Design
www.lacircus.com (323)751-3486

Christiansen Amusements　　　　　　　**(800) 300-6114**
Call for Appt
Carnival rides & games for all events & productions
info@amusements.com * www.amusements.com
Dapper Cadaver/Creatures & Cultures　　　**(818) 771-0818**
Sideshow props and poster art. Freakshow oddities and skeletons.
E.C. Prop Rentals　　　　　　　　　　**(818) 764-2008**
string lights & barricades
History For Hire, Inc.　　　　　　　　**(818) 765-7767**
Mardi Gras heads, trunks, bed of nails

L. A. Circus (323) 751-3486
Call for Appt, Los Angeles, CA, 90047
tentage, silent flags, circus posters, steam train, costumes, side show banner, circus dressing room, horses
circusinc@aol.com * www.lacircus.com

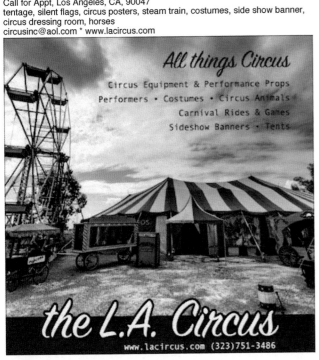

L. A. Party Works (888) 527-2789
9712 Alpaca St, S El Monte, CA, 91733
in Vancouver tel. 604-589-4101. booths, games, vendor carts & much more
partyworks@aol.com * www.partyworksusa.com
Lennie Marvin Enterprises, Inc. (Prop Heaven) (818) 841-5882
side show banners, games, machines, mechanical figures, cut-outs
RC Vintage, Inc. (818) 765-7107
Bumper cars, Clown Head Trash Cans Funhouse Mirrors, Carnival Games... String Lights

Carnival Games & Rides

See Also: Carnival Dressing/Supplies* Carousel Horses* Circus Equipment/Dressing/Costumes* Game Booths
Amusement Svcs/Candyland Amusements (818) 266-4056
18653 Ventura Blvd Ste 235, Tarzana, CA, 91356
Carnival games, carnival rides, carnival food stands, ticket booths. We are the owner, no middleman.
www.candylandamusements.com

Christiansen Amusements (800) 300-6114
Call for Appt
Carnival rides & games; Quality & Experience for all events & productions
info@amusements.com * www.amusements.com

L. A. Circus (323) 751-3486
Call for Appt, Los Angeles, CA, 90047
tunnel of love swan, Barker Booths, Morland photo booths, ticket booths, small carrousel horses, mary go rounds
circusinc@aol.com * www.lacircus.com

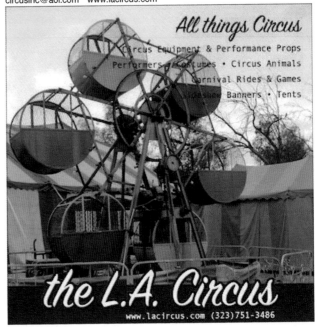

DISPLAY AD AND LISTINGS FOR THIS CATEGORY
CONTINUE ON THE FOLLOWING PAGE

L. A. Party Works (888) 527-2789
9712 Alpaca St, S El Monte, CA, 91733
in Vancouver tel. 604-589-4101. Carnival Games; dunk tanks, human bowling, crab races, zip lines & much more
partyworks@aol.com * www.partyworksusa.com

DUNK TANKS / RIDES / ZIP LINE / GAME BOOTHS / HIGH STRYKER / MORE

BOOK TODAY:
888-527-2789
partyworksusa.com

PARTYWORKS
I N T E R A C T I V E

Carousel Horses

Amusement Svcs/Candyland Amusements (818) 266-4056
18653 Ventura Blvd Ste 235, Tarzana, CA, 91356
carousel horses, carousel jets, carousel dragons, carousel cups, other rotating rides, tidal wave, ferris wheel, kite flyer, sizzler rock-o-plane
www.candylandamusements.com

Christiansen Amusements (800) 300-6114
Call for Appt
Carnival Ride Horses for photo or filming
info@amusements.com * www.amusements.com

Omega/Cinema Props (323) 466-8201
Large carousel animals to miniature toy carousel animals.

Universal Studios Property & Hardware Dept (818) 777-2784
Prop carousel horses of many shapes, types and sizes for rent.

Carpet & Flooring

See Also: Art Deco Carpet & Rugs Dirt Skins* Red Carpeting, Events/Premiers* Rugs* Sono Tubes* Studio Tile Flooring* Tile, Marble, Granite, Etc.*

FormDecor, Inc. (310) 558-2582
America's largest event rental supplier of 20th Century furniture and accessories for Modern and Mid-Century styles.

Linoleum City, Inc. (323) 469-0063
4849 Santa Monica Blvd, Hollywood, CA, 90029
Vinyl, Carpet, Linoleum, Hardwood, Laminate, Cork, Tile, Sisal, Seagrass, Bamboo, Area Rugs, Wall Cork, Dance Floors.
sales@linocity.com * www.linoleumcity.com

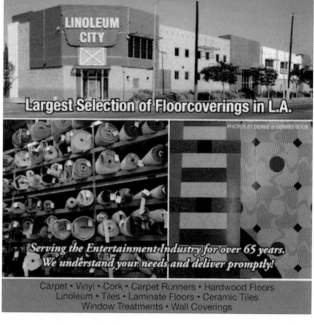

LINOLEUM CITY

Largest Selection of Floorcoverings in L.A.

Serving the Entertainment Industry for over 65 years. We understand your needs and deliver promptly!

Carpet • Vinyl • Cork • Carpet Runners • Hardwood Floors
Linoleum • Tiles • Laminate Floors • Ceramic Tiles
Window Treatments • Wall Coverings

Pacific Floor Company (818) 456-9415
9300 Oso Ave, Chatsworth, CA, 91311
Design to Build Performance Floor Contractor; Gym Flooring, Fitness Flooring, Dance Flooring, Designer Flooring, & more.
cglenn@pacificfloor.com * www.pacificfloor.com

Prop Services West (818) 503-2790

The Rug Warehouse (310) 838-0450
3270 Helms Ave, Los Angeles, CA, 90034
High quality area rugs & carpet. Contemporary, traditional, antique, kilims, shags, hides, custom options & more
www.therugwarehouse.com

Warner Bros. Drapery, Upholstery & Flooring (818) 954-1831
4000 Warner Blvd, Burbank, CA, 91522
All grades of residential & commercial carpet; Indoor/Outdoor; Linoleum; VCT Tile; installation
wbsfdrapery@warnerbros.com * www.wbdrapery.com

Carport Canopies

See: Awnings Canopies, Tents, Gazebos, Cabanas*

Carriages, Horse Drawn

Barton's Horse Drawn Carriages & Sleighs (626) 447-6693
Antique carriages/sleighs, transport to site, drivers provided, realistic brown prop horse on wheels, saddles, harnesses, 1800s-1900s

Harris Stage Lines (805) 237-1860
5995 N. River Rd, Paso Robles, CA 93446
horse drawn vehicles for hire: stagecoach, carriages, chariots.

Universal Studios Property & Hardware Dept (818) 777-2784
Horse drawn carriages, horse drawn chariots, and more for rent.

Warner Bros. Studios Property Department (818) 954-2181
Western carriages, Buggies, Covered Farm Wagons, Stagecoach wagons

Cars

See: Vehicle Preparation Services Vehicles*

Carts

See: Airport Dressing & Hangars Vendor Carts & Concession Counters*

Carved Figures

History For Hire, Inc.   (818) 765-7767
ship's figureheads
Modern Props   (323) 934-3000
contemporary figurines, futuristic figurines
Ob-jects   (818) 351-4200
Omega/Cinema Props   (323) 466-8201
Carved figurines from ancient to modern of various animals, sports and
religions.
Sony Pictures Studios-Prop House (Off Lot)   (310) 244-5999
Sword & Stone   (818) 562-6548
Universal Studios Property & Hardware Dept   (818) 777-2784
Carved figures of different backgrounds, ethnicities, and mediums for rent.
Used Church Items, Religious Rentals   (239) 992-5737
216 Cumer Road, McDonald, PA, 15057
Patron Saints, Angels, Jesus, Joseph, Mary, Wood & Plaster, Pietas, Stations
of the Cross, Scenes. All sizes.
warehouse@religiousrentals.com * www.religiousrentals.com
ZG04 DECOR   (818) 853-8040
Animal, Figurative, Relief, Tribal, African, Busts, Dogs, Horses, Male, Female

Cases

See Also: Briefcases Crates/ Vaults* Display Cases, Racks &
Fixtures (Store)* Futuristic Furniture, Props, Decorations* Luggage*
Musical Instrument Cases* Trophies/Trophy Cases*
Astro Audio Video Lighting, Inc.   (818) 549-9915
6615 San Fernando Rd, Glendale, CA, 91201
Road cases, lighting bags, Pro X Cases, Stand Cases, Turntable Cases,
Keyboard Bags and more for your traveling needs.
www.astroavl.com
E.C. Prop Rentals   (818) 764-2008
The Hand Prop Room LP.   (323) 931-1534
LCW Props   (818) 243-0707
Huge selection, Molded Cases, Anvil Cases, Pelican Cases, Road Cases,
Wood Cases, Any Kind.

Cash Registers

A. D. Business Solutions   (818) 765-5353
11412 Vanowen St, N. Hollywood, CA 91605
Cash registers, point of sale equipment, touch screens, credit card devices,
time card devices & more.
info@cashandcredit.com * www.cashandcredit.com
AIR Designs   (818) 768-6639
Period to Modern, Practical

American Cash Registers   (323) 664-4586
507 N Hoover St, Los Angeles, CA, 90004
sell, rent, lease & repair; cash registers & point of sale machines from 1900 to
present
erwin@american-pos.com * www.american-pos.com
The Hand Prop Room LP.   (323) 931-1534
period-modern
History For Hire, Inc.   (818) 765-7767
LCW Props   (818) 243-0707
Digital & Analog, Period - Present
RC Vintage, Inc.   (818) 765-7107
modern to early 1900s Brass and Contemporary
Sony Pictures Studios-Prop House (Off Lot)   (310) 244-5999
Universal Studios Property & Hardware Dept   (818) 777-2784
Vintage cash registers, modern cash registers, manual cash registers, electric
cash registers all for rent.

Casino Gaming Equipment

See: Gambling Equipment

Caskets

See Also: Cemetery Dressing Mortuary* Religious Articles*
ABC Caskets Factory   (323) 268-1783
1705 N Indiana St, Los Angeles, CA, 90063
Manufacture fine wood & metal caskets and funeral dressing; biers, carts,
skirts, church trucks, lowering devices & more
factorydirect@abettercasket.com * www.abettercasket.com

C. P. Valley   (323) 466-8201
Metal caskets, wooden coffins, toe pincher coffins, gothic coffins, pine coffins,
chrome plated caskets and more.
California Casket Co.   (310) 963-3905
12421 Venice Blvd Suite 1, Los Angeles, CA, 90066
Caskets, grave markers, flower arrangements, urns, also hearse rentals,
funeral supplies. Can rent
calcasket@aol.com * www.losangelesfuneralservice.com
Dapper Cadaver/Creatures & Cultures   (818) 771-0818
Modern wood & metal caskets, toe-pinchers and vintage coffins. Casket stands
and lecterns.
The Hand Prop Room LP.   (323) 931-1534
History For Hire, Inc.   (818) 765-7767
old, new, Dracula
LCW Props   (818) 243-0707
Wood, Metal, Military, Rigged
Sony Pictures Studios-Prop House (Off Lot)   (310) 244-5999
Universal Studios Property & Hardware Dept   (818) 777-2784
Metal caskets & wood caskets for rent.

Cat Scratching Post, Climbers, Condos & Beds

See: Pet Furniture, Houses, Clothing

Catering

See Also: Beer Equipment, Taps & Coolers* Events, Decorations, Supplies & Services* Food, Artificial Food* Food, Food Stylists

Along Came Mary Events (323) 931-9082
5265 W. Pico Blvd, Los Angeles, CA, 90019
Big Screen Cuisine Catering (818) 345-0009
6924 Canby Ave. Ste 109, Reseda, CA 91335
Catering for film/TV since 1989, quick turnaround
Bobby Weisman Caterers (818) 843-9999
736 S. Glenwood Pl, Burbank, CA, 91506
Serving the Entertainment Industry since 1984. Our mobile kitchens travel nationwide.
Command Performance Catering (800) 817-3232
5273 N. Commerce Ave, Unit # 6, Moorpark, CA, 93021
Java The Truck (310) 717-6967
345 Kansas St, El Segundo, CA 90245
Mobile coffee shop offering the widest selection around, 24/7. Self contained, 2 barristas, no setup time, blended drink
Michael's Epicurean (818) 360-7626
15411 Lassen Street, Los Angeles, CA, 91345
Full service catering & event planning
Rise & Shine Catering (310) 649-0906
7401 W 88th Pl, Los Angeles, CA, 90045
Breakfast & lunch catering. Film locations, office meetings, private events.
Someone's In The Kitchen (818) 343-5151
5973 Reseda Blvd, Tarzana, CA, 91356
Too Tasty Catering (818) 355-5431
Call For Arrangements Glendale, CA, 91201
Highest quality bistro gourmet food at affordable prices. All items hand-crafted from scratch.
www.tootasty-catering.com
Universal Studios Special Events (818) 777-9466
100 Universal City Plaza, Universal City, CA, 91608
www.universalstudiosspecialevents.com
Wolfgang Puck Catering (323) 491-1250
6801 Hollywood Blvd Ste 513, Hollywood, CA, 90028

Cats

See: Animals (Live), Services, Trainers & Wranglers

Catwalks

See: Grating, Grated Flooring, Catwalks

Cauldrons

See: Occult/Spiritual/Metaphysical

Cellular Phones

See: Telephones, Cellular

Cemetery Dressing

See Also: Caskets* Florists/Floral Design* Morgue* Mortuary

Dapper Cadaver/Creatures & Cultures (818) 771-0818
Tombstones, monuments, obelisks & crypts. Angels, crosses & military. Cemetery combos. Custom tombstone engraving.
Green Set, Inc. (818) 764-1231
high quality tombstones, urns decorative and plain, many grave markers, cemetery walls
The Hand Prop Room LP. (323) 931-1534
caskets, prop headstones, fake bats
History For Hire, Inc. (818) 765-7767
headstones
Jackson Shrub Supply, Inc. (818) 982-0100
over 200 units in top quality fiberglass, grave markers, headstones, funeral dressing
LCW Props (818) 243-0707
Tombstones Real & Fake, Caskets, Coffins
Sony Pictures Studios-Prop House (Off Lot) (310) 244-5999
Universal Studios Graphic Design & Sign Shop (818) 777-2350
custom tombstones
Universal Studios Property & Hardware Dept (818) 777-2784
Prop tombstones and other cemetery dressing for rent.

Centrifuges

LCW Props (818) 243-0707
Large & Small, Working, Rigged
Universal Studios Property & Hardware Dept (818) 777-2784
Prop centrifuges for rent.

Ceramic Casting & Manufacturing

See: Prop Design & Manufacturing* Prop Reproduction & Fabrication* Staff Shops

Ceramics

See: Decorative Accessories* Pottery* Urns

Certificates

See Also: Art, Supplies & Stationery* Office Equipment & Dressing

C. P. Valley (323) 466-8201
Various certificates; birth certificates, award certificates, professional certificates, graduation certificates and more.
The Earl Hays Press (818) 765-0700
services the Industry only. every kind of form you can think of
The Hand Prop Room LP. (323) 931-1534
printed graphics, office dressing
History For Hire, Inc. (818) 765-7767
custom mfg.
Hollywood Cinema Arts, Inc. (818) 504-7333
Thousands of Certificates in ornate custom frames to standard black frames.
Hollywood Studio Gallery (323) 462-1116
100s to choose from,custom-medical-miltary,school,etc
LCW Props (818) 243-0707
Custom Graphics, Legal, Sports, Diplomas, Dentistry, Medical, Professional
Omega/Cinema Props (323) 466-8201
Medical certificates, diplomas, dental certificates, achievement certificates and much more!
On Set Graphics (661) 233-6786
Web Based Business
100% cleared office certificates for everything from medical certificates and dental certificates to participation awards.
info@onsetgraphics.com * www.onsetgraphics.com
Prop Services West (818) 503-2790
Sony Pictures Studios-Prop House (Off Lot) (310) 244-5999
large selection
Universal Studios Graphic Design & Sign Shop (818) 777-2350
custom
Universal Studios Property & Hardware Dept (818) 777-2784
Prop certificates for rent; graduation diplomas, medical certification and more.

Chain & Rope

See Also: Camouflage Nets* Cargo Nets
Alley Cats Studio Rentals (818) 982-9178
all widths,lengths,styles rope; fake & real chain
Castex Rentals (323) 462-1468
1044 N. Cole Ave, Hollywood, CA, 90038
rope boxes, rolls, hanks of sash, sash cord, mason line, manilla rope
service@castexrentals.com * www.castexrentals.com
E.C. Prop Rentals (818) 764-2008
wide assortment
The Hand Prop Room LP. (323) 931-1534
period-modern
History For Hire, Inc. (818) 765-7767
rope & chain
LCW Props (818) 243-0707
Large Selection Of Assorted Sizes & Styles. Boating, Industrial, Sporting
Pacific Fibre & Rope Co. (800) 825-7673
903 Flint Ave, Wilmington, CA, 90748
rope manufacturing, all kinds, as much as you need, hwr fittings, tools, nets,
but no chains, rope
moreinfo@pacificfibre.com * www.pacificfibre.com

PACIFIC FIBRE ROPE CO. INC. EST. 1978
We've sold over 25 million miles of rope.
You can be assured: We know rope!

ROPE NETTING LADDERS HARDWARE
CUSTOM ROPE DESIGN & PRODUCTS
www.pacificfibre.com

Sony Pictures Studios-Prop House (Off Lot) (310) 244-5999
faux chains, real chains, chain sleeve

Chain Hoists

See Also: Automotive/Garage Equip. & Parts* Construction Site
Equipment* Rigging, Equipment or Services
AIR Designs (818) 768-6639
Block & Tackle Engine Hoists
Astro Audio Video Lighting, Inc. (818) 549-9915
6615 San Fernando Rd, Glendale, CA, 91201
Chain hoists and rope hoists for rigging.
www.astroavl.com
E.C. Prop Rentals (818) 764-2008
large & small, also A frames

Chain Link Fence

See: Fences

Chainmail

See: Armor, Chainmail, Suits of Armor

Chair Covers

See: Events, Decorations, Supplies & Services* Slipcovers*
Upholstery Materials/Services

Chair Risers

See: Audience Seating* Stages, Portable & Steel Deck

Chairs

See Also: Benches* Chairs, Senate Chamber (Sets)* Director's
Chairs, Bags, Pouches* Folding Chairs/Tables* Furniture,
Outdoor/Patio* Futons & Bean Bag Chairs* Opera Chairs*
Slipcovers* Stools
Advanced Liquidators Office Furniture (818) 763-3470
new & used, all quality levels, huge variety of models, designers, upholstery,
costs, purpose, and types.
AIR Designs (818) 768-6639
Restaurant/Bar, Coffee Shop, Fast Food, Bistro, Cafeteria, Interior & Exterior
Bridge Furniture & Props Los Angeles (818) 433-7100
We carry modern & traditional furniture, lighting, accessories, cleared art,&
rugs. Items are online for easy shopping.

BRIDGE LA
FURNITURE & PROPS
3210 Vanowen St.
Burbank, CA 91505
BridgeProps.com
Tel: 818.433.7100

C. P. Two (323) 466-8201
All kinds of chairs from patio and restaurant to folding and beach.
C. P. Valley (323) 466-8201
All kinds of chairs from patio and restaurant to folding and beach.

**DISPLAY ADS AND LISTINGS FOR THIS CATEGORY
CONTINUE ON THE FOLLOWING PAGE**

Castle Antiques & Design   (855) 765-5800
11924 Vose St, N Hollywood, CA, 91605
Chairs of all kinds including seats, benches, chairs, stools, sofas for rent and purchase.
info@castleantiques.net * www.castleprophouse.com

Dozar Office Furnishings   (310) 559-9292
9937 Jefferson Blvd, Culver City, CA, 90232
Rentals X22. Office chairs, arm chairs, reception chairs, executive chairs, waiting room chairs, wheel chairs
dozarrents@aol.com * www.dozarrents.com

E.C. Prop Rentals   (818) 764-2008
high multiples, industrial, metal/wood/castered/stool/etc.

Faux Library Studio Props, Inc.   (818) 765-0096
luxury chairs, high end chairs, classical chairs, desk chairs, posh chairs, elegant chairs, residential office chairs

FormDecor, Inc.   (310) 558-2582
America's largest event rental supplier of 20th Century furniture and accessories for Modern and Mid-Century styles.

LCW Props   (818) 243-0707
Stacking, Upholstered, Futuristic, Office, Rocket Chairs

Lennie Marvin Enterprises, Inc. (Prop Heaven)   (818) 841-5882
cafe seating, restaurant chairs, contemporary chairs, high qty.

Little Bohemia Rentals   (818) 853-7506
11940 Sherman Rd, N Hollywood, CA, 91605
Vintage to contemp %u2013lounge, club, cigar, reclining, bergere, Danish modern, leather, slipper, high back, chair & ottoman
sales@wearelittlebohemia.com * www.wearelittlebohemia.com

Lux Lounge EFR   (888) 247-4411
106 1/2 Judge John Aiso St #318, Los Angeles, CA, 90012
Many Chairs: Classic Chairs, Contemporary Chairs, Armless Chairs, Lounge Chairs, Ghost Chairs
info@luxloungeefr.com * www.luxloungeefr.com

Modern Props   (323) 934-3000
contemporary chairs, futuristic chairs, multiples chairs

Modernica Props   (323) 664-2322
classic, modern, contemporary, multiples

NEST Studio Rentals, Inc.   (818) 942-0339
contemporary, upholstered, dining, office

Ob-jects   (818) 351-4200
decorative, contemporary, traditional, upholstery, dining chairs, ottomans, loveseats, sofas, settees, sectionals

Omega/Cinema Props   (323) 466-8201
All kinds of chairs from patio and restaurant to folding and beach.

Prop Services West   (818) 503-2790

Sony Pictures Studios-Prop House (Off Lot)   (310) 244-5999
large selection/multiples, adirondack chairs, armchairs, chair backs, folding bamboo chairs, benches, beach chairs, more

Taylor Creative Inc.   (888) 245-4044
We offer a large selection of dining and lounge chairs, perfect for conferences, movie premieres, and social affairs.

TR Trading Company   (310) 329-9242
15604 S Broadway, Gardena, CA, 90248
85,000 sq/ft of items, selection and inventory changes weekly
sales@trtradingcompany.com * www.trtradingcompany.com

Universal Studios Property & Hardware Dept   (818) 777-2784
All kinds of chairs of different styles and time periods for rent.

Warner Bros. Studios Property Department   (818) 954-2181
Dining, Wingback, Patio, Upholstered, folding, stacking, side, bentwood, Bank of England, Barcelona, executive

ZG04 DECOR   (818) 853-8040
Seating, Benches, Club Chairs, Side, Client, Dining, Desk, Swivel, Vanity, Folding Chairs, Event Seating, Multiples

Chairs, Senate Chamber (Sets)

Sony Pictures Studios-Prop House (Off Lot)   (310) 244-5999

Chalk Boards

See Also: Office Equipment & Dressing* School Supplies, Desks & Dressing

E.C. Prop Rentals   (818) 764-2008
castered & wall-mount

The Hand Prop Room LP.   (323) 931-1534
wall mounted chalkboards, rolling chalkboards, dry erase boards, chalk, chalk erasers

History For Hire, Inc.   (818) 765-7767
rolling & wall-mount

LCW Props   (818) 243-0707
Many Sizes, Green, Black, White Boards, Freestanding

Prop Services West   (818) 503-2790

RC Vintage, Inc.   (818) 765-7107
including stand up menu chalk boards,

Sony Pictures Studios-Prop House (Off Lot)   (310) 244-5999
all sizes

Universal Studios Property & Hardware Dept   (818) 777-2784
Chalkboards for rent; from standing blackboards to wall mounted chalkboards.

Chandeliers

Castle Antiques & Design (855) 765-5800
11924 Vose St, N Hollywood, CA, 91605
Candelabras and chandeliers for rent or purchase.
info@castleantiques.net * www.castleprophouse.com

Lux Lounge EFR (888) 247-4411
106 1/2 Judge John Aiso St #318, Los Angeles, CA, 90012
Chandeliers: Custom made Chandeliers, Classic Chandeliers, Crystal
Chandeliers, Luxury Chandeliers, Pendant Chandeliers
info@luxloungeefr.com * www.luxloungeefr.com

Omega/Cinema Props (323) 466-8201
Period to contemporary chandeliers.

Pasadena Antiques & Design (626) 389-3938
330 S. Fair Oaks Avenue, Pasadena, CA 91105
Antique & Mid-Century Chandeliers of all descriptions.
roy@antiquesofpasadena.com * www.antiquesofpasadena.com

Prop Services West (818) 503-2790

Rapport International Furniture (323) 930-1500
435 N La Brea Ave, Los Angeles, CA, 90036
Dozens of elegant, contemporary, modern and luxury chandelier pieces to
choose from.
rapport@rapportusa.com * www.rapportfurniture.com

ShopWildThings (928) 855-6075
2880 Sweetwater Ave, Lake Havasu City, AZ, 86406
Event Decor, Beaded Curtains, Chain Curtains, String Curtains & Columns,
Crystal Columns. Reliable service & delivery.
help@shopwildthings.com * www.shopwildthings.com

Sony Pictures Studios-Fixtures (310) 244-5996
5933 W Slauson Ave, Culver City, CA, 90230
period to present day, large sel,art deco, brass, candle, chinese, crystal,
contemporary, court room, crystal, empire style, french, georgian, mission,
morrocan, novelty, period, spanish, traditional, victorian, western
www.sonypicturesstudios.com

Sony Pictures Studios-Prop House (Off Lot) (310) 244-5999
period chandeliers to modern chandeliers, chandelier shipping boxes

Susanne Hollis, Inc. (626) 441-0346
230 Pasadena Ave, South Pasadena, CA, 91030
20th - 17th century Antiques, Accessories, and Fine Art from around the world
in our 19,000sqft. warehouse and showrooms
sales@susannehollis.com * www.susannehollis.com

Sword & Stone (818) 562-6548

Universal Studios Property & Hardware Dept (818) 777-2784
Chandeliers of different sizes and time periods. Gold chandeliers, plain
chandeliers, crystal chandeliers & more.

Used Church Items, Religious Rentals (239) 992-5737
216 Cumer Road, McDonald, PA, 15057
Large Gothic Chandeliers, Wall Scones, Hanging, Wall Mount, Sanctuary
Lights, Votive Stands and Votive Lights.
warehouse@religiousrentals.com * www.religiousrentals.com

Warner Bros. Studios Property Department (818) 954-2181
Hanging, ballroom, crystal, antique, Entryway chandeliers, floor standing,
period, hallway, ornate

ZG04 DECOR (818) 853-8040
Classic Chandeliers, Crystal Chandeliers, Contemporary Chandeliers,
Traditional Chandeliers

Change Machines

See: Vending Machines

Chapel

See: Church, Chapel, Synagogue, Mosque

Charities & Donations

Amusement Svcs/Candyland Amusements (818) 266-4056
18653 Ventura Blvd Ste 235, Tarzana, CA, 91356
Games, rides, food stands, ticket booths. We are the owner, no middleman.
www.candylandamusements.com

Habitat for Humanity of Greater Los Angeles (424) 246-3637
8739 E Artesia Blvd, Bellflower, CA, 90706
Habitat's ReStores are home-improvement thrift stores, helping to fund our
mission. Free pick-up, tax-deductible.
www.ShopHabitat.org

Hollywood Cinema Production Resources (310) 258-0123
any props/set material, will pick up, charity donation

The ReUse People (818) 244-5635
3015 Dolores St, Los Angeles, CA, 90065
We accept almost all types of building supplies and offer tax-deductible
donation receipts.
JefCockerell@TheReUsePeople.org * www.TheReUsePeople.org

Charters

See: Aircraft, Charters & Aerial Services* Nautical/Marine Services &
Charters* Trains

Chase Lights

Astro Audio Video Lighting, Inc. (818) 549-9915
6615 San Fernando Rd, Glendale, CA, 91201
Various chase lights for purchase or rent including DJ effects and more.
www.astroavl.com

Sony Pictures Studios-Fixtures (310) 244-5996
5933 W Slauson Ave, Culver City, CA, 90230
period to present day
www.sonypicturesstudios.com

Universal Studios Property & Hardware Dept (818) 777-2784
Various chase light strings for different occasions.

Chastity Belts

See: Goth/Punk/Bondage/Fetish/Erotica Etc.* Wardrobe,
Antique/Historical

Check-out Stands

See: Grocery Check-out Stands (Complete)

Chemical Lab

See: Lab Equipment

Chestnut Carts/Machines

See: Vendor Carts & Concession Counters

Chicago Themed Parties

See: Events, Decorations, Supplies & Services* Events,
Design/Planning/Production* Travel (City/Country) Themed Events

Chicken Feeders

See: Farm Equipment & Dressing

Children's & Baby Clothing

See Also: Children/Baby Accessories & Bedroom

The Costume House (818) 508-9933
christening gowns, school clothes

Sony Pictures Studios-Wardrobe (310) 244-5995
alterations, call (310) 244-7260

Universal Studios Costume Dept (818) 777-2722
Rental, mfg., & alterations

Western Costume Co. (818) 760-0900

Children/Baby Accessories & Bedroom

See Also: School Supplies, Desks & Dressing* Toys & Games

Art By Kidz (818) 240-6650
Call for Appt, Glendale, CA, 91207
100s of ORIGINAL CHILDRENS 2D & 3D ARTWORKS for rent at low flat rates
based on size. Cleared copyright, located in Glendale.
www.artbykidz.com

C. P. Two (323) 466-8201
Kids toys, sleighs, rocking horses, infant carriers, kids bikes, kids wagons, baby
changing tables and much more.

The Hand Prop Room LP. (323) 931-1534

History For Hire, Inc. (818) 765-7767
period carriages, strollers, toys, accessories

Hollywood Studio Gallery (323) 462-1116
prints-mounted unicorn head

Modern Props (323) 934-3000
contemporary and futuristic, furniture to accessories, small collection

NEST Studio Rentals, Inc. (818) 942-0339
furniture, toys, accessories; many cleared items

Omega/Cinema Props (323) 466-8201
Baby accessories and children accessories from toys to lunch boxes.

Prop Services West (818) 503-2790

Sony Pictures Studios-Prop House (Off Lot) (310) 244-5999
crib, bed, stroller, car seat, plus accessories, baby bath, baby bottle warmer,
baby car items, baby monitor, bassinet

Universal Studios Property & Hardware Dept (818) 777-2784
Children and baby accessories for the bedroom.

Chimes & Bells

The Hand Prop Room LP.	(323) 931-1534
LCW Props	(818) 243-0707

Many Sizes & Styles

Omega/Cinema Props   (323) 466-8201
Decorative bells, functional bells, cow bells, brass desk bells, school bells, copper bells, wind chimes and more.

Sony Pictures Studios-Prop House (Off Lot)   (310) 244-5999
chimes, counter bell, cow bell, dinner bell, entry bell, gong, religious bell, school bell, ship bell, summons bell, warning bell

Universal Studios Property & Hardware Dept   (818) 777-2784
Wind chimes, servants bells and much more for rent.

Chimney Parts & Tops

See: Rooftop Dressing

China Hat Lights

See Also: Caged Vapor Proof Lights* Lamp Posts & Street Lights* Lamp Shades* Lamps* Lanterns* Light Fixtures* Light Fixtures, Period* Lighting, Industrial* Warehouse Dressing

AIR Designs   (818) 768-6639
Post-Mount, Hanging, Wall-Mounted, Assorted Styles

Alley Cats Studio Rentals   (818) 982-9178
Gooseneck china hat lights & hanging china hat lights.

E.C. Prop Rentals   (818) 764-2008
1000 inventory, many styles, practical, w/optional piping for all

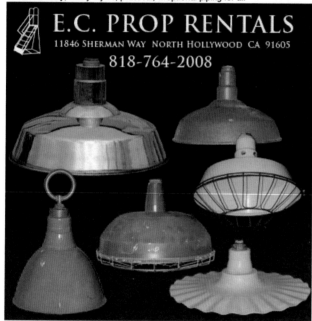

E.C. PROP RENTALS
11846 SHERMAN WAY NORTH HOLLYWOOD CA 91605
818-764-2008

The Hand Prop Room LP.	(323) 931-1534
Modern Props	(323) 934-3000

contemporary china hat lights

Sony Pictures Studios-Fixtures   (310) 244-5996
5933 W Slauson Ave, Culver City, CA, 90230
period to present day
www.sonypicturesstudios.com

Universal Studios Property & Hardware Dept   (818) 777-2784
Various china hat lights and china hat lamps for rent.

Chinese Art & Artifacts

See: Asian Antiques, Furniture, Art & Artifacts

Chinese Fly Streamers

See: Asian Antiques, Furniture, Art & Artifacts* Flags/Banners

Chinese Pots

See: Pottery

Choir Risers

See: Audience Seating* Stages, Portable & Steel Deck

Christmas

See Also: Candles* Costume Rental Houses* Costumes* Events, Decorations, Supplies & Services* Events, Design/Planning/Production* Holiday Theme Events* Sleds* Sleighs* Snow, Artificial & Real* Soldier Toys & Drums* Thrones* Toys & Games* Wrapped Prop Gift Packages

Almost Christmas Prop Shoppe   (954) 914-0469
5057 Lankershim Blvd, N. Hollywood, CA, 91601
Christmas decor.

Bob Gail Special Events   (310) 202-5200
Christmas in July? No problem! With our huge inventory of Christmas and Winter Props you can have Christmas year round.

Flower Art   (323) 935-6800
5859 West 3rd Street, Los Angeles, CA, 90036
If you need a little Xmas (even in July), let us transform your sets into a Xmas wonderland w/trees, garlands wreaths!
info@flowerartla.com * http://www.flowerartla.com

FROST   (310) 704-8812
Call for Appointment, 21515 Madrona Ave, Torrance, CA 90503
Holiday decor, specializing in large scale trees, Santa sets, ornaments. Professional installations.
mdisplay@yahoo.com * www.frostchristmasprops.com

Green Set, Inc.   (818) 764-1231
Christmas trees live/artif., lights, decor, sleighs, snowman, soldiers, smalls, outdoor and indoor dressing

The Hand Prop Room LP.   (323) 931-1534
Sleighs, decorations, lights, toys

History For Hire, Inc.   (818) 765-7767
thrones, multiples of toys; Santa's workshop dressing

Jackson Shrub Supply, Inc.   (818) 982-0100
Xmas trees, snowmen, toy soldiers, reindeer, Santa throne, Santa sleigh, Christmas decorations, string lights

LCW Props   (818) 243-0707
Decorations Big & Small, Inflatables, Lighting, Reindeer, Penguins

Modern Props   (323) 934-3000
contemporary christmas dressing & period christmas dressing

Moskatel's   (213) 689-4590
733 S San Julian St, Los Angeles, CA, 90014

Omega/Cinema Props (323) 466-8201
Christmas swag, christmas trees, nutcrackers, tree toppers, christmas stockings, christmas ornaments and much more.
ShopWildThings (928) 855-6075
2880 Sweetwater Ave, Lake Havasu City, AZ, 86406
Event Decor, Beaded Curtains, Chain Curtains, String Curtains & Columns, Crystal Columns. Reliable service & delivery.
help@shopwildthings.com * www.shopwildthings.com
Sony Pictures Studios-Fixtures (310) 244-5996
5933 W Slauson Ave, Culver City, CA, 90230
period to present day, indoor/ext. lights/christmas decorations
www.sonypicturesstudios.com
Sony Pictures Studios-Prop House (Off Lot) (310) 244-5999
christmas decorations, tree ornaments, wreaths, floral arrangements, christmas trees
Stats Floral Supply (626) 795-9308
120 S Raymond Ave, Pasadena, CA, 91105
Universal Studios Property & Hardware Dept (818) 777-2784
lights, decorations, props, Santa throne

Church, Chapel, Synagogue, Mosque

See Also: Clerical, Judicial, Academic Gowns/Apparel Religious Articles*
LCW Props (818) 243-0707
Bibles, Hymn Books, Crosses, Pews, Sound Equipment, Lighting
Omega/Cinema Props (323) 466-8201
Church organs, church pews, church lecterns, church benches, church artwork, bimahs, and much more.
RJR Props (404) 349-7600
Church podiums and church pews for rent.
Universal Studios Property & Hardware Dept (818) 777-2784
Church props, synagogue props and mosque props of all time periods for rent.
Used Church Items, Religious Rentals (239) 992-5737
216 Cumer Road, McDonald, PA, 15057
Catholic Statues, Crucifixes, Censors, Vestments, Votive Stands, Candelabras, Podiums, Hanging Lights, Baptismals.
warehouse@religiousrentals.com * www.religiousrentals.com
Warner Bros. Studios Property Department (818) 954-2181
Religious smalls, candle holders, religious panels, pictures, statues, crosses

Cigar Store Indian

See Also: Smoking Products
The Hand Prop Room LP. (323) 931-1534
Omega/Cinema Props (323) 466-8201
Tobacco Indian figures, cigar store Indian statue, tobacco Indian statues
RC Vintage, Inc. (818) 765-7107
Large 7 feet, a couple models
Universal Studios Property & Hardware Dept (818) 777-2784
Cigar store Indian statue

Cigar/Tobacco Products

See: Smoking Products

Cigarette Machines

See: Vending Machines

Cinder Block

See: Concrete Block, Brick, Gravel, Sand, Rocks, Etc.

Circus Equipment/Dressing/Costumes

See Also: Animal Cages Animals (Live), Services, Trainers & Wranglers* Balloons & Balloon Sculptures* Calliopes* Carnival Dressing/Supplies* Carnival Games & Rides* Carriages, Horse Drawn* Clowns* Vendor Carts & Concession Counters* Wagons*
Artistic Carnival & Circus Design (323) 751-3486
Circus & carnival dressing, costumes, consulting services
Dapper Cadaver/Creatures & Cultures (818) 771-0818
Sideshow gaffs & oddities: feejee mermaids, etc. Fortune teller cabinet & decor. Scary clown & dark ride props.
History For Hire, Inc. (818) 765-7767
trunks, animal stands, etc.

L. A. Circus (323) 751-3486
Call for Appt, Los Angeles, CA, 90047
classic/traditional to contemporary to avant garde, incl the Roschu circus props, side show wagons, tokens
circusinc@aol.com * www.lacircus.com

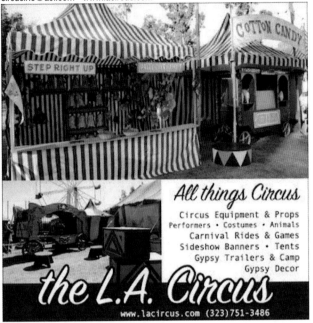

All things Circus
Circus Equipment & Props
Performers • Costumes • Animals
Carnival Rides & Games
Sideshow Banners • Tents
Gypsy Trailers & Camp
Gypsy Decor
the L.A. Circus
www.lacircus.com (323)751-3486

L. A. Party Works (888) 527-2789
9712 Alpaca St, S El Monte, CA, 91733
in Vancouver tel. 604-589-4101. trapeze to tightropes, snake lady, magicians and clowns
partyworks@aol.com * www.partyworksusa.com
Modern Props (323) 934-3000
side show backdrops, circus banners
RC Vintage, Inc. (818) 765-7107
side show posters & accessories only

Cities Themed Parties

See: Events, Decorations, Supplies & Services Events, Design/Planning/Production* Themed Environment Construction* Travel (City/Country) Themed Events*

Civil War Era

See Also: Firearms, Gunsmith, Firearm Choreography Military Props & Equipment* Prop Reproduction & Fabrication* Wardrobe, Antique/Historical* Weaponry, Historical*
Caravan West Productions (661) 268-8300
35660 Jayhawker Rd, Aqua Dulce, CA, 91390
weapons, saddlery, costumes, props, rolling stock & buckaroos
caravanwest@earthlink.net * www.caravanwest.com
Fall Creek Corporation (765) 482-1861
PO Box 92, Whitestown, IN, 46075
Civil War era, military & civilian. high quality uniforms, equip., weapons, rifles; muskets, tentage, misc.
ajfulks@fcsutler.com * www.fcsutler.com
The Hand Prop Room LP. (323) 931-1534
Confederate weaponry and union weaponry, all kinds of costuming dressing for soldiers of the time.
History For Hire, Inc. (818) 765-7767
Lots! Can outfit 100s of soldiers
Sony Pictures Studios-Prop House (Off Lot) (310) 244-5999
Sword & Stone (818) 562-6548

Clapboards

See: Slates/Clapboards

Classroom

See: Chalk Boards School Supplies, Desks & Dressing*

Cleaners & Cleaning Services

See Also: Vacuum Cleaners

Crime Scene Clean Up　　　　　　　　**(888) 431-7233**
We come to you - biohazard disposal, Los Angeles, CA, 90630
Trauma scene management, licensed, bonded, insured O.S.H.A./Haz-Mat
certified, Dept. of Health #TSW-003

Milt & Edie's　　　　　　　　　　**(818) 846-4734**
4021 W Alameda at Pass, Burbank, CA, 91505
2-Hour cleaning & shirt laundry available 24/7/365 at no extra charge. Tailoring
& Alterations available 24/7/365.
info@miltandedies.com * www.miltandedies.com

MiLT & EDiE'S DRYCLEANERS & Tailoring Center
OPEN **24** HOURS A DAY, **7** DAYS A WEEK,
365 DAYS A YEAR...
including Holidays!
WE SPECIALIZE IN COUTURE GARMENTS AND COSTUMES.
2-Hour cleaning & shirt laundry available 24 hours a day, 7 days a week... at no extra charge!
Tailors Available 24/7/365!
(818) 846-4734
4021 W. Alameda Ave. at Pass Ave. • Burbank, CA 91505
www.MiltandEdies.com

Sunset Laundraclean　　　　　　　　**(323) 653-2360**
8201 Melrose Ave, Los Angeles, CA, 90046
Dry cleaning & laundry, 24 hr service, pickup/del for studios only

Cleaning Supplies

See: Expendables

Clear Vinyl

See Also: Floor, Ground & Surface Protection Wall Coverings*

Linoleum City, Inc.　　　　　　　　**(323) 469-0063**
4849 Santa Monica Blvd, Hollywood, CA, 90029
Clear Vinyl, Vinyl Runners, Rubber Runner, Diamond Plate Vinyl, Embossed
Flooring, Clear Carpet Runners, Entrance Mats
sales@linocity.com * www.linoleumcity.com

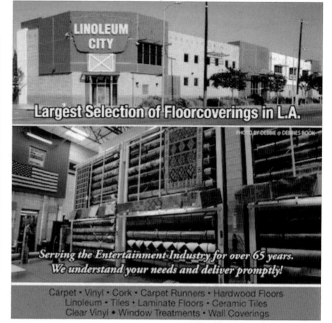

LINOLEUM CITY
Largest Selection of Floorcoverings in L.A.
*Serving the Entertainment Industry for over 65 years.
We understand your needs and deliver promptly!*
Carpet • Vinyl • Cork • Carpet Runners • Hardwood Floors
Linoleum • Tiles • Laminate Floors • Ceramic Tiles
Clear Vinyl • Window Treatments • Wall Coverings

Clearances

See: Art For Rent Art, Artists For Hire* Private Investigations*
Research, Advisors, Consulting & Clearances*

Cleared Art

See: Art For Rent Art, Artists For Hire* Paintings/Prints*
Photographs* Research, Advisors, Consulting & Clearances*
Sculpture*

Clerical, Judicial, Academic Gowns/Apparel

Alpha Robes　　　　　　　　　　**(314) 921-7777**
1310 Hialeah Pl, Florissant, MO, 63033
Robes: children's choir, judicial, baptismal, paraments, vestments, stoles,
accessories

C. M. Almy & Son, Inc.　　　　　　**(800) 225-2569**
228 Sound Beach Ave, Old Greenwich, CT, 06870
Mfg.-all denominations, stock & custom. vestments, clothing for clergy & choir

The Costume House　　　　　　　**(818) 508-9933**
priest robes, judges robes

Cotter Church Supplies　　　　　**(213) 385-3366**
1701 James M. Wood Blvd, Los Angeles, CA, 90015

Sony Pictures Studios-Wardrobe　　**(310) 244-5995**
alterations, call (310) 244-7260

Universal Studios Costume Dept　　**(818) 777-2722**
Rental, mfg., & alterations

Victorious Robes　　　　　　　　**(800) 866-2630**
123 Washington St, Bolivar, TN, 38008
robes: childrens choir, judicial, baptismal, custom, paraments, vestments,
accessories, stoles

Western Costume Co.　　　　　　　**(818) 760-0900**

Climate Control

See: Air Conditioning & Heating, Production/Event Heaters, Indoor*
Heaters, Outdoor* Plumbing Fixtures, Heating/Cooling Appliances*

Clocks

See Also: Watches & Pocket Watches

AIR Designs (818) 768-6639
Kitchen, Restaurant, Diner, Auto

Castle Antiques & Design (855) 765-5800
11924 Vose St, N Hollywood, CA, 91605
Many clock sets, wall clocks, and desk clocks for rent or purchase.
info@castleantiques.net * www.castleprophouse.com

E.C. Prop Rentals (818) 764-2008
industrial, school, dual-face, multiples + time clocks

Feldmar Watch & Clock Center (310) 274-8016
9000 W. Pico Blvd, Los Angeles, CA, 90035
Repairs

The Hand Prop Room LP. (323) 931-1534
period-present, novelty

History For Hire, Inc. (818) 765-7767
desk, wall, time clocks

LCW Props (818) 243-0707
Digital, Analog, Period - Present, Large & Small, Programmable, Rigged

Mandex LED Displays (800) 473-5623
2350 Young Ave, Thousand Oaks, CA, 91360
LED Displays & Sign Rentals nationwide, all configurations, tickers, flexible panels, big LED Digital Countdown Clocks.
alan@ledsignage.com * www.ledsignage.com

Modern Props (323) 934-3000
contemporary clocks, futuristic clocks, household clocks, commercial clocks

NEST Studio Rentals, Inc. (818) 942-0339
wall, mantel, desk, novelty, kitchen

Ob-jects (818) 351-4200
decorative

Omega/Cinema Props (323) 466-8201
Period clocks to contemporary clocks; wall clocks, grandfather clocks, modern clocks, mid-century modern clocks and more.

Pasadena Antique Warehouse (626) 404-2422
1609 East Washington Blvd., Pasadena, CA, 91104
Vintage and Antique grandfather, wall, mantle, and cuckoo clocks. Antique clock radios.
pasadenaantiquewarehouse@gmail.com * www.pasadenaantiquewarehouse.com

Prop Services West (818) 503-2790

RC Vintage, Inc. (818) 765-7107
40s, 50s & 60s & time clocks Herman Miller

Sony Pictures Studios-Prop House (Off Lot) (310) 244-5999
large selection, chess timers, contessa clock, desk clocks, hourglass clocks, mantle clocks, oversized clocks, radio clocks

Universal Studios Property & Hardware Dept (818) 777-2784
All kinds of clock prop rentals

Clowns

See Also: Carnival Dressing/Supplies Circus Equipment/Dressing/Costumes* Make-up & Hair, Supplies & Services*

Bubba's Clown Supplies (904) 272-5878
P.O. Box 65039, Orange Park, FL, 32065
face paint, noses, horns, wigs, circus music, apparel

Clown Supplies Inc. (603) 435-8812
Website only.
catalog sales; clown make-up, noses, wigs, hats, buttons, props, sound makers, books, magic tricks, gag books
www.clownsupplies.com

Dapper Cadaver/Creatures & Cultures (818) 771-0818
Lifesize scary clown character props.

Priscilla Mooseburger Originals (800) 973-6277
116 Division St West, Maple Lake, MN, 55358
custom tailored clown costumes, make-up supplies

Spear's Specialty Shoe Co. (413) 739-5693
12 Orlando St, Springfield, MA, 01108
custom made clown shoes & street shoes, also slap gloves & Santa boots & belts

Clump Grass

See: Greens

Clutter

See: Salvage, Rubble, Clutter & Trash (Prop)

CNC Router & Laser Etching Services

See Also: Prop Design & Manufacturing Water Jet CNC Services*

Beyond Image Graphics (818) 547-0899
1853 Dana St, Glendale, CA, 91201
Over 10 years servicing the film industry, and businesses with top quality prints and signs. CNC Routing.
rafi@beyondimagegraphics.com * www.beyondimagegraphics.com

Bill Ferrell Co. (818) 767-1900
10556 Keswick St, Sun Valley, CA, 91352
CNC routing; CAD drawing; Fabrication
www.billferrell.com

Charisma Design Studio, Inc. (818) 252-6611
8414 San Fernando Road, Sun Valley, CA, 91352
Bring sketches to life! Glass Etching and waterjet, experienced cutting services
info@charismadesign.com * www.charismadesign.com

D'ziner Sign Co. (323) 467-4467
801 Seward Street, Los Angeles, CA 90038
Props, 3D carving
sales@dzinersign.com * www.dzinersign.com

**DISPLAY ADS AND LISTINGS FOR THIS CATEGORY
CONTINUE ON THE FOLLOWING PAGE**

EFX- Event Special Effects   (626) 888-2239
125 Railroad Ave, Monrovia, CA, 91016
Custom Fabrication- CNC- Plasma Table- Pipe & Ring Benders- 3D Renderings
info@efxla.com * www.efxla.com

Flix FX Inc.   (818) 765-3549
7327 Lankershim Blvd #4, N Hollywood, CA, 91605
CNC machining, CNC wood & plastic routing, CNC tube & profile bending
info@flixfx.com * www.flixfx.com

The Hand Prop Room LP.   (323) 931-1534
CNC Machine, CAD Drawing, 3D Rapid Prototyping, Laser engraving

HPR Custom   (323) 931-1534
5700 Venice Blvd, Los Angeles, CA, 90019
Design, CAD drawings, fabrication, laser cutting and laser etching.
www.hprcustom.com

Jet Sets   (818) 764-5644
6910 Farmdale Ave, N Hollywood, CA, 91605
set construction, custom props, scenic painting, special effects, set illustration, 3D Router Cutting
dougmorris@jetsets.com * www.jetsets.com

Warner Bros. Design Studio Scenic Art & Sign Shop   (818) 954-1815
4000 Warner Blvd, Burbank, CA, 91522
graphic design and production studio for signs & scenic art; digital printing to hand-painted
wbsigns@warnerbros.com * www.wbsignandscenic.com

Worlds of Wow   (817) 380-4215
2126 Hamilton Rd, Argyle, TX, 76226
Advanced CNC routing services.
www.worldsofwow.com

Coal

See: Concrete Block, Brick, Gravel, Sand, Rocks, Etc.

Coat Racks

See: Office Equipment & Dressing* Prop Houses

Coca Cola Memorabilia

AIR Designs   (818) 768-6639
Neon, Signage, Vending Machines, Clocks, Soda Dispensers

The Hand Prop Room LP.   (323) 931-1534
signs, bottles

History For Hire, Inc.   (818) 765-7767
coolers, bottles, other brands

LCW Props   (818) 243-0707
Period Pieces, Large Quantity Of Soda Bottles & Glasses, Lighting

RC Vintage, Inc.   (818) 765-7107
signs & machines 40s, 50s & 60s, coca cola machines

Cockpits

See: Airport Dressing & Hangars* Space Shuttle/Space Hardware

Cocktails

See: Food, Artificial Food

Coffee House

See Also: Cafe Tables/Chairs/Umbrellas* Delicatessen Equipment

AIR Designs   (818) 768-6639
Cappuccino Machines/Equipment, Signs, Neon Displays, Counters, Tables & Chairs

The Hand Prop Room LP.   (323) 931-1534
cappucino machines, display, dressing, coffee grinders

History For Hire, Inc.   (818) 765-7767

Lennie Marvin Enterprises, Inc. (Prop Heaven)   (818) 841-5882
cappuccino machines, espresso machines, signs, counter/back bar/cases/tables/stools

Modern Props   (323) 934-3000
contemporary/household & commercial cappuccino machines

New Frontier Coffee   (310) 839-3423
5890 Blackwelder Street, Culver City, CA 90232
We have a tremendous amount of coffee related equipment. New and vintage, prop and functional.
newfrontiercoffee@gmail.com * www.nfcoffee.com

RC Vintage, Inc.   (818) 765-7107
Cappuccino Machines, Coffee Machines Espresso, contemporary, Grinders. Carts. Bean bags Faux. Displays

Sony Pictures Studios-Prop House (Off Lot)   (310) 244-5999
coffee grinders

Universal Studios Property & Hardware Dept   (818) 777-2784
Coffee house dressing including signage, furniture & appliances.

Coffee Mugs

See: Promotional Items & Materials

Coffins, Wooden & Period

See: Caskets* Cemetery Dressing* Prop Houses* Religious Articles

Coin Op Rides, Machines & Cranes

See: Arcade Equipment, Games & Rides* Vending Machines

Coin-op Photo Booths

See: Photo Booths

Coins & Currency

See: Money (Prop)

Collars & Cuffs

See: Wardrobe, Accessories

Collectibles

See Also: Coca Cola Memorabilia* Comic Books & Comic Book Racks* Memorabilia & Novelties* Pepsi Memorabilia* Prop Houses* Sports Fan Items, Memorabilia, Photographs

AIR Designs   (818) 768-6639
Toys, Signs, Auto, Pedal Cars, smalls

Castle Antiques & Design   (855) 765-5800
11924 Vose St, N Hollywood, CA, 91605
Collectibles from almost all eras in time for rent or purchase.
info@castleantiques.net * www.castleprophouse.com

The Hand Prop Room LP.   (323) 931-1534
period-present, radios, clocks, sports, electronics

History For Hire, Inc.   (818) 765-7767

LCW Props   (818) 243-0707
Coins, Stamps, Bronzes, Metals, Rocks, Call Us First

Modern Props   (323) 934-3000
contemporary/futuristic/electronic

Off The Wall   (310) 652-1185
737 N. La Cienega, Los Angeles, CA 90069
unusual antiques of early 20th C., Art Deco to mid-century

Sony Pictures Studios-Prop House (Off Lot)   (310) 244-5999
coin collection, gems, minerals, insect collections, spoon collections

Used Church Items, Religious Rentals   (239) 992-5737
216 Cumer Road, McDonald, PA, 15057
Vintage Religious Catholic and Christian Antiques and Collectibles from Rosary Beads to Cathedral Stained Glass Windows
warehouse@religiousrentals.com * www.religiousrentals.com

Color Keyed Backgrounds

See: Green Screens, Blue Screens* Fabrics* Paint & Painting Supplies

Columns

See Also: Architectural Pieces & Artifacts* Scenery/Set Rentals* Statuary

American Wood Column Corp.   (718) 782-3163
913 Grand St, Brooklyn, NY, 11211-2785
catalog sales; large sel. of millwork, architectural/decorative small finials to tall columns, plain to ornate, custom t

Bob Gail Special Events   (310) 202-5200
Bob Gail has an extensive list of themed props for movie sets, events, and tradeshows for rental in CA and Las Vegas.

C. P. Valley   (323) 466-8201
Antique columns to vintage columns; English Victorian columns, oak columns, pine columns, and more.

Green Set, Inc.   (818) 764-1231
Columns, Pedestals & Balustrades, Banister sectionals, specialized capitals, Ionic, Corinthian, Doric, and statue

Jackson Shrub Supply, Inc.   (818) 982-0100
Corinthian columns, Ionic columns, modern columns, many others 8'-12' tall, fiberglass columns, and more.

LCW Props   (818) 243-0707
Roman, Futuristic, Faux

Modern Props   (323) 934-3000
Roman-present, fiberglass

MODRoto   (888) 724-1228
16404 Knott Ave, La Mirada, CA, 90638
plastic, also pedestals, lightbases, colonnades, arches for wedding & events

Sword & Stone   (818) 562-6548

Warner Bros. Studios Staff Shop   (818) 954-2269
Manufacturer of exterior & interior details used for the creation of sets in all architectural styles & eras.

Comic Books & Comic Book Racks

See Also: Collectibles* Magazines & Magazine/Newspaper Racks

AIR Designs (818) 768-6639
Display Stands, Racks, Old & New Comic Books

The Earl Hays Press (818) 765-0700
services the Industry only. mockups/classics

The Hand Prop Room LP. (323) 931-1534
in stock & will fabricate, Vintage comic books, vintage DC Comics

Hi De Ho Comics & Books with Pictures (310) 394-2820
1431 Lincoln Blvd, Santa Monica, CA, 90401
Southern California's first & best. comic books

History For Hire, Inc. (818) 765-7767
custom mfg.

Meltdown (323) 851-7223
7522 W Sunset Blvd, Los Angeles, CA, 90046
comic books

RC Vintage, Inc. (818) 765-7107
40s, 50s & 60s comic books, wall & standing racks, full set of matching racks

Sony Pictures Studios-Prop House (Off Lot) (310) 244-5999

Universal Studios Property & Hardware Dept (818) 777-2784
Comic book racks and comic book store dressing.

Computer Graphics

See: Graphics, Digital & Large Format Printing

Computer Software & Services

See Also: Computers

Di-No Computers-Service Dept (626) 795-6674
2817 E Foothill, Pasadena, CA 91107
sales & repair; Pasadena's premier Apple specialist

Hi-Tech Computer Rental (818) 841-0677
172 W Verdugo Ave, Burbank, CA, 91502
Mac, PC, peripherals

LCW Props (818) 243-0707
Product Boxes For Software, Custom Graphics, Playback Software, Media Players

Computers

See Also: Control Boards

Airwaves Wireless (818) 501-8200
13400 Riverside Dr. # 103 Sherman Oaks, CA 91423
Cellular phones, cellphones, tablets, laptops, iPhones, iPads, dummy phones, walkies, Wi-Fi, satellite phones, macbooks
anita@airwaveswireless.com * www.airwaveswireless.com

C. P. Valley (323) 466-8201
Computers, computer accessories, and computer parts.

The Earl Hays Press (818) 765-0700
services the Industry only. stock & custom-made fake screens

The Hand Prop Room LP. (323) 931-1534

LCW Props (818) 243-0707
Large Selection Of New & Old, Servers Of Any Kind, Custom, Working, Rigged, Our Specialty Is Servers

SERVER RACKS ARE OUR SPECIALTY!
6439 San Fernando Rd. Glendale, CA 91201
Phone: 818-243-0707 - www.lcwprops.com

Modern Props (323) 934-3000
contemporary laptops, flat-screen LCDs

RJR Props (404) 349-7600
Computers and computer props are our specialty. Over 5000 computers, accessories and more for rent from new to old.

Sony Pictures Studios-Prop House (Off Lot) (310) 244-5999

Universal Studios Property & Hardware Dept (818) 777-2784
Many prop computers and computer parts for rent

Woody's Electrical Props (818) 503-1940
period to futuristic. mockups & will fabricate any design. Fantasy sets, military sets, industrial sets, air tower

Concert Lighting

See: Lighting & Sound, Concert/Theatrical/DJ/VJ

Concert Staging

See: Audience Seating* Stages, Portable & Steel Deck

Concession Equipment

See: Carnival Dressing/Supplies* Vending Machines* Vendor Carts & Concession Counters

Concession Stands/Carts

See: Vendor Carts & Concession Counters

Concrete Block, Brick, Gravel, Sand, Rocks, Etc.

See Also: Building Supply, Lumber, Hardware, Etc.* Tile, Marble, Granite, Etc.

Ace Brick & Patio (818) 781-1755
6023 Sepulveda Blvd, Van Nuys, CA, 91411
also fireplaces, BBQ's & mantels

American Builders Supply (818) 768-3176
8563 San Fernando Rd, Sun Valley, CA, 91352
block, brick, pavers, stone, sand, gravel, boulders

Angelus Block Co., Inc (818) 767-8576
11374 Tuxford St, Sun Valley, CA, 91352
mfg., every kind of cinder block, paving block, 7 plants in L.A.

Arroyo Building Materials (818) 365-6170
890 Arroyo St, San Fernando, CA, 91340
new/used brick, block, stone, sand, gravel, boulders

Balboa Brick & Supply Co. (818) 785-7492
16755 Roscoe Blvd, North Hills, CA, 91343
concrete, masonry, brick, stone, sand, stucco

California Quarry Products (661) 942-3992
42057 3rd St. East, Lancaster, CA, 93535
we deliver. gravel, rocks, sand, landscape supplies

Central Valley Builders Supply (818) 343-3838
7030 Reseda Blvd, Reseda, CA, 91335
also loc in Van Nuys & North Hills comprehensive: sand, gravel, rock, cinderblock, brick, etc.

Classical Building Arts (626) 575-3516
9516 Gidley St, Temple City, CA, 91780
stone, brick, masonry material

Green Set, Inc. (818) 764-1231
gravel, sand, rocks; also prop rocks

Hanson Aggregates (626) 856-6710
13550 E Live Oak Ave, Irwindale, CA, 91706
aggregates in large quantity, rocks to fine sand

Hub Construction Specialties (818) 547-3364
5310 San Fernando Rd, Glendale, CA, 91203
concrete specialists

Jackson Shrub Supply, Inc. (818) 982-0100
desert, mountain peaks, outcroppings, river rock, pebbles, walls, coal

La Canada Rustic Stone Co. (626) 798-7876
1385 Lincoln Ave, Pasadena, CA, 91103
wall/volcanic rock, sand, cement, brick/block, great flagstone

Pennsylvania Builders Supply (323) 957-7620
6659 Santa Monica Blvd, Los Angeles, CA, 90038
block, brick, brick veneer, sand, gravel, cement

Prime Building Materials (818) 765-6767
6900 Lankershim Blvd, N Hollywood, CA, 91605
brick, block, stone, sand, gravel, Mexican pavers

Sepulveda Building Materials (310) 436-1400
359 E Gardena Blvd, Gardena, CA, 90248
block, brick, sand, gravel, cement, slate, boulders

Condom Machines

See: Vending Machines

Condoms

See: Goth/Punk/Bondage/Fetish/Erotica Etc.

Conduit

See: Electrical/Electronic Supplies & Services

Cones, Traffic

See: Traffic/Road Signs, Lights, Safety Items

Confetti

See Also: Events, Decorations, Supplies & Services

Astro Audio Video Lighting, Inc. (818) 549-9915
6615 San Fernando Rd, Glendale, CA, 91201
Confetti canons/confetti machines available/confetti launchers
www.astroavl.com

Bill Ferrell Co. (818) 767-1900
10556 Keswick St, Sun Valley, CA, 91352
Confetti, streamers & die-cut shapes in tissue & metallic color combinations.
Cannon systems & continuous flow launchers
www.billferrell.com

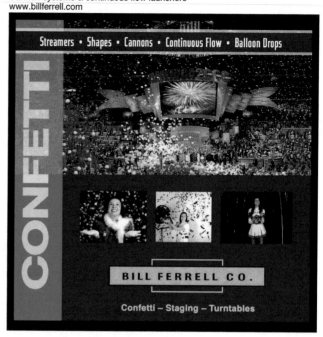

CONFETTI & FOG FX Special Effects Company (786) 308-7063
2739 W 79 St Bay, #12, Hialeah, FL 33016
www.caffx.com

EFX- Event Special Effects (626) 888-2239
125 Railroad Ave, Monrovia, CA, 91016
Double Barrel Cannon- Continuous Feed Unit- Confetti
info@efxla.com * www.efxla.com

J & M Special Effects, Inc. (718) 875-0140
524 Sackett St, Brooklyn, NY 11217
confetti, confetti cannons, confetti blasters, confetti blowers, icicles, bubbles, floating bubbles, snow dressing products
info@jmfx.net * www.jmfx.net

L. A. Party Works (888) 527-2789
9712 Alpaca St, S El Monte, CA, 91733
Confetti canons and more. If in Vancouver tel. 604-589-4101
partyworks@aol.com * www.partyworksusa.com

Universal Studios Property & Hardware Dept (818) 777-2784
Confetti including jumbo bags of confetti and plastic boxes full of confetti.

Construction Materials

See: Architectural Pieces & Artifacts* Building Supply, Lumber, Hardware, Etc.* Columns* Concrete Block, Brick, Gravel, Sand, Rocks, Etc.* Electrical/Electronic Supplies & Services* Glass & Mirrors* Metal Suppliers* Metalworking, Welding & Structural* Moulding, Wood* Paint & Painting Supplies* Paneling, Veneers & Laminates* Plastics, Materials & Fabrication* Plumbing Fixtures, Heating/Cooling Appliances* Tile, Marble, Granite, Etc.

Construction Site Equipment

See Also: Barricades Traffic/Road Signs, Lights, Safety Items*
Welding Equipment/Stations*

AIR Designs (818) 768-6639
Tools, Port-A-Potty, Manhole, Skirt, Barricades, Cones, Mesh, Construction Dressing

Alley Cats Studio Rentals (818) 982-9178
street construction props, cement mixer, Caltrans blinking arrow, porta potties

E.C. Prop Rentals (818) 764-2008
tools & equip., cement mixers, barricades, signage, K-rails, etc

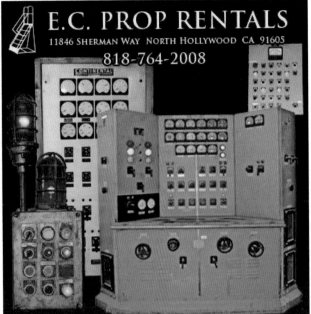

The Hand Prop Room LP. (323) 931-1534
barricades, traffic, road signs, safety items

LCW Props (818) 243-0707
Hoses, Barricades, Cones, Lights, Signs, Deliniators

Consulting Services

See: Art, Artists For Hire Research, Advisors, Consulting & Clearances* Search Tools, Directories, Libraries*

Contact Paper

See: Wall Coverings Window Treatments*

Control Boards

See Also: Computers Electronic Equipment (Dressing)*

E.C. Prop Rentals (818) 764-2008
extensive sel., including stainless w/ lights/buttons/switches

History For Hire, Inc. (818) 765-7767
radio station, recording studio, TVs, big sel.

LCW Props (818) 243-0707
Working & Rigged, Many Sizes & Styles, Period - Present

Modern Props (323) 934-3000
contemporary/futuristic-radio stations to space

Woody's Electrical Props (818) 503-1940
period to futuristic. electronic panels,read-outs. Fantasy sets, military sets, industrial sets, air tower/mission contr

Control Panels/Boxes

See Also: Electronic Equipment (Dressing) Instrument Panels*

E.C. Prop Rentals (818) 764-2008
stainless & painted-wide sel.

The Hand Prop Room LP. (323) 931-1534
past-future,mfg., electronic, real/dummy

Jadis (310) 396-3477
2701 Main St, Santa Monica, CA, 90405
Steampunk style large panels with vintage switches and gauges on casters. Army surplus and electronic frequency panels.
jadis1@gmail.com * www.jadisprops.com

LCW Props (818) 243-0707
Another Specialty. We Can Rig, Create, Any Of Our Very Large Selection

**DISPLAY ADS AND LISTINGS FOR THIS CATEGORY
CONTINUE ON THE FOLLOWING PAGE**

Modern Props (323) 934-3000
contemporary/futuristic/electronic
RJR Props (404) 349-7600
Large control panels, industrial control panels, futuristic control panels and more for rent.
Sony Pictures Studios-Prop House (Off Lot) (310) 244-5999
control panels, breakers boxes, electronic control boxes, electronic alarms, electronic equipment, electronic gauge, and more
Universal Studios Property & Hardware Dept (818) 777-2784
Many prop control panels and control boxes for rent.
Woody's Electrical Props (818) 503-1940
period to futuristic. will design & build. Fantasy sets, military sets, industrial sets, air tower, electrical panels

Convenience Store Racks

See: Display Cases, Racks & Fixtures (Store)* Store Shelf Units & Shelving

Conventions

See: Trade Shows & Conventions

Conveyor Equipment

AIR Designs (818) 768-6639
Straight, Curved, Grocery & Warehouse
Bill Ferrell Co. (818) 767-1900
10556 Keswick St, Sun Valley, CA, 91352
Gravity & motorized conveyors/treadmills. Easy variable speed & reversing controllers or computer-controlled automation.
www.billferrell.com
E.C. Prop Rentals (818) 764-2008
working electric, gravity feed, skate wheel, roller bar
LCW Props (818) 243-0707
Conveyors, Gravity, Electronic, Rigged
Machinery & Equipment Co., Inc. (909) 599-3916
115 N Cataract Ave, San Dimas, CA, 91773
Over 3 acres of industrial processing equip., such as kettles, mixers, tanks, conveyors & other stainless machinery for
sherri@machineryandequipment.com * www.machineryandequipment.com

Cooking Equipment

AIR Designs (818) 768-6639
Commercial Stoves, Ovens, Ranges, Fryers, Counters, Sinks, Mixers, Restaurant Kitchen Props
History For Hire, Inc. (818) 765-7767
vintage
LCW Props (818) 243-0707
Large Outdoor BBQ's, Pots & Pans, Home & Commercial
Modern Props (323) 934-3000
contemporary/futuristic, household & commercial
Prop Services West (818) 503-2790
Sony Pictures Studios-Prop House (Off Lot) (310) 244-5999
Universal Studios Property & Hardware Dept (818) 777-2784
All kinds of cooking equipment props for rent.

Cool Suits

See: Environmental (Cool/Heat) Suits

Copy Machines

See Also: Office Equipment & Dressing
C. P. Valley (323) 466-8201
Copy machines/copier machines from various times and manufacturers.
Cal Business Systems & Supply (310) 470-3435
1920 Pandora Ave, Ste 7, Los Angeles, CA, 90025
short term rentals, 1 day to a year, copiers, faxes, supplies & service
LCW Props (818) 243-0707
Large Selection Of Big & Small, Rigged, Non Working
Steven Enterprises (800) 491-8785
17952 Skypark Circle Unit E, Irvine, CA, 92614
Wide Format Printers. Rent/Buy. Authorized Dealer: HP, KIP, Canon, Oce, Epson. We service & supply everything we install
sales@plotters.com * www.plotters.com
Universal Studios Property & Hardware Dept (818) 777-2784
Prop photocopy machines of various sizes and types for rent.

Cork Inlay Work

See: Carpet & Flooring

Coroner

See: Morgue

Corsets

See: Goth/Punk/Bondage/Fetish/Erotica Etc.* Underwear & Lingerie, Bloomers, Corsets, Etc.

Cosmetics

See: Beauty Salon* Make-up & Hair, Supplies & Services

Costume Jewelry

See: Jewelry, Costume

Costume Rental Houses

See Also: Costume/Wardrobe/Sewing Supplies* Costumes* Costumes, International/Ethnic* Masks* Wardrobe* Wardrobe, Accessories* Wardrobe, Antique/Historical* Wardrobe, Construction & Alterations* Wardrobe, Contemporary* Wardrobe, International/Ethnic* Wardrobe, Vintage
Action Sets and Props / WonderWorks, Inc. (818) 992-8811
7231 Remmet Ave, Canoga Park, CA, 91303
Space shuttle & station, space suit, specialty props, miniatures, mechanical effects, cityscape, miniature buildings
www.wonderworksweb.com

Spacecraft • Spacesuits • Sets • Miniatures • SFX • Props
Photography • Museum Design • Architectural • Vehicles
WonderWorks INC
Serving Aerospace, Film, Entertainment & Education for a Third Of A Century

Adele's of Hollywood (323) 663-2231
5034 Hollywood Blvd, Hollywood, CA, 90027
American Costume Corp. (818) 764-2239
12980 Raymer St, N. Hollywood, CA, 91605
1770s through 1970s
Bill Hargate Costumes (323) 876-4432
1117 N Formosa Ave, Hollywood, CA 90046
Broadway Costumes, Inc. (312) 829-6400
1100 W. Cermak, Chicago, IL, 60608
Chicago's oldest & largest costume house
The Costume House (818) 508-9933
7324 Greenbush Ave, North Hollywood, CA, 91605
www.valentinoscostumes.com
Costume Rentals Corporation (818) 753-3700
11149 Vanowen St, N. Hollywood, CA, 91605
motion picture supplier & special order items
The Costume Shoppe (818) 244-1161
746 W. Doran St, Glendale, CA, 91203
Open Wed.-Sat. all periods, military, walk arounds
Global Effects, Inc. (818) 503-9273
7115 Laurel Canyon Blvd, N Hollywood, CA, 91605
science fiction, fantasy, armor, hazmat & historical
office@globaleffects.com * www.globaleffects.com
Helen Uffner Vintage Clothing LLC (718) 937-0220
30-10 41st Avenue, 3rd Floor, Long Island City, NY, 11101
authentic 1850-1973 M/W/children apparel & accessories

International Costume, Inc. (310) 320-6392
1423 Marcelina Ave, Torrance, CA, 90501
Make Believe, Inc. (310) 396-6785
3240 Pico Blvd, Santa Monica, CA, 90405
We also sell masks, wigs, theatrical makeup & access. period, novelty & character, accessories
Motion Picture Costume Company (818) 557-1247
3811 Valhalla Dr, Burbank, CA, 91505
uniforms & civilian wardrobe, 1775 to present
Oregon Shakespeare Festival Costume Rentals (541) 482-2111
408 Talent Ave, Talent, OR 97540 x308
Full-service costume rental facility featuring quality garments constructed by the Oregon Shakespeare Festival
costumerentals@osfashland.org * www.osfcostumerentals.org
Palace Costume & Prop Co. (323) 651-5458
835 N Fairfax Ave, Los Angeles, CA, 90046
1850s-1980s, European, ethnic
Returner Rentals (818) 506-7695
4019 Tujunga Ave, Studio City, CA, 91604
Roxy Deluxe (818) 487-7800
11311 Hartland St, N Hollywood, CA, 91605
Sony Pictures Studios-Wardrobe (310) 244-5995
5933 W Slauson Ave, Culver City, CA, 90230
alterations, call (310) 244-7260
www.sonypicturesstudios.com
StarMakers Costumes and Parties (626) 797-6384
605 N Lake Avenue, Pasadena, CA 91101
Costumes for kids, adults, Renaissance, mascots, Victorian, wigs, make-up, masks, Star Wars, theater, TV, film, schools
contact@StarMakersCostumes.com * www.StarMakersCostumes.com
Theatrix Costume House (800) 977-8749
165 Geary Ave 2nd Fl, Toronto, Ontario, M6H 2B8
Over 25,000 theatrical costumes in stock, tens of thousands of accessories, custom tailoring & services
Universal Studios Costume Dept (818) 777-2722
100 Universal City Plaza, Universal City, CA, 91608
Rental, mfg., & alterations
universal.costume@nbcuni.com * www.filmmakersdestination.com
Warner Bros. Studios Costume Dept (818) 954-1297
4000 Warner Blvd, Burbank, CA, 91522
Collection of period & contemporary costumes for rent categorized by era, decade and style.
wbsfcostumedesk@warnerbros.com * www.wbcostumedept.com

Western Costume Co. (818) 760-0900
11041 Vanowen St, N Hollywood, CA, 91605

Costume/Wardrobe/Sewing Supplies

See Also: Feathers* Fur, Artificial & Real* Patterns* Sewing Equipment & Workrooms* Trims, Fringe, Tassels, Beading Etc.
Acme Display Fixture & Packaging (888) 411-1870
3829 S Broadway St., Los Angeles, CA 90037
Complete store setups: garment racks, displays/display cases, counters, packaging, shelving, hangers, mannequins
sales@acmedisplay.com * www.acmedisplay.com
Beadcats (503) 625-2323
P.O. Box 2840, Wilsonville, OR, 97070-2840
catalog sales; glass seed beads size 6-24, supplies, Czech pressed glass shaped beads, books, needles, thread
The Button Store (323) 658-5473
8344 W 3rd St, Los Angeles, CA, 90048
a large collection from Europe to Far East. huge sel, every kind of button
Dharma Trading Co. (800) 542-5227
1604 4th St, San Rafael, CA 94901
catalog sales; fabric painting/dyeing supplies/tools, plain rayon garments suitable for painting/dyeing
H. E. Goldberg & Co. (800) 722-8201
9050 Martin Luther King Jr. Way, South Seattle, WA, 98118
catalog sales; sewing skins, pelts
Hedgehog Handworks (888) 670-6040
8616 La Tijera Ste 303, Westchester, CA, 90045
catalog sales; unusual needlework supplies, books on historical sewing, needlepoint & costuming topics
Hyman Hendler & Sons, Inc (212) 240-8393
142 W 38th Street, New York, NY, 10018
ribbons, lace, sequins, trims, millinery supplies + more
Lacis (510) 843-7178
2982 Adeline St, Berkeley, CA, 94703
trims, laces, costume supplies, reference books, website has useful links
L'Atelier (310) 540-4440
1722 South Catalina Ave, Redondo Beach, CA, 90277
open 10-5 Tues-Sat; 2nd location in Redondo Beach. knitting yarn
Manhattan Wardrobe Supply (212) 268-9993
245 West 29th St., 8th Floor, New York, NT 10001
all credit cards accepted, wardrobe expendables, costume expendables
info@wardrobesupplies.com * www.wardrobesupplies.com
Newark Dressmaker Supply (800) 736-6783
PO Box 4099, Bethlehem, PA, 18018
catalog sales; sewing supplies, fabrics, threads, trims, notions, zippers, patterns
Renaissance Ribbons (530) 692-0842
9690 Stackhouse Ln, Oregon House, CA, 95962
catalog sales; ribbons, trims, metallic lace for trims & for costumes, notions, upholstery & more, wholesale only
Sculptural Arts Coating, Inc. (800) 743-0379
PO Box 10546, Greensboro, NC, 27404
Mfg. of "Sculpt or Coat" nontoxic plastic cream for making props, scenery, puppets, masks, costumes, arch. elements
Testfabrics, Inc. (570) 603-0432
415 Delaware Ave, West Pittston, PA, 18643
catalog sales; synthetic & natural fabrics without additives, conservation uses: restoration/conservation/storage
Wawak Corporation (800) 654-2235
1059 Powers Rd, Conklin, NY, 13748
catalog sales; sewing supplies & tools, cleaning supplies & tools
Zipperstop (888) 947-7872
27 Allen St, New York, NY, 10002
catalog sales; YKK zippers, ship worldwide, all major credit cards, no minimum

Costumes

See Also: Animal Costumes & Walk Around Characters Holiday
Costumes* Masks* Native American* Puppets, Marionettes,
Automata, Animatronics* Wardrobe*

Adele's of Hollywood	**(323) 663-2231**
American Conservatory Theater	**(415) 439-2379**

By appt only, San Francisco, CA, 94108

Art, Models & Props, Inc. **(951) 206-9156**
1725 Marengo Ave, Pasadena, CA, 91103
Custom design/fabr. Old World to Sci-Fi, Fantasy. See ad in "Prop Design &
Manufacturing"
modelsandprops@msn.com * www.artmodeltech.com

Artistic Carnival & Circus Design **(323) 751-3486**
Circus & carnival dressing, costumes, consulting services

Broadway Costumes, Inc. **(312) 829-6400**
Chicago's oldest & largest costume house

Costume Co-Op **(818) 752-7522**
11501 Chandler Blvd, N. Hollywood, CA, 91601
Full service costume shop, alterations and made-to-order for the Film & TV
industry. No inventory sales or rentals.

The Costume House **(818) 508-9933**
theatrical, authentic 1880-1980 & Renaissance costumes

Costumes & Creatures **(612) 378-2561**
504 Malcom Ave. SE #200, Minneapolis, MN, 55414
full service costume/mascot design & fabrication. custom full body costumes

Global Effects, Inc. **(818) 503-9273**
medieval replicas, science fiction costumes, futuristic costumes, space suits,
horror costumes, fantasy costumes

Hollywood Toys & Costumes **(800) 554-3444**
6600 Hollywood Blvd, Hollywood, CA, 90028
Halloween, kids & adults

JFF Uniforms-Costumes **(310) 320-1327**
557 Van Ness Ave, Torrance, CA, 90501
Custom garments 1-10,000 pcs made from sketch or sample. Period, military,
modern & more.

L. A. Circus **(323) 751-3486**
Call for Appt, Los Angeles, CA, 90047
Circus, Vegas Showgirl, performance costumes, clown outfits, dressing tents,
circus dressing rooms, circus linens
circusinc@aol.com * www.lacircus.com

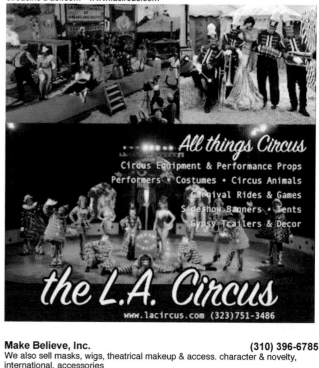

Make Believe, Inc. **(310) 396-6785**
We also sell masks, wigs, theatrical makeup & access. character & novelty,
international, accessories

Margaretrose Custom Clothing Design **(323) 852-4787**
1355 South Genesee Ave, Los Angeles, CA, 90019
made-to-order design, construction, pattern making, period & modern

Norcostco **(800) 220-6920**
825 Rhode Island Ave S, Golden Valley, MN, 55426
multiple sales office locations around the U.S. period production, classics,
musicals, opera

Oregon Shakespeare Festival Costume Rentals **(541) 482-2111
x308**
Full-service costume rental facility featuring quality garments constructed by
the Oregon Shakespeare Festival

Returner Rentals **(818) 506-7695**

Sony Pictures Studios-Wardrobe **(310) 244-5995**
alterations, call (310) 244-7260

StarMakers Costumes and Parties **(626) 797-6384**
Costumes for kids, adults, Renaissance, mascots, Victorian, wigs, make-up,
masks, Star Wars, theater, TV, film, schools

Sword & Stone **(818) 562-6548**

Tech Works FX Studios **(504) 722-1504**
13405 Seymour Meyers Blvd. #5, Covington, LA, 70433
Specializes in Costume Design, Creature Suits, Make Up FX, Monsters and
Custom Characters.
info@techworksstudios.com * www.techworksstudios.com

Universal Studios Costume Dept **(818) 777-2722**
Rental, mfg., & alterations

Ursula's Costumes, Inc. **(310) 582-8230**
2516 Wilshire Blvd, Santa Monica, CA, 90403
party costumes, wigs, masks, hats

Warner Bros. Studios Costume Dept **(818) 954-1297**
Collection of period & contemporary costumes for rent categorized by era,
decade and style.

Western Costume Co. **(818) 760-0900**

Costumes, International/Ethnic

See Also: Wardrobe, International/Ethnic

The Costume House	(818) 508-9933
JFF Uniforms-Costumes	(310) 320-1327

557 Van Ness Ave, Torrance, CA, 90501
Custom garments 1-10,000 pcs made from sketch or sample. Period, military, modern & more.

OPFOR Solutions, Inc (747) 666-7367
8100 Remmet Ave Unit #6, Canoga Park, CA, 91304
Opfor Solutions, Inc. brings you ethnic/military apparel from countries such as - Afghanistan, Iraq, Libya & more.
moe@opforsolutions.com * www.opforsolutions.com

OPFOR SOLUTIONS INC.

INTERNATIONAL MILITARY COSTUMES · TRADITIONAL COSTUMES
PROPS · ATMOSPHERICS

MIDDLE EAST · SOUTH AFRICA · SOUTH AMERICA · ASIA

Sony Pictures Studios-Wardrobe	(310) 244-5995

alterations, call (310) 244-7260

Universal Studios Costume Dept	(818) 777-2722

Rental, mfg., & alterations

Warner Bros. Studios Costume Dept	(818) 954-1297

Headpieces, Tribal, Folk, Latin, Islander, Grass Skirts, Polar, Middle Eastern

Western Costume Co.	(818) 760-0900

Cotton Candy Machines

See: Vendor Carts & Concession Counters

Counters

See Also: Cafeteria Counter/Line* Display Cases, Racks & Fixtures (Store)* Kitchen Counters & Cabinets* Lunch Counters* Vendor Carts & Concession Counters

Acme Display Fixture & Packaging (888) 411-1870
3829 S Broadway St., Los Angeles, CA 90037
Complete store setups: garment racks, displays/display cases, counters, packaging, shelving, hangers, mannequins
sales@acmedisplay.com * www.acmedisplay.com

AIR Designs (818) 768-6639
Airline, Bus Station, Auto Parts, Restaurant, Coffee Shop, Diner, Reception, Convenience Store

C. P. Valley (323) 466-8201
Deli counters, restaurant counters, diner counters, meat counters, capuccino counter cart, receptionist counters and more.

FormDecor, Inc. (310) 558-2582
America's largest event rental supplier of 20th Century furniture and accessories for Modern and Mid-Century styles.

LCW Props (818) 243-0707
Desks, Airport, Digital, LED, Medical, Office

Lennie Marvin Enterprises, Inc. (Prop Heaven) (818) 841-5882
deli, coffee house, bakery, market, conv. store, diner, kitchen

Sony Pictures Studios-Prop House (Off Lot) (310) 244-5999
display

Country Themed Parties

See: Events, Backings & Scenery* Events, Decorations, Supplies & Services* Events, Design/Planning/Production* Travel (City/Country) Themed Events

Courier Services

See: Messenger & Courier Services

Courtroom Furniture & Dressing

See Also: Scenery/Set Rentals

Alpha Companies - Spellman Desk Co. (818) 504-9090
judges benches, tables, Bank of England chairs, benches, flag posts, flags

C. P. Valley (323) 466-8201

The Earl Hays Press (818) 765-0700
services the Industry only. signage

Faux Library Studio Props, Inc. (818) 765-0096
clean quality legal book shelves, and legal office dressing including statuary, furniture, books, signs and more

The Hand Prop Room LP. (323) 931-1534
stenograph, block, hand props

History For Hire, Inc. (818) 765-7767

RJR Props (404) 349-7600
Courtroom benches, stenographers typewriter and more for rent.

Sony Pictures Studios-Prop House (Off Lot) (310) 244-5999

Universal Studios Property & Hardware Dept (818) 777-2784
Courtroom props and dressing for rent.

Warner Bros. Studios Property Department (818) 954-2181
Courtroom benches, law books, courtroom smalls, podiums, seating

Coverlets

See: Linens, Household

Cowboy Dressing

See: Horse Saddles & Tack* Horses, Horse Equipment, Livestock* Western Wear

Cowboy Hats & Boots

See: Western Wear

Craft Supplies

See: Hobby & Craft Supplies

Cranes

See: Ladders* Scaffolding/Lighting Towers* Heavy Machinery, Equipment & Specialists

Crash Dummies

See: Dummies, Fall & Crash

Crash Pads

See: Fall Pads & Crash Pads

Crates/ Vaults

See Also: Barrels & Drums, Wood/Metal/Plastic* Boxes* Produce Crates

AIR Designs (818) 768-6639
Fruit, Produce, Wine, Milk, Shipping Large & Small

Alley Cats Studio Rentals (818) 982-9178
wood, metal, plastic

Basaw Manufacturing, Inc. (818) 765-6650
7300 Varna, N Hollywood, CA, 91605
Basaw builds crates to order, large inventory in stock. all sizes & kinds, high multiples
fredy@basaw.com * www.basaw.com

www.basaw.com
(818) 765-6650
BASAW manufacturing
performance crating solutions

C. P. Valley (323) 466-8201
Many crates of various sizes and types. Wooden crates, weathered crates, plastic crates and much more.

E.C. Prop Rentals (818) 764-2008
wood & fiberglass, good multiples, many castered

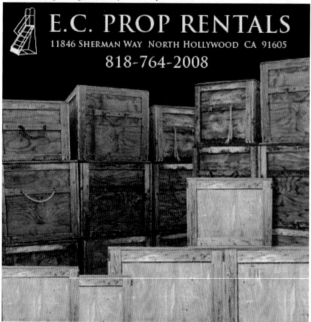

E.C. PROP RENTALS
11846 SHERMAN WAY NORTH HOLLYWOOD CA 91605
818-764-2008

History For Hire, Inc. (818) 765-7767
LCW Props (818) 243-0707
Largest Selection Around. Crates Of Any Size & Shape. Wood, Plastic, Vault Storage and Marine Shipping Crates.

L.C.W. PROPS
CALL US FIRST!
HUGE SELECTION
6439 San Fernando Rd. Glendale, CA 91201
Phone: 818-243-0707 - www.lcwprops.com

Sony Pictures Studios-Prop House (Off Lot) (310) 244-5999
Universal Studios Property & Hardware Dept (818) 777-2784
Many kinds of prop crates and vaults for rent.

Credit Card Imprint Machine

AIR Designs (818) 768-6639
Card Machines, ATM Pin Pads, Card Swipes

ATM Cash Connect/Financial Product, Inc. (818) 848-1025
624 S San Fernando Blvd, Burbank, CA, 91502
ATMs: all models, full function, custom paint/enclosures/screens manipulate cash dispensing, other bank machines
www.financialproductinc.com

C. P. Valley (323) 466-8201
Credit card machines, credit card imprint machines, credit card scanners, credit card readers and more.

Faux Library Studio Props, Inc. (818) 765-0096
Credit card imprint machines for rent or purchase.

The Hand Prop Room LP. (323) 931-1534
Digital credit card readers, vintage credit card imprint machine, card swipe machine, vintage card swipe machine

History For Hire, Inc. (818) 765-7767

LCW Props (818) 243-0707
Card Imprinters, POS, Credit Card Terminals, Credit Card Readers, Credit Card Machines

RC Vintage, Inc. (818) 765-7107
Plug in electric credit card readers/credit card machines

Sony Pictures Studios-Prop House (Off Lot) (310) 244-5999
Universal Studios Property & Hardware Dept (818) 777-2784
Many kinds of prop credit card imprint machines and readers for rent.

Crime Scene Cleanup

See: Sanitation, Waste Disposal

Crowd Control: Barricades, Turnstiles Etc.

See Also: Barricades
E.C. Prop Rentals   **(818) 764-2008**
wood & metal, turnstiles, stanchions, high multiples

History For Hire, Inc.   **(818) 765-7767**
old style wood
Lavi Industries   **(888) 285-8605**
27810 Avenue Hopkins, Valencia, CA, 91355
mfg: retractable tape posts, stanchions & rope, railing systems rail & panels, turnstiles; hotel, restaurant, bank/theat
LCW Props   **(818) 243-0707**
Barricades, Steel & Wood, Stanchions, Turnstile, Large Selection
Universal Studios Property & Hardware Dept   **(818) 777-2784**
Prop barricades and turnstiles for rent.

Crowd Stand-ups & Cutouts

See: Audience Cutouts & Stand-Ups

Crowns & Tiaras

See Also: Headwear - Hats, Bonnets, Caps, Helmets Etc.
The Costume House   **(818) 508-9933**
tiaras & crowns
The Hand Prop Room LP.   **(323) 931-1534**
Sony Pictures Studios-Prop House (Off Lot)   **(310) 244-5999**
crowns & tiaras
Sword & Stone   **(818) 562-6548**
in stock & custom fabricated with jewels & etching

Crucifixes & Crosses

See: Religious Articles

Cruise Ship Themed Parties

See: Events, Backings & Scenery* Events, Decorations, Supplies & Services* Events, Design/Planning/Production* Nautical Dressing & Props

Cryogenic Equipment

E.C. Prop Rentals   **(818) 764-2008**
nitrogen tanks & many stainless pieces
EFX- Event Special Effects   **(626) 888-2239**
125 Railroad Ave, Monrovia, CA, 91016
Cryo Guns- Cryo Cannons- Cyrogenics- Tanks
info@efxla.com * www.efxla.com
LCW Props   **(818) 243-0707**
Largest Selection Around, Tanks, Equipment, Hoses, Machines, Come Here First

Crystal Balls

See Also: Gypsy Wagon* Occult/Spiritual/Metaphysical
The Hand Prop Room LP.   **(323) 931-1534**
Modern Props   **(323) 934-3000**
solid glass crystal balls
Sony Pictures Studios-Prop House (Off Lot)   **(310) 244-5999**
Universal Studios Property & Hardware Dept   **(818) 777-2784**
Many crystal ball props for rent in different colors and sizes.

Crystal Stemware

See Also: Bars, Nightclubs, Barware & Dressing* Glassware/Dishes
The Hand Prop Room LP.   **(323) 931-1534**
Modern Props   **(323) 934-3000**
contemporary/futuristic, multiples
Omega/Cinema Props   **(323) 466-8201**
Wine glasses, champagne glasses and martini glasses.
Sony Pictures Studios-Prop House (Off Lot)   **(310) 244-5999**
Warner Bros. Studios Property Department   **(818) 954-2181**
Crystal wine glasses, champagne flutes, champagne glasses, water glasses, assorted crystal glasses

Crystals

See: Gems, Minerals & Crystals

Cue Cards

See: Expendables* Teleprompting

Curtain/Drape Tracks & Platforms

See: Theatrical Draperies, Hardware & Rigging

Curtains

See: Drapery & Curtains* Events, Backings & Scenery* Theatrical Draperies, Hardware & Rigging* Window Treatments

Custom Props & Fabrication

See: Art For Rent* Art, Artists For Hire* Fiberglass Products/Fabrication* Furniture, Custom-made/Reproduction* Metalworking, Decorative* Metalworking, Welding & Structural* Prop Design & Manufacturing* Prop Reproduction & Fabrication* Scenery/Set Construction* Vacu-forms/Vacu-forming

Cut Outs, Audience

See: Audience Cutouts & Stand-Ups

Cycle Exercisers

See: Exercise & Fitness Equipment

Daggers

See: Swords & Swordplay* Weaponry, Historical* Weaponry, Medieval* Weapons

Dance Equipment

See: Ballet Barres & Dance Mirrors* Dance Floors

Dance Floors

See Also: Ballet Barres & Dance Mirrors
Astro Audio Video Lighting, Inc.   **(818) 549-9915**
6615 San Fernando Rd, Glendale, CA, 91201
Dance floors and dance floor rentals for any event.
www.astroavl.com
C. P. Valley   **(323) 466-8201**
Oak dance floors, dance floor sectionals, modular dance floors.
Dance Equipment International   **(800) 626-9258**
2103 Lincoln Ave, Ste C, San Jose, CA, 95125
Marley type dance floors, hardwood sprung dance floor systems

**DISPLAY ADS AND LISTINGS FOR THIS CATEGORY
CONTINUE ON THE FOLLOWING PAGE**

L. A. Party Works   **(888) 527-2789**
9712 Alpaca St, S El Monte, CA, 91733
Portable dance floors/panel flooring including traditional and LED dance floors.
partyworks@aol.com * www.partyworksusa.com

888-527-2789
partyworksusa.com

ALLOWING INFINITE COMBINATIONS AND IMMERSIVE CAPABILITIES.
MULTIPLE COLORS, SHAPES AND SIZES

PARTYWORKS
I N T E R A C T I V E

Linoleum City, Inc.   **(323) 469-0063**
4849 Santa Monica Blvd, Hollywood, CA, 90029
Dance floors, stage floors, smooth floors, shiny floors, studio tiles, solid color vinyl, paint back vinyl.
sales@linocity.com * www.linoleumcity.com

Dance Wear

Dance Distributors   **(800) 333-2623**
213 Scranton Carbondale Highway, Scranton, PA 18508
catalog sales; dance wear, shoes and tights

Discount Dance Supply   **(800) 328-7107**
1501 N. Raymond Ave. Anaheim, CA 92801
catalog sales; dance wear, tights, warmups, shoes

N2N Bodywear   **(213) 748-1797**
1358 S Flower St, Los Angeles, CA, 90015
men's erotic wear, swimwear, underwear. contemp. men's dance & athletic wear

Sony Pictures Studios-Wardrobe   **(310) 244-5995**
alterations, call (310) 244-7260

Danish Modern

See: Furniture, Mid-Century Modern

Darkroom

See: Camera Equipment* Photographic Processing

Darts & Dartboards

See Also: Prop Houses* Sporting Goods & Services
Billiards & Barstools   **(818) 897-5772**
12367 Foothill Blvd, Sylmar, CA 91342
The Hand Prop Room LP.   **(323) 931-1534**
History For Hire, Inc.   **(818) 765-7767**

Day Of The Dead

See: Mexican Decorations

Decontamination Suits

See: Protective Apparel

Decorative Accessories

See Also: Antiques & Antique Decorations* Art For Rent*
Candelabras* Carved Figures* Collectibles* Linens, Household*
Memorabilia & Novelties* Prop Houses* Religious Articles* Sculpture
Badia Design, Inc.   **(818) 762-0130**
5420 Vineland Ave, N. Hollywood, CA, 91601
Moroccan Home Decor and Accessories including Moroccan furniture, rugs, lamps, light fixtures and more.
info@badiadesign.com * www.badiadesign.com

Bassman-Blaine   **(213) 748-5909**
1933 S. Broadway, #1005, Los Angeles, CA 90007
Boxes, trays, hurricanes, sculptures, porcelain, ceramics, bar accessories, containers, baskets, vases, & much more.
lashowroom@bassman-blaine.com * www.bassmanblainelamart.com

Bridge Furniture & Props Los Angeles   **(818) 433-7100**
We carry modern & traditional furniture, lighting, accessories, cleared art,& rugs. Items are online for easy shopping.

Castle Antiques & Design   **(855) 765-5800**
11924 Vose St, N Hollywood, CA, 91605
bowls, vases, tea sets, urns, ewers, cassolettes, inkwells, candelabras, glass cups, crystal cups, paintings, pillows
info@castleantiques.net * www.castleprophouse.com

Eric's Architectural Salvage, Wells Antique Tile   **(213) 413-6800**
2110 W Sunset Blvd, Los Angeles, CA, 90026
We have the largest selection of antique pottery and tile in the world.
ericstiques@aol.com * www.ericsarchitecturalsalvage.com

Faux Library Studio Props, Inc.   **(818) 765-0096**
wide selection of high-end, fresh, quality accessories to accompany book shelves, table tops and desk tops, choice ornamentation

FormDecor, Inc.   **(310) 558-2582**
America's largest event rental supplier of 20th Century furniture and accessories for Modern and Mid-Century styles.

Galerie Sommerlath - French 50s 60s   **(310) 838-0102**
9608 Venice Blvd, Culver City, CA, 90232
10,000 sq ft Mid-Century - 80s furniture, lighting & accessories
info@french50s60s.com * http://www.galeriesommerlath.com

The Hand Prop Room LP.   **(323) 931-1534**
fabulous silver collection and more

Hollywood Cinema Arts, Inc.   **(818) 504-7333**
Thousands of small props from the unusual to the ordinary.

Kitsch N Sync Props   **(323) 343-1190**
Specializing in 70's and 80's props. Large collection of cameras, electronics, phones, art, games, stereos, & much more.

L. A. Mart   **(800) 526-2784**
1933 S Broadway, Los Angeles, CA, 90007
400+ showrooms in 725K sqft; giftware, merchandise, furnishings accessories to registered buyers. Call for directory.

Little Bohemia Rentals   **(818) 853-7506**
11940 Sherman Rd, N Hollywood, CA, 91605
Antique through contemporary smalls.
sales@wearelittlebohemia.com * www.wearelittlebohemia.com

Modern Props   **(323) 934-3000**
Hand props and decorative accessories of a wide assortment. We can fabricate too!

Modernica Props   **(323) 664-2322**

NEST Studio Rentals, Inc.   **(818) 942-0339**
large selection; many cleared items

N.S. Aerospace Props   **(818) 765-1087**
7429 Laurel Canyon Blvd, North Hollywood, CA 91605
Rocket Engines, Rocket Components, Hardware, Fittings and Industrial parts for various time periods, consultations too.
nortonsalesm@aol.com * www.nortonsalesinc.com

Ob-jects   **(818) 351-4200**

OK   **(323) 653-3501**
8303 W 3rd St, Los Angeles, CA, 90048
unique home decor & gifts, will carry Studio accounts

Omega/Cinema Props   **(323) 466-8201**
Many kinds of decorative accessories from dishes, canisters, centerpieces and much more.

Pasadena Antiques & Design   **(626) 389-3938**
330 S. Fair Oaks Avenue, Pasadena, CA 91105
Antique and Mid Century Accessories. A huge selection in 21,600 sq. ft.
roy@antiquesofpasadena.com * www.antiquesofpasadena.com

Prop Services West   **(818) 503-2790**
brass, porcelain, etc.

Rapport International Furniture   **(323) 930-1500**
435 N La Brea Ave, Los Angeles, CA, 90036
Choose from handcrafted vases, artwork, throws and much more. All the flourishes needed to pull a room together.
rapport@rapportusa.com * www.rapportfurniture.com

Retro Gallery (323) 936-5261
1100 S La Brea Ave, Los Angeles, CA, 90019
20th C glass lamps, vases, objets d'art, primarily European

RJR Props (404) 349-7600
All kinds of decorative accessories and decorative props for rent.

ShopWildThings (928) 855-6075
2880 Sweetwater Ave, Lake Havasu City, AZ, 86406
Event Decor, Beaded Curtains, Chain Curtains, String Curtains & Columns, Crystal Columns. Reliable service & delivery.
help@shopwildthings.com * www.shopwildthings.com

Sony Pictures Studios-Prop House (Off Lot) (310) 244-5999
Animal figurines, figurine sets, human figurines, fine china cups, fine china dinner plate, fine china serving dishes, and more

Susanne Hollis, Inc. (626) 441-0346
230 Pasadena Ave, South Pasadena, CA, 91030
20th - 17th century Antiques, Accessories, and Fine Art from around the world in our 19,000sqft. warehouse and showrooms
sales@susannehollis.com * www.susannehollis.com

Sword & Stone (818) 562-6548

Universal Studios Property & Hardware Dept (818) 777-2784
Prop decorative accessories for rent, from smalls to large.

Used Church Items, Religious Rentals (239) 992-5737
216 Cumer Road, McDonald, PA, 15057
Baptismal Fonts, Votive stands, Banners, Stands, Statues, Crucifixes, Lights, Cruets, Vestments, Altars, Angels.
warehouse@religiousrentals.com * www.religiousrentals.com

Warner Bros. Studios The Collection (818) 954-2181
4000 Warner Blvd, Burbank, CA, 91522
High end fixtures, smalls, rugs, desk accessories, linens, pillows, frames, gadgets, kitchen dressing
wbsfproperty@warnerbros.com * www.wbpropertydept.com

ZG04 DECOR (818) 853-8040
Smalls, Ceramics, Porcelain and Ceramics, Multi Cultural, Eclectic, Tribal & Folk, Antique

Decoys

See: Fishing Equipment & Tackle Sporting Goods & Services*

Deep Fryer

AIR Designs (818) 768-6639
Period to Modern, Baskets, Restaurant and Smaller

Omega/Cinema Props (323) 466-8201
Residential deep fryers & commercial deep fryers

Universal Studios Property & Hardware Dept (818) 777-2784
Prop commercial deep fryers, deep fryer baskets, and more for rent.

Delicatessen Equipment

See Also: Cafe Tables/Chairs/Umbrellas Coffee House* Display Cases, Racks & Fixtures (Store)* Food, Artificial Food* Restaurant Kitchens/Equip./Supplies* Shopping Bags (Silent)*

AIR Designs (818) 768-6639
Display Cases, Fake Food, Scales, Jars, Glass Door Coolers, Deli Slicers, Meat Saw, Food Props

C. P. Valley (323) 466-8201
Deli counter, refrigerated meat cases, meat trays, prop meat slices, deli meats

The Hand Prop Room LP. (323) 931-1534
dressing, signage, accessories, replica food

History For Hire, Inc. (818) 765-7767

LCW Props (818) 243-0707
Signs, Take A Ticket, Display Counters, Fake Meats & Cheeses

Lennie Marvin Enterprises, Inc. (Prop Heaven) (818) 841-5882
period/modern, cases, fake food, compl. deli dressing

Sony Pictures Studios-Prop House (Off Lot) (310) 244-5999

Universal Studios Property & Hardware Dept (818) 777-2784
Prop deli equipment, butcher meat carts, meat slicers, sandwich boards, dressing and more for rent.

Dentist Equipment

See Also: Medical Equip/Furniture, Graphics/Supplies

A-1 Medical Integration (818) 753-0319
Medical devices for Set Decoration & Property, from minor procedures to detailed hospital units.

Alpha Companies - Spellman Desk Co. (818) 504-9090
The #1 source for medical equipment in the Industry.

C. P. Valley (323) 466-8201
Vintage dentist equipment and chairs, dental xray machine, dental instruments and more.

Dapper Cadaver/Creatures & Cultures (818) 771-0818
Mouth gags, tooth extruders, stainless steel instruments & instrument trays. Open-mouth prop heads. Replica teeth.

Estrada Dental Supply (909) 989-2088
8556 Red Oak St, Rancho Cucamonga, CA 91730
1890 to present, consulting on dentist procedures
HANKIE1@dslextreme.com * www.estradadental.com

The Hand Prop Room LP. (323) 931-1534

LCW Props (818) 243-0707
Chairs, Signs, Certificates, Tools, Lighting

Universal Studios Property & Hardware Dept (818) 777-2784
Prop dental equipment for rent

Department Store

See Also: Cash Registers Counters* Credit Card Imprint Machine* Display Cases, Racks & Fixtures (Store)* Jewelry, Fine/Reproduction* Prop Houses* Security Walk-Through & Baggage Alarms* Shopping Bags (Silent)* Shopping Carts* Steel Folding Gates & Roll-Up Doors* Store Shelf Units & Shelving* Surveillance Equipment* Wardrobe*

Acme Display Fixture & Packaging (888) 411-1870
3829 S Broadway St., Los Angeles, CA 90037
Complete store setups: garment racks, displays/display cases, counters, packaging, shelving, hangers, mannequins
sales@acmedisplay.com * www.acmedisplay.com

Lennie Marvin Enterprises, Inc. (Prop Heaven) (818) 841-5882
extensive; fixtures, equipment, products, & more

RJR Props (404) 349-7600
Credit card terminals, receipt printers, barcode scanners and more for rent.

Designers

See: Art, Artists For Hire Events, Design/Planning/Production* Graphics, Digital & Large Format Printing* Prop Design & Manufacturing* Prop Reproduction & Fabrication* Scenery/Set Construction* Staff Shops* Themed Environment Construction*

Desk Dressing

See Also: Globes, World Map* Maps* Office Equipment & Dressing*
Office Supplies* Paperwork, Documents & Letters, Office

Advanced Liquidators Office Furniture   **(818) 763-3470**
phones, etc. desktop office equipment, desktop smalls, many desktop items for
business or home desks

Alpha Companies - Spellman Desk Co.   **(818) 504-9090**
Phones, computers, staples, stack trays, desk pads

C. P. Valley   **(323) 466-8201**
Desk dressing of all kinds including vertical file organizers, letter trays, post it
note dispensers and more

Dozar Office Furnishings   **(310) 559-9292**
9937 Jefferson Blvd, Culver City, CA, 90232
Rentals X22. Desks, book stops, desk clocks, battery clocks, speakers, desk
art, artistic paper weights
dozarrents@aol.com * www.dozarrents.com

The Earl Hays Press   **(818) 765-0700**
services the Industry only. in-stock forms, certificates, paperwork per-present

E.C. Prop Rentals   **(818) 764-2008**
lamps/file holders/letter trays/smalls

Faux Library Studio Props, Inc.   **(818) 765-0096**
1000's of desktop items, even the desks, vintage desk set, retro desk sets

The Hand Prop Room LP.   **(323) 931-1534**
desk access., phones, adding machines, typewriters

History For Hire, Inc.   **(818) 765-7767**
period

LCW Props   **(818) 243-0707**
Anything You Need, Large Quantities, Everything

Modern Props   **(323) 934-3000**
contemporary/futuristic desk dressing, artificial plants, and more

Omega/Cinema Props   **(323) 466-8201**
Paperweights, ink stands, calculators, letter trays, typewriters, memo pads,
pencil cups, ink wells and more.

Prop Services West   **(818) 503-2790**

Sony Pictures Studios-Prop House (Off Lot)   **(310) 244-5999**
writing desks and dressing

TR Trading Company   **(310) 329-9242**
15604 S Broadway, Gardena, CA, 90248
85,000 sq/ft of items, selection and inventory changes weekly. hundreds of
desk accessories
sales@trtradingcompany.com * www.trtradingcompany.com

Warner Bros. Studios Property Department   **(818) 954-2181**
Blotters & Desk Pads, Desktop Accessories, Letter Trays & Sorters, Magazine
Files, Pencil Cups

ZG04 DECOR   **(818) 853-8040**
Globes, Paperwork, Binders, Books, Desk Smalls, Blotters, Desk-Sets,
Desk-Frames, Note-pads, Calendars, Desk-Clocks

Desks

See: Lab Equipment* Office Furniture* School Supplies, Desks &
Dressing

Dessert Carts

See: Restaurant Furniture & Dressing* Vendor Carts & Concession
Counters

Detectives

See: Private Investigations

Detour Signs

See: Traffic/Road Signs, Lights, Safety Items

Diapers & Rags

See: Expendables

Digital Device Imaging, D.D.I.

See: Video 24fps / Sync System / D.D.I.

Digital Imaging

See: Art, Artists For Hire* Graphics, Digital & Large Format Printing*
Signs

Dimensional Signage

See: Graphics, Digital & Large Format Printing* Signs

Diner Restaurant

See: Restaurant Furniture & Dressing* Restaurant
Kitchens/Equip./Supplies

Dinosaurs

See Also: Bones, Skulls & Skeletons* Fossils

Dapper Cadaver/Creatures & Cultures   **(818) 771-0818**
Dinosaur skulls, skeletons, bones and teeth. Lifelike dinosaur statues and fossil panels. T-rex skeleton.

Kokoro Dinosaurs   **(818) 704-9094**
21211 Oxnard St, Woodland Hills, CA, 91367
prehistoric mammals, dinosaurs, giant insects, display exhibits, lifesize/large, animated/robotic also

LM Treasures   **(626) 252-7354**
10557 Juniper Ave Unit A, Fontana, CA 92337
We acquire a variation of extraordinary dinosaurs ranging from life size 7000 lbs. Mammoths to Baby Triceratops at 5 lbs.
lmtreasures.ll@gmail.com * www.lifesizestatues.net

Universal Studios Property & Hardware Dept   **(818) 777-2784**
Assorted prop dinosaur rentals from fossils to stuffed animals.

Director's Chairs, Bags, Pouches

See Also: Folding Chairs/Tables

C. P. Two   **(323) 466-8201**
Tall directors chairs, folding directors chairs, wooden directors chairs, metal directors chairs

Castex Rentals   **(323) 462-1468**
1044 N. Cole Ave, Hollywood, CA, 90038
authorized dealer to the Industry, replacement directors chair seats & backs, Hollywood chairs, director chairs
service@castexrentals.com * www.castexrentals.com

The Hand Prop Room LP.   **(323) 931-1534**
in-house fab., logos for chair backs

History For Hire, Inc.   **(818) 765-7767**
period, current, all eras

Sony Pictures Studios-Prop House (Off Lot)   **(310) 244-5999**

Universal Studios Property & Hardware Dept   **(818) 777-2784**
Many types and sizes of directors chairs, including side pouches.

Directories

See: Search Tools, Directories, Libraries

Dirt Skins

Green Set, Inc.   **(818) 764-1231**

Jackson Shrub Supply, Inc.   **(818) 982-0100**
sheets of... dirt! Dirk skins as well as cam skins

LCW Props   **(818) 243-0707**
large quantities

Disc Jockey Dj/Vj Booths

See: Audio Equipment* Events, Entertainment* Lighting & Sound, Concert/Theatrical/DJ/VJ* Radio/TV Station

Disco Balls & Lighting Fixtures

See: Mirror Balls/Drivers

Disco Floors

See: Dance Floors

Dishes

See: Glassware/Dishes

Display Cases, Racks & Fixtures (Store)

See Also: Candy Racks* Comic Books & Comic Book Racks* Hat Racks* Magazines & Magazine/Newspaper Racks* Market Equipment/Fixtures* Store Shelf Units & Shelving

10 Karat Rentals   **(818) 635-4124**
7100 Tujunga (At R.C. Vintage), N. Hollywood, CA 91605
10karatrentals@gmail.com

Acme Display Fixture & Packaging   **(888) 411-1870**
3829 S Broadway St., Los Angeles, CA 90037
Complete store setups: garment racks, displays/display cases, counters, packaging, shelving, hangers, mannequins
sales@acmedisplay.com * www.acmedisplay.com

GARMENT RACKS · STEAMERS · FORMS · MANNEQUINS · JEWELRY DISPLAYS
STORE COUNTERS · PACKAGING · GONDOLA SYSTEMS · DISPLAY CASES

AIR Designs   **(818) 768-6639**
Mini Mart, Grocery Wire Racks/Glass Display Cases

Alley Cats Studio Rentals   **(818) 982-9178**

Books For Libraries, Inc.   **(800) 321-5596**
28064 Ave Standford Unit L, Santa Clarita, CA, 91355
Metal cantilever library shelving or wooden modular shelving
JStitz@pacbell.net * www.booksforlibraries.com

C. P. Valley   **(323) 466-8201**
Market display cases, residential display cases, commercial display cases, retail display cases, and more.

Custom Acrylic Fabrication Corp.   **(310) 844-7640**
13004 S. Figueroa, Los Angeles, CA, 90061
cut to size acrylic, display cases, next day service

The Hand Prop Room LP.   **(323) 931-1534**
jewelry cases, jewelry display cases, jewelry stands, wardrobe racks, antique hat stands

Henry Hanger Company   **(877) 436-7952**
3101 S. Hill St, Los Angeles, CA, 90007
many styles of clothing hangers

LCW Props   **(818) 243-0707**
Wardrobe Racks, Kiosks, Counters, Tables

Modern Props   **(323) 934-3000**
contemporary/futuristic

RC Vintage, Inc.   **(818) 765-7107**
40s, 50s & 60s Department Store..

Sony Pictures Studios-Prop House (Off Lot)   **(310) 244-5999**
retail display cases, jewelry display cases, candy display cases, wine racks, dish racks, magazine racks, postcard racks, more

Universal Studios Property & Hardware Dept   **(818) 777-2784**
Present to period prop display cases, racks & fixtures for rent.

Display Food

See: Food, Artificial Food* Food, Food Stylists

Diving Equipment

See: Nautical Dressing & Props* Nautical/Marine Services & Charters* Sporting Goods & Services* Wetsuits, Diving/Surfing

DJ/VJ Booths & Equipment

See: Events, Entertainment* Radio/TV Station* Lighting & Sound, Concert/Theatrical/DJ/VJ* Audio Equipment

Dock Cleats

See: Nautical Dressing & Props

Doctor's Bags

The Hand Prop Room LP.	(323) 931-1534
period-present	
History For Hire, Inc.	(818) 765-7767
Omega/Cinema Props	(323) 466-8201
Period doctors bags and vintage doctors bags.	
Sony Pictures Studios-Prop House (Off Lot)	(310) 244-5999
Universal Studios Property & Hardware Dept	(818) 777-2784
Prop doctors bags for rent.	

Doctors Office

See: Dentist Equipment* Doctor's Bags* Gurneys* Hospital Equipment* Medical Equip/Furniture, Graphics/Supplies* Stretchers* X-ray Machine* X-ray Viewer* X-rays* Waiting Room* Emergency Room* Exam Room

Documents

See: Book Covers & Bookbinding* Books, Real/Hollow & Faux Books* Graphics, Digital & Large Format Printing* Paperwork, Documents & Letters, Office

Doghouses

See: Garden/Patio* Pet Furniture, Houses, Clothing

Dogs

See: Animals (Live), Services, Trainers & Wranglers

Dogsleds

See Also: Animals (Live), Services, Trainers & Wranglers* Christmas* Sleds

LCW Props	(818) 243-0707
Period, Wood	
Universal Studios Property & Hardware Dept	(818) 777-2784
Prop dog sleds for rent.	

Dollhouses

See Also: Dolls* Toys & Games

The Hand Prop Room LP.	(323) 931-1534
design & mfg. dollhouses, antique dollhouse, vintage dollhouse, wooden dollhouse, dollhouse furniture	
Merritt Productions, Inc.	(818) 760-0612
10845 Vanowen St, North Hollywood, CA 91605	
specialty props, miniatures, sculpture, mech effects, set const.	
www.merrittproductions.com	
My Doll's House	(310) 320-4828
1218 El Prado Ave Ste 136, Torrance, CA 90501	
Dollhouses, Dollhouse Kits, Room Boxes, Miniatures, Collectibles, Accessories, Tools and Supplies	
margiesminiatures@gmail.com * www.mydollshouse.com	
Omega/Cinema Props	(323) 466-8201
Various doll houses	
Prop Services West	(818) 503-2790
Universal Studios Property & Hardware Dept	(818) 777-2784
Many kinds of prop doll houses and doll house furniture for rent.	

Dollies

See: Camera Equipment* Furniture Dollies, Pads & Hand Trucks

Dolls

See Also: Children/Baby Accessories & Bedroom* Dollhouses* Soldier Toys & Drums* Toys & Games

Dolls By Sandra	(818) 343-4842
7700 Rhea Ave, Reseda, CA, 91335	
All dolls, modern, antique & portrait, doll repairs & doll refurbishment	
The Hand Prop Room LP.	(323) 931-1534
History For Hire, Inc.	(818) 765-7767
vintage	
Modern Props	(323) 934-3000
large selection of antique chalk dolls	
Monique Trading Corp.	(510) 887-6200
27317 Industrial Blvd, Hayward, CA, 94545	
catalog sales; parts only; doll wigs, eyes, eyelashes, stands website links to many other doll sites	
Ob-jects	(818) 351-4200
Omega/Cinema Props	(323) 466-8201
Dolls of many kinds including stuffed dolls, russian stacking dolls, wooden dolls, paper dolls and more.	
Prop Services West	(818) 503-2790
RC Vintage, Inc.	(818) 765-7107
Vintage Dolls Turn of the Century	
Sony Pictures Studios-Prop House (Off Lot)	(310) 244-5999
large selection, for all ages	
Universal Studios Property & Hardware Dept	(818) 777-2784
Prop period dolls to contemporary dolls for rent.	

Donations

See: Charities & Donations

Doors

See Also: Architectural Pieces & Artifacts* Salvage, Architectural

Charisma Design Studio, Inc.	(818) 252-6611
8414 San Fernando Road, Sun Valley, CA, 91352	
custom metal/glass/wood functional art	
info@charismadesign.com * www.charismadesign.com	
Coppa Woodworking, Inc.	(310) 548-5332
1231 Paraiso Ave, San Pedro, CA, 90731	
catalog sales; old fashioned wood screen doors	
The ReUse People	(818) 244-5635
3015 Dolores St, Los Angeles, CA, 90065	
Hundreds of doors to choose from.	
JefCockerell@TheReUsePeople.org * www.TheReUsePeople.org	

Dori Poles

See: Events, Decorations, Supplies & Services

Drafting Equipment & Supplies

See Also: Blueprint Equipment & Supplies* Graphics, Digital & Large Format Printing* Miniatures/Models* Office Equipment & Dressing* Plotters & Plotting Services

The Hand Prop Room LP.	(323) 931-1534
T-squares, micrometers, antique drafting tables, drafting tools	
History For Hire, Inc.	(818) 765-7767
Hopper's Office & Drafting Furniture	(323) 254-7362
2901 Fletcher Dr, Los Angeles, CA, 90065	
Prop rentals for art/drafting room. Over 100 Drafting tables, flat files, stools, & all drafting equipment.	
www.draftingfurniture.com	
Modern Props	(323) 934-3000
contemporary/futuristic	
The Rational Past	(310) 476-6277
By Appointment, West Los Angeles, CA	
Authentic science, industrial, technical antiques & collectibles. Many professions & eras represented. See web site.	
info@therationalpast.com * www.therationalpast.com	
Repro-Graphic Supply	(818) 771-9066
9838 Glenoaks Blvd, Sun Valley, CA, 91352	
drafting & engineering supplies, equipment & service, all Ind.'s. See Display Ad in Blueprint Equipment	
info@reprographicsupply.com * www.reprographicsupply.com	
Steven Enterprises	(800) 491-8785
17952 Skypark Circle Unit E, Irvine, CA, 92614	
Wide Format Printers. Rent/Buy. Authorized Dealer: HP, KIP, Canon, Oce, Epson. We service & supply everything we install	
sales@plotters.com * www.plotters.com	

Drapery & Curtains

See Also: Flameproofing* Hampers, Theatrical* Rigging, Equipment or Services* Stanchions & Rope* Theatrical Draperies, Hardware & Rigging* Window Treatments

Astro Audio Video Lighting, Inc. (818) 549-9915
6615 San Fernando Rd, Glendale, CA, 91201
www.astroavl.com

Contempo Window Fashions (818) 768-1773
11760 Roscoe Blvd Unit E, Sun Valley, CA, 91352
Wholesale manufacturing of draperies and bedding to the trade.
contempowindows@att.net * www.contempowindowfashions.com

Fox Studios Production Services (310) 369-4636
10201 W. Pico Blvd, Los Angeles, CA, 90035

NEST Studio Rentals, Inc. (818) 942-0339
multiple 84" and 95" contemporary panels

Omega/Cinema Props (323) 466-8201
Drapery rentals and drapery sales, manufacturing, Local 44. Custom drapery shop.

ShopWildThings (928) 855-6075
2880 Sweetwater Ave, Lake Havasu City, AZ, 86406
Event Decor, Beaded Curtains, Chain Curtains, String Curtains & Columns, Crystal Columns. Reliable service & delivery.
help@shopwildthings.com * www.shopwildthings.com

Sony Pictures Studios-Linens, Drapes, Rugs (310) 244-5999
5933 W Slauson Ave, Culver City, CA, 90230
large selection of drapes & curtains, sheers
www.sonypicturesstudios.com

Sony Pictures Studios-Prop House (Off Lot) (310) 244-5999
Drapes, placemats, curtain sheer panels, domestic drapery, velvet theatre drapes, drapery trim, domestic drape tassels, more

Strickland's Window Coverings (800) 279-0944
2817 N. 23rd Street, Wilmington, NC 28401
Strickland's Window Coverings Set Services has been providing window coverings to the film industry for over 26 years.
laurasalo@stricklandswindowcoverings.com *
www.stricklandswindowcoverings.com

Universal Studios Drapery Dept (818) 777-2761
manufacturing

Warner Bros. Drapery, Upholstery & Flooring (818) 954-1831
4000 Warner Blvd, Burbank, CA, 91522
Window treatments, vintage, period, modern, deco, curtains, beaded curtains, theatrical draperies
wbsfdrapery@warnerbros.com * www.wbdrapery.com

WB DRAPERY DEPARTMENT
WBDrapery.com
"The icing on the set"
818.954.4426

ZG04 DECOR (818) 853-8040
Custom made Drapery, Stage Curtains, Curtains, Sheers, Custom Drapery, Pillows, Table-linens, Bedding

Drapery Hardware

See: Drapery & Curtains* Rigging, Equipment or Services* Theatrical Draperies, Hardware & Rigging

Drawings

See: Art For Rent* Calligraphy* Paintings/Prints

Dress Forms

See Also: Mannequins

C. P. Valley (323) 466-8201
Dress forms of many kinds.

The Hand Prop Room LP. (323) 931-1534
dress forms, rolling dress forms, antique dress forms, vintage dress forms, full size dress forms, cloth dress forms

History For Hire, Inc. (818) 765-7767
character

LCW Props (818) 243-0707
Multiple Sizes

Sony Pictures Studios-Prop House (Off Lot) (310) 244-5999

Universal Studios Property & Hardware Dept (818) 777-2784
Prop sewing dress forms, display dress forms, mens dress forms and womens dress forms for rent.

Drink & Beverage Machines/Carts

See: Beer Equipment, Taps & Coolers* Fountains, Drinking (Wall & Stand)* Soda Fountain Dressing* Vending Machines* Vendor Carts & Concession Counters

Drinking Fountains

See: Fountains, Drinking (Wall & Stand)* Soda Fountain Dressing

Drones, UAVs & UASs

AeroVironment, Inc (626) 357-9983
181 W. Huntington Dr., Suite 202, Monrovia, CA 91016
Committed to creating and delivering powerful new Unmanned Aircraft and Electric Vehicle solutions.
evscs@avinc.com * www.avinc.com

Drone Dudes - Aerial Cinematography Specialists (866) 856-8465
Call for Appt.
Every system we design and flight we take is driven by our love of cutting-edge cinema, music and new adventures.
bookings@dronedudes.com * www.dronedudes.com

DroneFly.com (805) 480-4033
2630 Townsgate Road Suite I, Westlake Village, CA 91361
A leader in the drone Aerospace Industry for both professional and recreational uses. We also offer full service repairs.
contact@dronefly.com * www.dronefly.com

3D Robotics (858) 225-1414
1608 4th Street, Suite 410, Berkeley, CA 94710
3DR has the resources to become the first company to truly and fully integrate drones and smartphones.
pr@3drobotics.com * www.3drobotics.com

Drops

See: Backings* Graphics, Digital & Large Format Printing* Scenery/Set Construction* Theatrical Draperies, Hardware & Rigging

Drugstore/Apothecary

See Also: Candy Jars* Cash Registers* Counters* Credit Card Imprint Machine* Display Cases, Racks & Fixtures (Store)* Prop Products & Packages* Security Walk-Through & Baggage Alarms* Soda Fountain Dressing* Steel Folding Gates & Roll-Up Doors* Store Shelf Units & Shelving

C. P. Valley (323) 466-8201
Apothecary dressing, glass bottles, labeled bottles, amber glass bottles, clear glass bottles, ceramic bottles and more.

Dapper Cadaver/Creatures & Cultures (818) 771-0818
1800s to present. Apothecary jars, specimens, glassware, labware, instruments & decor. Vintage pharmacy to meth lab.

The Earl Hays Press (818) 765-0700
services the Industry only. apothecary paper & plastic repro. vintage labels

The Hand Prop Room LP. (323) 931-1534
period-present, glasses, bottles, beakers, signage

History For Hire, Inc. (818) 765-7767

LCW Props (818) 243-0707
Huge Selection Of Apothecary Jars, Pill Bottles, Fake Drugs, Meth lab Dressing, Kilos Cocaine, Marijuana

RC Vintage, Inc. (818) 765-7107
period jars & 40s, 50s & 60s dressing of all kinds

Sony Pictures Studios-Prop House (Off Lot) (310) 244-5999
apothecary, butter jar, candy jars, cookie jars, decorative jars, honeypot, ginger jars, jelly jars, jam jars, spice jars

Universal Studios Property & Hardware Dept (818) 777-2784
Prop apothecary dressing and drugstore dressing for rent.

Vermont Country Store (802) 824-3184
657 Main St, Weston, VT, 05161
Catalog: hard-to-find household furnishings, clothing, food & personal care items just like old-fashioned drugstore

Drums

See: Barrels & Drums, Wood/Metal/Plastic* Crates/ Vaults* Musical Instruments* Tanks* Wine Kegs

Dry Cleaners (Dressing)

See Also: Vacuum Cleaners

Lennie Marvin Enterprises, Inc. (Prop Heaven)   **(818) 841-5882**
storefront setup, steamers

Dry Cleaning Services

See: Cleaners & Cleaning Services* Laundry Carts

Dry Ice

See: Ice & Ice Sculpture

Dryers

See: Cleaners & Cleaning Services* Washing Machines/Dryers

Dulling Spray

See: Expendables

Dumbbells

See: Exercise & Fitness Equipment* Weightlifting Equipment

Dummies

See: Magicians & Props, Supplies, Dressing* Mannequins* Puppets, Marionettes, Automata, Animatronics

Dummies, Fall & Crash

Dapper Cadaver/Creatures & Cultures   **(818) 771-0818**
Poseable stunt dummies and fall dummies. Male and female. Lifelike and corpse. Wounded, burn and custom FX.
Elden Designs   **(323) 550-8922**
2767 W. Broadway, Eagle Rock, CA, 90041
crash test dummies, NO fall dummies
The Hand Prop Room LP.   **(323) 931-1534**
History For Hire, Inc.   **(818) 765-7767**
fall type
Leavittation, Inc.   **(661) 252-7551**
25982 Sand Canyon Rd, Santa Clarita, CA, 91387
articulated crash dummies & puppeteering,crash & stunt pads
Sony Pictures Studios-Prop House (Off Lot)   **(310) 244-5999**
Universal Studios Property & Hardware Dept   **(818) 777-2784**
Various prop dummies, dummy body parts, and more of different sizes, types and gender for rent.

Dumpsters

See: Alley Dressing* Construction Site Equipment

Dungeon

See: Medieval

Dunk Tanks

See: Carnival Games & Rides

Duplicating

See: Copy Machines* Photographic Processing

Dutch Shoes

See: Shoes, Boots & Footwear

Duvet

See: Linens, Household

Duvetyne

See Also: Expendables* Fire Extinguishers, Practical & Prop* Flameproofing

Castex Rentals   **(323) 462-1468**
1044 N. Cole Ave, Hollywood, CA, 90038
call for sizes, sales by the roll, duvetyne backings for rent
service@castexrentals.com * www.castexrentals.com
Fore-Peak   **(323) 460-4192**
1040 N. Las Palmas Ave, Los Angeles, CA, 90038
plus muslin, black net, china silk, grid cloth, velour

DVD Rental/Sales Store

See: Video Rental/Sales Store* Video Store Dressing

Dyeing

See: Fabric Dyeing/Tie Dyeing/Painting/Aging* Paint & Painting Supplies

Early American Furniture

See: Furniture, Early American/Colonial

Earthquake Monitoring Equipment

See: Lab Equipment

Easels

See Also: Art For Rent* Art, Artists For Hire* Art, Supplies & Stationery

Astro Audio Video Lighting, Inc.   **(818) 549-9915**
6615 San Fernando Rd, Glendale, CA, 91201
www.astroavl.com
The Hand Prop Room LP.   **(323) 931-1534**
Large and small, wall-mounted & on wheels
History For Hire, Inc.   **(818) 765-7767**
wood, brass
LCW Props   **(818) 243-0707**
Wood, Metal
Modern Props   **(323) 934-3000**
contemporary/futuristic, wood, aluminum, metal, walnut, acrylic, adjustable, moving, large, small, sturdy, versatile.
Sony Pictures Studios-Prop House (Off Lot)   **(310) 244-5999**
Sword & Stone   **(818) 562-6548**
Universal Studios Property & Hardware Dept   **(818) 777-2784**
Various prop easels for rent.

Editing Equipment & Services

Christy's Editorial Film & Video   **(818) 845-1755**
3625 W. Pacific Ave, Burbank, CA, 91505
film & digital editing supplies & equipment
History For Hire, Inc.   **(818) 765-7767**
period, film & video
LCW Props   **(818) 243-0707**
Large Selection, Boards, Switchers, Custom Graphics, Audio Mixing
NBCUniversal StudioPost Editorial Facilities   **(818) 777-4728**
100 Universal City Plaza, Universal City, CA, 91608
170 Editorial Rooms and Suites, Exceptional 24 Hour Technical Support, Nationwide delivery and service.
www.filmmakersdestination.com

Egg Crate Bottom Fluorescents

See Also: Light Fixtures
E.C. Prop Rentals (818) 764-2008
all working, high multiples in many styles

E.C. PROP RENTALS
11846 SHERMAN WAY NORTH HOLLYWOOD CA 91605
818-764-2008

LCW Props (818) 243-0707
large sel. of lighting
Universal Studios Property & Hardware Dept (818) 777-2784
Prop egg crate bottom fluorescent lights for rent.

Egyptian Dressing

Dapper Cadaver/Creatures & Cultures (818) 771-0818
Prop mummies, realistic mummified corpses and mummy characters. Egyptian statues. Obelisks and sarcophagi.
Green Set, Inc. (818) 764-1231
from dessert plants to Egyptian tomb dressing, many models of Egyptian statuary with some Egyptian furniture
The Hand Prop Room LP. (323) 931-1534
statues, mummy, masks, figures etc.
History For Hire, Inc. (818) 765-7767
mummy, smalls & fans
LM Treasures (626) 252-7354
10557 Juniper Ave Unit A, Fontana, CA 92337
Anything needed to help start the party such as animals, Egyptian Kings, Gods, and Sarcophaguses.
lmtreasures.ll@gmail.com * www.lifesizestatues.net
Omega/Cinema Props (323) 466-8201
Egyptian figurings, Egyptian busts, Egyptian books, Egyptian prints, Egyptian sculptures and much more.
Sword & Stone (818) 562-6548
Universal Studios Property & Hardware Dept (818) 777-2784
Prop Egyptian statues, props, weapons and more for rent.
Warner Bros. Studios Property Department (818) 954-2181
Egyptian Sculptures, Sarcophagus, Sphinx figures, Mummy statues, Egyptian Style Urns

Egyptian Themed Parties

See: Costume Rental Houses Events, Decorations, Supplies & Services* Events, Design/Planning/Production* Historical Era Themed Events* Wardrobe, Antique/Historical*

Electric Chairs

See Also: Jail Cell Dressing Torture Equipment*
Dapper Cadaver/Creatures & Cultures (818) 771-0818
Realistic electric chairs, interrogation chairs and restraint chairs.
History For Hire, Inc. (818) 765-7767
very authentic
Universal Studios Property & Hardware Dept (818) 777-2784
Prop electric chairs for rent

Electric Meters

See: Gas & Electric Meters

Electrical/Electronic Supplies & Services

See Also: Breaker Boxes Computers* Control Panels/Boxes* Expendables* Insulators* Power Generation/Distribution*
All Electronics Corporation (818) 997-1806
14928 Oxnard St, Van Nuys, CA, 91411
components retail store; new, used & industrial surplus
Antique Electronic Supply (480) 820-5411
6221 South Maple Ave, Tempe, AZ, 85283
catalog sales; electronic repair, parts & service for old radios, TVs, amps, speakers, record players, phones
Apex Jr. (818) 248-0416
1450 West 228th St. #4, Torrance, CA 90501
new & used surplus components, wire, control panels
Astro Audio Video Lighting, Inc. (818) 549-9915
6615 San Fernando Rd, Glendale, CA, 91201
Electronic equipment of all kinds. Equipment for lighting, music and more. Electronics repair also available.
www.astroavl.com
E.C. Prop Rentals (818) 764-2008
industrial & SS, wide sel wire & components
Electronic City (818) 632-4494
22287 Mulholland Highway #197, Calabasas, CA 91302
extensive inventory, esp. surveillance related
History For Hire, Inc. (818) 765-7767
LCW Props (818) 243-0707
Large Selection Of Electrical Panels, Boxes, Conduit, Breakers, Rigged

Electron Microscope

E.C. Prop Rentals (818) 764-2008
also other lab equip/dressing
LCW Props (818) 243-0707
Microscopes, Large & Small

Electronic Appliances

See: Appliances Computers* Fans-Table, Floor or Ceiling* Radios* Stereo Equipment* Telephones, Cellular* Televisions*

Electronic Dart Board

See: Arcade Equipment, Games & Rides

Electronic Equipment (Dressing)

See Also: Control Boards Game Show Electronics & Equipment* Mission Control Consoles* Read-outs*
Alley Cats Studio Rentals (818) 982-9178
insulators, gauges, fuse boxes
Apex Electronics (818) 767-7202
8909 San Fernando Rd, Sun Valley, CA, 91352
Electronic & aircraft salvage parts for props & dressing, wire & cable
apexsurplus@sbcglobal.net
Astro Audio Video Lighting, Inc. (818) 549-9915
6615 San Fernando Rd, Glendale, CA, 91201
Electronic dressing and electronic equipment available for many themes including events.
www.astroavl.com
E.C. Prop Rentals (818) 764-2008
control boxes, consoles, electrical paneling
The Hand Prop Room LP. (323) 931-1534
Kitsch N Sync Props (323) 343-1190
Specializing in 70's and 80's props. Large collection of cameras, electronics, phones, art, games, stereos, & much more.

**DISPLAY ADS AND LISTINGS FOR THIS CATEGORY
CONTINUE ON THE FOLLOWING PAGE**

LCW Props (818) 243-0707
Large Selection Of Elevator Panels, Brass, Stainless, Floor Indicators, Call Buttons

6439 San Fernando Rd. Glendale, CA 91201
Phone: 818-243-0707 - www.lcwprops.com

LCW Props (818) 243-0707
Large Selection Of Elevator Panels, Brass, Stainless, Floor Indicators, Call Buttons

6439 San Fernando Rd. Glendale, CA 91201
Phone: 818-243-0707 - www.lcwprops.com

Modern Props (323) 934-3000
Contemporary & futuristic rentals, we also fabricate electronics

RJR Props (404) 349-7600
Hundreds of control panels, dials, gauges, indicator lights and electronic assemblies from new styles to vintage & retro.

Sony Pictures Studios-Prop House (Off Lot) (310) 244-5999
antenna, battery, binoculars, cable boxes, bull horn, car radio, tape player, CB Radio, CD Player, DVD Player, flash camera

Woody's Electrical Props (818) 503-1940
period to futuristic. digital counters & dressing. Fantasy sets, military sets, industrial sets, air tower

Elevator Dressing

See Also: Hardware, Decorative
Elevator Research & Mftg. Corp. (213) 746-1914
1417 Elwood St, Los Angeles, CA, 90021
elevator pushbuttons, panels & related equip.
www.elevatorresearch.com

The Hand Prop Room LP. (323) 931-1534
hdw., decorative, panels/controls w/mfg.

Modern Props (323) 934-3000
contemporary/futuristic elevator

RJR Props (404) 349-7600
Elevator control panels w/ working lights, exterior elevator panels; working elevator button panels, elevator arrows.

Sony Pictures Studios-Prop House (Off Lot) (310) 244-5999

Universal Studios Property & Hardware Dept (818) 777-2784

Warner Bros. Studios Hardware Rentals (818) 954-1335
4000 Warner Blvd., Bldg. 44 Burbank, CA 91522
Door Knobs & Plates, Hinges, Window Fixtures, Elevator Panels, Train & Boat Accessories
wbsfconstructionservices@warnerbros.com * www.wbsf.com

Embalming

See: Mortuary

Emblems

See: Badges, Patches & Buttons Flags/Banners*

Embroidery, Screen Printing, Etc.

See Also: Fabric Dyeing/Tie Dyeing/Painting/Aging Promotional
Items & Materials*

Big 10 Industries, Inc. (310) 280-1610
149 S. Barrington Ave, Ste 812, Los Angeles, CA, 90049
embroidery, screen printing on clothing & all promotional items

House of Embroidery (323) 469-4666
5273 Fountain Ave, Los Angeles, CA, 90029
By Appt. Only, custom-made embroidery for the entertainment & interior design
industries

Imprint Revolution (310) 474-4472
10675 W Pico Blvd, Los Angeles, CA, 90064
Heat transfer, silk-screen, embroidery, custom garments, no minimums, rush
svc avail.

L. A. Party Works (888) 527-2789
9712 Alpaca St, S El Monte, CA, 91733
in Vancouver tel. 604-589-4101. custom T-shirts
partyworks@aol.com * www.partyworksusa.com

Quickdraw (310) 477-6770
2244 Federal Ave, Los Angeles, CA, 90064
custom embroidery & screen printing for clothing, bags, etc.

Wizard (323) 656-0287
13248 Victory Blvd, Valley Glen, CA 91401
Screen printing, heat transfers, direct to garment printer, embroidery, digital
printing, sports & team apparel
debbie@thewizard.tv * www.thewizard.tv

Emergency Room

See Also: Ambulance/Paramedic Hospital Equipment* Medical
Equip/Furniture, Graphics/Supplies* Stretchers* Nurses Station*
Waiting Room* Intensive Care Unit / NICU (Natal Intensive Care
Unit)* Exam Room*

A-1 Medical Integration (818) 753-0319
Medical devices for Set Decoration & Property, from minor procedures to
detailed hospital units.

Alpha Companies - Spellman Desk Co. (818) 504-9090
The #1 source for medical equipment in the industry.

Emissions Analyzers

AIR Designs (818) 768-6639
Period to Modern, Smog Machines

Alley Cats Studio Rentals (818) 982-9178

LCW Props (818) 243-0707
Smog Machine, Garage Tools

Engraving

See Also: Sign Painters Signs* Trophies/Trophy Cases*

Art, Signs & Graphics (818) 503-7997
6939 Farmdale Ave, N Hollywood, CA, 91605
props, banners, vinyl graphics, vehicle graphics, 3D router cut letters & logos
jessee@artsignsandgraphics.com * www.artsignsandgraphics.com

D'ziner Sign Co. (323) 467-4467
801 Seward Street, Los Angeles, CA 90038
plastic/metal name plates, desk signs, badges
sales@dzinersign.com * www.dzinersign.com

The Earl Hays Press (818) 765-0700
services the Industry only. traditional to modern, paper & plastic

Nights of Neon (818) 756-4791
13815 Saticoy St, Van Nuys, CA 91402
Computerized table router for engraving.
contact@nightsofneon.com * www.nightsofneon.com

Sword & Stone (818) 562-6548
Same-day electrochemical metal etching & plating

WestOn Letters (818) 503-9472
7259 N. Atoll Ave, N. Hollywood, CA, 91605
Serving the signage needs of the entertainment industry since the 1960s
sales@westonletters.com * www.WestonLetters.com

Environmental (Cool/Heat) Suits

Global Effects, Inc. (818) 503-9273
cool suits convenient hook up / disconnect for filming, heat suits are waterproof
and perform in underwater shots

Equestrian

See: Horse Saddles & Tack Horses, Horse Equipment, Livestock*
Western Dressing* Western Wear*

Erotica

See: Goth/Punk/Bondage/Fetish/Erotica Etc. Leather (Clothing,
Accessories, Materials)*

Espresso/Expresso

See: Coffee House

Etching

See: Glass & Mirrors Prop Design & Manufacturing*

Events, Backings & Scenery

See Also: Backings Scenery/Set Construction* Scenic Artists*

ShopWildThings (928) 855-6075
2880 Sweetwater Ave, Lake Havasu City, AZ, 86406
Event Decor, Beaded Curtains, Chain Curtains, String Curtains & Columns,
Crystal Columns. Reliable service & delivery.
help@shopwildthings.com * www.shopwildthings.com

Events, Decorations, Supplies & Services

See Also: Badges, Patches & Buttons Balloons & Balloon
Sculptures* Carnival Dressing/Supplies* Catering* Columns*
Confetti* Flags/Banners* Florists/Floral Design* Folding
Chairs/Tables* Inflatables, Custom* Linens, Household* Mirror
Balls/Drivers* Neon Lights & Signs* Prop Houses* Pyrotechnics* Red
Carpeting, Events/Premiers* Vendor Carts & Concession Counters*
Wedding Props* Food, Food Stylists*

A-Packaged Parties, Inc. (818) 710-1222
6635 Independence Ave, Canoga Park, CA, 91303
Event planning, party rentals, props, decorating services, specializing in more
than 300 elegant linens & chair covers
info@a-packagedparties.com * www.a-packagedparties.com

Aah-Inspiring Balloons (562) 494-7605
Call for an Appointment.
After 14 years in the TV and Film Industry, Aah-Inspiring Balloon Decor has
been seen in over 200 TV shows and Films.
aahinspiring1@aol.com * www.aahinspiringballoons.com

AIR Designs (818) 768-6639
Diner, NASCAR, Automotive, Street Dressing, Seating

DISPLAY ADS AND LISTINGS FOR THIS CATEGORY
CONTINUE ON THE FOLLOWING PAGE

Arc de Belle   (855) 332-3553
Call for Consultation
Unique brand of Wedding/Event Arches, Gazebos, Chuppah, Column &
Canopy Rentals. Themed Photo Booths & Vintage Airstream
info@arcdebelle.com * www.arcdebelle.com

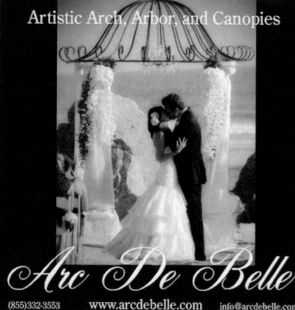

Astro Audio Video Lighting, Inc.   (818) 549-9915
6615 San Fernando Rd, Glendale, CA, 91201
Event decorations and event supplies for concerts, festivals and parties.
www.astroavl.com

Benson's Tropical Sea Imports   (714) 841-3399
7442 Vincent Cir, Huntington Beach, CA 92648
tropical, nautical, & Mexican decor
sales@bensonsimport.com * www.bensonsimport.com

Bill Ferrell Co.   (818) 767-1900
10556 Keswick St, Sun Valley, CA, 91352
Stages, ramps, risers, handicap lifts, turntables, winches, computer controls,
custom sets, props, confetti, balloons.
www.billferrell.com

Bob Gail Special Events   (310) 202-5200
Bob Gail has an extensive list of themed props for movie sets, events, and
tradeshows for rental in CA and Las Vegas.

Carving Ice & Big on Snow   (714) 224-1455
900 S Placentia Ave Ste B, Placentia, CA, 92870
You're the best at what you do & so are we. Carving Ice & Blowing Snow for
the TV & film industries for over 20 years.
info@carvingice.com * www.carvingice.com

Dapper Cadaver/Creatures & Cultures   (818) 771-0818
Halloween party central. Monsters, gore, skeletons, tombstones, caskets,
candelabras & decor. Haunted mansion to zombie.

Fiesta Parade Floats   (626) 610-0974
16016 Avenida Padilla Suite B, Irwindale, CA, 91702
parade floats, props & displays

Flower Art   (323) 935-6800
5859 West 3rd Street, Los Angeles, CA, 90036
Award-winning, full-service floral design for movie/television sets. Located near
The Grove. SDSA members since 1994
info@flowerartla.com * http://www.flowerartla.com

FormDecor, Inc.   (310) 558-2582
America's largest event rental supplier of 20th Century furniture and
accessories for Modern and Mid-Century styles.

FROST   (310) 704-8812
Call for Appointment, 21515 Madrona Ave, Torrance, CA 90503
Christmas decor prop rentals and installations for all your holiday events and
productions!
mdisplay@yahoo.com * www.frostchristmasprops.com

Green Set, Inc.   (818) 764-1231
theme decor. Arbors & Arches, Gazebos, Lattice, Trellis

History For Hire, Inc.   (818) 765-7767
decorations, accessories

Jackson Shrub Supply, Inc.   (818) 982-0100

Jet Sets   (818) 764-5644
6910 Farmdale Ave, N Hollywood, CA, 91605
set construction, custom props, scenic painting, special effects, set illustration,
research library for clients
dougmorris@jetsets.com * www.jetsets.com

L. A. Circus   (323) 751-3486
Call for Appt, Los Angeles, CA, 90047
canvas tents, circus tents, clown mannequins, fake carnival animals: elephant,
zebra, lion, horse, ferris wheel
circusinc@aol.com * www.lacircus.com

L. A. Party Works   (888) 527-2789
9712 Alpaca St, S El Monte, CA, 91733
Vancouver (604) 589-4101. Event supplies; carnival, circus, competitive
athletic, misting fans, virtual reality & more
partyworks@aol.com * www.partyworksusa.com

Lennie Marvin Enterprises, Inc. (Prop Heaven)   (818) 841-5882
props & dressing, 50s, Halloween, birthday, etc.

LM Treasures   (626) 252-7354
10557 Juniper Ave Unit A, Fontana, CA 92337
Anything needed to help start the party such as animals, celebrities, or pirates
will truly make it a night to remember.
lmtreasures.ll@gmail.com * www.lifesizestatues.net

Lux Lounge EFR   (888) 247-4411
106 1/2 Judge John Aiso St #318, Los Angeles, CA, 90012
We%u2019ll add the extra touch of luxury to your event with our custom
designs and event decorations.
info@luxloungeefr.com * www.luxloungeefr.com

Mandex LED Displays   (800) 473-5623
2350 Young Ave, Thousand Oaks, CA, 91360
LED Displays & Sign Rentals nationwide, all configurations, tickers, flexible
panels, big LED Digital Countdown Clocks.
alan@ledsignage.com * www.ledsignage.com

Oceanic Arts   (562) 698-6960
theme decor for Hawaiian, Tropical, Nautical, Polynesian, Island, Carved,
Rattan, Tapa, Tiki, Luau and more

Phoenix Decorating Co., Inc.   (626) 793-3174
835 S Raymond Ave, Pasadena, CA, 91105
parade float builder

Sandy Rose Floral, Inc   (818) 980-4371
6850 Vineland Ave Unit C, N Hollywood, CA, 91605
fresh & artificial florals, custom & prefab rentals, call 24 hrs.
www.sandyrose.com

ShopWildThings (928) 855-6075
2880 Sweetwater Ave, Lake Havasu City, AZ, 86406
Event Decor, Beaded Curtains, Chain Curtains, String Curtains & Columns,
Crystal Columns. Reliable service & delivery.
help@shopwildthings.com * www.shopwildthings.com

Sony Pictures Studios-Prop House (Off Lot) (310) 244-5999
conduit, pin spotlights, voltage transformer
Taylor Creative Inc. (888) 245-4044
Our collection is designed for the event industry; perfect for premieres, product
launches, galas, and social affairs.
Universal Studios Property & Hardware Dept (818) 777-2784
Provides an array of event locations and services creating an exciting and
unique environment for any occasion.
Universal Studios Special Events (818) 777-9466
100 Universal City Plaza, Universal City, CA, 91608
www.universalstudiosspecialevents.com

Events, Design/Planning/Production

See Also: Bleachers & Grandstand Seating* Canopies, Tents,
Gazebos, Cabanas* Floor, Ground & Surface Protection* Grip
Equipment* Insurance* Lighting & Sound, Concert/Theatrical/DJ/VJ*
Lighting, LED, Fiber Optic & Specialty* Limousine Service* Prop
Design & Manufacturing* Research, Advisors, Consulting &
Clearances* Rigging, Equipment or Services* Sanitation, Waste
Disposal* Searchlights/Skytrackers, Architectural Lights* Security
Devices or Services* Special Effects, Equipment & Supplies* Stage
Turntables* Stages, Portable & Steel Deck* Trade Shows &
Conventions* Transportation, Trucking and/or Storage* Truss
Amusement Svcs/Candyland Amusements (818) 266-4056
18653 Ventura Blvd Ste 235, Tarzana, CA, 91356
We own our carnival equipment, games, rides and attractions; we set up. Street
Fairs, commercial shoots, Carnivals, Corporate picnics
www.candylandamusements.com
Astro Audio Video Lighting, Inc. (818) 549-9915
6615 San Fernando Rd, Glendale, CA, 91201
We provide event planning & event design as well as concert planning &
concert design.
www.astroavl.com
Bob Gail Special Events (310) 202-5200
As professional event planners, Bob Gail Special Events ensures that every
facet is professionally coordinated.
Create a Scene! & Hooray 4 Holidays! (323) 978-0883
Call for Appointment or to Place an Order
Provides services, coordinating, design work & supplies for your special event
needs.
Events@CreateaScene.net * www.CreateaScene.net
EFX- Event Special Effects (626) 888-2239
125 Railroad Ave, Monrovia, CA, 91016
Event Design- Layouts- 3D Renderings- Management- Acitvations- Tours
info@efxla.com * www.efxla.com

Entertainment Design Corp. (310) 641-9300
5455 Wilshire Blvd. Ste 910 Los Angeles, CA 90036
stadium shows, corporate events, awards shows, TV & film
Flower Art (323) 935-6800
5859 West 3rd Street, Los Angeles, CA, 90036
Award-winning, full-service floral design for movie/television sets. Located near
The Grove. SDSA members since 1994
info@flowerartla.com * http://www.flowerartla.com
L. A. Party Works (888) 527-2789
9712 Alpaca St, S El Monte, CA, 91733
in Vancouver tel. 604-589-4101. pre/post event PR, design to implementation
partyworks@aol.com * www.partyworksusa.com
Lux Lounge EFR (888) 247-4411
106 1/2 Judge John Aiso St #318, Los Angeles, CA, 90012
Event Design, Event Planning, Event Production: We work with you to ensure
your event looks amazing!
info@luxloungeefr.com * www.luxloungeefr.com
Miziker Entertainment Group (818) 558-1888
4110 Riverside Dr, Burbank, CA, 91505
Concept, design, production & operations for shows, compelling places &
experiences
Paradigm Shift Worldwide (818) 831-3005
17326 Devonshire St, Northridge, CA, 91325
all aspects of event design & production, specializing in media events &
publicity stunts
Premier Displays & Exhibits (562) 755-1668
11261 Warland Dr, Cypress, CA, 90630
Full service exhibit house providing turnkey services for trade shows, events,
meetings, & permanent installations.
Route 66 Productions, Inc. (310) 823-2066
Web Based Business
full service production of corporate events: development, design, scripting &
implementation of events & media
whitneyr@artdimensionsonline.com
Sandy Rose Floral, Inc (818) 980-4371
6850 Vineland Ave Unit C, N Hollywood, CA, 91605
Fresh & artificial florals, floral props, custom & prefab rentals, call 24 hours.
www.sandyrose.com
Tractor Vision Scenery & Rentals (323) 235-2885
340 E Jefferson Blvd. Los Angeles, CA 90011
Specializing in entertainment, trade shows, & events, we bring your projects to
life with precision, speed & personality
sets@tractorvision.com * www.tractorvision.com
Universal Studios Special Events (818) 777-9466
100 Universal City Plaza, Universal City, CA, 91608
www.universalstudiosspecialevents.com
The Vox Group (310) 535-5510
1334 Parkview Ave Ste 100, Manhattan Beach, CA, 90266
Full service event marketing, production, management, and entertainment

Events, Destinations

See Also: Locations, Insert Stages & Small Theatres*
Stages/Studios, Film/TV/Theatre/Events
Aquarium of the Pacific (562) 590-3100
100 Aquarium Way, Long Beach, CA, 90802
call Group Sales for location shoots, (562) 951-1684
Cabrillo Marine Aquarium (310) 548-7562
3720 Stephen M White Dr, San Pedro, CA, 90731
Castle Park (951) 785-3000
3500 Polk St, Riverside, CA, 92505
miniature golf, arcade, haunted house, etc.
Descanso Gardens (818) 949-4200
1418 Descanso Dr, La Canada, CA, 91011
contact "filming/rentals dept"
Disneyland (714) 781-4565
1313 S. Harbor Blvd, Anaheim, CA, 92803
Disney's California Adventure (714) 781-4636
1600 Disneyland Dr, Anaheim, CA, 92803
The Hollywood Museum (323) 464-7776
1660 N. Highland Ave, Hollywood, CA, 90028
events & location space
The Japanese Garden (818) 756-8166
6100 Woodley Ave, Van Nuys, CA, 91406
Knott's Berry Farm (714) 220-5200
8039 Beach Blvd, Buena Park, CA, 90620
Legoland California (760) 918-5346
1 Legoland Drive, Carlsbad, CA, 92008

LISTINGS FOR THIS CATEGORY CONTINUE ON THE
FOLLOWING PAGE

Monterey Bay Aquarium (831) 648-4888
886 Cannery Row, Monterey, CA, 93940
Newfornia Event Center (323) 789-6288
7000 S Western Avenue, Los Angeles, CA, 90047
Event Venue with Multi-purpose Rooms, a Commercial Kitchen, Dance floor,
Reception area, Stage, Dj booth and Bar area.
newforniaeventcenter@gmail.com * www.newfornia-events.com
Raging Waters (909) 802-2200
111 Raging Waters Dr, San Dimas, CA, 91773
RMS Queen Mary (562) 435-3511
1126 Queens Hwy, Long Beach, CA, 90802
End of the 710 Fwy, in the water
San Diego Zoo's Wild Animal Park (760) 747-8702
2920 Zoo Dr, San Diego, CA, 90023
Sea World San Diego (800) 257-4268
500 Sea World Dr, San Diego, CA, 92109
Six Flags Hurricane Harbor (661) 255-4100
26101 Magic Mountain Pkwy, Valencia, CA, 91355
Six Flags Magic Mountain (661) 255-4100
26101 Magic Mountain Pkwy, Valencia, CA, 91355
Sony Pictures Studios-Events (310) 244-4456
10202 W Washington Blvd, Los Angeles, CA, 90232
www.sonypicturesstudios.com
Universal Studios Hollywood (800) 892-1979
100 Universal City Plaza, Universal City, CA, 91608
www.filmmakersdestination.com
Universal Studios Special Events (818) 777-9466
100 Universal City Plaza, Universal City, CA, 91608
www.universalstudiosspecialevents.com

Events, Entertainment

See Also: Animal Costumes & Walk Around Characters Arcade
Equipment, Games & Rides* Carnival Games & Rides* Clowns*
Events, Mobile Marketing* Magicians & Props, Supplies, Dressing*
Video Games*
Arcade Amusements (866) 576-8878
802 West Washington Ave Ste E, Escondido, CA, 92025-1644
Planning a Party? How about having some games there? How about 10? How
about 20? How about... Well, you get the idea.
phil@arcadeamusements.com * www.arcadeamusements.com
Bob Gail Special Events (310) 202-5200
For over three decades, Bob Gail Special Events has provided entertainment at
the most prestigious events in the country
Christiansen Amusements (800) 300-6114
Call for Appt
Carnival rides & games for all events & productions
info@amusements.com * www.amusements.com
L. A. Circus (323) 751-3486
Call for Appt, Los Angeles, CA, 90047
canvas tents, circus tents, clown mannequins, fake carnival animals: elephant,
zebra, lion, horse, ferris wheel
circusinc@aol.com * www.lacircus.com
L. A. Party Works (888) 527-2789
9712 Alpaca St, S El Monte, CA, 91733
in Vancouver tel. 604-589-4101
partyworks@aol.com * www.partyworksusa.com
Owen Magic Supreme (626) 969-4519
734 N McKeever Ave, Azusa, CA, 91702
magic effects, consulting techniques, props, spec. effects
alanz@owenmagic.com * www.owenmagic.com
Quantum Rock Enterprises (310) 378-2171
PO Box 4032, Palos Verdes, CA, 90274
Rock climbing walls, mobile/indoor/outdoor up to 24', realistic, safety
staff/training/insurance, full service, easy set
www.quantumrock.com

Events, Mobile Marketing

Craftsmen Industries (800) 373-3575
3101 Elm Point Industrial Dr, Saint Charles, MO, 63301
design & build mobile trailers/vehicles, portable displays
EEI Global (248) 608-7500
1400 South Livernois, Rochester Hills, MI 48307
full svc. touring & mobile marketing, vehicle construction, exhibit fabrication
EFX- Event Special Effects (626) 888-2239
125 Railroad Ave, Monrovia, CA, 91016
Custom Fabrication- Marketing- Tours- Tour Management- Activations
info@efxla.com * www.efxla.com
Featherlite, Inc. (800) 800-1230
P.O. Box 320, Hwy 63 & 9, Cresco, IA, 52136
design & build custom mobile trailers for events, and for special services &
communications

L. A. Party Works (888) 527-2789
9712 Alpaca St, S El Monte, CA, 91733
in Vancouver tel. 604-589-4101. vehicles & props for marketing, promotions,
public relations
partyworks@aol.com * www.partyworksusa.com
MKTG (212) 366-3428
75 9th Avenue 3rd Floor, New York, NY, 10011
award-winning event & entertainment marketing solutions
Spevco, Inc. (336) 924-8100
8118 Reynolda Rd, Pfafftown, NC, 27040
custom vehicle design & construction
Turtle Transit (978) 365-9300
6 Fox Rd, Hudson, MA, 01749
custom built trailers & morphed vehicles, event props, vehicle wraps

Exam Room

See Also: Ambulance/Paramedic Dentist Equipment* Doctor's Bags*
Hospital Equipment* Medical Equip/Furniture, Graphics/Supplies*
X-ray Machine* X-ray Viewer* X-rays* Waiting Room* Intensive Care
Unit / NICU (Natal Intensive Care Unit)* Emergency Room*
Radiology*
A-1 Medical Integration (818) 753-0319
Medical devices for Set Decoration & Property, from minor procedures to
detailed hospital units.
Alpha Companies - Spellman Desk Co. (818) 504-9090
The #1 source for medical equipment in the industry.

Exercise & Fitness Equipment

See Also: Ballet Barres & Dance Mirrors Boxing, Wrestling, Mixed
Martial Arts (MMA)* Fall Pads & Crash Pads* Gymnasium &
Gymnastic Equipment* Massage Tables* Weightlifting Equipment*
Athletic Room (818) 764-9801
12750 Raymer St, N Hollywood, CA, 91605
Treadmills, Gym, Yoga, Boxing, ND Balls, mats, Golf, Surfboards, Tennis,
Soccer, Football, Basketball, Baseball, Hockey.
athleticroom@mac.com * www.athleticroomprops.net
C. P. Valley (323) 466-8201
Weight machines, bar bells, exercise machines, medicine balls, exercise mats,
gym mats, exercise balls and more.
Curtis Gym Equipment (818) 897-2804
10275 Glenoaks Blvd, Ste #7, Pacoima, CA, 91331
Prop Rentals and Servicing. Fitness Machines, Gymnastics & Weightlifting.
Fake & Real Weights
curtisgymequipment@hotmail.com

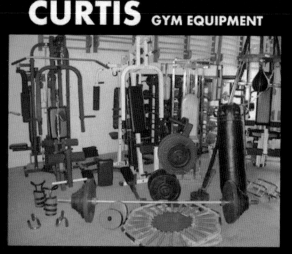

CURTIS GYM EQUIPMENT

RENTALS & SALES • REAL & PROPS
COMPLETE SET-UP & SERVICE

The Hand Prop Room LP. (323) 931-1534
all types, prop weights
History For Hire, Inc. (818) 765-7767
period, smalls

Hollywood Gym Rentals   (310) 663-6161
200 West Chevy Chase Drive Unit B, Glendale, CA 91204
Hollywood Gym Rentals specializes in short and long term rentals of fitness
equipment in the Los Angeles area.
chris@hollywoodgymrentals.com * www.hollywoodgymrentals.com

Castex Rentals   (323) 462-1468
1044 N. Cole Ave, Hollywood, CA, 90038
tape, layout board, gels, seamless paper, gloves, knives, furniture pads etc.
service@castexrentals.com * www.castexrentals.com

LCW Props   (818) 243-0707
Power Rack, Dumbbells, Fake & Real Weight Plates, Ropes, Sled, Benches,
Medicine Balls, Agility Ladders

Modern Props   (323) 934-3000
contemporary/electronic

Norbert's Athletic Products   (800) 779-1904
431 Figueroa St. Wilmington, CA 90744
We specialize in matting and equipment for gymnastics, cheer, dance, yoga,
stunt and martial arts.
info@norberts.net * www.norberts.net

Sony Pictures Studios-Prop House (Off Lot)   (310) 244-5999
exercise benches, sports benches, boxing equipment, exercise equipment, fall
pads, gym bags, jump ropes, massage tables

Exit Alarm

See: Security Walk-Through & Baggage Alarms

Expendables

See Also: Adhesives, Glues & Tapes Duvetyne* Firearms,
Gunsmith, Firearm Choreography* Flameproofing* Floor, Ground &
Surface Protection* Grip Equipment* Janitorial Supplies* Plastics,
Materials & Fabrication* Rubber Stamps*

Absolute Packaging   (800) 567-9190
11940 Sherman Road, N. Hollywood, CA 91605
std/custom, boxes, wardrobe, custom foam, bubble wrap, tape, shipping boxes
www.absolutepackagingsupply.com

Anytime   (323) 461-8483
expendables, digital & Chromakey tapes & paint
anytimerentals@hotmail.com

The Battery Hut   (818) 558-6740
913 South Victory Blvd, Burbank, CA 91502
for all your battery needs; also take old batteries for disposal

Bear Forest Products, Inc   (951) 727-1767
4685 Brookhollow Circle, Riverside, CA, 92509
Spray adhesives for wood and paneling.
matto@bearfp.com * www.bearfp.com

Cinelease/Expendables Plus   (818) 841-8282
5375 W. San Fernando Rd, Los Angeles, CA, 90039
expendables, grip/lighting equip., truck packages

Expendable Supply Store/Hollywood Rentals   (800) 233-7830
12800 Foothill Blvd, Sylmar, CA, 91342

Expendables Plus   (718) 609-6464
32 Eagle St Ste 1. Brooklyn, NY 11222
expendables only

Expendables Recycler   (818) 901-9796
5812 Columbus Ave, Van Nuys, CA, 91411
sell & buy surplus grip/electric/camera expendables, please call before visiting
us, thanks!

Feature Systems, Inc.   (201) 531-2299
223 Veteran's Blvd, Canstadt, NJ, 07072
grip/lighting, expendables/supplies, generators, trucks

The Hand Prop Room LP.   (323) 931-1534
extensive

Harris Industries, Inc.   (800) 222-6866
5181 Argosy Ave, Huntington Beach, CA, 92649
Tapes; safety, caution, anti-skid, barricade, flagging, custom

Highline Stages   (212) 206-8280
440 W. 15th Street, New York City, NY, 10011
expendables, lighting, generators, grip equip.

Imperial Paper Co.   (818) 769-4400
5733-37 Cahuenga Blvd, N Hollywood, CA, 91601
Wardrobe, tape, cushioning, foam, bubblewrap, custom & stock shipping
boxes. Tape machines, stretch wrappers, void fill
www.imperialpaper.com

Mole-Richardson Co.   (323) 851-0111
937 N Sycamore Ave, Hollywood, CA, 90038
Ask for Studio Depot

Mutual Hardware Corp.   (718) 361-2480
36-27 Vernon Blvd, Long Island City, NY, 11106
catalog sales; hardware, scenic materials, lighting, rigging

New Mexico Lighting & Grip Co.   (505) 227-2500
5650 University Blvd SE Bldg 2, Albuquerque, NM, 85107
Grip & rigging equip. & services, lighting & sound. Expendable store
www.newmexicolightingandgrip.com

Norcostco   (800) 220-6920
825 Rhode Island Ave S, Golden Valley, MN, 55426
multiple sales office locations around the U.S. full stock of theatrical
expendables

**DISPLAY ADS AND LISTINGS FOR THIS CATEGORY
CONTINUE ON THE FOLLOWING PAGE**

North Hollywood Hardware, Inc. (818) 980-2453
11847 Ventura Blvd, Studio City, CA, 91604
Fittings, pipes, faucets, etc. and knowledgeable staff
nohohardware@gmail.com * www.ehardware2go.com

Pacific Fibre & Rope Co. (800) 825-7673
903 Flint Ave, Wilmington, CA, 90748
rope manufacturing, all kinds, as much as you need, hwr fittings, tools, nets,
but no chains, rope
moreinfo@pacificfibre.com * www.pacificfibre.com

PACIFIC FIBRE ROPE CO. INC. EST. 1928
We've sold over 25 million miles of rope.
You can be assured: We know rope!

ROPE NETTING LADDERS HARDWARE
CUSTOM ROPE DESIGN & PRODUCTS
www.pacificfibre.com

Pacific Northwest Theatre Associates (800) 622-7850
2414 SW Andover C100, Seattle, WA, 98106
catalog sales; theatrical supplies, make-up, expendables, rigging, drops,
lighting, sound, effects

Panavision (Hollywood) (323) 464-3800
6735 Selma Ave, Hollywood, CA, 90028
expendables, plus camera equip., HD 900R, F23, Varicam

Prop Trx (818) 445-1480
Call to page me for appointment, Simi Valley, CA, 93063
Where's My Cupholder for directors chairs & silent shopping bags.
timschultz1@mac.com * www.proptrx.com

Quixote (504) 266-2297
10289 Airline Hwy, St. Rose LA 70087
Grip, Electric, Camera, Art Department, Grip Tape, Gels, Foam Core, Online
orders, Petty Cash Envelopes.
nola@quixote.com * www.quixote.com

Quixote Studio Store (323) 960-9191
1000 N Cahuenga, Hollywood, CA, 90038
Expendables sales & production supply rentals

R. S. Hughes (818) 686-9111
10639 Glenoaks Blvd, Pacoima, CA, 91331
industrial supplies, many brands

Set Wear (818) 340-0540
9027 Canoga Ave Ste K, Chatsworth, CA, 91311
Work gloves (incl. Hot Hand gloves), tool pouches/belts, accessories

Sugru 011 44 20 7998-0022
FormFormForm Ltd, Units 1&2, 47-49 Tudor Road, London, E9 7SN, United
Kingdom
Self-setting rubber that can be formed by hand. Turns into a strong, flexible
silicone rubber overnight.
linda@sugru.com * www.sugru.com

TMB (818) 899-8818
527 Park Ave, San Fernando, CA, 91340
in NJ: (201) 896-8600, elect. connectors, cabling, grip/lighting components

Warner Bros. Studios Mill Store (818) 954-4444
4000 Warner Blvd, Burbank, CA, 91522
Production expendables & production supplies to the entertainment community
at great prices
wbsfmillstore@warnerbros.com * www.wbmillstore.com

Xeno-Lights (212) 941-9494
1 Worth Street, New York City, NY, 10013
expendables, plus grip/lighting equip.

Experiential Marketing

See: Events, Mobile Marketing

Exterior Locations

See: Locations, Insert Stages & Small Theatres* Backlots/Standing
Sets

Eyewear, Glasses, Sunglasses, 3D

See Also: Wardrobe, Accessories

The Costume House (818) 508-9933
vintage

The Hand Prop Room LP. (323) 931-1534
period-futuristic

History For Hire, Inc. (818) 765-7767
period glasses, 3D glasses, lots of sunglasses

Meow (562) 438-8990
2210 E 4th St, Long Beach, CA, 90814
original "never worn" men's, women's, kids, 1950-70s frames

Sony Pictures Studios-Prop House (Off Lot) (310) 244-5999
large selection, glasses & sunglasses, eyepatches, eye patches, face sheild,
glasses cases, eyeglasses, goggles, monocles

Universal Studios Property & Hardware Dept (818) 777-2784
All kinds of eyewear props and accessories for rent.

EZ UP

See: Canopies, Tents, Gazebos, Cabanas

Fabric Dyeing/Tie Dyeing/Painting/Aging

See Also: Embroidery, Screen Printing, Etc.

Almore Dye House (818) 506-5444
6850 Tujunga Ave, N. Hollywood, CA, 91605

A Dyeing Art/Studio 2 (818) 246-5440
Call for Appt.
cater specifically to the Industry

Melissa Binder (818) 535-7085
By Appt, aging, dyeing, painting, ask for credits

Fabricators

See: Art For Rent* Art, Artists For Hire* Fiberglass
Products/Fabrication* Furniture, Custom-made/Reproduction*
Metalworking, Decorative* Metalworking, Welding & Structural* Prop
Design & Manufacturing* Prop Reproduction & Fabrication*
Scenery/Set Construction* Vacu-forms/Vacu-forming

Fabrics

See Also: Canvas* Costume/Wardrobe/Sewing Supplies* Leather (Clothing, Accessories, Materials)* Linens, Household* Linens, Tabletop & Events* Upholstery Materials/Services

American Silk Mills **(305) 308-9411**
2300 Chestnut Street 4th floor, Philadelphia, PA, 19103
United States manufacturer of the most exquisite textiles since 1896.
adriano.salucci@americansilk.com * www.sensuede.com

AntiqueFabric.com **(208) 921-6603**
3713 Woody Dr, Boise, ID, 83703
antique fabrics in stock, mid 1800s to 1960s
fabric@antiquefabric.com * www.antiquefabric.com
Britex Fabrics **(415) 392-2910**
146 Geary St, San Francisco, CA, 94108
fashion & home decorating fabrics, trims, 30,000 buttons, yarn & accessories
Calico Corners **(818) 766-1120**
12717 Ventura Blvd, Studio City, CA, 91604
upholstery, drapery, upholstering, open 7 days

Diamond Foam & Fabric Co. **(323) 931-8148**
611 S La Brea Ave, Los Angeles, CA, 90036
decorative fabrics & foam for upholstery, drapery & slipcovers, custom sewing on premises
www.diamondfoamandfabric.com

F & S Fabrics **(310) 475-1637**
10629 W. Pico Blvd, Los Angeles, CA, 90064
Call (310) 441-2477 for upholstery fabrics
Home Fabrics **(213) 689-9600**
910 S. Wall St, Los Angeles, CA, 90015
decorative drapery & upholstery at wholesale prices
International Silks & Woolens **(323) 653-6453**
8347 Beverly Blvd, Los Angeles, CA, 90048
notions, fabric & patterns, drapery & upholstery

**DISPLAY ADS AND LISTINGS FOR THIS CATEGORY
CONTINUE ON THE FOLLOWING PAGE**

Download our tablet-friendly
eBook
FREE from Lulu.com

Leather Corral Inc   (818) 764-7880
13052 Raymer St., North Hollywood, CA, 91605
Excellent source for vinyls, leathers and other fabrics.
leathercorral@yahoo.com * www.leathercorral.com

Michael Levine, Inc.   (213) 622-6259
920 S Maple Ave, Los Angeles, CA, 90015
Fabric for apparel & the home, and yarn, trims & buttons

Morgan Fabrics   (323) 583-9981
4265 Exchange Ave, Los Angeles, CA, 90058
Upholstery & drapery fabrics, full rolls only

National Fiber Technology, LLC   (978) 686-2964
15 Union St, Lawrence, MA, 01840
catalog sales; hair & fur fabrics for wigs, headdresses, 'make-up' hair, & animal costumes, wigs custom made.

Oriental Silk Co.   (323) 651-2323
8377 Beverly Blvd, Los Angeles, CA, 90048
Finest imported silks, woolens, and linens from China & Orient Open Mon - Fri 9 to 5
kenwong@orientalsilk.com * www.orientalsilk.com

ORIENTAL SILK Co. IMPORTS

Finest Imported Silks, Woolens, Porcelains, and Linens from China and the Orient

Outdoor Wilderness Fabrics, Inc.   (800) 693-7467
123 E Simplot Blvd, Caldwell, ID, 83605
fleece, cordura, pack cloth, ripstop, waterproof/breathables, meshes, hardware & zippers

ShopWildThings   (928) 855-6075
2880 Sweetwater Ave, Lake Havasu City, AZ, 86406
Event Decor, Beaded Curtains, Chain Curtains, String Curtains & Columns, Crystal Columns. Reliable service & delivery.
help@shopwildthings.com * www.shopwildthings.com

Sommer's Plastics Products   (973) 777-7888
31 Styertowne Rd, Clifton, NJ, 07012
Mfg., wide sel plastic fabrics, pleathers, fake furs, metallic, stretch, for set decoration or costumes
www.sommers.com

Testfabrics, Inc.   (570) 603-0432
415 Delaware Ave, West Pittston, PA, 18643
catalog sales; synthetic & natural fabrics without additives, conservation uses: restoration/conservation/storage

Warner Bros. Drapery, Upholstery & Flooring   (818) 954-1831
4000 Warner Blvd, Burbank, CA, 91522
Sunbrella, damasks, velour, linens, cottons, sheers, lace, jacquards & prints
wbsfdrapery@warnerbros.com * www.wbdrapery.com

Factory/Industrial

See Also: Conveyor Equipment* Loading Dock Dressing* Warehouse Dressing

AIR Designs   (818) 768-6639
Drums, Lighting, Work Benches, Crates, Tools, Equipment

Alley Cats Studio Rentals   (818) 982-9178
drums, gauges, pallets, pulleys

E.C. Prop Rentals   (818) 764-2008
"1-stop shop" examples: food processing, machine/wood/metal shop

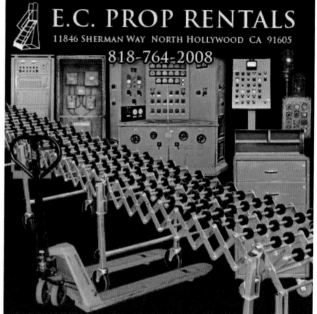

E.C. PROP RENTALS
11846 SHERMAN WAY NORTH HOLLYWOOD CA 91605
818-764-2008

LCW Props   (818) 243-0707
From Shelving To Products To Equipment

Machinery & Equipment Co., Inc.   (909) 599-3916
115 N Cataract Ave, San Dimas, CA, 91773
Over 3 acres of industrial processing equip., such as kettles, mixers, tanks, conveyors & other stainless machinery for
sherri@machineryandequipment.com * www.machineryandequipment.com

Fake Food

See: Food, Artificial Food

Fall Pads & Crash Pads

See Also: Dummies, Fall & Crash

The Hand Prop Room LP.   (323) 931-1534
many sizes and types

L. A. Party Works   (888) 527-2789
9712 Alpaca St, S El Monte, CA, 91733
AIR BAR Free fall air bag/fall bag for stunts and gags.
partyworks@aol.com * www.partyworksusa.com

Norbert's Athletic Products   (800) 779-1904
431 Figueroa St. Wilmington, CA 90744
We specialize in all sizes and styles of matting and landing pads including stunt pads, crash pads, and custom pads.
info@norberts.net * www.norberts.net

Fans, Hand

See: Wardrobe

Fans-Table, Floor or Ceiling

See Also: Air Conditioning & Heating, Production/Event* Special
Effects, Equipment & Supplies

AIR Designs	**(818) 768-6639**
Shop Fans, Fans on Stands	
Alley Cats Studio Rentals	**(818) 982-9178**
industrial, period & modern (no ceiling fans)	
E.C. Prop Rentals	**(818) 764-2008**
industrial desk/floor/ceiling/wall	
The Hand Prop Room LP.	**(323) 931-1534**
table, desk, wall period-present	
History For Hire, Inc.	**(818) 765-7767**
table & floor	
LCW Props	**(818) 243-0707**
Large Industrial, Rolling, Desk, Ceiling	
Modern Props	**(323) 934-3000**
contemporary/futuristic, table, floor, ceiling, large fan racks,	
Omega/Cinema Props	**(323) 466-8201**
Table fans, floor fans, ceiling fans, oscillating fans, box fans, portable fans and more.	
RC Vintage, Inc.	**(818) 765-7107**
Vintage 40s, 50s & 60s/desk, floor, ceiling Working Condition	
Sony Pictures Studios-Fixtures	**(310) 244-5996**
5933 W Slauson Ave, Culver City, CA, 90230	
period to present day, ceiling fans	
www.sonypicturesstudios.com	
Sony Pictures Studios-Prop House (Off Lot)	**(310) 244-5999**
box fans, ceiling fans, clip-on fans, electric fans, floor fans, industrial fans, table fans	
Universal Studios Property & Hardware Dept	**(818) 777-2784**
Period to present prop floor fans, table table, ceiling fans for rent.	

Fantasy Props, Costumes, or Decorations

See Also: Aliens* Events, Backings & Scenery* Events, Decorations,
Supplies & Services* Events, Design/Planning/Production* Futuristic
Furniture, Props, Decorations

Bob Gail Special Events	**(310) 202-5200**
Create a fantasy world with our Fairytale Props. Invite the Giant Dragon, Unicorns and many more!	
The Hand Prop Room LP.	**(323) 931-1534**
Hollywood Studio Gallery	**(323) 462-1116**
photos, drawings, prints, 3D models	
LM Treasures	**(626) 252-7354**
10557 Juniper Ave Unit A, Fontana, CA 92337	
Everything needed to create your own fantasy story ranging from the Knight in shining Armor to the wizard and dragon.	
lmtreasures.ll@gmail.com * www.lifesizestatues.net	
Modern Props	**(323) 934-3000**
furniture, sculpture, accessories & more	
ShopWildThings	**(928) 855-6075**
2880 Sweetwater Ave, Lake Havasu City, AZ, 86406	
Event Decor, Beaded Curtains, Chain Curtains, String Curtains & Columns, Crystal Columns. Reliable service & delivery.	
help@shopwildthings.com * www.shopwildthings.com	
Sword & Stone	**(818) 562-6548**

Farm Equipment & Dressing

See Also: Animals (Live), Services, Trainers & Wranglers* Cattle &
Drums, Wood/Metal/Plastic* Carriages, Horse Drawn* Horse Saddles
& Tack* Horses, Horse Equipment, Livestock* Milk Bottles & Cans*
Tools* Wagons* Weather Vanes

C. P. Valley	**(323) 466-8201**
Plows, carts, milk cans, burlap bags and burlap sacks, water pumps, farm tools, hay	
The Hand Prop Room LP.	**(323) 931-1534**
History For Hire, Inc.	**(818) 765-7767**
Sony Pictures Studios-Prop House (Off Lot)	**(310) 244-5999**

Farriers

See: Blacksmith Shop/Foundry

Fast Food Equipment

See: Restaurant Kitchens/Equip./Supplies* Vendor Carts &
Concession Counters

Faux Books

See: Books, Real/Hollow & Faux Books

Fax Machines

See: Business Machines* Office Equipment & Dressing

Feathers

American Plume	**(800) 521-1132**
11 Skyine Drive East, Unit 2, Clarks Summit, PA 18411	
Boas/jackets/theatrical division in NYC; (800) 962-8544. feather boas, fans, gloves	
The Feather Place	**(213) 291-3253**
719 S Los Angeles St Ste 620, Los Angeles, CA, 90014	
Feather masks, boas, headdresses, wings, wigs, fans, jackets, loose feathers; peacock, pheasant, ostrich, & much more	
www.featherplace.com	
Gettinger Feather Corp.	**(212) 695-9470**
16 West 36th St, New York, NY, 10018	
catalog sales; raw & colored fancy feathers & plumes, also boas, fans & masks	
Hollywood Fancy Feather	**(818) 765-1767**
12140 Sherman Way, N. Hollywood, CA, 91605	
loose, packaged, dyed, boas, strings, marabou fans, naturals, peacocks, skins	
Mother Plucker Feather Co., Inc.	**(213) 637-0411**
2511 W 3rd St, Los Angeles, CA, 90057	

Fences

See Also: Barricades* Steel Folding Gates & Roll-Up Doors* Wood
Shop

Alley Cats Studio Rentals	**(818) 982-9178**
huge selection, self-standing chain link panels, chain link fences	
C & C Fence Co., Inc.	**(818) 983-1959**
12822 Sherman Way, N. Hollywood, CA, 91605	
chain link panel rentals, gate rentals, barbed wire and razor ribbon, install/remove/repair, fence rentals, fence props, electric iron gates	
candcfence@gmail.com * www.candcfence.com	
CI-Fabrics, Inc.	**(619) 661-7166**
2325 Marconi Ct, San Diego, CA, 92154	
wind screen, crowd control, sports event boundary fabric, shade cloth, sight barriers, bulk bags	
E.C. Prop Rentals	**(818) 764-2008**
chainlink/expanded metal, sections, orange plastic rolls	
Green Set, Inc.	**(818) 764-1231**
Metal Fences, Wooden Fences, Bamboo Fencing	
Jackson Shrub Supply, Inc.	**(818) 982-0100**
LCW Props	**(818) 243-0707**
Chain link, Stand Alone	

Fencing Equipment

See: Sporting Goods & Services* Swords & Swordplay

Ferrellels

See: Stages, Portable & Steel Deck

Fetish

See: Goth/Punk/Bondage/Fetish/Erotica Etc.* Leather (Clothing,
Accessories, Materials)

Fiberglass Products/Fabrication

See Also: Prop Reproduction & Fabrication* Scenery/Set
Construction* Staff Shops* Themed Environment Construction

California Art Products	**(818) 762-4276**
11125 Vanowen St, N. Hollywood, CA, 91605	
trees, rocks, animals, urns, fanciful architectural elements	
Green Set, Inc.	**(818) 764-1231**
Palm trunks, Cypress swamp trunks, tree trunks, we are devoted to having it, finding it, or creating it! too!	
Jackson Shrub Supply, Inc.	**(818) 982-0100**
The Mannequin Gallery	**(818) 834-5555**
12350 Montague St Ste E, Pacoima, CA, 91331	
sculpture, molding, and reproduction	
shelley@mannequingallery.com * www.mannequingallery.com	
Projex International	**(661) 268-0999**
9555 Hierba Rd, Agua Dulce, CA, 91390	
fiberglass & steelwork for Film & TV props, scenic, FX, many credits	
Universal Studios Property & Hardware Dept	**(818) 777-2784**
Fiberglass props for rent, from statues and pottery to furniture and fake produce.	
Warner Bros. Studios Staff Shop	**(818) 954-2269**
Manufacturer of exterior & interior details used for the creation of sets in all architectural styles & eras.	

Field Striping & Lining

See: Sporting Goods & Services* Sports/Athletic Field
Lining/Graphics

Fiesta Dinnerware

The Homer Laughlin China Co.   (800) 452-4462
672 Fiesta Dr, Newell, WV, 26050
Made in the USA since 1871
Ob-jects   (818) 351-4200
Ceramic bowls, contemporary bowls,
Sony Pictures Studios-Prop House (Off Lot)   (310) 244-5999
large selection

Fifties Furniture

See: Furniture, Mid-Century Modern

Fifties Theme Parties

See: Costume Rental Houses* Costumes* Events, Backings & Scenery* Events, Decorations, Supplies & Services* Events, Design/Planning/Production* Historical Era Themed Events* Wardrobe, Vintage

Fifty-five Gal. Bar-B-Que Drum

See: Barbecues

Filing Cabinets

See Also: Office Equipment & Dressing* Police Office Dressing
Advanced Liquidators Office Furniture   (818) 763-3470
Large selection, various quantities, pkg deals avail.
C. P. Valley   (323) 466-8201
All kinds of filing cabinets; steel filing cabinets, wood filing cabinets, plastic filing cabinets and more.
Dozar Office Furnishings   (310) 559-9292
9937 Jefferson Blvd, Culver City, CA, 90232
Rentals X22. Bookcases, mobile pedestals, vertical file cabinets, lateral file cabinets, storage cabinets
dozarrents@aol.com * www.dozarrents.com
LCW Props   (818) 243-0707
Large Selection, Lateral, Upright, Wood, Metal, Locking
Modern Props   (323) 934-3000
contemporary filing cabinets, various sizes, purposes, colors, veneered and plated. Small collection.
Prop Services West   (818) 503-2790
RC Vintage, Inc.   (818) 765-7107
40s Wooden and Metal
Sony Pictures Studios-Prop House (Off Lot)   (310) 244-5999
Warner Bros. Studios Property Department   (818) 954-2181
Lateral, Filing, Metal, Wood, Rolling, office, school, multiples, vintage, multiple drawers, period

Film Commissions

Assn. of Film Commissioners Int'l.   (323) 461-2324
9595 Wilshire Blvd. ste. 900 Beverly Hills, CA 90212
web site links to Film Commissions world wide.
California Film Commission   (323) 860-2960
7080 Hollywood Blvd Ste 900, Hollywood, CA, 90028
www.film.ca.gov
Film L. A. Inc.   (213) 977-8600
6255 W Sunset Blvd 12th Floor, Hollywood, CA, 90028
Hollywood liaison of California Film Commission
www.filmlainc.com

Film Reels

See Also: Video Camera Equipment & Services* Video Equipment
The Hand Prop Room LP.   (323) 931-1534

Finials, Decorative

See: Lamps

Fire Extinguishers, Practical & Prop

See Also: Expendables* Fire Hoses (Prop)
AIR Designs   (818) 768-6639
Period to New, Handheld, 2-wheeled Carts
Alley Cats Studio Rentals   (818) 982-9178
modern, antique, brass
C. P. Two   (323) 466-8201
Fire extinguishers; period fire extinguishers, historical fire extinguishers, and modern fire extinguishers.
E.C. Prop Rentals   (818) 764-2008
wide sel. w/wall boxes; also alarm boxes, fire pulls, signage

---

The Hand Prop Room LP.   (323) 931-1534
rigged, prop/rubber
History For Hire, Inc.   (818) 765-7767
brass, most eras
LCW Props   (818) 243-0707
Real & Fake, Rubber, Large Selection
Mike Green Fire Equipment Co.   (818) 989-3322
11916 Valerio St, N Hollywood, CA, 91605
Affordable/dependable refill great pricing - large inventory, next day delivery to most areas.
info@mgfire.com * www.Mgfire.com

Modern Props   (323) 934-3000
contemporary/futuristic, red silver, yellow, white, industrial sized nozzles,
Sony Pictures Studios-Prop House (Off Lot)   (310) 244-5999
bracket extinguishers, extinguisher cases, fire extinguishers
Universal Studios Property & Hardware Dept   (818) 777-2784
Prop fire extinguishers, vintage fire extinguishers, modern fire extinguishers and more for rent.

Fire Hoses (Prop)

C. P. Two   (323) 466-8201
Fire hoses of many kinds: Wall mounted fire hoses, fire hose reels, fire hose steel box, fire hose nozzles and more.
E.C. Prop Rentals   (818) 764-2008
good multiples w/boxes & reels
The Hand Prop Room LP.   (323) 931-1534
History For Hire, Inc.   (818) 765-7767
LCW Props   (818) 243-0707
Large Quantities, With Or Without Nozzles, Boxes, Pulls, Extinguishers
Mike Green Fire Equipment Co.   (818) 989-3322
11916 Valerio St, N Hollywood, CA, 91605
Large inventory, great pricing, next day delivery to most areas.
info@mgfire.com * www.Mgfire.com
Sony Pictures Studios-Prop House (Off Lot)   (310) 244-5999
fire alarm boxes, fire bells, fire stand pipe, fire hydrants
Universal Studios Property & Hardware Dept   (818) 777-2784
Prop fire hoses, fire hose wheels, fire hose cabinets, fire hose valves and more for rent.

Fire Hydrants

See: Street Dressing

Fire Retardants

See: Fire Extinguishers, Practical & Prop* Flameproofing

Fire Sprinklers

See: Fire Extinguishers, Practical & Prop* Fire Hoses (Prop)*
Flameproofing* Plumbing Fixtures, Heating/Cooling Appliances

Fire Suits

See: Costume Rental Houses* Flameproofing* Protective Apparel

Fire Trucks

See: Vehicles

Firearms, Gunsmith, Firearm Choreography

See Also: Civil War Era* Non-Guns & Non-Pyro Flashes* Weaponry,
Historical* Weapons* Western Wear

Caravan West Productions   **(661) 268-8300**
35660 Jayhawker Rd, Aqua Dulce, CA, 91390
Old West, exact reproduction all types, plain & fancy, gunsmiths too. Over 1000
guns from 1820s-1900s. 650 gun belts.
caravanwest@earthlink.net * www.caravanwest.com

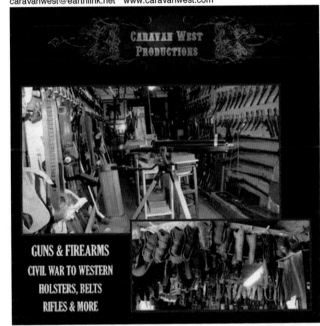

The Hand Prop Room LP.   **(323) 931-1534**
weapons, arsenal, handguns, rifles, fully automatic weapons, semi automatic
weapons, antique handguns, six shooters
History For Hire, Inc.   **(818) 765-7767**
replicas only, flintlock to M-16
I.T.T.S.   **(310) 446-1390**
P.O. Box 149 S. Barrington Ave, Los Angeles, CA, 90049
technical consulting, weapons choreography
LCW Props   **(818) 243-0707**
Period - Present, Fake Guns, Futuristic Guns
RJR Props   **(404) 349-7600**
Prop guns; prop handguns, prop AK47s, prop M4 assault rifles, prop M16
assault rifles, plastic guns & realistic guns.
Tactical Edge Group   **(706) 638-8499**
382 Beard Dr, Trion, GA, 30753
weapons specialists for film, TV; tech advisors military, law enforcement

Fireman Uniforms, Hats & Equipment

See Also: Alarms* Duvetyne* Fire Extinguishers, Practical & Prop*
Fire Hoses (Prop)* Flameproofing* Hoses
Allstar Fire Equipment, Inc.   **(626) 652-0900**
12328 Lower Azusa Rd, Arcadia, CA, 91006
fireman & hazmat apparel & gear
The Hand Prop Room LP.   **(323) 931-1534**
axes, wrenches, gear, badges, air tanks, fireman tools
LCW Props   **(818) 243-0707**
Equipment, Hoses, Nozzles, Extinguishers, Hats, Boots
Western Costume Co.   **(818) 760-0900**

Fireplaces & Mantels/Screens/Tools/Andirons

See Also: Blacksmith Shop/Foundry* Furnaces* Heaters, Indoor*
Heaters, Outdoor
Antiquarian Traders   **(310) 247-3900**
4851 S. Alameda Street, Los Angeles, CA 90048
American Victorian, Marble mantels, and bronze figurative andirons
antiques@antiquariantraders.com * www.antiquariantraders.com
Castle Antiques & Design   **(855) 765-5800**
11924 Vose St, N Hollywood, CA, 91605
We have fireplaces and screens along with an array of furniture to mix and
match with it, and accessories to top it off
info@castleantiques.net * www.castleprophouse.com
Encino Fireplace Shop   **(818) 881-4684**
17954 Ventura Blvd, Encino, CA, 91316
variety; free standing, glass, brass, custom made
Modern Props   **(323) 934-3000**
contemporary fireplaces, small collection.
Omega/Cinema Props   **(323) 466-8201**
Fireplaces and fireplace accessories. Various fireplace screens and fireplace
mantels.
Prop Services West   **(818) 503-2790**
RC Vintage, Inc.   **(818) 765-7107**
vintage fireplace, vintage furnaces, stand up fireplaces, house warmers, wood
burners, single room fireplaces
Sony Pictures Studios-Prop House (Off Lot)   **(310) 244-5999**
andirons, bellows, coal braziers, coal scuttles, fireplaces, screens & tools
Sword & Stone   **(818) 562-6548**
Universal Studios Property & Hardware Dept   **(818) 777-2784**
All things mantel and fireplace props for rent.
Universal Studios Special Effects Equip.   **(818) 777-3333**
special effects setups

Fireworks

See: Pyrotechnics

First Aid Kits

See: Ambulance/Paramedic* Medical Equip/Furniture,
Graphics/Supplies

Fish

See: Aquariums & Tropical Fish

Fish Wranglers

See: Aquariums & Tropical Fish

Fish, Artificial & Rubber

See Also: Aquariums & Tropical Fish
AIR Designs   **(818) 768-6639**
Fake Lobster, Fake Crab, Fake Fish, Etc.
The Hand Prop Room LP.   **(323) 931-1534**
taxidermy, asst. types/sizes
Lennie Marvin Enterprises, Inc. (Prop Heaven)   **(818) 841-5882**
taxidermy, assorted types & sizes
Sony Pictures Studios-Prop House (Off Lot)   **(310) 244-5999**
Universal Studios Property & Hardware Dept   **(818) 777-2784**
Prop fake fish and artificial fish for rent.
Universal Studios Special Effects Equip.   **(818) 777-3333**
shark fins, heads

Fishing Equipment & Tackle

See Also: Fish, Artificial & Rubber* Lobster/Fish Traps
Bob Marriott's Flyfishing Store   **(800) 535-6633**
2700 W Orangethorpe Ave, Fullerton, CA, 92833
all flyfishing, 30K+ inventory items, 325 pg catalog avail.
Fishermen's Spot   **(818) 785-7306**
14411 Burbank Blvd, Van Nuys, CA, 91401
fly fishing & fishing tackle collectibles
The Hand Prop Room LP.   **(323) 931-1534**
full outfitting
History For Hire, Inc.   **(818) 765-7767**

LISTINGS FOR THIS CATEGORY CONTINUE ON THE
FOLLOWING PAGE

Johnny's Sports Shop   **(626) 797-8839**
1402 Lincoln Ave, Pasadena, CA, 91103
all tackle, some camping, float tubes, live bait worms
Sony Pictures Studios-Prop House (Off Lot)   **(310) 244-5999**
Tally Ho Marine Salvage & Decor   **(310) 548-5273**
406 22nd St, San Pedro, CA, 90731
If we don't have it & can't find it, we can build it. boats, nautical, block & tackle
sets, barrels, rope
Turner's Outdoorsman   **(626) 578-0155**
835 S Arroyo Pkwy, Pasadena, CA, 91105
fishing equip. tackle, firearms; Reseda store (818) 996-5033
Universal Studios Property & Hardware Dept   **(818) 777-2784**
All things fishing props from saltwater to freshwater for rent.

Fishnets

See: Camouflage Nets* Cargo Nets* Fishing Equipment & Tackle*
Hosiery* Nautical Dressing & Props

Fitness Equipment

See: Exercise & Fitness Equipment* Massage Tables* Medical
Equip/Furniture, Graphics/Supplies

Fixtures, Display

See: Display Cases, Racks & Fixtures (Store)* Store Shelf Units &
Shelving

Fixtures, Lighting

See: Light Fixtures

Fixtures, Plumbing

See: Plumbing Fixtures, Heating/Cooling Appliances

Flagpoles

AIR Designs   **(818) 768-6639**
8' to 35' Poles, Flags
E.C. Prop Rentals   **(818) 764-2008**
aluminum sectional, free standing & wall-mount

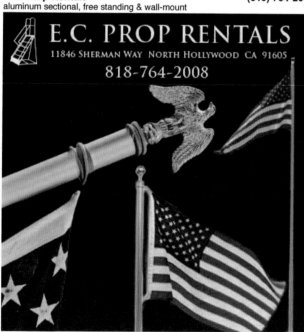

History For Hire, Inc.   **(818) 765-7767**
inside & military style
LCW Props   **(818) 243-0707**
Aluminum, Large & Small, Flags, Ornate
Modern Props   **(323) 934-3000**
contemporary/futuristic, wall and free standing, with United States flag optional

Sony Pictures Studios-Linens, Drapes, Rugs   **(310) 244-5999**
5933 W Slauson Ave, Culver City, CA, 90230
Large flagpoles and pennants
www.sonypicturesstudios.com
Universal Studios Property & Hardware Dept   **(818) 777-2784**
Prop flagpoles; wall mounted flag poles, standing flag poles, and flag pole
bases all for rent.

Flags/Banners

See Also: Flagpoles* Signs* Windsocks
AAA Flag & Banner Mfg Co   **(310) 836-3341**
8937 National Blvd, Los Angeles, Los Angeles, CA 90034
Full Color Custom Printing - Backdrops, Banners, Signs, Posters, Flags, Wall
and Window Graphics. Any size and Quantity.
fred@aaaflag.com * www.aaaflag.com
Art, Signs & Graphics   **(818) 503-7997**
6939 Farmdale Ave, N Hollywood, CA, 91605
props, banners, vinyl graphics, vehicle graphics, 3D router cut letters & logos
jessee@artsignsandgraphics.com * www.artsignsandgraphics.com
Beyond Image Graphics   **(818) 547-0899**
1853 Dana St, Glendale, CA, 91201
Custom Banners, Back Lit Prints, Vinyl Graphics, Vinyl Lettering, Design &
Layout, Printed Banners.
rafi@beyondimagegraphics.com * www.beyondimagegraphics.com

D'ziner Sign Co.   **(323) 467-4467**
801 Seward Street, Los Angeles, CA 90038
vinyl/paper, all sizes up to 20' by 200'
sales@dzinersign.com * www.dzinersign.com
The Hand Prop Room LP.   **(323) 931-1534**
countries, circus, graphic reprod.
History For Hire, Inc.   **(818) 765-7767**
Huge selection presidential, army, etc.
L. A. Circus   **(323) 751-3486**
Call for Appt, Los Angeles, CA, 90047
silent flags, antique sideshow banners, side show banners, circus banners,
circus wagons: many types
circusinc@aol.com * www.lacircus.com
LCW Props   **(818) 243-0707**
Large Selection, Countries, Sports Banners, UN, Swags
Modern Props   **(323) 934-3000**
United States flags framed and on stands, flag bearing figurines
Omega/Cinema Props   **(323) 466-8201**
Many flags from armed forces flags to state flags and country flags.
Presidential flags & various American Flags.

Perry Flag Headquarters   (818) 526-0019
1924 W Olive Ave, Burbank, CA, 91506
flags & flagpoles, distributors & manufacturers
flagheadquarters@att.net

Sony Pictures Studios-Linens, Drapes, Rugs   (310) 244-5999
5933 W Slauson Ave, Culver City, CA, 90230
all nations flags & state flags
www.sonypicturesstudios.com

Sword & Stone   (818) 562-6548
Medieval & Renaissance

Universal Studios Graphic Design & Sign Shop   (818) 777-2350
design, large format printing to 100" wide, & full service sign

Universal Studios Property & Hardware Dept   (818) 777-2784
Various country, state, and religious flags in different sizes and shapes all for rent.

Warner Bros. Design Studio Scenic Art & Sign Shop   (818) 954-1815
4000 Warner Blvd, Burbank, CA, 91522
graphic design and production studio for signs & scenic art; digital printing to hand-painted
wbsigns@warnerbros.com * www.wbsignandscenic.com

Warner Bros. Drapery, Upholstery & Flooring   (818) 954-1831
4000 Warner Blvd, Burbank, CA, 91522
Flags; Flag poles; Banners; Medieval Banners; Butterflies; Futuristic; Custom manufacturing
wbsfdrapery@warnerbros.com * www.wbdrapery.com

WestOn Letters   (818) 503-9472
7259 N. Atoll Ave, N. Hollywood, CA, 91605
Serving the signage needs of the entertainment industry since the 1960s
sales@westonletters.com * www.WestonLetters.com

Flameproofing

See Also: Duvetyne* Fire Extinguishers, Practical & Prop* Protective Apparel

Fabric Flameproofing Company Inc.   (323) 245-1701
835 Milford St, Glendale, CA, 91203
fabrics, costumes, drapery, scenic backdrops, flame retardant

Green Set, Inc.   (818) 764-1231
flameproofing plants, including a wide variety of cacti, dessert plants, and of course succulents galore!

Jackson Shrub Supply, Inc.   (818) 982-0100
Flameproofing materials, flame retardant trees, flame retardant Xmas trees, fire retardant brush, succulents

Flash Bulbs

See: Camera Equipment

Flashlights

See: Camping Equipment* Sporting Goods & Services

Flea Markets

See: Swap Meets, Southern California

Flight Suits

See: Military Surplus/Combat Clothes, Field Gear

Floats, Nautical

See: Nautical Dressing & Props

Floats, Parade

See: Events, Decorations, Supplies & Services

Flocking

See: Fabrics* Wall Coverings

Floor, Ground & Surface Protection

See Also: Clear Vinyl* Duvetyne* Expendables* Flameproofing

Elasco Guard   (800) 827-7887
18081 Redondo Circle Ste D, Huntington Beach, CA 92648
mfg of polyurethane products, esp. cableguards

SVE Portable Roadway Systems, Inc.   (800) 762-8267
6128-F Brookshire Blvd, Charlotte, NC, 28216
MUD-TRAKS for protecting ground surface from tire ruts

Terraplas USA Inc.   (903) 983-2111
1104 W State Highway 31, Kilgore, TX, 75662
turf protection from heavy crowd traffic on large or small areas

Flooring

See: Carpet & Flooring* Dirt Skins* Floor, Ground & Surface Protection* Grating, Grated Flooring, Catwalks* Plastics, Materials & Fabrication* Red Carpeting, Events/Premiers* Rugs* Studio Tile Flooring* Tile, Marble, Granite, Etc.

Floral Foam

See: Foam

Florists/Floral Design

See Also: Flower Carts* Flowers, Dried* Flowers, Silk & Plastic* Greens

Create a Scene! & Hooray 4 Holidays!   (323) 978-0883
Call for Appointment or to Place an Order
Custom Floral & Event Decor for your Film and/or Event Production setting.
Events@CreateaScene.net * www.CreateaScene.net

Floral Design by Daves Flowers   (323) 666-4391
4738 Hollywood Blvd, Los Angeles, CA, 90027
In business for over 40 years. We listen and create, deliver everywhere - LA, Santa Barbara, San Diego
davesflowers@aol.com * www.davesflowers.com

DISPLAY ADS AND LISTINGS FOR THIS CATEGORY CONTINUE ON THE FOLLOWING PAGE

Flower Art (323) 935-6800
5859 West 3rd Street, Los Angeles, CA, 90036
Award-winning, full-service floral design for movie/television sets. Located near The Grove. SDSA members since 1994
info@flowerartla.com * http://www.flowerartla.com

Sandy Rose Floral, Inc (818) 980-4371
6850 Vineland Ave Unit C, N Hollywood, CA, 91605
fresh & artificial florals, custom & prefab rentals, call 24 hrs. Set Florist.
www.sandyrose.com

Flower Carts

See Also: Florists/Floral Design* Flowers, Silk & Plastic

AIR Designs (818) 768-6639
Vendor Carts, Glass Cases, Stands/Display

Bob Gail Special Events (310) 202-5200
Carts come in many shapes and sizes and we have a wide variety of exactly that to choose from!

The Hand Prop Room LP. (323) 931-1534
metal flower cart, wooden flower cart, flower baskets, silk flowers, artificial flowers, outfitted flower cart

History For Hire, Inc. (818) 765-7767

Jackson Shrub Supply, Inc. (818) 982-0100
flower shop decor, wood flower carts, flower vendor carts, multi-tier flower carts, flower sales station props

Sandy Rose Floral, Inc (818) 980-4371
6850 Vineland Ave Unit C, N Hollywood, CA, 91605
custom wood & wood/chalkboard
www.sandyrose.com

Sony Pictures Studios-Prop House (Off Lot) (310) 244-5999

Flower Shop

See Also: Flower Carts* Flowers, Silk & Plastic

Jackson Shrub Supply, Inc. (818) 982-0100
Flower shop decor, wood flower carts, flower vendor carts, flower sales station props.

Lennie Marvin Enterprises, Inc. (Prop Heaven) (818) 841-5882

Flowers, Dried

Omega/Cinema Props (323) 466-8201
Various dried flowers

Sony Pictures Studios-Prop House (Off Lot) (310) 244-5999
dried flowers, dried floral arrangements

Flowers, Silk & Plastic

Alpha Companies - Spellman Desk Co. (818) 504-9090
silk florals, silk plants

Benson's Tropical Sea Imports (714) 841-3399
7442 Vincent Cir, Huntington Beach, CA 92648
tropical palms & banana trees, plants & flowers, vines, leis
sales@bensonsimport.com * www.bensonsimport.com

Flower Art (323) 935-6800
5859 West 3rd Street, Los Angeles, CA, 90036
Award-winning, full-service floral design for movie/television sets. Located near The Grove. SDSA members since 1994
info@flowerartla.com * http://www.flowerartla.com

Green Set, Inc. (818) 764-1231
Fruit, veggies, vines, cornstalks, floral arrangements real and faux. Great for flower shop dressing & florist dressing.

Jackson Shrub Supply, Inc. (818) 982-0100
suburban, classic, exotic; bushes, leaves, vintage-flowers, silk greens

Omega/Cinema Props (323) 466-8201
Various plastic flowers and silk flowers.

Prop Services West (818) 503-2790

Sandy Rose Floral, Inc (818) 980-4371
6850 Vineland Ave Unit C, N Hollywood, CA, 91605
Huge collection, vintage plastics, custom & prefab silks
www.sandyrose.com

Sony Pictures Studios-Prop House (Off Lot) (310) 244-5999
Plastic floral, silk floral, plastic flowers, silk flowers

Universal Studios Property & Hardware Dept (818) 777-2784
Prop artificial floral arrangements, artificial plants, silk flowers, plastic flowers and more for rent.

Fluorescent Fixtures

See: Light Fixtures

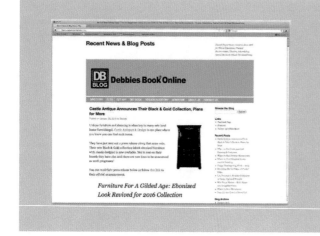

Find out what's new

DB Blog
Debbies Book

check us out online or
download our free mobile app

Foam

See Also: Architectural Pieces & Artifacts Rubber & Foam Rubber*

Advanced Foam, Inc. (310) 515-0617
1745 W. 134th St, Gardena, CA, 90249

Astro Audio Video Lighting, Inc. (818) 549-9915
6615 San Fernando Rd, Glendale, CA, 91201
Foam machines for parties and events.
www.astroavl.com

Atlas Foam Products (818) 837-3626
12836 Arroyo St, Sylmar, CA, 91342
foam, sheets, small-large, cust. shape/size, floral foam

Charisma Design Studio, Inc. (818) 252-6611
8414 San Fernando Road, Sun Valley, CA, 91352
cutting, sculpting & fabrication
info@charismadesign.com * www.charismadesign.com

DeRouchey Foam (888) 959-4852
13618 Vaughn Street, San Fernando, CA, 91340
We offer a full line of foam sculpting materials and services. Urethane, EPS,
HardCoat, Foam Adhesive. 24/7 Service.
dustin@derofoam.com * www.derofoam.com

Diamond Foam & Fabric Co. (323) 931-8148
611 S La Brea Ave, Los Angeles, CA, 90036
decorative fabrics & foam for upholstery, drapery & slipcovers, custom sewing
on premises
www.diamondfoamandfabric.com

EFX- Event Special Effects (626) 888-2239
125 Railroad Ave, Monrovia, CA, 91016
Foam Party- Foam Cannon- Foam Machines- Fluid
info@efxla.com * www.efxla.com

Foam Sales & Marketing (818) 558-5717
1005 W. Isabel St, Burbank, CA, 91506
rigid foam sheets, bead foam blocks, bead board

Williams Foam (818) 833-4343
12961 San Fernando Rd, Sylmar, CA, 91342
foam fabrication, custom work, polyethylene & polystyrene

Foam Core Board

See: Expendables Paper* Styrofoam*

Fog Machines

See Also: Special Effects, Equipment & Supplies Special Effects,
Lighting & Lasers*

Astro Audio Video Lighting, Inc. (818) 549-9915
6615 San Fernando Rd, Glendale, CA, 91201
Dry ice fog machines and fluid fog machines for events and concerts including
remote controlled fog machines.
www.astroavl.com

Castex Rentals (323) 462-1468
1044 N. Cole Ave, Hollywood, CA, 90038
Mole, Roscoe, D50 Hazers, fog juice, indoor fog machines & outdoor fog
machines
service@castexrentals.com * www.castexrentals.com

CONFETTI & FOG FX Special Effects Company (786) 308-7063
2739 W 79 St Bay, #12, Hialeah, FL 33016
www.caffx.com

EFX- Event Special Effects (626) 888-2239
125 Railroad Ave, Monrovia, CA, 91016
Fog Machines- Fog- Haze- Low Lye- Dry Ice- DNG- Fluid
info@efxla.com * www.efxla.com

L. A. Party Works (888) 527-2789
9712 Alpaca St, S El Monte, CA, 91733
Fog machines fore rent
partyworks@aol.com * www.partyworksusa.com

Special Effects Unlimited, Inc. (323) 466-3361
1005 N. Lillian Way, Hollywood, CA, 90038
many kinds
www.specialeffectsunlimited.com

Universal Studios Special Effects Equip. (818) 777-3333
bee smokers to fog guns & supplies

Folding Chairs/Tables

See Also: Chairs

Advanced Liquidators Office Furniture (818) 763-3470
many colors and models of folding chairs including padded seats and/or
padded backs. Folding tables with many high end finishes

C. P. Two (323) 466-8201
Many folding chairs, wooden folding chairs, metal folding chairs, retro folding
chairs and modern folding chairs.

C. P. Valley (323) 466-8201

Castex Rentals (323) 462-1468
1044 N. Cole Ave, Hollywood, CA, 90038
4', 6', 8' tables folding tables, folding chairs
service@castexrentals.com * www.castexrentals.com

Dozar Office Furnishings (310) 559-9292
9937 Jefferson Blvd, Culver City, CA, 90232
Rentals X22. Portable chairs, portable tables, folding tables, folding chairs, card
tables and more available.
dozarrents@aol.com * www.dozarrents.com

History For Hire, Inc. (818) 765-7767
chairs, card tables

LCW Props (818) 243-0707
Many, Plastic, Wood, Different Sizes, Beer Pong

Omega/Cinema Props (323) 466-8201
Many folding chairs from modern to period. Many folding tables from modern to
period.

Universal Studios Property & Hardware Dept (818) 777-2784
Many kinds of folding chairs in multiples for rent.

Folding Screens

See: Screens, Folding

Folk Art

See: Art, Tribal & Folk

Food or Beverage Carts

See: Airport Dressing & Hangars Vendor Carts & Concession
Counters*

Food Processing Plant

See: Factory/Industrial

Food, Artificial Food

See Also: Beer Equipment, Taps & Coolers Catering* Ice Cubes,
Plastic* Soda Fountain Dressing*

C. P. Valley (323) 466-8201
Artificial food from fake cakes to produce crates, fake crab, and bread baskets.

Exotic Cakes (323) 938-2286
1066 S. Fairfax Ave, Los Angeles, CA, 90019
www.exoticcakes.com

Fosselmans Ice Cream Co. (626) 282-6533
1824 W. Main St, Alhambra, CA, 91801
best ice cream in L.A.

Galco's Soda Pop Stop (323) 255-7115
5702 York Blvd, Los Angeles, CA, 90042
100s of rare, regional, imported & half-forgotten soft drinks

Grand Central Market (213) 624-2378
317 S. Broadway, Los Angeles, CA, 90013
fresh & preserved foods from all over the world

Green Set, Inc. (818) 764-1231
Artificial Fruit & Artificial Vegetables, Oversized Fruits & Oversized Vegetables

The Hand Prop Room LP. (323) 931-1534
fruit to bakery goods in stock, will design & mfg.

Hollywood Cinema Arts, Inc. (818) 504-7333
Hundreds of pristine artificial food items.

Iwasaki Images of America (310) 225-2727
16927 S Main St Unit C, Gardena, CA, 90248

Jack's Wholesale Candy & Toy (213) 622-9287
777 S Central Ave, Los Angeles, CA 90021
Bulk candy, vending candy, American candy, novelty candy, pinata candy,
Mexican candy

Jackson Shrub Supply, Inc. (818) 982-0100
fake fruit, fake vegetables, fake gourds, fake corn stalks, fake seaweed,
oversized fruits, oversized vegetables

Jaqki's Cake Creations (818) 769-4967
12032 Burbank Blvd, North Hollywood, CA, 91607
Wedding cakes & custom cakes made fresh or props rental/purchase. We have
80 prop wedding cake styles to choose from.
cakesbyjaqki@yahoo.com * www.jaqkiscakes.com

LCW Props (818) 243-0707
Fake Food, Cheeses, Meats, Fruits & Vegetables

Lennie Marvin Enterprises, Inc. (Prop Heaven) (818) 841-5882
prop vegetables, fruits, meat, baked goods, cold meats, sushi, wedding cake

LM Treasures (626) 252-7354
10557 Juniper Ave Unit A, Fontana, CA 92337
Fruits, vegetables, ice cream, pizza, hotdogs are all pieces used to make a
statement when working in the food industry.
lmtreasures.ll@gmail.com * www.lifesizestatues.net

New Rule FX (818) 387-6450
7751 Densmore Ave, Van Nuys, CA 91406
Fake bread, Prop Party Cakes, Prop Birthday Cakes, Prop Chocolate Candies,
Plastic Ice Cubes, and more.
ryan@newrulefx.com * www.NewRuleFX.com

Real Sodas In Real Bottles (310) 327-1700
2140 W 139th St, Gardena, CA, 90249
nostalgic, no longer made & hard to find sodas, will deliver

Sony Pictures Studios-Prop House (Off Lot) (310) 244-5999
fake bread, fake candy, fake casserole, fake cheeses, fake
chickens, fake cooked foods, fake crabs

Universal Studios Property & Hardware Dept (818) 777-2784
Prop foods/fake foods for rent.

Food, Food Stylists

See Also: Beer Equipment, Taps & Coolers* Catering* Events, Decorations, Supplies & Services* Vendor Carts & Concession Counters

Exotic Cakes   **(323) 938-2286**
1066 S. Fairfax Ave, Los Angeles, CA, 90019
custom erotic cakes, sculptured & airbrushed protrait cakes, wedding cakes, real or prop
www.exoticcakes.com

Food Art L.A.   **(323) 791-2591**
Los Angeles, CA, 90019
"Food Stylist to the Stars" TV - Film - Print - Commercial
foodartla@mac.com * www.FoodArtLA.com

Gourmet Proppers   **(818) 566-4140**
Call for Appointment
Culinery producer & food stylist for camera ready edible food in cooking segments/demos, film, TV & commercials
bonnie@gourmetproppers.com * www.gourmetproppers.com

Jaqki's Cake Creations   **(818) 769-4967**
12032 Burbank Blvd, North Hollywood, CA, 91607
Wedding cakes & custom cakes made fresh or props rental/purchase. We have 80 prop wedding cake styles to choose from.
cakesbyjaqki@yahoo.com * www.jaqkiscakes.com

Foosball

See: Game Tables & Equipment

Foosball Game Table

See: Arcade Equipment, Games & Rides

Foot Wear

See: Shoes, Boots & Footwear

Formal Wear

See Also: Wedding Attire

The Costume House   **(818) 508-9933**
frock coats, morning coats, 1950s & 1970s tuxedoes

Sony Pictures Studios-Wardrobe   **(310) 244-5995**
alterations, call (310) 244-7260

Universal Studios Costume Dept   **(818) 777-2722**
Rental, mfg., & alterations

Western Costume Co.   **(818) 760-0900**

Forties Furniture

See: Furniture, Mid-Century Modern

Forties Theme Parties

See: Costume Rental Houses* Costumes* Events, Backings & Scenery* Events, Decorations, Supplies & Services* Events, Design/Planning/Production* Historical Era Themed Events* Wardrobe, Vintage

Fortune-Teller & Zoltar Mahines

See Also: Carnival Dressing/Supplies* Carnival Games & Rides

L. A. Party Works   **(888) 527-2789**
9712 Alpaca St, S El Monte, CA, 91733
Fortune-teller machine/Zoltars fortune machine
partyworks@aol.com * www.partyworksusa.com

RC Vintage, Inc.   **(818) 765-7107**
4 fortune-teller machines including Zoltar machines, female fortune-teller and a period fortune teller machines.

Fortuneteller

See: Fortune-Teller & Zoltar Mahines* Tarot Cards* Gypsy Wagon* Crystal Balls* Astrological

Fossils

See Also: Bones, Skulls & Skeletons* Dinosaurs

Dapper Cadaver/Creatures & Cultures   **(818) 771-0818**
Standalone fossil replicas and fossil panels. Dinosaur fossils, ice age fossils and fantasy dragon fossils.

Geological Tools & Outfitter, LLC   **(435) 225-6421**
71 N. 200 W, Brigham City, UT, 84302
Fossil collecting & geology tools & equipment

Sword & Stone   **(818) 562-6548**

Wonders of the World & Beyond   **(310) 393-4700**
1460 Lincoln Blvd, Santa Monica, CA, 90401
4-8 pm Mon-Sat, but appt preferred; real fossils, minerals lrg crystals, reprod. ancient jewelry, lrg insect specimens

Foundry Dressing

See: Blacksmith Shop/Foundry

Fountain Pens

See: Pens, Fountain

Fountains, Decorative & Garden

See Also: Garden/Patio* Statuary

Badia Design, Inc.   **(818) 762-0130**
5420 Vineland Ave, N. Hollywood, CA, 91601
Moroccan Outdoor Furniture including fountains, mosaic table tops wrought iron and more.
info@badiadesign.com * www.badiadesign.com

Bob Gail Special Events   **(310) 202-5200**
Create a park scene or a courtyard with our Fountain and Garden Props!

Castle Antiques & Design   **(855) 765-5800**
11924 Vose St, N Hollywood, CA, 91605
Decorative fountains and garden fountains for rent or purchase.
info@castleantiques.net * www.castleprophouse.com

Green Set, Inc.   **(818) 764-1231**
Eiffel tower, animal fountains, statue fountains, Greek fountains, Asian fountains, multiple tier, mini and massive

Jackson Shrub Supply, Inc.   **(818) 982-0100**
Egyptian decor, fiberglass fountains, aluminum fountains, clay fountains, and wishing wells, bird baths

Potted   **(323) 665-3801**
3158 Los Feliz Blvd, Los Angeles, CA, 90039
Decorative garden accessories, furniture, fountains, statues and pots
info@pottedstore.com * www.pottedstore.com

San Gabriel Nursery & Florist   **(626) 286-0787**
632 S San Gabriel Blvd, San Gabriel, CA, 91776
large sel statuary & fountains, also plants

Fountains, Drinking (Wall & Stand)

See Also: Water Coolers

AIR Designs   **(818) 768-6639**
Wall & Stand, Period & Present, Some Rigged

Alley Cats Studio Rentals   **(818) 982-9178**
Free standing drinking fountains and wall mounted drinking fountains available.

C. P. Valley   **(323) 466-8201**
Wall mounted drinking fountains and standing drinking fountains, period to modern.

E.C. Prop Rentals   **(818) 764-2008**
porcelain/metal, period/contemp

History For Hire, Inc.   **(818) 765-7767**

LCW Props   **(818) 243-0707**
Water Coolers, Wall Mount Fountains, Freestanding, Office, School, Prison

Modern Props   **(323) 934-3000**
contemporary/modern, garden and public water fountains.

RC Vintage, Inc.   **(818) 765-7107**
period & modern units Prison Type, public drinking fountains, park drinking fountains, office drinking fountains

Sony Pictures Studios-Fixtures   **(310) 244-5996**
5933 W Slauson Ave, Culver City, CA, 90230
period to present day
www.sonypicturesstudios.com

Universal Studios Property & Hardware Dept   **(818) 777-2784**
Prop standing drinking fountains & prop wall mounted drinking fountains for rent.

Fountains, Soda

See: Soda Fountain Dressing

Frames, Eyeglass

See: Eyewear, Glasses, Sunglasses, 3D

Framing, Picture

See: Picture Frames* Art & Picture Framing Services

Freezers

See: Market Equipment/Fixtures* Refrigerators* Restaurant Kitchens/Equip./Supplies

French Decorations

Bob Gail Special Events (310) 202-5200
Take a trip to Paris with our French-Paris Props and make your guests say "C'est magnifique!"

Castle Antiques & Design (855) 765-5800
11924 Vose St, N Hollywood, CA, 91605
French decor/French decorations for rent or purchase.
info@castleantiques.net * www.castleprophouse.com

Universal Studios Property & Hardware Dept (818) 777-2784
French decorative props for rent.

French Themed Parties

See: Events, Decorations, Supplies & Services* Events, Design/Planning/Production* Travel (City/Country) Themed Events

Frock Coats

See: Formal Wear* Wardrobe, Antique/Historical

Fun House Mirrors

See Also: Carnival Dressing/Supplies

Get The Picture (323) 931-5794
137 S. La Brea Ave, Los Angeles, CA, 90036
manufacturer, several styles & made to order

Lennie Marvin Enterprises, Inc. (Prop Heaven) (818) 841-5882
quantity available

RC Vintage, Inc. (818) 765-7107
carnival mirrors, misshaping mirrors, distortion mirrors

Funeral Dressing

See: Caskets* Cemetery Dressing* Florists/Floral Design* Morgue* Mortuary* Vehicles

Fur Garments

See Also: Fur, Artificial & Real* Leather (Clothing, Accessories, Materials)

Donna Salyers' Fabulous Furs (859) 291-3300
25 W. Robbins, Covington, KY, 41011
catalog sales; faux fur, fabric by the yard

Roxy Deluxe (818) 487-7800
vintage women/men/child

Sword & Stone (818) 562-6548

Western Costume Co. (818) 760-0900

Fur, Artificial & Real

See Also: Leather (Clothing, Accessories, Materials)

The Indian Store (760) 639-5309
1950 Hacienda Dr, Vista, CA, 92081
beads, jewelry findings, fur, feather, leather, rawhide, pottery finished artifacts, many books on Indian lore/tribes

Sword & Stone (818) 562-6548

Furnaces

See Also: Heaters, Indoor* Plumbing Fixtures, Heating/Cooling Appliances

E.C. Prop Rentals (818) 764-2008
mock coal/wood-burning & large factory-size boilers, all castered

LCW Props (818) 243-0707
Industrial, Steampunk, Brownstone, Commercial

Furniture & Art, Repair & Restoration

Adams Wood Products (423) 587-2942
5436 Jeffry Ln, Morristown, TN, 37813
catalog sales; wood furniture components & assembly kits

Advanced Liquidators Office Furniture (818) 763-3470
repair kits, quick and no hassle - apply and let dry kits to fix almost any upholstery, including stains and chips

Castle Antiques & Design (855) 765-5800
11924 Vose St, N Hollywood, CA, 91605
Furniture repair and furniture restoration available.
info@castleantiques.net * www.castleprophouse.com

Pasadena Antique Warehouse (626) 404-2422
1609 East Washington Blvd., Pasadena, CA, 91104
Furniture repair and creation, with a specialty in wood furniture.
pasadenaantiquewarehouse@gmail.com * www.pasadenaantiquewarehouse.com

Van Dyke's Restorers (800) 558-1234
PO Box 52, Louisiana, MO, 63353
catalog sales; woodworking and antique restoration supplies. antique furniture repair parts/hardware/locks/supplies

Warner Bros. Studios Cabinet & Furniture Shop (818) 954-1339
Antique restoration, repair, refinishing and/or replication of period to contemporary furniture.

Furniture Dollies, Pads & Hand Trucks

Alley Cats Studio Rentals (818) 982-9178
wood, metal, period hand trucks

Castex Rentals (323) 462-1468
1044 N. Cole Ave, Hollywood, CA, 90038
Super shelves, truck shelves, racks, furniture dollies, magliners, furniture pads, ratchets, rope
service@castexrentals.com * www.castexrentals.com

E.C. Prop Rentals (818) 764-2008
wide sel. & period stevedore dollies

The Hand Prop Room LP. (323) 931-1534

History For Hire, Inc. (818) 765-7767
dollies, pads, hand trucks

Imperial Paper Co. (818) 769-4400
5733-37 Cahuenga Blvd, N Hollywood, CA, 91601
Wardrobe, tape, cushioning, foam, bubblewrap, custom & stock shipping boxes.
www.imperialpaper.com

Universal Studios Property & Hardware Dept (818) 777-2784
Furniture dollies, furniture pads & hand trucks for rent

Furniture For Pets

See: Pet Furniture, Houses, Clothing

Furniture Oil & Polish

See: Expendables

Furniture, Antique

See: Antiques & Antique Decorations* Furniture, Custom-made/Reproduction

Furniture, Art Deco

Antiquarian Traders (310) 247-3900
4851 S. Alameda Street, Los Angeles, CA 90048
Unique Collection of Art Deco Furniture, living, dining and bedroom suites
antiques@antiquariantraders.com * www.antiquariantraders.com

Castle Antiques & Design (855) 765-5800
11924 Vose St, N Hollywood, CA, 91605
Art deco furniture and Hollywood Regency styles for rent and purchase.
info@castleantiques.net * www.castleprophouse.com

FormDecor, Inc. (310) 558-2582
America's largest event rental supplier of 20th Century furniture and accessories for Modern and Mid-Century styles.

LM Treasures (626) 252-7354
10557 Juniper Ave Unit A, Fontana, CA 92337
This includes a wide range of distinctively different pieces such as Lip Wall Decor, Venice Face Masks, & lady lamps.
lmtreasures.ll@gmail.com * www.lifesizestatues.net

DISPLAY ADS AND LISTINGS FOR THIS CATEGORY CONTINUE ON THE FOLLOWING PAGE

Modern Props   (323) 934-3000
furniture & accessories. Sofas, club chairs, desks, bars, tables, floor lamps, sculptures, clocks, sconces.

Omega/Cinema Props   (323) 466-8201
Art deco chairs, art deco tables. art deco vanities, art deco night stands, art deco coffee tables, and more.
RC Vintage, Inc.   (818) 765-7107
art deco chairs, fine crafted chairs, fancy tables, art deco counters, art deco sofas, comfy chairs, art deco living room sets
Sony Pictures Studios-Prop House (Off Lot)   (310) 244-5999
furniture & lamps
Susanne Hollis, Inc.   (626) 441-0346
230 Pasadena Ave, South Pasadena, CA, 91030
20th - 17th century Antiques, Accessories, and Fine Art from around the world in our 19,000sqft. warehouse and showrooms
sales@susannehollis.com * www.susannehollis.com
Warner Bros. Studios Property Department   (818) 954-2181
High end art deco furniture

Furniture, Arts & Crafts

C. P. Two   (323) 466-8201
Different types of furniture from the Craftsman style. Craftsman furniture/Craftsman bedroom furniture.
Modern Props   (323) 934-3000
Craftsman furniture
Prop Services West   (818) 503-2790
Sony Pictures Studios-Prop House (Off Lot)   (310) 244-5999
Susanne Hollis, Inc.   (626) 441-0346
230 Pasadena Ave, South Pasadena, CA, 91030
20th - 17th century Antiques, Accessories, and Fine Art from around the world in our 19,000sqft. warehouse and showrooms
sales@susannehollis.com * www.susannehollis.com

Furniture, Asian

See: Asian Antiques, Furniture, Art & Artifacts

Furniture, Baby/Children

See Also: Children/Baby Accessories & Bedroom
C. P. Two   (323) 466-8201
Lots of childrens furniture and baby furniture. Baby furniture including changing tables, baby cribs and more.
Kids Cottage Furniture   (818) 783-3055
14444 Ventura Blvd, Sherman Oaks, CA, 91423
Kids bedroom furniture and kids bedroom accessories
kidscottagefurniture@gmail.com * http://kidscottagefurniture.com
Prop Services West   (818) 503-2790
Susanne Hollis, Inc.   (626) 441-0346
230 Pasadena Ave, South Pasadena, CA, 91030
20th - 17th century Antiques, Accessories, and Fine Art from around the world in our 19,000sqft. warehouse and showrooms
sales@susannehollis.com * www.susannehollis.com

Furniture, Biedermeier

Omega/Cinema Props   (323) 466-8201
All kinds of furniture, including bierdermeier
Prop Services West   (818) 503-2790
Susanne Hollis, Inc.   (626) 441-0346
230 Pasadena Ave, South Pasadena, CA, 91030
20th - 17th century Antiques, Accessories, and Fine Art from around the world in our 19,000sqft. warehouse and showrooms
sales@susannehollis.com * www.susannehollis.com

Furniture, Contemporary

Advanced Liquidators Office Furniture   (818) 763-3470
Large selection of high-end furniture, from executive quarters to secretary furniture. Innovative furniture for today
Bassman-Blaine   (213) 748-5909
1933 S. Broadway, #1005, Los Angeles, CA 90007
NOIR/cFc, Arteriors, and World's Away w/ variety of styles; Tables/Chairs, Consoles, Chests/Bookcases, upholstery & more
lashowroom@bassman-blaine.com * www.bassmanblainelamart.com
Blueprint Furniture   (310) 657-4315
8600 Pico Blvd. Los Angeles, CA 90035
Modern furniture lighting accessories early classic bauhaus mid-century contemporary design. Good studio rental history.
www.blueprintfurniture.com

Bridge Furniture & Props Los Angeles   **(818) 433-7100**
We carry modern & traditional furniture, lighting, accessories, cleared art,& rugs. Items are online for easy shopping.

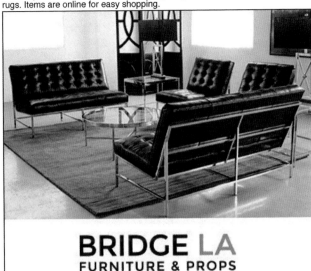

BRIDGE LA
FURNITURE & PROPS

3210 Vanowen St.   BridgeProps.com
Burbank, CA 91505   Tel: 818.433.7100

Castle Antiques & Design   **(855) 765-5800**
11924 Vose St, N Hollywood, CA, 91605
20th century furniture, modern furniture and contemporary furniture for purchase or rent.
info@castleantiques.net * www.castleprophouse.com

Dozar Office Furnishings   **(310) 559-9292**
9937 Jefferson Blvd, Culver City, CA, 90232
Rentals X22. Contemporary furniture for the office and at home.
dozarrents@aol.com * www.dozarrents.com

Faux Library Studio Props, Inc.   **(818) 765-0096**
Modern desks; glass desks and wooden desks

FormDecor, Inc.   **(310) 558-2582**
America's largest event rental supplier of 20th Century furniture and accessories for Modern and Mid-Century styles.

Ikea   **(818) 842-4532**
600 N. San Fernando Blvd, Burbank, CA, 91502

Little Bohemia Rentals   **(818) 853-7506**
11940 Sherman Rd, N Hollywood, CA, 91605
sofas, chairs, coffee tables, end tables, dining sets, headboards, nightstands, desks, shelving, vanities, benches
sales@wearelittlebohemia.com * www.wearelittlebohemia.com

Lux Lounge EFR   **(888) 247-4411**
106 1/2 Judge John Aiso St #318, Los Angeles, CA, 90012
Contemporary furniture including contemporary chairs, contemporary sofas, and contemporary tables.
info@luxloungeefr.com * www.luxloungeefr.com

MidcenturyLA   **(818) 509-3050**
5333 Cahuenga Blvd, N. Hollywood, CA, 91601
Danish Modern furniture, both newly refinished and original vintage condition. Lighting, cleared photography, & ceramics
midcenturyla@midcenturyla.com * www.midcenturyla.com

MIDCENTURYLA

5333 CAHUENGA BLVD NORTH HOLLYWOOD 91601
818.509.3050 WWW.MIDCENTURYLA.COM
7 DAYS A WEEK 10-5
FURNITURE, LIGHTING, & MORE
RENTALS & PURCHASES

Modern Props   **(323) 934-3000**
furniture, lamps, art, prints & accessories

Modernica Props   **(323) 664-2322**
huge inventory of 50s-70s furniture & decor, multiples up to 500

NEST Studio Rentals, Inc.   **(818) 942-0339**
living, dining, den, home office, bedroom

Ob-jects   **(818) 351-4200**
upholstery, coffee tables, end tables, sofa tables

Omega/Cinema Props   **(323) 466-8201**

DISPLAY ADS AND LISTINGS FOR THIS CATEGORY
CONTINUE ON THE FOLLOWING PAGE

Prop Services West (818) 503-2790

Welcome to our NoHo location!

www.PropServicesWest.com

Smartphone & Tablet Search-Friendly:)

818.503.2790
7040 Laurel Canyon Blvd., NoHo 91605

Rapport International Furniture (323) 930-1500
435 N La Brea Ave, Los Angeles, CA, 90036
Rapport Furniture features contemporary and modern furnishings for the home and office plus media storage & accessories.
rapport@rapportusa.com * www.rapportfurniture.com

Sony Pictures Studios-Prop House (Off Lot) (310) 244-5999
contemporary cabinets, china cabinets, computer cabinets, credenzas, entertainment centers, hutch cabinets

Susanne Hollis, Inc. (626) 441-0346
230 Pasadena Ave, South Pasadena, CA, 91030
20th - 17th century Antiques, Accessories, and Fine Art from around the world in our 19,000sqft. warehouse and showrooms
sales@susannehollis.com * www.susannehollis.com

Taylor Creative Inc. (888) 245-4044
Our modern furniture rentals are ideally suited for photo shoots, film and TV sets, press events, and social affairs.

Universal Studios Property & Hardware Dept (818) 777-2784
Contemporary furniture; contemporary chairs, contemporary tables, contemporary artwork and more for rent.

Warner Bros. Studios Property Department (818) 954-2181
Contemporary bar stools, bistro tables, stacking chairs, ottomans, chaises, hanging fixtures & accessories

Warner Bros. Studios Property Dept. - Atlanta, GA (404) 878-0002
3645 Southside Industrial Pkwy., Atlanta, GA 30354
Contemporary furniture collection at our Atlanta Prop House location.
nikki.giovacchini@warnerbros.com * www.WBPropertyAtlanta.com

Warner Bros. Studios The Collection (818) 954-2181
4000 Warner Blvd, Burbank, CA, 91522
High end Contemporary, industrial, modern, rustic & one-of-a-kind items, Oval Office Set Dressing Items
wbsfproperty@warnerbros.com * www.wbpropertydept.com

ZG04 DECOR (818) 853-8040
Iconic Design, Classic-Modern, Mid-Century Furniture

search by
Company Name

Find it fast **DB** Debbies Book®

Furniture, Custom-made/Reproduction

Antiquarian Traders   (310) 247-3900
4851 S. Alameda Street, Los Angeles, CA 90048
Large selection of American Victorian, Art Deco, Art Nouveau & European
Furniture, great variety of all styles and scale
antiques@antiquariantraders.com * www.antiquariantraders.com

Castle Antiques & Design   (855) 765-5800
11924 Vose St, N Hollywood, CA, 91605
Custom furniture/custom-made furniture in many styles and colors including
distressed finishes and bleached finishes.
info@castleantiques.net * www.castleprophouse.com

Dan Parish LTD   (909) 284-9227
533 Magnolia Ave, Ontario CA 91762
Source for interior designers to create their vision without limitation. 30 years
experience producing custom furniture.
dan@danparishltd.com * www.danparishltd.com

Dan Parish Ltd
INSPIRED ARTISAN FURNITURE

Creating Your Vision
Without Limitations

Evans Family Barrels   (818) 523-8174
7918 Fairchild Ave, Canoga Park, CA, 91306
Solid oak wine barrel furniture: tables, chairs, cabinets, pet furniture, home and
business decor, swings
evansbarrels@gmail.com * www.EvansFamilyBarrels.com

House of Brienza, Inc   (310) 839-9254
2358 S. Robertson Blvd, Los Angeles, CA, 90034
also hand-painted furniture; refinishing conservancy, caning & rush work

Larry St. John & Co.   (310) 630-5828
17021 S Broadway, Gardena, CA, 90248
Custom, heavily discounted, locally made, quality hardwood & reclaimed wood
furniture, sofa sectionals and classic cars! Custom Furniture
info@larrystjohn.com * www.larrystjohn.com

LM Treasures   (626) 252-7354
10557 Juniper Ave Unit A, Fontana, CA 92337
All our items are hand painted and crafted to provide each customer with their
own personally unique piece.
lmtreasures.ll@gmail.com * www.lifesizestatues.net

Lux Lounge EFR   (888) 247-4411
106 1/2 Judge John Aiso St #318, Los Angeles, CA, 90012
Custom furniture design & custom furniture production: Anything you can
imagine, we can create.
info@luxloungeefr.com * www.luxloungeefr.com

Pasadena Antique Warehouse   (626) 404-2422
1609 East Washington Blvd., Pasadena, CA, 91104
Bring in any photo, and we will make you a custom piece or fix a piece of
furniture that has seen better days.
pasadenaantiquewarehouse@gmail.com *
www.pasadenaantiquewarehouse.com

Stephen Kenn   (503) 330-5550
1250 Long Beach Ave #120, Los Angeles, CA, 90021
Stephen Kenn is available for custom design work, and The Inheritance
Collection is available for purchase or rental.
contact@stephenkenn.com * www.stephenkenn.com

Streamline Custom Upholstery Inc.   (562) 531-9119
11920 Garfield Ave, South Gate, CA, 90280
High end custom upholstery and reproductions, sofas, beds, slipcovers,
indoor/outdoor cushions. 30 years experience.
streamline562@yahoo.com

Susanne Hollis, Inc.   (626) 441-0346
230 Pasadena Ave, South Pasadena, CA, 91030
20th - 17th century Antiques, Accessories, and Fine Art from around the world
in our 19,000sqft. warehouse and showrooms
sales@susannehollis.com * www.susannehollis.com

Warner Bros. Studios Cabinet & Furniture Shop   (818) 954-1339
Custom manufacturing & installation of cabinets & furniture to your
specifications. Design services available.

ZG04 DECOR   (818) 853-8040
Custom Made Upholstery, Wood & Metal furniture, Made to order

Furniture, Early American/Colonial

Advanced Liquidators Office Furniture   (818) 763-3470
almost any wood style, veneered, metallic and other table top textures, colonial
chairs and furniture, large variety

Castle Antiques & Design   (855) 765-5800
11924 Vose St, N Hollywood, CA, 91605
Continental furniture and colonial American furniture for rent or purchase.
info@castleantiques.net * www.castleprophouse.com

Ob-jects   (818) 351-4200

Omega/Cinema Props   (323) 466-8201

Susanne Hollis, Inc.   (626) 441-0346
230 Pasadena Ave, South Pasadena, CA, 91030
20th - 17th century Antiques, Accessories, and Fine Art from around the world
in our 19,000sqft. warehouse and showrooms
sales@susannehollis.com * www.susannehollis.com

Universal Studios Property & Hardware Dept   (818) 777-2784
Colonial furniture; colonial chairs, colonial tables, colonial artwork and more for
rent.

Warner Bros. Studios Property Department   (818) 954-2181
Chest of drawers, bedside cabinets, arm chairs, court cabinets, panels

Furniture, Eclectic

See Also: Furniture, Contemporary* Furniture, Custom-made/Reproduction

Blackman-Cruz (323) 466-8600
836 N. Highland Ave, Los Angeles, CA, 90036
unusual furniture, antique & contemp. & arch. elements
Design Mix Furniture (323) 939-7500
442 S La Brea Ave, Los Angeles, CA, 90036
Global imports of Indian, Indonesian, Chinese, African, Moroccan art, acc., antiques, reprod. & Industrial Furniture
www.mixfurniture.com
Galerie Sommerlath - French 50s 60s (310) 838-0102
9608 Venice Blvd, Culver City, CA, 90232
10,000 sq ft Mid-Century - 80s furniture, lighting & accessories
info@french50s60s.com * http://www.galeriesommerlath.com
Malabar Coast Living (323) 634-0800
500 N. La Brea Ave, Los Angeles, CA, 90036
Furniture Store featuring Vintage, Rustic, Indian, Balinese, Chinese, Tibetan, Thai, Asian, African and Moroccan Items.
info@malabarcoastliving.com * www.malabarcoastliving.com
Prop Services West (818) 503-2790
Sony Pictures Studios-Prop House (Off Lot) (310) 244-5999
all periods, couches, chairs, bedframes, storage cabinets, liquor cabinets
Susanne Hollis, Inc. (626) 441-0346
230 Pasadena Ave, South Pasadena, CA, 91030
20th - 17th century Antiques, Accessories, and Fine Art from around the world in our 19,000sqft. warehouse and showrooms
sales@susannehollis.com * www.susannehollis.com
Warisan (323) 938-3960
1274 Center Court Dr Ste 110, Covina, CA, 91724
Warner Bros. Studios Property Department (818) 954-2181
One of a kind eclectic furniture, hand props & light fixtures
Warner Bros. Studios The Collection (818) 954-2181
4000 Warner Blvd, Burbank, CA, 91522
wbsfproperty@warnerbros.com * www.wbpropertydept.com
ZG04 DECOR (818) 853-8040
Pedestals, Plant-stands, Bamboo, Teak, Japanese Tansu, Folding Screens, Bars, Easels, Coat racks

Furniture, English/French Country

Advanced Liquidators Office Furniture (818) 763-3470
Castle Antiques & Design (855) 765-5800
11924 Vose St, N Hollywood, CA, 91605
English furniture and French furniture for rent or purchase.
info@castleantiques.net * www.castleprophouse.com
Omega/Cinema Props (323) 466-8201
Prop Services West (818) 503-2790
Susanne Hollis, Inc. (626) 441-0346
230 Pasadena Ave, South Pasadena, CA, 91030
20th - 17th century Antiques, Accessories, and Fine Art from around the world in our 19,000sqft. warehouse and showrooms
sales@susannehollis.com * www.susannehollis.com
Unique Antiques & Collectibles (805) 499-2222
2357 Michael Drive, Newbury Park, CA, 91320
Authentic antique furniture from Italy, France, & England. Furniture & accessories from 1700's, 1800's & early 1900's.
diamond-m-enterprises@live.com * www.uniqueantiquesandcollectibles.com
Warner Bros. Studios Property Department (818) 954-2181
Occasional tables and chairs, Oak furniture, English cottage style furniture, pillows and floor coverings

Furniture, Forties/Fifties/Sixties

See: Furniture, Mid-Century Modern

Furniture, French Period (Louis to Empire)

Castle Antiques & Design (855) 765-5800
11924 Vose St, N Hollywood, CA, 91605
French period furniture for rent or purchase.
info@castleantiques.net * www.castleprophouse.com
Omega/Cinema Props (323) 466-8201
Susanne Hollis, Inc. (626) 441-0346
230 Pasadena Ave, South Pasadena, CA, 91030
20th - 17th century Antiques, Accessories, and Fine Art from around the world in our 19,000sqft. warehouse and showrooms
sales@susannehollis.com * www.susannehollis.com

Unique Antiques & Collectibles (805) 499-2222
2357 Michael Drive, Newbury Park, CA, 91320
Authentic antique furniture from Italy, France, & England. Furniture & accessories from 1700's, 1800's & early 1900's.
diamond-m-enterprises@live.com * www.uniqueantiquesandcollectibles.com
Universal Studios Property & Hardware Dept (818) 777-2784
French period furniture; French period chairs, French period tables, French period artwork and more for rent.
Warner Bros. Studios Property Department (818) 954-2181
Antique furniture, fixtures and floor coverings, large selection

Furniture, Functional Art

Charisma Design Studio, Inc. (818) 252-6611
8414 San Fernando Road, Sun Valley, CA, 91352
custom metal/glass/wood/stone mixed media
info@charismadesign.com * www.charismadesign.com
Gallery of Functional Art (310) 829-6990
2525 Michigan Ave E3, Santa Monica, CA, 90404
furniture & lighting & objects by artists

Furniture, Futuristic

See: Futuristic Furniture, Props, Decorations

Furniture, Gothic

Omega/Cinema Props (323) 466-8201
Susanne Hollis, Inc. (626) 441-0346
230 Pasadena Ave, South Pasadena, CA, 91030
20th - 17th century Antiques, Accessories, and Fine Art from around the world in our 19,000sqft. warehouse and showrooms
sales@susannehollis.com * www.susannehollis.com
Universal Studios Property & Hardware Dept (818) 777-2784
Gothic furniture; Gothic chairs, Gothic tables, Gothic artwork and more for rent.
Warner Bros. Studios Property Department (818) 954-2181

Furniture, Hand-Painted

See Also: Furniture, Custom-made/Reproduction

Prop Services West (818) 503-2790

Furniture, Home Office

See: Office Furniture

Furniture, Indian (Far East)

See: Asian Antiques, Furniture, Art & Artifacts

Furniture, Indonesian

See: Asian Antiques, Furniture, Art & Artifacts

Furniture, Industrial

See Also: Furniture, Eclectic* Furniture, Functional Art

Design Mix Furniture (323) 939-7500
442 S La Brea Ave, Los Angeles, CA, 90036
Global imports of Indian, Indonesian, Chinese, African, Moroccan art, acc., antiques, reprod. & Industrial Furniture
www.mixfurniture.com
Modern Props (323) 934-3000
Warner Bros. Studios Property Dept. - Atlanta, GA (404) 878-0002
3645 Southside Industrial Pkwy., Atlanta, GA 30354
Industrial furniture and industrial decorations at our Atlanta Prop House location.
nikki.giovacchini@warnerbros.com * www.WBPropertyAtlanta.com
Warner Bros. Studios The Collection (818) 954-2181
4000 Warner Blvd, Burbank, CA, 91522
wbsfproperty@warnerbros.com * www.wbpropertydept.com

Furniture, Iron

See: Wrought Iron Furniture & Decorations

Furniture, Japanese

See: Asian Antiques, Furniture, Art & Artifacts* Shoji Screens

Furniture, Kitchen/Dining Room

Advanced Liquidators Office Furniture	(818) 763-3470
Bridge Furniture & Props Los Angeles	(818) 433-7100

We carry modern & traditional furniture, lighting, accessories, cleared art,& rugs. Items are online for easy shopping.

Little Bohemia Rentals	(818) 853-7506

11940 Sherman Rd, N Hollywood, CA, 91605
Vintage and Contemporary 4 - 10 person Dining and Dinette Sets, mix and match. Serving and barware.
sales@wearelittlebohemia.com * www.wearelittlebohemia.com

Modernica Props	(323) 664-2322
NEST Studio Rentals, Inc.	(818) 942-0339
Omega/Cinema Props	(323) 466-8201
Prop Services West	(818) 503-2790
Sony Pictures Studios-Prop House (Off Lot)	(310) 244-5999
Warner Bros. Studios Property Department	(818) 954-2181

Kitchen & Dining room tables, side chairs, ottomans, sofas, cabinets, dressers, corner cabinets, display cabinets

Furniture, Medical

See: Medical Equip/Furniture, Graphics/Supplies* Exam Room

Furniture, Mexican

C. P. Two	(323) 466-8201
Sony Pictures Studios-Prop House (Off Lot)	(310) 244-5999

Furniture, Mid-Century Modern

Alpha Companies - Spellman Desk Co.	(818) 504-9090

Eames Furniture, Le Corbusier Furniture, Barcelona Furniture, Haller Furniture, Aeron Furniture, Danish Modern Furniture

Blueprint Furniture	(310) 657-4315

8600 Pico Blvd. Los Angeles, CA 90035
Modern furniture lighting accessories early classic bauhaus mid-century contemporary design. Good studio rental history.
www.blueprintfurniture.com

Castle Antiques & Design	(855) 765-5800

11924 Vose St, N Hollywood, CA, 91605
Mid-century modern furniture and vintage furniture for rent and purchase
info@castleantiques.net * www.castleprophouse.com

Chez Camille	(310) 854-3565

810 N. La Cienega, Los Angeles, CA, 90069
chairs, tables, sofas, light fixtures & lamps, accessories

Eric's Architectural Salvage, Wells Antique Tile	(213) 413-6800

2110 W Sunset Blvd, Los Angeles, CA, 90026
The new Architectural Salvage store in Los Angeles that you haven't been to yet.
ericstiques@aol.com * www.ericsarchitecturalsalvage.com

Faux Library Studio Props, Inc.	(818) 765-0096

mid century modern furniture, Danish modern furniture

FormDecor, Inc.	(310) 558-2582

America's largest event rental supplier of 20th Century furniture and accessories for Modern and Mid-Century styles.

Galerie Sommerlath - French 50s 60s	(310) 838-0102

9608 Venice Blvd, Culver City, CA, 90232
10,000 sq ft Mid-Century - 80s furniture, lighting & accessories
info@french50s60s.com * http://www.galeriesommerlath.com

Little Bohemia Rentals	(818) 853-7506

11940 Sherman Rd, N Hollywood, CA, 91605
American, European, Danish and Scandinavian designs of the 50s, 60s and 70s.
sales@wearelittlebohemia.com * www.wearelittlebohemia.com

MidcenturyLA	(818) 509-3050

5333 Cahuenga Blvd, N. Hollywood, CA, 91601
Wide range of Mid-Century, Danish Modern, vintage furniture, lighting, pottery, & cleared photography. Rental & purchase
midcenturyla@midcenturyla.com * www.midcenturyla.com

MIDCENTURYLA

5333 CAHUENGA BLVD NORTH HOLLYWOOD 91601
818.509.3050 WWW.MIDCENTURYLA.COM
7 DAYS A WEEK 10-5
FURNITURE, LIGHTING, & MORE
RENTALS & PURCHASES

LISTINGS FOR THIS CATEGORY CONTINUE ON THE FOLLOWING PAGE

Modern Props   (323) 934-3000
furniture & accessories
Modernica Props   (323) 664-2322
wide range of colors, classic items, accents; mid-century
Omega/Cinema Props   (323) 466-8201
Pasadena Antiques & Design   (626) 389-3938
330 S. Fair Oaks Avenue, Pasadena, CA 91105
Mid Century Modern Furniture and Mid Century Modern Accessories.
roy@antiquesofpasadena.com * www.antiquesofpasadena.com
Prop Services West   (818) 503-2790
Rapport International Furniture   (323) 930-1500
435 N La Brea Ave, Los Angeles, CA, 90036
For over 67 years Rapport Furniture has specialized in contemporary and
modern European and designer furnishings.
rapport@rapportusa.com * www.rapportfurniture.com
RC Vintage, Inc.   (818) 765-7107
furniture to household items, more
Susanne Hollis, Inc.   (626) 441-0346
230 Pasadena Ave, South Pasadena, CA, 91030
20th - 17th century Antiques, Accessories, and Fine Art from around the world
in our 19,000sqft. warehouse and showrooms
sales@susannehollis.com * www.susannehollis.com
Taylor Creative Inc.   (888) 245-4044
Our modern furniture collection features pieces by iconic designers Philippe
Starck, Frank Gehry, and Verner Panton.
Universal Studios Property & Hardware Dept   (818) 777-2784
Mid-century furniture; Mid-century chairs, Mid-century tables, Mid-century
artwork and more for rent.
Warner Bros. Studios Property Department   (818) 954-2181
Chairs, sofas, tables, styles from 1940's, 1950's & 1960's
Warner Bros. Studios Property Dept. - Atlanta, GA   (404) 878-0002
3645 Southside Industrial Pkwy., Atlanta, GA 30354
Mid-century modern furniture collection at our Atlanta Prop House location.
nikki.giovacchini@warnerbros.com * www.WBPropertyAtlanta.com
Warner Bros. Studios The Collection   (818) 954-2181
4000 Warner Blvd, Burbank, CA, 91522
wbsfproperty@warnerbros.com * www.wbpropertydept.com

Furniture, Middle Eastern

Badia Design, Inc.   (818) 762-0130
5420 Vineland Ave, N. Hollywood, CA, 91601
Hanging wall lamps, ceiling lanterns, camel bone metal horn mirror,
info@badiadesign.com * www.badiadesign.com
Omega/Cinema Props   (323) 466-8201
Susanne Hollis, Inc.   (626) 441-0346
230 Pasadena Ave, South Pasadena, CA, 91030
20th - 17th century Antiques, Accessories, and Fine Art from around the world
in our 19,000sqft. warehouse and showrooms
sales@susannehollis.com * www.susannehollis.com
Universal Studios Property & Hardware Dept   (818) 777-2784
Middle Eastern furniture; Middle Eastern chairs, Middle Eastern tables, Middle
Eastern artwork and more for rent.
Warner Bros. Studios Property Department   (818) 954-2181

Furniture, Moroccan

See Also: African/Oceanic Decorative Items
Badia Design, Inc.   (818) 762-0130
5420 Vineland Ave, N. Hollywood, CA, 91601
Badia Design Inc. offers a wide variety of Moroccan Furniture Los Angeles,
home decor, chandeliers, tables and much more.
info@badiadesign.com * www.badiadesign.com

Design Mix Furniture   (323) 939-7500
442 S La Brea Ave, Los Angeles, CA, 90036
Global imports of Indian, Indonesian, Chinese, African, Moroccan art, acc.,
antiques, reprod. & Industrial Furniture
www.mixfurniture.com
Little Bohemia Rentals   (818) 853-7506
11940 Sherman Rd, N Hollywood, CA, 91605
Antique furnishings of Morocco.
sales@wearelittlebohemia.com * www.wearelittlebohemia.com
Susanne Hollis, Inc.   (626) 441-0346
230 Pasadena Ave, South Pasadena, CA, 91030
20th - 17th century Antiques, Accessories, and Fine Art from around the world
in our 19,000sqft. warehouse and showrooms
sales@susannehollis.com * www.susannehollis.com
Warner Bros. Studios Property Department   (818) 954-2181

Furniture, Office

See: Office Furniture

Furniture, Outdoor/Patio

See Also: Cafe Tables/Chairs/Umbrellas* Garden/Patio

AIR Designs (818) 768-6639
Tables, Benches, Umbrella Tables, Lawn Chairs, Fast Food, 50's to Modern

All Patio (866) 217-4252
12863 Foothill Blvd, Sylmar, CA, 91342
restoration/repair, new/used, umbrellas, glass tops, vintage, relacing, restrapping, powder coating

Alley Cats Studio Rentals (818) 982-9178
metal shell-back chairs, picnic tables w/metal umbrellas, folding chairs and beach chairs

C. P. Two (323) 466-8201
Outdoor furniture from porch swings to patio furniture.

Design Mix Furniture (323) 939-7500
442 S La Brea Ave, Los Angeles, CA, 90036
Global imports of Indian, Indonesian, Chinese, African, Moroccan art, acc., antiques, reprod. & Industrial Furniture
www.mixfurniture.com

E.C. Prop Rentals (818) 764-2008
picnic tables/benches, fiberglass or aluminum

Fishbecks (626) 796-9255
150 S. Raymond, Pasadena, CA, 91105
In Pasadena since 1899

FormDecor, Inc. (310) 558-2582
America's largest event rental supplier of 20th Century furniture and accessories for Modern and Mid-Century styles.

L. A. Party Works (888) 527-2789
9712 Alpaca St, S El Monte, CA, 91733
Outdoor furniture including benches, patio chairs/patio furniture, picnic tables for adults/kids and more.
partyworks@aol.com * www.partyworksusa.com

LCW Props (818) 243-0707
Outdoor Kitchen BBQ, Chairs, Tables

Lux Lounge EFR (888) 247-4411
106 1/2 Judge John Aiso St #318, Los Angeles, CA, 90012
Outdoor Furniture including Patio Sets & Umbrellas
info@luxloungeefr.com * www.luxloungeefr.com

Prop Services West (818) 503-2790

RC Vintage, Inc. (818) 765-7107
Vintage Folding Chairs. BBQ's Ice Chests. Patio sets

Sony Pictures Studios-Prop House (Off Lot) (310) 244-5999
multiples, period/present, lawn chairs, picnic tables, furniture

Streamline Custom Upholstery Inc. (562) 531-9119
11920 Garfield Ave, South Gate, CA, 90280
High end custom indoor and outdoor cushions and daybeds. Upholstery and reupholstery. 30 years experience.
streamline562@yahoo.com

Universal Studios Property & Hardware Dept (818) 777-2784
Outdoor furniture/patio furniture; patio chairs, patio tables, picnic tables and more for rent.

Warner Bros. Studios Property Department (818) 954-2181
Outdoor furniture, garden furniture, bamboo furniture, flags, gardening tools, hand trucks

Furniture, Pine

Omega/Cinema Props (323) 466-8201
Prop Services West (818) 503-2790

Furniture, Plexi/Lucite

FormDecor, Inc. (310) 558-2582
America's largest event rental supplier of 20th Century furniture and accessories for Modern and Mid-Century styles.

Little Bohemia Rentals (818) 853-7506
11940 Sherman Rd, N Hollywood, CA, 91605
Charles Hollis Jones and Karl Springer designs.
sales@wearelittlebohemia.com * www.wearelittlebohemia.com

Lux Lounge EFR (888) 247-4411
106 1/2 Judge John Aiso St #318, Los Angeles, CA, 90012
Plastic Furniture and Decoration: Custom Bars, LED Furniture and more.
info@luxloungeefr.com * www.luxloungeefr.com

Omega/Cinema Props (323) 466-8201

Taylor Creative Inc. (888) 245-4044
We offer a large selection of Lucite and Plexi products, from Ghost chairs and stools to Plexi bars and display pieces.

Universal Studios Property & Hardware Dept (818) 777-2784
Lucite furniture/plexi furniture; lucite chairs, lucite tables, plexi chairs, plexi tables and more for rent.

Furniture, Rattan & Wicker

C. P. Two (323) 466-8201
Rattan chairs and wicker chairs, rattan baskets and wicker baskets, and more.

Lux Lounge EFR (888) 247-4411
106 1/2 Judge John Aiso St #318, Los Angeles, CA, 90012
Wicker Furniture and Rattan Furniture rentals.
info@luxloungeefr.com * www.luxloungeefr.com

Modern Props (323) 934-3000
Furniture, screens, dividers

Omega/Cinema Props (323) 466-8201

Pier 1 Imports (Hollywood) (323) 466-3443
5711 Hollywood Blvd, Hollywood, CA, 90028

Prop Services West (818) 503-2790

Sony Pictures Studios-Prop House (Off Lot) (310) 244-5999

Taylor Creative Inc. (888) 245-4044
At Taylor Creative Inc. our extensive outdoor collection offers clients a number of all-weather lounge furnishings.

Universal Studios Property & Hardware Dept (818) 777-2784
Rattan furniture & wicker furniture; wicker chairs, wicker tables, rattan chairs, rattan tables and more for rent.

Warner Bros. Studios Property Department (818) 954-2181
Tables, chairs, cabinets, sofas, ottomans, bars and hand props

Furniture, Restaurant

See: Restaurant Furniture & Dressing

Furniture, Rustic

C. P. Two (323) 466-8201
C. P. Valley (323) 466-8201
Evans Family Barrels (818) 523-8174
7918 Fairchild Ave, Canoga Park, CA, 91306
Solid oak wine barrel furniture: tables, chairs, cabinets, pet furniture, home and business decor, swings
evansbarrels@gmail.com * www.EvansFamilyBarrels.com

Omega/Cinema Props (323) 466-8201

Prop Services West (818) 503-2790

Sony Pictures Studios-Prop House (Off Lot) (310) 244-5999

Susanne Hollis, Inc. (626) 441-0346
230 Pasadena Ave, South Pasadena, CA, 91030
20th - 17th century Antiques, Accessories, and Fine Art from around the world in our 19,000sqft. warehouse and showrooms
sales@susannehollis.com * www.susannehollis.com

Universal Studios Property & Hardware Dept (818) 777-2784
Rustic furniture; rustic chairs, rustic tables and more for rent.

Warner Bros. Studios Property Department (818) 954-2181
Rustic tables, chairs, ottomans, desks, decorative items

Furniture, Southwest

Little Bohemia Rentals (818) 853-7506
11940 Sherman Rd, N Hollywood, CA, 91605
Southwest style furniture
sales@wearelittlebohemia.com * www.wearelittlebohemia.com

Omega/Cinema Props (323) 466-8201

Pasadena Antiques & Design (626) 389-3938
330 S. Fair Oaks Avenue, Pasadena, CA 91105
California Rancho & Rustic Furnishings.
roy@antiquesofpasadena.com * www.antiquesofpasadena.com

Sony Pictures Studios-Prop House (Off Lot) (310) 244-5999

Furniture, Spanish

Castle Antiques & Design (855) 765-5800
11924 Vose St, N Hollywood, CA, 91605
Spanish furniture for rent and purchase.
info@castleantiques.net * www.castleprophouse.com

Omega/Cinema Props (323) 466-8201

Pasadena Antiques & Design (626) 389-3938
330 S. Fair Oaks Avenue, Pasadena, CA 91105
Spanish Revival & Colonial Furniture & Accessories. Iron & Wood.
roy@antiquesofpasadena.com * www.antiquesofpasadena.com

Susanne Hollis, Inc. (626) 441-0346
230 Pasadena Ave, South Pasadena, CA, 91030
20th - 17th century Antiques, Accessories, and Fine Art from around the world in our 19,000sqft. warehouse and showrooms
sales@susannehollis.com * www.susannehollis.com

Warner Bros. Studios Property Department (818) 954-2181

Furniture, Tenement Tacky Motel

C. P. Two	**(323) 466-8201**
Tenement furniture and dressing from chairs to sconces.	
Omega/Cinema Props	**(323) 466-8201**
Prop Services West	**(818) 503-2790**
Sony Pictures Studios-Prop House (Off Lot)	**(310) 244-5999**
Universal Studios Property & Hardware Dept	**(818) 777-2784**
Tenement tacky furniture; tenement tacky chairs, tenement tacky tables, tenement tacky artwork and more for rent.	
Warner Bros. Studios Property Department	**(818) 954-2181**
Distressed furniture pieces	

Furniture, Traditional

Advanced Liquidators Office Furniture	**(818) 763-3470**
Alpha Companies - Spellman Desk Co.	**(818) 504-9090**
Chippendale, Queen Anne, Regency, Sheraton	
Bridge Furniture & Props Los Angeles	**(818) 433-7100**
We carry modern & traditional furniture, lighting, accessories, cleared art,& rugs. Items are online for easy shopping.	
Castle Antiques & Design	**(855) 765-5800**
11924 Vose St, N Hollywood, CA, 91605	
Traditional furniture, period European furniture, for rent and purchase.	
info@castleantiques.net * www.castleprophouse.com	

35,000 sq. ft. Showroom

♦♦♦♦

11924 Vose St. N. Hollywood, CA 91605

♦♦♦♦

(855) 765-5800

(818) 300-9909

avoosh@msn.com

CASTLE
ANTIQUES & DESIGN

www.castleantiques.net

Dozar Office Furnishings	**(310) 559-9292**
9937 Jefferson Blvd, Culver City, CA, 90232	
Rentals X22. Traditional furniture for the home and office.	
dozarrents@aol.com * www.dozarrents.com	
Ob-jects	**(818) 351-4200**
Omega/Cinema Props	**(323) 466-8201**
Antique furniture, vintage furniture, rustic furniture, wicker furniture, chairs, stools, tables	
Prop Services West	**(818) 503-2790**

Welcome to our NoHo location!

www.PropServicesWest.com

Smartphone & Tablet Search-Friendly:)

818.503.2790
7040 Laurel Canyon Blvd., NoHo 91605

Sony Pictures Studios-Prop House (Off Lot)	**(310) 244-5999**
Susanne Hollis, Inc.	**(626) 441-0346**
230 Pasadena Ave, South Pasadena, CA, 91030	
20th - 17th century Antiques, Accessories, and Fine Art from around the world in our 19,000sqft. warehouse and showrooms	
sales@susannehollis.com * www.susannehollis.com	
Universal Studios Property & Hardware Dept	**(818) 777-2784**
Traditional furniture; traditional chairs, traditional tables, traditional artwork and more for rent.	
Warner Bros. Studios Property Department	**(818) 954-2181**
Traditional tables, chairs, end tables, cabinets	
ZG04 DECOR	**(818) 853-8040**

Furniture, Transitional

See: Furniture, Contemporary* Furniture, Traditional* Furniture, English/French Country* Furniture, Eclectic* Asian Antiques, Furniture, Art & Artifacts

Furniture, Unfinished

See Also: Furniture, Custom-made/Reproduction
Castle Antiques & Design **(855) 765-5800**
11924 Vose St, N Hollywood, CA, 91605
Unfinished furniture/unpainted furniture for rent or purchase.
info@castleantiques.net * www.castleprophouse.com

Furniture, Used/Second Hand

See Also: Thrift Shops
Advanced Liquidators Office Furniture **(818) 763-3470**
chairs / desk / filing cabs / partitions / executive sets / package deals
Castle Antiques & Design **(855) 765-5800**
11924 Vose St, N Hollywood, CA, 91605
Used furniture/second hand furniture for rent or purchase.
info@castleantiques.net * www.castleprophouse.com
LCW Props **(818) 243-0707**
Large Selection. Hoarder Houses, Debris, Junk Yards
Sony Pictures Studios-Prop House (Off Lot) **(310) 244-5999**
TR Trading Company **(310) 329-9242**
15604 S Broadway, Gardena, CA, 90248
85,000 sq/ft of items, selection and inventory changes weekly.
sales@trtradingcompany.com * www.trtradingcompany.com
Universal Studios Property & Hardware Dept **(818) 777-2784**
Used furniture; used chairs, used tables, second hand chairs, second hand tables and more for rent.

Furniture, Victorian

Antiquarian Traders **(310) 247-3900**
4851 S. Alameda Street, Los Angeles, CA 90048
Fully restored and original condition dining suites, desks, Wooton desks bedroom suites and parlor furniture.
antiques@antiquariantraders.com * www.antiquariantraders.com
Castle Antiques & Design **(855) 765-5800**
11924 Vose St, N Hollywood, CA, 91605
Victorian furniture for rent or purchase.
info@castleantiques.net * www.castleprophouse.com
Omega/Cinema Props **(323) 466-8201**
Susanne Hollis, Inc. **(626) 441-0346**
230 Pasadena Ave, South Pasadena, CA, 91030
20th - 17th century Antiques, Accessories, and Fine Art from around the world in our 19,000sqft. warehouse and showrooms
sales@susannehollis.com * www.susannehollis.com
Unique Antiques & Collectibles **(805) 499-2222**
2357 Michael Drive, Newbury Park, CA, 91320
Authentic antique furniture from Italy, France, & England. Furniture & accessories from 1700's, 1800's & early 1900's.
diamond-m-enterprises@live.com * www.uniqueantiquesandcollectibles.com
Universal Studios Property & Hardware Dept **(818) 777-2784**
Victorian furniture; Victorian chairs, Victorian tables, Victorian artwork and more for rent.

Furniture, Western

C. P. Valley **(323) 466-8201**
antique furniture, vintage furniture, rustic furniture, wicker furniture, chairs, stools, tables
Sony Pictures Studios-Prop House (Off Lot) **(310) 244-5999**
Universal Studios Property & Hardware Dept **(818) 777-2784**
Western furniture; Western chairs, Western tables, Western artwork and more for rent.

Futons & Bean Bag Chairs

Omega/Cinema Props **(323) 466-8201**
bean bag chairs
Prop Services West **(818) 503-2790**
bean bag chairs
RC Vintage, Inc. **(818) 765-7107**
bean bag chairs in many colors
Sony Pictures Studios-Prop House (Off Lot) **(310) 244-5999**
bean bag chairs

Futuristic Furniture, Props, Decorations

See Also: Aliens* Fantasy Props, Costumes, or Decorations* Graphics, Digital & Large Format Printing* NASA Dressing* Paintings/Prints* Space Shuttle/Space Hardware* Space Suits* Spaceship Computer Panel
The Hand Prop Room LP. **(323) 931-1534**
LCW Props **(818) 243-0707**
Our Specialty. We Have A Large Selection Of Many Kinds. Rigged, Large & Small Futuristic Props
Modern Props **(323) 934-3000**
furniture, lamps, art/sculptures, accessories
Omega/Cinema Props **(323) 466-8201**
Taylor Creative Inc. **(888) 245-4044**
Our rental collection boasts a line of innnovative products, from sleek Lucite sofas to glowing benches and ottomans.

Futuristic Themed Parties

See: Costume Rental Houses* Costumes* Events, Decorations, Supplies & Services* Events, Design/Planning/Production* Fantasy Props, Costumes, or Decorations* Prop Houses

Gambling Equipment

See Also: Game Tables & Equipment* Poker Tables
C. P. Valley **(323) 466-8201**
Gambling tables/casino tables for poker, roulette and blackjack. Raffle drum and wheel of fortune.
Dealer Dolls **(866) 96-Dolls**
#258 / 20058 Ventura Blvd, Woodland Hills, CA, 91364
info@dealerdolls.com * www.dealerdolls.com
The Hand Prop Room LP. **(323) 931-1534**
L. A. Party Works **(888) 527-2789**
9712 Alpaca St, S El Monte, CA, 91733
in Vancouver tel. 604-589-4101, casino tables, black jack tables, poker tables
partyworks@aol.com * www.partyworksusa.com

RC Vintage, Inc. **(818) 765-7107**
Vintage Poker Tables, Craps, Roulette, Wheel Of Fortune, Large Selection: Stools Casino Signs Blazing 777 and more.
Sony Pictures Studios-Prop House (Off Lot) **(310) 244-5999**
casino equipment, playing cards, cribbage equipment, dice cups, dice, dominoes case, lotto games, poker chips, raffle equipment

Game Booths

See Also: Carnival Games & Rides
Amusement Svcs/Candyland Amusements   **(818) 266-4056**
18653 Ventura Blvd Ste 235, Tarzana, CA, 91356
Games, rides, food stands, ticket booths. We are the owner, no middleman.
dunk tanks, machine gun alley, basketball, water race, game tents
www.candylandamusements.com
C. P. Valley   **(323) 466-8201**
Christiansen Amusements   **(800) 300-6114**
Call for Appt
Major carnival games for all events & productions
info@amusements.com * www.amusements.com
L. A. Party Works   **(888) 527-2789**
9712 Alpaca St, S El Monte, CA, 91733
in Vancouver tel. 604-589-4101
partyworks@aol.com * www.partyworksusa.com

Game Show Electronics & Equipment

CBS Electronics   **(323) 575-2645**
7800 Beverly Blvd Rm M162, Los Angeles, CA, 90036
our specialty; custom, arbitrarily complicated
L. A. Party Works   **(888) 527-2789**
9712 Alpaca St, S El Monte, CA, 91733
in Vancouver tel. 604-589-4101
partyworks@aol.com * www.partyworksusa.com

888-527-2789
partyworksusa.com

CUSTOM GAME SHOWS / STAGING / CUSTOM SOFTWARE / CUSTOM BRANDING

PARTYWORKS
I N T E R A C T I V E

Game Tables & Equipment

See Also: Poker Tables* Pool/Billiard Tables & Accessories
Amusement Svcs/Candyland Amusements   **(818) 266-4056**
18653 Ventura Blvd Ste 235, Tarzana, CA, 91356
Games, rides, food stands, ticket booths. We are the owner, no middleman.
Many game booths, game exhibits and game kiosks
www.candylandamusements.com
Lennie Marvin Enterprises, Inc. (Prop Heaven)   **(818) 841-5882**
blackjack, roulette, baccarat, craps, poker tables, Texas Hold'em, per-mod.

Games

See: Arcade Equipment, Games & Rides* Events, Entertainment*
Sporting Goods & Services* Sports & Games Themed Events* Toys
& Games

Garage Dressing

See: Automotive/Garage Equip. & Parts* Motorcycles

Garden/Patio

See Also: Canopies, Tents, Gazebos, Cabanas* Fountains,
Decorative & Garden* Furniture, Outdoor/Patio* Greens* Heaters,
Outdoor* Lawn Mowers* Statuary
Alley Cats Studio Rentals   **(818) 982-9178**
tools, lawnmowers, hoes
Bear Forest Products, Inc   **(951) 727-1767**
4685 Brookhollow Circle, Riverside, CA, 92509
Wood lattices and plastic lattices.
matto@bearfp.com * www.bearfp.com
Bridge Furniture & Props Los Angeles   **(818) 433-7100**
We carry modern & traditional furniture, lighting, accessories, cleared art,&
rugs. Items are online for easy shopping.
E.C. Prop Rentals   **(818) 764-2008**
tools, lawn mowers, garden "Vermont" carts, tool carts, hoses & chairs
Evans Family Barrels   **(818) 523-8174**
7918 Fairchild Ave, Canoga Park, CA, 91306
Solid oak wine barrel furniture: tables, chairs, cabinets, pet furniture, home and
business decor, swings
evansbarrels@gmail.com * www.EvansFamilyBarrels.com
Green Set, Inc.   **(818) 764-1231**
Baskets, Brass Planters, Ceramic Pots, Faux Pots, Planter Boxes, Terra Cotta
History For Hire, Inc.   **(818) 765-7767**
garden tools, whirligigs
Jackson Shrub Supply, Inc.   **(818) 982-0100**
8'-12' Japanese style garden bridges, garden decorations, fencing, fountains,
and more.
LCW Props   **(818) 243-0707**
Umbrellas, Tables & Chairs
Little Bohemia Rentals   **(818) 853-7506**
11940 Sherman Rd, N Hollywood, CA, 91605
Faux and Live succulents and indoor/house plants. Potted outdoor plants.
Hanging plants.
sales@wearelittlebohemia.com * www.wearelittlebohemia.com
Ob-jects   **(818) 351-4200**
furniture
Potted   **(323) 665-3801**
3158 Los Feliz Blvd, Los Angeles, CA, 90039
Decorative garden accessories, furniture, fountains, statues and pots
info@pottedstore.com * www.pottedstore.com
Prop Services West   **(818) 503-2790**
Scavenger's Paradise   **(818) 843-5257**
3425 W. Magnolia Blvd, Burbank, CA 91505
antique wrought iron gates & fence, vintage fountains, garden pots/statuary
gilliamgreyson@sbcglobal.net * www.scavengersparadise.com
Sony Pictures Studios-Prop House (Off Lot)   **(310) 244-5999**
tools, mowers, furniture, bird baths, chainsaws, garden tools, lawnmowers,
patio torches, power tools, rakes, and more
Universal Studios Property & Hardware Dept   **(818) 777-2784**
Gardening tools, patio furniture, lawn mowers, bird baths, and more for rent.

Gargoyles

See: Architectural Pieces & Artifacts

Garment Racks

Acme Display Fixture & Packaging (888) 411-1870
3829 S Broadway St., Los Angeles, CA 90037
Complete store setups: garment racks, displays/display cases, counters,
packaging, shelving, hangers, mannequins
sales@acmedisplay.com * www.acmedisplay.com
C. P. Valley (323) 466-8201
Castex Rentals (323) 462-1468
1044 N. Cole Ave, Hollywood, CA, 90038
rolling collapsible wardrobe racks, steamers, irons, hangers, schmere kits, top
stick, sewing supplies, garment racks
service@castexrentals.com * www.castexrentals.com
History For Hire, Inc. (818) 765-7767
empty/full rolling racks, period

Gas & Electric Meters

Alley Cats Studio Rentals (818) 982-9178
gas, different styles
E.C. Prop Rentals (818) 764-2008
residential/commercial several types
LCW Props (818) 243-0707
Both Gas & Electric Meters, Period - Present, Residential, Commercial
Universal Studios Property & Hardware Dept (818) 777-2784
Prop gas meters and prop electric meters for rent.

Gas Cans

AIR Designs (818) 768-6639
1920's to Present, Vintage Gas Cans, Modern Gas Cans
Alley Cats Studio Rentals (818) 982-9178
E.C. Prop Rentals (818) 764-2008
wide selection
The Hand Prop Room LP. (323) 931-1534
period-present, asst. styles/sizes
History For Hire, Inc. (818) 765-7767
all types
LCW Props (818) 243-0707
Large Selection
Sony Pictures Studios-Prop House (Off Lot) (310) 244-5999

Gas Furnaces

See: Furnaces

Gas Logs

See: Fireplaces & Mantels/Screens/Tools/Andirons

Gas Pumps/Islands, Gas Station

See Also: Automotive/Garage Equip. & Parts
AIR Designs (818) 768-6639
1920's-Present, signage, Gas Station & Mini Mart, Full Dressing
Alley Cats Studio Rentals (818) 982-9178
20s to present day (digital) large selection, service station props
C. P. Valley (323) 466-8201

Gates

See: Fences Steel Folding Gates & Roll-Up Doors*

Gators

See: Grip Equipment

Gauges

Alley Cats Studio Rentals (818) 982-9178
huge selection!
E.C. Prop Rentals (818) 764-2008
wide selection
History For Hire, Inc. (818) 765-7767
Jadis (310) 396-3477
2701 Main St, Santa Monica, CA, 90405
Vintage gauges and porcelain insulators.
jadis1@gmail.com * www.jadisprops.com
LCW Props (818) 243-0707
Huge Selection, Military, Airplane, Industrial, PSI, MPH, Weather
Universal Studios Property & Hardware Dept (818) 777-2784
All kinds of prop gauges for rent.

Geiger Counter

See: Mining & Prospecting Equipment

Gems, Minerals & Crystals

See Also: Jewelry, Fine/Reproduction
Little Bohemia Rentals (818) 853-7506
11940 Sherman Rd, N Hollywood, CA, 91605
Various polished and raw minerals and crystals.
sales@wearelittlebohemia.com * www.wearelittlebohemia.com
Sword & Stone (818) 562-6548
Wonders of the World & Beyond (310) 393-4700
1460 Lincoln Blvd, Santa Monica, CA, 90401
4-8 pm Mon-Sat, but appt preferred; real fossils, minerals lrg crystals, reprod.
ancient jewelry, lrg insect specimens

General Store

See Also: Cash Registers Counters* Display Cases, Racks &
Fixtures (Store)*
AIR Designs (818) 768-6639
Counters, Coolers, Racks, Produce, Food, Signs, Hardware
C. P. Valley (323) 466-8201
coffee grinders, scales, dry goods, butter churns, jars
History For Hire, Inc. (818) 765-7767
lots of products
RC Vintage, Inc. (818) 765-7107
General Store Dressing, Pawnshop Dressing, many cases, shelving and racks,
general store smalls, shelf fillers, cash registers
Sony Pictures Studios-Prop House (Off Lot) (310) 244-5999
Universal Studios Property & Hardware Dept (818) 777-2784
General store dressing and general store props for rent.

Generators

See Also: Power Generation/Distribution
Astro Audio Video Lighting, Inc. (818) 549-9915
6615 San Fernando Rd, Glendale, CA, 91201
Power generators of various sizes for rent.
www.astroavl.com
Castex Rentals (323) 462-1468
1044 N. Cole Ave, Hollywood, CA, 90038
portable Honda generators 9 amp-60 amp, ac cords
service@castexrentals.com * www.castexrentals.com
E.C. Prop Rentals (818) 764-2008
non-working prop, portable
**Filmmaker Production Services Company -
Atlanta** (404) 815-5202
219 Armour Drive NE, Atlanta, GA, 30324
Grip & rigging equip. & services, lighting & sound
http://www.filmmakerproductionservices.com
**Filmmaker Production Services Company -
Chicago** (678) 628-1997
2558 W 16th Street Dock #4, Chicago, IL, 60608
Grip & rigging equip. & services, lighting & sound
http://www.filmmakerproductionservices.com
LCW Props (818) 243-0707
Industrial, Residential, Commercial, Back Up

Genetic Lab

See: Lab Equipment

German Themed Parties

See: Events, Decorations, Supplies & Services Events,
Design/Planning/Production* Travel (City/Country) Themed Events*

Gift Wrapping

See Also: Boxes* Packing/Packaging Supplies, Services* Wrapped Prop Gift Packages

Acme Display Fixture & Packaging (888) 411-1870
3829 S Broadway St., Los Angeles, CA 90037
Complete store setups: garment racks, displays/display cases, counters, packaging, shelving, hangers, mannequins
sales@acmedisplay.com * www.acmedisplay.com

History For Hire, Inc. (818) 765-7767
also mfg.

Mail Boxes & Accessories (818) 843-5803
827 Hollywood Way, Burbank, CA, 91505
P.O. Box rentals, UPS, Fed-X, notary, bus cards, supplies, prop boxes, prop gift wrapping

Gilding Materials & Services

See: Metal Plating, Coating, Polishing

Glass & Mirrors

See Also: Breakaways (Glass, Props, Scenery)* Fun House Mirrors* Mirrors, Framed Decorative Furnishings

Acme Display Fixture & Packaging (888) 411-1870
3829 S Broadway St., Los Angeles, CA 90037
Complete store setups: garment racks, displays/display cases, counters, packaging, shelving, hangers, mannequins
sales@acmedisplay.com * www.acmedisplay.com

Angelus Block Co., Inc (818) 767-8576
11374 Tuxford St, Sun Valley, CA, 91352
mfg. glass block

Antiqued Mirrors (818) 767-6188
12970 Branford St, Unit L, Arleta, CA, 91331
re-silver old mirrors & mfg new antiqued mirrors

Bassman-Blaine (213) 748-5909
1933 S. Broadway, #1005, Los Angeles, CA 90007
Featuring mirrors & decorative wall decor from Arteriors, Mirror Image Home, NOIR/cFc and World's Away.
lashowroom@bassman-blaine.com * www.bassmanblainelamart.com

Campbell Custom Glass (323) 735-0021
6234 S. Gramercy Pl, Los Angeles, CA, 90047
custom & mfg.

Castle Antiques & Design (855) 765-5800
11924 Vose St, N Hollywood, CA, 91605
Mirrors, crystal cups, glass cups, cut glass, crystal, stained glass for rent or purchase.
info@castleantiques.net * www.castleprophouse.com

E.C. Prop Rentals (818) 764-2008
dance studio mirrors, castered

Hollywood Glass (323) 661-7774
5119 Hollywood Blvd, Los Angeles, CA, 90027

Knickerbocker Plate Glass (212) 247-8500
79 New York Ave, Westbury, NY 11590
furnish & install commercial & residential

Lux Lounge EFR (888) 247-4411
106 1/2 Judge John Aiso St #318, Los Angeles, CA, 90012
Mirror decorations, Vanity Mirrors, Mirrored Furniture, Glass tables
info@luxloungeefr.com * www.luxloungeefr.com

Manhattan Shade & Glass (212) 288-5616
1299 3rd Avenue, New York City, NY, 10021

Motion Picture Glass (818) 885-8700
18135 Napa St, Northridge, CA, 91325
Wholesale glass supply, custom design, engineering & installation

Prop Services West (818) 503-2790

Ruben's Glass & Mirrors (323) 937-7519
616 S La Brea Ave, Los Angeles, CA, 90036
shower doors to store front windows

Superior Glass Service (323) 663-1165
3923 W Sunset Blvd, Los Angeles, CA, 90029
custom frameless glass projects

Glass & Mirrors, Art/Finishing/Etching/Etc.

Antiquarian Traders (310) 247-3900
4851 S. Alameda Street, Los Angeles, CA 90048
Collection of Tiffany and grand scale stained glass
antiques@antiquariantraders.com * www.antiquariantraders.com

Art, Models & Props, Inc. (951) 206-9156
1725 Marengo Ave, Pasadena, CA, 91103
custom works of art. See ad in "Prop Design & Manufacturing"
modelsandprops@msn.com * www.artmodeltech.com

Charisma Design Studio, Inc. (818) 252-6611
8414 San Fernando Road, Sun Valley, CA, 91352
museum quality glass etching & shaping
info@charismadesign.com * www.charismadesign.com

Glass Door Coolers

AIR Designs (818) 768-6639
Single, Double, Triple, Mini-Mart, Period-Present

Modern Props (323) 934-3000

Glass Tinting

See: Glass & Mirrors, Art/Finishing/Etching/Etc.

Glasses

See: Eyewear, Glasses, Sunglasses, 3D

Glassware/Dishes

See Also: Bottles* Crystal Stemware* Fiesta Dinnerware* Pewter & Pewterware* Prop Houses* Restaurant Kitchens/Equip./Supplies

AIR Designs (818) 768-6639

Bargain Fair (Mid-City) (323) 965-2227
4635 W Pico Blvd, Los Angeles, CA, 90019
corner of Fairfax; dinnerware, glassware, silverware, cookware & more at unbelievable prices, open 7 days
sheida@bargainfair.com * www.bargainfair.com

The Hand Prop Room LP. (323) 931-1534
Baccarat crystal glasses, cut glass, crystal glasses, rock glasses, bar glasses, high ball glasses, brandy snifters

History For Hire, Inc. (818) 765-7767

Little Bohemia Rentals (818) 853-7506
11940 Sherman Rd, N Hollywood, CA, 91605
Vintage glassware/vintage dishes and contemporary glassware/contemporary dishes.
sales@wearelittlebohemia.com * www.wearelittlebohemia.com

Modern Props (323) 934-3000
contemporary/futuristic, multiples

Ob-jects (818) 351-4200

Omega/Cinema Props (323) 466-8201

Prop Services West (818) 503-2790

RC Vintage, Inc. (818) 765-7107
diner dressing to household, crystal cups, glass cups, glass mugs, vintage restaurant dishes,

Sony Pictures Studios-Prop House (Off Lot) (310) 244-5999
multiples, lg. selection pewter to ceramic

The Surface Library (323) 546-9314
1106 N. Hudson Ave, 2nd Floor, Los Angeles, CA 90038
A curated prop house specializing in surfaces and table top props for food, product, and lifestyle shoots.
info@thesurfacelibrary.com * www.thesurfacelibrary.com

Universal Studios Property & Hardware Dept (818) 777-2784
All kinds of glassware and dishware for rent.

Warner Bros. Studios Property Department (818) 954-2181
Large variety and styles of glassware & dishes, crystal stemware, restaurant supplies, multiples

Glitter

See: Hobby & Craft Supplies

Globes, World Map

See Also: Maps

The Hand Prop Room LP. (323) 931-1534
table & floor, Old World, universe

History For Hire, Inc. (818) 765-7767

Modern Props (323) 934-3000
desk & floor-standing, oversized metallic cage globes. armillary globes, brass planet systems, ringed systems.

Prop Services West (818) 503-2790

RC Vintage, Inc. (818) 765-7107

Sony Pictures Studios-Prop House (Off Lot) (310) 244-5999
world globes

Gloves

See: Protective Apparel* Sporting Goods & Services* Wardrobe, Accessories

Glue

See: Expendables

Gobos/Projection

See Also: Lighting & Sound, Concert/Theatrical/DJ/VJ Lighting, LED, Fiber Optic & Specialty*

Astro Audio Video Lighting, Inc. **(818) 549-9915**
6615 San Fernando Rd, Glendale, CA, 91201
Gobos and gobo projectors available as well as gobo fabrication.
www.astroavl.com

Gold Leaf

See: Metal Plating, Coating, Polishing

Golf

See: Sporting Goods & Services

Gondolas

See: Boats & Water Sport Vehicles Ski Equipment* Nautical/Marine Services & Charters* Market Equipment/Fixtures* Display Cases, Racks & Fixtures (Store)* Balloon (Hot Air) Gondolas*

Goth/Punk/Bondage/Fetish/Erotica Etc.

See Also: Leather (Clothing, Accessories, Materials) Occult/Spiritual/Metaphysical* Special Effects, Make-up/Prosthetics* Tattoo & Body Piercing Equipment & Supplies* Steam Punk*

665 Leather **(310) 854-7276**
8722 Santa Monica Blvd, W. Hollywood, CA, 90069
Leather & fetish clothing & access., erotica, on-site manufacturing, repairs, alterations

The Costume House **(818) 508-9933**
club wear

Dapper Cadaver/Creatures & Cultures **(818) 771-0818**
Gothic and punk decor: decorative skulls, oddities, dark statues, etc. Bondage furniture: restraint chairs, beds, etc.

GoodGoth.com **(818) 771-0818**
Web Based Business
Gothic clothing & accessories, Hrs: M-F 10-4:30 EST
www.goodgoth.com

Hoss International **(213) 744-1364**
1030 S. Los Angeles St, 2nd Floor, Los Angeles, CA, 90015
specialty corsets & waist cinchers; custom & bridal too, corsetry in plus sizes

Necromance **(323) 934-8684**
7222 Melrose Ave, Los Angeles, CA, 90046
Goth jewelry & nasty looking access. some from real insects, incl. freeze dried rodents/bats, animals preserved in jars

The Pleasure Chest **(323) 650-1022**
7733 Santa Monica Blvd, W Hollywood, CA, 90046
Erotic goods, S&M items, toys, lubes, DVDs, over 10,000 items; also stores in NYC & Chicago

Sony Pictures Studios-Wardrobe **(310) 244-5995**
alterations, call (310) 244-7260

Sword & Stone **(818) 562-6548**
aluminum, steel, leather & chainmail chastity belts & corsets

Gourds

See: Pumpkins & Gourds

Gowns

See: Clerical, Judicial, Academic Gowns/Apparel Formal Wear* Wedding Attire*

Granite

See: Tile, Marble, Granite, Etc.

Graphics, Digital & Large Format Printing

See Also: Calligraphy Embroidery, Screen Printing, Etc.* Medical Equip/Furniture, Graphics/Supplies* Printing Presses* Promotional Items & Materials* Prop Houses* Signs*

AAA Flag & Banner Mfg Co **(310) 836-3341**
8937 National Blvd, Los Angeles, Los Angeles, CA 90034
Large Format Printing - Backdrops, Step & Repeat Press Walls, Prop Signage, Vehicle Wraps, Custom Graphics Solutions.
fred@aaaflag.com * www.aaaflag.com

ARC Imaging Resources **(800) 950-3729**
616 Monterey Pass Rd, Monterey Park, CA, 91754
CAD/Graphics Printers/Copiers/Scanners. Oce, Xerox, HP, Canon. We service & supply what we place.
mike.timchenko@e-arc.com * www.arcsupplies.com

Art, Signs & Graphics **(818) 503-7997**
6939 Farmdale Ave, N Hollywood, CA, 91605
props, banners, vinyl graphics, vehicle graphics, 3D router cut letters & logos, DVDs and CD cases
jessee@artsignsandgraphics.com * www.artsignsandgraphics.com

design & layout
large format graphics
dimensional signage
hand lettering
stage & location
banners & billboards
props & package
vehicle graphics &...

Artery Props **(877) 732-7733**
7684 Clybourn Ave 2nd Floor Unit C, Sun Valley, CA, 91352
100% cleared & owned artwork: posters, stickers, flyers, gold records, signs, CDs, DVDs, albums, mic flags & more.
info@arteryprops.com * www.arteryprops.com

DISPLAY ADS AND LISTINGS FOR THIS CATEGORY CONTINUE ON THE FOLLOWING PAGE

Beyond Image Graphics (818) 547-0899
1853 Dana St, Glendale, CA, 91201
Large Format Imaging, Canvas Printing, Canvas Stretching, Trade Show
Graphics, Exhibit Graphics, Custom Decals
rafi@beyondimagegraphics.com * www.beyondimagegraphics.com

D'ziner Sign Co. (323) 467-4467
801 Seward Street, Los Angeles, CA 90038
graphics design & 8' wide digital printing in house, rush orders
sales@dzinersign.com * www.dzinersign.com

CBS Graphics (323) 575-2617
7800 Beverly Blvd Room M-40, Los Angeles, CA, 90036
A full design and print facility catering to the Television, Commercial, and Retail
business industries.
Carson.Mazaros@cbs.com * www.cbs-graphics.com

The Earl Hays Press (818) 765-0700
services the Industry only. lrg sel & custom creation

EFX- Event Special Effects (626) 888-2239
125 Railroad Ave, Monrovia, CA, 91016
Step & Repeat Printing- Large Format- Decals- Signage- Poster- Mounting
info@efxla.com * www.efxla.com

FILM ART LA   **(323) 461-4900**
Culver City Warehouse at Jefferson & Hauser. Call for address.
digital reproductions of contemporary, period & graphic art. ORDER
ARTWORK ONLINE: Address for pick ups/returns only.
filmartla@gmail.com * www.artimagela.com

Flix FX Inc.   **(818) 765-3549**
7327 Lankershim Blvd #4, N Hollywood, CA, 91605
Vinyl graphics and 3D vacuum formed signs
info@flixfx.com * www.flixfx.com

Graphic Space Online   **(213) 321-3919**
Web-Based Only
Fabricated & licensed graphics available 24/7 online to download on automated
website.
theteam@graphicspaceonline.com * www.graphicspaceonline.com

The Hand Prop Room LP.   **(323) 931-1534**
in-house graphics dept.

History For Hire, Inc.   **(818) 765-7767**
Full service graphic shop for signs, labels, event tickets, and more.

HPR Graphics   **(323) 556-2694**
5674 Venice Blvd, Los Angeles, CA, 90019
Product labels, certificates, magazine covers, newspapers, antique graphics,
thermo printing, inkjet printing, and more.
hprcan@earthlink.net * www.hprgraphics.net

Jet Sets   **(818) 764-5644**
6910 Farmdale Ave, N Hollywood, CA, 91605
set construction, custom props, scenic painting, special effects, set illustration,
research library for clients
dougmorris@jetsets.com * www.jetsets.com

L. A. Party Works   **(888) 527-2789**
9712 Alpaca St, S El Monte, CA, 91733
Large Format Printing, Vehicle Printing & Wrapping, Canvas Printing, Trade
Show Graphics, Step & Repeats, Custom Decals
partyworks@aol.com * www.partyworksusa.com

Repro-Graphic Supply   **(818) 771-9066**
9838 Glenoaks Blvd, Sun Valley, CA, 91352
drafting & engineering supplies, equipment & service, all Ind.'s. large format
xerographics printing
info@reprographicsupply.com * www.reprographicsupply.com

Steven Enterprises   **(800) 491-8785**
17952 Skypark Circle Unit E, Irvine, CA, 92614
Wide Format Printers. Rent/Buy. Authorized Dealer: HP, KIP, Canon, Oce,
Epson. We service & supply everything we install
sales@plotters.com * www.plotters.com

LCW Props   **(818) 243-0707**
Custom Graphics Department. We Make Any Video Files Needed & Have A
Huge Stock

Nights of Neon   **(818) 756-4791**
13815 Saticoy St, Van Nuys, CA 91402
Full service sign shop, digital imaging, vinyl graphics, sheet graphics,
metal/posters
contact@nightsofneon.com * www.nightsofneon.com

DISPLAY ADS AND LISTINGS FOR THIS CATEGORY
CONTINUE ON THE FOLLOWING PAGE

Tractor Vision Scenery & Rentals (323) 235-2885
340 E Jefferson Blvd. Los Angeles, CA 90011
Specializing in entertainment, trade shows, & events, we bring your projects to life with precision, speed & personality
sets@tractorvision.com * www.tractorvision.com

Universal Studios Graphic Design & Sign Shop (818) 777-2350
design, large format printing to 100" wide, & full service sign

Warner Bros. Design Studio Scenic Art & Sign Shop (818) 954-1815
4000 Warner Blvd, Burbank, CA, 91522
graphic design and production studio for signs & scenic art; digital printing to hand-painted
wbsigns@warnerbros.com * www.wbsignandscenic.com

Warner Bros. Studios Production Sound & Video (818) 954-2511
4000 Warner Blvd, Burbank, CA, 91522
A/V Equipment Rental, Design, Presentations, Install & Support; Visual Display Creation; Communication
wbsfproductionsound@warnerbros.com * www.wbsoundandvideo.com

Warner Bros. Studios Property Department (818) 954-2181
2 LF 16', any size matl, backlit, see-through, seaming, design/install

WestOn Letters (818) 503-9472
7259 N. Atoll Ave, N. Hollywood, CA, 91605
Serving the signage needs of the entertainment industry since the 1960s
sales@westonletters.com * www.WestonLetters.com

Grass Mats

See Also: Greens

Benson's Tropical Sea Imports (714) 841-3399
7442 Vincent Cir, Huntington Beach, CA 92648
lauhalla, bacbac, sea grass, pandan, tatami, lampac, abaca, etc.
sales@bensonsimport.com * www.bensonsimport.com

Green Set, Inc. (818) 764-1231
Artificial Grasses & Artificial Turf, Grass Mats. Fake Grass, Fake Turf

Jackson Shrub Supply, Inc. (818) 982-0100
all sizes, as well as artificial grass, grassmats

Linoleum City, Inc. (323) 469-0063
4849 Santa Monica Blvd, Hollywood, CA, 90029
Astro turf, indoor/outdoor carpet, grass turf, walk off mats, coco brush, green turf, blue turf, black turf, white turf, grass tex.
sales@linocity.com * www.linoleumcity.com

Universal Studios Property & Hardware Dept (818) 777-2784
Grass mats, golf mats and tatamis for rent.

Grass, Sisal

See: Carpet & Flooring

Grating, Grated Flooring, Catwalks

E.C. Prop Rentals (818) 764-2008
steel & plastic floor grate sections

Grating Pacific, Inc. (800) 321-4314
3651 Sausalito St, Los Alamitos, CA, 90720
Steel, aluminum, fiberglass gratings. Fabricated or stock sizes.

Grave Markers

See: Cemetery Dressing

Gravel

See: Concrete Block, Brick, Gravel, Sand, Rocks, Etc.* Greens

Grease Boards

See: Office Equipment & Dressing* School Supplies, Desks & Dressing

Great Room

See: Antiques & Antique Decorations* Decorative Accessories* Furniture, Eclectic* Prop Houses* Rugs* Taxidermy, Hides/Heads/Skeletons

Grecian Themed Parties

See: Costume Rental Houses* Events, Decorations, Supplies & Services* Events, Design/Planning/Production* Events, Entertainment* Historical Era Themed Events* Wardrobe, Antique/Historical

Green Beds

See: Grip Equipment* Scenery/Set Rentals* Stages, Portable & Steel Deck

Green Rooms/Stage Client Areas

See: Office Furniture

Green Screens, Blue Screens

See Also: Backings* Light Fixtures* Sewing Services, Industrial

Art, Models & Props, Inc. (951) 206-9156
1725 Marengo Ave, Pasadena, CA, 91103
on-site filming of custom special effects. See ad in "Prop Design & Manufacturing"
modelsandprops@msn.com * www.artmodeltech.com

Composite Components Co. (323) 257-1163
134 N. Avenue 61, Ste 103, Los Angeles, CA, 90042
screens, costumes, fabric, paint, fluorescent lights

Fore-Peak (323) 460-4192
1040 N. Las Palmas Ave, Los Angeles, CA, 90038
chromakey blue/green, also red/yellow/orange/white

LCW Props (818) 243-0707
Blue, Green, White. Stands & Lighting Too

The Rag Place, Inc. (818) 765-3338
13160 Raymer St, N Hollywood, CA, 91605
fabrics, grip backings, nets, silks, solid muslin, chromakey, grip

Ragtime Rentals (323) 769-0650
11970 Borden Ave, San Fernando, CA, 91340
backings: solids, muslins, nets, gridcloths, grip equip., chromakey fabric, paint, tape; truss frames w/rigging

Warner Bros. Studios Grip Department (818) 954-1590
4000 Warner Blvd, Burbank, CA, 91522
Production, rigging & construction grip equipment, canvas shop, steel scaffolding rentals/services
www.wbgripdept.com

Greenhouses & Growing Systems

See Also: Greens* Marijuana Plants, Dispensary Dressing & Hydroponics

Turner Greenhouses (800) 672-4770
PO Box 1260, Goldsboro, NC, 27533
catalog sales; hobby greenhouses & related accessories

Greens

See Also: Cactus, Live & Artificial* Concrete Block, Brick, Gravel, Sand, Rocks, Etc.* Dirt Skins* Florists/Floral Design* Flowers, Dried* Fountains, Decorative & Garden* Grass Mats* Pumpkins & Gourds* Pumpkins, Artificial* Marijuana Plants, Dispensary Dressing & Hydroponics

American Foliage & Design Group, Inc. (212) 741-5555
122 West 22nd St, New York, NY, 10011
greens, trees, dirt, sand, rocks, snow, fountains, special EFX, fiberglass

Benson's Tropical Sea Imports (714) 841-3399
7442 Vincent Cir, Huntington Beach, CA 92648
tropical palm & banana trees, plants/flowers, bamboo & thatching
sales@bensonsimport.com * www.bensonsimport.com

Breaux's Arts (323) 221-8071
2222 Foothill Blvd E154, La Canada, CA, 91011
Call for Appt. Unusual, hard to find plant & natural materials, horticultural & botanical research
breauxarts@sbcglobal.net * http://bit.ly/BreauxArts

Flower Art (323) 935-6800
5859 West 3rd Street, Los Angeles, CA, 90036
Award-winning, full-service floral design for movie/television sets. Located near The Grove. SDSA members since 1994
info@flowerartla.com * http://www.flowerartla.com

Green Set, Inc. (818) 764-1231
Collected Materials, Cut Brush, Moss, Straw & Hay, Vines. live & artificial, full nursery facilities

Jackson Shrub Supply, Inc. (818) 982-0100
giant Sequoias, Cypress tropical, live/custom made palms, bushes

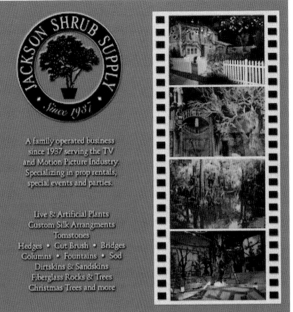

LCW Props (818) 243-0707
dirt skins, lots

NatureMaker (800) 872-1889
6225 El Camino Real Ste 110, Carlsbad, CA, 92009
custom fabricators of steel art trees

Oceanic Arts (562) 698-6960
bamboo poles, 3/4" to 6" dia., bamboo fencing, thatch, mattings

Pacific Earth Resources (805) 987-8456
305 W Hueneme Rd, Camarillo, CA, 93012
sod farm

Rainforest Flora, Inc. (310) 370-8044
19121 Hawthorne Blvd, Torrance, CA, 90503
largest supplier of exotic tropicals, bromeliads, and air plants

Sandy Rose Floral, Inc (818) 980-4371
6850 Vineland Ave Unit C, N Hollywood, CA, 91605
Fresh & artificial florals, custom & prefab rentals, call 24 hrs
www.sandyrose.com

Grip Equipment

See Also: Expendables* Lighting & Sound, Concert/Theatrical/DJ/VJ* Rigging, Equipment or Services* Stage Lighting, Film/Video/TV

Alan Gordon Enterprises, Inc. (323) 466-3561
5625 Melrose Ave, Los Angeles, CA, 90038
grip, lighting, camera & audio equip.

Bill Ferrell Co. (818) 767-1900
10556 Keswick St, Sun Valley, CA, 91352
Camera risers, Steel Deck and Ferrellel Decks.
www.billferrell.com

Birns & Sawyer, Inc. (323) 466-8211
5275 Craner Ave, North Hollywood, CA 91601
film & video cameras, accessories, lighting/grip, expendables, for lighting & grip rental call (818) 766-2525

Castex Rentals (323) 462-1468
1044 N. Cole Ave, Hollywood, CA, 90038
full line of grip equipment, boom arms, lights, reflectors, steel deck
service@castexrentals.com * www.castexrentals.com

Cineworks Lighting & Grip (818) 252-0001
8125 Lankershim Blvd, N. Hollywood, CA 91605
Hot lighting, grip equipment, grip trucks, car mounts, specialty items, expendables, kinoflos
cineworks@cineworksinc.com * www.cineworksinc.com

Expendable Supply Store/Hollywood Rentals (800) 233-7830
12800 Foothill Blvd, Sylmar, CA, 91342
grip & lighting, power generators, power & climate control

LISTINGS FOR THIS CATEGORY CONTINUE ON THE FOLLOWING PAGE

Feature Systems, Inc. (201) 531-2299
223 Veteran's Blvd, Canstadt, NJ, 07072
grip/lighting, expendables/supplies, generators, trucks
Filmmaker Production Services Company - Atlanta (404) 815-5202
219 Armour Drive NE, Atlanta, GA, 30324
Grip & rigging equip. & services, lighting & sound
http://www.filmmakerproductionservices.com
Filmmaker Production Services Company - Chicago (678) 628-1997
2558 W 16th Street Dock #4, Chicago, IL, 60608
Grip & rigging equip. & services, lighting & sound
http://www.filmmakerproductionservices.com
Highline Stages (212) 206-8280
440 W. 15th Street, New York City, NY, 10011
expendables, lighting, generators, grip equip.
History For Hire, Inc. (818) 765-7767
period
New Mexico Lighting & Grip Co. (505) 227-2500
5650 University Blvd SE Bldg 2, Albuquerque, NM, 85107
Grip & rigging equip. & services, lighting & sound
www.newmexicolightingandgrip.com
Paladin Group, Inc. (323) 874-7758
7351 Santa Monica Blvd, Hollywood, CA, 90046
grip equipment & stage lighting
Paskal Lighting (818) 896-5233
12685 Van Nuys Blvd, Pacoima, CA, 91321
grip/lighting equip. & expendables
Ragtime Rentals (323) 769-0650
11970 Borden Ave, San Fernando, CA, 91340
backings: solids, muslins, nets, gridcloths, grip equip., chromakey fabric, paint, tape; truss frames w/rigging
Source Lighting & Grip Rentals, Inc. (323) 463-5555
1111 N Beachwood Dr, Hollywood, CA, 90038
Grip trucks, generators, lighting equipment, stages
Universal Studios Grip Dept (818) 777-2291
100 Universal City Plaza, Universal City, CA, 91608
Extensive inventory of quality grip equipment incl. digital screens, steel deck & more
universal.grip@nbcuni.com * www.filmmakersdestination.com
Warner Bros. Studios Grip Department (818) 954-1590
4000 Warner Blvd, Burbank, CA, 91522
Production, rigging & construction grip equipment, canvas shop, steel scaffolding rentals/services
www.wbgripdept.com

Grocery Check-out Stands (Complete)

AIR Designs (818) 768-6639
Supermarket Dual Conveyor, Matching Pair
Lennie Marvin Enterprises, Inc. (Prop Heaven) (818) 841-5882

Grocery Store

See: Market Equipment/Fixtures* Prop Houses* Prop Products & Packages* Scales* Shopping Bags (Silent)

Grocery Store Produce Scales

See: Scales

Grooming

See: Make-up & Hair, Supplies & Services* Shaving, Old Fashion, Non-Electric

Ground & Floor Protection

See: Floor, Ground & Surface Protection

Guard Shacks

See Also: Street Dressing
AIR Designs (818) 768-6639
Clean/Rustic, Electric Toll Gate Mech. Arms, Lights, Pylons, Signage
E.C. Prop Rentals (818) 764-2008
multiple styles, castered, lighted, practical parking arms

Guillotines

Dapper Cadaver/Creatures & Cultures (818) 771-0818
Guillotines. Severed heads, decapitated bodies and blood. More torture equipment: gibbets, stocks, etc.
History For Hire, Inc. (818) 765-7767
Sword & Stone (818) 562-6548
Universal Studios Property & Hardware Dept (818) 777-2784
Guillotine with wooden frame and fake blade, magician's guillotine and miniature guillotines for rent.

Gumball Machines

See: Vending Machines

Guns/Gunsmith

See: Firearms, Gunsmith, Firearm Choreography* Non-Guns & Non-Pyro Flashes* Weapons* Western Wear

Gurneys

See Also: Hospital Equipment* Military Props & Equipment* Intensive Care Unit / NICU (Natal Intensive Care Unit)* Emergency Room
A-1 Medical Integration (818) 753-0319
Medical devices for Set Decoration & Property, from minor procedures to detailed hospital units.
Alpha Companies - Spellman Desk Co. (818) 504-9090
period to contemporary from the #1 source for medical equipment in the Industry.
C. P. Valley (323) 466-8201
Vintage gurneys to modern gurneys.
Dapper Cadaver/Creatures & Cultures (818) 771-0818
Hospital gurneys and ambulance gurneys.
The Hand Prop Room LP. (323) 931-1534
History For Hire, Inc. (818) 765-7767
period, hospital, ambulance
LCW Props (818) 243-0707
Stainless Steel, Morgue Dressing, Hospital
Universal Studios Property & Hardware Dept (818) 777-2784
Medical gurneys, emergency gurneys and morgue gurneys for rent.

Gym & Tumbling Mats

See: Fall Pads & Crash Pads* Gymnasium & Gymnastic Equipment

Gym Equipment

See: Exercise & Fitness Equipment* Gymnasium & Gymnastic Equipment

Gym Floors

See: Carpet & Flooring* Gymnasium & Gymnastic Equipment

Gym Lights

See Also: Egg Crate Bottom Fluorescents* Light Fixtures* Lighting, Industrial

Alley Cats Studio Rentals   **(818) 982-9178**
working, goosenecks, poles, single
E.C. Prop Rentals   **(818) 764-2008**
working, many china hat & high bay styles

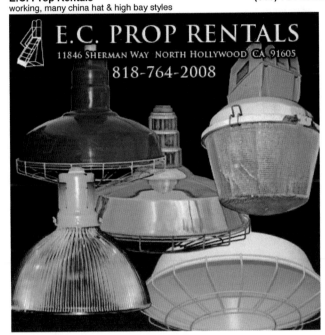

E.C. PROP RENTALS
11846 SHERMAN WAY NORTH HOLLYWOOD CA 91605
818-764-2008

LCW Props   **(818) 243-0707**
Overhead, Fire, Exit, Industrial
Sony Pictures Studios-Fixtures   **(310) 244-5996**
5933 W Slauson Ave, Culver City, CA, 90230
period to present day
www.sonypicturesstudios.com

Gymnasium & Gymnastic Equipment

See Also: Ballet Barres & Dance Mirrors* Boxing, Wrestling, Mixed Martial Arts (MMA)* Exercise & Fitness Equipment* Fall Pads & Crash Pads* Lockers* Weightlifting Equipment

C. P. Valley   **(323) 466-8201**
Gym mats and gym chairs
Curtis Gym Equipment   **(818) 897-2804**
10275 Glenoaks Blvd, Ste #7, Pacoima, CA, 91331
Prop Rentals and Servicing. Complete Setups. Fitness Machines, Gymnastics & Weightlifting. Fake & Real Weights
curtisgymequipment@hotmail.com
E.C. Prop Rentals   **(818) 764-2008**
lights, lockers, benches, towel carts, basketball scoreboard etc
The Hand Prop Room LP.   **(323) 931-1534**
Pommel horse, jump rope, basketball hoops, basketball backboards, spring boards, wall clocks, countdown timers
Hollywood Gym Rentals   **(310) 663-6161**
200 West Chevy Chase Drive Unit B, Glendale, CA 91204
Hollywood Gym Rentals specializes in short and long term rentals of fitness equipment in the Los Angeles area.
chris@hollywoodgymrentals.com * www.hollywoodgymrentals.com

Gypsy Wagon

L. A. Circus   **(323) 751-3486**
Call for Appt, Los Angeles, CA, 90047
Many gypsy wagons
circusinc@aol.com * www.lacircus.com
Universal Studios Property & Hardware Dept   **(818) 777-2784**
Wagons for rent, perfect for all your gypsy needs!

Hair

See: Beauty Salon* Make-up & Hair, Supplies & Services* Wigs

Hair Dryers

See: Beauty Salon

Hair Ornaments

See: Wardrobe, Accessories

Hairpieces

See: Wigs

Halliburton Cases

See: Futuristic Furniture, Props, Decorations

Halloween Dressing & Accessories

See Also: Haunted House* Holiday Costumes* Horror/Monster Dressing* Pumpkins & Gourds* Pumpkins, Artificial

AA Surplus Sales Co., Inc.   **(323) 526-3622**
2940 E. Olympic Blvd, Los Angeles, CA, 90023
Military Uniforms, Ghillie Suits, Footware and Accesories for the whole family in used and new condition
surplusking@hotmail.com * www.aasurplus.com/
Bob Gail Special Events   **(310) 202-5200**
We have a haunted mansion full of Coffins, Skeletons, Monsters, and more to make even Herman Munster run away in fear!
Dapper Cadaver/Creatures & Cultures   **(818) 771-0818**
Halloween prop central. Monsters, gore, skeletons, tombstones, caskets, candelabras & decor. Haunted mansion to zombie.

DAPPER CADAVER
Halloween Props & Decorations
7648 San Fernando Rd., Sun Valley, CA 91352
(818) 771-0818 | www.dappercadaver.com

Green Set, Inc.   **(818) 764-1231**
skeletons, tombstones, scarecrows and many other scary figures and evil figures, even gargoyles
The Hand Prop Room LP.   **(323) 931-1534**
skeletons, skulls, cauldrons, chains, masks
History For Hire, Inc.   **(818) 765-7767**
Jackson Shrub Supply, Inc.   **(818) 982-0100**
L. A. Party Works   **(888) 527-2789**
9712 Alpaca St, S El Monte, CA, 91733
in Vancouver tel. 604-589-4101
partyworks@aol.com * www.partyworksusa.com
Universal Studios Property & Hardware Dept   **(818) 777-2784**
Halloween props, Halloween dressing, and Halloween accessories for rent.

Halloween Make-up

See: Special Effects, Make-up/Prosthetics

Halloween Themed Parties

See: Events, Decorations, Supplies & Services Events, Design/Planning/Production* Holiday Theme Events*

Hampers, Theatrical

iWeiss Theatrical Solutions	(888) 325-7192
815 Fairview Ave #10, Fairview, NJ 07022	
Universal Studios Property & Hardware Dept	(818) 777-2784
Theatrical hampers, commercial hampers for rent.	

Hand Bags

See: Leather (Clothing, Accessories, Materials) Wardrobe, Accessories*

Hand Lettering

See: Calligraphy Signs*

Hand Trucks

See: Furniture Dollies, Pads & Hand Trucks

Handcuffs

See: Police Equipment

Handrails

See: Audience Seating Moulding, Wood* Scenery/Set Construction*

Hangar

See: Airport Dressing & Hangars

Hangers

See: Display Cases, Racks & Fixtures (Store)

Hard Hats

See: Headwear - Hats, Bonnets, Caps, Helmets Etc. Traffic/Road Signs, Lights, Safety Items* Uniforms, Trades/Professional/Sports*

Hardware Store Dressing

See Also: Cash Registers Counters* Credit Card Imprint Machine* Display Cases, Racks & Fixtures (Store)* Shopping Bags (Silent)*

Acme Display Fixture & Packaging	(888) 411-1870
3829 S Broadway St., Los Angeles, CA 90037	
Complete store setups: garment racks, displays/display cases, counters, packaging, shelving, hangers, mannequins	
sales@acmedisplay.com * www.acmedisplay.com	
History For Hire, Inc.	(818) 765-7767
LCW Props	(818) 243-0707
A Huge Selection Of Hardware Store, Shelves With Product, Tools, POS Systems, Security	
Lennie Marvin Enterprises, Inc. (Prop Heaven)	(818) 841-5882
product/fixtures, period to modern, signage too	
Sony Pictures Studios-Prop House (Off Lot)	(310) 244-5999
Misc hardware equipment/supplies, lock plates, brackets	

Hardware, Construction

See: Building Supply, Lumber, Hardware, Etc.

Hardware, Decorative

See Also: Expendables

Atlas Homewares	(818) 240-3500
1310 Cypress Ave, Los Angeles, CA, 90065	
decorative hardware, knobs, pulls, knockers, house numbers	
C. P. Valley	(323) 466-8201
The Craftsmen Hardware Co.	(660) 376-2481
P.O. Box 161, Marceline, MO, 64658	
Hand-hammered copper hardware in the Arts & Crafts style	
Crown City Hardware Co.	(626) 794-1188
1047 N. Allen Ave, Pasadena, CA, 91104	
decorative & period hardware; ask for our 400 pg. catalog	
Design Hardware	(323) 930-1330
6053 West 3rd St, Los Angeles, CA, 90036	
all types of hardware, will do custom	
Designer Door & Window	(818) 841-3181
1037 N Victory Place, Burbank, CA 91502	
decorative hardware & moldings	
History For Hire, Inc.	(818) 765-7767
LCW Props	(818) 243-0707
Very large selection of marine hardware.	
Liz's Antique Hardware	(323) 939-4403
453 S. La Brea Ave, Los Angeles, CA, 90036	
All kinds of vintage and contemporary hardware & lighting from Victorian through to modern.	
shop@lahardware.com * www.lahardware.com	
Ohio Travel Bag	(800) 800-1941
6481 Davis Industrial Pkwy, Solon, OH, 44139	
luggage, purse, trunk, case, saddlery, etc. all components	
www.ohiotravelbag.com	
Omega/Cinema Props	(323) 466-8201
door & window hardware, registers	
Omnia	(800) 310-7960
5 Cliffside Dr PO Box 330, Cedar Grove, NJ, 07009	
ornate brass & S.S. architectural trim, bath & cabinet, locks & latches	
The Reggio Register Co.	(800) 880-3090
31 Jytek Rd, Leominster, MA, 01453	
catalog sales; cast iron, brass, alum., zinc & wood grills & registers for contemp. & traditional homes	
Restoration Hardware	(626) 795-7234
127 W Colorado Blvd, Pasadena, CA, 91105	
Rompage Hardware	(323) 467-2129
1801 N Western Ave, Los Angeles, CA, 90027	
Sword & Stone	(818) 562-6548
Universal Studios Property & Hardware Dept	(818) 777-2784
Decorative hardware for rent.	
Van Dyke's Restorers	(800) 558-1234
PO Box 52, Louisiana, MO, 63353	
catalog sales; woodworking and antique restoration supplies. antique reprod. hardware, locks	
Warner Bros. Studios Hardware Rentals	(818) 954-1335
4000 Warner Blvd., Bldg. 44 Burbank, CA 91522	
Door Knobs & Plates, Hinges, Window Fixtures, Elevator Panels, Train & Boat Accessories	
wbsfconstructionservices@warnerbros.com * www.wbsf.com	

Harness Carriage

See: Carriages, Horse Drawn Horses, Horse Equipment, Livestock*

Harpoons

See: Nautical Dressing & Props

Hat Blocks & Hat Boxes

California Millinery Supply Co.	(213) 622-8746
721 S. Spring St, Los Angeles, CA, 90014	
hat blocks, hat boxes, hat frames & hat-making supplies	
The Hand Prop Room LP.	(323) 931-1534
History For Hire, Inc.	(818) 765-7767
hat boxes	
Universal Studios Property & Hardware Dept	(818) 777-2784
Hat blocks & hat boxes for rent.	
Western Costume Co.	(818) 760-0900

Hat Pins

See: Wardrobe, Accessories

Hat Racks

See Also: Display Cases, Racks & Fixtures (Store)* Hat Blocks & Hat Boxes* Headwear - Hats, Bonnets, Caps, Helmets Etc.* Store Shelf Units & Shelving

C. P. Valley	(323) 466-8201
History For Hire, Inc.	(818) 765-7767

wall & floor

Omega/Cinema Props	(323) 466-8201
Prop Services West	(818) 503-2790
Sony Pictures Studios-Prop House (Off Lot)	(310) 244-5999

hat racks and coat stands, wall hooks

Universal Studios Property & Hardware Dept	(818) 777-2784

Hat racks from different time periods and styles for rent.

Hats

See: Headwear - Hats, Bonnets, Caps, Helmets Etc.

Haunted House

See Also: Cemetery Dressing* Halloween Dressing & Accessories* Horror/Monster Dressing* Special Effects, Equipment & Supplies

CONFETTI & FOG FX Special Effects Company (786) 308-7063
2739 W 79 St Bay, #12, Hialeah, FL 33016
www.caffx.com

Dapper Cadaver/Creatures & Cultures (818) 771-0818
Haunted house prop central. Monsters, zombies, bodies, gore, skeletons, tombstones & decor. Custom fabrication & FX.

History For Hire, Inc. (818) 765-7767
Universal Studios Property & Hardware Dept (818) 777-2784
Haunted house dressing for rent, haunted house props.

Hawaiian Dressing

See Also: Carved Figures* Costume Rental Houses* Events, Decorations, Supplies & Services* Greens* Jungle Dressing* Light Fixtures, South Seas* Prop Houses* Tikis & Tropical Dressing

Benson's Tropical Sea Imports (714) 841-3399
7442 Vincent Cir, Huntington Beach, CA 92648
bamboo, thatching, carvings/masks, birds/fish, tikis, torches, spears
sales@bensonsimport.com * www.bensonsimport.com

Bob Gail Special Events (310) 202-5200
Whether a corporate luau or a tiki-themed birthday party, spend the night in paradise with our Hawaiian props!
History For Hire, Inc. (818) 765-7767

LCW Props (818) 243-0707
Nets, Shells, Surf Boards, Nautical

Oceanic Arts (562) 698-6960
Raincape thatching - 7 sizes, Bamboo Poles 3/4" to 6" diameter, Mattings, Tikis, Tropical Lights, and more.

Hay

See: Greens

Hazardous Waste Removal

See: Sanitation, Waste Disposal

Headdresses

American Plume (800) 521-1132
11 Skyine Drive East, Unit 2, Clarks Summit, PA 18411
Boas/jackets/theatrical division in NYC; (800) 962-8544. Vegas showgirl, wild natural

The Hand Prop Room LP. (323) 931-1534
Western Costume Co. (818) 760-0900

Headstones

See: Cemetery Dressing

Headwear - Hats, Bonnets, Caps, Helmets Etc.

See Also: Formal Wear* Military Surplus/Combat Clothes, Field Gear* Sporting Goods & Services* Uniforms, Trades/Professional/Sports

AIR Designs (818) 768-6639
Racing Helmets, Hard Hats

California Millinery Supply Co. (213) 622-8746
721 S. Spring St, Los Angeles, CA, 90014

The Costume House (818) 508-9933
1870s-1970s, top hats, bonnets, derby, fedoras

Lynda Burdick Millinery (323) 662-7612
938 Parkman Ave, Los Angeles, CA, 90026
baby & children's hats

Sony Pictures Studios-Wardrobe (310) 244-5995
alterations, call (310) 244-7260. wide variety sizes, styles, periods

Sword & Stone (818) 562-6548
helmets of all styles & materials

Tarpy Tailors (310) 645-4694
9100 S Sepulveda Blvd Ste 103, Los Angeles, CA, 90045
airline pilot, all airlines

Universal Studios Costume Dept (818) 777-2722
Rental, mfg., & alterations

Health Club Equipment/Dressing

See: Exercise & Fitness Equipment* Gymnasium & Gymnastic Equipment

Hearses

See: Vehicles

Heat Suits

See: Environmental (Cool/Heat) Suits

Heaters, Indoor

See Also: Furnaces

Castex Rentals   **(323) 462-1468**
1044 N. Cole Ave, Hollywood, CA, 90038
electric dish heaters, propane blower heaters, indoor heaters
service@castexrentals.com * www.castexrentals.com

E.C. Prop Rentals   **(818) 764-2008**
overhead and floor models, radiators

LCW Props   **(818) 243-0707**
Space Heaters, Wall Heaters

RC Vintage, Inc.   **(818) 765-7107**
Faux Radiators Wall type

Sony Pictures Studios-Prop House (Off Lot)   **(310) 244-5999**
Universal Studios Property & Hardware Dept   **(818) 777-2784**
Indoor heaters for rent from wall mounted to portable.

Heaters, Outdoor

Castex Rentals   **(323) 462-1468**
1044 N. Cole Ave, Hollywood, CA, 90038
propane dolly heaters, blower heaters, umbrella heaters, outdoor heaters
service@castexrentals.com * www.castexrentals.com

E.C. Prop Rentals   **(818) 764-2008**
contemp. propane

LCW Props   **(818) 243-0707**
Space Heaters, Wall Heaters, Patio Style

Universal Studios Property & Hardware Dept   **(818) 777-2784**
Outdoor heaters and outdoor space heaters.

Heavy Machinery, Equipment & Specialists

See Also: Construction Site Equipment* Machine Shop & Machinery* Welding Equipment/Stations

BHC Crane LLC   **(310) 830-6450**
2190 W Willow St, Long Beach, CA, 90810
30-300 ton mobile crane & boomtruck rentals, trucking & storage at our 3 acre facility along the 103 fwy, Long Beach, CA
www.bhccrane.com

Helicopters

See: Aircraft, Charters & Aerial Services

Helium Equipment

See: Balloons & Balloon Sculptures

Helmets

See: Headwear - Hats, Bonnets, Caps, Helmets Etc.* Military Surplus/Combat Clothes, Field Gear* Sporting Goods & Services* Uniforms, Trades/Professional/Sports

Hides

See: Costume/Wardrobe/Sewing Supplies* Leather (Clothing, Accessories, Materials)* Taxidermy, Hides/Heads/Skeletons

High Chairs

See: Children/Baby Accessories & Bedroom

Highway Safety Items

See: Barricades* Crowd Control: Barricades, Turnstiles Etc.* Traffic/Road Signs, Lights, Safety Items

Hip Hop

See: Bling

Historical & Antique Reproductions

See: Civil War Era* Egyptian Dressing* Prop Reproduction & Fabrication* Weaponry, Historical* Weaponry, Medieval

Historical Era Themed Events

See Also: Costume Rental Houses* Events, Backings & Scenery* Events, Decorations, Supplies & Services* Events, Design/Planning/Production* Wardrobe, Antique/Historical

Bob Gail Special Events   **(310) 202-5200**
Vintage never goes out of style. Bring an old fashioned flare to your event or theatrical set with our vintage props.

Hoarder Dressing

See: Furniture, Used/Second Hand* Salvage, Rubble, Clutter & Trash (Prop)* Salvage, Architectural* Paperwork, Documents & Letters, Office* Newspapers (Prop)* Boxes* Bag Lady Carts

Hobby & Craft Supplies

See Also: Art, Supplies & Stationery* Model Ships/Planes/Trains/Autos Etc.* Scrapbooks

Burbank's House of Hobbies   **(818) 848-3674**
911 South Victory Blvd, Burbank, CA 91502
Plastic model kits, built up display airplanes (military and commercial), automobiles in all scales, pinewood derby kits

The Caning Shop   **(800) 544-3373**
926 Gilman St (at 8th), Berkeley, CA, 94710
caning/basketry/gourd crafting supplies, tools, books

Craft Depot   **(213) 627-5232**
401 East 7th St, Los Angeles, CA, 90014

Hedgehog Handworks   **(888) 670-6040**
8616 La Tijera Ste 303, Westchester, CA, 90045
catalog sales; unusual needlework supplies, books on historical sewing, needlepoint & costuming topics

Kit Kraft, Inc.   **(818) 509-9739**
12109 Ventura Pl, Studio City, CA, 91604
crafts, models, art materials

Moskatel's   **(213) 689-4590**
733 S San Julian St, Los Angeles, CA, 90014

ShopWildThings   **(928) 855-6075**
2880 Sweetwater Ave, Lake Havasu City, AZ, 86406
Event Decor, Beaded Curtains, Chain Curtains, String Curtains & Columns, Crystal Columns. Reliable service & delivery.
help@shopwildthings.com * www.shopwildthings.com

Stats Floral Supply   **(626) 795-9308**
120 S Raymond Ave, Pasadena, CA, 91105

Utrecht Manufacturing Corp.   **(310) 479-1416**
11531 Santa Monica Blvd, Los Angeles, CA, 90025
art supply, 30+ stores in US, call (800) 223-9132

Hockey Equipment

See: Ice Skating Surfaces* Sporting Goods & Services

Holiday Costumes

See Also: Costume Rental Houses
The Costume House   **(818) 508-9933**
Mardi Gras costumes, Halloween costumes, Christmas Costumes, Christmas
Tree Costume, Santa Claus Costume
Halloween Club   **(714) 367-0859**
14447 Firestone Blvd. La Mirada, CA 90638
Costumes, masks, props, make-up & all related accessories
Sony Pictures Studios-Wardrobe   **(310) 244-5995**
alterations, call (310) 244-7260
Warner Bros. Studios Costume Dept   **(818) 954-1297**
Santa Suits, Elves, Patriotic, Bunnies, Valentine, St. Patricks Day

Holiday Theme Events

See Also: Christmas* Events, Decorations, Supplies & Services*
Events, Design/Planning/Production* Events, Entertainment*
Halloween Dressing & Accessories* Holiday Costumes
Bob Gail Special Events   **(310) 202-5200**
Bob Gail's event planners will provide the perfect spirit with Christmas and
winter props, decor and entertainment.
Create a Scene! & Hooray 4 Holidays!   **(323) 978-0883**
Call for Appointment or to Place an Order
Full Production Services & Holiday Decor
Events@CreateaScene.net * www.CreateaScene.net

FROST   **(310) 704-8812**
Call for Appointment, 21515 Madrona Ave, Torrance, CA 90503
Holiday decor, specializing in large scale trees, Santa sets, ornaments.
Professional installations.
mdisplay@yahoo.com * www.frostchristmasprops.com
The Hand Prop Room LP.   **(323) 931-1534**
ShopWildThings   **(928) 855-6075**
2880 Sweetwater Ave, Lake Havasu City, AZ, 86406
Event Decor, Beaded Curtains, Chain Curtains, String Curtains & Columns,
Crystal Columns. Reliable service & delivery.
help@shopwildthings.com * www.shopwildthings.com

Hollywood Themed Parties

See: Events, Decorations, Supplies & Services* Events,
Design/Planning/Production* Travel (City/Country) Themed Events

Holsters

See: Wardrobe, Accessories* Western Wear

Home Office Furniture

See: Office Furniture

Homeland Security

See: Research, Advisors, Consulting & Clearances* Security Devices
or Services* Security Walk-Through & Baggage Alarms* Surveillance
Equipment

Honeywagon Waste Removal

See: Production Vehicles/Trailers* Sanitation, Waste Disposal

Hoop Skirts

See: Wardrobe, Antique/Historical

Horror/Monster Dressing

Dapper Cadaver/Creatures & Cultures   **(818) 771-0818**
Horror prop central. Crime to supernatural. Bodies, gore, blood, fake weapons,
bones, torture & oddities. Custom FX.
The Hand Prop Room LP.   **(323) 931-1534**
LCW Props   **(818) 243-0707**
Frankenstein Lair, Steam Punk, Van Helsing, Dracula's Castle, Torture
Equipment
Universal Studios Property & Hardware Dept   **(818) 777-2784**
Horror props and monster props for rent.

Horror/Monster Make-up

See: Special Effects, Make-up/Prosthetics

Horse Drawn Carriages

See: Carriages, Horse Drawn

Horse Saddles & Tack

See Also: Western Dressing* Western Wear

Broken Horn Saddlery (626) 337-4088
1022 Leorita St, Baldwin Park, CA, 91706
10-6 Wed.- Sat. 10-5 Sun. Closed Mon & Tues. feed, tack, saddles, clothing-English & Western

C. P. Two (323) 466-8201

Caravan West Productions (661) 268-8300
35660 Jayhawker Rd, Aqua Dulce, CA, 91390
Old West, historically accurate & museum quality.
caravanwest@earthlink.net * www.caravanwest.com

Da Moor's (818) 242-2841
1532 Riverside Dr, Glendale, CA, 91201
feed, clothing, tack

The Hand Prop Room LP. (323) 931-1534
saddles, saddlebags, bedrolls, tack, feedbags

History For Hire, Inc. (818) 765-7767
Western & military saddles & tack, vintage

Sony Pictures Studios-Prop House (Off Lot) (310) 244-5999

Weaver Leather (800) 932-8371
PO Box 68, Mt Hope, OH, 44660-0068
catalog sales; leather, leather working tools, machinery. tack & saddle making/repair supplies & tools

Horse/Bull, Mechanical (Riding Simulators)

L. A. Party Works (888) 527-2789
9712 Alpaca St, S El Monte, CA, 91733
in Vancouver tel. 604-589-4101
partyworks@aol.com * www.partyworksusa.com

Horses, Horse Equipment, Livestock

See Also: Animals (Live), Services, Trainers & Wranglers* Blacksmith Shop/Foundry* Carriages, Horse Drawn* Horse Saddles & Tack* Wagons* Western Dressing* Western Wear

Caravan West Productions (661) 268-8300
35660 Jayhawker Rd, Aqua Dulce, CA, 91390
horses, rolling stock, accurate recreations back to Civil War
caravanwest@earthlink.net * www.caravanwest.com

Harry Patton Horseshoeing Supplies (626) 359-8018
223 W. Maple Ave, Monrovia, CA, 91016
blacksmith shop avail. as location; horseshoeing supplies, can locate farriers

Movin' On Livestock (661) 252-8654
20527 Soledad St, Canyon Country, CA, 91351
livestock, many wagons & stagecoaches, jail wagon too

Horticulturalists

See: Greens

Hoses

Alley Cats Studio Rentals (818) 982-9178

E.C. Prop Rentals (818) 764-2008
Stainless braid, fire, water, air, industrial

History For Hire, Inc. (818) 765-7767

LCW Props (818) 243-0707
Large Selection, Any Size, Color, Style

Rubber Supply (310) 355-1500
12600 Chadron Ave, Hawthorne, CA, 90250

Sony Pictures Studios-Prop House (Off Lot) (310) 244-5999

Universal Studios Property & Hardware Dept (818) 777-2784
All kinds of hoses; fire hoses, garden hoses, pneumatic hoses, aquarium hoses, welding hose for rent.

Hosiery

The Costume House (818) 508-9933
men's tights, seamed hose

Sony Pictures Studios-Wardrobe (310) 244-5995
alterations, call (310) 244-7260

Hospital Equipment

See Also: Ambulance/Paramedic* Anesthesia Equipment* Gurneys* Lab Equipment* Medical Equip/Furniture, Graphics/Supplies* Morgue* MRI (Magnetic Resonance Imaging)* Uniforms, Trades/Professional/Sports* Wheelchairs

A-1 Medical Integration (818) 753-0319
Medical devices for Set Decoration & Property, from minor procedures to detailed hospital units.

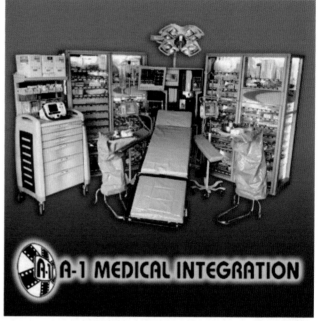

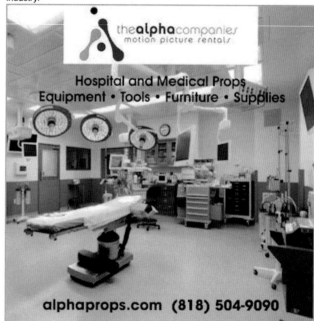

Alpha Companies - Spellman Desk Co. (818) 504-9090
period to contemporary from the #1 source for medical equipment in the industry.

Angelus Medical & Optical Co., Inc. (310) 769-6060
13007 S Western Ave, Gardena, CA, 90249
O.R., surgery tables, lights, cabinets
www.angelusmedical.com

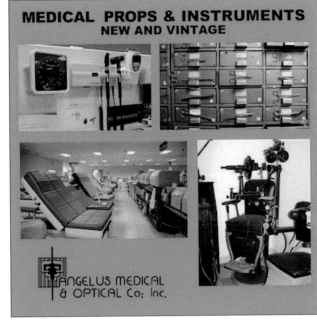

MEDICAL PROPS & INSTRUMENTS
NEW AND VINTAGE

ANGELUS MEDICAL
& OPTICAL Co, Inc.

C. P. Valley (323) 466-8201
Period to modern hospital dressing and equipment.
The Hand Prop Room LP. (323) 931-1534
past-present, gurney
History For Hire, Inc. (818) 765-7767
period
LCW Props (818) 243-0707
Whole Hospital Room Setup, Linen Carts, Gurneys, Graphics, Heart Monitors,
IV Poles
RJR Props (404) 349-7600
Exam room, hospital sets, ER/OR hospital beds, hospital curtains, hospital
furniture, hospital props and more.
Universal Studios Property & Hardware Dept (818) 777-2784
All things hospital equipment and hospital dressing for rent.

Hot Dog Carts

See: Vendor Carts & Concession Counters

Hotel, Motel, Inn, Lodge

See Also: Furniture, Tenement Tacky Motel* Prop Houses
C. P. Two (323) 466-8201
The Earl Hays Press (818) 765-0700
services the Industry only. paper plastic signage
The Hand Prop Room LP. (323) 931-1534
luggage, carts, signs, phones, electr. devices
History For Hire, Inc. (818) 765-7767
maid carts, keys, keywall, switchboards
Hollywood Studio Gallery (323) 462-1116
signage
Omega/Cinema Props (323) 466-8201
Prop Services West (818) 503-2790
RC Vintage, Inc. (818) 765-7107
40s-60s fixtures to signage, Bad Art
Sony Pictures Studios-Prop House (Off Lot) (310) 244-5999
Universal Studios Property & Hardware Dept (818) 777-2784
Hotel props & motel props; hotel keys, hotel signage, hotel pouf and more for
rent. Many multiples.

Hotspots, Wireless

See: Wi-Fi Boxes

Hub Caps

See: Automotive/Garage Equip. & Parts

Human Anatomy

See: Anatomical Charts & Models* Bones, Skulls & Skeletons*
Medical Equip/Furniture, Graphics/Supplies

Hurdles

See: Track & Field Equipment

Hypodermics

See: Medical Equip/Furniture, Graphics/Supplies

Need a

Find it here **DB** Debbies Book®

Ice & Ice Sculpture

See Also: Snow, Artificial & Real* Special Effects, Equipment &
Supplies
Carving Ice & Big on Snow (714) 224-1455
900 S Placentia Ave Ste B, Placentia, CA, 92870
You're the best at what you do & so are we. Carving Ice & Blowing Snow for
the TV & film industries for over 20 years.
info@carvingice.com * www.carvingice.com

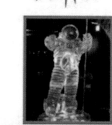

714 - 224 - 1455

Newhall Ice Company (661) 259-0893
22502 5th St, Newhall, CA, 91321
Bulk ice & dry ice, ice sculpture, machine made snow at your site
Union Ice Co. / Arctic Glacier (323) 277-1000
2970 East 50th St, Vernon, CA, 90058
Van Nuys store (888) 830-8383; 24X7, M.P. catering, cubes custom carving,
crushed ice, dry ice, real snow FX

Ice Chests

See Also: Refrigerators* Sporting Goods & Services
Alley Cats Studio Rentals (818) 982-9178
period, modern
Castex Rentals (323) 462-1468
1044 N. Cole Ave, Hollywood, CA, 90038
coolers, water coolers, coffee makers, galvanized tubs, coffee thermos,
Gatorade coolers, ice chests
service@castexrentals.com * www.castexrentals.com
The Hand Prop Room LP. (323) 931-1534
period-present
History For Hire, Inc. (818) 765-7767
period, modern, rigged
Sony Pictures Studios-Prop House (Off Lot) (310) 244-5999

Ice Cream Carts & Bikes

See: Vendor Carts & Concession Counters

Ice Cubes, Plastic

See Also: Ice Chests* Ice & Ice Sculpture
The Hand Prop Room LP. (323) 931-1534
prop ice cubes, acrylic prop ice cubes, acrylic ice cubes, prop broken glass,
prop ice blocks, silicone glass
Omega/Cinema Props (323) 466-8201
Plastic ice cubes
Universal Studios Property & Hardware Dept (818) 777-2784
Prop ice cubes/plastic ice cubes for rent.

Ice Machines

See Also: Snow, Artificial & Real* Special Effects, Equipment &
Supplies
AIR Designs (818) 768-6639
Outdoor & Indoor Machines, Ice Machines, Bar
Alley Cats Studio Rentals (818) 982-9178
C. P. Valley (323) 466-8201
Ice machines for rent
RC Vintage, Inc. (818) 765-7107
Bad Condition, restaurant ice machines, bar ice machines, industrial ice
machines for business
Universal Studios Property & Hardware Dept (818) 777-2784
Prop ice machines, commercial ice machines and restaurant ice machines for
rent.

Ice Skates

See: Sporting Goods & Services

Ice Skating Surfaces

Willy Bietak Productions, Inc (310) 576-2400
1404 3rd Street Promenade #200, Santa Monica, CA, 90401
portable, plastic, any size, luge tracks, hockey & curling rinks

Independence Day

See: Holiday Costumes* Holiday Theme Events* Pyrotechnics

Indian Clubs

See: Gymnasium & Gymnastic Equipment

Indian Rugs, Furniture, Artifacts

See: Asian Antiques, Furniture, Art & Artifacts* Native American*
Rugs* Western Dressing

Industrial Dressing

See: Break Room* Factory/Industrial* Grating, Grated Flooring,
Catwalks* Scales

Industrial Lighting

See: Lighting, Industrial

Inflatable People

See: Audience Cutouts & Stand-Ups

Insects

See: Animals (Live), Services, Trainers & Wranglers* Insects,
Artificial

Insects, Artificial

See: Animals (Live), Services, Trainers & Wranglers

Insert Stages

See: Locations, Insert Stages & Small Theatres

Instant Rust

See: Paint & Painting Supplies

Instrument Cases

See: Musical Instrument Cases

Instrument Panels

See Also: Control Boards* Control Panels/Boxes*
Electrical/Electronic Supplies & Services* Electronic Equipment
(Dressing)* Space Shuttle/Space Hardware* Spaceship Computer
Panel
E.C. Prop Rentals (818) 764-2008
industrial, stainless
LCW Props (818) 243-0707
Working, Large Selection, Period - Present
Modern Props (323) 934-3000
Fabricated contemporary electonic racks, futuristic electronic racks, consoles
and sci-fi equipment.

Instruments

See: Dentist Equipment* Lab Equipment* Medical Equip/Furniture,
Graphics/Supplies* Musical Instruments* Nautical Dressing & Props*
Science Equipment* Surveying Equipment

Insulators

Alley Cats Studio Rentals	**(818) 982-9178**
ceramic, glass, all sizes	
E.C. Prop Rentals	**(818) 764-2008**
also power pole transformers, crossbars, 16' tall poles	
History For Hire, Inc.	**(818) 765-7767**
w/posts	
Universal Studios Property & Hardware Dept	**(818) 777-2784**
Prop insulators, electrical insulators and more for rent.	

Insurance

Abacus Insurance Brokers	**(424) 214-3700**
2512 Wilshire Blvd, Santa Monica, CA, 90403	
entertainment industry products, special event coverage	
Heffernan Insurance Brokers	**(213) 622-6500**
811 Wilshire Blvd Ste 810, Los Angeles, CA, 90017	
Insurance West Corp.	**(805) 579-1900**
2450 Tapo St, Simi Valley, CA, 93063	
40 years of motion picture insurance excellence. From cameras, sound equip, cranes to post-production & pyrotechnics.	
bsulzinger@insurancewest.com * www.insurancewest.com	

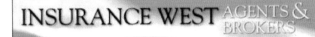

United Agencies Inc., Insurance	**(800) 800-5880**
100 N 1st Street Ste 301, Burbank, CA, 91502	
entertainment industry coverage; also in Las Vegas	
Wells Fargo Insurance Services	**(818) 464-9300**
15303 Ventura Blvd 7th Floor, Sherman Oaks, CA, 91403	
custom-designed packages for production & special events	

Intensive Care Unit / NICU (Natal Intensive Care Unit)

See Also: Hospital Equipment Medical Equip/Furniture, Graphics/Supplies* Stretchers* Emergency Room*

A-1 Medical Integration	**(818) 753-0319**
Medical devices for Set Decoration & Property, from minor procedures to detailed hospital units.	
Alpha Companies - Spellman Desk Co.	**(818) 504-9090**
The #1 source for medical equipment in the industry.	
Sony Pictures Studios-Prop House (Off Lot)	**(310) 244-5999**
neonatal ICU, nursery tubs, nursery wheels, operating room, oxygen tank	

Interactive Equipment

See: Video Games

Intercoms

C. P. Valley	**(323) 466-8201**
E.C. Prop Rentals	**(818) 764-2008**
wall-mount & free standing, apartment style & entrance keypads	

History For Hire, Inc.	**(818) 765-7767**
period	
LCW Props	**(818) 243-0707**
Large Selection, Emergency, Video, Phone	
RJR Props	**(404) 349-7600**
Prop intercoms; apartment intercoms, parking deck intercoms, security intercoms, vintage intercoms, antique intercoms	
Sony Pictures Studios-Fixtures	**(310) 244-5996**
5933 W Slauson Ave, Culver City, CA, 90230	
period to present day	
www.sonypicturesstudios.com	
Universal Studios Property & Hardware Dept	**(818) 777-2784**
Many kinds of intercoms for rent, from period to modern.	

Investigation

See: Private Investigations Research, Advisors, Consulting & Clearances*

Irish, All Things Irish

See Also: Pub Signs

Lennie Marvin Enterprises, Inc. (Prop Heaven)	**(818) 841-5882**
Irish pub signage, equip., neon, glassware & more	
NEST Studio Rentals, Inc.	**(818) 942-0339**

Ironwork & Iron Furniture

See: Bedroom Furniture & Decorations Furniture, Outdoor/Patio* Furniture, Rustic* Metalworking, Decorative* Wrought Iron Furniture & Decorations*

Jacks

See: Automotive/Garage Equip. & Parts

Jacuzzis

See: Salon & Spa Equipment Spas & Jacuzzis*

Jail Cell Dressing

Alley Cats Studio Rentals	**(818) 982-9178**
sinks, toilets, beds, tables, benches with handcuff bar	
E.C. Prop Rentals	**(818) 764-2008**
wall-mounted bunks, stools/tables, jail & prison signage, sink/toilet unit, jail bars	

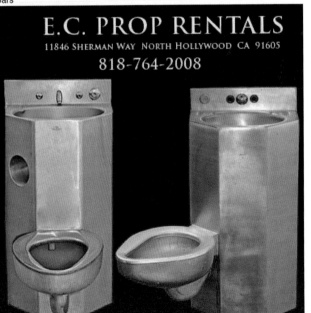

RJR Props	**(404) 349-7600**
Prison beds, prison toilets, prison phones, prison cameras, and more.	
Sony Pictures Studios-Prop House (Off Lot)	**(310) 244-5999**
prison tables, prison toilets, jail bathrooms	
Universal Studios Property & Hardware Dept	**(818) 777-2784**
Props for jail cell dressing, prison dressing for rent.	

Janitorial Supplies

See Also: Expendables* Vacuum Cleaners

Absolute Packaging (800) 567-9190
11940 Sherman Road, N. Hollywood, CA 91605
facility maintenance & safety, chemicals, liners, floor & carpet care, paper & dispenser.
www.absolutepackagingsupply.com

C. P. Valley (323) 466-8201
Janitorial bins, mops, brooms, dust pans, laundry wringers, mop buckets, scrub brushes, and supplies.

E.C. Prop Rentals (818) 764-2008
carts, cleaning tools & supplies & clutter

The Hand Prop Room LP. (323) 931-1534
complete setups, carts, fully outfitted

History For Hire, Inc. (818) 765-7767
vintage

LCW Props (818) 243-0707
Janitor Carts, Tools, Mops

Sony Pictures Studios-Prop House (Off Lot) (310) 244-5999
janitorial equipment, janitorial carts, laundry baskets, janitorial cleaning supplies

Universal Studios Property & Hardware Dept (818) 777-2784
Janitor props; janitor carts, housekeeping carts and utility carts for rent.

Japanese Antiques

See: Asian Antiques, Furniture, Art & Artifacts

Jet Skis

See: Boats & Water Sport Vehicles* Sporting Goods & Services

Jewelry Display Cases

See: Display Cases, Racks & Fixtures (Store)

Jewelry Store

C. P. Valley (323) 466-8201
The Hand Prop Room LP. (323) 931-1534
RC Vintage, Inc. (818) 765-7107
jewelry display cases stocked with jewelry see our Web Page

Jewelry, Costume

See Also: Bling* Goth/Punk/Bondage/Fetish/Erotica Etc.* Wardrobe, Accessories

10 Karat Rentals (818) 635-4124
7100 Tujunga (At R.C. Vintage), N. Hollywood, CA 91605
10karatrentals@gmail.com

Catherine Nash's Closet (520) 620-6613
1102 W. Huron St, Tucson, AZ, 85745
wholesale to Industry only: costume jewelry 1860s-1970s

The Costume House (818) 508-9933
1900s to 1980s, necklaces, pins, earrings, bracelets

The Hand Prop Room LP. (323) 931-1534
costume jewelry, vintage costume jewelry, fake pearls, pearl necklaces, costume jewelry pins, rhinestone jewelry, rhinestone broaches

Hollywood Cinema Arts, Inc. (818) 504-7333
For costume jewelry that looks real, situated in a completely rentable jewelry store.

Palace Costume & Prop Co. (323) 651-5458
11th to 20th C. & ethnic

Playclothes (818) 557-8447
3100 W Magnolia Blvd, Burbank, CA, 91505
Men & Women's-1940s-1980s w/ original displays

RC Vintage, Inc. (818) 765-7107
Large Selection of Costume Jewelry!

Repeat Performance (323) 938-0609
Web Based Business
whitneyr@artdimensionsonline.com * www.rpvintage.com

Sony Pictures Studios-Prop House (Off Lot) (310) 244-5999
necklaces, bracelets, earrings, crystal drops, crystal chains, african jewelry, brooch pins, cameo, change purse, and more

Sony Pictures Studios-Wardrobe (310) 244-5995
alterations, call (310) 244-7260

Universal Studios Costume Dept (818) 777-2722
Rental, mfg., & alterations

Universal Studios Property & Hardware Dept (818) 777-2784
Lots of costume jewelry/prop jewelry for rent.

Warner Bros. Studios Costume Dept (818) 954-1297
Necklaces, Bracelets, Earrings, Rings, Beads, Cuffs, Vintage, Chokers, Tiaras, Clips

Western Costume Co. (818) 760-0900

Jewelry, Fine/Reproduction

See Also: Bling* Gems, Minerals & Crystals* Jewelry, Costume* Prop Design & Manufacturing

10 Karat Rentals (818) 635-4124
7100 Tujunga (At R.C. Vintage), N. Hollywood, CA 91605
10karatrentals@gmail.com

1928 Jewelry Company (818) 841-1928
3000 W. Empire Ave, Burbank, CA, 91504
fashion jewelry, custom antiq. reprod., open to public

The Costume House (818) 508-9933
reproductions

The Hand Prop Room LP. (323) 931-1534
designer watches, reproduction designer jewelry, reproduction designer diamond necklaces, velvet jewelry boxes

Harry Winston Jewelers (310) 271-8554
310 N Rodeo Dr, Beverly Hills, CA, 90210
also salons in NY, Europe, Japan

L. Wilmington & Co. (213) 624-8314
611 Wilshire Blvd, #1116, Los Angeles, CA, 90017
Jewelry mfg, numerous Industry credits; custom designs, able to copy most anything, military/championship/class rings
lwilco@pacbell.net * www.lwilmington.com

Martin Katz, Ltd (310) 276-7200
9540 Brighton Way, Beverly Hills, CA, 90210
ready-made, custom, estate & fine jewelry, will design to suit, all pieces made in Paris

Regency Jewelry Co., Inc. (323) 655-2573
8129 W 3rd St, Los Angeles, CA, 90048
Jewelry & jewelry repair

Sword & Stone (818) 562-6548
custom-made, silver, gold, bronze, gem cutting

Judaica

See: Religious Articles

Judge/Jury Props

See: Courtroom Furniture & Dressing

Judging Systems

See: Game Show Electronics & Equipment* Scoreboards & Scoring Systems

Juggling

See: Carnival Dressing/Supplies* Clowns* Magicians & Props, Supplies, Dressing* Toys & Games

Jukeboxes, Music/Dance Machines

See Also: Bars, Nightclubs, Barware & Dressing

AIR Designs (818) 768-6639
40's-Now, Table & Floor Models

C. P. Two (323) 466-8201
Jukeboxes from many time periods.

The Hand Prop Room LP. (323) 931-1534
floor, tabletop

RC Vintage, Inc. (818) 765-7107
Working/Nonworking 40s-present/ CD Jukebox, variety, vintage jukeboxes

Sony Pictures Studios-Prop House (Off Lot) (310) 244-5999

Jungle Dressing

See Also: Animals (Live), Services, Trainers & Wranglers* Greens* Tikis & Tropical Dressing

Benson's Tropical Sea Imports (714) 841-3399
7442 Vincent Cir, Huntington Beach, CA 92648
masks, spears, carvings, bamboo & thatching
sales@bensonsimport.com * www.bensonsimport.com

Bob Gail Special Events (310) 202-5200
Take your guests on a jungle safari or create a zoo with our wide variety of Jungle and Animal Props!

History For Hire, Inc. (818) 765-7767

Oceanic Arts (562) 698-6960
thatch & hut roofing, bamboo, alligators, birds, shields, masks

Jungle Gym

See: Playground Equipment

Jungle Themed Parties

See: Events, Decorations, Supplies & Services* Events, Design/Planning/Production* Greens* Jungle Dressing* Taxidermy, Hides/Heads/Skeletons* Themed Environment Construction* Tikis & Tropical Dressing* Travel (City/Country) Themed Events

Junk Removal

See: Sanitation, Waste Disposal

Junkyard

See: Architectural Pieces & Artifacts Salvage, Rubble, Clutter & Trash (Prop)*

Kayaks

See: Boats & Water Sport Vehicles

Key Boxes & Racks

AIR Designs	**(818) 768-6639**
Valet & Industrial	
E.C. Prop Rentals	**(818) 764-2008**
Wall-Mounted Boxes & Wall-Mounted Boards with Keys, Valet Stands	
LCW Props	**(818) 243-0707**
Valet Stands, Locking Key Boxes	
Universal Studios Property & Hardware Dept	**(818) 777-2784**
Key boxes, key racks, valet boxes and valet racks for rent.	

Keyboards

See: Pianos & Keyboard Instruments

Keying Backgrounds

See: Fabrics Paint & Painting Supplies*

Keys & Locks

See Also: Lockers

Antrim's Security Co.	**(626) 795-8661**
2051 E. Foothill Blvd., Pasadena, CA, 91107	
Door Keyper, Inc.	**(626) 794-6940**
942 N Amelia Ave, San Dimas, CA, 91773	
large master key systems	
History For Hire, Inc.	**(818) 765-7767**
Keedex Lock Museum	**(714) 993-4300**
510 Cameron St, Placentia, CA, 92870	
By Appt. Only, Mon-Thurs, lock & key museum, extensive collection for research	
LCW Props	**(818) 243-0707**
Selection For Hardware Store, Hotel, Digital Locks, Safes	
Lockmasters Security Institute	**(866) 574-8724**
200 John C Watts Dr, Nicholasville, KY, 40356	
Harry C. Miller lock collection (museum), items dating to 1300s, research source for covert entry methods/lock drilling	
Sony Pictures Studios-Prop House (Off Lot)	**(310) 244-5999**
key holders and keys, combination locks	
Sword & Stone	**(818) 562-6548**
Universal Studios Property & Hardware Dept	**(818) 777-2784**
Many kinds of keys and locks for rent.	

Kids

See: Children's & Baby Clothing Children/Baby Accessories & Bedroom* Game Tables & Equipment* Hobby & Craft Supplies* Sporting Goods & Services* Sportswear* Toys & Games* Video Games*

Kilims

See: Rugs

Kiosks

See Also: Magazines & Magazine/Newspaper Racks Newspapers (Prop)* Newsstands (Prop)*

AIR Designs	**(818) 768-6639**
Newspaper, Food, Mall, Coffee, Flower	
Alley Cats Studio Rentals	**(818) 982-9178**
new, green wood, dressed, newspaper kiosk	
E.C. Prop Rentals	**(818) 764-2008**
park/college courtyard style kiosks	
LCW Props	**(818) 243-0707**
Large & Small. Mall, Merchandise, Airport Kiosks, Information, Video Kiosks	
Lennie Marvin Enterprises, Inc. (Prop Heaven)	**(818) 841-5882**
mall directory, mall vending, phone, etc.	
Modern Props	**(323) 934-3000**
ATM, airport or bus terminal, e-ticket, security entry, shopping mall directory, fabricate universal kiosk	
RC Vintage, Inc.	**(818) 765-7107**
ticket counters, mini bars, ticket kiosks, food kiosks, beverage kiosks, nameless kiosks, with chair sets, public buffet lines	

Kitchen Appliances

See: Appliances Cooking Equipment* Kitchen Dressing* Refrigerators* Stoves*

Kitchen Counters & Cabinets

C. P. Two	**(323) 466-8201**
The Kitchen Store	**(310) 839-5215**
6322 W Slauson Ave, Culver City, CA, 90230	
Our Studio Division provides expedited delivery of residential and commercial building materials for your design needs.	
www.studiosupplier.com	
RC Vintage, Inc.	**(818) 765-7107**
Kitchen Counters and Stoves and Fridges	
The ReUse People	**(818) 244-5635**
3015 Dolores St, Los Angeles, CA, 90065	
Contemporary, vintage and antique.	
JefCockerell@TheReUsePeople.org * www.TheReUsePeople.org	
Warner Bros. Studios Cabinet & Furniture Shop	**(818) 954-1339**
Custom manufacturing and installation of cabinets, built-ins countertops. Wood & laminate finishes.	

Kitchen Dressing

See Also: Appliances Cooking Equipment* Food, Artificial Food* Glassware/Dishes* Linens, Household*

C. P. Two	**(323) 466-8201**
The Hand Prop Room LP.	**(323) 931-1534**
period-present	
History For Hire, Inc.	**(818) 765-7767**
period	
Hollywood Studio Gallery	**(323) 462-1116**
wall dressing only	
LCW Props	**(818) 243-0707**
Large Quantity, Appliances, Pots & Pans, Outdoor Kitchen BBQ, Utensils	
Modern Props	**(323) 934-3000**
contemporary/futuristic, appliances, dishes & more	
Modern-Aire Ventilating Corp.	**(818) 765-9870**
7319 Lankershim Blvd, N Hollywood, CA, 91605	
Range hoods only, many styles/materials	
NEST Studio Rentals, Inc.	**(818) 942-0339**
household, large sel., gourmet to family	
Ob-jects	**(818) 351-4200**
dressing for gourmet kitchen, countertops/appl "Kitchenaid"	
Omega/Cinema Props	**(323) 466-8201**
Prop Services West	**(818) 503-2790**
RC Vintage, Inc.	**(818) 765-7107**
40s, 50s & 60s Flatware,and Wall Art, Blenders, Toasters, Sink Units Cookie Jars!	
Sony Pictures Studios-Prop House (Off Lot)	**(310) 244-5999**
large bowls, bread plates, butter plates, butter dishes w cover, cake plates, centerpieces, coffee server, dessert bowls	
Universal Studios Property & Hardware Dept	**(818) 777-2784**
All kinds of kitchen props and kitchen dressing for rent.	
Warner Bros. Studios Property Department	**(818) 954-2181**
Appliances, faux food, linens, table dressing, cooking equipment, toasters, kitchen smalls, table linens	
ZG04 DECOR	**(818) 853-8040**
Dishes, Cookware, Flatware	

Kites

See: Hobby & Craft Supplies Sporting Goods & Services* Toys & Games* Windsocks*

Kludge Dressing

See: Control Panels/Boxes Foam* Futuristic Furniture, Props, Decorations* Lab Equipment* Pallets* Plastics, Materials & Fabrication* Science Equipment*

Knick-knacks (Nick-nacks)

See: Prop Houses Decorative Accessories*

Knickers

See Also: Wardrobe, Antique/Historical
The Costume House (818) 508-9933
colonial & 1930s golfing
Sony Pictures Studios-Wardrobe (310) 244-5995
alterations, call (310) 244-7260
Western Costume Co. (818) 760-0900

Knitting Supplies

See: Costume/Wardrobe/Sewing Supplies

Knives

See Also: Kitchen Dressing Swords & Swordplay* Weaponry,
Historical* Weaponry, Medieval* Weapons*
Dapper Cadaver/Creatures & Cultures (818) 771-0818
Plastic knives and foam knives. Machetes, cleavers, etc. More fake weapons.
Emerson Knives (310) 539-5633
1234 254th St., Harbor City, CA 90710
Emerson Knives are the only choice of Elite Military and U.S. Covert Units.
They are truly, "Famous In the Worst Places"
eknives@aol.com * www.emersonknives.com

The Hand Prop Room LP. (323) 931-1534
period-present, custom manufacturing
History For Hire, Inc. (818) 765-7767
period, all types
Prop Services West (818) 503-2790
Sony Pictures Studios-Prop House (Off Lot) (310) 244-5999
Sword & Stone (818) 562-6548
custom-made swords, knives & axes

Lab Equipment

See Also: Cryogenic Equipment Electron Microscope* Hospital
Equipment* Scales* Science Equipment*
A-1 Medical Integration (818) 753-0319
Medical devices for Set Decoration & Property, from minor procedures to
detailed hospital units. Various lab equipment
Alpha Companies - Spellman Desk Co. (818) 504-9090
Complete hi-end lab dressing: tables, clean room, microscopes, refrigeration,
fume hoods, cryogenics, analyzers and more

C. P. Valley (323) 466-8201
Lab equipment, machines, glassware, and scales.
Dapper Cadaver/Creatures & Cultures (818) 771-0818
Period to modern. Laboratory glassware, specimen jars, lab instruments &
scientific models. Forensic to high school lab.
E.C. Prop Rentals (818) 764-2008
stainless tables, racks & carts
The Hand Prop Room LP. (323) 931-1534
beakers, Bunson burners, beaker racks, glass jars, formaldehyde jars,
formaldehyde jars with specimens, lab tools, lab trays, lab utensils
History For Hire, Inc. (818) 765-7767
period
Kinemetrics, Inc. (626) 795-2220
222 Vista Ave, Pasadena, CA, 91107
mfr. seismic equip., will rent/repair, equip & software

LCW Props (818) 243-0707
Our Specialty, Glassware, Equipment, DNA, Analyzers, Desks, Cryogenic, Any Kind

Modern Props (323) 934-3000
flumed hooded cabinets on casters, contemporary/futuristic-beakers to microscopes, petri dishes, glass jars, vials, vial holders
Universal Studios Property & Hardware Dept (818) 777-2784
Prop lab equipment for rent.

Lab Wear

See: Protective Apparel

Labels

See: Graphics, Digital & Large Format Printing Product Labels*

Laces & Trims

See: Costume/Wardrobe/Sewing Supplies

Ladders

See Also: Scaffolding/Lighting Towers
Alley Cats Studio Rentals (818) 982-9178
wood, metal, fire escape
C. P. Valley (323) 466-8201
prop ladders
Castex Rentals (323) 462-1468
1044 N. Cole Ave, Hollywood, CA, 90038
Fiberglass double sided "A" frame ladders, fiberglass extension ladders
service@castexrentals.com * www.castexrentals.com
E.C. Prop Rentals (818) 764-2008
Rooftop Access Ladders, Wood Ladders, Metal Ladders, A-Frame Ladders, Extension Ladders, Warehouse Ladders, Rolling Ladders.
LCW Props (818) 243-0707
Rolling Industrial, Step Ladders, Construction, Extension
Sony Pictures Studios-Prop House (Off Lot) (310) 244-5999
Universal Studios Property & Hardware Dept (818) 777-2784
All kinds of ladders for all your laddering needs.

Laminates

See: Paneling, Veneers & Laminates

Laminating & Mounting

See Also: Art & Picture Framing Services
Art, Signs & Graphics (818) 503-7997
6939 Farmdale Ave, N Hollywood, CA, 91605
props, banners, vinyl graphics, vehicle graphics, 3D router cut letters & logos
jessee@artsignsandgraphics.com * www.artsignsandgraphics.com
Beyond Image Graphics (818) 547-0899
1853 Dana St, Glendale, CA, 91201
rafi@beyondimagegraphics.com * www.beyondimagegraphics.com

D'ziner Sign Co. (323) 467-4467
801 Seward Street, Los Angeles, CA 90038
various backgrounds & laminating material up to 60" wide
sales@dzinersign.com * www.dzinersign.com
Dennis Bolton Enterprises, Inc. (818) 982-1800
7285 Coldwater Cyn Ave, N.Hollywood, CA, 91605
Warner Bros. Design Studio Scenic Art & Sign Shop (818) 954-1815
4000 Warner Blvd, Burbank, CA, 91522
graphic design and production studio for signs & scenic art; digital printing to hand-painted
wbsigns@warnerbros.com * www.wbsignandscenic.com

Lamp Posts & Street Lights

See Also: Billboards & Billboard Lights* Bulkhead Lights* China Hat Lights* Lanterns* Light Fixtures* Light Fixtures, Period* Neon Lights & Signs* Searchlights/Skytrackers, Architectural Lights* Street Dressing* Street Dressing, Exterior Signs

AIR Designs (818) 768-6639
Street, Parking Lot, Traffic, Acorn, Cobras, Railroad

Alley Cats Studio Rentals (818) 982-9178
extra tall cobra head lights, acorn lights, billboard lights, Victorian, parking lot lamp posts

E.C. Prop Rentals (818) 764-2008
alum. cobra head poles, candy cane china hats, acorn, mushroom top

E.C. PROP RENTALS
11846 SHERMAN WAY NORTH HOLLYWOOD CA 91605
818-764-2008

Green Set, Inc. (818) 764-1231
party lights & lot lights, street lamp posts, and street light sets. high end to period to modern, for any street

Jackson Shrub Supply, Inc. (818) 982-0100
Victorian lamp posts, single globe lamp posts, multiple globe lamp posts, poles, street lamps

LCW Props (818) 243-0707
Period - Present, Mercury Vapors, Cobra Heads

Lennie Marvin Enterprises, Inc. (Prop Heaven) (818) 841-5882
per-mod., practical lamp posts, traffic lights, large qty avail.

Need a

Find it here **DB** Debbies Book®

Main Street Lighting (330) 723-4431
1080 Industrial Pkwy, Medina, OH, 44256
Nostalgic, ornamental-posts, fixtures, bollards, & brackets
tracyr@mainstreetlighting.com * www.mainstreetlighting.com

MAIN STREET · LIGHTING, INC. ·
Nostalgic, Lightweight, Fiberglass and Aluminum Lamp Posts and Luminaires
Accessories & Bollards

Omega/Cinema Props (323) 466-8201
Lamp posts and street lights

RC Vintage, Inc. (818) 765-7107
traditional lamp posts to wharf dock lights

Sony Pictures Studios-Prop House (Off Lot) (310) 244-5999
lamp posts

Universal Studios Property & Hardware Dept (818) 777-2784
Prop street lamps and street light dressing from many periods and styles for rent.

Lamp Shades

See Also: China Hat Lights* Lamps

The Hand Prop Room LP. (323) 931-1534

LCW Props (818) 243-0707
futuristic, ultra modern, period

Prop Services West (818) 503-2790

Sony Pictures Studios-Prop House (Off Lot) (310) 244-5999

Warner Bros. Studios Property Department (818) 954-2181
Assorted lamp shades, fabric, metal, glass, wood shades

Lamps

See Also: Lamp Posts & Street Lights* Lamp Shades* Lanterns* Light Fixtures* Restaurant Table Lamps

Badia Design, Inc. (818) 762-0130
5420 Vineland Ave, N. Hollywood, CA, 91601
brass chandelier, Moroccan hanging lamps, Henna lamps, metal and bones lamps, copper lamps, brass lamps
info@badiadesign.com * www.badiadesign.com

Bassman-Blaine (213) 748-5909
1933 S. Broadway, #1005, Los Angeles, CA 90007
Table & floor lamps, chandeliers, pendants & more, from Arteriors, NOIR/cFc, World's Away, & Gallery Designs.
lashowroom@bassman-blaine.com * www.bassmanblainelamart.com

Blueprint Furniture (310) 657-4315
8600 Pico Blvd. Los Angeles, CA 90035
Modern furniture lighting accessories early classic bauhaus mid-century contemporary design. Good studio rental history.
www.blueprintfurniture.com

Bridge Furniture & Props Los Angeles (818) 433-7100
We carry modern & traditional furniture, lighting, accessories, cleared art,& rugs. Items are online for easy shopping.

Castle Antiques & Design　　　　　　(855) 765-5800
11924 Vose St, N Hollywood, CA, 91605
Lamps of many kinds over different time periods for rent or purchase.
info@castleantiques.net * www.castleprophouse.com

Dozar Office Furnishings　　　　　　(310) 559-9292
9937 Jefferson Blvd, Culver City, CA, 90232
Rentals X22. Goose neck table lamps, desk lamps, floor lamps, modern lamps,
lamp shades, adjustable lamps & more.
dozarrents@aol.com * www.dozarrents.com

Faux Library Studio Props, Inc.　　　(818) 765-0096
variety of desk and floor lamps, vintage floor lamps, vintage table lamps, retro
floor lamps, many shapes sizes and colors

FormDecor, Inc.　　　　　　　　　　(310) 558-2582
America's largest event rental supplier of 20th Century furniture and
accessories for Modern and Mid-Century styles.

Fortune Trading Co & Import Bazaar　(323) 222-6287
483 Gin Ling Way (Old Chinatown), Los Angeles, CA, 90012
1000s of copies of many styles of paper lanterns, masks. Costumes, lions,
dragons, gongs, scrolls, Oriental gift items
fortunetradingco@gmail.com

Galerie Sommerlath - French 50s 60s　(310) 838-0102
9608 Venice Blvd, Culver City, CA, 90232
10,000 sq ft Mid-Century - 80s furniture, lighting & accessories
info@french50s60s.com * http://www.galeriesommerlath.com

The Hand Prop Room LP.　　　　　　(323) 931-1534
all periods

Hollywood Cinema Arts, Inc.　　　　(818) 504-7333
From standard lamps to one of a kind lamps. HCA has them all.

Little Bohemia Rentals　　　　　　　(818) 853-7506
11940 Sherman Rd, N Hollywood, CA, 91605
Vintage and Contemporary lighting. Table and floor lamps.
sales@wearelittlebohemia.com * www.wearelittlebohemia.com

Lux Lounge EFR　　　　　　　　　　(888) 247-4411
106 1/2 Judge John Aiso St #318, Los Angeles, CA, 90012
Event Lamps and Decorations.
info@luxloungeefr.com * www.luxloungeefr.com

MidcenturyLA　　　　　　　　　　　(818) 509-3050
5333 Cahuenga Blvd, N. Hollywood, CA, 91601
Huge selection of vintage lamps: ceramic, glass, brass, wide array of colors
and styles. Rental & purchases.
midcenturyla@midcenturyla.com * www.midcenturyla.com

Modern Props　　　　　　　　　　　(323) 934-3000
contemporary/futuristic, wall sconces and floor, sculptural lamps.

Modernica Props　　　　　　　　　　(323) 664-2322
floor & table styles from the 20th century

NEST Studio Rentals, Inc.　　　　　(818) 942-0339
large sel. of contemp. shaded pairs, desk & floor lamps: many cleared items

Ob-jects　　　　　　　　　　　　　(818) 351-4200
designer/contemporary/traditional

Omega/Cinema Props　　　　　　　(323) 466-8201
Decorative vintage, antique, and historical to modern sconces.

Pasadena Antiques & Design　　　　(626) 389-3938
330 S. Fair Oaks Avenue, Pasadena, CA 91105
Lamps , Sconces & Chandeliers.
roy@antiquesofpasadena.com * www.antiquesofpasadena.com

Prop Services West　　　　　　　　(818) 503-2790

RC Vintage, Inc.　　　　　　　　　(818) 765-7107
40s, 50s & 60s Large selection of lighting. Desk,Table Floor, Sconces, Check
web site ..rcvintage.com

ShopWildThings　　　　　　　　　　(928) 855-6075
2880 Sweetwater Ave, Lake Havasu City, AZ, 86406
Event Decor, Beaded Curtains, Chain Curtains, String Curtains & Columns,
Crystal Columns. Reliable service & delivery.
help@shopwildthings.com * www.shopwildthings.com

Sony Pictures Studios-Fixtures　　　(310) 244-5996
5933 W Slauson Ave, Culver City, CA, 90230
period to present day, all styles,wall,floor
www.sonypicturesstudios.com

Sony Pictures Studios-Prop House (Off Lot)　(310) 244-5999
gothic style lamp, hurricane lamp, lanterns, light bulb, light wheel, night light,
novelty lamp, oil lamp, and MORE

Taylor Creative Inc.　　　　　　　　(888) 245-4044
We offer a variety of table lamps, floor lamps, and pendant lighting in addition
to our light up furniture collections.

Universal Studios Property & Hardware Dept　(818) 777-2784
Prop lamps, sconces and lamp shades for rent.

Warner Bros. Studios Property Department　(818) 954-2181
Table, desk, standing, floor, hanging, metal, wood, ornate, overhead, eclectic

Landscaping/Plants

See: Greens

Lanterns

See Also: Candelabras* Candles* Lamps

Badia Design, Inc.　　　　　　　　(818) 762-0130
5420 Vineland Ave, N. Hollywood, CA, 91601
Moroccan hanging lanterns, Henna lanterns, metal and bones lanterns, copper
lanterns, brass lanterns,
info@badiadesign.com * www.badiadesign.com

C. P. Valley　　　　　　　　　　　(323) 466-8201
Barn lanterns, nautical lanterns, camping lanterns

Dapper Cadaver/Creatures & Cultures　(818) 771-0818
Vintage & decorative inspired lanterns.

E.C. Prop Rentals　　　　　　　　　(818) 764-2008
Kerosene Lanterns, Battery Operated Lanterns, Construction Lanterns, Vintage
'Ball-Shaped' Lanterns.

FormDecor, Inc.　　　　　　　　　　(310) 558-2582
America's largest event rental supplier of 20th Century furniture and
accessories for Modern and Mid-Century styles.

Fortune Trading Co & Import Bazaar　(323) 222-6287
483 Gin Ling Way (Old Chinatown), Los Angeles, CA, 90012
1000s of copies of many styles of paper lanterns, masks. Costumes, lions,
dragons, gongs, scrolls, Oriental gift items
fortunetradingco@gmail.com

The Hand Prop Room LP.　　　　　　(323) 931-1534
nautical, railroad, barns, camping, gas, kerosene, rigged

History For Hire, Inc.　　　　　　　(818) 765-7767
multiples, vintage

LCW Props　　　　　　　　　　　　(818) 243-0707
Large Selection Of Lighting

Omega/Cinema Props　　　　　　　(323) 466-8201

Sony Pictures Studios-Fixtures　　　(310) 244-5996
5933 W Slauson Ave, Culver City, CA, 90230
period to present day
www.sonypicturesstudios.com

Universal Studios Property & Hardware Dept　(818) 777-2784
Lanterns from different styles, countries, and periods for rent.

Warner Bros. Studios Property Department　(818) 954-2181
Table lanterns, hanging lanterns, camping lanterns, metal lanterns, outdoor
lanterns, Asian lanterns

Large Format Printing

See: Graphics, Digital & Large Format Printing

Large Screen Displays

See: Video Equipment

Las Vegas Themed Parties

See: Events, Decorations, Supplies & Services* Events,
Design/Planning/Production* Gambling Equipment* Game Tables &
Equipment* Travel (City/Country) Themed Events

Lasers

See: Lab Equipment* Light Fixtures* Lighting & Sound,
Concert/Theatrical/DJ/VJ* Special Effects, Lighting & Lasers*
Ultraviolet Products

Latex Make-up

See: Make-up & Hair, Supplies & Services* Special Effects,
Make-up/Prosthetics

Lattices

See: Garden/Patio* Greens

Laundromat

See: Dry Cleaners (Dressing)* Laundry Carts* Vending Machines*
Washing Machines/Dryers

Laundry Carts

C. P. Valley　　　　　　　　　　　(323) 466-8201
Laundry carts, white canvas laundry carts

E.C. Prop Rentals　　　　　　　　　(818) 764-2008
canvas, vinyl, multiple sizes

History For Hire, Inc.　　　　　　　(818) 765-7767
canvas

Lava Lamps

See: Lamps* Light Fixtures* Light Fixtures, Period

Law Books

See: Books, Real/Hollow & Faux Books* Courtroom Furniture & Dressing* Prop Houses

Lawn Chairs

See: Furniture, Outdoor/Patio

Lawn Mowers

Alley Cats Studio Rentals	**(818) 982-9178**
gas, pushers, edgers	
C. P. Valley	**(323) 466-8201**
E.C. Prop Rentals	**(818) 764-2008**
gas, weed whackers	
The Hand Prop Room LP.	**(323) 931-1534**
History For Hire, Inc.	**(818) 765-7767**
push & power	
Sony Pictures Studios-Prop House (Off Lot)	**(310) 244-5999**
Universal Studios Property & Hardware Dept	**(818) 777-2784**
Various lawn mowers for rent.	

Layout Board

See: Expendables* Floor, Ground & Surface Protection

Leather (Clothing, Accessories, Materials)

See Also: Fabrics* Fur Garments* Fur, Artificial & Real* Native American* Western Wear

gbb Custom Leather **(818) 768-1135**
11754 Roscoe Blvd, Studio 5, Sun Valley, CA, 91352
Specializing in Film & Television prop & wardrobe pieces. Also, doubles, back-ups; fast turnaround.

The Hide House **(800) 453-2847**
595 Monroe St, Napa, CA 94995
all type leathers, findings, tools, thread, no finished items, "hair on" rugs, will rent for set dressing

Montana Leather Company **(800) 527-0227**
2015 1st Ave, N Billings, MT, 59101
catalog sales; footwear components & leathers

Sword & Stone **(818) 562-6548**
custom made wardrobe, masks, accessories

Western Costume Co. **(818) 760-0900**

Leaves

See: Flowers, Dried* Greens

Lecterns

See: Podiums & Lecterns

LED's, LED Color Changers

See: Lighting, LED, Fiber Optic & Specialty

Legal Documents

See: Courtroom Furniture & Dressing* Research, Advisors, Consulting & Clearances

Leis

See: Events, Decorations, Supplies & Services* Tikis & Tropical Dressing

Lemonade Fountains

See: Soda Fountain Dressing

Lettering

See: Calligraphy* Graphics, Digital & Large Format Printing* Signs

Letters

See: Graphics, Digital & Large Format Printing* Mail & Mail Room* Paperwork, Documents & Letters, Office* Signs

Library Books

See: Books, Real/Hollow & Faux Books* Prop Houses* Research, Advisors, Consulting & Clearances* Search Tools, Directories, Libraries

License Plates

AIR Designs **(818) 768-6639**
California & Out-of-State, Metal & Plastic
Alley Cats Studio Rentals **(818) 982-9178**
variety state and era, metal
C. P. Valley **(323) 466-8201**
The Earl Hays Press **(818) 765-0700**
services the Industry only. paper, plastic or metal
The Hand Prop Room LP. **(323) 931-1534**
made-to-order
HPR Graphics **(323) 556-2694**
5674 Venice Blvd, Los Angeles, CA, 90019
Government license plates, metal plates, vacuum forming, foreign license plates, commercial license plates, and more.
hprcan@earthlink.net * www.hprgraphics.net
LCW Props **(818) 243-0707**
Period - Present
Sony Pictures Studios-Prop House (Off Lot) **(310) 244-5999**
cardboard set license plates, metal set license plates, license plate tags
Universal Studios Property & Hardware Dept **(818) 777-2784**
License plate rentals from many locations, time periods, and vehicles.

Life Vests, Jackets & Rings

See: Airport Dressing & Hangars* Nautical Dressing & Props

Lifts

See: Construction Site Equipment* Ladders* Scaffolding/Lighting Towers

Light Bulbs

See: Candelabras* Candles* Chandeliers* Chase Lights* Egg Crate Bottom Fluorescents* Expendables* Gym Lights* Lamp Posts & Street Lights* Lamp Shades* Lamps* Lanterns* Light Fixtures* Light Fixtures, Period* Light Fixtures, South Seas* Light Strings* Lighting & Sound, Concert/Theatrical/DJ/VJ* Lighting, Industrial* Lighting, LED, Fiber Optic & Specialty* Neon Lights & Signs* Special Effects, Lighting & Lasers* Stage Lighting, Film/Video/TV* Ultraviolet Products

Light Fixtures

See Also: Billboards & Billboard Lights* Bulkhead Lights* Caged Vapor Proof Lights* Candelabras* Candles* Chandeliers* Chase Lights* China Hat Lights* Egg Crate Bottom Fluorescents* Gym Lights* Lamp Posts & Street Lights* Lamp Shades* Lamps* Lanterns* Light Fixtures, Period* Light Fixtures, South Seas* Light Strings* Lighting & Sound, Concert/Theatrical/DJ/VJ* Lighting Control Boards* Lighting, Industrial* Lighting, LED, Fiber Optic & Specialty* Mirror Balls/Drivers* Neon Lights & Signs* Restaurant Table Lamps* Searchlights/Skytrackers, Architectural Lights* Special Effects, Lighting & Lasers* Stage Lighting, Film/Video/TV* Ultraviolet Products

AIR Designs **(818) 768-6639**
China Hats, Warehouse Lights, Restaurant Lights, Pendants
Alley Cats Studio Rentals **(818) 982-9178**
china hats & vapor lights, cobra lights, fluorescents, street light poles
Alpha Companies - Spellman Desk Co. **(818) 504-9090**
Desk Lamps, Table Lamps, Floor Lamps, Office Lighting
Antiquarian Traders **(310) 247-3900**
4851 S. Alameda Street, Los Angeles, CA 90048
Varied collection of American and European chandeliers, sconces, torchieres crystal and bronze.
antiques@antiquariantraders.com * www.antiquariantraders.com
Architectural Lighting & Design **(213) 742-8800**
1933 S. Broadway, Ste 1204, Los Angeles, CA, 90007
Open to the Trade only
Badia Design, Inc. **(818) 762-0130**
5420 Vineland Ave, N. Hollywood, CA, 91601
Moroccan Lighting Fixtures are elegantly designed from a combination of brass, metal, copper, glass and tin.
info@badiadesign.com * www.badiadesign.com
Bridge Furniture & Props Los Angeles **(818) 433-7100**
We carry modern & traditional furniture, lighting, accessories, cleared art,& rugs. Items are online for easy shopping.
Castle Antiques & Design **(855) 765-5800**
11924 Vose St, N Hollywood, CA, 91605
Light fixtures of many periods for rent or purchase.
info@castleantiques.net * www.castleprophouse.com

Davis Fluorescent Lighting   (310) 836-4860
8530 Venice Blvd (in rear), Los Angeles, CA, 90034
Fluorescent & HID light fixtures, fluorescent bulbs/fluorescent light bulbs for indoor/outdoor, rentals and purchases.
davisfluorescent@sbcglobal.net

E.C. Prop Rentals   (818) 764-2008
fluorescents, wall sconces, china hats, ext. lighting, industrial

Flix FX Inc.   (818) 765-3549
7327 Lankershim Blvd #4, N Hollywood, CA, 91605
Custom light fixture fabrication
info@flixfx.com * www.flixfx.com

FormDecor, Inc.   (310) 558-2582
America's largest event rental supplier of 20th Century furniture and accessories for Modern and Mid-Century styles.

LCW Props   (818) 243-0707
Large Selection, Industrial, Residential, Commercial

Modern Props   (323) 934-3000
Contemporary lighting and futuristic lighting, chandeliers to lamps

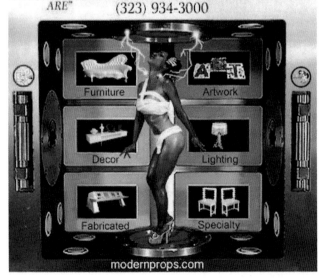

NEST Studio Rentals, Inc.   (818) 942-0339
wall sconces, contemp. hanging styles

Ob-jects   (818) 351-4200
contemporary/traditional designer sconces

Omega/Cinema Props   (323) 466-8201

Prop Services West   (818) 503-2790

Rapport International Furniture   (323) 930-1500
435 N La Brea Ave, Los Angeles, CA, 90036
Dozens of elegant, contemporary, modern and designer lighting fixtures, including floor lamps and pendants.
rapport@rapportusa.com * www.rapportfurniture.com

RC Vintage, Inc.   (818) 765-7107
large selection 40s to present, huge sel. contemporary lighting

7100 TUJUNGA AVE
North Hollywood, 91605
E-MAIL
rcvintage@aol.com

California USA
Telephone: 818.765.7107
Fax: 818.765.7197
www.rcvintage.com

Sony Pictures Studios-Fixtures   (310) 244-5996
5933 W Slauson Ave, Culver City, CA, 90230
period to present day, all styles, wall, floor, commercial, drag racing lights, fluorescent, fake fire machine
www.sonypicturesstudios.com

Sony Pictures Studios-Prop House (Off Lot)   (310) 244-5999
vapor lights, light bulb socket extensions, sign lights, work lights, security lights, sconces

Universal Studios Property & Hardware Dept   (818) 777-2784
Light fixtures from all time periods, styles, and sizes.

Warner Bros. Studios Property Department   (818) 954-2181
Vapor lights, street lights, disco lights, decorative lights, coach lights, pole lights, security lights

Warner Bros. Studios Property Dept. - Atlanta, GA   (404) 878-0002
3645 Southside Industrial Pkwy., Atlanta, GA 30354
Many kinds of lights and light fixtures at our Atlanta Prop House location.
nikki.giovacchini@warnerbros.com * www.WBPropertyAtlanta.com

ZG04 DECOR   (818) 853-8040
Modern Contemporary Lighting, Traditional Eclectic Lighting, Mid Century Lighting, Art Deco Lighting, Vintage Lighting

Light Fixtures, Period

See Also: Antiques & Antique Decorations

Alley Cats Studio Rentals — (818) 982-9178
ornate carriage street lights, vintage street lights

Antiquarian Traders — (310) 247-3900
4851 S. Alameda Street, Los Angeles, CA 90048
Varied collection of American and European chandeliers, sconces, torchieres
crystal and bronze.
antiques@antiquariantraders.com * www.antiquariantraders.com

Castle Antiques & Design — (855) 765-5800
11924 Vose St, N Hollywood, CA, 91605
Period light fixtures for rent and purchase.
info@castleantiques.net * www.castleprophouse.com

E.C. Prop Rentals — (818) 764-2008
working, industrial, incandescent & fluorescent, many types

Main Street Lighting — (330) 723-4431
1080 Industrial Pkwy, Medina, OH, 44256
Nostalgic, ornamental-posts, fixtures, bollards, & brackets
tracyr@mainstreetlighting.com * www.mainstreetlighting.com

MidcenturyLA — (818) 509-3050
5333 Cahuenga Blvd, N. Hollywood, CA, 91601
Huge array of mid-century ceiling lights, pendants, table lamps, and desk
lamps. Most inventory is in store not online.
midcenturyla@midcenturyla.com * www.midcenturyla.com

Pasadena Antique Warehouse — (626) 404-2422
1609 East Washington Blvd., Pasadena, CA, 91104
Large selection of chandeliers and lights. Crystal, electric, and colored glass.
pasadenaantiquewarehouse@gmail.com *
www.pasadenaantiquewarehouse.com

Sony Pictures Studios-Fixtures — (310) 244-5996
5933 W Slauson Ave, Culver City, CA, 90230
period to present day
www.sonypicturesstudios.com

Sword & Stone — (818) 562-6548

Universal Studios Property & Hardware Dept — (818) 777-2784
Period light fixture rentals

Warner Bros. Studios Property Department — (818) 954-2181

Light Fixtures, South Seas

See Also: Lamp Posts & Street Lights Lanterns*

Benson's Tropical Sea Imports — (714) 841-3399
7442 Vincent Cir, Huntington Beach, CA 92648
bamboo, seashell & tapa lamps
sales@bensonsimport.com * www.bensonsimport.com

Oceanic Arts — (562) 698-6960
pufferfish lights, glass floats in nets, tapa cloth & more

Sony Pictures Studios-Fixtures — (310) 244-5996
5933 W Slauson Ave, Culver City, CA, 90230
period to present day
www.sonypicturesstudios.com

Universal Studios Property & Hardware Dept — (818) 777-2784
South sea light fixture rentals.

Warner Bros. Studios Property Department — (818) 954-2181

Light Strings

See Also: Chase Lights Lighting, LED, Fiber Optic & Specialty*
Neon Lights & Signs*

Amusement Svcs/Candyland Amusements — (818) 266-4056
18653 Ventura Blvd Ste 235, Tarzana, CA, 91356
www.candylandamusements.com

E.C. Prop Rentals — (818) 764-2008
construction, carnival, Christmas tree lot, some cages & shades

RC Vintage, Inc. — (818) 765-7107
Various String lights motion animated. Strip Club. Flashing and preset, exterior
string lights, in many Colors!

ShopWildThings — (928) 855-6075
2880 Sweetwater Ave, Lake Havasu City, AZ, 86406
Event Decor, Beaded Curtains, Chain Curtains, String Curtains & Columns,
Crystal Columns. Reliable service & delivery.
help@shopwildthings.com * www.shopwildthings.com

Sony Pictures Studios-Fixtures — (310) 244-5996
5933 W Slauson Ave, Culver City, CA, 90230
period to present day
www.sonypicturesstudios.com

Universal Studios Property & Hardware Dept — (818) 777-2784
Light string rentals, Christmas lights and more.

Warner Bros. Studios Property Department — (818) 954-2181

Lighters

See: Smoking Products

Lighting & Sound, Concert/Theatrical/DJ/VJ

See Also: Events, Design/Planning/Production Events,
Entertainment* Lighting Control Boards* Mirror Balls/Drivers* Rock 'n'
Roll Lighting & Sound* Scaffolding/Lighting Towers*
Searchlights/Skytrackers, Architectural Lights* Special Effects,
Lighting & Lasers* Stage Lighting, Film/Video/TV* Stages, Portable &
Steel Deck*

Astro Audio Video Lighting, Inc. — (818) 549-9915
6615 San Fernando Rd, Glendale, CA, 91201
Sound & lighting, all sizes, concert/stage/club/church/school/DJ and staging
www.astroavl.com

Barbizon Lighting Co. — (866) 502-2724
456 W. 55th St, New York, NY, 10019
catalog sales; lighting & rigging equipment, see web site for locations

Coast Recording Audio Props — (818) 755-4692
10715 Magnolia Blvd, N Hollywood, CA, 91601
DJ Setup, Sound Board for Concert and Theatre.
props@coastrecording.com * www.coastrecordingprops.com

Derksen USA, Inc. — (916) 988-0390
4934 Pathway Ct. Fair Oaks, CA 95528
custom gobos delivered anywhere in 14 days or less

EFX- Event Special Effects — (626) 888-2239
125 Railroad Ave, Monrovia, CA, 91016
Stage Lighting- LED Screens- Event Lighting
info@efxla.com * www.efxla.com

History For Hire, Inc. — (818) 765-7767
vintage lighting, dimmers

Mac Tech LED Lighting — (818) 777-1281
3900 Lankershim Blvd, Universal City, CA, 91608
Uses 30-70% less power than equivalent conventional production lighting -
Superior quality of light for stage & location
info@mactechled.com * www.mactechled.com

Musson Theatrical TV Film — (800) 843-2837
890 Walsh Avenue, Santa Clara, CA, 95050
catalog sales; lighting, sound, expendables

New Mexico Lighting & Grip Co.   (505) 227-2500
5650 University Blvd SE Bldg 2, Albuquerque, NM, 85107
Grip & rigging equip. & services, lighting & sound
www.newmexicolightingandgrip.com

Strong International, Inc.   (402) 453-4444
13710 FNB Parkway Ste 400, Omaha, NE, 68154
Digital lighting, entertainment lighting, cinema projection equipment

Tobins Lake Sales   (888) 525-3753
3313 Yellowstone Dr, Ann Arbor, MI, 48105
installation too

Universal Studios Set Lighting Dept   (818) 777-2291
100 Universal City Plaza, Universal City, CA, 91608
Extensive inventory of quality stage & location lighting
universal.setlighting@nbcuni.com * www.filmmakersdestination.com

Lighting Control Boards

See Also: Control Boards Electronic Equipment (Dressing)*
Astro Audio Video Lighting, Inc.   (818) 549-9915
6615 San Fernando Rd, Glendale, CA, 91201
Lighting control boards, lighting control systems, DMX lighting controllers, light control boards and more.
www.astroavl.com

E.C. Prop Rentals   (818) 764-2008
props-2 castered Mole Richardson units

History For Hire, Inc.   (818) 765-7767
period, motion picture & theatrical

LCW Props   (818) 243-0707
A Specialty Of Ours, Rigged, Period - Present

Lighting Services, Special Effects

See: Lighting, LED, Fiber Optic & Specialty Special Effects, Lighting & Lasers*

Lighting, Industrial

See Also: Caged Vapor Proof Lights China Hat Lights* Egg Crate Bottom Fluorescents* Light Fixtures*
AIR Designs   (818) 768-6639
Warehouse Lights, Yard Lights, Work Lights

Alley Cats Studio Rentals   (818) 982-9178
Fluorescents, Egg Crate Fluorescents, and more

E.C. Prop Rentals   (818) 764-2008
7000 incandescent & fluorescent, many styles/multiples

E.C. PROP RENTALS
11846 SHERMAN WAY NORTH HOLLYWOOD CA 91605
818-764-2008

LCW Props   (818) 243-0707
Large Selection Of Industrial Lighting, mercury Vapor, HPS, Flourescent

Lighting, LED, Fiber Optic & Specialty

See Also: Gobos/Projection Lighting & Sound, Concert/Theatrical/DJ/VJ*
Astro Audio Video Lighting, Inc.   (818) 549-9915
6615 San Fernando Rd, Glendale, CA, 91201
LED lighting and specialty lighting for concerts, festivals and events.
www.astroavl.com

Charisma Design Studio, Inc.   (818) 252-6611
8414 San Fernando Road, Sun Valley, CA, 91352
custom LED & fiber optic lights
info@charismadesign.com * www.charismadesign.com

EFX- Event Special Effects   (626) 888-2239
125 Railroad Ave, Monrovia, CA, 91016
LED Stage Lighting- LED Screens- Event Lighting
info@efxla.com * www.efxla.com

Filmmaker Production Services Company - Atlanta   (404) 815-5202
219 Armour Drive NE, Atlanta, GA, 30324
Grip & rigging equip. & services, lighting & sound
http://www.filmmakerproductionservices.com

Filmmaker Production Services Company - Chicago   (678) 628-1997
2558 W 16th Street Dock #4, Chicago, IL, 60608
Grip & rigging equip. & services, lighting & sound
http://www.filmmakerproductionservices.com

Lazarus Lighting Design, Inc   (800) 553-5554
14701 Arminta St, Van Nuys, CA, 91402
custom fiber optic signs systems. no LEDs.

Mac Tech LED Lighting   (818) 777-1281
3900 Lankershim Blvd, Universal City, CA, 91608
Uses 30-70% less power than equivalent conventional production lighting - Superior quality of light for stage & location
info@mactechled.com * www.mactechled.com

Mandex LED Displays   (800) 473-5623
2350 Young Ave, Thousand Oaks, CA, 91360
LED Displays & Sign Rentals nationwide, all configurations, tickers, flexible panels, big LED Digital Countdown Clocks.
alan@ledsignage.com * www.ledsignage.com

ShopWildThings   (928) 855-6075
2880 Sweetwater Ave, Lake Havasu City, AZ, 86406
Event Decor, Beaded Curtains, Chain Curtains, String Curtains & Columns, Crystal Columns. Reliable service & delivery.
help@shopwildthings.com * www.shopwildthings.com

Universal Studios Set Lighting Dept   (818) 777-2291
100 Universal City Plaza, Universal City, CA, 91608
Extensive inventory of quality stage & location lighting
universal.setlighting@nbcuni.com * www.filmmakersdestination.com

Lime Wash

See: Paint & Painting Supplies

Limousine Service

AM-PM Limousine Service   (800) 995-AMPM
W. Hollywood, CA, 90046
flat rates to all airports, beautiful cars & great rates

Ascot Limousine Service   (310) 559-5959
375 E. Beach Ave. Inglewood 90302
Limos, sedans, SUVs, vans

Avalon Transportation   (800) 528-2566
5534 Westlawn Ave, Los Angeles, CA 90066
Flat rate airport service, sedans, limos

Limousine Connection   (818) 766-4311
5118 Vineland Ave, N Hollywood, CA, 91601
Flat rate airport service, limos, sedans & stretches

Linens, Household

See Also: Slipcovers

Badia Design, Inc.   **(818) 762-0130**
5420 Vineland Ave, N. Hollywood, CA, 91601
Moroccan kilim pillows also, traditional designs
info@badiadesign.com * www.badiadesign.com

GBS Linens   **(714) 778-6448**
305 N. Muller, Anaheim, CA, 92801
Wholesale specialty linens.

History For Hire, Inc.   **(818) 765-7767**
huge selection of blankets, also quilts

International Down & Linen   **(310) 657-8243**
8687 Melrose Ave B368, Los Angeles, CA, 90069
luxury linens, custom sewing & embroidery, custom sized pillows & comforters,
silk bedding

Little Bohemia Rentals   **(818) 853-7506**
11940 Sherman Rd, N Hollywood, CA, 91605
Blankets, throws, tablecloths.
sales@wearelittlebohemia.com * www.wearelittlebohemia.com

Ob-jects   **(818) 351-4200**
antique/Aubusson contemp/country pillows; Beacon/chenille throws, fine sel
American quilts

Omega/Cinema Props   **(323) 466-8201**
lrg sel bedding, blankets, quilts, decorative pillows, will also fabricate

Pier 1 Imports (Hollywood)   **(323) 466-3443**
5711 Hollywood Blvd, Hollywood, CA, 90028

Prop Services West   **(818) 503-2790**
decorative pillows

The Rug Warehouse   **(310) 838-0450**
3270 Helms Ave, Los Angeles, CA, 90034
Handmade decorative area rugs, pillows and carpet. Contemporary, traditional,
antique, kilims, custom options & more
www.therugwarehouse.com

Sony Pictures Studios-Linens, Drapes, Rugs   **(310) 244-5999**
5933 W Slauson Ave, Culver City, CA, 90230
tablecloths, napkins, decorative pillows, bedding/pillows, bedroom dress,
kitchen, and bath
www.sonypicturesstudios.com

Sony Pictures Studios-Prop House (Off Lot)   **(310) 244-5999**
bedspreads for queen, king, twin, and full; airplane blankets, period blankets,
prison blankets, dust comforter, and more

Universal Studios Property & Hardware Dept   **(818) 777-2784**
Household linens from different time period for rent.

Warner Bros. Drapery, Upholstery & Flooring   **(818) 954-1831**
4000 Warner Blvd, Burbank, CA, 91522
Bedding; Comforters; Pillows; Duvets; Table cloths; Napkins; Runners; Picnic;
Towels; Blankets
wbsfdrapery@warnerbros.com * www.wbdrapery.com

Warner Bros. Studios Property Department   **(818) 954-2181**
Table linens, towels, sheets, napkins, see WBSF Drapery Department

ZG04 DECOR   **(818) 853-8040**
Bedding, Bathroom Linens, Kitchen linens, Blankets

Linens, Tabletop & Events

See Also: Events, Decorations, Supplies & Services* Linens,
Household

Omega/Cinema Props   **(323) 466-8201**

Resource One   **(818) 343-3451**
6900 Canby Ave Ste 106, Reseda, CA, 91325
upscale table linens, unusual combinations, custom fabr.

Lingerie

See: Underwear & Lingerie, Bloomers, Corsets, Etc.

Linoleum

See: Carpet & Flooring

Liquid Iron

See: Paint & Painting Supplies

Liquor Bottles

AIR Designs   **(818) 768-6639**
Liquor, Wine, Beer, Champagne, Large Quantity, Multiples of Cleared

The Hand Prop Room LP.   **(323) 931-1534**
period-modern, breakaway, cust. labels

History For Hire, Inc.   **(818) 765-7767**
all periods

LCW Props   **(818) 243-0707**
New, Old, We Own The Recycling Center Next Door. Unlimited Quantity,
Cleared

Modern Props   **(323) 934-3000**
contemporary, multiples

Omega/Cinema Props   **(323) 466-8201**
Decanters of many kinds, scotch bottles, rye bottles, bourbon bottles and
more.

RC Vintage, Inc.   **(818) 765-7107**
Large Assortment, faux liquor bottles, bar shelf liquor bottles

Sony Pictures Studios-Prop House (Off Lot)   **(310) 244-5999**

Universal Studios Property & Hardware Dept   **(818) 777-2784**
Liquor bottle rentals from all time periods and locales.

Liquor Store

See: Drugstore/Apothecary

Livestock

See: Animals (Live), Services, Trainers & Wranglers* Horses, Horse
Equipment, Livestock* Western Dressing

Loading Dock Dressing

See Also: Barrels & Drums, Wood/Metal/Plastic* Crates/ Vaults*
Furniture Dollies, Pads & Hand Trucks* Nautical Dressing & Props*
Pallets* Warehouse Dressing

Alley Cats Studio Rentals   **(818) 982-9178**
pallets, drums, hand carts, coastal signage

E.C. Prop Rentals   **(818) 764-2008**
1-stop shop for crates, drums, dollies, pallets, jacks, signage

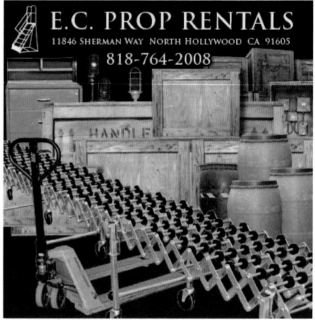

The Hand Prop Room LP.   **(323) 931-1534**
drums, crates, pallets, dollies, carts

LCW Props   **(818) 243-0707**
Crates, Drums, Pallet Jacks, Forklifts, Dollies, Signage

Lobby Cards

See: Posters, Art/Movie/Travel/Wanted Etc.* Signs

Lobby Seating

See Also: Dentist Equipment* Hotel, Motel, Inn, Lodge* Medical Equip/Furniture, Graphics/Supplies
Alpha Companies - Spellman Desk Co. **(818) 504-9090**
medical office seating, dentists office seating, hotel lobby seating
ZG04 DECOR **(818) 853-8040**
Benches, Club-chairs, Sofas, Multiples

Lobster/Fish Traps

Alley Cats Studio Rentals **(818) 982-9178**
wood, metal, slat, also have cargo nets
Benson's Tropical Sea Imports **(714) 841-3399**
7442 Vincent Cir, Huntington Beach, CA 92648
lobster, crabs & shellfish
sales@bensonsimport.com * www.bensonsimport.com
History For Hire, Inc. **(818) 765-7767**

Locations

See: Locations, Insert Stages & Small Theatres

Locations, Insert Stages & Small Theatres

See Also: Events, Destinations* Stages, Road Tour Rehearsal* Stages/Studios, Film/TV/Theatre/Events* Backlots/Standing Sets
Aero Mock-Ups **(888) 662-5877**
full service aviation prop house. airplane cabins on site. Airline sets, Unsupervised sets, cockpit door and wall
AIR Designs **(818) 768-6639**
Middleton Ranch, 120 Acre Filming Location, 30's Gas Station, Modern Gas Station, Diner, Convenience Store
Air Hollywood - Prop House & Standing Sets **(818) 890-0444**
757, 737, 767, private jets, departure lounge security, aviation themed studio, airport terminal, TSA sets

The Brig Parking Lot **(310) 709-3540**
1515 Abbot Kinney Blvd #200, Venice, CA, 90291
6700 sf 30 cars, Only large surface lot in the heart of Abbot Kinney for parking catering craft wardrobe. Vintage mural.
pariswst@gte.net
Caravan West Productions **(661) 268-8300**
35660 Jayhawker Rd, Aqua Dulce, CA, 91390
8-building frontier town for print works. 2,488 acres in the 30 mile zone. Miles of dirt roads.
caravanwest@earthlink.net * www.caravanwest.com

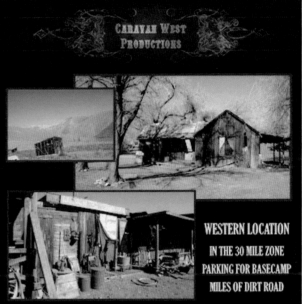

DISPLAY ADS AND LISTINGS FOR THIS CATEGORY
CONTINUE ON THE FOLLOWING PAGE

Fortune Trading Co & Import Bazaar   (323) 222-6287
483 Gin Ling Way (Old Chinatown), Los Angeles, CA, 90012
1000s of copies of many styles of paper lanterns, masks. Costumes, lions, dragons, gongs, scrolls, Oriental gift items
fortunetradingco@gmail.com

International Printing Museum   (714) 529-1832
315 Torrance Blvd, Carson, CA, 90745
antique printing/office equipment 1450-1980. old presses, machines, complete shops
www.printmuseum.org

Koch's Movie Ranch   (661) 268-1341
7650 Soledad Canyon Road, Acton, CA 93510
Locations: House, Cabin, Mineshaft, Cave, Barn, Outhouse, Restaurant, 70,000 gallon pond w/ waterfall & gazebo, Church
customerservice@kochs.com * www.kochsmovieranch.com

Koch's Movie Ranch
www.kochsmovieranch.com
(661) 268-1341 (661) 433-2854
7650 Soledad Canyon Road, Acton, CA

Living Art Aquatic Design, Inc.   (310) 822-7484
2301 South Sepulveda Blvd, Los Angeles, CA, 90064
One of a kind 2000 sq ft aquarium showroom and aquarium store for saltwater fish and freshwater fish.
ron@aquatic2000.com * www.aquatic2000.com

Local # 399 Studio Transportation Drivers   (818) 985-7374
4747 Vineland Ave, N Hollywood, CA, 91602
Teamsters Local 399. Hire an experienced and knowledgeable location manager!
www.ht399.org

MorguePropRentals.com   (818) 957-2178
5134 Valley Blvd, Los Angeles, CA, 90032
set-up for lighting/cameras, morgue, period medical lab
info@1800autopsy.com * www.morgueproprentals.com

Rancho Santa Ana Botanic Garden   (909) 625-8767
1500 N College Ave, Claremont, CA, 91711
86 acre garden, native Cal. plants, herbarium, call X251 for visit info

Repro-Graphic Supply   (818) 771-9066
9838 Glenoaks Blvd, Sun Valley, CA, 91352
Bar Location, Restaurant Location, and House Location. See Display Ad in Blueprint Equipment
info@reprographicsupply.com * www.reprographicsupply.com

Sketch Paper Design   (818) 442-0284
7771 Lemona Ave, Van Nuys, CA, 91405
White Cyc stage that can be painted depending on production's needs, stage for rent
info@sketchpaperdesign.com * www.sketchpaperdesign.com

Sword & Stone   (818) 562-6548
medieval rooms & blacksmith workshop location

Universal Studios Stages & Backlot   (818) 777-3000
100 Universal City Plaza, Universal City, CA, 91608
Universal Studios backlot
universal.locations@nbcuni.com * www.filmmakersdestination.com

Lockers

See Also: School Supplies, Desks & Dressing
Alley Cats Studio Rentals   (818) 982-9178
locker room, locker row units, blue, silver etc

C. P. Valley   (323) 466-8201
School lockers, gym lockers, footlockers, hallway lockers, wood lockers, metal lockers, public lockers, coin-op lockers

E.C. Prop Rentals   (818) 764-2008
School Lockers, Gym Lockers, Locker Room, Pro-Sports, Coin-Op, larport Lockers, Bus Station, Multiples, Some Castered.

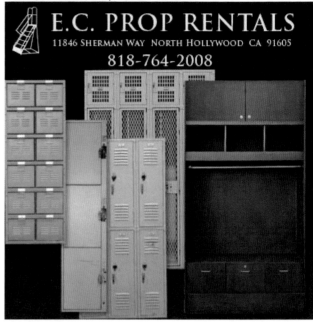

E.C. PROP RENTALS
11846 SHERMAN WAY NORTH HOLLYWOOD CA 91605
818-764-2008

Engineered Storage Systems, Inc   (626) 330-2233
161 Mercury Circle, Pamona, CA, 91768
Lockers of all shapes and sizes, huge warehouse.
www.engineeredstorage.com

Engineered Storage Systems
1038 W. Kirkwall Road
Azusa, CA 91702
engineeredstorage.com

FormDecor, Inc.   (310) 558-2582
America's largest event rental supplier of 20th Century furniture and accessories for Modern and Mid-Century styles.

LCW Props (818) 243-0707
Large Selection, School, Industrial, Wood, Metal, Military

6439 San Fernando Rd. Glendale, CA 91201
Phone: 818-243-0707 - www.lcwprops.com

RJR Props (404) 349-7600
High school lockers, gym lockers for rent.
Sony Pictures Studios-Prop House (Off Lot) (310) 244-5999
small, bus depot, locker room dressing
Warner Bros. Studios Property Department (818) 954-2181
Gym lockers, school lockers, storage lockers, Doctors lounge lockers, metal and office lockers, multiples of lockers

Locks & Locksmith

See: Keys & Locks

Lodge

See: Hotel, Motel, Inn, Lodge

Logo Design

See: Graphics, Digital & Large Format Printing* Signs

Lubricants

See: Expendables

Luggage

See Also: Briefcases* Steamer Trunks* Trunks
Air Hollywood - Prop House & Standing Sets (818) 890-0444
Vintage luggage, modern luggage, many pieces
C. P. Valley (323) 466-8201
The Hand Prop Room LP. (323) 931-1534
History For Hire, Inc. (818) 765-7767
huge selection
Innerspace Cases Unltd. (818) 767-3030
11555 Cantara St, N. Hollywood, CA, 91605
custom protective cases for film, music, video, medical, sports equipment
LCW Props (818) 243-0707
Period, Cases & Crates
Sony Pictures Studios-Prop House (Off Lot) (310) 244-5999
backpacks, briefcases, garment bags, gun cases, messenger bags, shoulder bags
Universal Studios Property & Hardware Dept (818) 777-2784
Luggage rentals; from period to modern.
Warner Bros. Studios Property Department (818) 954-2181
Assorted Suitcases, Briefcase, Luggage Caddy, Carry On luggage, Garment Bags, luggage racks, trunks

Luggage Carts

Air Hollywood - Prop House & Standing Sets (818) 890-0444
Airport terminal, carts, luggage, airport; Smarte Cartes, with name clearance
C. P. Valley (323) 466-8201
E.C. Prop Rentals (818) 764-2008
several styles

The Hand Prop Room LP. (323) 931-1534
airport, hotel, train station
History For Hire, Inc. (818) 765-7767
train, plane, airport
LCW Props (818) 243-0707
We Have Clean Cleared Luggage Carts
Sony Pictures Studios-Prop House (Off Lot) (310) 244-5999
Universal Studios Property & Hardware Dept (818) 777-2784
Hotel luggage carts and airport luggage carts for rent.

Lumber

See: Building Supply, Lumber, Hardware, Etc.

Lunch Boxes

The Hand Prop Room LP. (323) 931-1534
period-present
History For Hire, Inc. (818) 765-7767
vintage
RC Vintage, Inc. (818) 765-7107
40s, 50s & 60s striped, metal, kids, big, small and locked lunch boxes. with art, or plain for work
Sony Pictures Studios-Prop House (Off Lot) (310) 244-5999
metal, plastic
Universal Studios Property & Hardware Dept (818) 777-2784
Adult lunchboxes and kids lunchboxes from period to modern.

Lunch Counters

AIR Designs (818) 768-6639
Diner Restaurant, Cafeteria
C. P. Two (323) 466-8201
assortment & period
RC Vintage, Inc. (818) 765-7107
40s, 50s & 60s diner and restaurant counters, break room counters, wall pieces with counters

Lunch Room

See: Break Room

Machine Shop & Machinery

See Also: Automotive/Garage Equip. & Parts* Factory/Industrial* Tools* Welding Equipment/Stations* Heavy Machinery, Equipment & Specialists
E.C. Prop Rentals (818) 764-2008
power & hand tools, tables, cabinets, signage
Machinery & Equipment Co., Inc. (909) 599-3916
115 N Cataract Ave, San Dimas, CA, 91773
Over 3 acres of industrial processing equip., such as kettles, mixers, tanks, conveyors & other stainless machinery for
sherri@machineryandequipment.com * www.machineryandequipment.com
Sword & Stone (818) 562-6548

Magazines & Magazine/Newspaper Racks

See Also: Comic Books & Comic Book Racks* Display Cases, Racks & Fixtures (Store)* Newspapers (Prop)* Newsstands* Newsstands (Prop)* Store Shelf Units & Shelving
AIR Designs (818) 768-6639
Stands, Racks, Dressed, Indoor & Outdoor, Bundled Newspaper, Crates of Magazines
Alley Cats Studio Rentals (818) 982-9178
period, modern magazine racks
Book Castle, Inc. (818) 845-1563
212 N. San Fernando Blvd, Burbank, CA, 91502
vintage magazines & newspapers, no racks, back-issue magazines, old newspapers. Industry experience for 30 years.
www.bookcastlesmovieworld.com
C. P. Valley (323) 466-8201
Magazine racks, newspaper racks, bundled newspapers, metal racks, steel racks, metal racks and more.
The Earl Hays Press (818) 765-0700
The Industry only. vintage-modern custom design, also have generic prints, labels. Hundreds ready, we'll make anything.
The Hand Prop Room LP. (323) 931-1534
History For Hire, Inc. (818) 765-7767
magazines & racks, custom
LCW Props (818) 243-0707
Unlimited Quantity Of Newspaper & Magazines
Prop Services West (818) 503-2790
Sony Pictures Studios-Prop House (Off Lot) (310) 244-5999
magazines & racks
Warner Bros. Studios Property Department (818) 954-2181
Magazine stands, metal newspaper racks, period/vintage racks, standing magazine racks & stands

Magicians & Props, Supplies, Dressing

See Also: Occult/Spiritual/Metaphysical

Don Wayne Magic, Inc.　　　　　　　　(818) 763-3192
10907 Magnolia Blvd, Ste 467, N. Hollywood, CA, 91601
We are technical magic consultants.

The Hand Prop Room LP.　　　　　　　(323) 931-1534
magic cases, ventriloquist dummies

L. A. Party Works　　　　　　　　　　(888) 527-2789
9712 Alpaca St, S El Monte, CA, 91733
in Vancouver tel. 604-589-4101. custom built medium to large scale illusions
partyworks@aol.com * www.partyworksusa.com

Owen Magic Supreme　　　　　　　　(626) 969-4519
734 N McKeever Ave, Azusa, CA, 91702
magic effects, consulting techniques, props, spec. effects
alanz@owenmagic.com * www.owenmagic.com

Show Fx, Inc.　　　　　　　　　　　(562) 903-7285
13165 Sandoval St, Santa Fe Springs, CA, 90670
stock magic illusions & custom build

The Society of American Magicians　(303) 362-0575
PO Box 505, Parker, CO, 80134
advances magic as a performing art, contact performers via links to local
chapters on their website
www.magicsam.com

Universal Studios Property & Hardware Dept　(818) 777-2784
Magician props, magician supplies, and magician dressing for rent.

Mail & Mail Room

See Also: Post Office Scales*

Advanced Liquidators Office Furniture　(818) 763-3470
Wide variety of office dressing, and office furniture fit to satisfy the look of any
type of business office.

C. P. Valley　　　　　　　　　　　　(323) 466-8201
Mail carts, mail baskets, mail cabinets, shipping boxes, sorting shelves, mail
sorter and more.

E.C. Prop Rentals　　　　　　　　　(818) 764-2008
canvas & wire carts, sorting units, tables, racks, shelving

Faux Library Studio Props, Inc.　　　(818) 765-0096
Mail room dressing and faux mail dressing for rent.

History For Hire, Inc.　　　　　　　　(818) 765-7767

LCW Props　　　　　　　　　　　　(818) 243-0707
Mail Sorters, Mailboxes, Cleared Mail, Postage Scales

Sony Pictures Studios-Prop House (Off Lot)　(310) 244-5999
mail & other dressing

Universal Studios Property & Hardware Dept　(818) 777-2784
Mail only for rent.

Mailboxes

AIR Designs　　　　　　　　　　　　(818) 768-6639
USPS Mailboxes, Storage Boxes, Package Drop Off

Alley Cats Studio Rentals　　　　　　(818) 982-9178
Blue U.S. Mail, green relay, rural boxes on posts

C. P. Valley　　　　　　　　　　　　(323) 466-8201
Post office mailboxes, residential mailboxes, wall mounted mail boxes,
apartment mailboxes, standup mailboxes and more.

E.C. Prop Rentals　　　　　　　　　(818) 764-2008
rural & apartment type, several styles, multiples

History For Hire, Inc.　　　　　　　　(818) 765-7767
home & street

Jackson Shrub Supply, Inc.　　　　　(818) 982-0100
mail boxes

LCW Props　　　　　　　　　　　　(818) 243-0707
Large Selection. Apartment, Office, Slots, Hotel, Mail Sorters

RC Vintage, Inc.　　　　　　　　　　(818) 765-7107
Modern US POST OFFICE DROP BOX!

Sony Pictures Studios-Prop House (Off Lot)　(310) 244-5999

Universal Studios Property & Hardware Dept　(818) 777-2784
Mailboxes from different time periods and styles for rent.

Warner Bros. Studios Property Department　(818) 954-2181
Outdoor mailboxes, rural mail boxes, wood & metal mail boxes, standing
mailboxes, rustic mailboxes

Make-up & Hair, Supplies & Services

See Also: Expendables* Production Vehicles/Trailers* Salon & Spa Equipment* Special Effects, Make-up/Prosthetics* Tattoos (Temporary) Body/Face Painting* Wigs

Alcone Co. (718) 361-8373
5-45 49th Avenue, Long Island City, NY, 11101
technical supply catalog for animal glue, paints, etc. & make-up catalog for theatrical make-up & supplies

Ball Beauty Supply (323) 655-2330
1535 S. La Cienega Blvd., Los Angeles, CA, 90035
beauty supply shop

Ben Nye Co. Inc. (310) 839-1984
3655 Lenawee Ave, Los Angeles, CA, 90016
Mfg., call for local dealer referral

Bobbe Joy Make-up Studio (310) 275-3505
350 N. Bedford Dr, Beverly Hills, CA 90210
Bobbe Joy make-up, custom made cosmetics

Cinema Secrets, Inc. (818) 846-0579
4400 Riverside Dr, Burbank, CA, 91505
huge sel.

Frends Beauty Supply (818) 769-3834
5244 Laurel Canyon Blvd, N. Hollywood, CA, 91607
theatrical & special FX make-up

Fun Corner (888) 885-7648
426 W. Baseline, San Bernardino, CA, 92410
Ben Nye dealer-Moulage

GlenPro Beauty Center (818) 244-1776
717 E. California Ave, Glendale, CA, 91206
beauty supply shop

The Hand Prop Room LP. (323) 931-1534
period-present

History For Hire, Inc. (818) 765-7767
most eras through 1970s

Industry Hair (818) 562-1858
4313 Riverside Dr, Burbank, CA, 91505
Hair only, no make-up

Kryolan Corporation (800) 579-6526
134 9th St, 1st floor, San Francisco, CA, 94103
catalog sales; make-up supplies

Larchmont Beauty Supply (323) 461-0162
208 N Larchmont Blvd, Los Angeles, CA, 90004
beauty supply shop

Lorac Cosmetics, Inc (818) 678-3939
29025 Avenue Penn, Valencia, CA, 91355
ask for Product Placement

M.A.C. (310) 271-9137
133 N Robertson Blvd, Los Angeles, CA, 90048
M.A.C. make-up

Make-Up Center (212) 977-9494
Web Based Business
Mail order & web services only. cosmetics & theatrical make-up
www.make-up-center.com

Melrose Beauty Center (323) 852-6910
7617 Melrose Ave, Los Angeles, CA, 90046
beauty supply shop

Naimie's Beauty Supply (818) 655-9933
12640 Riverside Dr, Valley Village, CA, 91607
Studio services (818) 655-9922

Senna Cosmetics (661) 257-3662
28042 Avenue Stanford Ste A, Valencia, CA, 91355

Ursula's Costumes, Inc. (310) 582-8230
2516 Wilshire Blvd, Santa Monica, CA, 90403

Wilshire Beauty Supply (323) 937-2001
5401 Wilshire Blvd, Los Angeles, CA, 90036

Make-up Schools

Dinair Airbrush Make-up & Institute (818) 780-4777
6215 Laurel Canyon Blvd, N. Hollywood, CA, 91606

The Joe Blasco Make-up Center (323) 467-4949
1285 N Valdivia Way, Palm Springs, CA, 92262

Make-Up Designory (MUD) (818) 729-9420
129 S San Fernando Blvd, Burbank, CA, 91502
Los Angeles School of Make-Up, Inc.

Make-up Tables & Mirrors

C. P. Valley (323) 466-8201
Makeup tables, makeup displays, makeup bottles, makeup mirrors.

Castex Rentals (323) 462-1468
1044 N. Cole Ave, Hollywood, CA, 90038
portable wood/metal make-up tables, make-up mirrors and full length mirrors, salon chairs, portable dressing rooms
service@castexrentals.com * www.castexrentals.com

History For Hire, Inc. (818) 765-7767
lots

Lennie Marvin Enterprises, Inc. (Prop Heaven) (818) 841-5882
quantities avail.

Prop Services West (818) 503-2790

Universal Studios Property & Hardware Dept (818) 777-2784
Makeup tables and makeup tables with mirrors for rent.

Mall Carts

See: Vendor Carts & Concession Counters

Man Hole Covers

See: Alley Dressing* Street Dressing

Manicure & Pedicure Stations

See: Beauty Salon

Mannequins

See Also: Anatomical Charts & Models* Dress Forms* Puppets, Marionettes, Automata, Animatronics* Robots

Acme Display Fixture & Packaging (888) 411-1870
3829 S Broadway St., Los Angeles, CA 90037
Complete store setups: garment racks, displays/display cases, counters, packaging, shelving, hangers, mannequins
sales@acmedisplay.com * www.acmedisplay.com

C. P. Valley (323) 466-8201
Mannequins of assorted sizes and styles.

LCW Props (818) 243-0707
White Store Mannequins, Limbs Too

Lennie Marvin Enterprises, Inc. (Prop Heaven) (818) 841-5882
per-mod., full body & torso, child/adult w/clothing

**DISPLAY ADS AND LISTINGS FOR THIS CATEGORY
CONTINUE ON THE FOLLOWING PAGE**

The Mannequin Gallery (818) 834-5555
12350 Montague St Ste E, Pacoima, CA, 91331
modern mannequins & vintage mannequins, custom mannequins
shelley@mannequingallery.com * www.mannequingallery.com

Mannequin Rentals, Sales, Repairs and Custom Work

Modern Props (323) 934-3000
traditional mannequins, fantasy, real people, exotic humans, futuristic, hi-tech, modern, conventional, small collection

RC Vintage, Inc. (818) 765-7107
50s & 60s, and new ones too, can change position, flesh colored, cloth colored, bust only, full figured mannequins

Rubens Display World (909) 923-5671
1482 E Francis St, Ontario, CA, 91761
custom forms to mannequins, basic/complex, period/contemp
www.rubensdisplay.com

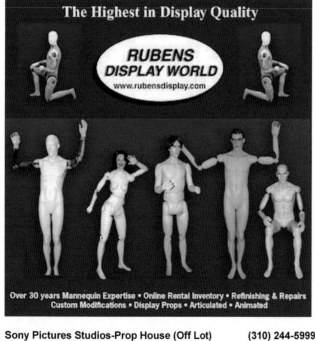

The Highest in Display Quality

RUBENS DISPLAY WORLD
www.rubensdisplay.com

Over 30 years Mannequin Expertise • Online Rental Inventory • Refinishing & Repairs
Custom Modifications • Display Props • Articulated • Animated

Sony Pictures Studios-Prop House (Off Lot) (310) 244-5999
base mannequins, dummy mannequins, display mannequins

Sword & Stone (818) 562-6548

Universal Studios Property & Hardware Dept (818) 777-2784
Different kinds of mannequins, mannequin parts and sizes for rent from different time periods.

Mantels

See: Fireplaces & Mantels/Screens/Tools/Andirons

Maps

See Also: Globes, World Map

C. P. Valley (323) 466-8201

Clearedart.com/El Studio Granados (818) 240-4421
958 Verdugo Circle Dr, Glendale, CA, 91206
"Age of Exploration" ancient-styled maps and charts. Period treasure maps, and hand-props. Custom work.
fineart@elstudiogranados.com * www.clearedart.com

D'ziner Sign Co. (323) 467-4467
801 Seward Street, Los Angeles, CA 90038
print mockups of any kind
sales@dzinersign.com * www.dzinersign.com

Faux Library Studio Props, Inc. (818) 765-0096
globes and wall maps, some cleared

The Hand Prop Room LP. (323) 931-1534
antique-present, standing, wall, desk, book, travel, academic

History For Hire, Inc. (818) 765-7767
rental & custom

Hollywood Studio Gallery (323) 462-1116
rental only

Rand McNally (800) 275-7263
9855 Woods Dr. Skokie, IL, 60077
mfg. of maps, atlas, travel videos. Truck GPS, RV GPS, more

Sony Pictures Studios-Prop House (Off Lot) (310) 244-5999
maps, wall maps

Universal Studios Property & Hardware Dept (818) 777-2784
Maps from different time periods, countries and styles for rent.

Marble

See: Tile, Marble, Granite, Etc.

Mardi Gras

See: Carnival Dressing/Supplies* Events, Decorations, Supplies & Services* Events, Design/Planning/Production* Holiday Costumes* Holiday Theme Events* Masks* Travel (City/Country) Themed Events

Marijuana Plants, Dispensary Dressing & Hydroponics

See Also: Greenhouses & Growing Systems* Greens

Jackson Shrub Supply, Inc. (818) 982-0100
Marijuana field set with bamboo, silk marijuana bush, silk marijuana bush on bamboo pole

LCW Props (818) 243-0707
Marijuana, Nutrients, Lights, Tables, Scales, Jars, Bags of Marijuana, Containers, Counters, Signage, Edibles

L.C.W. PROPS
PLANTS OF ALL SIZES GROW OPERATION
DISPENSARY GOODS
6439 San Fernando Rd. Glendale, CA 91201
Phone: 818-243-0707 - www.lcwprops.com

Marine

See: Nautical Dressing & Props* Nautical/Marine Services & Charters* Tikis & Tropical Dressing

Marionettes

See: Puppets, Marionettes, Automata, Animatronics

Market Equipment/Fixtures

See Also: Bakery* Cash Registers* Credit Card Imprint Machine* Delicatessen Equipment* Display Cases, Racks & Fixtures (Store)* Graphics, Digital & Large Format Printing* Grocery Check-out Stands (Complete)* Produce Carts* Produce Crates* Produce Stands* Prop Houses* Prop Products & Packages* Shopping Bags (Silent)* Shopping Carts* Signs* Store Shelf Units & Shelving

AIR Designs (818) 768-6639
Shelving, Racks, Counters, Coolers, Freezers, Large Selection, Period to Present

C. P. Valley (323) 466-8201
Market fixtures, produce boxes, farmers market dressing, butchers scale, produce scales, grocery store baskets and more.

Lennie Marvin Enterprises, Inc. (Prop Heaven) (818) 841-5882
gondolas, shelving, signage, fixtures, products, foods, more

Marquees

See Also: Canopies, Tents, Gazebos, Cabanas* Neon Lights & Signs* Signs

Alley Cats Studio Rentals (818) 982-9178
theater marquee sign, seating

Martial Arts

See: Boxing, Wrestling, Mixed Martial Arts (MMA)

Mascot Character

See: Animal Costumes & Walk Around Characters

Mascots

See: Animal Costumes & Walk Around Characters

Masks

See Also: Art, Tribal & Folk* Leather (Clothing, Accessories, Materials)

American Plume (800) 521-1132
11 Skyine Drive East, Unit 2, Clarks Summit, PA 18411
Boas/jackets/theatrical division in NYC; (800) 962-8544. highest quality feather masks

Clearedart.com/El Studio Granados (818) 240-4421
958 Verdugo Circle Dr, Glendale, CA, 91206
100s of multi-media masks, from miniature to large-sized, in Native American, Guatemalan, and contemporary styles.
fineart@elstudiogranados.com * www.clearedart.com

Fortune Trading Co & Import Bazaar (323) 222-6287
483 Gin Ling Way (Old Chinatown), Los Angeles, CA, 90012
1000s of copies of many styles of paper lanterns, masks. Costumes, lions, dragons, gongs, scrolls, Oriental gift items
fortunetradingco@gmail.com

The Hand Prop Room LP. (323) 931-1534
tribal, paper mache, porcelain

Hollywood Studio Gallery (323) 462-1116
Asian, South American, African

Make-up Effects Laboratories (818) 982-1483
7110 Laurel Canyon Blvd Bldg E, N Hollywood, CA, 91605
latex, silicone, foam, cast from your choice of model

Oceanic Arts (562) 698-6960
Carved Wood masks, 22 Authentic styles and some one of a kind. South Pacific, New Guinea, and African.

Omega/Cinema Props (323) 466-8201

Prop Services West (818) 503-2790
ethnic decorative masks

Sony Pictures Studios-Prop House (Off Lot) (310) 244-5999

Sony Pictures Studios-Wardrobe (310) 244-5995
alterations, call (310) 244-7260

Southern Importers (713) 524-8236
4825 San Jacinto St, Houston, TX, 77004-5620
catalog sales; mask foundations & plastic animal masks

Sword & Stone (818) 562-6548
leather, feather, aluminum, steel, bronze

The Theater Maskery (360) 297-4160
PO Box 421, Indianola, WA, 98342
mask makers & mask theater instructors

Universal Studios Property & Hardware Dept (818) 777-2784
Many prop masks for different time periods and cultures for rent.

Warner Bros. Studios Costume Dept (818) 954-1297
Mardi Gras, Feathered, Jeweled, Venetian, Masquerade, Opera

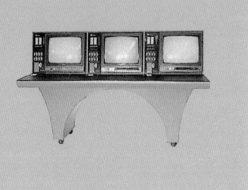

Massage Rollers

See: Exercise & Fitness Equipment* Gymnasium & Gymnastic Equipment

Massage Tables

See Also: Medical Equip/Furniture, Graphics/Supplies

E.C. Prop Rentals (818) 764-2008
several styles

L. A. Party Works (888) 527-2789
9712 Alpaca St, S El Monte, CA, 91733
Multiple massage tables and masseuse talent for rent.
partyworks@aol.com * www.partyworksusa.com

Modern Props (323) 934-3000
contemporary

Universal Studios Property & Hardware Dept (818) 777-2784
Massage chairs and massage tables for rent.

Mats

See: Fall Pads & Crash Pads* Gymnasium & Gymnastic Equipment

Mechanic Shop

See: Automotive/Garage Equip. & Parts

Mechanical Bull/Bronco

See: Events, Entertainment* Horse/Bull, Mechanical (Riding Simulators)* Western Theme Events

Mechanical Effects

See Also: Confetti* Pyrotechnics

Action Sets and Props / WonderWorks, Inc. (818) 992-8811
Space shuttle & station, space suit, specialty props, miniatures, mechanical effects, cityscape, miniature buildings

Bill Ferrell Co. (818) 767-1900
10556 Keswick St, Sun Valley, CA, 91352
Turntables, lifts, winches, conveyors; moving props, sets. Simple or automated. We design, fabricate, install, operate.
www.billferrell.com

Charisma Design Studio, Inc. (818) 252-6611
8414 San Fernando Road, Sun Valley, CA, 91352
custom mechanical effects & fabrication
info@charismadesign.com * www.charismadesign.com

CONFETTI & FOG FX Special Effects Company (786) 308-7063
2739 W 79 St Bay, #12, Hialeah, FL 33016
www.caffx.com

EFX- Event Special Effects (626) 888-2239
125 Railroad Ave, Monrovia, CA, 91016
Snow- Confetti- Cryo- Bubbles- Fog- Foam- Fluid- Lighting- Fabrication
info@efxla.com * www.efxla.com

Flix FX Inc. (818) 765-3549
7327 Lankershim Blvd #4, N Hollywood, CA, 91605
Custom mechanical EFX fabrication-motorized, pneumatic, hydraulic, RC
info@flixfx.com * www.flixfx.com

The Hand Prop Room LP. (323) 931-1534
HPR Custom (323) 931-1534
5700 Venice Blvd, Los Angeles, CA, 90019
Remote control, wireless, electronics, digital, fabrication, and mechanical effect manufacturing
www.hprcustom.com

Jet Effects (818) 764-5644
6910 Farmdale Ave, N Hollywood, CA, 91605
custom mechanical effects fabrication
tito@jeteffects.net * www.jeteffects.net

Rando Productions, Inc (818) 982-4300
11939 Sherman Rd, N Hollywood, CA, 91605
turntables, lifts, rolling rooms, gimbals, hydraulics

Special Effects Unlimited, Inc. (323) 466-3361
1005 N. Lillian Way, Hollywood, CA, 90038
turntables, gimbals, special purpose rigging
www.specialeffectsunlimited.com

Warner Bros. Studios Special Effects & Prop Shop (818) 954-1365
4000 Warner Blvd, Burbank, CA, 91522
Consultation, Script Break-down, Equipment Rentals, Expendable Sales, Picture Car Prep, Action Props
www.wbspecialeffects.com

Media Storage

See: Archiving Media/Records Management

Medical Books

See: Books, Real/Hollow & Faux Books* Prop Houses* Exam Room

Medical Equip/Furniture, Graphics/Supplies

See Also: Ambulance/Paramedic* Anesthesia Equipment* Bones, Skulls & Skeletons* Dentist Equipment* Doctor's Bags* Hospital Equipment* Lab Equipment* Morgue* Scales* Stretchers* Uniforms, Trades/Professional/Sports* Wheelchairs* X-rays* Nurses Station* Waiting Room* Birthing Room* Intensive Care Unit / NICU (Natal Intensive Care Unit)* Emergency Room* Radiology* Exam Room* Lobby Seating

A-1 Medical Integration (818) 753-0319
Medical devices for Set Decoration & Property, from minor procedures to detailed hospital units.

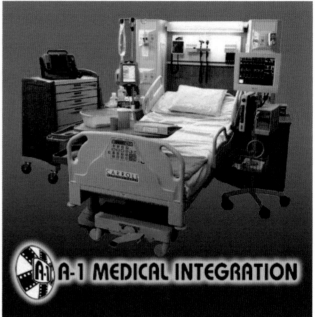

AA Surplus Sales Co., Inc. (323) 526-3622
2940 E. Olympic Blvd, Los Angeles, CA, 90023
Military field operating tables, field nurse stations, military bunk beds, scrubs, field hospital beds & stretchers
surplusking@hotmail.com * www.aasurplus.com/

Alpha Companies - Spellman Desk Co. (818) 504-9090
The #1 source for medical equipment in the industry.

Angelus Medical & Optical Co., Inc. (310) 769-6060
13007 S Western Ave, Gardena, CA, 90249
emergency equipment, physical therapy, opthalmic, etc.
www.angelusmedical.com

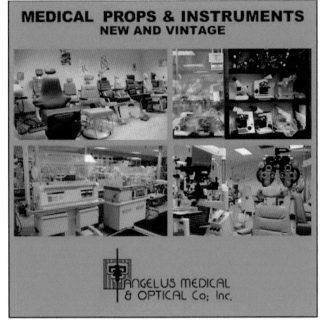

MEDICAL PROPS & INSTRUMENTS
NEW AND VINTAGE

ANGELUS MEDICAL & OPTICAL Co; Inc.

C. P. Valley (323) 466-8201
Range of medical equipment from defibrillators to thermovision oscilloscopes.
Dapper Cadaver/Creatures & Cultures (818) 771-0818
Medical equipment: gurneys, mayo stands & autopsy equipment. Stainless
steel instruments & trays. Anatomical models.
E.C. Prop Rentals (818) 764-2008
first aid kits & signage
The Hand Prop Room LP. (323) 931-1534
stretchers, gurney, first aid, doctor's bags, no furniture
History For Hire, Inc. (818) 765-7767
LCW Props (818) 243-0707
Large Selection Of Medical Files, Equipment, Supplies, Custom Graphics
Modern Props (323) 934-3000
contemp./futuristic furniture & dressing
RJR Props (404) 349-7600
Medical props, ER props, ICU props and OR props for rent.
Sony Pictures Studios-Prop House (Off Lot) (310) 244-5999
xray viewers, bandages, bio hazard container, blood pressure equipment,
bones, medical bottles, patient charts, and more
Universal Studios Property & Hardware Dept (818) 777-2784
A lot of prop medical equipment for rent.
Warner Bros. Studios Property Department (818) 954-2181
Medical equipment, Aspirator, Newborn Hospital Bed, rolling bedside trays,
bladder pumps, x-ray machines

Medical Examiner

See: Morgue* Exam Room

Medical Library

See: Books, Real/Hollow & Faux Books

Medicine Balls

See: Gymnasium & Gymnastic Equipment

Medieval

See Also: Armor, Chainmail, Suits of Armor* Blacksmith
Shop/Foundry* Goth/Punk/Bondage/Fetish/Erotica Etc.* Historical
Era Themed Events* Lanterns* Leather (Clothing, Accessories,
Materials)* Swords & Swordplay* Torture Equipment* Wardrobe,
Antique/Historical* Weaponry, Historical* Weaponry, Medieval
Bob Gail Special Events (310) 202-5200
Go back to Medieval times with Knights, Dragons, Castles,Thrones, Armor and
More!
The Hand Prop Room LP. (323) 931-1534
armor, swords, shields, custom mfg.
Historic Enterprises, Inc. (760) 789-2299
17228 Voorhes Lane, Ramona, CA, 92065
custom fab, replicas, specialty/stunt props, horse equip, tents
History For Hire, Inc. (818) 765-7767
good selection
Hollywood Studio Gallery (323) 462-1116
swords, shields, armor
Omega/Cinema Props (323) 466-8201
Sony Pictures Studios-Prop House (Off Lot) (310) 244-5999
medieval swords, medieval shields, medieval knives, medieval cauldrons,
lanterns
Sword & Stone (818) 562-6548
iron maiden, ball & chain, shackles, dungeon dressing
Universal Studios Property & Hardware Dept (818) 777-2784
Medieval props of various kinds for rent.

Megaphones

The Hand Prop Room LP. (323) 931-1534
History For Hire, Inc. (818) 765-7767
all types
LCW Props (818) 243-0707
Handheld, Police, Cheerleader, Working
Sony Pictures Studios-Prop House (Off Lot) (310) 244-5999
Universal Studios Property & Hardware Dept (818) 777-2784
Prop megaphones for rent.

Memorabilia & Novelties

See Also: Coca Cola Memorabilia* Collectibles* Promotional Items &
Materials* Prop Houses* Sports Fan Items, Memorabilia,
Photographs
History For Hire, Inc. (818) 765-7767
LCW Props (818) 243-0707
Sporting, Old Periodicals, Photos
Pasadena Antique Warehouse (626) 404-2422
1609 East Washington Blvd., Pasadena, CA, 91104
Sports, military, and Americana memorabilia. Comic books, model cars, and
toys.
pasadenaantiquewarehouse@gmail.com *
www.pasadenaantiquewarehouse.com
RC Vintage, Inc. (818) 765-7107
period to present Toys and TV items from the past
Universal Studios Property & Hardware Dept (818) 777-2784
Prop novelties and prop memorabilia for rent.

Menus

See Also: Graphics, Digital & Large Format Printing
AIR Designs (818) 768-6639
Restaurant, Bakery, Diner, Coffee Shop, Neon's, Menu Boards
C. P. Valley (323) 466-8201
Chalkboard menus, vinyl menus, menu racks, menu holders, vintage menu
signs, standing menu boards, french menu sign
The Earl Hays Press (818) 765-0700
services the Industry only. ready-made or custom designed menus.
The Hand Prop Room LP. (323) 931-1534
custom design
History For Hire, Inc. (818) 765-7767
rental & custom
Kater-Crafts Bookbinders (562) 692-0665
4860 Gregg Rd, Pico Rivera, CA, 90660
Custom menu covers. Industry credits. any size/style binding.
sales@katercrafts.com * www.katercrafts.com
LCW Props (818) 243-0707
Selection Of Restaurant Menus For Indoor & Outdoor
RC Vintage, Inc. (818) 765-7107
40s, 50s & 60s Diner style. Drive Thru Menu Signs w speaker box
Sony Pictures Studios-Prop House (Off Lot) (310) 244-5999
Universal Studios Graphic Design & Sign Shop (818) 777-2350
custom
Universal Studios Property & Hardware Dept (818) 777-2784
Prop menus for various restaurants for rent.

Mercury Glass

See: Antiques & Antique Decorations* Decorative Accessories

Merry-go-round

See: Carnival Games & Rides* Carousel Horses* Playground Equipment

Messenger & Courier Services

See Also: Walkie-Talkies

Lightning Messenger Express (818) 754-1234
5503 Cahuenga Blvd Ste 100, N Hollywood, CA, 91601
Pickup & delivery for greater LA area, plus Orange Cty, San Diego
Pacific Couriers (714) 278-6100
1706 Orangethorpe, Fullerton, CA, 92833
Messenger svcs for entire LA studio zone
Sunrise Delivery Service (818) 789-5121
13351-D Riverside Dr #672, Sherman Oaks, CA, 91423
24 By 7 delivery, online realtime delivery tracking

Metal Detectors

See Also: Mining & Prospecting Equipment* Police Equipment* Security Walk-Through & Baggage Alarms

Air Hollywood - Prop House & Standing Sets (818) 890-0444
Airport Security sets, TSA sets and props available incl. metal detector walk-through machines, x-rays & body scanners
Faux Library Studio Props, Inc. (818) 765-0096
Metal detectors for rent
The Hand Prop Room LP. (323) 931-1534
LCW Props (818) 243-0707
Our Specialty. We Have A Large Selection Of Many Kinds. Rigged, Large & Small

Metal Plating, Coating, Polishing

See Also: Paint & Painting Supplies

Artcraft (818) 845-9292
76 E. Santa Anita Ave, Burbank, CA, 91502
on metals or non-metallic props, electroforming
Astro Plating (818) 781-1463
8136 Lankershim Blvd, North Hollywood CA, 91605
Barry Avenue Plating Co. (310) 478-0078
2210 Barry Ave, Los Angeles, CA, 90064
Charisma Design Studio, Inc. (818) 252-6611
8414 San Fernando Road, Sun Valley, CA, 91352
custom fabrication, metal plating & polishing
info@charismadesign.com * www.charismadesign.com
F & H Plating (818) 765-1221
12023 Vose St, N. Hollywood, CA, 91605
nickle, brass, copper, gold, silver, tin, small items
Faith Plating (323) 582-5400
4330 District Blvd. Vernon, CA 90058
chrome plating, esp. auto, motorcycle
LNL Anodizing (818) 768-9224
9900 Glenoaks Blvd, Unit 3, Sun Valley, CA, 91352
plating, antiquing, anodizing, sand blasting
Pyramid Powder Coating (818) 768-5898
12251 Montague St, Pacoima, CA, 91331
custom colors, production runs, sandblasting, powder coating
Sepp Leaf Products (212) 683-2840
381 Park Avenue South #1301, New York City, NY, 10016
Metal leaf materials & brushes. Edible gold & silver leaf.
Sword & Stone (818) 562-6548

Metal Shop

See Also: Factory/Industrial* Tools

E.C. Prop Rentals (818) 764-2008
power & hand tools, welding equipment, tables, cabinets, signage
Sword & Stone (818) 562-6548
Warner Bros. Studios Metal Shop (818) 954-1265
4000 Warner Blvd, Burbank, CA, 91522
Custom metal fabrication creating anything from structural steel elements to intricate custom furniture
wbsfconstructionservices@warnerbros.com * www.wbmetalshop.com

Metal Suppliers

See Also: Grating, Grated Flooring, Catwalks

Alameda Pipe (310) 532-7911
14500 Avalon Blvd, Gardena, CA, 90248
new/used steel/non-ferrous, wide variety of forms
Bobco Metals (888) 304-5927
2000 S. Alameda St, Los Angeles, CA, 90058
steel, brass, copper, aluminum, power tools, welding supplies
Borrmann Metal Center (818) 846-7171
110 W. Olive Ave, Burbank, CA, 91502
Burbank Metal Supply (818) 846-4333
3207 N. San Fernando Blvd, Burbank, CA, 91504
aluminum distributors
Coast Aluminum (562) 946-6061
10628 Fulton Wells Ave, Santa Fe Springs, CA 90670
aluminum, brass, stainless, custom shapes
Hadco Aluminum (800) 221-0344
120 Spagnoli Rd., Melville, NY 11747
plate, sheet, wire, rod, bar, extrusions, tube, pipe, fittings
Industrial Metal Supply Co. (818) 729-3333
8300 San Fernando Rd, Sun Valley, CA, 91352
ferrous/non-ferrous, speedrail products
M & K Metal (310) 327-9011
14400 S Figueroa St, Gardena, CA, 90248
ferrous/non-ferrous, variety of stock
McNichols (562) 921-3344
14108 Arbor Pl, Cerritos, CA, 90703
Metal Depot (562) 921-2524
14334 E Firestone Blvd, La Mirada, CA, 90638
Phillip's Steel (562) 435-7571
1368 W Anaheim St, Long Beach, CA, 90813
Since 1915. steel, aluminum, stainless, brass, sheet, plate, angle, channel, tubing, beams, tools, fabrication
Premier Steel (800) 220-9940
1330 N Knollwood, Anaheim, CA, 92801
structural steel, stainless, aluminum
Totten Tubes (800) 882-3748
500 Danlee St, Azusa, CA, 91702
steel distributor, wide variety tubing & finishing svcs
Tube Service (800) 776-8823
9351 S Norwalk Blvd, Santa Fe Springs, CA, 90670
alum. & steel pipe/tubing

Metalworking, Decorative

See Also: Prop Design & Manufacturing* Sculpture* Wrought Iron Furniture & Decorations

Charisma Design Studio, Inc. (818) 252-6611
8414 San Fernando Road, Sun Valley, CA, 91352
custom all metals, functional art & arch. pcs, water jet cutting
info@charismadesign.com * www.charismadesign.com
Martin Iron Design (818) 760-3636
10750 Cumpston St, N Hollywood, CA, 91601
custom made Rod Iron furniture and chandeliers by your design.
Sword & Stone (818) 562-6548
wrought iron, sheet metal fab, etching, plating, embossing
Universal Studios Property & Hardware Dept (818) 777-2784
Decorative metalworking and decorative metal items for rent.
Warner Bros. Studios Metal Shop (818) 954-1265
4000 Warner Blvd, Burbank, CA, 91522
Custom metal fabrication creating anything from structural steel elements to intricate custom furniture
wbsfconstructionservices@warnerbros.com * www.wbmetalshop.com

Metalworking, Welding & Structural

See Also: Welding Equipment/Stations

Alameda Pipe (310) 532-7911
14500 Avalon Blvd, Gardena, CA, 90248
cutting, beveling, straightening, buffing, welding
Chamber Sheet Metal (818) 346-5685
7026 Deering Ave, Canoga Park, CA, 91303
only sheet metal fabrication & A/C ducts
EFX- Event Special Effects (626) 888-2239
125 Railroad Ave, Monrovia, CA, 91016
Custom Fabrication- CNC- Plasma Table- Pipe & Ring Benders- 3D Renderings
info@efxla.com * www.efxla.com
Flix FX Inc. (818) 765-3549
7327 Lankershim Blvd #4, N Hollywood, CA, 91605
Machining, tube & pipe bending, cutting & finishing, welding (certified)
info@flixfx.com * www.flixfx.com
The Hand Prop Room LP. (323) 931-1534

HPR Custom (323) 931-1534
5700 Venice Blvd, Los Angeles, CA, 90019
Steel fabrication, MIG welding, TIG welding, ARC welding, water jet cutting, and CNC machining.
www.hprcustom.com

Jet Effects (818) 764-5644
6910 Farmdale Ave, N Hollywood, CA, 91605
custom fabrication & complete fabrication shop
tito@jeteffects.net * www.jeteffects.net

Jet Sets (818) 764-5644
6910 Farmdale Ave, N Hollywood, CA, 91605
set construction, custom props, scenic painting, special effects, set illustration, research library for clients
dougmorris@jetsets.com * www.jetsets.com

Pipeworks Fabrication (562) 432-6826
1471 Cota Ave, Long Beach, CA, 90813

Robert James Company (415) 420-4011
2110 West 20th St, Los Angeles, CA, 90018
Specializing in large-scale steel sculpture; proficient in architectural, structural, and creative steel fabrication.
rob@robertjamesstudio.com * www.robertjamesstudio.com

www.robertjamessf.com

Sword & Stone (818) 562-6548
sheet metal, wrought iron, & welding

Tractor Vision Scenery & Rentals (323) 235-2885
340 E Jefferson Blvd. Los Angeles, CA 90011
Specializing in entertainment, trade shows, & events, we bring your projects to life with precision, speed & personality
sets@tractorvision.com * www.tractorvision.com

Warner Bros. Studios Metal Shop (818) 954-1265
4000 Warner Blvd, Burbank, CA, 91522
Custom metal fabrication creating anything from structural steel elements to intricate custom furniture
wbsfconstructionservices@warnerbros.com * www.wbmetalshop.com

Metaphysical

See: Astrological Occult/Spiritual/Metaphysical*

Meters

See: Electronic Equipment (Dressing) Gas & Electric Meters*

Mexican Decorations

See Also: Pottery

Benson's Tropical Sea Imports (714) 841-3399
7442 Vincent Cir, Huntington Beach, CA 92648
sombreros, serapes, instruments, masks, & thatching
sales@bensonsimport.com * www.bensonsimport.com

Bob Gail Special Events (310) 202-5200
Create a Mexican Fiesta or a Spanish style Mission scene with our Mexican, Spanish, and Cuban Props!

The Hand Prop Room LP. (323) 931-1534
period-present

History For Hire, Inc. (818) 765-7767
period

Lennie Marvin Enterprises, Inc. (Prop Heaven) (818) 841-5882
street vendor carts

Omega/Cinema Props (323) 466-8201
Mexican decor from folk art and pottery to rugs and chairs.

Sony Pictures Studios-Prop House (Off Lot) (310) 244-5999

Universal Studios Property & Hardware Dept (818) 777-2784
Many Mexican themed decorations available for rent.

Mexican Pottery

See: Pottery

Mexican Themed Parties

See: Costume Rental Houses Events, Decorations, Supplies & Services* Events, Design/Planning/Production* Mexican Decorations* Travel (City/Country) Themed Events*

Microphones

See Also: Audio Equipment Radio/TV Station*

Astro Audio Video Lighting, Inc. (818) 549-9915
6615 San Fernando Rd, Glendale, CA, 91201
Wireless microphones and wired microphones, handheld microphones and microphone receivers.
www.astroavl.com

C. P. Valley (323) 466-8201

Coast Recording Audio Props (818) 755-4692
10715 Magnolia Blvd, N Hollywood, CA, 91601
Microphones from the 20s to the present. Prop microphones
props@coastrecording.com * www.coastrecordingprops.com

The Hand Prop Room LP. (323) 931-1534
period-present, hand-held, stand, personal

History For Hire, Inc. (818) 765-7767
biggest selection there is

LCW Props (818) 243-0707
DJ, Boom, Radio, Stage, Headsets

Modern Props (323) 934-3000
non-functional set dressing only

Sony Pictures Studios-Prop House (Off Lot) (310) 244-5999

Universal Studios Property & Hardware Dept (818) 777-2784
Many kinds of microphones from different time periods and uses for rent.

Microscopes

See: Electron Microscope Lab Equipment* Medical Equip/Furniture, Graphics/Supplies*

Mid-Century Furnishings

See: Furniture, Mid-Century Modern

Military Props & Equipment

See Also: Camouflage Nets Canopies, Tents, Gazebos, Cabanas* Civil War Era* Police Car, Police Motorcycle* Police Equipment* Stretchers* Weapons*

AA Surplus Sales Co., Inc. (323) 526-3622
2940 E. Olympic Blvd, Los Angeles, CA, 90023
U.S. military tents, clothing, footwear & field gear, military shipping containers, bunk beds
surplusking@hotmail.com * www.aasurplus.com/

American Military Museum (626) 442-1776
1918 N. Rosemead Blvd, S. El Monte, CA, 91733

At The Front Militaria (270) 384-1965
430 Rose Ln, Columbia, KY, 42728
WW II re-enactor uniforms/equip. web site has extensive links to related resources

C. P. Valley (323) 466-8201

E.C. Prop Rentals (818) 764-2008
missile containers, ammo boxes, checkpoint barricades, tarps

Emerson Knives (310) 539-5633
1234 254th St., Harbor City, CA 90710
Emerson Knives are the only choice of Elite Military and U.S. Covert Units. They are truly, "Famous In the Worst Places"
eknives@aol.com * www.emersonknives.com

DISPLAY ADS AND LISTINGS FOR THIS CATEGORY CONTINUE ON THE FOLLOWING PAGE

Fall Creek Corporation (765) 482-1861
PO Box 92, Whitestown, IN, 46075
Civil War era, military & civilian. Civil War era
reproductions ajfulks@fcsutler.com * www.fcsutler.com

Fall Creek Suttlery

CIVIL WAR

1860s reproduction military and civilian
clothing, tents, shoes, equipment, books,
weapons, insignia, leather goods, and
embroideries of all kinds.

Serving the Historical
and Entertainment
communities since 1978

The Hand Prop Room LP. (323) 931-1534
History For Hire, Inc. (818) 765-7767
Large accurate selection of military leather work
Hollywood Studio Gallery (323) 462-1116
framed medals, photos, posters only
Landser Outfitters, LLC (877) 499-1939
26741 Portola Pkwy Ste 1E411, Foothill Ranch, CA, 92610
WW II German Third Reich / uniforms equipment
sales@landser.com * www.landser.com
LCW Props (818) 243-0707
A Specialty Of Ours, Rigged, Period - Present, Camo, Weapons, Field Gear,
Cases & Ammo Crates, Missiles, Bombs & Marine
RDD U.S.A. Inc. (213) 742-0666
4638 E Washington Blvd., Commerce, CA 90040
field gear, military equipment, tents
www.rddusa.com
RJR Props (404) 349-7600
Military electronics, military communications sets,military tactical electronics,
military telemetry units and more.
Sony Pictures Studios-Prop House (Off Lot) (310) 244-5999
military helmets, military supplies, ammo belts, ammo crates, ammo tins, army
tents, bombs, explosives, cannons, more
Supply Sergeant (323) 849-3744
503 N. Victory Blvd, Burbank, CA 91502
Military movie props including ancient Greek/Roman armor & helmets as well
as modern military surplus & military gear.
david@jacksgt.com * www.supplysergeantshop.com
Surplus City (530) 534-9956
4514 Pacific Heights Rd, Oroville, CA, 95965
Military museum rentals
Sword & Stone (818) 562-6548

Universal Studios Property & Hardware Dept (818) 777-2784
Military equipment and military props for rent.

Military Surplus/Combat Clothes, Field Gear

See Also: Civil War Era* Costume Rental Houses* Uniforms, Military
AA Surplus Sales Co., Inc. (323) 526-3622
2940 E. Olympic Blvd, Los Angeles, CA, 90023
U.S. military tents, military bunk beds, stretchers, clothing, footwear & field
gear, camping equipment, knives, childre
surplusking@hotmail.com * www.aasurplus.com/

At The Front Militaria (270) 384-1965
430 Rose Ln, Columbia, KY, 42728
WW II re-enactor uniforms/equip. web site has extensive links to related
resources
California Surplus Mart (323) 465-5525
6263 Santa Monica Blvd, Los Angeles, CA, 90038
Army/Navy & camping gear & work clothes & boots
The Duffle Bag (845) 878-7106
1270 Route 311, Patterson, NY, 12563
U.S./foreign WW I-current, clothes/insignia/gear, 10-5 M-F or by appt
Golden West Supply Army/Navy Supply (626) 357-0711
626 S. Myrtle Ave, Monrovia, CA, 91016
surplus, pins, badges, etc., also backpacking/camping
History For Hire, Inc. (818) 765-7767
"surplus" items, no clothing
KSI NYC (212) 757-5670
319 West 42nd Street, New York City, NY, 10036
a real military surplus store, well stocked, good sel., American & German, some
British WWII
LCW Props (818) 243-0707
Camo Nets, Artillery, Field Radios
Omaha's Original Surplus (817) 332-1493
2413 White Settlement Rd, Fort Worth, TX, 76107
your source for original Vietnam gear, vast inventory of genuine military
surplus, an authentic Army/Navy store
RDD U.S.A. Inc. (213) 742-0666
4638 E Washington Blvd., Commerce, CA 90040
military clothing & equipment, field gear, tents
www.rddusa.com

MILITARY SURPLUS NEW & USED SINCE 1985

Tents & Tarps Military Clothing & Props Camouflage Nets Field Gear
www.rdusa.com
www.americawear.com

Supply Sergeant (323) 849-3744
503 N. Victory Blvd, Burbank, CA 91502
Army surplus, military clothes, army clothes, navy surplus, navy clothes,
military gear, camping gear, camping equipment
david@jacksgt.com * www.supplysergeantshop.com

Milk Bottles & Cans

The Hand Prop Room LP. (323) 931-1534
bottles & cans
History For Hire, Inc. (818) 765-7767
cans & bottles
LCW Props (818) 243-0707
Unlimited Quantity, We Own The Recycling Center Next Door
Sony Pictures Studios-Prop House (Off Lot) (310) 244-5999
cans & bottles
Universal Studios Property & Hardware Dept (818) 777-2784
Prop milk bottles and prop milk cans for rent.

Milk Crates

See: Expendables

Milk Paint

See: Paint & Painting Supplies

Milk Vending Machines

See: Vending Machines

Millinery

See: Headwear - Hats, Bonnets, Caps, Helmets Etc.

Milling, Custom

See: Moulding, Wood* Staff Shops

Mini-blinds

See: Window Treatments

Mini-mart

See: Cash Registers* Counters* Credit Card Imprint Machine* Display Cases, Racks & Fixtures (Store)* Food, Artificial Food* General Store* Graphics, Digital & Large Format Printing* Steel Folding Gates & Roll-Up Doors* Store Shelf Units & Shelving* Surveillance Equipment

Miniatures/Models

See Also: Dollhouses* Dolls* Model Ships/Planes/Trains/Autos Etc.* Prop Design & Manufacturing* Puppets, Marionettes, Automata, Animatronics

Action Sets and Props / WonderWorks, Inc.   **(818) 992-8811**
Space shuttle & station, space suit, specialty props, miniatures, mechanical effects, cityscape, miniature buildings

Art, Models & Props, Inc.   **(951) 206-9156**
1725 Marengo Ave, Pasadena, CA, 91103
Custom design/fabr. all categories. See ad in "Prop Design & Manufacturing"
modelsandprops@msn.com * www.artmodeltech.com

Culver Architects Inc.   **(310) 721-9867**
Call for Appointment, Playa del Rey, CA, 90293
Rentals of architecture models & landscape/interior design renderings, drawings, material samples, drafting tools, art.
ron@culverarchitects.com * www.carcinc.com/C_ARC/model_rentals.html

Glenn R. Johnson Scale Models   **(714) 538-9429**
1060 N. Batavia St., Unit C, Orange, CA 92867
Scale models, oversize/miniature, fabrication for architecture, Film, TV, Tradeshows, developers, realistic/fantasy
info@grjmodels.com * www.grjmodels.com

History For Hire, Inc.   **(818) 765-7767**
tract houses

IDF Studio Scenery   **(818) 982-7433**
6844 Lankershim Blvd, North Hollywood, CA 91605
Custom fabrication of miniatures & props
info@idfstudioscenery.com * www.idfstudioscenery.com

Jet Sets   **(818) 764-5644**
6910 Farmdale Ave, N Hollywood, CA, 91605
set construction, custom props, scenic painting, special effects, set illustration, research library for clients
dougmorris@jetsets.com * www.jetsets.com

LCW Props   **(818) 243-0707**
Anatomical Models, DNA, Elements

Merritt Productions, Inc.   **(818) 760-0612**
10845 Vanowen St, North Hollywood, CA 91605
specialty props, miniatures, sculpture, mech effects, set const. A whole city of miniature buildings.
www.merrittproductions.com

My Doll's House   **(310) 320-4828**
1218 El Prado Ave Ste 136, Torrance, CA 90501
Dollhouses, Dollhouse Kits, Room Boxes, Miniatures, Collectibles, Accessories, Tools and Supplies
margiesminiatures@gmail.com * www.mydollshouse.com

Sketch Paper Design   **(818) 442-0284**
7771 Lemona Ave, Van Nuys, CA, 91405
info@sketchpaperdesign.com * www.sketchpaperdesign.com

Tractor Vision Scenery & Rentals   **(323) 235-2885**
340 E Jefferson Blvd. Los Angeles, CA 90011
Specializing in entertainment, trade shows, & events, we bring your projects to life with precision, speed & personality
sets@tractorvision.com * www.tractorvision.com

ZG04 DECOR   **(818) 853-8040**
Scale Models: Speed Boat Models, Sail Boat Ship Models, Car Models, Airplane Models, Architectural Models

Mining & Prospecting Equipment

Black Cat Mining   **(541) 622-8225**
710 Rossanley Dr, Medford, OR 97501
everything for prospecting & rock hounding

Keene Engineering, Inc.   **(818) 993-0411**
8940 Lurline, Chatsworth, CA, 91311
Dredges, hydraulic systems, and related mining equip., website lists dealer network

Universal Studios Property & Hardware Dept   **(818) 777-2784**
Gold mining pans, mining ore buckets and more for rent.

Mirror Balls/Drivers

AIR Designs   **(818) 768-6639**
12" to 48"

Astro Audio Video Lighting, Inc.   **(818) 549-9915**
6615 San Fernando Rd, Glendale, CA, 91201
12" to 40" mirror balls; all sizes with motor drives for disco dudes & divas. Fixed & variable speeds
www.astroavl.com

History For Hire, Inc.   **(818) 765-7767**

LCW Props   **(818) 243-0707**
Complete DJ Setup, Disco Balls, Lighting

Omega/Cinema Props   **(323) 466-8201**

RC Vintage, Inc.   **(818) 765-7107**
Large assortment, disco balls, laser disco ball light

ShopWildThings   **(928) 855-6075**
2880 Sweetwater Ave, Lake Havasu City, AZ, 86406
Event Decor, Beaded Curtains, Chain Curtains, String Curtains & Columns, Crystal Columns. Reliable service & delivery.
help@shopwildthings.com * www.shopwildthings.com

Sony Pictures Studios-Fixtures   **(310) 244-5996**
5933 W Slauson Ave, Culver City, CA, 90230
period to present day, disco ball, electronic disco ball
www.sonypicturesstudios.com

Universal Studios Property & Hardware Dept   **(818) 777-2784**
Mirror balls and disco mirror balls for rent, in different sizes.

Mirrors, Framed Decorative Furnishings

See Also: Ballet Barres & Dance Mirrors* Bathroom Fixtures* Fun House Mirrors* Glass & Mirrors* Make-up Tables & Mirrors

Acme Display Fixture & Packaging   **(888) 411-1870**
3829 S Broadway St., Los Angeles, CA 90037
Complete store setups: garment racks, displays/display cases, counters, packaging, shelving, hangers, mannequins
sales@acmedisplay.com * www.acmedisplay.com

Antiquarian Traders   **(310) 247-3900**
4851 S. Alameda Street, Los Angeles, CA 90048
Unusual collection: Art, Tiffany stained glass, Murano glass, turn of the century embroideries, Victorian fashion print
antiques@antiquariantraders.com * www.antiquariantraders.com

Bridge Furniture & Props Los Angeles   **(818) 433-7100**
We carry modern & traditional furniture, lighting, accessories, cleared art,& rugs. Items are online for easy shopping.

Castle Antiques & Design   **(855) 765-5800**
11924 Vose St, N Hollywood, CA, 91605
Many decorative mirrors and framed mirrors for rent and purchase.
info@castleantiques.net * www.castleprophouse.com

The Hand Prop Room LP.   **(323) 931-1534**

Lux Lounge EFR   **(888) 247-4411**
106 1/2 Judge John Aiso St #318, Los Angeles, CA, 90012
Mirror Furniture/Mirrored Furniture Rentals
info@luxloungeefr.com * www.luxloungeefr.com

Ob-jects   **(818) 351-4200**

Omega/Cinema Props   **(323) 466-8201**

Prop Services West   **(818) 503-2790**

Rapport International Furniture   **(323) 930-1500**
435 N La Brea Ave, Los Angeles, CA, 90036
Choose from a variety of framed and unframed mirrors and accessories for home and office decor.
rapport@rapportusa.com * www.rapportfurniture.com

Sony Pictures Studios-Prop House (Off Lot)   **(310) 244-5999**
dance studio mirrors, standing mirrors, studio makeup mirrors, tabletop mirrors, wall mounted mirrors

U-Frame It Gallery   **(818) 781-4500**
6203 Lankershim Blvd, N Hollywood, CA, 91606
Framed mirrors, wide variety, custom framing
uframit@aol.com * www.uframeitgallery.com

Universal Studios Property & Hardware Dept   **(818) 777-2784**
Decorative mirrors and framed mirrors for rent.

ZG04 DECOR   **(818) 853-8040**
Wall Mirrors, Cheval Mirror, Bathroom - Mirrors, Standing, Hanging

Mission Control Consoles

See Also: Control Boards* Electronic Equipment (Dressing)
LCW Props (818) 243-0707
Large Selection Of Aerospace Panels, Rigged, Consoles, Boxes & Graphics
Woody's Electrical Props (818) 503-1940
period to futuristic. Apollo 13 is one of our successes! Fantasy sets, military sets, industrial sets, electrical panels

Model Makers

See: Miniatures/Models* Prop Design & Manufacturing* Puppets, Marionettes, Automata, Animatronics

Model Ships/Planes/Trains/Autos Etc.

See Also: Dollhouses* Hobby & Craft Supplies* Miniatures/Models* Prop Houses
Action Sets and Props / WonderWorks, Inc. (818) 992-8811
Space shuttle & station, space suit, specialty props, miniatures, mechanical effects, cityscape, miniature buildings
Antiquarian Traders (310) 247-3900
4851 S. Alameda Street, Los Angeles, CA 90048
Stunning collection of 19th century ship models and 20th ship models
antiques@antiquariantraders.com * www.antiquariantraders.com
Art, Models & Props, Inc. (951) 206-9156
1725 Marengo Ave, Pasadena, CA, 91103
Custom design/fabr. for special effects. See ad in "Prop Design & Manufacturing"
modelsandprops@msn.com * www.artmodeltech.com
The Hand Prop Room LP. (323) 931-1534
History For Hire, Inc. (818) 765-7767
model trains
Modern Props (323) 934-3000
variety of models including architectural buildings.
Pacmin (714) 447-4478
2021 Raymer Ave, Fullerton, CA, 92833
lrg sel aircraft, 10"-20' or more, airline, military, corporate custom build; NYC office (585) 226-8540
Prop Services West (818) 503-2790
Sony Pictures Studios-Prop House (Off Lot) (310) 244-5999
model airplanes, model bicycles, model canoes, model helicopters, model lighthouses, model motorcycles, model rockets, and more
The Train Shack (818) 842-3330
1030 N Hollywood Way, Burbank, CA, 91505
Universal Studios Property & Hardware Dept (818) 777-2784
Many kinds of models for rent.

Modular Work Stations

See: Office Furniture

Mold Making

See Also: Prop Design & Manufacturing* Sculpture* Statuary
Flix FX Inc. (818) 765-3549
7327 Lankershim Blvd #4, N Hollywood, CA, 91605
info@flixfx.com * www.flixfx.com
The Hand Prop Room LP. (323) 931-1534
HPR Custom (323) 931-1534
5700 Venice Blvd, Los Angeles, CA, 90019
Roto casting, 3D rapid prototyping, silicone molding, fiberglass molding, spin casting, and 3D modeling.
www.hprcustom.com
Reynolds Advanced Materials: Smooth-On Distributor (818) 358-6000
10856 Vanowen St, N. Hollywood, CA, 91605
Hollywood's F/X source for Liquid Rubbers, and Plastics. Lifecasting, F/X Makeup, Dragon Skin, Eco Flex and more.
LA@reynoldsam.com * www.moldmakingmaterials.com
Warner Bros. Studios Staff Shop (818) 954-2269
Manufacturer of exterior & interior details used for the creation of sets in all architectural styles & eras.

Money (Prop)

See Also: Bank Dressing
CONFETTI & FOG FX Special Effects Company (786) 308-7063
2739 W 79 St Bay, #12, Hialeah, FL 33016
www.caffx.com
The Earl Hays Press (818) 765-0700
Services the Industry only. U.S./foreign, old/new stage money, real looking money, fake money, and counterfeit money
The Hand Prop Room LP. (323) 931-1534
History For Hire, Inc. (818) 765-7767
paper money, coins, gold bricks, real period currency
LCW Props (818) 243-0707
Large Quantites, Fake Money, Coin, Bundles, Pallets Of Money, Gold Bars, Treasure
RJR Props (404) 349-7600
Prop money/stage money/fake money; legal fake money in all denominations and amounts including bags of cash & stacks.
Sony Pictures Studios-Prop House (Off Lot) (310) 244-5999
fake money, fake gold bars, fake silver bars
Universal Studios Property & Hardware Dept (818) 777-2784
Prop money, money bags, money bundles, money clips, money molds, prop gold ingots and more for rent.

Money Belts

See: Underwear & Lingerie, Bloomers, Corsets, Etc.

Monkey Cages

See: Animal Cages

Monsters

See: Aliens* Horror/Monster Dressing* Special Effects, Make-up/Prosthetics

Morgue

See Also: Cemetery Dressing* Mortuary
A-1 Medical Integration (818) 753-0319
Medical devices for Set Decoration & Property, from minor procedures to detailed hospital units.
Alpha Companies - Spellman Desk Co. (818) 504-9090
The #1 source for medical equipment in the industry.

Dapper Cadaver/Creatures & Cultures (818) 771-0818
Autopsy tables and instruments. Autopsy bodies with organs. Embalming
tables and pumps. Body bags, toe tags, etc.
LCW Props (818) 243-0707
Morgue Tables, Doors, Tools & Equipment
MorguePropRentals.com (818) 957-2178
5134 Valley Blvd, Los Angeles, CA, 90032
surg/pathology instrument props, set dressing, shooting loc.
info@1800autopsy.com * www.morgueproprentals.com

Mortuary

See Also: Caskets* Cemetery Dressing* Florists/Floral Design
Dapper Cadaver/Creatures & Cultures (818) 771-0818
Embalming tables, embalming pumps and instruments like trocars. Caskets
and lecterns.
MorguePropRentals.com (818) 957-2178
5134 Valley Blvd, Los Angeles, CA, 90032
prep room/embalming equip. & instruments
info@1800autopsy.com * www.morgueproprentals.com

Motel

See: Furniture, Tenement Tacky Motel* Hotel, Motel, Inn, Lodge

Motion Control

See Also: Mechanical Effects* Rigging, Equipment or Services
Bill Ferrell Co. (818) 767-1900
10556 Keswick St, Sun Valley, CA, 91352
Turntables, lifts, winches, conveyors; moving props, ramps, sets. Simple or
automated positioning and speed controls.
www.billferrell.com
CONFETTI & FOG FX Special Effects Company (786) 308-7063
2739 W 79 St Bay, #12, Hialeah, FL 33016
www.caffx.com
General Lift (310) 414-0717
111 Maryland St. El Segundo, CA 90245
variety of portable motion control systems for camera filming
Skjonberg Controls, Inc. (805) 650-0877
1363 Donlon St Ste 6, Ventura, CA, 93003

Motion Picture Camera Equipment

See Also: Camera Equipment* Video 24fps / Sync System / D.D.I.*
Video Camera Equipment & Services* Video Equipment
Birns & Sawyer, Inc. (323) 466-8211
5275 Craner Ave, North Hollywood, CA 91601
film & video cameras, accessories, lighting/grip, expendables, for lighting & grip
rental call (818) 766-2525
Panavision (818) 316-1000
6101 Variel Ave, Woodland Hills, CA, 91367
Cameras & film. Commercials, music videos, hair & make-up test, trailers
www.panavision.com

Panavision (Hollywood) (323) 464-3800
6735 Selma Ave, Hollywood, CA, 90028
expendables, plus camera equip., HD 900R, F23, Varicam. 16mm, 35mm,
HD900
RJR Props (404) 349-7600
News cameras for rent.
Slow Motion Inc.-Film & Digital (818) 982-4400
7211 Clybourn Ave, Sun Valley, CA, 91352
high speed cameras/lenses, underwater, sound cameras, carry many
brands/models

Motion Picture Production Equip., Period

See Also: Camera Equipment* Motion Picture Projectors
History For Hire, Inc. (818) 765-7767
most comprehensive selection there is
Universal Studios Property & Hardware Dept (818) 777-2784
Vintage and period motion picture equipment for rent.

Motion Picture Projectors

See Also: Camera Equipment* Film Reels
The Hand Prop Room LP. (323) 931-1534
period-present
History For Hire, Inc. (818) 765-7767
8mm, 16mm, 35mm, all levels
LCW Props (818) 243-0707
8mm, 16mm, 35mm Projectors

Motor Homes

See: RV Vehicles & Travel Trailers, Equip & Parts

Motorcycles

See Also: Police Car, Police Motorcycle* Vehicles
Alley Cats Studio Rentals (818) 982-9178
parts only, not complete cycles
Bartel's Harley Davidson (310) 823-1112
4141 Lincoln Blvd, Marina Del Rey, CA, 90292
motorcycles, clothing, collectibles, parts
Cornwell & Sheridan Picture Vehicles (310) 217-9060
15700 S Broadway, Gardena, CA, 90248
Convertibles, Coupes, Sedans, Limos, Motorcycles
www.old-cars.net
EagleRider Motorcycle Rental (310) 536-6777
11860 S La Cienega Blvd, Hawthorne, CA, 90250-3461 **x1169**
Motorcycles (All Models), Choppers, Customs, Sport Bikes, Dirt Bikes, ATV's,
Scooters, Parts, Damaged Bikes, Accessories
rent@eaglerider.com * www.eaglerider.com

DISPLAY ADS AND LISTINGS FOR THIS CATEGORY
CONTINUE ON THE FOLLOWING PAGE

Laidlaw's Harley-Davidson　　　　(626) 851-0412
1919 Puente Ave, Baldwin Park, CA, 91706
Sales, service & rentals

Los Angeles Motorcycle Salvage　　(323) 233-8792
425 E 58th Street, Los Angeles, CA, 90011
motorcycles & personal watercraft, pristine & damaged, high multiples, many models, parts galore, special projects
lasalvage@hotmail.com * www.losangelesmotorcyclesalvage.com

Motorcycles * Pristine & Damaged * Mutiples for Stunts
Parts Galore for Crash & Garage Scenes

Los Angeles Motorcycle Salvage

Michael Harper-Smith　　　　　(818) 705-8655
5375 Tampa Ave, Tarzana, CA, 91356
European picture vehicles
mharperxke@aol.com * www.eurofilmcars.com

MovieMoto.com　　　　　　(626) 359-0016
16015 Adelante St, Irwindale, CA, 91702
Rare, Odd, Classic, Exotic, Unknown MOTORCYCLE RENTALS. Specializing in Italian marks.
www.MovieMoto.com

MOVIEMOTO.com

Route 66 Riders　　　　　　(310) 578-0112
4161 Lincoln Blvd, Marina Del Rey, CA, 90292
Only Harleys

Moulding, Wood

See Also: Staff Shops

American Wood Column Corp.　　(718) 782-3163
913 Grand St, Brooklyn, NY, 11211-2785
catalog sales; large sel. of millwork, architectural/decorative small finials to tall columns, plain to ornate, custom t

Moulding Center　　　　　　(818) 985-5376
6501 Lankershim Blvd, N Hollywood, CA, 91606

National Hardwood Flooring & Moulding　(818) 988-9663
14959 Delano St, Van Nuys, CA, 91411
Flooring, moulding, custom milling, stains, finishes, abrasives, sundries, tools, fireplace mantels & stair components

Stock Components　　　　　　(818) 842-8139
161 W Cypress Ave, Burbank, CA, 91502
custom milling

Sunland Wood Products　　　　(818) 982-3110
7442 Varna Ave, N Hollywood, CA, 91605
custom, spindles, railings, std/cust doors & windows, etc.

Vintage Woodworks　　　　　(903) 356-2158
9195 Highway 34 S PO Box 39, Quinlan, TX, 75474
catalog sales; + online sales, old-fashioned interior/exterior details, mouldings, Victorian gingerbread, doors, porch p

Warner Bros. Studios Mill Store　　(818) 954-4444
4000 Warner Blvd, Burbank, CA, 91522
Production expendables & supplies to the entertainment community at great prices
wbsfmillstore@warnerbros.com * www.wbmillstore.com

Mounted Heads

See: Taxidermy, Hides/Heads/Skeletons

Mounting Services

See: Art & Picture Framing Services

Movie Lobby

See: Crowd Control: Barricades, Turnstiles Etc. Display Cases, Racks & Fixtures (Store)* Posters, Art/Movie/Travel/Wanted Etc.* Stanchions & Rope* Vendor Carts & Concession Counters*

Movie Posters

See: Memorabilia & Novelties Posters, Art/Movie/Travel/Wanted Etc.*

MRI (Magnetic Resonance Imaging)

Alpha Companies - Spellman Desk Co.　(818) 504-9090
various styles

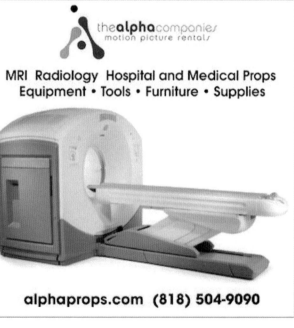

the**alpha**companies
motion picture rentals

MRI Radiology Hospital and Medical Props
Equipment • Tools • Furniture • Supplies

alphaprops.com (818) 504-9090

Muffler Man

See: Automotive/Garage Equip. & Parts

Mummies

See: Egyptian Dressing

Murals

See: Art, Artists For Hire* Backings* Scenic Artists* Wall Coverings

Music & Dance Machines

See: Jukeboxes, Music/Dance Machines

Music Stands

See Also: Music, Sheet

C. P. Two	(323) 466-8201
The Hand Prop Room LP.	(323) 931-1534
History For Hire, Inc.	(818) 765-7767
choices	
RC Vintage, Inc.	(818) 765-7107
1930s Big Band style, band stands	
Sony Pictures Studios-Prop House (Off Lot)	(310) 244-5999
sheet music stands, guitar stands	
Universal Studios Property & Hardware Dept	(818) 777-2784

Wooden musics stands, metal music stands, modern music stands and vintage music stands for rent.

Music, Sheet

See Also: Music Stands

The Hand Prop Room LP.	(323) 931-1534
History For Hire, Inc.	(818) 765-7767
rental & custom	
Hollywood Sheet Music	(818) 567-4338
323 S. Front St. Burbank, CA 91502	
Online sales only	
Sony Pictures Studios-Prop House (Off Lot)	(310) 244-5999

Musical Instrument Cases

See Also: Prop Houses

C. P. Two	(323) 466-8201
History For Hire, Inc.	(818) 765-7767
Sony Pictures Studios-Prop House (Off Lot)	(310) 244-5999

Musical Instruments

See Also: Beatles Musical Instruments* Calliopes* Chimes & Bells* Pianos & Keyboard Instruments* Prop Houses* Rock 'n' Roll Instruments

The Auditorium (877) 732-7733
7684 Clybourn Ave, 2nd Fl, Unit C, Sun Valley, CA 91352
We specialize in musical prop rentals and set dressing for media production.
info@auditoriumprops.com * www.auditoriumprops.com

Badia Design, Inc.	(818) 762-0130

5420 Vineland Ave, N. Hollywood, CA, 91601
Moroccan Musical Instrument including Moroccan ceramic drum, small iron castanets, Moroccan hand drum and more.
info@badiadesign.com * www.badiadesign.com

C. P. Two	(323) 466-8201

Wide range of instruments from rock and acoustic to traditional and classical.

C. P. Valley	(323) 466-8201

Upright pianos, grand pianos and more.

Doug Rowell, Sculptor	(818) 353-4607

Call for appt, Tujunga, CA, 91042
Wood, foam, metal, custom only, design/fabrication/any size job

The Hand Prop Room LP.	(323) 931-1534

all instruments

History For Hire, Inc.	(818) 765-7767

Huge selection of instruments from all periods, rock 'n' roll our specialty.

LCW Props	(818) 243-0707

Guitars, Some Percussion, Violins, Wind Instruments, Music Trays

Los Angeles Percussion Rentals	(310) 666-8152

26450 Ruether Ave Unit 208, Santa Clarita, CA, 91350
Drums, guitars, bass, keyboards, percussion & orchestra instruments (modern or vintage). For performance or prop use.
dan@lapercussionrentals.com * www.lapercussionrentals.com

Norman's Rare Guitars	(818) 344-8300

18969 Ventura Blvd, Tarzana, CA, 91356
vintage guitars

Omega/Cinema Props	(323) 466-8201

Pianos, church organs, mandolins and more.

Sony Pictures Studios-Prop House (Off Lot)	(310) 244-5999

Bagpipes, orchestral instruments, band instruments, folk instruments, pianos, organs percussion instruments and more

Universal Studios Property & Hardware Dept	(818) 777-2784

and cases

Muskets

See: Weaponry, Historical

Mutoscope

See: Arcade Equipment, Games & Rides

Name Badges

See: Badges, Patches & Buttons

Name Plates

The Earl Hays Press   **(818) 765-0700**
services the Industry only. paper or plastic already made
Sony Pictures Studios-Prop House (Off Lot)   **(310) 244-5999**
Universal Studios Property & Hardware Dept   **(818) 777-2784**
Prop name plates and name plate holders for rent.

NASA Dressing

See Also: Computers Science Equipment* Space Shuttle/Space
Hardware*
Action Sets and Props / WonderWorks, Inc.   **(818) 992-8811**
Space shuttle & station, space suit, specialty props, miniatures, mechanical
effects, cityscape, miniature buildings

Spacecraft • Spacesuits • Sets • Miniatures • SFX • Props
Photography • Museum Design • Architectural Vehicles

WonderWorks INC
Serving Aerospace, Film, Entertainment & Education for a Third Of A Century

Global Effects, Inc.   **(818) 503-9273**
space suits, lunar rover, space tools

NASCAR

See Also: Vehicles
AIR Designs   **(818) 768-6639**
Pit Carts, Equipment, Jacks, Tire Racks, Tires, & More
K4 Motorsports   **(818) 713-0552**
P.O. Box 8902, Calabasas, CA, 91372
Full NASCAR Racing Resources for Production, Features, T.V., and
Commercials; Race cars, haulers, pit equip., drivers.
www.k4motorsports.com

Native American

See Also: Archery Equipment, Training Baskets* Leather (Clothing,
Accessories, Materials)* Pottery* Rugs* Wardrobe,
Antique/Historical* Western Dressing*
Absaroka Western Designs   **(307) 455-2440**
1414 Warm Springs Dr, Dubois, WY, 82513
Lodgepole furniture, raw costuming/prop materials, also tanning & some
finished costumes
American Plume   **(800) 521-1132**
11 Skyine Drive East, Unit 2, Clarks Summit, PA 18411
Boas/jackets/theatrical division in NYC; (800) 962-8544. war bonnet, spirit
mask, dreamcatcher, mandela
Autry National Center   **(323) 667-2000**
4700 Western Heritage Way, Los Angeles, CA, 90027
Research room Ext 349, book, archival, artifact collection on the Native
American & history of Amer. West
Caravan West Productions   **(661) 268-8300**
35660 Jayhawker Rd, Aqua Dulce, CA, 91390
everything Native American, enough for a whole Indian village, trading post
caravanwest@earthlink.net * www.caravanwest.com
Crazy Crow Trading Post   **(800) 786-6210**
1801 N. Airport Dr, Pottsboro, TX 75076
Catalog; Native American & mountain man craft supplies, finished goods,
catalog is $5.
The Hand Prop Room LP.   **(323) 931-1534**
auth. antiques, headdresses, knives, beadwork, animal skins etc
History For Hire, Inc.   **(818) 765-7767**
Authentic antiques; baskets, beadwork, blankets
Hollywood Studio Gallery   **(323) 462-1116**
Western paintings, prints & masks
Indian Art Center   **(818) 763-3430**
12666 Ventura Blvd, Studio City, CA, 91604
Rugs & blankets, artifacts, jewelry
Indian Images   **(618) 664-3384**
203 Asbury Ave, Greenville, IL, 62246
High quality made-to-order costumes, props & set decoration of planes,
plateau, southwest & northeast woodlands indians.
The Indian Store   **(760) 639-5309**
1950 Hacienda Dr, Vista, CA, 92081
beads, jewelry findings, fur, feather, leather, rawhide, pottery finished artifacts,
many books on Indian lore/tribes

Nautical Dressing & Props

See Also: Boats & Water Sport Vehicles Caged Vapor Proof Lights*
Canvas* Chain & Rope* Fish, Artificial & Rubber* Pirate, Chests &
Treasures* Seashells*
Alley Cats Studio Rentals   **(818) 982-9178**
Extensive/all sizes, everything from anchors to shark diving cage including
bouys, wooden boats, and beach signage.
Benson's Tropical Sea Imports   **(714) 841-3399**
7442 Vincent Cir, Huntington Beach, CA 92648
lanterns, ship's wheels, rope, game fish, portholes, treasure chest
sales@bensonsimport.com * www.bensonsimport.com
Bob Gail Special Events   **(310) 202-5200**
Sail the high seas with our Nautical Props! Add a Sunken Shipwreck, Anchor,
Ship Steering Wheels to your themed event.
C. P. Valley   **(323) 466-8201**
The Hand Prop Room LP.   **(323) 931-1534**
ship parts & access., auth. artifacts
History For Hire, Inc.   **(818) 765-7767**
anchors,fish/cargo nets,life jacket/rings,portholes,ship's wheel
LCW Props   **(818) 243-0707**
Large Selection, Russian Sub, Regular Sub, Nets, Rope, Anchors, Outboard
Motors, Ship, Yacht & Pilot House Interiors
Lennie Marvin Enterprises, Inc. (Prop Heaven) **(818) 841-5882**
netting, fenders, ropes, lights, anchors, life jackets, portholes, etc.
LM Treasures   **(626) 252-7354**
10557 Juniper Ave Unit A, Fontana, CA 92337
Assorted Sand Dollars, starfish, & anchors are just a few items sold to help
recreate any type beach like theme in mind.
lmtreasures.ll@gmail.com * www.lifesizestatues.net
Oceanic Arts   **(562) 698-6960**
Rope Rigging, Belaying Pins, Cleats, Dead Eyes, Wood Block Pulleys, Barrels,
Used fish nets.
Prop Services West   **(818) 503-2790**

Sony Pictures Studios-Linens, Drapes, Rugs　　(310) 244-5999
5933 W Slauson Ave, Culver City, CA, 90230
fish nets
www.sonypicturesstudios.com
Sony Pictures Studios-Prop House (Off Lot)　　(310) 244-5999
nautical bells, boat bumpers, boat hooks, boat motors, buoys, anchors, life
jackets/rings, portholes, etc.
Tally Ho Marine Salvage & Decor　　(310) 548-5273
406 22nd St, San Pedro, CA, 90731
If we don't have it & can't find it, we can build it. anchors, fish nets, dock cleats,
lanterns, cargo & safety nets

Universal Studios Property & Hardware Dept　　(818) 777-2784
Nautical props and nautical dressing for rent; cargo nets,fish nets, life
jacket/rings, portholes, ship's wheel
Warner Bros. Studios Hardware Rentals　　(818) 954-1335
4000 Warner Blvd., Bldg. 44 Burbank, CA 91522
Door Knobs & Plates, Hinges, Window Fixtures, Elevator Panels, Train & Boat
Accessories
wbsfconstructionservices@warnerbros.com * www.wbsf.com

Nautical Themed Events

See: Events, Backings & Scenery Events, Decorations, Supplies &
Services* Events, Design/Planning/Production* Prop Houses*

Nautical/Marine Services & Charters

See Also: Wetsuits, Diving/Surfing
Aquavision　　(562) 433-2863
3708 E. 4th St, Long Beach, CA, 90814
picture & camera boats/crews, scouting, stunts, set medics lifeguards, safety
divers, marine prop fab., underwater sets
California Sailing Academy　　(310) 821-3433
14025 Panay Way, Marina Del Rey, CA, 90292
sail boats & sailing instruction, camera/film boats, actor instruction
Captain Nemo Underwater Operations　　(310) 626-7083
904 Silver Spur Rd, #386, Rolling Hills Estates, CA, 90274
scuba, safety divers, ALL diving equipment, long list of credits
Cinema Rentals, Inc　　(661) 222-7342
25876 The Old Rd #174, Stevenson Ranch, CA, 91381
picture boats/ships, marine filming equip., underwater cameras, unmanned
aerial filming equip.
Executive Yacht Management, Inc.　　(310) 306-2555
644 Venice Blvd, Marina Del Rey, CA, 90291
power & sail yachts, camera boats, marine coordination, technical advisors
info@yacht-management.com

HEF Pool Service Corp　　(818) 439-6234
6632 Hesperia Ave, Reseda, CA 91335
Portable filtration units, any size tank. Surface skimmers. Chemical balance to
Health Board specs. Onsite maintenance.
www.hefpool.com
Hornblower Cruises & Events　　(310) 301-6000
13755 Fiji Way, Marina Del Rey, CA, 90292
also loc in San Francisco, Berkeley, Newport Beach, San Diego
Living Art Aquatic Design, Inc.　　(310) 822-7484
2301 South Sepulveda Blvd, Los Angeles, CA, 90064
Water tanks.
ron@aquatic2000.com * www.aquatic2000.com
Nautical Film Services　　(562) 594-9276
PO Box 50066, Long Beach, CA, 90815
comprehensive marine services for film, TV, print ad photography, special
events
Offshore Grip Marine　　(310) 547-3515
22631 Pacific Coast Hwy #764, Malibu, CA, 90265
comprehensive svcs from picture & camera boats, to underwater services
(diving, rigging for stunts, etc.)
Outerside　　(615) 720-7011
Environmental & underwater photography

Neglige

See: Underwear & Lingerie, Bloomers, Corsets, Etc.

Neon Lights & Signs

See Also: Bars, Nightclubs, Barware & Dressing Carnival
Dressing/Supplies* Light Fixtures* Signs* Special Effects, Lighting &
Lasers*
AIR Designs　　(818) 768-6639
Large Selection, Auto, Bar, Diner, Restaurant, Ice Cream, Coffee
Alley Cats Studio Rentals　　(818) 982-9178
including night club decorations, coastal signage
C. P. Two　　(323) 466-8201
The Hand Prop Room LP.　　(323) 931-1534
lrg sel., creative, commercial
Heaven or Las Vegas Neon　　(310) 636-0081
11814 Jefferson Blvd, Culver City, CA 90230
Thousands of neon signs & neon props. Custom mfg, install, strike & delivery
services. CA Electric Sign Lic#931962
mail@rentneon.com * www.rentneon.com

**DISPLAY ADS AND LISTINGS FOR THIS CATEGORY
CONTINUE ON THE FOLLOWING PAGE**

Hollywood Neon, Inc (323) 227-6208
custom neon design
Lennie Marvin Enterprises, Inc. (Prop Heaven) (818) 841-5882
wide variety, commercial to art piece
Modern Props (323) 934-3000
contemporary
Nights of Neon (818) 756-4791
13815 Saticoy St, Van Nuys, CA 91402
Over 2,000 neon props in stock. Custom neon lighting and neon fabrication
done onsite.
contact@nightsofneon.com * www.nightsofneon.com

RC Vintage, Inc. (818) 765-7107
large selection of neon signs, Neon Clocks, and more
Sony Pictures Studios-Prop House (Off Lot) (310) 244-5999
neon dimmer switch, neon signs, neon transformer, neon lights, misc neon
supplies, neon shipping crate
Universal Studios Property & Hardware Dept (818) 777-2784
Bar, restaurant, hotel and clubs neon signs for rent.

Nets

See: Camouflage Nets* Cargo Nets* Military Surplus/Combat
Clothes, Field Gear* Nautical Dressing & Props* Sporting Goods &
Services

New Orleans/Mardi Gras Themed Parties

See: Costume Rental Houses* Events, Decorations, Supplies &
Services* Events, Design/Planning/Production* Masks* Travel
(City/Country) Themed Events

New York City Set Dressing & Props

AIR Designs (818) 768-6639
Trash Cans, Subway Entrance, Signage & More
Alley Cats Studio Rentals (818) 982-9178
newsracks, kiosks, subway & street signs, NY park bench, street vendors, food
carts, vendor carts, and much more.
Bob Gail Special Events (310) 202-5200
Bring the streets of the "Big Apple" to life with our many New York Props!
E.C. Prop Rentals (818) 764-2008
Orange/White Steam Vents, Newspaper Machines, Street Signage, Subway
Signage, Blue Police Barricades
The Hand Prop Room LP. (323) 931-1534
vendor carts, taxi, police, firemen, set-ups
History For Hire, Inc. (818) 765-7767
police, etc.
Lennie Marvin Enterprises, Inc. (Prop Heaven) (818) 841-5882
lights, benches, trash cans, parking pods, Central Park benches
Universal Studios Property & Hardware Dept (818) 777-2784
New York city set dressing and New York city props for rent.

New York Themed Parties

See: Events, Decorations, Supplies & Services* Events,
Design/Planning/Production* Statue Of Liberty* Travel (City/Country)
Themed Events

Newspapers (Prop)

The Earl Hays Press (818) 765-0700
The Industry only. old-modern, reproductions, any design, any language.
Original newspapers and custom newspapers.
History For Hire, Inc. (818) 765-7767
custom & stock items for sale
Timothy Hughes Rare & Early Newspapers (570) 326-1045
PO Box 3636, Williamsport, PA, 17701
buy/sell historic newspapers, 1600s to 1991, over 2 million original & historic
issues

Newsroom

E.C. Prop Rentals (818) 764-2008
desk & smalls, chairs, phones
History For Hire, Inc. (818) 765-7767
teletypes, typewriters, phones, etc.
LCW Props (818) 243-0707
News Desk, Monitors, Lighting, Paperwork
RJR Props (404) 349-7600
Newsroom cameras, newsroom pedestals, news crew cameras, ENV cameras
Universal Studios Property & Hardware Dept (818) 777-2784
Newsroom props and newsroom dressing for rent.

Newsstands

Above The Fold (323) 464-6397
226 N. Larchmont Blvd, Los Angeles, CA, 90004
King's Newsstand (323) 653-6793
8361 Beverly Blvd, Los Angeles, CA, 90048
RC Vintage, Inc. (818) 765-7107
Newspaper stands
Robertson Magazine (310) 205-8956
1414 S Robertson Blvd, Los Angeles, CA, 90035
Sherman Oaks Newsstand (818) 995-0632
14500 Ventura Blvd, Sherman Oaks, CA, 91403

Newsstands (Prop)

See Also: Kiosks* Magazines & Magazine/Newspaper Racks
AIR Designs (818) 768-6639
Full Size, Boxes, Books, Newspaper, Lottery Stands, Wall Units
Alley Cats Studio Rentals (818) 982-9178
magazine stands, newspaper racks
C. P. Valley (323) 466-8201
E.C. Prop Rentals (818) 764-2008
Newspaper Machines
History For Hire, Inc. (818) 765-7767
full or empty
LCW Props (818) 243-0707
Newspapers, Magazines, News Racks, Kiosks
Universal Studios Property & Hardware Dept (818) 777-2784
Prop newsstands, vending newsstands, and newsstand displays for rent.
Warner Bros. Studios Property Department (818) 954-2181
Outdoor newsstands, metal newsstands, vintage/period newsstands

Nightclubs

See: Banquets/Booths (Seating)* Bars, Nightclubs, Barware &
Dressing* Chairs* Liquor Bottles* Tables

Nightgowns

See: Sleepwear - Pajamas, Nightgowns, Etc.

Nodders

Modern Props (323) 934-3000
good selection
RC Vintage, Inc. (818) 765-7107
lots! baseball, football, dogs, cats, aliens, ducks, hula dancers, boxers, and
many more bobble heads!

Non-Guns & Non-Pyro Flashes

See Also: Firearms, Gunsmith, Firearm Choreography
CONFETTI & FOG FX Special Effects Company (786) 308-7063
2739 W 79 St Bay, #12, Hialeah, FL 33016
www.caffx.com
The Hand Prop Room LP. (323) 931-1534

Notions

See: Costume/Wardrobe/Sewing Supplies* Fabrics* Trims, Fringe, Tassels, Beading Etc.

Novelties

See: Magicians & Props, Supplies, Dressing* Memorabilia & Novelties

Nursery, Baby

See: Children/Baby Accessories & Bedroom* Hospital Equipment

Nurses Station

See Also: Medical Equip/Furniture, Graphics/Supplies

A-1 Medical Integration   (818) 753-0319
Medical devices for Set Decoration & Property, from minor procedures to detailed hospital units.

Alpha Companies - Spellman Desk Co.   (818) 504-9090
The #1 source for medical equipment in the industry.

Obstacle Courses

See: Fall Pads & Crash Pads* Ramps: Skateboard, BMX, Freestyle, etc.* Sports & Games Themed Events

Occult/Spiritual/Metaphysical

See Also: Astrological* Crystal Balls* Goth/Punk/Bondage/Fetish/Erotica Etc.* Tarot Cards

Psychic Eye Book Shops, Inc.   (818) 784-3797
13435 Ventura Blvd, Sherman Oaks, CA, 91423
new age, metaphysical, self help, occult, astrology, also several other stores in LA area

Dapper Cadaver/Creatures & Cultures   (818) 771-0818
Occult oddities. Witches, werewolf, & vampire props. Supernatural props from Egyptian to Voodoo. Apothecary props.

History For Hire, Inc.   (818) 765-7767
good selection

Sony Pictures Studios-Prop House (Off Lot)   (310) 244-5999

Universal Studios Property & Hardware Dept   (818) 777-2784
Voodoo dolls, voodoo props, witch props, spiritual props and more for rent.

Office Equipment & Dressing

See Also: Bulletin Boards* Business Machines* Certificates* Computers* Copy Machines* Desk Dressing* Drafting Equipment & Supplies* Fans-Table, Floor or Ceiling* Filing Cabinets* Fountains, Drinking (Wall & Stand)* Globes, World Map* Paperwork, Documents & Letters, Office* Safes/Vaults* Trash Cans & Waste Baskets* Typewriters* Water Coolers

Advanced Liquidators Office Furniture   (818) 763-3470
selection of used equipment, professional office furniture designer sets, many qualities, full range of office dressing

C. P. Valley   (323) 466-8201
executive boardroom desks, office desks

Copyrite Solutions   (818) 503-0015
12945 Sherman Way, Ste. 4, N. Hollywood, CA 91605
copiers, fax m/cs, typewriters, all supplies

Dozar Office Furnishings   (310) 559-9292
9937 Jefferson Blvd, Culver City, CA, 90232
Rentals X22: desks, tables, chairs, cabinets, office dressing, office accessories, office dressing, office smalls & more
dozarrents@aol.com * www.dozarrents.com

The Earl Hays Press   (818) 765-0700
services the Industry only

E.C. Prop Rentals   (818) 764-2008
industrial desks & smalls, comp. monitors/keyboards, chairs

Faux Library Studio Props, Inc.   (818) 765-0096
Home Office Dressing, Furniture Home Office, retro office dressing, vintage office dressing, period office dressing

The Hand Prop Room LP.   (323) 931-1534

History For Hire, Inc.   (818) 765-7767
all the smalls

Kitsch N Sync Props   (323) 343-1190
Specializing in 70's and 80's props. Large collection of cameras, electronics, phones, art, games, stereos, & much more.

LCW Props   (818) 243-0707
Desk Setups, Printers, Faxes, Copiers, Desks, Chairs, Large Selection Of Computers & Monitors

Modern Props   (323) 934-3000
contemporary/futuristic-furniture & accessories, including cleared photos, models, full sets, hi-tech, and other office amenities.

"WHERE OUR THINGS ARE" **MODERN PROPS** BRING YOUR CREATIVE IMAGINATION TO LIFE (323) 934-3000
Furniture — Artwork — Decor — Lighting — Fabricated — Specialty
modernprops.com

NEST Studio Rentals, Inc.   (818) 942-0339
home office/exec. furniture, lighting, desk sets, accessories

Prop Services West   (818) 503-2790

RJR Props   (404) 349-7600
Office dressing for up to 400 person bull pen/office; computers, phones, fax machines, copy machines, projectors & more.

Sony Pictures Studios-Prop House (Off Lot)   (310) 244-5999
paper cup dispenser, gooseneck desk fixture, memo holder, blueprint holder, map holder, brochure stand

Universal Studios Property & Hardware Dept   (818) 777-2784
Office dressing, office equipment, office props and more for rent.

Warner Bros. Studios Property Department   (818) 954-2181
Phones, partitions, desk dressing, smalls, assorted computer monitors & CPUs, fax machines, printers

Office Furniture

See Also: Business Machines Filing Cabinets* Office Equipment &
Dressing* Office Supplies*

Advanced Liquidators Office Furniture   (818) 763-3470
New/used: chairs, desks, filing cabinets, partitions executive sets. High end
office furniture for every job and person

Alpha Companies - Spellman Desk Co.   (818) 504-9090
desks, chairs, tables, sofas, traditional to contemporary. Hi-End office
furnishings.

Blueprint Furniture   (310) 657-4315
8600 Pico Blvd. Los Angeles, CA 90035
Modern furniture lighting accessories early classic bauhaus mid-century
contemporary design. Good studio rental history.
www.blueprintfurniture.com

C. P. Valley   (323) 466-8201

Dozar Office Furnishings   (310) 559-9292
9937 Jefferson Blvd, Culver City, CA, 90232
Rentals X22: desks, tables, chairs, cabinets, office dressing, office accessories,
office dressing, office smalls & more
dozarrents@aol.com * www.dozarrents.com

E.C. Prop Rentals   (818) 764-2008
office utility tables, chairs, phones, lighting, water coolers

Faux Library Studio Props, Inc.   (818) 765-0096
conference room to executive desks, vintage office furniture, retro office
furniture, mid century office furniture

FormDecor, Inc.   (310) 558-2582
America's largest event rental supplier of 20th Century furniture and
accessories for Modern and Mid-Century styles.

LCW Props   (818) 243-0707
Chairs, Desks, File Cabinets

Modern Props   (323) 934-3000
contemporary/futurisitic, desks, shelfs, cabinets, chairs, dividers, tables,
counters, executive and hi-tech, realistic to innovative.

Rapport International Furniture   (323) 930-1500
435 N La Brea Ave, Los Angeles, CA, 90036
Choose from modern and contemporary office sets, desks, chairs, shelving and
storage.
rapport@rapportusa.com * www.rapportfurniture.com

Sony Pictures Studios-Prop House (Off Lot)   (310) 244-5999
childrens desks, pedestal desks, reception desks, roll top desks, office desks,
laptop desks, and more

TR Trading Company (310) 329-9242
15604 S Broadway, Gardena, CA, 90248
85,000 sq/ft of items, selection and inventory changes weekly. extensive!
sales@trtradingcompany.com * www.trtradingcompany.com

Universal Studios Property & Hardware Dept (818) 777-2784
Executive office furniture and regular office furniture for rent.

Office Supplies

See Also: Art, Supplies & Stationery* Expendables
Repro-Graphic Supply (818) 771-9066
9838 Glenoaks Blvd, Sun Valley, CA, 91352
Pens/Rulers/Markers/Leads Clearprint/Vellums/Diazo Film Graphic/Sketch
Paper/Title Block Cutting Supplies/Tools/Boards
info@reprographicsupply.com * www.reprographicsupply.com

Oil Cans & Drums

AIR Designs (818) 768-6639
1 Quart to 55 Gallon Drum, Metal & Plastic
Alley Cats Studio Rentals (818) 982-9178
street propane tanks, yellow barrel containers
C. P. Valley (323) 466-8201
E.C. Prop Rentals (818) 764-2008
large sel., multiples
History For Hire, Inc. (818) 765-7767
LCW Props (818) 243-0707
55 Gallon Drums, 25 Gallon, Handheld, Garage, Industrial
Sony Pictures Studios-Prop House (Off Lot) (310) 244-5999
Universal Studios Property & Hardware Dept (818) 777-2784
Period oil cans to modern oil cans for rent.

On-Air Signs

C. P. Two (323) 466-8201
On the air signs, on air signs
History For Hire, Inc. (818) 765-7767
lots, choices
LCW Props (818) 243-0707
Selection Of On-Air Signs, Rigged
Modern Props (323) 934-3000
RC Vintage, Inc. (818) 765-7107
Universal Studios Property & Hardware Dept (818) 777-2784
Prop On Air signs for rent.

Opera Chairs

C. P. Two (323) 466-8201
Omega/Cinema Props (323) 466-8201
Universal Studios Property & Hardware Dept (818) 777-2784
Opera chairs/opera audience chairs for rent.
Warner Bros. Studios Property Department (818) 954-2181

Operating Room & Equipment

See Also: Hospital Equipment
A-1 Medical Integration (818) 753-0319
Medical devices for Set Decoration & Property, from minor procedures to
detailed hospital units.
Alpha Companies - Spellman Desk Co. (818) 504-9090
The #1 source for medical equipment in the industry.
Universal Studios Property & Hardware Dept (818) 777-2784
Operating room props and operating room equipment for rent.

Ophthalmic Equipment

See: Hospital Equipment* Medical Equip/Furniture,
Graphics/Supplies

Optical Lab Equipment

See: Eyewear, Glasses, Sunglasses, 3D* Hospital Equipment* Lab
Equipment* Medical Equip/Furniture, Graphics/Supplies

Orchid Plants

See: Greens

Organs

See: Body Parts* Musical Instruments

Oriental Dressing

See: Asian Antiques, Furniture, Art & Artifacts* Rickshaws

Oriental Themed Parties

See: Events, Decorations, Supplies & Services* Events,
Design/Planning/Production* Travel (City/Country) Themed Events

Outdoor Advertising

See: Billboards & Billboard Lights

Outer Space Themed Parties

See: Aliens* Costume Rental Houses* Costumes* Events,
Decorations, Supplies & Services* Events,
Design/Planning/Production* Fantasy Props, Costumes, or
Decorations* Special Effects, Make-up/Prosthetics

Outerwear

The Costume House	(818) 508-9933
men's & women's period coats & jackets, period furs	
Sony Pictures Studios-Wardrobe	(310) 244-5995
alterations, call (310) 244-7260	
Universal Studios Costume Dept	(818) 777-2722
Rental, mfg., & alterations	
Western Costume Co.	(818) 760-0900

Outrigger Canoes

See: Boats & Water Sport Vehicles

Oversized Props

Bob Gail Special Events	(310) 202-5200
Super-size your next event with an Oversized, Giant Prop. No matter the theme, we have something that will wow!	
Flix FX Inc.	(818) 765-3549
7327 Lankershim Blvd #4, N Hollywood, CA, 91605	
Oversized prop fabrication	
info@flixfx.com * www.flixfx.com	
The Hand Prop Room LP.	(323) 931-1534
crayons, pencils, etc.	
History For Hire, Inc.	(818) 765-7767
also undersized	
L. A. Party Works	(888) 527-2789
9712 Alpaca St, S El Monte, CA, 91733	
in Vancouver tel. 604-589-4101. for film, advertising, events, visual merchandising	
partyworks@aol.com * www.partyworksusa.com	

LCW Props	(818) 243-0707
Planets, Giant Pot, Chess Pieces, Getting New Stuff All The Time	
Lennie Marvin Enterprises, Inc. (Prop Heaven)	(818) 841-5882
teddy bears, baby pins, crayons, pens, etc.	
LM Treasures	(626) 252-7354
10557 Juniper Ave Unit A, Fontana, CA 92337	
8ft silver back gorillas & 13ft long pre-historic fish are some examples of how we range from small to very large items.	
lmtreasures.ll@gmail.com * www.lifesizestatues.net	
Modern Props	(323) 934-3000
crayons, combs, toys + more	
Prop Services West	(818) 503-2790

RC Vintage, Inc.	(818) 765-7107
We have lots of oversize props!	
Robert James Company	(415) 420-4011
2110 West 20th St, Los Angeles, CA, 90018	
Artist studio specializing in large-scale sculpture with turn key projects available at a moments notice or design/build	
rob@robertjamesstudio.com * www.robertjamesstudio.com	
ShopWildThings	(928) 855-6075
2880 Sweetwater Ave, Lake Havasu City, AZ, 86406	
Event Decor, Beaded Curtains, Chain Curtains, String Curtains & Columns, Crystal Columns. Reliable service & delivery.	
help@shopwildthings.com * www.shopwildthings.com	
Sony Pictures Studios-Prop House (Off Lot)	(310) 244-5999
oversized corn, oversized apple, oversized fork, oversized spoon, oversized pencil, and many more oversized props, more	
Universal Studios Property & Hardware Dept	(818) 777-2784
Oversized props for rent and fabrication	

Packaging Design

See: Graphics, Digital & Large Format Printing Product Labels*

Packing/Packaging Supplies, Services

See Also: Boxes Crates/ Vaults* Expendables* Gift Wrapping* Wrapped Prop Gift Packages*

Absolute Packaging	(800) 567-9190
11940 Sherman Road, N. Hollywood, CA 91605	
std/custom, boxes, wardrobe, custom foam, bubble wrap, tape. gift bags, shipping boxes	
www.absolutepackagingsupply.com	

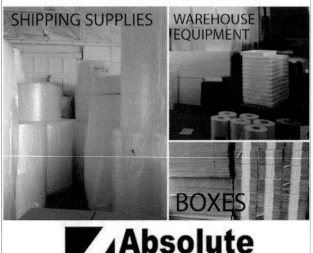

Banner Packing & Crating	(310) 276-0804
344 N. La Cienega, Los Angeles, CA, 90048	
Basaw Manufacturing, Inc.	(818) 765-6650
7300 Varna, N Hollywood, CA, 91605	
Basaw builds crates to order, large inventory in stock. domestic & export packaging, standard & specialized	
fredy@basaw.com * www.basaw.com	
Delta Packaging Co.	(310) 538-8700
14110 S. Broadway, Los Angeles, CA, 90061	
EPS foam boxes, liners, packing expendables esp. for produce, floral, biotech	
Imperial Paper Co.	(818) 769-4400
5733-37 Cahuenga Blvd, N Hollywood, CA, 91601	
Wardrobe, tape, cushioning, foam, bubblewrap, custom & stock shipping boxes.	
www.imperialpaper.com	

Paint & Painting Supplies

See Also: Expendables Prop & Set Design Supplies, Parts, Tools*
Ultraviolet Products*

Burbank Paint (818) 845-2684
548 S. San Fernando Blvd, Burbank, CA, 91502
specialty industrial paints

Day-Glo Corp. (800) 289-3294
4515 St. Clair Ave, Cleveland, OH, 44107
mfg. of Day-Glo paints, inks, plastics, coated papers/fabrics

Delta Creative (800) 842-4197
3225 Westech Drive, Norcross, GA, 30092
craft paint for ceramics, fabric

Dunn Edwards (800) 735-4632
7064 W. Sunset Blvd., Hollywood, CA 90028

G & M Paint & Supply (818) 771-0608
8011 Webb Ave, N. Hollywood, CA, 91605
automotive & industrial paints

Mann Brothers (323) 936-5168
758 N La Brea Ave, Los Angeles, CA, 90038

Mark's Paint Store (818) 766-3949
4830 Vineland Ave, N Hollywood, CA, 91601
special purpose paint store catering to the Industry

Newhall Paint Store, Inc. (661) 259-3454
24401 Main St, Newhall, CA, 91321
general purpose paint store in good location

North Hollywood Hardware, Inc. (818) 980-2453
11847 Ventura Blvd, Studio City, CA, 91604
Paint, stains, faux & spray finishes, computerized color matching. Grass paint
now available in wide range of sizes.
nohohardware@gmail.com * www.ehardware2go.com

Nova Color Artists Acrylic Paint (310) 204-6900
5894 Blackwelder St, Culver City, CA, 90232
mfr/retail special purpose acrylics, 80 colors, free price list & color chart, ship to
USA & Canada

Portola Paint & Glazes (323) 655-2211
8213 West 3rd St, Los Angeles, CA, 90048
Lime wash, Roman Clay, Wrought Iron, Royal Satin, Florentine glaze

Warner Bros. Studios Paint Department (818) 954-1817
4000 Warner Blvd, Bldg 47, Burbank, CA 91522
Supplier of all major paint, stain & finish brands, tools, brushes, rollers,
adhesives, tapes & more
wbsfconstructionservices@warnerbros.com * www.wbpaintdept.com

Paint Removal

See: Sanitation, Waste Disposal

Paintball

See: Sporting Goods & Services

Paintings/Prints

See Also: Art For Rent Art, Artists For Hire* Art, Tribal & Folk* Art &
Picture Framing Services* Posters, Art/Movie/Travel/Wanted Etc.*
Prop Houses*

Art Dimensions Inc. (310) 433-8934
Web Based Business
Cleared contemporary art for lease including paintings, prints, sculptures and
photography by more than 80 artists.
info@artdimensionsonline.com * www.artdimensionsonline.com

ART PIC (818) 503-5999
6826 Troost Ave, N Hollywood, CA, 91605
contemporary art, all mediums + sculpture, all art cleared
artpicla@mac.com * www.artpic2000.com

Artspace Warehouse (323) 936-7020
7358 Beverly Boulevard, Los Angeles, CA, 90036
Huge selection of cleared original art in stock for same day rent or sale at
affordable prices.
info@artspacewarehouse.com * www.artspacewarehouse.com

ART SPACE WARE HOUSE
spectacular ART | amazing SELECTION
GUILT-FREE prices | INTERNATIONAL artists

Bridge Furniture & Props Los Angeles (818) 433-7100
We carry modern & traditional furniture, lighting, accessories, cleared art,&
rugs. Items are online for easy shopping.

Clearedart.com/El Studio Granados (818) 240-4421
958 Verdugo Circle Dr, Glendale, CA, 91206
Multi-media variety of original paintings and prints in a multitude of styles and
techniques.
fineart@elstudiogranados.com * www.clearedart.com

FILM ART LA (323) 461-4900
Culver City Warehouse at Jefferson & Hauser. Call for address.
Film Art LA rents cleared art and creates digital, painted reproductions,
specialty prop art, portraits and paintings.
filmartla@gmail.com * www.artimagela.com

The Hand Prop Room LP. (323) 931-1534
1,000 cleared pcs

Hollywood Cinema Arts, Inc. (818) 504-7333
Nobody has more cleared painting/prints than HCA

Hollywood Studio Gallery (323) 462-1116
neo-classical to contemporary

LCW Props (818) 243-0707
Paintings, Photos, Sketches

Modern Props (323) 934-3000
cleared paintings and cleared prints, contemporary/futuristic large selection

NEST Studio Rentals, Inc. (818) 942-0339
cleared original paintings & prints in stock

Ob-jects (818) 351-4200
sets of architectural, floral & portraits

Omega/Cinema Props (323) 466-8201

Pasadena Antique Warehouse (626) 404-2422
1609 East Washington Blvd., Pasadena, CA, 91104
Paintings and prints of ceramics, still life studies, and portraits. Original
artwork.
pasadenaantiquewarehouse@gmail.com *
www.pasadenaantiquewarehouse.com

Prop Services West (818) 503-2790

Rapport International Furniture (323) 930-1500
435 N La Brea Ave, Los Angeles, CA, 90036
Choose from a variety of high quality prints, paintings and other accessories to
dress your rooms with authenticity.
rapport@rapportusa.com * www.rapportfurniture.com

LISTINGS FOR THIS CATEGORY CONTINUE ON THE
FOLLOWING PAGE

Retro-Reproductions (310) 659-7058
Web Based Business
Specialize in high quality digital prints & reproductions of vintage movie posters & photographs, ALL CLEARED
stage.door1969@gmail.com * www.retro-reproductions.com
Sony Pictures Studios-Prop House (Off Lot) (310) 244-5999
Temporary Contemporary Art (562) 900-6115
7815 Gazette Ave, Winnetka, CA 91306
Abstract Expressionism, Modern Art, Gallery Art, Kids Art, Tiki, Lowbrow, Street Art, Punk Rock, Skateboards
temporarycontemporaryart@gmail.com * www.temporarycontemporaryart.com
Universal Studios Property & Hardware Dept (818) 777-2784
Framed and unframed paintings and prints for rent.
Wallspace (323) 930-0471
607 N La Brea, Los Angeles, CA 90036
Contemporary abstract art gallery and photography. Available for rent and sale with permission to use on tv film & print
art@wallspacela.com * www.wallspacela.com
ZG04 DECOR (818) 853-8040
Abstract, Portrait, Landscape, Seascape, Botanical, Nude, Portraits, Figurative Drawings, Floral, Shadowboxes

Pajamas

See: Sleepwear - Pajamas, Nightgowns, Etc.

Pallets

Alley Cats Studio Rentals (818) 982-9178
wood & metal style, modern, crates
Basaw Manufacturing, Inc. (818) 765-6650
7300 Varna, N Hollywood, CA, 91605
Basaw builds crates to order, large inventory in stock. machinery/electronic crates
fredy@basaw.com * www.basaw.com
E.C. Prop Rentals (818) 764-2008
wood & plastic, also pallet jacks, good multiples
LCW Props (818) 243-0707
Large Selection, Wood, Metal, Plastic, Warehouse Dressing
Universal Studios Property & Hardware Dept (818) 777-2784
Pallets and pallet jacks for rent.

Paneling, Veneers & Laminates

See Also: Building Supply, Lumber, Hardware, Etc. Floor, Ground & Surface Protection*
Architectural Plywood (818) 255-1900
7104 Case Ave, N. Hollywood, CA, 91605
wholesale & retail; custom veneers only, lumber, plywood
Bear Forest Products, Inc (951) 727-1767
4685 Brookhollow Circle, Riverside, CA, 92509
Plywood, veneer, and wood paneling.
matto@bearfp.com * www.bearfp.com
California Panel & Veneer (562) 926-5834
14055 Artesia Blvd, Cerritos, CA, 90703
panel, veneer, laminates
General Veneer Manufacturing Co. (323) 564-2661
8652 Otis St, South Gate, CA, 90280
Breakaway balsa wood sheets & boards
balsasales@generalveneer.com * www.generalveneer.com
MacBeath Hardwood (877) 499-7350
2211 Ringwood Ave., San Jose, CA 95131
hardwood veneers, paneling, hardwood stock
Manhattan Laminates (212) 255-2522
624 W 52nd Street, New York City, NY, 10019
laminates
Phillip's Plywood (818) 897-7736
13599 Desmond St, Pacoima, CA, 91331
wholesaler of plywood, laminates & laminated panels
Wurth Louis and Company (800) 422-4389
895 Columbia St, Brea, CA, 92821
distribute Chemetal, metal laminates, solid metals, treefrog veneers, Nevamar laminates

Panty Hose

See: Hosiery

Paper

See Also: Art, Supplies & Stationery
Flax Art & Design (415) 552-2355
1699 Market St, San Francisco, CA, 94103
catalog sales; fine papers, printed, natural, textured, machine-milled, chiyogami, tissue & lace, many varieties/colors
Hiromi Paper, Inc. (310) 998-0098
2525 Michigan Ave, #G9, Santa Monica, CA, 90404
conservation, framing, art, decorative, stationary, acid-free, Japanese papers, book/paper making supplies, spec. orders
Kate's Paperie (800) 809-9880
188 Lafayette St, New York, NY, 10013
paper goods; 5 stores in NY

Paper, Seamless

See: Expendables

Paperwork, Documents & Letters, Office

Advanced Liquidators Office Furniture (818) 763-3470
C. P. Valley (323) 466-8201
paperwork & letters
The Earl Hays Press (818) 765-0700
Services the Industry only. paperwork; old-modern, repro. any design, any language.
Faux Library Studio Props, Inc. (818) 765-0096
desk plates, glass plaques, glass inscribed awards, over sized dollar bills, many colored file folders
The Hand Prop Room LP. (323) 931-1534
letters, paperwork
History For Hire, Inc. (818) 765-7767
anything done custom, paperwork to rent
HPR Graphics (323) 556-2694
5674 Venice Blvd, Los Angeles, CA, 90019
Law enforcement files, letterheads, business cards, identification, newspapers, certificates, diplomas, stocks and more.
hprcan@earthlink.net * www.hprgraphics.net
LCW Props (818) 243-0707
Our Specialty. Huge Quantities Of Any Kind. Medical, Legal, Office, Blueprints, Binders, Custom

6439 San Fernando Rd. Glendale, CA 91201
Phone: 818-243-0707 - www.lcwprops.com

Universal Studios Property & Hardware Dept (818) 777-2784
Prop office paperwork, prop documents, prop letters, prop office documents, prop paperwork; all for rent.

Parades

See: Events, Decorations, Supplies & Services Events, Design/Planning/Production* Events, Entertainment*

Paramedic Equipment

See: Ambulance/Paramedic

Parasols

See: Umbrellas, Hand & Parasols

Park Benches

See: Benches

Park Playground

See: Playground Equipment

Parking Meters & Sign Poles

AIR Designs	**(818) 768-6639**
Large Selection of Single & Double Meter, Sign Poles 4'-10'	
Alley Cats Studio Rentals	**(818) 982-9178**
Parking meters mounted on self-standing poles as well as new digital meters. Coin and credit card parking meters	
C. P. Valley	**(323) 466-8201**
Old fashioned parking meters and automatic parking meters	
E.C. Prop Rentals	**(818) 764-2008**
poles with bases, lrg multiples	
The Hand Prop Room LP.	**(323) 931-1534**
History For Hire, Inc.	**(818) 765-7767**
quantity in matching	
LCW Props	**(818) 243-0707**
Singles & Doubles	
Lennie Marvin Enterprises, Inc. (Prop Heaven)	**(818) 841-5882**
period/modern meters, parking poles/signs, NYC parking pods	
RC Vintage, Inc.	**(818) 765-7107**
free standing Digital, coin operated parking meters, vintage parking meters, period parking meters, multiple sizes	
Universal Studios Property & Hardware Dept	**(818) 777-2784**
Freestanding parking meters & coin operated parking meters from different periods and many street signs/sign poles for rent.	

Partitions

See: Office Furniture

Party Decorations & Design

See: Events, Decorations, Supplies & Services* Events, Design/Planning/Production* Events, Entertainment* Trade Shows & Conventions

Party Food Props

See: Food, Artificial Food

Patches

See: Badges, Patches & Buttons

Patio & Outdoor Furniture

See: Cafe Tables/Chairs/Umbrellas* Furniture, Outdoor/Patio

Patterns

See Also: Fabrics* Stage Lighting, Film/Video/TV* Lighting & Sound, Concert/Theatrical/DJ/VJ

Amazon Drygoods	**(812) 852-1780**
3788 Wilson St, Osgood, IN 47037	
catalog sales; 19 C. wardrobe/patterns, home access., books	
Hedgehog Handworks	**(888) 670-6040**
8616 La Tijera Ste 303, Westchester, CA, 90045	
catalog sales; unusual needlework supplies, books on historical sewing, needlepoint & costuming topics	

PDAs (Personal Digital Assistant)

See: Computers

Peanut Carts

See: Vendor Carts & Concession Counters

Pedal Cars/Toys

See: Toys & Games

Pedestals

See Also: Architectural Pieces & Artifacts* Columns

C. P. Two	**(323) 466-8201**
C. P. Valley	**(323) 466-8201**
Castle Antiques & Design	**(855) 765-5800**
11924 Vose St, N Hollywood, CA, 91605	
Various pedestals/prop pedestals for rent or purchase.	
info@castleantiques.net * www.castleprophouse.com	
The Hand Prop Room LP.	**(323) 931-1534**
Modern Props	**(323) 934-3000**
contemporary/futuristic	
Omega/Cinema Props	**(323) 466-8201**
Prop Services West	**(818) 503-2790**
Sony Pictures Studios-Prop House (Off Lot)	**(310) 244-5999**
Universal Studios Property & Hardware Dept	**(818) 777-2784**
Pedestals of various time periods and sizes for rent.	
Warner Bros. Studios Property Department	**(818) 954-2181**
Pedestal bases, column pedestals, classic pedestals, commode pedestals, figural pedestals, Asian, Syrian	

Pennants

See: Badges, Patches & Buttons* Flags/Banners

Penny Arcade

See: Arcade Equipment, Games & Rides* Vendor Carts & Concession Counters

Pens, Fountain

See Also: Art, Supplies & Stationery

The Hand Prop Room LP.	**(323) 931-1534**
antique, period pcs, lrg sel.	
History For Hire, Inc.	**(818) 765-7767**
all working	
Sony Pictures Studios-Prop House (Off Lot)	**(310) 244-5999**
Universal Studios Property & Hardware Dept	**(818) 777-2784**
Fountain pens of different time periods and styles for rent.	

Pepsi Memorabilia

AIR Designs	**(818) 768-6639**
Signage, Vending Machine	
History For Hire, Inc.	**(818) 765-7767**

Perfume Bottles

Badia Design, Inc.	**(818) 762-0130**
5420 Vineland Ave, N. Hollywood, CA, 91601	
info@badiadesign.com * www.badiadesign.com	
The Hand Prop Room LP.	**(323) 931-1534**
period-contemp	
History For Hire, Inc.	**(818) 765-7767**
many	
Modern Props	**(323) 934-3000**
contemporary, many sizes & styles	
Ob-jects	**(818) 351-4200**
Prop Services West	**(818) 503-2790**
Sony Pictures Studios-Prop House (Off Lot)	**(310) 244-5999**
Universal Studios Property & Hardware Dept	**(818) 777-2784**
Contemporary perfume bottles, period perfume bottles, decorative perfume bottles and more for rent.	

Periscopes

See: Military Props & Equipment

Personal Care

See: Make-up & Hair, Supplies & Services* Shaving, Old Fashion, Non-Electric

Pet Cemetery & Crematory Services

See Also: Cemetery Dressing* Mortuary* Taxidermy, Hides/Heads/Skeletons

Cal Pet Crematory	**(818) 983-2313**
9595 Glenoaks Blvd, P.O. Box 488, Sun Valley, CA 91353-0488	
Pet cremation services for small to medium pets as well as decorative urns and memorial stones.	
www.calpet.com	

Pet Furniture, Houses, Clothing

Alley Cats Studio Rentals   **(818) 982-9178**
1 dog house
Animal Stars   **(661) 424-1700**
16787 Sierra Hwy, Santa Clarita, CA, 91351
Luxury pet accessories, Swarovski crystal tags, collars, jewelry, clothing
Evans Family Barrels   **(818) 523-8174**
7918 Fairchild Ave, Canoga Park, CA, 91306
Solid oak wine barrel furniture: tables, chairs, cabinets, pet furniture, home and business decor, swings
evansbarrels@gmail.com * www.EvansFamilyBarrels.com
The Retro Kats   **(818) 834-5022**
Located in Sylmar, CA, 91342
Custom Luxury Cat Trees, Unique Cat Condos, Lush Faux Fur Cat Mats & Dog Mats, Artistically Designed Feline Furniture.
TheRetroKats@gmail.com * www.TheRetroKats.com
Universal Studios Property & Hardware Dept   **(818) 777-2784**
Cat scratching poles, cat scratching pads, dog houses and dog beds for rent.
Worldwise, Inc.   **(415) 721-7400**
160 Mitchell Boulevard, San Rafael, CA, 94903
pet furniture, plush toys, pet jewelry, pet beds, collars & leads

Pews

See: Church, Chapel, Synagogue, Mosque

Pewter & Pewterware

Gibson Pewter   **(603) 464-3410**
18 E. Washington Rd, Hillsborough, NH, 03244
Lead-free reproduction pewterware, tankards, plates, bowls, porringers, etc.
The Hand Prop Room LP.   **(323) 931-1534**
History For Hire, Inc.   **(818) 765-7767**
good sel.
Omega/Cinema Props   **(323) 466-8201**
Prop Services West   **(818) 503-2790**
Sword & Stone   **(818) 562-6548**

Pharmacy

See: Drugstore/Apothecary

Phonograph Records

See Also: Record/Video Store
Amoeba Music   **(323) 245-6400**
6400 Sunset Blvd, Hollywood, CA, 90028
big, changing sel. of hard-to-find collectible disks/records, also new & vintage rock posters & memorabilia
Astro Audio Video Lighting, Inc.   **(818) 549-9915**
6615 San Fernando Rd, Glendale, CA, 91201
Time code and control vinyl for DJ software including Serato systems and Traktor systems
www.astroavl.com
The Hand Prop Room LP.   **(323) 931-1534**
History For Hire, Inc.   **(818) 765-7767**
from wax cylinders to 78s, 45s, 33s
Omega/Cinema Props   **(323) 466-8201**
Phonograph record players, period and vintage.
Sony Pictures Studios-Prop House (Off Lot)   **(310) 244-5999**
Universal Studios Property & Hardware Dept   **(818) 777-2784**
Phonograph records for rent.

Phonographs

See Also: Audio Equipment Victrolas/Gramophones*
Astro Audio Video Lighting, Inc.   **(818) 549-9915**
6615 San Fernando Rd, Glendale, CA, 91201
Phonographs/record players for rent or purchase including DJ turntables; Technics, Pioneer & Numark.
www.astroavl.com
The Hand Prop Room LP.   **(323) 931-1534**
all periods
History For Hire, Inc.   **(818) 765-7767**
most eras
LCW Props   **(818) 243-0707**
Period - Present
Modern Props   **(323) 934-3000**
Omega/Cinema Props   **(323) 466-8201**
RC Vintage, Inc.   **(818) 765-7107**
40s, 50s, 60s & 70s, vintage brass phonographs, vintage record players, horn phonographs
Universal Studios Property & Hardware Dept   **(818) 777-2784**
Phonographs, victrolas, gramophones and more for rent.

Photo Albums

See: Scrapbooks

Photo Blow-ups

See Also: Graphics, Digital & Large Format Printing
Art, Signs & Graphics   **(818) 503-7997**
6939 Farmdale Ave, N Hollywood, CA, 91605
props, banners, vinyl graphics, vehicle graphics, 3D router cut letters & logos
jessee@artsignsandgraphics.com * www.artsignsandgraphics.com
D'ziner Sign Co.   **(323) 467-4467**
801 Seward Street, Los Angeles, CA 90038
standees
sales@dzinersign.com * www.dzinersign.com
Warner Bros. Studios Photo Lab   **(818) 954-7118**
4000 Warner Blvd, Burbank, CA 91522
A complete imaging resource serving the needs of the entertainment industry for over 85 years.
photolab@warnerbros.com * www.wbphotolab.com

Photo Booths

Arc de Belle   **(855) 332-3553**
Call for Consultation
Themed Photo Booth Canopies VIP Lounge Booth Photo Booth, Rentals
info@arcdebelle.com * www.arcdebelle.com
L. A. Party Works   **(888) 527-2789**
9712 Alpaca St, S El Monte, CA, 91733
in Vancouver tel. 604-589-4101
partyworks@aol.com * www.partyworksusa.com

VARIETY OF PHOTO BOOTHS / PROPS / CUSTOM BRANDING & MESSAGE ON UNIT & PHOTO PRINTS

PARTYWORKS INTERACTIVE

Lennie Marvin Enterprises, Inc. (Prop Heaven)   **(818) 841-5882**
coin-op. photo booths (non-op.)
Lucky Photo Booth   **(323) 229-9455**
4040 Farmouth Drive, Los Angeles, CA 90027
Lucky Photo Booth rents one of a kind Art Deco style booths that are custom designed by a portrait photographer.
www.luckyphotobooth.com
RC Vintage, Inc.   **(818) 765-7107**
arcade, period, coin-operated, 25 cent photo booths

Photographic Equipment

See: Camera Equipment

Photographic Processing

Warner Bros. Studios Photo Lab   **(818) 954-7118**
4000 Warner Blvd, Burbank, CA 91522
A complete imaging resource serving the needs of the entertainment industry
for over 85 years.
photolab@warnerbros.com * www.wbphotolab.com

Photographs

See Also: Memorabilia & Novelties Paintings/Prints* Art & Picture
Framing Services* Sports Fan Items, Memorabilia, Photographs*
ART PIC   **(818) 503-5999**
6826 Troost Ave, N Hollywood, CA, 91605
contemporary art, all mediums + sculpture, all art cleared
artpicla@mac.com * www.artpic2000.com
Bridge Furniture & Props Los Angeles   **(818) 433-7100**
We carry modern & traditional furniture, lighting, accessories, cleared art,&
rugs. Items are online for easy shopping.
Faux Library Studio Props, Inc.   **(818) 765-0096**
Art photos, cleared family photos and cleared police photos, framed and
unframed
FILM ART LA   **(323) 461-4900**
Culver City Warehouse at Jefferson & Hauser. Call for address.
Large Inventory of cleared art rentals 19th Century to Present. All types Art,
Photography and Sculpture High Rez images
filmartla@gmail.com * www.artimagela.com
The Hand Prop Room LP.   **(323) 931-1534**
Hollywood Studio Gallery   **(323) 462-1116**
cleared photos (b/w & color) large selection
LCW Props   **(818) 243-0707**
Period - Present
Little Bohemia Rentals   **(818) 853-7506**
11940 Sherman Rd, N Hollywood, CA, 91605
Cleared family photos, vintage and modern.
sales@wearelittlebohemia.com * www.wearelittlebohemia.com
Modern Props   **(323) 934-3000**
large collection of cleared modern photographs and cleared contemporary
photographs
NEST Studio Rentals, Inc.   **(818) 942-0339**
cleared, framed art photos, framed family photos
Ob-jects   **(818) 351-4200**
Pasadena Antique Warehouse   **(626) 404-2422**
1609 East Washington Blvd., Pasadena, CA, 91104
Antique prints and postcards, as well as contemporary photography prints.
pasadenaantiquewarehouse@gmail.com *
www.pasadenaantiquewarehouse.com
Retro-Reproductions   **(310) 659-7058**
Web Based Business
Specialize in high quality digital prints & reproductions of vintage movie posters
& photographs, ALL CLEARED
stage.door1969@gmail.com * www.retro-reproductions.com
Sony Pictures Studios-Prop House (Off Lot)   **(310) 244-5999**
Old black and white photographs, black and white photos
Superstock   **(800) 828-4545**
6620 Southpoint Dr South Ste 501, Jacksonville, FL, 32216
stock photography & fine art, licensing or royalty-free. Email
tom@superstock.com for contract information.
Universal Studios Property & Hardware Dept   **(818) 777-2784**
Framed photographs, unframed photographs, cleared photographs and more
for rent.
Wallspace   **(323) 930-0471**
607 N La Brea, Los Angeles, CA 90036
Contemporary abstract art gallery and photography. Available for rent and sale
with permission to use on tv film & print
art@wallspacela.com * www.wallspacela.com
Warner Bros. Studios Photo Lab   **(818) 954-7118**
4000 Warner Blvd, Burbank, CA 91522
A complete imaging resource serving the needs of the entertainment industry
for over 85 years.
photolab@warnerbros.com * www.wbphotolab.com

Physical Therapy

See: Weightlifting Equipment Traction Equipment* Massage Tables*
Exercise & Fitness Equipment* Medical Equip/Furniture,
Graphics/Supplies*

Pianos & Keyboard Instruments

C. P. Two   **(323) 466-8201**
C. P. Valley   **(323) 466-8201**
History For Hire, Inc.   **(818) 765-7767**
electric, upright, large selection
Hollywood Piano Rental Company   **(818) 954-8500**
323 S Front Street, Burbank, CA, 91502
Over 700 pianos in stock, all colors, sizes, periods. Tuning, piano services &
repairs, Piano moving (insured/bonded)
glennt@hollywoodpiano.com * www.hollywoodpiano.com
Universal Studios Property & Hardware Dept   **(818) 777-2784**
Many pianos of all styles for rent.

Picnic Tables

See: Furniture, Outdoor/Patio

Picture Frames

See Also: Photographs
The Hand Prop Room LP.   **(323) 931-1534**
selection in stock, custom framing
Hollywood Studio Gallery   **(323) 462-1116**
ornate, ready made or custom
Little Bohemia Rentals   **(818) 853-7506**
11940 Sherman Rd, N Hollywood, CA, 91605
Tabletop and Wall with Cleared photos and/or art.
sales@wearelittlebohemia.com * www.wearelittlebohemia.com
Ob-jects   **(818) 351-4200**
Omega/Cinema Props   **(323) 466-8201**
Prop Services West   **(818) 503-2790**
Sony Pictures Studios-Prop House (Off Lot)   **(310) 244-5999**
framed drawing, framed paintings, framed photographs, picture plaques, print /
litho, shadow box picture, picture stands
U-Frame It Gallery   **(818) 781-4500**
6203 Lankershim Blvd, N Hollywood, CA, 91606
classic frames to modern, laminating, restorations and more
uframit@aol.com * www.uframeitgallery.com

Universal Studios Property & Hardware Dept   **(818) 777-2784**
Different picture frames from styles and time periods for rent.
ZG04 DECOR   **(818) 853-8040**
Framed Art & Tabletop Frames

Picture Framing Services

See: Picture Frames* Art & Picture Framing Services

Picture Vehicles

See: Aircraft, Charters & Aerial Services* Ambulance/Paramedic* Jet Skis* Motorcycles* Nautical/Marine Services & Charters* Police Car, Police Motorcycle* RV Vehicles & Travel Trailers, Equip & Parts* Trains* Vehicle Preparation Services* Vehicles

Pictures

See: Paintings/Prints* Photographs* Posters, Art/Movie/Travel/Wanted Etc.* Sports Fan Items, Memorabilia, Photographs

Pilings

See: Nautical Dressing & Props

Pillows, Decorative

See Also: Linens, Household* Prop Houses
Bassman-Blaine (213) 748-5909
1933 S. Broadway, #1005, Los Angeles, CA 90007
Great source for accent pillows in designer quality fabrics, featuring 24x24s & assorted bolster/lumbar and accent sizes
lashowroom@bassman-blaine.com * www.bassmanblainelamart.com
Little Bohemia Rentals (818) 853-7506
11940 Sherman Rd, N Hollywood, CA, 91605
African Mud Cloth, Japanese Shibori, Indigo, Embroidered, Kilim, Vintage and Contemporary.
sales@wearelittlebohemia.com * www.wearelittlebohemia.com
Lux Lounge EFR (888) 247-4411
106 1/2 Judge John Aiso St #318, Los Angeles, CA, 90012
Decorative Pillows: Assorted Colored Pillows, Couch Throw Pillows, Sequin Pillows, Custom Design Pillows & More.
info@luxloungeefr.com * www.luxloungeefr.com
NEST Studio Rentals, Inc. (818) 942-0339
large selection
Prop Services West (818) 503-2790
Tara Design (310) 559-8272
3223 S La Cienega Boulevard, Los Angeles, CA, 90016
Our textiles are made from traditional Indian Saris and silks. We also carry bedding, curtains and rugs.
info@tara-design.com * www.tara-design.com
ZG04 DECOR (818) 853-8040
Modern, Contemporary, Traditional, Vintage

Pinata

See: Mexican Decorations

Pinball Machines

See Also: Arcade Equipment, Games & Rides
C. P. Two (323) 466-8201
L. A. Party Works (888) 527-2789
9712 Alpaca St, S El Monte, CA, 91733
in Vancouver tel. 604-589-4101
partyworks@aol.com * www.partyworksusa.com
LCW Props (818) 243-0707
Modern & High End Gaming Systems
RC Vintage, Inc. (818) 765-7107
arcade, modern to period, coin-operated Cleared, many models, large assortment

Pipe & Bases

See: Rigging, Equipment or Services* Theatrical Draperies, Hardware & Rigging

Pipes (Metal & Plastic)

Alley Cats Studio Rentals (818) 982-9178
PVC, metal w/valves, rooftop
E.C. Prop Rentals (818) 764-2008
large sel w/gate valves, many sizes & diameters
LCW Props (818) 243-0707
Large Selection Of Industrial, Plastic, Steel, Basement, Conduit

Pipes, Smoking

See: Smoking Products* Marijuana Plants, Dispensary Dressing & Hydroponics

Pirate, Chests & Treasures

Bob Gail Special Events (310) 202-5200
Need some Pirate Props that will make even Jack Sparrow proud? Choose Pirate Ships, Treasure Chests, and more!
Dapper Cadaver/Creatures & Cultures (818) 771-0818
Pirate props & pirate themed decorations. Mummies & skeletons. Standing gallows, gibbets & period torture devices.
The Hand Prop Room LP. (323) 931-1534
fully dressed
History For Hire, Inc. (818) 765-7767
outfitted
Lennie Marvin Enterprises, Inc. (Prop Heaven) (818) 841-5882
large/small chests, treasure, nautical dressing & more
LM Treasures (626) 252-7354
10557 Juniper Ave Unit A, Fontana, CA 92337
Life size pirates to cannons and treasure chests are all fun ways to spice up any dull room or yard.
lmtreasures.ll@gmail.com * www.lifesizestatues.net
Sony Pictures Studios-Prop House (Off Lot) (310) 244-5999
pirate treasure chests
Sword & Stone (818) 562-6548

Pitching Machine, Baseball

See: Baseball Pitching Machine

Pizza Ovens & Boxes

AIR Designs (818) 768-6639
Ovens, Signage, Paddles, Neon, Kitchen Equipment
C. P. Valley (323) 466-8201
Lennie Marvin Enterprises, Inc. (Prop Heaven) (818) 841-5882
boxes, pizza scoops, rotating pizza display oven countertop

Planters

See: Pottery

Plants

See: Greens

Plaques

See: Badges, Patches & Buttons* Engraving* Trophies/Trophy Cases

Plaster, Ornamental

See: Staff Shops

Plastic Food

See: Food, Artificial Food

Plastic Ice Cubes

See: Ice Cubes, Plastic

Plastic Snow

See: Snow, Artificial & Real

Plastics, Materials & Fabrication

See Also: Clear Vinyl* Flowers, Silk & Plastic* Foam* Ice Cubes,
Plastic* Rubber & Foam Rubber

Canal Plastic Center (212) 925-1032
345 Canal St, New York, NY, 10013
supply plastics

Gavrieli Plastic Supply (818) 982-0000
11733 Sherman Way, N. Hollywood, CA, 91605
small sheet form

Harrington Industrial Plastics (818) 780-5212
15000 Keswick St, Suite B, Van Nuys, CA, 91405
sheet form, tanks, pipes, grating, industrial shapes

LCW Props (818) 243-0707
Huge Selection Of Tubes, Tanks, Spheres

Living Art Aquatic Design, Inc. (310) 822-7484
2301 South Sepulveda Blvd, Los Angeles, CA, 90064
Custom acrylic work, forming, aquariums, Point of Purchase displays,
ReadyReef, nano cubes.
ron@aquatic2000.com * www.aquatic2000.com

Tanks • Custom Aquariums • Reefs • Saltwater • Freshwater • Ponds
RESIDENTIAL AND COMMERIAL • CUSTOM DESIGNS • INSTALLATION • MAINTENANCE • PROFESSIONAL STAFF

CREDITS:
Transformers 2
Ocean's Thirteen
Mission Impossible 3
Knocked Up

LIVING ART Aquatic
DESIGN, INC.

CREDITS:
Weeds
nip / tuck
Dexter
Fear Factor

M.A.S. Plastics (818) 997-8064
14229 Oxnard St, Van Nuys, CA, 91401
sheet plastic & display case fabrication, custom acrylic fabrication svcs.

Orange County Industrial Plastics (714) 632-9450
4811 E La Palma, Anaheim, CA, 92807
wide sel. sheet/rod/block; design & fabrication too

Plastic Depot (818) 843-3030
2907 N San Fernando Blvd, Burbank, CA, 91504
Fiberglass resins & cloths, silicone mold making materials

Plastic Mart (800) 200-4228
456 E Avenue K-4 Suite 9, Lancaster, CA, 93534
We stock material from .020" to 4.0"

Plastifab/Leed Plastics (909) 596-1927
1425 Palomares Ave, La Verne, CA, 91750
sheets, rods, tubes

PSI-Plastic Sales South (800) 257-7747
17622 Metzler Ln, Huntington Beach, CA, 92647
raw materials

Reynolds Advanced Materials: Smooth-On (818) 358-6000
Distributor
10856 Vanowen St, N. Hollywood, CA, 91605
Hollywood's F/X source for Liquid Rubbers, Plastics & more
LA@reynoldsam.com * www.moldmakingmaterials.com

Sabic Polymer Shapes (562) 942-9381
9905 Pioneer Blvd, Santa Fe Springs, CA, 90670
sheets, rods, tubes, films

Solter Plastics (310) 473-5115
12016 W Pico Blvd, Los Angeles, CA, 90064
sheet materials, unique colors & textures

TMX AIN Plastics (562) 623-4444
13338 Orden Dr, Santa Fe Springs, CA, 90670
sheets, rods, tubes

Vinyl Technology, Inc. (626) 443-5257
200 Railroad Ave, Monrovia, CA, 91016
plastic fabr., thermoforming, vacuum forming, berm liners very large
environmental protection shipping containers

Walco Materials Group/Fiberlay San Diego (760) 520-1020
5304 Custer St, San Diego, CA, 92110
liquid plastics, silicones

Platforms

See: Audience Seating* Stages, Portable & Steel Deck

Playground Equipment

Alley Cats Studio Rentals (818) 982-9178
jungle gym, swings, slides, monkey bars, merry-go-round, kids geo domes,
metal basketball rims, bicycle racks, benches

L. A. Steelcraft Products, Inc. (626) 798-7401
1975 N Lincoln Ave, Pasadena, CA, 91103
jungle gym, merry-go-round, slides, play barrels, teeter-totter, arch climbers,
hoppy animals, swings, etc.
www.lasteelcraft.com

Universal Studios Property & Hardware Dept (818) 777-2784
Jungle gyms, slides, swings, swing set, tether balls, school benches, etc. for
rent.

Worlds of Wow (817) 380-4215
2126 Hamilton Rd, Argyle, TX, 76226
Indoor soft contained playgrounds
www.worldsofwow.com

Plexi-Lucite Furniture

See: Furniture, Plexi/Lucite

Plexiglass

See: Plastics, Materials & Fabrication

Plotters & Plotting Services

See Also: Blueprint Equipment & Supplies* Computers* Graphics,
Digital & Large Format Printing

The Hand Prop Room LP. (323) 931-1534

Nights of Neon (818) 756-4791
13815 Saticoy St, Van Nuys, CA 91402
over 2,000 neon props in stock. plotting services
contact@nightsofneon.com * www.nightsofneon.com

Repro-Graphic Supply (818) 771-9066
9838 Glenoaks Blvd, Sun Valley, CA, 91352
equipment & service, all Ind.'s. OCE & HP wide format plotters. See Display Ad
in Blueprint Equipment
info@reprographicsupply.com * www.reprographicsupply.com

Steven Enterprises (800) 491-8785
17952 Skypark Circle Unit E, Irvine, CA, 92614
Wide Format Printers. Rent/Buy. Authorized Dealer: HP, KIP, Canon, Oce,
Epson. We service & supply everything we install
sales@plotters.com * www.plotters.com

Plumbing Fixtures, Heating/Cooling Appliances

See Also: Air Conditioning & Heating, Production/Event* Bathroom Fixtures* Factory/Industrial* Furnaces, Indoor* Jail Cell Dressing* Plastics, Materials & Fabrication* Sinks

Alley Cats Studio Rentals (818) 982-9178
Swamp coolers, plastic & metal valves, stainless steel sink, stainless steel prison toilet and prison sink unit

C. P. Valley (323) 466-8201

E.C. Prop Rentals (818) 764-2008
rooftop & window units, furnace/boiler, ducting/vents, fire sprinklers

LCW Props (818) 243-0707
Appliances, Parts, Tools, Empty Air Conditioners, Heaters, etc.

Mike Green Fire Equipment Co. (818) 989-3322
11916 Valerio St, N Hollywood, CA, 91605
Fire Sprinkler Systems; Fire Sprinkler design, Fire Sprinkler installation, Fire Sprinkler parts.
info@mgfire.com * www.Mgfire.com

The ReUse People (818) 244-5635
3015 Dolores St, Los Angeles, CA, 90065
Kitchen and bath sinks, faucets, toilets, bidets, both tubs, Jacuzzis, and more.
JefCockerell@TheReUsePeople.org * www.TheReUsePeople.org

Universal Studios Property & Hardware Dept (818) 777-2784
Prop plumbing fixtures for rent.

Universal Studios Special Effects Equip. (818) 777-3333
portable water heaters, water pumps

Pocket Watches

See: Watches & Pocket Watches

Podiums & Lecterns

See Also: Furniture, Plexi/Lucite* Game Show Electronics & Equipment* Teleprompting

C. P. Two (323) 466-8201
Valet parking podium

C. P. Valley (323) 466-8201
Podiums and lecterns from presidential to lecture hall.

The Hand Prop Room LP. (323) 931-1534

History For Hire, Inc. (818) 765-7767

L. A. Party Works (888) 527-2789
9712 Alpaca St, S El Monte, CA, 91733
in Vancouver tel. 604-589-4101. game show/party
partyworks@aol.com * www.partyworksusa.com

LCW Props (818) 243-0707
Futuristic, Lighting, Award Ceremony, Custom, Contemporary

Lennie Marvin Enterprises, Inc. (Prop Heaven) (818) 841-5882
business & church, acrylic lecterns

Modern Props (323) 934-3000
wood, metal, acrylic

Omega/Cinema Props (323) 466-8201

Prop Services West (818) 503-2790

Sony Pictures Studios-Prop House (Off Lot) (310) 244-5999
custom podiums, library podiums, office podiums, presidential podiums, lecterns

Universal Studios Property & Hardware Dept (818) 777-2784
Podiums of different styles and time periods for rent.

Used Church Items, Religious Rentals (239) 992-5737
216 Cumer Road, McDonald, PA, 15057
Walk in and Free Standing Podiums, Pulpits, Lecterns, Baptismals, Wood and Metal, Large and Small, Old to Modern.
warehouse@religiousrentals.com * www.religiousrentals.com

Poker Tables

See Also: Gambling Equipment

C. P. Valley (323) 466-8201
Poker tables for rent

Universal Studios Property & Hardware Dept (818) 777-2784
Poker tables for rent.

Police Barricades

See: Traffic/Road Signs, Lights, Safety Items

Police Car, Police Motorcycle

See Also: Siren Lights* Vehicles

The Earl Hays Press (818) 765-0700
The Industry only. Labels, signage paper/plastic. Police & fire department door skins & signage for picture vehicles.

The Hand Prop Room LP. (323) 931-1534
interior dressing, skins, vizbaps

Universal Studios Property & Hardware Dept (818) 777-2784
Police car rentals and police motorcycle rentals, contact Universal Studios Transportation.

Police Equipment

See Also: Badges, Patches & Buttons* Graphics, Digital & Large Format Printing* Military Props & Equipment* Military Surplus/Combat Clothes, Field Gear* Police Car, Police Motorcycle* Uniforms, Trades/Professional/Sports* Walkie-Talkies* Police Office Dressing

The Earl Hays Press (818) 765-0700
services the Industry only. 1000+ forms 1900 to present

E.C. Prop Rentals (818) 764-2008
squadroom & locker room dressing, lighted POLICE sign

The Hand Prop Room LP. (323) 931-1534
SWAT gear, arsenal, communication, fully outfitted

History For Hire, Inc. (818) 765-7767
Lots of police uniforms, hand cuffs, hard hats. 1880's - present police dressing and uniforms.

Hollywood Studio Gallery (323) 462-1116
pre-dressed bulletin boards posters,certificates,signs,maps

LCW Props (818) 243-0707
Helmets, Belts, Fake Guns, Taser, Batons, Handcuffs

RJR Props (404) 349-7600
Prop police equipment; police radios, police computers, police car consoles, police lights and much more.

Shomer-Tec (360) 733-6214
PO Box 28070, Bellingham, WA, 98228
catalog sales; badges/patches, handcuffs, metal detectors, covert ops equip. & SWAT gear; no guns

Sony Pictures Studios-Prop House (Off Lot) (310) 244-5999
Tasers, shotguns, police badges, police id holder, police belts, police belt accessories, body bags, radios more!

Universal Studios Property & Hardware Dept (818) 777-2784
All kinds of police gear, police props and police equipment for rent.

Police Expendable Supplies

See: Expendables

Police Office Dressing

See Also: Books, Real/Hollow & Faux Books* Courtroom Furniture & Dressing* Filing Cabinets* Office Furniture* Paperwork, Documents & Letters, Office* Police Equipment

Faux Library Studio Props, Inc. (818) 765-0096
desktop and cleared photos, police station dressing

The Hand Prop Room LP. (323) 931-1534

On Set Graphics (661) 233-6786
Web Based Business
Police Office Dressing including Coroners Office documents, Crime Scene Photos, Police Records, Missing Person and more.
info@onsetgraphics.com * www.onsetgraphics.com

RJR Props (404) 349-7600
Police office dressing including computers, phones, copiers, water coolers and police desk dressing.

Police Uniforms

See: Badges, Patches & Buttons* Police Car, Police Motorcycle* Police Equipment* Uniforms, Trades/Professional/Sports

Political Campaign Memorabilia

See: Memorabilia & Novelties

Polyester Fiber

See: Upholstery Materials/Services

Polynesian Dressing

See: Hawaiian Dressing* Jungle Dressing* Tikis & Tropical Dressing

Pom Pons

The Hand Prop Room LP.	(323) 931-1534
History For Hire, Inc.	(818) 765-7767

period & contemporary

National Spirit	(800) 527-4366

6745 Lenox Center Court Ste 300, Memphis, TN, 38115
custom, standard, small to large, metallic, streamers, etc.

Team Leader	(877) 365-7555

Call for Appt
Online uniform catalog. Will make custom pom pons.
www.teamleader.com

Universal Studios Property & Hardware Dept	(818) 777-2784

Various pom poms/pom pons for rent of many sizes and colors.

Pool/Billiard Tables & Accessories

See Also: Game Tables & Equipment

Adler Pool Tables	(310) 676-5331

3155 W. El Segundo Blvd, Hawthorne, CA 90250
pool table rental, billiard table rental, accessories, lamps, moving, restoring, sales
www.adlerpooltables.com

AIR Designs	(818) 768-6639

Tables, Lights, Signs, Racks & Props

C. P. Valley	(323) 466-8201
The Hand Prop Room LP.	(323) 931-1534

cues, racks, rubber pool balls

RC Vintage, Inc.	(818) 765-7107

Pool Tables w Pool Cues Stands, pool ball signs

Universal Studios Property & Hardware Dept	(818) 777-2784

Pool tables and pool table accessories for rent.

Pools

See: Swimming Pools

Popcorn & Machines

See: Vendor Carts & Concession Counters

Porcelain/Ceramics

See: Decorative Accessories* Pottery* Prop Houses* Urns

Portable Studio Lighting

See: Stage Lighting, Film/Video/TV

Portable Toilets

See: Production Vehicles/Trailers* Toilets, Portable Prop

Portapotty

See: Construction Site Equipment* Production Vehicles/Trailers* Toilets, Portable Prop

Portfolios

See: Book Covers & Bookbinding

Portholes

See: Nautical Dressing & Props

Post Office

See Also: Mail & Mail Room* Prop Houses

C. P. Valley	(323) 466-8201
History For Hire, Inc.	(818) 765-7767

hampers, bags, letter carrier bags, period maiboxes

LCW Props	(818) 243-0707

Postal Scales, Bins, Cleared Mail

Sony Pictures Studios-Prop House (Off Lot)	(310) 244-5999

Posters, Art/Movie/Travel/Wanted Etc.

See Also: Art For Rent* Graphics, Digital & Large Format Printing* Paintings/Prints* Signs

Artery Props	(877) 732-7733

7684 Clybourn Ave 2nd Floor Unit C, Sun Valley, CA, 91352
100% cleared & owned artwork: posters, stickers, flyers, gold records, signs, CDs, DVDs, albums, mic flags & more.
info@arteryprops.com * www.arteryprops.com

CANADIAN ART PRINTS & WINN DEVON ART GROUP	(800) 663-1166

UNIT 110 - 6311 Westminster Hwy, Richmond, BC, Canada, V7C 4V4
Clearable stocked posters with a wide variety of images. Printed canvas, and a selection framed art is available too.
sales@capandwinndevon.com * www.capandwinndevon.com

The Earl Hays Press	(818) 765-0700

services the Industry only. per/modern campaign,movie,travel,wanted,knockoff/real

Eddie Brandt's Saturday Matinee	(818) 506-4242

5006 Vineland Ave, N. Hollywood, CA, 91601
Tues.-Fri. 1:00-6:00 pm Sat. 8:30am - 5:00 pm. video rentals, vintage & hard to find photos, no posters

Faux Library Studio Props, Inc.	(818) 765-0096

large variety of art to travel posters, cleared

FILM ART LA	(323) 461-4900

Culver City Warehouse at Jefferson & Hauser. Call for address.
art, prop & poster research. ORDER ARTWORK ONLINE: Address for pick ups and returns only.
filmartla@gmail.com * www.artimagela.com

History For Hire, Inc.	(818) 765-7767

manufacturing

Hollywood Studio Gallery	(323) 462-1116

travel, many places, framed & unframed

Omega/Cinema Props	(323) 466-8201
On Set Graphics	(661) 233-6786

Web Based Business
Law enforcement paperwork, family photos, hotel paperwork, restaurant dressing, wanted posters and more.
info@onsetgraphics.com * www.onsetgraphics.com

Retro-Reproductions	(310) 659-7058

Web Based Business
Specialize in high quality digital prints & reproductions of vintage movie posters & photographs, ALL CLEARED
stage.door1969@gmail.com * www.retro-reproductions.com

Sony Pictures Studios-Prop House (Off Lot)	(310) 244-5999

foreign,govt.,movie,transportation,school,travel (many places)

Universal Studios Property & Hardware Dept	(818) 777-2784

Framed posters and unframed posters for rent.

Pot Belly Stoves

See: Stoves

Pottery

See Also: Statuary Urns*

Asian Ceramics, Inc. (626) 449-6800
2800 Huntington Dr, Duarte, CA 91010
Thailand, Vietnam, China, large & unique jars etc., planters, urns in stoneware, rustic & glazed finishes
sales@asian-ceramics.com * www.asian-ceramics.com

Badia Design, Inc. (818) 762-0130
5420 Vineland Ave, N. Hollywood, CA, 91601
Badia Design Inc. has a large selection of Moroccan clay pots that can be used for plants or any of your design needs.
info@badiadesign.com * www.badiadesign.com

C. P. Valley (323) 466-8201

Eric's Architectural Salvage, Wells Antique Tile (213) 413-6800
2110 W Sunset Blvd, Los Angeles, CA, 90026
We have the largest selection of antique tile and pottery in the world.
ericstiques@aol.com * www.ericsarchitecturalsalvage.com

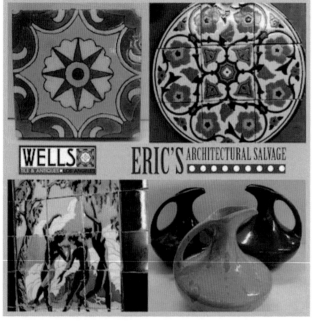

Galerie Sommerlath - French 50s 60s (310) 838-0102
9608 Venice Blvd, Culver City, CA, 90232
10,000 sq ft Mid-Century - 80s furniture, lighting & accessories
info@french50s60s.com * http://www.galeriesommerlath.com

The Hand Prop Room LP. (323) 931-1534
American, Asian, African, Mexican, Egyptian, American Indian

History For Hire, Inc. (818) 765-7767
Mexican, Egyptian, archaeology

Jackson Shrub Supply, Inc. (818) 982-0100
pots 4"-44" diameter, contemporary pottery, classical pottery, plastic pottery, fiberglass pottery

Little Bohemia Rentals (818) 853-7506
11940 Sherman Rd, N Hollywood, CA, 91605
Danish modern pottery, Japanese pottery, Art pottery, Studio pottery. Vintage pottery and Contemporary pottery.
sales@wearelittlebohemia.com * www.wearelittlebohemia.com

MidcenturyLA (818) 509-3050
5333 Cahuenga Blvd, N. Hollywood, CA, 91601
Nice selection of vintage ceramics and furniture. Most inventory is in store, not online. Rental and purchase.
midcenturyla@midcenturyla.com * www.midcenturyla.com

Omega/Cinema Props (323) 466-8201
pottery from around the world

Prop Services West (818) 503-2790

Sony Pictures Studios-Prop House (Off Lot) (310) 244-5999
large assortment styles & sizes

Universal Studios Property & Hardware Dept (818) 777-2784
Pottery from multiple styles & sizes for rent.

The Village Art Project Ceramic Studio (818) 985-9357
11602 Ventura Blvd, Studio City, CA, 91604
Custom ceramics, props, pottery & clay supplies. Classes and consulting as well.
www.thevillageartproject.com

Westmoore Pottery (910) 464-3700
4622 Busbee Rd, Seagrove, NC, 27341
17th, 18th, early 19th Century replicas

ZG04 DECOR (818) 853-8040
Vases, Vessels, Bowls, Arts & Crafts Pottery, Dishware

Pouffe (Hotel)

See: Hotel, Motel, Inn, Lodge

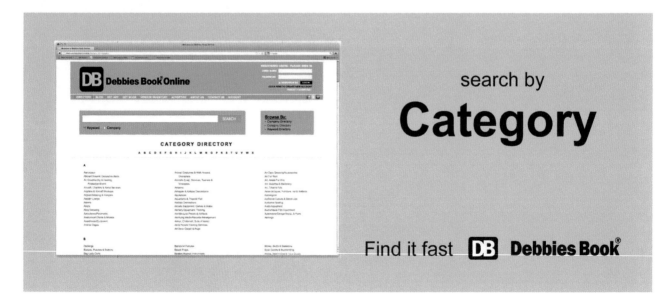

Power Generation/Distribution

See Also: Floor, Ground & Surface Protection* Generators
Ace Rentals (818) 255-5995
11950 Sherman Rd, N. Hollywood, CA, 91605
up to 500 KW generators, service, fueling, 24 Hrs.
Aggreko Event Services (818) 767-7288
13230 Cambridge St, Santa Fe Springs, CA 90670
big, quiet power, heating & HVAC systems, over 130 locations globally for
filming, tours, events
Astro Audio Video Lighting, Inc. (818) 549-9915
6615 San Fernando Rd, Glendale, CA, 91201
Power cords of many sizes, surge protectors of all types, and power generators
available; Power Distro 3kw-50kva
www.astroavl.com
Castex Rentals (323) 462-1468
1044 N. Cole Ave, Hollywood, CA, 90038
portable Honda generators 9 amp-60 amp, ac cords
service@castexrentals.com * www.castexrentals.com

Presentation Books

See: Research, Advisors, Consulting & Clearances

Press Equipment

The Hand Prop Room LP. (323) 931-1534
History For Hire, Inc. (818) 765-7767
all eras thru present day, biggest sel.

Press Room

See: Newsroom

Press Walls

See: Graphics, Digital & Large Format Printing

Pretzel Cart/Machines

See: Vendor Carts & Concession Counters

Primates

See: Animals (Live), Services, Trainers & Wranglers

Printing Presses

International Printing Museum (714) 529-1832
315 Torrance Blvd, Carson, CA, 90745
antique printing/office equipment 1450-1980. period printing, resource books,
period advertising, period artwork
www.printmuseum.org

Printing, 3-D, 3-Dimensional Printing

See Also: Prop & Set Design Supplies, Parts, Tools Prop Design &
Manufacturing* Prop Reproduction & Fabrication*
Kapow! 3D, LLC (310) 591-2964
1636 19th St, Santa Monica, CA, 90404
Kapow! 3D is a Santa Monica-based shop providing 3D Printing, Scanning, and
Modeling.
info@kapow3d.com * www.kapow3d.com
New Rule FX (818) 387-6450
7751 Densmore Ave, Van Nuys, CA 91406
Breakaway props-all types & categories Custom prop & FX design &
construction, 3D printing Prototypes, Molding & Casting
ryan@newrulefx.com * www.NewRuleFX.com

Printing, Digital & Large Format Printers

See: Graphics, Digital & Large Format Printing

Prints

See: Paintings/Prints

Prison Cell Dressing

See: Electric Chairs* Jail Cell Dressing

Private Investigations

Westside Detectives Inc. (323) 583-8660
6230 Wilshire Blvd #59, Los Angeles, CA, 90048
Investigations, trademark infringement, intellectual property investigations,
polygraph, bodyguards, background checks
www.westsidedetectives.com

Produce Carts

See Also: Produce Crates* Produce Stands
AIR Designs (818) 768-6639
Vegetable, Fruit, Flower, Farmers Market
Universal Studios Property & Hardware Dept (818) 777-2784
Produce carts from different time periods available for rent.

Produce Crates

See Also: Food, Artificial Food Grocery Check-out Stands
(Complete)* Produce Carts* Produce Stands* Food, Food Stylists*
Alley Cats Studio Rentals (818) 982-9178
w/artificial produce, wood
Sony Pictures Studios-Prop House (Off Lot) (310) 244-5999

Produce Stands

AIR Designs (818) 768-6639
Vegetable, Fruit, Signage, Farmers Market, Grocery Store
Alley Cats Studio Rentals (818) 982-9178
variety of food stands as well, with crates, fake food and umbrella tops.
C. P. Valley (323) 466-8201
Wooden produce stands
Lennie Marvin Enterprises, Inc. (Prop Heaven) (818) 841-5882
period & modern, wide variety, product too
Sony Pictures Studios-Prop House (Off Lot) (310) 244-5999
Universal Studios Property & Hardware Dept (818) 777-2784
Contemporary produce stand, produce crates & produce carts for rent.

Product Labels

See Also: Graphics, Digital & Large Format Printing* Prop Houses
Art, Signs & Graphics (818) 503-7997
6939 Farmdale Ave, N Hollywood, CA, 91605
props, banners, vinyl graphics, vehicle graphics, 3D router cut letters & logos
jessee@artsignsandgraphics.com * www.artsignsandgraphics.com
D'ziner Sign Co. (323) 467-4467
801 Seward Street, Los Angeles, CA 90038
labels & packaging
sales@dzinersign.com * www.dzinersign.com
The Earl Hays Press (818) 765-0700
services the Industry only. knockoff/real, custom design
Graphic Space Online (213) 321-3919
Web-Based Only
Fabricated & licensed graphics available 24/7 online to download on automated
website.
theteam@graphicspaceonline.com * www.graphicspaceonline.com
The Hand Prop Room LP. (323) 931-1534
in stock & custom
History For Hire, Inc. (818) 765-7767
custom graphics
HPR Graphics (323) 556-2694
5674 Venice Blvd, Los Angeles, CA, 90019
Beverage labels, food labels, food boxes, media packaging, cigarette
packaging, liquor labels, beer labels and more.
hprcan@earthlink.net * www.hprgraphics.net
Sony Pictures Studios-Prop House (Off Lot) (310) 244-5999
Universal Studios Graphic Design & Sign Shop (818) 777-2350
package design & point of sale display signage
Warner Bros. Design Studio Scenic Art & Sign (818) 954-1815
Shop
4000 Warner Blvd, Burbank, CA, 91522
graphic design and production studio for signs & scenic art; digital printing to
hand-painted
wbsigns@warnerbros.com * www.wbsignandscenic.com

Product Placement

AIM Productions (718) 729-9288
34-12 36th Street, Suite 228, Astoria, NY, 11106
an entertainment marketing company
LCW Props (818) 243-0707
Let Us Help You Find Anything You Need

Production Vehicles/Trailers

See Also: Vehicles

D. Aguiar Productions (310) 925-0967
P.O. Box 1473, Chino Hills, CA, 91709
talent, wardrobe, production, make-up/hair trailers & motorhomes

Easy Rider Productions, Inc. (818) 822-8782
23919 Newhall Ave, Newhall, CA 91321
trailers: 2 room talent, 6 & 8 station make-up/wardrobe, 4, 5 & 8 room
honeywagons, generators, work vehicles.

Hollywood Honeywagon & Prod. Vehicles (818) 763-1966
11160 Victory Blvd, N. Hollywood, CA, 91606
Prod. trailers & motorhomes, 2 & 3 room star trailers, 4-9 room honeywagons,
make-up/wardrobe, upscale portable toilets

Star Waggons Production Trailers (818) 367-5946
Los Angeles, New Orleans, Atlanta, Albuquerque
dressing room trailers

Stardeck Industries (310) 650-7046
1275 Railroad St, Carona, CA, 92882
Prod. trailers with pop-outs & skydecks, honeywagons, motorhomes

Touring Video, Inc. (818) 953-8700
827 Hollywood Way Ste 424, Burbank, CA, 91505
studio recording, corp. production, webcasting, concert tours

Universal Studios Transportation (818) 777-2966
100 Universal City Plaza, Universal City, CA, 91608
Production vehicles, trailers, SUVs, vans & more
universal.transpo@nbcuni.com * www.filmmakersdestination.com

Western Studio Service, Inc. (818) 842-9272
4561 Colorado Blvd, Los Angeles, CA, 90039
We have the largest fleet of custom trailers to transport scenery of all sizes and
heights. All trailers for rent too!
www.westernstudioservice.com

Projectors

See: Motion Picture Projectors

Promotional Items & Materials

See Also: Badges, Patches & Buttons Embroidery, Screen Printing,
Etc.* Graphics, Digital & Large Format Printing*

Aah-Inspiring Balloons (562) 494-7605
Call for an Appointment.
After 14 years in the TV and Film Industry, Aah-Inspiring Balloon Decor has
been seen in over 200 TV shows and Films.
aahinspiring1@aol.com * www.aahinspiringballoons.com

Kater-Crafts Bookbinders (562) 692-0665
4860 Gregg Rd, Pico Rivera, CA, 90660
Custom work. Presentation binders, folders, portfolios, boxes, foil stamping.
sales@katercrafts.com * www.katercrafts.com

Prompting

See: Teleprompting

Prop & Set Design Supplies, Parts, Tools

See Also: CNC Router & Laser Etching Services Metal Plating,
Coating, Polishing* Paint & Painting Supplies* Plastics, Materials &
Fabrication* Scenery/Set Construction* Special Effects,
Make-up/Prosthetics* Ultraviolet Products* Water Jet CNC Services*

CONFETTI & FOG FX Special Effects Company (786) 308-7063
2739 W 79 St Bay, #12, Hialeah, FL 33016
www.caffx.com

E. B. Bradley (800) 533-3030
5602 Bickett St, Vernon, CA 90058
6 Loc., B2B, don't sell to general public, tools & hardware, carry Wilsonart
metallic finish laminates

Flanders Control Cables (626) 303-0700
859 Meridian St, Duarte, CA 91010
small dia. cables, housings, fittings for wire control mechanisms

General Veneer Manufacturing Co. (323) 564-2661
8652 Otis St, South Gate, CA, 90280
Breakaway balsa wood sheets & boards
balsasales@generalveneer.com * www.generalveneer.com

Grainger (818) 253-7970
7565 N. Lockheed Dr, Burbank, CA, 91505
catalog sales; industrial supplies, tools, etc.

Heatshrink.com (801) 621-1501
2752 South 1900 West, Ogden, UT, 84401
heatshrink tubing

K. R. Anderson Co. (714) 549-1343
2655 S Orange Ave, Santa Ana, CA, 92707
mold making materials & tools, several locations

Konica Minolta Sensing Americas, Inc. (888) 473-2656
101 Williams Dr, Ramsey, NJ, 07446
Non-contact 3D digitizing scanners

LCW Props (818) 243-0707
huge sel machine parts, great prop starters

Leica Geosystems HDS, Inc. (925) 790-2300
4550 Norris Canyon Rd, San Ramon, CA, 94586
Scene, structure & site scanning hardware & software

LM Treasures (626) 252-7354
10557 Juniper Ave Unit A, Fontana, CA 92337
Life Size & Oversized Fiberglass Resin Statues of Many Kinds
lmtreasures.ll@gmail.com * www.lifesizestatues.net

Mike Green Fire Equipment Co. (818) 989-3322
11916 Valerio St, N Hollywood, CA, 91605
Large inventory of new and used fire alarm cabinets & fire protection devices.
info@mgfire.com * www.Mgfire.com

Montroy Supply (800) 666-8769
1601 S Maple Ave, Montebello, CA, 90640   x1000
sign & graphics mfg. materials, supplies, equip.

My Doll's House (310) 320-4828
1218 El Prado Ave Ste 136, Torrance, CA 90501
Dollhouses, Dollhouse Kits, Room Boxes, Miniatures, Collectibles,
Accessories, Tools and Supplies
margiesminiatures@gmail.com * www.mydollshouse.com

Ohio Travel Bag (800) 800-1941
6481 Davis Industrial Pkwy, Solon, OH, 44139
1000s of hard-to-find fasteners & decorative hdw parts
www.ohiotravelbag.com

Prop Masters, Inc. (818) 846-3915
2721 Empire Ave, Burbank, CA, 91504
casting & mold making materials

Quixote (504) 266-2297
10289 Airline Hwy, St. Rose LA 70087
Set building, gloves, Construction, glues, tape, expendables, lumber, power tools, delivers, online orders.
nola@quixote.com * www.quixote.com

Reynolds Advanced Materials: Smooth-On (818) 358-6000
Distributor
10856 Vanowen St, N. Hollywood, CA, 91605
Hollywood's F/X source for Liquid Rubbers, Plastics & more
LA@reynoldsam.com * www.moldmakingmaterials.com

Roland DGA Corp. (800) 542-2307
Web Based Business
A business resource. Special purpose 2D/3D scanning, milling, engraving, printing devices; use web site to locate nearest dealer
http://www.rolanddga.com

Sculptural Arts Coating, Inc. (800) 743-0379
PO Box 10546, Greensboro, NC, 27404
Mfg. of "Sculpt or Coat" nontoxic plastic cream for making props, scenery, puppets, masks, costumes, arch. elements

ShopWildThings (928) 855-6075
2880 Sweetwater Ave, Lake Havasu City, AZ, 86406
Event Decor, Beaded Curtains, Chain Curtains, String Curtains & Columns, Crystal Columns. Reliable service & delivery.
help@shopwildthings.com * www.shopwildthings.com

Specialty Coatings & Chemicals (818) 983-0055
7360 Varna Ave, N Hollywood, CA, 91605
special coatings, paints & dyes

Wurth Louis and Company (800) 422-4389
895 Columbia St, Brea, CA, 92821
distribute Chemetal, metal laminates, solid metals, treefrog veneers, Nevamar laminates

Prop Breakaways

See: Breakaways (Glass, Props, Scenery)

Prop Builders

See: Architectural Pieces & Artifacts Fiberglass Products/Fabrication* Prop Design & Manufacturing* Prop Reproduction & Fabrication* Scenery/Set Construction* Vacu-forms/Vacu-forming*

Prop Design & Manufacturing

See Also: Animal Costumes & Walk Around Characters Art, Artists For Hire* CNC Router & Laser Etching Services* Fiberglass Products/Fabrication* Food, Artificial Food* Metalworking, Decorative* Metalworking, Welding & Structural* Miniatures/Models* Prop Reproduction & Fabrication* Robots* Scenery/Set Construction* Sculpture* Staff Shops* Vacu-forms/Vacu-forming* Water Jet CNC Services*

Action Sets and Props / WonderWorks, Inc. (818) 992-8811
Space shuttle & station, space suit, specialty props, miniatures, mechanical effects, cityscape, miniature buildings

Art, Models & Props, Inc. (951) 206-9156
1725 Marengo Ave, Pasadena, CA, 91103
Custom design/fabr. all categories, tiny to giant sized.
modelsandprops@msn.com * www.artmodeltech.com

Arteffex/Dann O'Quinn (818) 506-5358
911 Mayo St, Los Angeles, CA, 90042
acfx@att.net

CBS Electronics (323) 575-2645
7800 Beverly Blvd Rm M162, Los Angeles, CA, 90036
Complete carpentry shop and fabrication shop.

The Character Shop (805) 306-9441
4735 Industrial St #4B-G, Simi Valley, CA, 93063
Extraordinary Custom Animatronic Animals & Creatures, Puppets, Marionettes, Replicas, Robots, Props, Art Installations
lazzwaldo@mac.com * www.character-shop.com

Charisma Design Studio, Inc. (818) 252-6611
8414 San Fernando Road, Sun Valley, CA, 91352
metal/glass/wood/stone, 12'X6' CNC water jet cutter, custom art
info@charismadesign.com * www.charismadesign.com

Charisma Design Studio, Inc.
CNC WATERJET CUTTING
GLASS ETCHING   SIGN FABRICATION
PROP FABRICATION
www.charismadesign.com

Dapper Cadaver/Creatures & Cultures (818) 771-0818
Custom bodies, stunt dummies, horror & supernatural characters, body parts, tombstones and fake animals.

Decker Studios Art Foundry (818) 503-9913
7400 Ethel Ave, N. Hollywood, CA, 91605
Open 11-3; fine arts & sculpture casting, mold making, restorations, small scale to large public space pieces

EFX- Event Special Effects (626) 888-2239
125 Railroad Ave, Monrovia, CA, 91016
Custom Fabrication- CNC- Plasma Table- Pipe & Ring Benders- 3D Renderings
info@efxla.com * www.efxla.com

Elden Designs (323) 550-8922
2767 W. Broadway, Eagle Rock, CA, 90041
custom props for TV/film & commercials & print advertising

Flix FX Inc. (818) 765-3549
7327 Lankershim Blvd #4, N Hollywood, CA, 91605
Mechanical EFX, CNC routing, sculpting, vacuforming & Prop Making
info@flixfx.com * www.flixfx.com

FormDecor, Inc. (310) 558-2582
America's largest event rental supplier of 20th Century furniture and accessories for Modern and Mid-Century styles.

FXperts, Inc. (818) 767-0883
11352 Goss St, Sun Valley, CA, 91352
custom props, sets, special visual effects

Global Effects, Inc. (818) 503-9273
medieval props, futuristic props, fantasy props, science fiction props, space suits

Global Entertainment Industries, Inc. (818) 567-0000
2948 N. Ontario St, Burbank, CA, 91504
molds, sculpting, miniatures

Grant McCune Design, Inc (818) 779-1920
6836 Valjean Ave, Van Nuys, CA, 91406
full svc model building, metal/wood/paint shops, filming stage

The Hand Prop Room LP. (323) 931-1534
in-house, custom, mfg. & design, leather, wood, metal

DISPLAY ADS AND LISTINGS FOR THIS CATEGORY CONTINUE ON THE FOLLOWING PAGE

HPR Custom (323) 931-1534
5700 Venice Blvd, Los Angeles, CA, 90019
3D modeling, woodworking, CNC machining, CAD drawings, water jet cutting, metal working, custom electronics and more.
www.hprcustom.com

J & M Special Effects, Inc. (718) 875-0140
524 Sackett St, Brooklyn, NY 11217
Formerly Jauchem & Meeh. effects design
info@jmfx.net * www.jmfx.net

Jet Sets (818) 764-5644
6910 Farmdale Ave, N Hollywood, CA, 91605
set construction, custom props, scenic painting, special effects, set illustration, Hero prop fabrication
dougmorris@jetsets.com * www.jetsets.com

L. A. Party Works (888) 527-2789
9712 Alpaca St, S El Monte, CA, 91733
in Vancouver tel. 604-589-4101
partyworks@aol.com * www.partyworksusa.com

Merritt Productions, Inc. (818) 760-0612
10845 Vanowen St, North Hollywood, CA 91605
specialty props, miniatures, sculpture, mech effects, set const.
www.merrittproductions.com

MovieMoto.com (626) 359-0016
16015 Adelante St, Irwindale, CA, 91702
A manufacturer of Model Airplane Engines, a mechanical engineering company, and can design and make anything, literally.
www.MovieMoto.com

New Deal Studios, Inc. (310) 578-9929
15392 Cobalt St, Los Angeles, CA, 91342
Design miniatures, photography, digital & visual effects & stage rental

New Rule FX (818) 387-6450
7751 Densmore Ave, Van Nuys, CA 91406
Breakaway props-all types & categories Custom prop & FX design & construction, 3D printing Prototypes, Molding & Casting
ryan@newrulefx.com * www.NewRuleFX.com

Nights of Neon (818) 756-4791
13815 Saticoy St, Van Nuys, CA 91402
over 2,000 neon props in stock. custom neon prop design
contact@nightsofneon.com * www.nightsofneon.com

RJR Props (404) 349-7600
Can design props and manufacture props including printing fake money.

Robert James Company (415) 420-4011
2110 West 20th St, Los Angeles, CA, 90018
Creative fabrication shop specializing in large-scale sculpture and unique steel designs for event and set production.
rob@robertjamesstudio.com * www.robertjamesstudio.com

Sets, Etc.-Bob Pinkos Services (925) 432-1083
270 E 15th St, Pittsburg, CA, 94565
cust. sets, displays, props, 3-D signs, models, prototypes, backdrops, illusions, quality prof. corp. art svcs since 198

Sketch Paper Design (818) 442-0284
7771 Lemona Ave, Van Nuys, CA, 91405
Wood, Metal, Plastic, Foam Custom Designed Props, any size, any idea
info@sketchpaperdesign.com * www.sketchpaperdesign.com

Sword & Stone (818) 562-6548
metal, wood, glass, wrought iron, 1-day custom etching

Tech Works FX Studios (504) 722-1504
13405 Seymour Meyers Blvd. #5, Covington, LA, 70433
Specializes in Mechanical Props, Fabrication and Design, Molding and casting and Robotics.
info@techworksstudios.com * www.techworksstudios.com

Tractor Vision Scenery & Rentals (323) 235-2885
340 E Jefferson Blvd. Los Angeles, CA 90011
Specializing in entertainment, trade shows, & events, we bring your projects to life with precision, speed & personality
sets@tractorvision.com * www.tractorvision.com

Universal Studios Graphic Design & Sign Shop (818) 777-2350
the complete range of materials & applications for graphics work

Universal Studios Staff Shop (818) 777-2337

Warner Bros. Studios Special Effects & Prop Shop (818) 954-1365
4000 Warner Blvd, Burbank, CA, 91522
Consultation, Script Break-down, Equipment Rentals, Expendable Sales, Picture Car Prep, Action Props
www.wbspecialeffects.com

Woody's Electrical Props (818) 503-1940
period to futuristic. design/build panels, consoles, sound mix boards more

Prop Custom Design
Rental & Custom Fabrication of Control Panels & Consoles

Electronic Dressing For:
Antique/Modern Industrial Sets
Mission Control & Air Tower
Computer Room
Military Sets
Fantasy Sets

NEW LOCATION ON CRAMER

WOODY'S ELECTRICAL PROPS

Worlds of Wow (817) 380-4215
2126 Hamilton Rd, Argyle, TX, 76226
Custom foam designed, hard-coated, painted and finished environments.
wwww.worldsofwow.com

Prop Food

See: Food, Artificial Food Food, Food Stylists*

Prop Houses

See Also: Prop & Set Design Supplies, Parts, Tools* Prop Design & Manufacturing* Prop Reproduction & Fabrication* Scenery/Set Construction

A-1 Medical Integration   **(818) 753-0319**
7344 Laurel Canyon Blvd, North Hollywood, CA, 91605
Medical devices for Set Decoration & Property, from minor procedures to detailed hospital units.
a1medwarehouse@aol.com * www.a1props.com

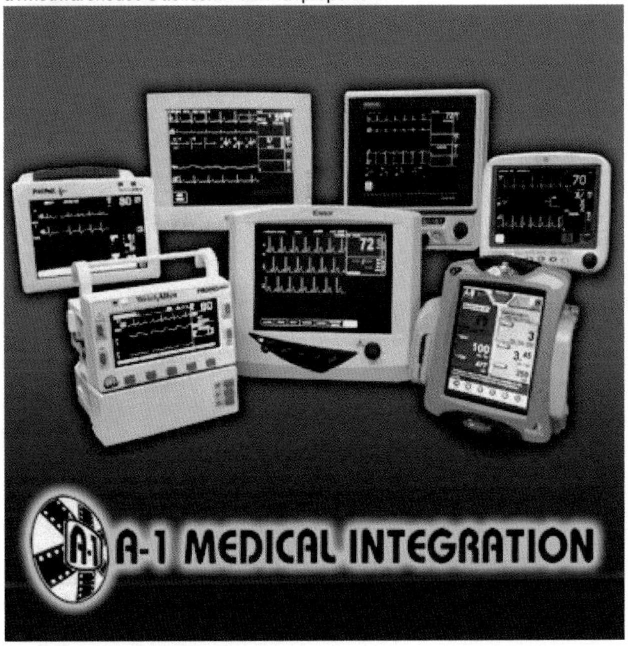

Advanced Liquidators Office Furniture   **(818) 763-3470**
11151 Vanowen St., N. Hollywood, CA, 91605
Specializes in new and used office furniture as well as studio rentals.
sales@advancedliquidators.com * www.advancedliquidators.com

Aero Mock-Ups   **(888) 662-5877**
13126 Saticoy St, N Hollywood, CA, 91605
full service aviation prop house. Complete airplane interiors & airport dressing, model airplanes
info@aeromockups.com * www.aeromockups.com

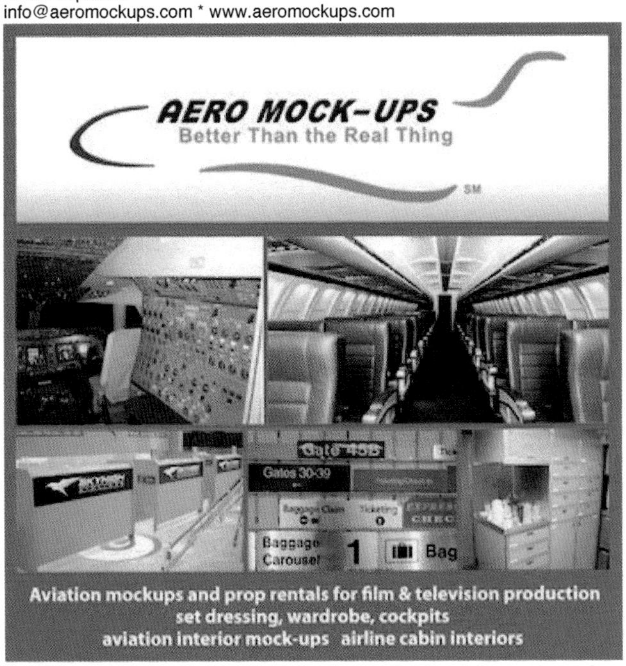

Aviation mockups and prop rentals for film & television production
set dressing, wardrobe, cockpits
aviation interior mock-ups   airline cabin interiors

AIR Designs   **(818) 768-6639**
11900 Wicks St, Sun Valley, CA, 91352
Auto, Gas, Racing, Fast Food, Coffee, Diner, Cafeteria, Store, Street, Vendor Carts & More.
info@airdesigns.net * www.airdesigns.net

Debbies Book®

Mobile App

Desktop Website

Print Book

BLOG
Blog

Mobile Web

eBook

PROP HOUSES

Air Hollywood - Prop House & Standing Sets   (818) 890-0444
13240 Weidner St, Los Angeles, CA, 91331
Aviation-themed props and set dressing. We have thousands of items available
to dress Airport Terminals.
info@airhollywood.com * www.airhollywood.com

Alley Cats Studio Rentals   (818) 982-9178
7101 Case Ave, N Hollywood, CA, 91605
alleycatsprops@gmail.com * www.alleycatsprops.com

Alpha Companies - Spellman Desk Co.   (818) 504-9090
7990 San Fernando Rd, Sun Valley, CA, 91352
The #1 source for medical equipment in the industry.
rentals@alphaprops.com * www.alphaprops.com

Arenson Prop Center   (917) 210-2562
396 Tenth Avenue, New York, NY, 10001
info@aof.com

Artkraft Taxidermy Rentals   (818) 505-8425
10847 Vanowen St., N. Hollywood, CA 91605
Taxidermied animals of all kinds: birds, fish, mammals, and much more from
Africa, North America, and exotic locales.
info@artkrafttaxidermy.com * www.artkrafttaxidermy.net

MUSEUM QUALITY TAXIDERMIED ANIMALS - FROM ANTELOPES TO ZEBRAS
ESTABLISHED 1969 HOLLYWOOD, CA

Bob Gail Special Events   (310) 202-5200
3321 La Cienega Pl, Los Angeles, CA, 90016
Bob Gail has an extensive list of themed props for movie sets, events, and
tradeshows for rental in CA and Las Vegas.
eSales@BobGail.com * www.bobgail.com

Bridge Furniture & Props Los Angeles   (818) 433-7100
3210 Vanowen St, Burbank, CA, 91505
We carry modern & traditional furniture, lighting, accessories, cleared art,&
rugs. Items are online for easy shopping.
la@bridgeprops.com * http://la.bridgeprops.com

BRIDGE LA
FURNITURE & PROPS

3210 Vanowen St.   BridgeProps.com
Burbank, CA 91505   Tel: 818.433.7100

C. P. Two   (323) 466-8201
5755 Santa Monica Blvd, Los Angeles, CA, 90038
www.omegacinemaprops.com

C. P. Valley   (323) 466-8201
7545 N. San Fernando Road, Burbank, CA, 91505
www.omegacinemaprops.com

Dapper Cadaver/Creatures & Cultures   (818) 771-0818
7648 San Fernando Rd, Sun Valley, CA, 91352
Specializes in horror, science, medical, crime, oddity & Halloween props.
Custom fabrication & FX. Rent & buy online.
info@dappercadaver.com * www.dappercadaver.com

The Earl Hays Press   (818) 765-0700
10707 Sherman Way, Sun Valley, CA, 91352
services the Industry only
ehp@la.twcbc.com * www.theearlhayspress.com

E.C. Prop Rentals   **(818) 764-2008**
11846 Sherman Way, N Hollywood, CA, 91605
Factory, Industrial, Loading Dock, Warehouse, Locker Room, Garage,
Street/Alley, Shipping Yard
ecprops@aol.com * www.ecprops.com

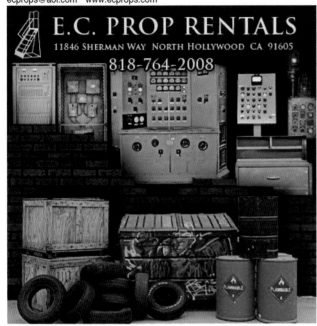

Eccentric Trading Company Ltd.   **011 44 20**
Unit 2 Frogmore Estate, Acton Lane, London NW10 7NQ   **8453-1125**
www.eccentrictrading.com
Eclectic/Encore Props   **(212) 645-8880**
47-51 33rd St, Long Island City, NY 11101
sbieler@eclecticprops.com * www.eclecticprops.com
The Farley Group   **011 44 20**
1-17 Brunel Rd, London, W3 7XR UK   **8749-9925**
props@farley.co.uk * www.farley.co.uk
Faux Library Studio Props, Inc.   **(818) 765-0096**
7100 Case Avenue, N Hollywood, CA, 91605
large selection of hollow books, office furniture, desk dressing, decorative
accessories and of course books
fauxlibrary@sbcglobal.net

FormDecor, Inc.   **(310) 558-2582**
14371 Industry Circle, La Mirada, CA, 90638
America's largest event rental supplier of 20th Century furniture and
accessories for Modern and Mid-Century styles.
info@formdecor.com * www.formdecor.com
Green Set, Inc.   **(818) 764-1231**
11617 Dehougne St, N Hollywood, CA, 91605
www.greenset.com
The Hand Prop Room LP.   **(323) 931-1534**
5700 Venice Blvd, Los Angeles, CA, 90019
Large Prop House for prop rentals, prop weapons, custom graphic design &
custom graphic printing, expendables and more.
info@hpr.com * www.hpr.com

From over 1,000,000 props on hand,
to our exciting and creative graphics
department, along with our custom
manufacturing facility we are able
to service any type of production.

History For Hire, Inc.   **(818) 765-7767**
7149 Fair Ave, N Hollywood, CA, 91605
info@historyforhire.com * www.historyforhire.com
Hollywood Cinema Arts, Inc.   **(818) 504-7333**
8110 Webb Ave, N. Hollywood, CA, 91605
Hollywood Cinema Arts, "The Pro's Prop House."
hollywoodcinemaarts@gmail.com * www.hcarts.com
Hollywood Cinema Production Resources   **(310) 258-0123**
9700 S. Sepulveda Blvd, Los Angeles, CA, 90045
props@hollywoodcpr.org * www.hollywoodcpr.org
Hollywood Studio Gallery   **(323) 462-1116**
1035 Cahuenga Blvd, Hollywood, CA, 90038
hsginfo@hollywoodstudiogallery.com * www.hollywoodstudiogallery.com
Independent Studio Services, Inc   **(818) 951-5600**
9545 Wentworth St, Sunland, CA, 91040
www.issprops.com
Jackson Shrub Supply, Inc.   **(818) 982-0100**
11505 Vanowen St, N Hollywood, CA, 91605
Plant rentals, shrub rentals, tree rentals. Christmas decorations and Halloween
decorations and more.
gary@jacksonshrub.com * www.jacksonshrub.com
Kitsch N Sync Props   **(323) 343-1190**
5290 Valley Blvd Unit #1, Los Angeles, CA, 90032
Specializing in 70's and 80's props. Large collection of cameras, electronics,
phones, art, games, stereos, & much more.
kitschnsyncprops@gmail.com * www.kitschnsyncprops.com

LCW Props (818) 243-0707
6439 San Fernando Rd, Glendale, CA, 91201
LCW Is Your 1-Stop Shop For Almost Anything. We Work With Any Budget.
props@lcwprops.com * www.lcwprops.com

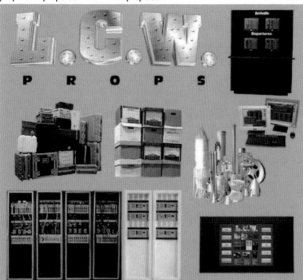

6439 San Fernando Rd. Glendale, CA 91201
Phone: 818-243-0707 - www.lcwprops.com

Lennie Marvin Enterprises, Inc. (Prop Heaven) (818) 841-5882
3110 Winona Ave, Burbank, CA, 91504
catering to the entertainment industry
info@propheaven.com * www.propheaven.com

Modern Props (323) 934-3000
5500 W Jefferson Blvd, Los Angeles, CA, 90016
Modern Props, Contemporary Props, Futuristic Props, & Electronic Props
ken@modernprops.com * www.modernprops.com

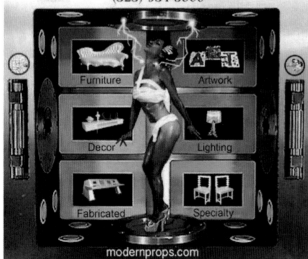

"WHERE **MODERN PROPS** OUR THINGS BRING YOUR CREATIVE IMAGINATION TO LIFE ARE" (323) 934-3000

Furniture | Artwork | Decor | Lighting | Fabricated | Specialty

modernprops.com

Modernica Props (323) 664-2322
2805 Gilroy Street, Los Angeles, CA, 90039
huge inventory 50s-70s furniture & decor, multiples up to 500
www.modernicaprops.net

NEST Studio Rentals, Inc. (818) 942-0339
7007 Lankershim Blvd, N Hollywood, CA, 91605
contemporary furniture, rugs, lighting, art, drapery, smalls
sales@neststudiorentals.net * www.neststudiorentals.net

Ob-jects (818) 351-4200
10623 Keswick St, Sun Valley, CA, 91352
fred@ob-jects.com * www.ob-jects.com

Oceanic Arts (562) 698-6960
12414 Whittier Blvd, Whittier, CA, 90602-1017
We Rent and We Sell Hawaiian, Polynesian, Tropical, and Nautical Decor.
oceanicarts@earthlink.net * www.oceanicarts.net

Omega/Cinema Props (323) 466-8201
5857 Santa Monica Blvd, Los Angeles, CA, 90038
www.omegacinemaprops.com

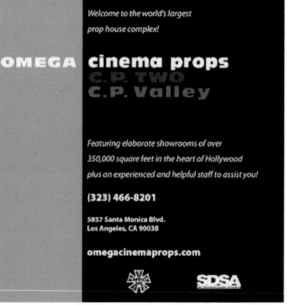

Welcome to the world's largest prop house complex!

OMEGA cinema props C.P. TWO C.P. Valley

Featuring elaborate showrooms of over 350,000 square feet in the heart of Hollywood plus an experienced and helpful staff to assist you!

(323) 466-8201

5857 Santa Monica Blvd.
Los Angeles, CA 90038

omegacinemaprops.com

Pinacoteca Picture Props (818) 764-2722
7120 Case Ave, N Hollywood, CA, 91605
Cleared art, linens, furniture & custom framing
sales@pinaprops.com * www.pinaprops.com

Premiere Props. (818) 768-3800
11500 Sheldon St, Sun Valley, CA, 91352

Prop Mart, Inc. (773) 772-7775
2343 W St Paul Ave, Chicago, IL, 60647
table top, mainly commercials; dishes, linens, flatware, more

Prop Services West   (818) 503-2790
7040 Laurel Canyon Blvd, North Hollywood, CA 91605
www.propserviceswest.com

Propabilities   (773) 278-2384
1517 N Elston, Chicago, IL, 60642
hand props, set dressing, furniture, smalls, park benches, photo surfaces

propNspoon / Props for Today   (212) 244-9600
32-00 Skillman Ave, 3rd Floor, Long Island City, NY, 11101

RC Vintage, Inc.   (818) 765-7107
7100 Tujunga Ave, N Hollywood, CA, 91605
specializing in 40s, 50s, 60s & 70s
rcvintage@aol.com * www.rcvintage.com

RJR Props   (404) 349-7600
5300 Westpark Drive SW, Ste B, Atlanta, CA 30336
RJR Props can provide working realistic Props for your feature film, show, commercial, music video, or event.
rjrelectronics@aol.com * www.rjrprops.com

Seasons Textiles Ltd   011 44 20
9 Gorst Road, London NW10 6LA   8965-6161
enquiries@seasonstextiles.net * www.seasonstextiles.co.uk

Sony Pictures Studios-Prop House (Off Lot)   (310) 244-5999
5933 W Slauson Ave, Culver City, CA, 90230
www.sonypicturesstudios.com

Sony Pictures Studios-Wardrobe   (310) 244-5995
5933 W Slauson Ave, Culver City, CA, 90230
alterations, call (310) 244-7260
www.sonypicturesstudios.com

Sword & Stone   (818) 562-6548
723 N Victory Blvd, Burbank, CA, 91502
medieval & fantasy props
tony@swordandstone.com * www.swordandstone.com

Taylor Creative Inc.   (888) 245-4044
1220 West Walnut St, Los Angeles, CA, 90220
Set decorators look to Taylor Creative Inc. to furnish their film and television shoots on both the East and West Coast.
info@taylorcreativeinc.com * www.taylorcreativeinc.com

Technical Props, Inc.   (818) 761-4993
6811 Farmdale Ave, North Hollywood, CA, 91605
www.techpropsinc.com

Trading Post Ltd.   011 44 20
1-3 Beresford Avenue, Wembley, Middlesex, HA0 1NU   8903-3727
info@tradingposthire.co.uk * www.tradingposthire.co.uk

Trevor Howsam Ltd   011 44 20
182 Acton Lane, Park Royal, London NW10 7NH   8838-6166
props@trevorhowsam.co.uk * www.retrowallpaper.co.uk

Universal Studios Drapery Dept   (818) 777-2761
100 Universal City Plaza, Universal City, CA, 91608
universal.property@nbcuni.com * www.filmmakersdestination.com

Universal Studios Graphic Design & Sign Shop   (818) 777-2350
100 Universal City Plaza, Universal City, CA, 91608
universal.signshop@nbcuni.com * www.filmmakersdestination.com

Universal Studios Property & Hardware Dept   (818) 777-2784
100 Universal City Plaza, Universal City, CA, 91608
One of the oldest prop houses with departments for everything from conceptualizing to finalizing your project.
universal.property@nbcuni.com * www.filmmakersdestination.com

Universal Studios Special Effects Equip.   (818) 777-3333
100 Universal City Plaza, Universal City, CA, 91608
universal.property@nbcuni.com * www.filmmakersdestination.com

Universal Studios Staff Shop   (818) 777-2337
100 Universal City Plaza, Universal City, CA, 91608
staff.shop@nbcuni.com * www.filmmakersdestination.com

Warner Bros. Studios Cabinet & Furniture Shop   (818) 954-1339
4000 Warner Blvd, Burbank, CA, 91522
Custom Cabinetry & Furniture, Furniture Repair & Refinishing, Special Set Construction Antique Restoration.
wbsfproperty@warnerbros.com * www.wbcabinetshop.com

Warner Bros. Studios Property Department   (818) 954-2181
4000 Warner Blvd, Burbank, CA, 91522
wbsfproperty@warnerbros.com * www.wbpropertydept.com

Warner Bros. Studios Staff Shop   (818) 954-2269
4000 Warner Blvd, Burbank, CA, 91522
Manufacturer of exterior & interior details used for the creation of sets in all architectural styles & eras.
wbsfconstructionservices@warnerbros.com * www.wbstaffshop.com

Woody's Electrical Props   (818) 503-1940
5323 Craner Ave., North Hollywood, CA 91601-3313
Period to futuristic. Electronic equipment. Custom built to specifications.
Electrical paneling
woody@woodysprops.com * www.woodysprops.com

Zap Props   (773) 376-2278
3611 S Loomis Pl, Chicago, IL, 60609
hand props, set dressing, street dressing, big & small

ZG04 DECOR   (818) 853-8040
12224 Montague Street, Sun Valley, CA, 91331
Rental & Sale
saul@zg04decor.com * www.zg04decor.com

Prop Locators

See: Research, Advisors, Consulting & Clearances

Prop Products & Packages

See Also: Product Labels

The Earl Hays Press (818) 765-0700
services the Industry only. in stock & custom, we can do anything!

Graphic Space Online (213) 321-3919
Web-Based Only
Fabricated & licensed graphics available 24/7 online to download on automated website.
theteam@graphicspaceonline.com * www.graphicspaceonline.com

The Hand Prop Room LP. (323) 931-1534
in stock & custom

History For Hire, Inc. (818) 765-7767
big selection, also custom

Omega/Cinema Props (323) 466-8201
Prop cans, prop jars, prop boxes and more. Vintage to contemporary.

Warner Bros. Design Studio Scenic Art & Sign Shop (818) 954-1815
4000 Warner Blvd, Burbank, CA, 91522
graphic design and production studio for signs & scenic art; digital printing to hand-painted
wbsigns@warnerbros.com * www.wbsignandscenic.com

Prop Reproduction & Fabrication

See Also: Fiberglass Products/Fabrication* Furniture, Custom-made/Reproduction* Metalworking, Decorative* Metalworking, Welding & Structural* Prop Design & Manufacturing* Scenery/Set Construction* Staff Shops* Vacu-forms/Vacu-forming

Art, Models & Props, Inc. (951) 206-9156
1725 Marengo Ave, Pasadena, CA, 91103
See ad in "Prop Design & Manufacturing"
modelsandprops@msn.com * www.artmodeltech.com

Charisma Design Studio, Inc. (818) 252-6611
8414 San Fernando Road, Sun Valley, CA, 91352
metal/glass/wood/stone
info@charismadesign.com * www.charismadesign.com

Dapper Cadaver/Creatures & Cultures (818) 771-0818
Custom fabrication and prop making. Specializing in bodies and body parts. Animals and taxidermy.

The Earl Hays Press (818) 765-0700
services the Industry only. anything with printing or graphics on it

EFX- Event Special Effects (626) 888-2239
125 Railroad Ave, Monrovia, CA, 91016
Custom Fabrication- CNC- Plasma Table- Pipe & Ring Benders- 3D Renderings
info@efxla.com * www.efxla.com

Fall Creek Corporation (765) 482-1861
PO Box 92, Whitestown, IN, 46075
Civil War era, military & civilian. Civil War era reproductions, rifles, muskets, civil war clothing
ajfulks@fcsutler.com * www.fcsutler.com

Flix FX Inc. (818) 765-3549
7327 Lankershim Blvd #4, N Hollywood, CA, 91605
Sculpting, molding, casting, digitizing & vacuum forming up to 5' x 10'
info@flixfx.com * www.flixfx.com

The Hand Prop Room LP. (323) 931-1534

History For Hire, Inc. (818) 765-7767
the best for vintage

HPR Custom (323) 931-1534
5700 Venice Blvd, Los Angeles, CA, 90019
Machining, woodworking, CNC machining, CAD drawings, water jet cutting, welding, metal working and more.
www.hprcustom.com

JMK Sculpture Inc. (818) 298-1415
820 N Buena Vista St, Burbank, CA, 91505
Custom sculpture, Fabricator, custom PROPS, Fiberglass, hard-coated foam and more! **[See our display ad in Sculpture]**
jeff@jmksculpture.com * www.jmksculpture.com

LM Treasures (626) 252-7354
10557 Juniper Ave Unit A, Fontana, CA 92337
Our products can vary in many different ways from casual items for your house to extravagant pieces to help a business.
lmtreasures.ll@gmail.com * www.lifesizestatues.net

Modern Props (323) 934-3000
Prop fabrication and fabricated props, fabricated electronic dressing, prop fabricators

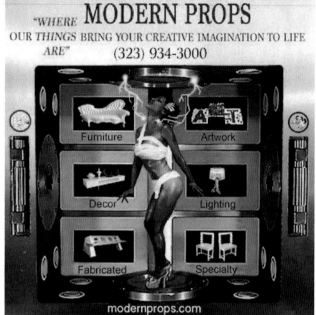

New Rule FX (818) 387-6450
7751 Densmore Ave, Van Nuys, CA 91406
Breakaway props-all types & categories Custom prop & FX design & construction, 3D printing Prototypes, Molding & Casting
ryan@newrulefx.com * www.NewRuleFX.com

Nights of Neon (818) 756-4791
13815 Saticoy St, Van Nuys, CA 91402
over 2,000 neon props in stock. custom neon props
contact@nightsofneon.com * www.nightsofneon.com

Sketch Paper Design (818) 442-0284
7771 Lemona Ave, Van Nuys, CA, 91405
Wood, Metal, Plastic, Foam Custom Designed Props
info@sketchpaperdesign.com * www.sketchpaperdesign.com

Sword & Stone (818) 562-6548

Warner Bros. Studios Metal Shop (818) 954-1265
4000 Warner Blvd, Burbank, CA, 91522
Custom metal fabrication creating anything from structural steel elements to intricate custom furniture
wbsfconstructionservices@warnerbros.com * www.wbmetalshop.com

Woody's Electrical Props (818) 503-1940
Period to futuristic. Design & build panels, consoles, sound mix boards and more

Property Master Storage Rooms

Western Studio Service, Inc.   (818) 842-9272
4561 Colorado Blvd, Los Angeles, CA, 90039
personal lockups to store kits, supplies, ladders, tools, etc. with 24/7 access.
www.westernstudioservice.com

WESTERN STUDIO SERVICE

Set Transportation / Storage	Prop. Lock-Ups
Production Facilities	Trailer Rentals
24/7 Service / Access	Scene Docks
Vaults	Local 399 & 80
Production Parking	Yard Storage

www.WesternStudioService.com

"We're Not the Only Way, We're Just the Best Way"

Prosthetics

See: Medical Equip/Furniture, Graphics/Supplies Special Effects,*
Make-up/Prosthetics

Protective Apparel

See Also: Duvetyne Flameproofing*
Allstar Fire Equipment, Inc.   (626) 652-0900
12328 Lower Azusa Rd, Arcadia, CA, 91006
fireman & hazmat apparel & gear
E.C. Prop Rentals   (818) 764-2008
industrial gloves, glasses, goggles, aprons, facemasks
LCW Props   (818) 243-0707
Fire Suits, Radiation Suits
R. S. Hughes   (818) 686-9111
10639 Glenoaks Blvd, Pacoima, CA, 91331
industrial suits, hats, gloves, shoes
Warner Bros. Studios Costume Dept   (818) 954-1297
HazMat suits from "Outbreak"

Pub Signs

Lennie Marvin Enterprises, Inc. (Prop Heaven)   (818) 841-5882
neon & old, vast selection
Universal Studios Property & Hardware Dept   (818) 777-2784
Pub signs for rent for pub dressing.

Pulleys

See: Rigging, Equipment or Services

Pumping Services

See: Sanitation, Waste Disposal

Pumpkins & Gourds

See Also: Greens Halloween Dressing & Accessories* Pumpkins,*
Artificial
The Pumpkin Patch   (909) 795-8733
32335 Live Oak Canyon Rd. Redlands, CA, 92373
seasonal, pumpkins, gourds, Xmas trees, kid rides, live entertainment

Pumpkins, Artificial

See Also: Halloween Dressing & Accessories
Green Set, Inc.   (818) 764-1231
Artificial Fruits and Artificial Vegetables

Jackson Shrub Supply, Inc.   (818) 982-0100
small artificial pumpkins & large artificial pumpkins, plain artificial pumpkins,
carved artificial pumpkins, & lighted
Universal Studios Property & Hardware Dept   (818) 777-2784
Artificial pumpkins/fake pumpkins from jack-o-lanterns to gourds for rent.

Puppets, Marionettes, Automata, Animatronics

See Also: Mannequins Robots* Special Effects, Make-up/Prosthetics*
Amalgamated Dynamics, Inc.   (818) 882-8638
20100 Plummer St, Chatsworth, CA, 91311
design & build custom animatronics/creatures
Anatomorphex/The Sculpture Studio   (818) 768-2880
8210 Lankershim Blvd Ste 14, N. Hollywood, CA, 91605
design/build realistic animals, creatures, body doubles
Animal Firm   (830) 324-6578
Call for information. custom built realistic & fantasy animals, animal costumes
AnimatronicBear.com   (714) 768-5809
765 South James Rd, Unit A8, Columbus, OH 43227 USA
Photo-realistic animal doubles for hire for film & live events
info@animatronicbear.com * www.animatronicbear.com
Art, Models & Props, Inc.   (951) 206-9156
1725 Marengo Ave, Pasadena, CA, 91103
Custom design/fabr. computer control to puppeteer. See ad in "Prop Design &
Manufacturing"
modelsandprops@msn.com * www.artmodeltech.com
Bali & Beyond   (818) 837-9485
11856 Balboa Blvd #318, Granada Hills, CA 91344
Balinese, Javanese, Contemporary and Made to Order shadow puppets
Bob Baker Marionettes   (213) 250-9995
1345 W First St, Los Angeles, CA, 90026
marionette performer, plus lrg collection marionettes
The Character Shop   (805) 306-9441
4735 Industrial St #4B-G, Simi Valley, CA, 93063
Extraordinary Custom Animatronic Animals & Creatures, Puppets, Marionettes,
Replicas, Robots, Props, Special Makeup FX
lazzwaldo@mac.com * www.character-shop.com
Chiodo Bros Productions, Inc   (818) 842-5656
511 5th St, Suite A, San Fernando, CA, 91340
animatronix, puppets, special effects for TV/film
Flix FX Inc.   (818) 765-3549
7327 Lankershim Blvd #4, N Hollywood, CA, 91605
Puppet & animatronic construction & SAG puppeteers
info@flixfx.com * www.flixfx.com
Folkmanis Puppets   (800) 654-8922
1219 Park Ave, Emeryville, CA 94608
Huge collection, award winning hand puppets, website lists contact info for
large projects & retail sales & small events
www.folkmanis.com
The Fratello Marionettes   (925) 984-3401
696 San Ramon Valley Blvd, Ste 200, Danville, CA, 94526
cust marionettes, Pelham puppet collection, performance company
The Frisch Marionette Co.   (513) 451-8875
P.O. Box 58505, Cincinatti, OH, 45258
custom build marionettes, performance company
Grey Seal Puppets, Inc.   (704) 521-2878
814 Pinckney St, McClellanville, SC, 29458
puppet character design, performance company, contact via web site
Handemonium   (301) 257-5135
in-stock & custom celebrity look-alike hand puppets
Jim Henson's Creature Shop   (323) 802-1500
1416 N. La Brea Ave, Hollywood, CA, 90028
puppets & animatronics, also HQ, NY & London loc.
Legacy Effects   (818) 782-0870
340 Parkside Drive, San Fernando, CA, 91340
LifeFormations   (419) 352-2101
2029 Woodbridge Blvd, Bowling Green, OH, 43402
Characters, scenery, props & support media, for exhibits & theme parks
Masters FX, Inc.   (818) 834-3000
10316 Norris Ave Unit C, Arleta, CA, 91331
animatronic & rod puppets, realistic animals, demons, aliens
Michael Curry Design   (503) 543-4010
50759 Dike Rd, Scappoose, OR, 97056
design/build/perform puppets, costume mechanics, effects for theater, theme
park, film, exhibits, live performance
Puppet Studio   (818) 506-7374
10903 Chandler Blvd, N Hollywood, CA, 91601
character design, hand/rod/animatronic, motion FX, live shows
Puppeteers Of America   (612) 821-2382
310 East 38th St, Suite 127, Minneapolis, MN, 55409
website links to many resources, incl. local/regional guilds, (like LA, OC, NYC)
which in turn list performers within th
www.puppeteers.org

LISTINGS FOR THIS CATEGORY CONTINUE ON THE
FOLLOWING PAGE

Puppets on the Pier (415) 781-4435
Pier 39, space H-4, San Francisco, CA, 94133
lrg sel Folkmanis puppets, European made marionettes
Rene and His Artists Productions (818) 848-6809
707 S Main St, Burbank, CA, 91506
vent puppets, marionettes, animatronics, walkaround characters
Sally Corporation (904) 355-7100
745 W Forsyth St, Jacksonville, FL, 32204
custom animatronics: human, animal, fantasy, plus animated shows & dark ride adventures
Tech Works FX Studios (504) 722-1504
13405 Seymour Meyers Blvd. #5, Covington, LA, 70433
Specializes in Animatronic Animals, Creatures, Robots, Puppets, Costumes and Special FX Make Up.
info@techworksstudios.com * www.techworksstudios.com
UNIMA-USA (404) 873-3089
1404 Spring St NW, Atlanta, GA, 30309
Has Puppetry Yellow Pages resource directory & Puppetry International, nationally dist. periodical
Wayne Martin Puppets (617) 733-9418
24 Pine Ridge Way, Carver, MA, 02330
Entertainment performance company; also design/build for TV, film & commercials

Purses

See: Wardrobe, Accessories

Pyrotechnics

See Also: Non-Guns & Non-Pyro Flashes* Special Effects, Equipment & Supplies* Special Effects, Lighting & Lasers
Atlas Pyrovision Productions (603) 532-8324
P.O. Box 498, Jaffrey, NH, 03452
fireworks productions
CONFETTI & FOG FX Special Effects Company (786) 308-7063
2739 W 79 St Bay, #12, Hialeah, FL 33016
www.caffx.com
Fireworks America (800) 464-7976
P.O. Box 488, Lakeside, CA, 92040
indoor/outdoor displays & effects, pull permits, insurance, prof. technicians
J & M Special Effects, Inc. (718) 875-0140
524 Sackett St, Brooklyn, NY 11217
Formerly Jauchem & Meeh. torches & flash equip., pyro supplies, licensed pyrotechnicians
info@jmfx.net * www.jmfx.net
Jet Effects (818) 764-5644
6910 Farmdale Ave, N Hollywood, CA, 91605
atmospheric & pyro effects, bullet hits, fire & explosions
tito@jeteffects.net * www.jeteffects.net
Lantis Fireworks & Lasers (800) 443-3040
P.O. Box 491, Draper, UT, 84020
fireworks displays & technicians, multimedia spectaculars, indoor/outdoor & close proximity
Phantom Fireworks (775) 537-1737
921 South Highway 160, Pahrump, NV, 89048
wholesale fireworks suppliers, many locations in U.S.
Pyro Spectaculars by Souza (888) 477-7976
3196 N Locust, Rialto, CA, 92377
fireworks choreography & effects, mfg custom effects for stage, film, TV, events
Spectrum Effects, Inc. (661) 510-5633
Call for Appt.
Zambelli Fireworks Internationale (800) 322-7142
PO Box 986, Shafter, CA, 93263
www.zambellifireworks.com

Quiet Bags

See: Grocery Check-out Stands (Complete)

Quilts

See: Linens, Household

Racks

See: Display Cases, Racks & Fixtures (Store)* Warehouse Dressing

Radiators (Household)

C. P. Two (323) 466-8201
Prop radiators for rent
E.C. Prop Rentals (818) 764-2008
NYC apartment style, heater panels, large sel.
History For Hire, Inc. (818) 765-7767
lightweight

LCW Props (818) 243-0707
Large Selection Of Real & Fake Radiators
RC Vintage, Inc. (818) 765-7107
40s, 50s & 60s Wallmount Faux, stand up radiators, many styles, vintage heaters.
Sony Pictures Studios-Prop House (Off Lot) (310) 244-5999
Universal Studios Property & Hardware Dept (818) 777-2784
Many kinds of radiators from fiberglass radiators to functional radiators for rent.

Radio/TV Station

See Also: Audio Equipment* Microphones* On-Air Signs* Video Camera Equipment & Services
Coast Recording Audio Props (818) 755-4692
10715 Magnolia Blvd, N Hollywood, CA, 91601
Everything for a complete Radio Station - One stop shopping! Radio station dressing, tv station dressing, station props
props@coastrecording.com * www.coastrecordingprops.com
History For Hire, Inc. (818) 765-7767
the most complete selection there is
LCW Props (818) 243-0707
Desks, Signs, Mixing Boards, Microphones, Media, AV Server Racks, etc
Modern Props (323) 934-3000
consoles, racks of tape machines, large selection
Omega/Cinema Props (323) 466-8201
RJR Props (404) 349-7600
TV station dressing and radio station dressing available for rent.
Sony Pictures Studios-Prop House (Off Lot) (310) 244-5999
on the air sign
Woody's Electrical Props (818) 503-1940
Period to futuristic. Digital counters & dressing.

Radiology

See Also: MRI (Magnetic Resonance Imaging)* Waiting Room
Alpha Companies - Spellman Desk Co. (818) 504-9090
The #1 source for medical equipment in the industry.

Radios

See Also: Audio Equipment* Televisions* Walkie-Talkies
Antique Radio Store (858) 268-4155
8280 Clairmont Mesa Blvd, #114, San Diego, CA, 92111
Sales & repair of antique radios - 1920-1960 vintage, hours M & W 5-7 PM, Sat 9-4
C. P. Two (323) 466-8201
Prop radios: Period radios to contemporary radios.
Ham Radio Outlet (800) 854-6046
1525 West Magnolia Blvd, Burbank, CA, 91506
Various radios including amateur radios, shortwave radios and more.
The Hand Prop Room LP. (323) 931-1534
period-present
History For Hire, Inc. (818) 765-7767
antique to present
LCW Props (818) 243-0707
Military, Transistor, Boom Box, Period - Present
Modern Props (323) 934-3000
contemporary/futuristic & period
Ob-jects (818) 351-4200
Old Time Replications (818) 786-2500
Call for appointment, Van Nuys, CA, 91411
old radio, TV knobs, escutcheons, pushbuttons, grills, handles, etc.
Prop Services West (818) 503-2790
40s-70s
RC Vintage, Inc. (818) 765-7107
period, 30s to 60s, tabletop & floor Large Selection Vintage Wooden, boom boxes, transistor radios, stereos
RJR Props (404) 349-7600
Handheld radios, car radios, military radios and more for rent.
Sony Pictures Studios-Prop House (Off Lot) (310) 244-5999
antique to present
Universal Studios Property & Hardware Dept (818) 777-2784
Prop radios from period to present for rent.
Warner Bros. Studios Property Department (818) 954-2181
Portable radios, shortwave radios, clock radios, 2-way radios, transistor radios Period radios, radio cabinets

Railroad Crossing Signal

AIR Designs (818) 768-6639
Matching Crossing Signals
Alley Cats Studio Rentals (818) 982-9178
lights, signs

Railroads

See: Trains

Ramps, Automobile

E.C. Prop Rentals (818) 764-2008
drive-up ramps, bottle jacks, hydraulic jacks, large sel.

Ramps: Skateboard, BMX, Freestyle, etc.

See Also: Scenery/Set Construction
Keen Ramps (562) 715-8643
3914 Cherry Ave Unit D, Long Beach, CA, 90807
Skateboard/BMX/bike/scooter ramp rentals: half pipe, mini ramp, quarter pipe,
rail, launch, grind box & custom obstacles
info@keenramps.com * www.keenramps.com

KEEN RAMPS
THE ORIGINAL
SKATER BUILT & APPROVED

Skate & Action Sports Ramps
Quarter Pipes • Half Pipes • Boxes • Custom

Spohn Ranch, Inc. (626) 330-5803
6824 S Centinela Ave, Los Angeles, CA, 90230
Bike & skateboard performance ramps. Skate equipment and BMX equipment.

Ranch

See: Horse Saddles & Tack Horses, Horse Equipment, Livestock*
Locations, Insert Stages & Small Theatres* Wagons* Western
Dressing*

Ranges

See: Stoves

Rapper Jewelry

See: Bling

Read-outs

See Also: Game Show Electronics & Equipment
CBS Electronics (323) 575-2645
7800 Beverly Blvd Rm M162, Los Angeles, CA, 90036
variety; bulb, video, etc.
L. A. Party Works (888) 527-2789
9712 Alpaca St, S El Monte, CA, 91733
in Vancouver tel. 604-589-4101
partyworks@aol.com * www.partyworksusa.com
LCW Props (818) 243-0707
Digital, LED, Analog, Medical, Office, etc

Record/Video Store

See: Video Rental/Sales Store Video Store Dressing*

Recording Studio (Prop)

See Also: Audio Equipment
Coast Recording Audio Props (818) 755-4692
10715 Magnolia Blvd, N Hollywood, CA, 91601
Everything for a Complete Recording Studio - One stop shopping! used and
new sound studio props
props@coastrecording.com * www.coastrecordingprops.com
The Hand Prop Room LP. (323) 931-1534
History For Hire, Inc. (818) 765-7767
the best selection

Records Management

See: Archiving Media/Records Management

Records, Phonograph

See: Phonograph Records

Recycling Services

See Also: Charities & Donations Sanitation, Waste Disposal*
EcoSet ReDirect (323) 669-0697
3423 Casitas Ave, Los Angeles, CA, 90039
One-stop drop-off solution for reusable production and event discards. We
specialize in scenic builds and custom pieces.
www.ecosetconsulting.com/redirect
L. A. Recycling Center (323) 221-9188
1000 N Main St, Los Angeles, CA, 90012
Don't take electronics. Mon-Fri, 7:30-4:30, Sat 7:30-3:00
Westside Metal Recycling (818) 243-6965
6449 San Fernando Rd, Glendale, CA, 91201
Since 1946, full recycling, hauling, clean-up, buyer all metal. Ewaste/computer
disposal, equipment, machinery.
www.westsidemetalrecycling.com

Find it in DB Debbies Book®

Mobile App   **Desktop Website**   **Blog**   **Print Book**   **Mobile Web**   **eBook**

Red Carpeting, Events/Premiers

Astro Audio Video Lighting, Inc. (818) 549-9915
6615 San Fernando Rd, Glendale, CA, 91201
Event red carpeting, rope & stanchions, step & repeats and lighting
www.astroavl.com
Bob Gail Special Events (310) 202-5200
Bob Gail has a huge inventory of special events equipment perfect for any premier event!
EFX- Event Special Effects (626) 888-2239
125 Railroad Ave, Monrovia, CA, 91016
Step & Repeat Printing- Carpet- Lighting- Stanchion & Rope- Printing
info@efxla.com * www.efxla.com
Linoleum City, Inc. (323) 469-0063
4849 Santa Monica Blvd, Hollywood, CA, 90029
Largest selection and always in stock. Red carpet runners, solid carpet runners, premier red carpet.
sales@linocity.com * www.linoleumcity.com

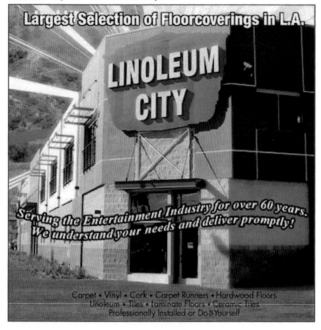

Reference Material/Library

See: Private Investigations* Research, Advisors, Consulting & Clearances* Search Tools, Directories, Libraries

Refrigerators

AIR Designs (818) 768-6639
Single Door Units Period to Present, Home Industrial, Mini Bar, Commercial
Alley Cats Studio Rentals (818) 982-9178
Angel Appliances (877) 262-6435
8545 Sepulveda Blvd, Sepulveda, CA, 91343
cut-aways, customized, practical, classic-current, chest freezer
props@angelappliances.com * www.angelappliances.com/rentals.php

C. P. Two (323) 466-8201
Period refrigerators to modern residential refrigerators; Commercial refrigerators, double door refrigerators & more.
LCW Props (818) 243-0707
Commercial, Industrial, Laboratory
Modern Props (323) 934-3000
contemporary/commercial
Ob-jects (818) 351-4200
Sub Zero (gourmet refrigerators only)
RC Vintage, Inc. (818) 765-7107
40s, 50s & 60s Asst Colors, vintage home refrigerators, diner refrigerators, bar refrigerators, display refrigerators, coolers
Sony Pictures Studios-Prop House (Off Lot) (310) 244-5999
Universal Studios Property & Hardware Dept (818) 777-2784
Prop refrigerators from period to modern for rent.

Registers

See: Hardware, Decorative

Religious Articles

See Also: Church, Chapel, Synagogue, Mosque* Clerical, Judicial, Academic Gowns/Apparel
Abi's Judaica & Gifts (818) 705-4573
18369 Ventura Blvd, Tarzana, CA, 91356
Cotter Church Supplies (213) 385-3366
1701 James M. Wood Blvd, Los Angeles, CA, 90015
Also, church & chapel, statuary
The Hand Prop Room LP. (323) 931-1534
period-present, worldwide sel.
History For Hire, Inc. (818) 765-7767
Hollywood Studio Gallery (323) 462-1116
stations of the cross
LCW Props (818) 243-0707
Bibles, Hymnal Books, Crosses, Urns, Candelabras, Pews, Chalice, Caskets
Ob-jects (818) 351-4200
Omega/Cinema Props (323) 466-8201

Scavenger's Paradise (818) 843-5257
3425 W. Magnolia Blvd, Burbank, CA 91505
Baptismals, votive racks, crosses, crucifix, holy fonts, art & statuary
gilliamgreyson@sbcglobal.net * www.scavengersparadise.com
Sony Pictures Studios-Prop House (Off Lot) (310) 244-5999
religious crosses, religious shrines, religious wall decorations
Universal Studios Property & Hardware Dept (818) 777-2784
Many religious articles and pieces for rent.
Used Church Items, Religious Rentals (239) 992-5737
216 Cumer Road, McDonald, PA, 15057
Statues, Lights, Chandeliers, Podiums, Lecterns, Votive Stands, Crucifixes,
Kneelers, Vestments, Chalices, Altars
warehouse@religiousrentals.com * www.religiousrentals.com
Warner Bros. Studios Property Department (818) 954-2181
Alters, candle holders, crucifixs, statues, kneelers, menorahs, candelabras,
incense holders

Relocation Services

See: Transportation, Trucking and/or Storage

Renaissance Themed Parties

See: Costume Rental Houses Events, Decorations, Supplies &
Services* Events, Design/Planning/Production* Events,
Entertainment* Historical Era Themed Events* Wardrobe,
Antique/Historical*

Reproductions

See: Prop Reproduction & Fabrication

Reptiles

See: Animals (Live), Services, Trainers & Wranglers

Research, Advisors, Consulting & Clearances

See Also: Art, Artists For Hire Private Investigations* Search Tools,
Directories, Libraries*
Act One Script Clearance, Inc. (818) 240-2416
230 N. Maryland Ave, Ste 201, Glendale, CA, 91206
Script research. clearances
Brand Library & Art Center (818) 548-2051
1601 W. Mountain St, Glendale, CA, 91201
Burbank Central Library (818) 238-5600
110 N. Glenoaks Blvd, Burbank, CA, 91502
Warner Research Library
Caravan West Productions (661) 268-8300
35660 Jayhawker Rd, Aqua Dulce, CA, 91390
Old West back to Civil War and trained Old West crew
caravanwest@earthlink.net * www.caravanwest.com
The Costume House (818) 508-9933
books, magazines, patterns, photo collection
Front Sight Firearms Training Institute (800) 987-7719
1 Front Sight Road, Pahrump, NV, 89061
firearms, firearm choreography, location filming, actor training
The Hand Prop Room LP. (323) 931-1534
on-site research library
History For Hire, Inc. (818) 765-7767
research & consulting, no clearances
Kansas Cosmosphere & Space Center (800) 397-0330
1100 N Plum, Hutchinson, KS, 67501-1499
U.S. Space Program equipment
Kitsch N Sync Props (323) 343-1190
Specializing in 70's and 80's props. Large collection of cameras, electronics,
phones, art, games, stereos, & much more.
Michael Dempsey (805) 345-0006
27 years experience as historical re-enactor, clothing, housewares, arms, camp
goods, mid-1600s to Civil War
appeldempsey@aol.com
MorguePropRentals.com (818) 957-2178
5134 Valley Blvd, Los Angeles, CA, 90032
script writing assist., autopsy, mortuary, crime scene, etc.
info@1800autopsy.com * www.morgueproprentals.com
SCA Marketplace (800) 789-7486
P.O. Box 360789, Milpitas, CA, 95036
catalog sales; books/patterns for historical clothing, artifacts from around the
world, website has useful links
Smithsonian Institution (202) 633-1000
PO Box 37012 SI Bldg Room 153 MR 010, Washington, DC, 20013
all museum info; image research, printing & photographic svcs.
www.si.edu
Sony Pictures Studios-Wardrobe (310) 244-5995
alterations, call (310) 244-7260

Sword & Stone (818) 562-6548
medieval period, over 5,000 reference books in our library
Warner Bros. Studios Research Library (818) 977-5050
10671 Lanark St, Sun Valley, CA, 91352
visual, historical, factual, architectural research. Research for film, TV,
commercials, and other creative artists

Resource Books

See: Search Tools, Directories, Libraries

Restaurant Bar

See: Bars, Nightclubs, Barware & Dressing Cafe
Tables/Chairs/Umbrellas* Jukeboxes, Music/Dance Machines* Liquor
Bottles*

Restaurant Furniture & Dressing

See Also: Banquets/Booths (Seating) Bars, Nightclubs, Barware &
Dressing* Cafe Tables/Chairs/Umbrellas* Counters* Salad Bars*
AIR Designs (818) 768-6639
Complete Dressing for Restaurant, Diner, Fast Food, Coffee Shop, Pizzeria
C. P. Valley (323) 466-8201
Period to modern restaurant chairs and restaurant tables.
History For Hire, Inc. (818) 765-7767
period
Hollywood Studio Gallery (323) 462-1116
signage, wall food/beverage pictures
LCW Props (818) 243-0707
Commercial, Industrial, Tables, Appliances, Chairs, Menus, POS Systems
Lennie Marvin Enterprises, Inc. (Prop Heaven) (818) 841-5882
all furniture/dressing/equip. for complete diner/restaurant
LM Treasures (626) 252-7354
10557 Juniper Ave Unit A, Fontana, CA 92337
We carry an extensive assortment of Restaurant furnishings including menu
board holders, butler statues, and wall decor.
lmtreasures.ll@gmail.com * www.lifesizestatues.net
Modern Props (323) 934-3000
contemp/futuristic, furniture, cabinets & more
RC Vintage, Inc. (818) 765-7107
40s, 50s & 60s, Chairs, Tables, Booths, Stools, Bar sets, Diner Counters
RJR Props (404) 349-7600
Restaurant props and restaurant dressing for rent.
Sony Pictures Studios-Prop House (Off Lot) (310) 244-5999
Restaurant Lamp, cash caddy, waitress tray, waitress station rail, cafeteria tray,
change dispenser, coffee bean dispenser
Universal Studios Property & Hardware Dept (818) 777-2784
Restaurant furniture, restaurant props and dressing for rent.

Restaurant Kitchens/Equip./Supplies

See Also: Bars, Nightclubs, Barware & Dressing Cafeteria
Counter/Line* Cooking Equipment* Credit Card Imprint Machine*
Deep Fryer* Food, Artificial Food* Glass Door Coolers*
Glassware/Dishes* Lunch Counters* Menus* Pizza Ovens & Boxes*
Restaurant Furniture & Dressing* Vendor Carts & Concession
Counters* Food, Food Stylists*
AIR Designs (818) 768-6639
Complete Dressing for Restaurant, Diner, Fast Food, Coffee Shop, Pizzeria
Bargain Fair (Beverly/Fairfax) (323) 655-2227
7901 Beverly Blvd, Los Angeles, CA, 90048
corner of Fairfax; dinnerware, glassware, silverware, cookware & more at
unbelievable prices, open 7 days
sheida@bargainfair.com * www.bargainfair.com
Bargain Fair (Mid-City) (323) 965-2227
4635 W Pico Blvd, Los Angeles, CA, 90019
located in Mid-City; dinnerware, glassware, silverware, cookware & more at
unbelievable prices, open 7 days
sheida@bargainfair.com * www.bargainfair.com
C. P. Valley (323) 466-8201
Restaurant sinks, restaurant counters, restaurant workspaces, restaurant
dishware, meat grinders and cookware.
E.C. Prop Rentals (818) 764-2008
stainless sinks & tables, freezer barrier curtain, exhaust fan
History For Hire, Inc. (818) 765-7767
LCW Props (818) 243-0707
Commercial, Industrial, Tables, Appliances, Chairs, Menus, POS Systems
Prop Services West (818) 503-2790
RC Vintage, Inc. (818) 765-7107
40s, 50s & 60s, large sel., & fast food equipment Drive Up Window order Menu
Board.....
Universal Studios Property & Hardware Dept (818) 777-2784
Restaurant kitchen dressing and commercial kitchen dressing for rent.

Restaurant Table Lamps

RC Vintage, Inc. (818) 765-7107
wide variety Contemporary Lamps!

Restoration & Repair

See: Furniture & Art, Repair & Restoration

Retractable Syringes

See: Medical Equip/Furniture, Graphics/Supplies

Retractable Tape Posts

See: Crowd Control: Barricades, Turnstiles Etc.* Stanchions & Rope

Rickshaws

C. P. Valley (323) 466-8201
History For Hire, Inc. (818) 765-7767
Universal Studios Property & Hardware Dept (818) 777-2784
Rickshaws for rent.
Warner Bros. Studios Property Department (818) 954-2181
Wicker rickshaws, rickshaws

Rigging, Equipment or Services

See Also: Motion Control* Nautical Dressing & Props* Theatrical
Draperies, Hardware & Rigging
A1-STUNTWORLD inc (310) 666-3004
Hollywood, CA 90028
stunt coordinators, stunt performers, master stunt riggers, stunt equipment
rental (large inventory), skydiver/parachut
www.stuntworldinc.com
Action Specialists (661) 775-8530
25620 Rye Canyon Rd, Unit E Valencia, CA 91355
stunt rigging, coordination, setup, rig rentals, fire gel sales, cell (818) 915-4691
Art, Models & Props, Inc. (951) 206-9156
1725 Marengo Ave, Pasadena, CA, 91103
Stunt custom design/fabr. aerial, water, harness, props. See ad in "Prop Design
& Manufacturing"
modelsandprops@msn.com * www.artmodeltech.com
Astro Audio Video Lighting, Inc. (818) 549-9915
6615 San Fernando Rd, Glendale, CA, 91201
Trusses, truss bases, box trusses, rigging trick lines, pipe and bases,
cheesebrough clamps and more available.
www.astroavl.com
Beckman Rigging/BRS Rigging (310) 532-3933
13516 Mariposa Ave, Gardena, CA 90247
Stunt rentals; 24/7 services for rigging, mobile fab. show design, stunt
coordination, motion control, robotics, stages
rigyou@mac.com * www.brsrigging.com
Branam Enterprises (818) 885-6474
9152 Independence Ave., Chatsworth, CA 91311
flying, rigging & truss systems provider/fabricator
Castex Rentals (323) 462-1468
1044 N. Cole Ave, Hollywood, CA, 90038
backings, frames, stands, rigging equipment, scratch pads
service@castexrentals.com * www.castexrentals.com
Eagle Studio Services (805) 701-7269
aerial rigging, ground support, motion control, film, TV, live events & tours
Filmmaker Production Services Company - (404) 815-5202
Atlanta
219 Armour Drive NE, Atlanta, GA, 30324
Grip & rigging equip. & services, lighting & sound
http://www.filmmakerproductionservices.com
Filmmaker Production Services Company - (678) 628-1997
Chicago
2558 W 16th Street Dock #4, Chicago, IL, 60608
Grip & rigging equip. & services, lighting & sound
http://www.filmmakerproductionservices.com
Fourth Cub Productions (661) 297-7747
aviation, car, theatrical lighting, film & TV, special events
Foy Inventerprises (702) 454-3300
3275 E. Patrick Lane, Las Vegas, NV, 89120
live performance, theatrical flying effects
Jet Effects (818) 764-5644
6910 Farmdale Ave, N Hollywood, CA, 91605
specialty rigging for film & TV
tito@jeteffects.net * www.jeteffects.net

Leavittation, Inc. (661) 252-7551
25982 Sand Canyon Rd, Santa Clarita, CA, 91387
extensive stunt equipment/rigging,crash & stunt pad rentals
Lowy Enterprises (310) 763-1111
1970 E Gladwick St, Rancho Dominguez, CA, 90220
webbing, fasteners, Velcro, cord, soft goods, parachutes
Matt Sweeney Special Effects, Inc. (818) 902-9354
14201 Bessemer St, Van Nuys, CA 91401
stunt equip, sheaves, pulleys, snatch blocks, flying rigs
New Mexico Lighting & Grip Co. (505) 227-2500
5650 University Blvd SE Bldg 2, Albuquerque, NM, 85107
Grip & rigging equip. & services, lighting & sound
www.newmexicolightingandgrip.com
Peak Trading Corporation (800) 952-7325
43 Basin Rd #1, West Hurley, NY, 12491
catalog sales; cable, chain, rope, hardware, hoists, harnesses, tools
Sapsis Rigging, Inc. (800) 727-7471
3883 Ridge Ave, Philadelphia, PA, 19132
Universal Studios Grip Dept (818) 777-2291
100 Universal City Plaza, Universal City, CA, 91608
Extensive inventory of quality grip equipment incl. digital screens, steel deck &
more
universal.grip@nbcuni.com * www.filmmakersdestination.com
Ver Sales (818) 567-3000
2509 N Naomi St, Burbank, CA, 91504
rigging for rafting, mountain climbing, hang gliding, sailing; also safety items,
fall protection equipment & classes
Warner Bros. Studios Grip Department (818) 954-1590
4000 Warner Blvd, Burbank, CA, 91522
Production, rigging & construction grip equipment, canvas shop, steel
scaffolding rentals/services
www.wbgripdept.com
West EFX, Inc. (818) 762-1059
11635 Sheldon St, Sun Valley, CA, 91352
equip. rentals, lrg scale cust. FX, flying/rigging, crash & burn
ZFX Inc. (502) 637-2500
611 Industry Rd, Louisville, KY, 40208
Flying effects for live performance, film & TV; equipment, choreography

Risers

See: Audience Seating* Stages, Portable & Steel Deck

Road Signs

See: Railroad Crossing Signal* Traffic/Road Signs, Lights, Safety
Items

Robes

See: Clerical, Judicial, Academic Gowns/Apparel* Costume Rental
Houses* Costumes

Robots

See Also: Factory/Industrial* Mannequins* Puppets, Marionettes,
Automata, Animatronics
Advanced Animations (802) 746-8974
P.O. Box 34, Route 107, Stockbridge, VT, 05772
rentals for trade shows, cust. design for theme parks
Art, Models & Props, Inc. (951) 206-9156
1725 Marengo Ave, Pasadena, CA, 91103
Custom design/fabr., computerized, prototype. See ad in "Prop Design &
Manufacturing"
modelsandprops@msn.com * www.artmodeltech.com
E.C. Prop Rentals (818) 764-2008
robotic arms, battery powered
Flix FX Inc. (818) 765-3549
7327 Lankershim Blvd #4, N Hollywood, CA, 91605
Radio controlled robots & robotic arms & SAG puppeteers
info@flixfx.com * www.flixfx.com
Florida Robotics (407) 568-6146
P.O. Box 565, Christmas, FL, 32709
"live" robots for events, trade shows, road shows, animatronic characters
available
LCW Props (818) 243-0707
Large Selection Of Rigged Robotics. Arms, Battle Bots, Large & Small
Tech Works FX Studios (504) 722-1504
13405 Seymour Meyers Blvd. #5, Covington, LA, 70433
Specializes in Robots for Rental, Custom Robots, Robot Suits and Costumes
and Animatronics.
info@techworksstudios.com * www.techworksstudios.com

Rock 'n' Roll Instruments

See Also: Musical Instruments
History For Hire, Inc.   (818) 765-7767
all periods-the biggest selection!
LCW Props   (818) 243-0707
call for styles and latest models

Rock 'n' Roll Lighting & Sound

See Also: Lighting & Sound, Concert/Theatrical/DJ/VJ
Astro Audio Video Lighting, Inc.   (818) 549-9915
6615 San Fernando Rd, Glendale, CA, 91201
48 ch mixers, speaker stacks, pro lighting, staging, rigging, line array speakers
www.astroavl.com

Rock 'n' Roll Staging

See Also: Audience Seating Mechanical Effects* Stages, Portable &
Steel Deck*
Astro Audio Video Lighting, Inc.   (818) 549-9915
6615 San Fernando Rd, Glendale, CA, 91201
Rock and roll staging, rock and roll festival staging; stairs, rails, ramps, drum
risers, gogo boxes
www.astroavl.com
Bill Ferrell Co.   (818) 767-1900
10556 Keswick St, Sun Valley, CA, 91352
Stages, risers, guardrails, ramps, turntables, winches, scissor and handicap
lifts, computer automation, confetti FX.
www.billferrell.com

Rock Climbing Walls

See: Events, Entertainment

Rocking Chairs

See: Chairs

Rocks

See: Concrete Block, Brick, Gravel, Sand, Rocks, Etc. Greens*

Roll-Up Doors

See: Steel Folding Gates & Roll-Up Doors

Roman Themed Parties

See: Columns Costume Rental Houses* Events, Decorations,
Supplies & Services* Events, Destinations* Events, Entertainment*
Wardrobe, Antique/Historical*

Rooftop Dressing

See Also: Satellite Dishes Weather Vanes*
Alley Cats Studio Rentals   (818) 982-9178
vents, turbines, rooftop A/C, skylights, swamp coolers, antennas, satellite
dishes, signs
E.C. Prop Rentals   (818) 764-2008
gutted castered swamp coolers & AC units, vents, ducting, ladders, lighting
LCW Props   (818) 243-0707
Large Selection, Vents, AC's, Roof Antennas, High Voltage, Transistors

Rope

See: Chain & Rope Expendables* Nautical Dressing & Props*

Rope Ladders

See: Nautical Dressing & Props

Rowboats & Oars

See: Boats & Water Sport Vehicles

Rowing Machines

See: Exercise & Fitness Equipment

Rubber & Foam Rubber

See Also: Plastics, Materials & Fabrication Special Effects,
Make-up/Prosthetics*
American Rubber & Supply Co.   (818) 782-8234
15849 Stagg St, Van Nuys, CA, 91406
sheet, sponge, matting & mats, extrusion, tubing, foam, all rainwear, and some
other finished products
Canal Rubber Supply Co.   (800) 444-6483
329 Canal Street, New York City, NY, 10013
wide variety, sheet, foam, mats, flooring, hoses, tubing, sponge
Reynolds Advanced Materials: Smooth-On   (818) 358-6000
Distributor
10856 Vanowen St, N. Hollywood, CA, 91605
Hollywood's F/X source for Liquid Rubbers, Plastics & more
LA@reynoldsam.com * www.moldmakingmaterials.com

Rubber Stamps

See: Art, Supplies & Stationery Office Equipment & Dressing*

Rubble

See: Salvage, Rubble, Clutter & Trash (Prop)

Ruby Dressing

See: Alley Dressing

Rugs

See Also: Art Deco Carpet & Rugs Carpet & Flooring* Red
Carpeting, Events/Premiers* Sono Tubes*
Antiquarian Traders   (310) 247-3900
4851 S. Alameda Street, Los Angeles, CA 90048
Great collection of rugs
antiques@antiquariantraders.com * www.antiquariantraders.com
Bassman-Blaine   (213) 748-5909
1933 S. Broadway, #1005, Los Angeles, CA 90007
We stock many styles & materials; contemporary 5x8 & 8x10 rugs, ottoman
poufs & decorative pillows from Jaipur Rugs.
lashowroom@bassman-blaine.com * www.bassmanblainelamart.com
Bridge Furniture & Props Los Angeles   (818) 433-7100
We carry modern & traditional furniture, lighting, accessories, cleared art,&
rugs. Items are online for easy shopping.
David's Rug Gallery   (310) 657-4623
505 N La Cienega Blvd, Los Angeles, CA, 90048
new/old/antiques, Persian, Chinese, Pakistani & Indian, Turkish
davidsrug@yahoo.com * http://bit.ly/DavidsRugGallery

DAVID'S RUG GALLERY Est. 1956

**DISPLAY ADS AND LISTINGS FOR THIS CATEGORY
CONTINUE ON THE FOLLOWING PAGE**

FormDecor, Inc. (310) 558-2582
America's largest event rental supplier of 20th Century furniture and
accessories for Modern and Mid-Century styles.

Linoleum City, Inc. (323) 469-0063
4849 Santa Monica Blvd, Hollywood, CA, 90029
Area rugs, carpet runners, custom area rugs, sisal rugs, seagrass rugs,
binding, serging, many custom sizes and styles.
sales@linocity.com * www.linoleumcity.com

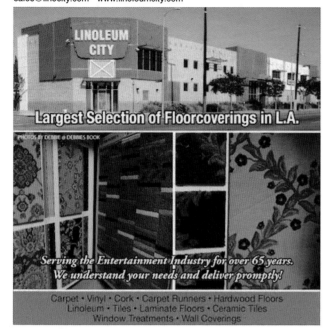

Little Bohemia Rentals (818) 853-7506
11940 Sherman Rd, N Hollywood, CA, 91605
Kilims, Flatweaves, Flokatis, Persians. Vintage rugs and Contemporary rugs.
sales@wearelittlebohemia.com * www.wearelittlebohemia.com

Mehraban Oriental Rugs (310) 657-4400
545 N La Cienega Ave, Los Angeles, CA, 90048
antique/reprod. ethnic, kilims, Oriental, Persian, Iran, Gabbehs

Modern Props (323) 934-3000
contemporary

Modernica Props (323) 664-2322
over 200 50s-70s pop, period & shag rugs

NEST Studio Rentals, Inc. (818) 942-0339
contemporary, traditional, sizes to 9' by 12'

Ob-jects (818) 351-4200
Americana, ethnic, Aubusson, needlepoint, modern, Navajo, Oriental

Omega/Cinema Props (323) 466-8201
Oriental rugs & more

Prop Services West (818) 503-2790
braided/rag/hooked,ethnic tribal,Oriental,Persian,Navajo,runners

The Rug Warehouse (310) 838-0450
3270 Helms Ave, Los Angeles, CA, 90034
High quality area rugs & carpet. Contemporary, traditional, antique, kilims,
shags, hides, custom options & more
www.therugwarehouse.com

Sony Pictures Studios-Linens, Drapes, Rugs (310) 244-5999
5933 W Slauson Ave, Culver City, CA, 90230
Throw rungs, runner rugs, and area rugs
www.sonypicturesstudios.com

Sony Pictures Studios-Prop House (Off Lot) (310) 244-5999
runner rugs, doormats, floor matting, throw rugs, bath mats

Universal Studios Drapery Dept (818) 777-2761
area rug

Universal Studios Property & Hardware Dept (818) 777-2784
Many rugs for rent; period-modern, Oriental to European, kilims,
handmade/hooked

Warner Bros. Drapery, Upholstery & Flooring (818) 954-1831
4000 Warner Blvd, Burbank, CA, 91522
Commercial; Plush & composite: Binding; Cleaning & Repair
wbsfdrapery@warnerbros.com * www.wbdrapery.com

Warner Bros. Studios Property Department (818) 954-2181
Area rugs, Persian rugs, shag rugs, outdoor rugs, tiger rugs, rug beaters

Y & B Bolour (310) 274-6719
321 S Robertson Blvd, Los Angeles, CA, 90048
European, handmade/hooked, kilims, Oriental, Persian

ZG04 DECOR (818) 853-8040
Area Rugs, Runners, Modern Rugs, Contemporary Rugs, Traditional Rugs,
Antique Rugs

Runners

See: Rugs

RV Vehicles & Travel Trailers, Equip & Parts

Arc de Belle (855) 332-3553
Call for Consultation
Vintage Airstream Trailer 1964 Travel Trailer Rentals
info@arcdebelle.com * www.arcdebelle.com

L. A. Circus (323) 751-3486
Call for Appt, Los Angeles, CA, 90047
Airstream trailers only
circusinc@aol.com * www.lacircus.com

Silver Trailer - Vintage Airstream Rentals & Props (530) 295-9299
California / Las Vegas
Silver Trailer is a vintage trailer rental company specializing in Airstream trailers
and props.
studio@silvertrailer.com * www.SilverTrailer.com

Sacks

See: Expendables* Packing/Packaging Supplies, Services

Saddles

See: Horse Saddles & Tack

Safes/Vaults

C. P. Two	**(323) 466-8201**
Real safes/real vaults & prop safes/prop vaults	
C. P. Valley	**(323) 466-8201**
Prop safes and prop vaults	
Dean Security Safe Company	**(818) 997-1234**
8616 Woodman Ave, Arleta, CA, 91331	
largest selection of safes	
Dozar Office Furnishings	**(310) 559-9292**
9937 Jefferson Blvd, Culver City, CA, 90232	

Rentals X22. Fire safes, combination safes/combo safes, sandstone safes, key safes, fire safes. Dimensions chart online.
dozarrents@aol.com * www.dozarrents.com

Faux Library Studio Props, Inc.	**(818) 765-0096**
Safe boxes only, hidden books, hidden money, book boxes, book safes	
History For Hire, Inc.	**(818) 765-7767**
vintage	
LCW Props	**(818) 243-0707**
Large Selection Of Large & Small Safes, Military, Rigged Safe Doors, Vault Doors	
RJR Props	**(404) 349-7600**
Prop safes and prop vaults; giant vaults, lock dials and more.	
Santa Monica Lock & Safe Company, Inc	**(310) 450-5101**
2208 Pico Blvd, Santa Monica, CA, 90405	
Sony Pictures Studios-Prop House (Off Lot)	**(310) 244-5999**
safe front, home style safe, rolling safe, coin banks, combination locks	
Universal Studios Property & Hardware Dept	**(818) 777-2784**
Many kinds of prop safes for rent.	

Safety

See: Floor, Ground & Surface Protection* Nautical Dressing & Props* Protective Apparel* Research, Advisors, Consulting & Clearances* Traffic/Road Signs, Lights, Safety Items* Uniforms, Trades/Professional/Sports

Sails & Sail Makers

See: Boats & Water Sport Vehicles* Canvas* Nautical Dressing & Props

Saint Patrick's Day

See: Events, Decorations, Supplies & Services* Events, Entertainment* Holiday Costumes* Holiday Theme Events* Irish, All Things Irish

Salad Bars

AIR Designs	**(818) 768-6639**
Large & Small Bars, Salsa Bars	
C. P. Valley	**(323) 466-8201**
Salad bars of different sizes	

Salon & Spa Equipment

See Also: Barber Shop* Beauty Salon* Spas & Jacuzzis

Lennie Marvin Enterprises, Inc. (Prop Heaven)	**(818) 841-5882**
full salon & manicure stations	
Modern Props	**(323) 934-3000**

Salvage, Architectural

See Also: Architectural Pieces & Artifacts

Scavenger's Paradise	**(818) 843-5257**
3425 W. Magnolia Blvd, Burbank, CA 91505	

vintage doors, windows, leaded & stained glass, columns, fireplace surround
gilliamgreyson@sbcglobal.net * www.scavengersparadise.com

Salvage, Rubble, Clutter & Trash (Prop)

See Also: Alley Dressing* Sanitation, Waste Disposal

AIR Designs	**(818) 768-6639**
Auto, Drums, Tires, Junkyard Dressing, etc.	
E.C. Prop Rentals	**(818) 764-2008**
shapes, textures galore, pipe, tires, drums, spools, carts etc.	

LCW Props	**(818) 243-0707**

Our Specialty! Large Selections Of Any Kind of clean trash, Own A Recyling Center, Our Inventory Cannot Be Matched

6439 San Fernando Rd. Glendale, CA 91201
Phone: 818-243-0707 - www.lcwprops.com

Tally Ho Marine Salvage & Decor	**(310) 548-5273**
406 22nd St, San Pedro, CA, 90731	
If we don't have it & can't find it, we can build it. marine	
Universal Studios Property & Hardware Dept	**(818) 777-2784**
Prop trash for rent.	

Sand

See: Concrete Block, Brick, Gravel, Sand, Rocks, Etc.* Greens

Sandbags

See: Greens

Sandwich Board Store Sign

AIR Designs	**(818) 768-6639**
Assorted Sizes, Types, Curb Signs	
D'ziner Sign Co.	**(323) 467-4467**
801 Seward Street, Los Angeles, CA 90038	
sandwich signs, directional signs	
sales@dzinersign.com * www.dzinersign.com	

Sanitation, Waste Disposal

See Also: Charities & Donations* Recycling Services

Andy Gump Temporary Site Services	**(800) 992-7755**
26954 Ruether Ave, Santa Clarita, CA, 91351	
State of the art equipment to meet all your sanitation needs, incl. trailers that productions can take along with them	
BCS Recycling Specialists	**(818) 341-4820**
8745 Remmet Ave, Canoga Park, CA, 91304	
Call first: computer parts, scrap metals, cellular phones	
EcoSet ReDirect	**(323) 669-0697**
3423 Casitas Ave, Los Angeles, CA, 90039	
One-stop drop-off solution for reusable production and event discards. We specialize in scenic builds and custom pieces.	
www.ecosetconsulting.com/redirect	
L & M Stripping	**(818) 983-1200**
14232 Aetna St, Van Nuys, CA, 91401	
paint & rust removal from metal, but not wood	
LCW Props	**(818) 243-0707**
Trash bins, Roll-Off Containers, Recycling Bins, Yard Waste	
Patriot Environmental Services	**(800) 624-9136**
2600 Springbrook Ave Unit 107, Saugus, CA, 91350	
will come to stage or location, assist with permits, emergency response service	
Waste Management, Inc	**(713) 512-6200**
1001 Fannin St Ste 4000, Houston, TX, 77002	
Phone number is main office, call for local numbers	

Santa Sleigh

See: Sleighs

Santa Thrones

See: Christmas

Sash Cord

See: Expendables

Sashes, Window

See: Window Treatments

Satellite Dishes

E.C. Prop Rentals (818) 764-2008
prop only, multiple sizes, wall mount and pole mount
LCW Props (818) 243-0707
Large Selection. From 12" To 16', All Kinds

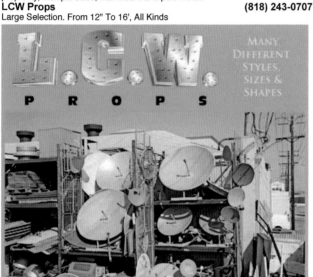

MANY DIFFERENT STYLES, SIZES & SHAPES

6439 San Fernando Rd. Glendale, CA 91201
Phone: 818-243-0707 - www.lcwprops.com

Modern Props (323) 934-3000
8' dia.
Universal Studios Property & Hardware Dept (818) 777-2784
Different satellite dishes, commercial to residential for rent.
Woody's Electrical Props (818) 503-1940
Period to futuristic. Large & small.

Satellites

See: Space Shuttle/Space Hardware

Sawdust

See: Greens

Scaffolding/Lighting Towers

See Also: Ladders* Lighting & Sound, Concert/Theatrical/DJ/VJ*
Rigging, Equipment or Services
E.C. Prop Rentals (818) 764-2008
castered alum. painter's scaffolds
Mike Brown Grandstands (800) 266-2659
2300 Pomona Blvd, Pomona, CA, 91768
and camera towers/platforms

Scale Models

See: Dollhouses* Miniatures/Models* Model
Ships/Planes/Trains/Autos Etc.* Prop Design & Manufacturing* Toys
& Games

Scales

AIR Designs (818) 768-6639
Grocery Store Scales, Deli Scales, Vending Vending Scales, Industrial Scales
Alley Cats Studio Rentals (818) 982-9178
contemporary scales, antique scales, grocery store scales, produce scales, and
carnival scales
C. P. Valley (323) 466-8201
Scales of varying sizes and industries.
E.C. Prop Rentals (818) 764-2008
several styles; lollipop, desktop & floor models
The Hand Prop Room LP. (323) 931-1534
period-present
History For Hire, Inc. (818) 765-7767
LCW Props (818) 243-0707
Postal, Industrial, Commercial, Part Scales, Gram Scales, Platform Scales
Omega/Cinema Props (323) 466-8201
Contemporary and antique household scales including bathroom scales and
kitchen scales.
Sony Pictures Studios-Prop House (Off Lot) (310) 244-5999
Baby scales, weight sets, balance scales, bathroom scales, beam scales,
commercial scales, hanging scales, and more
Universal Studios Property & Hardware Dept (818) 777-2784
Prop scales; period and antique for rent.

Scenery Trailer Rentals

See: Production Vehicles/Trailers

Scenery/Set Construction

See Also: Architectural Pieces & Artifacts* Backings* CNC Router &
Laser Etching Services* Columns* Events, Backings & Scenery*
Fiberglass Products/Fabrication* Graphics, Digital & Large Format
Printing* Hardware, Decorative* Moulding, Wood* Prop & Set Design
Supplies, Parts, Tools* Staff Shops* Themed Environment
Construction* Water Jet CNC Services
41 Sets (323) 860-2442
1040 N. Los Palmas Ave, Bldg 42, Los Angeles, CA, 90038
Full service Art Department, set creation and design for your production
info@41sets.com * www.41sets.com
A & D Scenery (702) 362-9404
3200 Sirius Ave, Ste F, Las Vegas, NV, 89102
fabrication, scenic & exhibit design, staging, turntables
Art, Models & Props, Inc. (951) 206-9156
1725 Marengo Ave, Pasadena, CA, 91103
See ad in "Prop Design & Manufacturing"
modelsandprops@msn.com * www.artmodeltech.com
California Theaming, Inc. (626) 303-2349
404 W. Evergreen Ave, Monrovia, CA, 91016
themed architectural facades, set pieces
Carthay Set Services (818) 762-3566
5539 Riverton Ave, N. Hollywood, CA, 91601
sets, props, billboards, small to large scale
Chris G TV inc. (323) 954 0759
11930 Wicks St, Sun Valley, CA 91352
Providing Scenery Rentals, set construction and custom work to the Film and
TV industry. Delivery available.
chrisg@chrisg.tv * www.chrisg.tv
Continental Scenery (818) 404-3418
Call for Appt
film, TV, theater, outdoor themed environments
Global Entertainment Industries, Inc. (818) 567-0000
2948 N. Ontario St, Burbank, CA, 91504
indoor/outdoor themed displays & facades, set building
IDF Studio Scenery (818) 982-7433
6844 Lankershim Blvd, North Hollywood, CA 91605
Custom Construction, Scenic Painting, welding & extensive rental inventory,
architectural details and pieces
info@idfstudioscenery.com * www.idfstudioscenery.com

Ironwood (818) 265-2055
1514 Flower St, Glendale, CA, 91201
small set pcs to very large metal fab & arch. pcs, sculptures

Jet Sets (818) 764-5644
6910 Farmdale Ave, N Hollywood, CA, 91605
set construction, custom props, scenic painting, special effects, set illustration, research library for clients
dougmorris@jetsets.com * www.jetsets.com

Merritt Productions, Inc. (818) 760-0612
10845 Vanowen St, North Hollywood, CA 91605
specialty props, miniatures, sculpture, mech effects, set const.
www.merrittproductions.com

OPFOR Solutions, Inc (747) 666-7367
8100 Remmet Ave Unit #6, Canoga Park, CA, 91304
Opfor Solutions, Inc. brings you ethnic/military apparel from countries such as - Afghanistan, Iraq, Libya & more.
moe@opforsolutions.com * www.opforsolutions.com

Pizzazz Scenic Contractors, Inc. (904) 641-1239
1354 Wigmore St, Jacksonville, FL, 32206
Design & build themed environments, scenic art, sculptures, signage, & architectural elements

Sally Corporation (904) 355-7100
745 W Forsyth St, Jacksonville, FL, 32204
custom animatronics: human, animal, fantasy, plus animated shows & dark ride adventures

Scenic Express (323) 254-4351
3019 Andrita St, Los Angeles, CA, 90065
Specialize in scenics, prop/set construction, displays and production.

Schmidli Backdrops LA (323) 938-2098
5830 W Adams Blvd, Culver City, CA, 90232
High end texture & scenic backdrops for Film/TV & photography. Full installation service & custom paintings.
backdrops@schmidli.com * www.schmidli.com

Sketch Paper Design (818) 442-0284
7771 Lemona Ave, Van Nuys, CA, 91405
Custom Designed Scenery, Faux facade installation and removal
info@sketchpaperdesign.com * www.sketchpaperdesign.com

Tractor Vision Scenery & Rentals (323) 235-2885
340 E Jefferson Blvd. Los Angeles, CA 90011
Specializing in entertainment, trade shows, & events, we bring your projects to life with precision, speed & personality
sets@tractorvision.com * www.tractorvision.com

Tribal Scenery (818) 558-4045
3216 Vanowen St, Burbank, CA, 91505
scenic painting, set design & construction

Universal Studios Graphic Design & Sign Shop (818) 777-2350
dimensional set pieces & architectural elements

Universal Studios Staff Shop (818) 777-2337

Warner Bros. Studios Construction Services (818) 954-7820
4000 Warner Blvd, Burbank, CA, 91522
Concept, Design, Fabrication of Interior & Exterior Standing Sets, Facades, Exhibits, Road Shows
wbsfconstructionservices@warnerbros.com * www.wbsf.com

Worlds of Wow (817) 380-4215
2126 Hamilton Rd, Argyle, TX, 76226
CUSTOM SCENIC FABRICATION
www.worldsofwow.com

Scenery/Set Rentals

See Also: Architectural Pieces & Artifacts* Backings* Columns*
Scenery/Set Construction

Chris G TV inc. (323) 954 0759
11930 Wicks St, Sun Valley, CA 91352
Providing Scenery Rentals and custom work to the Film and TV industry.
Delivery available.
chrisg@chrisg.tv * www.chrisg.tv

IDF Studio Scenery (818) 982-7433
6844 Lankershim Blvd, North Hollywood, CA 91605
Extensive rental inventory of set walls, windows, doors, fireplaces, etc.
info@idfstudioscenery.com * www.idfstudioscenery.com

LCW Props (818) 243-0707
Backdrops, Some Set Walls

Merritt Productions, Inc. (818) 760-0612
10845 Vanowen St, North Hollywood, CA 91605
specialty props, miniatures, sculpture, mech effects, set const.
www.merrittproductions.com

NBCUniversal Television Asset Center (818) 777-5163
11625 Hart St, N Hollywood, CA, 91605
Hundreds of complete sets and open stock pieces available for rent from our
expanding inventory.
becky.casey@nbcuni.com * http://nbcutvassetcenter.com

Sketch Paper Design (818) 442-0284
7771 Lemona Ave, Van Nuys, CA, 91405
Custom Designed Scenery, Faux facade installation and removal, we have our
own set for rent
info@sketchpaperdesign.com * www.sketchpaperdesign.com

Tractor Vision Scenery & Rentals (323) 235-2885
340 E Jefferson Blvd. Los Angeles, CA 90011
Specializing in entertainment, trade shows, & events, we bring your projects to
life with precision, speed & personality
sets@tractorvision.com * www.tractorvision.com

Warner Bros. Design Studio Scenic Art & Sign (818) 954-1815
Shop
4000 Warner Blvd, Burbank, CA, 91522
hand-painted art to grand-format digital printing for backings, billboards, murals
and portraits
wbsigns@warnerbros.com * www.wbsignandscenic.com

Scenery/Set Storage

Consolidated Scenic Services, Inc.   **(818) 409-3354**
4000 Chevy Chase Dr, Los Angeles, CA 90039
www.consolidatedscenicservices.com
SAUGUS STATION STORAGE   **(661) 253-0944**
25655 Springbrook Ave Bld 24, Santa Clarita, CA, 91350
Secure storage for sets, props, vehicles & containers. Up to 35' clear. Low
rates-helpful staff. Studio/freeway close.
SaugusStation@gmail.com * www.saugusstationstorage.com
Scenic Expressions   **(818) 409-3354**
4000 Chevy Chase Dr, Los Angeles, CA, 90039
mark@scenicexpressions.com * www.scenicexpressions.com
Tractor Vision Scenery & Rentals   **(323) 235-2885**
340 E Jefferson Blvd. Los Angeles, CA 90011
Specializing in entertainment, trade shows, & events, we bring your projects to
life with precision, speed & personality
sets@tractorvision.com * www.tractorvision.com
Western Studio Service, Inc.   **(818) 842-9272**
4561 Colorado Blvd, Los Angeles, CA, 90039
Full service storage using union crews to properly store stock sets and set dec.
safely & securely.
www.westernstudioservice.com

Scenic Artists

See Also: Backings* Guilds, Unions, Societies, Associations
Jet Sets   **(818) 764-5644**
6910 Farmdale Ave, N Hollywood, CA, 91605
set construction, custom props, scenic painting, special effects, set illustration,
research library for clients
dougmorris@jetsets.com * www.jetsets.com
Tractor Vision Scenery & Rentals   **(323) 235-2885**
340 E Jefferson Blvd. Los Angeles, CA 90011
Specializing in entertainment, trade shows, & events, we bring your projects to
life with precision, speed & personality
sets@tractorvision.com * www.tractorvision.com
Warner Bros. Design Studio Scenic Art & Sign   **(818) 954-1815**
Shop
4000 Warner Blvd, Burbank, CA, 91522
hand-painted art to grand-format digital printing for backings, billboards, murals
and portraits
wbsigns@warnerbros.com * www.wbsignandscenic.com

School Lockers

See: Lockers

School Supplies, Desks & Dressing

See Also: Bulletin Boards Chalk Boards* Lockers* Playground
Equipment*
Advanced Liquidators Office Furniture   **(818) 763-3470**
Large sel. used tanker desks, lockers, package deals available.
Alley Cats Studio Rentals   **(818) 982-9178**
student desks, school desks, student lockers, school lockers

Alley Cats Props

PHOTO BY DEBBIE @ DEBBIES BOOK

www.alleycatsprops.com

Art By Kidz   **(818) 240-6650**
Call for Appt, Glendale, CA, 91207
100s of ORIGINAL CHILDRENS 2D & 3D ARTWORKS for rent at low flat rates
based on size. Cleared copyright, located in Glendale.
www.artbykidz.com
C. P. Valley   **(323) 466-8201**
school desks, school supplies, school dressing, school accessories
The Earl Hays Press   **(818) 765-0700**
services the Industry only. test papers, report cards + more!
E.C. Prop Rentals   **(818) 764-2008**
hallway, shop, gym & locker room dressing
The Hand Prop Room LP.   **(323) 931-1534**
period-present dressing
History For Hire, Inc.   **(818) 765-7767**
supplies & dressing
Lakeshore Learning Materials   **(310) 559-9630**
8888 Venice Blvd, Los Angeles, CA, 90034
toys, furniture, school supplies
LCW Props   **(818) 243-0707**
School Desks, Chairs, Science Projects, Chalk & White Boards
On Set Graphics   **(661) 233-6786**
Web Based Business
100% cleared kids artwork, school tests, college flyers, and more.
info@onsetgraphics.com * www.onsetgraphics.com
Prop Services West   **(818) 503-2790**
TR Trading Company   **(310) 329-9242**
15604 S Broadway, Gardena, CA, 90248
85,000 sq/ft of items, selection and inventory changes weekly
sales@trtradingcompany.com * www.trtradingcompany.com
Universal Studios Property & Hardware Dept   **(818) 777-2784**
School lockers, desks, maps, flags and more for rent.

Science Equipment

See Also: Lab Equipment
C. P. Valley (323) 466-8201
science equipment for rent
Dapper Cadaver/Creatures & Cultures (818) 771-0818
Period to modern. Anatomical models, specimen jars, fossils & dinosaurs. Lab equipment, instruments & medical props.
E.C. Prop Rentals (818) 764-2008
lots of stainless shapes, racks, tables, cabinets, lights, smalls
The Hand Prop Room LP. (323) 931-1534
lab glassware
History For Hire, Inc. (818) 765-7767
vintage
Jadis (310) 396-3477
2701 Main St, Santa Monica, CA, 90405
Period laboratory dressing, Tesla coils, vintage quack medical and optical equipment.
jadis1@gmail.com * www.jadisprops.com
LCW Props (818) 243-0707
Glassware, Test Equipment, DNA, Analyzers, Microscopes, Instrumentation
Lynn Harding Antique Instruments (805) 646-0204
103 W Aliso St, Ojai, CA, 93023
lab, medical, pharmacy, nautical, surveyor, models, planetarium, natural history
Modern Props (323) 934-3000
contemporary/futuristic-beakers to microscopes, petri dishes, glass jars, vials, vial holders, more
The Rational Past (310) 476-6277
By Appointment, West Los Angeles, CA
Authentic science, industrial, technical antiques & collectibles. Many professions & eras represented. See web site.
info@therationalpast.com * www.therationalpast.com
Universal Studios Property & Hardware Dept (818) 777-2784
Science equipment and science props for rent.

Science Fiction

See: Aliens* Costumes* Fantasy Props, Costumes, or Decorations* Futuristic Furniture, Props, Decorations* Goth/Punk/Bondage/Fetish/Erotica Etc.* Prop Design & Manufacturing* Space Shuttle/Space Hardware* Space Suits* Spaceship Computer Panel* Special Effects, Electronic* Special Effects, Equipment & Supplies* Special Effects, Make-up/Prosthetics

Sconces

See: Lamps* Light Fixtures

Scoreboards & Scoring Systems

See Also: Clocks* Game Show Electronics & Equipment
CBS Electronics (323) 575-2645
7800 Beverly Blvd Rm M162, Los Angeles, CA, 90036
Custom electronics only.
E.C. Prop Rentals (818) 764-2008
working wall-mounted basketball scoreboard, lights
L. A. Party Works (888) 527-2789
9712 Alpaca St, S El Monte, CA, 91733
Working shot clocks, working scoreboards, working timing devices and more.
partyworks@aol.com * www.partyworksusa.com

LCW Props (818) 243-0707
Working Scoreboards, Just About Any Sport
Modern Props (323) 934-3000
8' long scoreboards and 12' long scoreboards, for set dressing only.
RC Vintage, Inc. (818) 765-7107
Basketball, and Baseball, shot clocks, full display score boards, electrical scoreboards

Scrapbooks

See Also: Hobby & Craft Supplies* Prop Houses
Gibbs Bookbinding (214) 673-0329
140 S Mariposa, Los Angeles, CA, 90004
Custom books and boxes of all sizes. Leather, cloth, and paper, in current or historic/aged styles. Fast turnaround.
stephaniegibbs@gmail.com * www.GibbsBookbinding.com
The Hand Prop Room LP. (323) 931-1534
will fabricate
History For Hire, Inc. (818) 765-7767
outfitted & empty
Kater-Crafts Bookbinders (562) 692-0665
4860 Gregg Rd, Pico Rivera, CA, 90660
Custom work. Scrapbooks, albums, portfolios, binders, journals, foil stamping.
sales@katercrafts.com * www.katercrafts.com
Universal Studios Property & Hardware Dept (818) 777-2784
Prop scrapbooks for rent.

Screens, Folding

Badia Design, Inc. (818) 762-0130
5420 Vineland Ave, N. Hollywood, CA, 91601
info@badiadesign.com * www.badiadesign.com
Bridge Furniture & Props Los Angeles (818) 433-7100
We carry modern & traditional furniture, lighting, accessories, cleared art,&
rugs. Items are online for easy shopping.
Modern Props (323) 934-3000
Chinese, Deco, futuristic & more
Ob-jects (818) 351-4200
antique, contemporary
Omega/Cinema Props (323) 466-8201
Prop Services West (818) 503-2790
Sony Pictures Studios-Prop House (Off Lot) (310) 244-5999
divider screens, dressing screens, hanging panels, medical screens, paneled
screens, Oriental screens, decorative screens
Universal Studios Property & Hardware Dept (818) 777-2784
Various prop folding screens for rent.
Warner Bros. Studios Property Department (818) 954-2181
1 Panel Screens, 2 Panel Screens, 3 Panel Screens, Asian screens, Moroccan
screens, rolling screens

Scuba & Wetsuits

See: Wetsuits, Diving/Surfing

Sculpture

See Also: Art For Rent Art, Artists For Hire* Balloons & Balloon
Sculptures* Carved Figures* Decorative Accessories* Ice & Ice
Sculpture* Mold Making* Prop Design & Manufacturing* Statuary*
Art, Models & Props, Inc. (951) 206-9156
1725 Marengo Ave, Pasadena, CA, 91103
Custom design/fabr. all categories, tiny to giant sized. See ad in "Prop Design
& Manufacturing"
modelsandprops@msn.com * www.artmodeltech.com
ART PIC (818) 503-5999
6826 Troost Ave, N Hollywood, CA, 91605
contemporary art, all mediums + sculpture, all art cleared
artpicla@mac.com * www.artpic2000.com
Charisma Design Studio, Inc. (818) 252-6611
8414 San Fernando Road, Sun Valley, CA, 91352
metal/glass/wood/stone, esthetic & functional
info@charismadesign.com * www.charismadesign.com
Clearedart.com/El Studio Granados (818) 240-4421
958 Verdugo Circle Dr, Glendale, CA, 91206
Multi-media sculptures and carvings in many styles and mediums,
works-in-progress
fineart@elstudiogranados.com * www.clearedart.com
Cope Studios: The Haven (818) 913-7187
926 Western Ave Ste A & B, Glendale, CA, 91201
Our studio ranges from creating high end realistic figurative sculpture and
drawings to a vast range of painting styles.
figurativesculptor@hotmail.com * www.copestudios.com
DeRouchey Foam (888) 959-4852
13618 Vaughn Street, San Fernando, CA, 91340
We offer a full line of foam sculpting materials and services. Urethane, EPS,
HardCoat, Foam Adhesive. 24/7 Service.
dustin@derofoam.com * www.derofoam.com
Doug Rowell, Sculptor (818) 353-4607
Call for appt, Tujunga, CA, 91042
Wood, foam, metal, custom only, design/fabrication/any size job
FILM ART LA (323) 461-4900
Culver City Warehouse at Jefferson & Hauser. Call for address.
large selection of contemporary sculpture; ORDER ARTWORK ONLINE:
Address for pick ups and returns only.
filmartla@gmail.com * www.artimagela.com
The Hand Prop Room LP. (323) 931-1534
art pcs, theme, busts

JMK Sculpture Inc. (818) 298-1415
820 N Buena Vista St, Burbank, CA, 91505
Custom sculpture, Fabricator, custom PROPS, Fiberglass (FRP), hard-coated
foam, and more! Job done right and on time.
jeff@jmksculpture.com * www.jmksculpture.com

On Time and On Budget
Quick Turnarounds Welcome
No Job Too Big Or Too Small

The Mannequin Gallery (818) 834-5555
12350 Montague St Ste E, Pacoima, CA, 91331
inventory & custom work
shelley@mannequingallery.com * www.mannequingallery.com
Merritt Productions, Inc. (818) 760-0612
10845 Vanowen St, North Hollywood, CA 91605
specialty props, miniatures, sculpture, mech effects, set const.
www.merrittproductions.com
Modern Props (323) 934-3000
all periods
Ob-jects (818) 351-4200
Omega/Cinema Props (323) 466-8201
Prop Services West (818) 503-2790
Robert James Company (415) 420-4011
2110 West 20th St, Los Angeles, CA, 90018
Steel artist studio producing large-scale sculpture; mosaics, flowers, organic,
objective works.
rob@robertjamesstudio.com * www.robertjamesstudio.com
Sculptors Pride Inc. (626) 720-7275
Web Based Business
Architectural design, iron shop, architectural sculpture, artificial rockwork
design/fab.
ironsculpture@yahoo.com * www.customforgediron.com
Sculpture by Bruce Gray (323) 223-4059
688 South Avenue 21, Los Angeles, CA, 90031
standing sculptures, wall sculptures, abstract, figurative, modern art, kinetic art,
mobiles, rolling ball machines, rub
bruce@brucegray.com * www.brucegray.com
Sword & Stone (818) 562-6548
Universal Studios Property & Hardware Dept (818) 777-2784
Many sculptures and fake sculptures for rent. Sculpture fabrication also
available.
Warner Bros. Studios Property Department (818) 954-2181
Animal sculptures, Black moor Sculptures, Bronze & wood Sculpture, Buddha
Sculpture, Eiffel Tower Sculpture
ZG04 DECOR (818) 853-8040
Bronzes, Steel, Wood Carvings & Stone Carvings

Seagrass Floor Covering

See: Carpet & Flooring

Search Tools, Directories, Libraries

Corbin Ball Associates (360) 734-8756
506 14th St, Bellingham, WA, 98225
Hosts web's most comprehensive site about meeting planning and events technology

Debbies Book®, Inc (626) 797-7699
Call for Appt., Altadena, CA 91003
A resource directory for professionals in the fields of Film & Television, Photography, Event and more!
info@debbiesbook.com * www.debbiesbook.com

Directory of Major Malls (800) 898-MALL
P.O. Box 837, Nyack, NY, 10960
Details, contacts, tenants lists for the major shopping centers and malls in the US and Canada.

Entertainment Resources & Marketing Association (310) 452-0426
2315 28th Street, Suite 204, Santa Monica, CA 90405
ERMA is an association of marketing, product placement, and brand integration professionals.
michael@erma.org

International Fashion Publications (213) 622-5663
110 E 9th St Ste AL19 (Lobby), Los Angeles, CA, 90079
apparel mfg contacts directory

The Internet Movie Database (213) 622-5663
web directory of movie/TV history, facts, news and also sales of DVDs, tickets, showtimes & more
www.imdb.com

L. A. Public Library (213) 228-7000
630 W 5th St, Los Angeles, CA, 90071
Also, website has links to contact info for all neighborhood libraries

Library of Congress (202) 707-5000
101 Independence Ave SE Washington, DC 20540
Phone # is for general information

New York Production Guide (203) 299-1330
50 Washington St Ste 703, South Norwalk, CT, 06854
best New York area production resource reference

ProductionHUB.com (877) 629-4122
Guide, directory and jobs for film and video
www.productionhub.com

Thomas Industrial Network (800) 699-9822
5 Penn Plaza, New York, NY, 10001
Web directory of 1000s of manufacturers

Variety 411 (800) 699-9822
11175 Santa Monica Blvd Ste 8, Los Angeles, CA, 90025
resources for preproduction & postproduction. LA411 (So. California) & NY411 (NYC region)
411update@variety.com * www.variety411.com

Virtual Library Museum Page (800) 699-9822
Web Based Business
A distributed web directory of museums, libraries & galleries worldwide
http://bit.ly/Virtual-Library

Visual Profile Books (212) 279-7000 ex 319
389 5th Avenue Ste 1105, New York City, NY, 10016
from outside U.S., call (212) 279-7000. Books on Interior Design, Architecture, Visual Merchandising
www.visualreference.com

World Wide Arts Resources (646) 455-1425
PO Box 150, Granville, OH, 43023
Art marketplace, art news & research, links to art museums & galleries worldwide

Searchlights/Skytrackers, Architectural Lights

See Also: Special Effects, Lighting & Lasers

Antiquarian Traders (310) 247-3900
4851 S. Alameda Street, Los Angeles, CA 90048
Amazing collection of grand scale lighting, multiples available, courtroom fixtures, etc
antiques@antiquariantraders.com * www.antiquariantraders.com

Syncrolite L.P. (214) 350-7696
2025 Royal Ln Ste 370, Dallas, TX, 75220
automated Xenon lighting systems, skylights

Seashells

See Also: Nautical Dressing & Props Tikis & Tropical Dressing*

Alley Cats Studio Rentals (818) 982-9178
large selection

Benson's Tropical Sea Imports (714) 841-3399
7442 Vincent Cir, Huntington Beach, CA 92648
seashells, starfish, etc. from India, Philippines, Thailand, Mexico
sales@bensonsimport.com * www.bensonsimport.com

The Hand Prop Room LP. (323) 931-1534

History For Hire, Inc. (818) 765-7767

Oceanic Arts (562) 698-6960
shells, pufferfish, fish nets & related items

Omega/Cinema Props (323) 466-8201

Prop Services West (818) 503-2790

Universal Studios Property & Hardware Dept (818) 777-2784
Prop seashells and natural seashells for rent.

Seating

See: Audience Seating Benches* Chairs* Theater Seating*

Security Devices or Services

See Also: Metal Detectors Police Equipment* Private Investigations* Security Walk-Through & Baggage Alarms* Surveillance Equipment*

Andrews International (818) 487-4060
455 N. Moss St. Burbank, CA 91502
Full service security company specializing in the Entertainment Industry.

LCW Props (818) 243-0707
Wide Selection, Homeland Security, High Tech Devices Of All Kinds

Security Fencing

See: Fences

Security Walk-Through & Baggage Alarms

AIR Designs (818) 768-6639
Walk-Through & Baggage Security Detectors

Air Hollywood - Prop House & Standing Sets (818) 890-0444
We have many Airport Security / TSA / Terminal and Body Scanner sets available.

LCW Props (818) 243-0707
Large Selection Of Walk Through Metal Detectors. Beautiful Baggage X-Ray Machines

Modern Props (323) 934-3000
walk-thru metal detectors baggage X-ray/conveyor & more

Seismic Equipment

See: Lab Equipment

Septic Tank Pumping

See: Sanitation, Waste Disposal

Serving Tables

AIR Designs (818) 768-6639
Hot & Cold, Many Sizes/Types

Set Boxes

See Also: Taco Carts (Propmaster & Set)

Universal Studios Property & Hardware Dept (818) 777-2784
Set boxes of various sizes and types for rent.

Set Construction

See: Scenery/Set Construction Scenic Artists*

Sewing Equipment & Workrooms

Omega/Cinema Props (323) 466-8201
drapery mfg. workroom

Sewing Machines

History For Hire, Inc. (818) 765-7767
Kato's Sewing Machine Co. (213) 626-6026
604 E 1st St, Los Angeles, CA, 90012
Commercial/domestic sales/repair, by appt. only
Omega/Cinema Props (323) 466-8201
Antique and modern sewing machines.
Universal Studios Property & Hardware Dept (818) 777-2784
Many sewing machines from all time periods for rent.
Weaver Leather (800) 932-8371
PO Box 68, Mt Hope, OH, 44660-0068
catalog sales; leather, leather working tools, machinery. leather working

Sewing Services, Industrial

See Also: Tarps, Covers, Custom Sewing
EIDE Industries, Inc (562) 402-8335
16215 Piuma Ave, Cerritos, CA, 90703
Custom mfg. of awnings, canopies, tents, covers, cabanas, tension structures;
industrial sewing services

Sewing Supplies

See: Costume/Wardrobe/Sewing Supplies

Shackles

The Hand Prop Room LP. (323) 931-1534
fake, real, rigged, custom mfg.
History For Hire, Inc. (818) 765-7767
real, fake, rigged
LCW Props (818) 243-0707
Handcuffs, Iron Shackles
Sword & Stone (818) 562-6548
ball & chain, shackles, dungeon dressing
Universal Studios Property & Hardware Dept (818) 777-2784
Prop shackles of different time periods for rent.

Shark Diving Cage

See: Nautical Dressing & Props

Shaving, Old Fashion, Non-Electric

The Hand Prop Room LP. (323) 931-1534
History For Hire, Inc. (818) 765-7767

Sheet Music

See: Music, Sheet

Shelving

See: Display Cases, Racks & Fixtures (Store)* Store Shelf Units & Shelving* Warehouse Dressing

Ship Models

See: Model Ships/Planes/Trains/Autos Etc.

Ship Wheels

See: Nautical Dressing & Props

Shipping

See: Packing/Packaging Supplies, Services* Transportation, Trucking and/or Storage

Shipping Supplies

See: Boxes* Expendables* Packing/Packaging Supplies, Services* Transportation, Trucking and/or Storage

Shoe Boxes

C. P. Valley (323) 466-8201
History For Hire, Inc. (818) 765-7767
big selection
Universal Studios Property & Hardware Dept (818) 777-2784
Prop shoe boxes for rent from different time periods.

Shoe Lifts, Men's

See: Shoes, Boots & Footwear

Shoe Shine Boxes, Chairs & Stands

AIR Designs (818) 768-6639
Open & Covered Units, Period to Present, Vending & Buffing Machine
C. P. Valley (323) 466-8201
The Hand Prop Room LP. (323) 931-1534
period
History For Hire, Inc. (818) 765-7767
RC Vintage, Inc. (818) 765-7107
period shoe shine stations
Universal Studios Property & Hardware Dept (818) 777-2784
Prop shoe polish, shoe shine brushes, shoe shine kits, shoe shine stands and
shoe shine boxes for rent.
Warner Bros. Studios Property Department (818) 954-2181

Shoe Store

See Also: Cash Registers* Counters* Credit Card Imprint Machine* Shoe Boxes* Shoes, Boots & Footwear* Shopping Bags (Silent)
Acme Display Fixture & Packaging (888) 411-1870
3829 S Broadway St., Los Angeles, CA 90037
Complete store setups: garment racks, displays/display cases, counters,
packaging, shelving, hangers, mannequins
sales@acmedisplay.com * www.acmedisplay.com
History For Hire, Inc. (818) 765-7767
Lennie Marvin Enterprises, Inc. (Prop Heaven) (818) 841-5882
product, signage, fitting stools, Brannock device & displays
Universal Studios Property & Hardware Dept (818) 777-2784
Shoe display stands, shoe forms, decorative shoe display boxes, shoe display
feet and mannequin shoe stands for rent.

Shoe Stretchers

See: Shoes, Boots & Footwear

Shoes, Boots & Footwear

See Also: Military Surplus/Combat Clothes, Field Gear* Sportswear* Uniforms, Military* Uniforms, Trades/Professional/Sports* Western Wear
American Duchess Company (775) 238-3674
Web Based Business
American Duchess offers fine ladies' historically accurate reproduction shoes &
accessories based on original examples.
info@americanduchess.com * www.americanduchess.com
Birkenstock USA, LP (415) 884-3315
8171 Redwood Blvd Novato, CA 94945
product placement: ask for "PR"
Champion Dance Shoes (323) 874-8704
3383 Barham Blvd, Los Angeles, CA, 90068
shoes for ballroom, ballet, swing, Latin, salsa, jazz,tango, tap
The Costume House (818) 508-9933
repro lace-up 1890s woman's boots up to size 11 & men's knee-high boots
Early Halloween (212) 691-2933
130 West 25th St, 11th Floor, New York, NY, 10001
vintage 1900-1970
E.C. Prop Rentals (818) 764-2008
rubber boots & boot racks
Glamour Uniform Shop (323) 666-2122
4951 W. Sunset Blvd, Los Angeles, CA, 90027
nurses, restaurant, mechanics, maids uniforms
History For Hire, Inc. (818) 765-7767
wooden shoes, shoe stretchers, for dressing
Lady Studio (323) 461-1765
6500 Hollywood Blvd, Los Angeles, CA, 90028
exotic platforms, stiletto heels, etc.
Professional Uniforms (818) 242-3404
1102 E Colorado St, Glendale, CA, 91205
nursing
Re-Mix Vintage Shoes (323) 936-6210
7384 Beverly Blvd, Los Angeles, CA, 90036
reproduction M/W styles, 30s to 70s, also unused deadstock
Screaming Mimi's (212) 677-6464
382 Lafayette St, New York, NY, 10003
vintage clothing for men & women 1940s - 1980s

LISTINGS FOR THIS CATEGORY CONTINUE ON THE FOLLOWING PAGE

Sony Pictures Studios-Prop House (Off Lot)   (310) 244-5999
Shoe shine brushes, shoe care buffer, shoe foot sizer, shoe horns, shoe polish, shoe shine kits, shoe care supplies, more
Sony Pictures Studios-Wardrobe   (310) 244-5995
alterations, call (310) 244-7260. variety of styles/periods shoes/boots
Universal Studios Costume Dept   (818) 777-2722
Rental, mfg., & alterations
Warner Bros. Studios Costume Dept   (818) 954-1297
High Heels, Flats, Sneakers, Saddle Shoes, Open Toed, Sling Backs, Wedges, Business, Loafers, Boots
Western Costume Co.   (818) 760-0900
Willie's Shoe Service   (323) 463-5011
1174 S La Brea Ave, Los Angeles, CA, 90019
shoe lifts, shoe stretchers, shoe repairing & dyeing, shoe shines & custom-made shoes

Shoji Screens

See Also: Asian Antiques, Furniture, Art & Artifacts
L. A. Shoji & Decorative Products Inc.   (323) 732-9161
4848 W Jefferson Blvd, Los Angeles, CA, 90016
McMullen's Japanese Antiques   (805) 278-2288
2001 Williams Dr #400, Oxnard, CA, 93030
antique furniture, access., folding screens, kimonos, folk arts, architectural pcs. Open Thur-Sat or by appt.
Warner Bros. Studios Property Department   (818) 954-2181
tatami mats

Shopping Bags (Silent)

The Hand Prop Room LP.   (323) 931-1534
Prop Trx   (818) 445-1480
Call to page me for appointment, Simi Valley, CA, 93063
Bags w/handles lunch bags, dept. store & more
timschultz1@mac.com * www.proptrx.com

Shopping Carts

AIR Designs   (818) 768-6639
Large Quantity Carts, Corrals, Signage, Chrome & Plastic
E.C. Prop Rentals   (818) 764-2008
assorted generic for alleyway
History For Hire, Inc.   (818) 765-7767
old-style
LCW Props   (818) 243-0707
Plastic, Metal, bag Lady, Debris, Recyclables
Universal Studios Property & Hardware Dept   (818) 777-2784
Prop shopping carts of various kinds for rent.

Shower Doors

See: Glass & Mirrors

Shower Trailers

See: Production Vehicles/Trailers

Showers

See: Bathroom Fixtures* Production Vehicles/Trailers

Shutters

See: Window Treatments

Side Saddle Riding Habits

See: Western Wear

Sidewalk Dressing

See: Alarms* Alley Dressing* Bag Lady Carts* Billboards & Billboard Lights* Bus Shelter* Fences* Guard Shacks* Kiosks* Lamp Posts & Street Lights* Mailboxes* Marquees* Parking Meters & Sign Poles* Sandwich Board Store Sign* Signs* Steel Folding Gates & Roll-Up Doors* Street Dressing* Telephone Poles Prop* Traffic/Road Signs, Lights, Safety Items* Vendor Carts & Concession Counters

Sign Painters

Warner Bros. Design Studio Scenic Art & Sign Shop   (818) 954-1815
4000 Warner Blvd, Burbank, CA, 91522
graphic design and production studio for signs & scenic art; digital printing to hand-painted
wbsigns@warnerbros.com * www.wbsignandscenic.com

Sign Posts

AIR Designs   (818) 768-6639
4' to 10' Multiples
Alley Cats Studio Rentals   (818) 982-9178
metal, wood, self-standing, menu boards, traffic light poles
E.C. Prop Rentals   (818) 764-2008
good multiples, various heights w/bases

Signals

See: Nautical Dressing & Props* Traffic/Road Signs, Lights, Safety Items

Signs

See Also: Engraving* Flags/Banners* Graphics, Digital & Large Format Printing* Laminating & Mounting* Lighting, LED, Fiber Optic & Specialty* Neon Lights & Signs* On-Air Signs* Paintings/Prints* Parking Meters & Sign Poles* Pub Signs* Read-outs* Sandwich Board Store Sign* Sign Painters* Signs, Foreign* Street Dressing, Exterior Signs* Traffic/Road Signs, Lights, Safety Items
AAA Flag & Banner Mfg Co   (310) 836-3341
8937 National Blvd, Los Angeles, CA 90034
Full Color Custom Printing - Backdrops, Banners, Signs, Posters, Flags, Wall and Window Graphics. Any size and Quantity.
fred@aaaflag.com * www.aaaflag.com
AIR Designs   (818) 768-6639
Restaurant, Diner, Coffee Shop, Traffic, Directional, Period, Neon
Air Hollywood - Prop House & Standing Sets   (818) 890-0444
100s of signs, airport-oriented, light boxes
Alley Cats Studio Rentals   (818) 982-9178
street, hwy, gas station, produce, construction, hotel neon, coast signs, bus stop, bench ads, menu boards, men working etc
Art, Signs & Graphics   (818) 503-7997
6939 Farmdale Ave, N Hollywood, CA, 91605
props, banners, vinyl graphics, vehicle graphics, 3D router cut letters & logos
jessee@artsignsandgraphics.com * www.artsignsandgraphics.com
Artery Props   (877) 732-7733
7684 Clybourn Ave 2nd Floor Unit C, Sun Valley, CA, 91352
100% cleared & owned artwork: banners, lawn signs, mic flags, signs, flyers, posters, CDs, DVDs, albums, stickers & more
info@arteryprops.com * www.arteryprops.com
Beyond Image Graphics   (818) 547-0899
1853 Dana St, Glendale, CA, 91201
Dimensional Signage, Custom Die-Cut Standees, Die Cut Standees, Backlit prints
rafi@beyondimagegraphics.com * www.beyondimagegraphics.com

Big Apple Visual Group   (212) 629-3650
247 West 35th St, New York, NY, 10001
24-hour rush service available

Charisma Design Studio, Inc.   (818) 252-6611
8414 San Fernando Road, Sun Valley, CA, 91352
high-end artistic metal/plastic/glass/neon/wood/stone
info@charismadesign.com * www.charismadesign.com

D'ziner Sign Co.   (323) 467-4467
801 Seward Street, Los Angeles, CA 90038
2000 fonts, symbols, aging, banners, vehicle wraps
sales@dzinersign.com * www.dzinersign.com

E.C. Prop Rentals   (818) 764-2008
street, loading dock, warehouse, factory, military, lab, automotive, exit, no
smoking

The Hand Prop Room LP.   (323) 931-1534
neon, custom design

Heaven or Las Vegas Neon   (310) 636-0081
11814 Jefferson Blvd, Culver City, CA 90230
Thousands of neon signs & neon props. Custom mfg, install, strike & delivery
services. CA Electric Sign Lic#931962
mail@rentneon.com * www.rentneon.com

History For Hire, Inc.   (818) 765-7767
Jet Sets   (818) 764-5644
6910 Farmdale Ave, N Hollywood, CA, 91605
set construction, custom props, scenic painting, special effects, set illustration
dougmorris@jetsets.com * www.jetsets.com
LCW Props   (818) 243-0707
Neon, Lighting Signs, Traffic, Lab, Medical, Foreign - Chinese, Arabic, German,
Airport, Lots Of Others Too...
Mandex LED Displays   (800) 473-5623
2350 Young Ave, Thousand Oaks, CA, 91360
LED Displays & Sign Rentals nationwide, all configurations, tickers, flexible
panels, big LED Digital Countdown Clocks.
alan@ledsignage.com * www.ledsignage.com
Metromedia Technologies   (800) 999-4668
370 Amapola Ave, Torrance, CA, 90501
Outdoor signage
Nights of Neon   (818) 756-4791
13815 Saticoy St, Van Nuys, CA 91402
over 2,000 neon props in stock. neon, wood, foam, vinyl, sheet metal, computer
table router
contact@nightsofneon.com * www.nightsofneon.com
RC Vintage, Inc.   (818) 765-7107
signs & sign poles Highway Signs. Neon signs and A frame signs
Sign Comm   (213) 383-2111
3214 Beverly Blvd, Los Angeles, CA, 90057
signs, banners, digital printing
Sony Pictures Studios-Prop House (Off Lot)   (310) 244-5999
A-Frames, advertisement signage, airport signs, award signs, bulletin board
signs, caution signs, certificates, more
Tractor Vision Scenery & Rentals   (323) 235-2885
340 E Jefferson Blvd. Los Angeles, CA 90011
Specializing in entertainment, trade shows, & events, we bring your projects to
life with precision, speed & personality
sets@tractorvision.com * www.tractorvision.com
Universal Studios Graphic Design & Sign Shop   (818) 777-2350
specialty prop signage, design, large fmt printing up to 100" wide
Universal Studios Property & Hardware Dept   (818) 777-2784
Many signs for rent as well as sign fabrication.

**DISPLAY ADS AND LISTINGS FOR THIS CATEGORY
CONTINUE ON THE FOLLOWING PAGE**

Warner Bros. Design Studio Scenic Art & Sign Shop　　(818) 954-1815
4000 Warner Blvd, Burbank, CA, 91522
graphic design and production studio for signs & scenic art; digital printing - hand-painted; sign printing & graphics
wbsigns@warnerbros.com * www.wbsignandscenic.com

WestOn Letters　　(818) 503-9472
7259 N. Atoll Ave, N. Hollywood, CA, 91605
Serving the signage needs of the entertainment industry since the 1960s
sales@westonletters.com * www.WestonLetters.com

Serving the signage needs of the
entertainment industry since the 1960s
Custom Cut Acrylic Letters – SAME DAY
Thousands of letters IN STOCK
3D Letters – Foam, Plastic, Metal, etc
Changeable Letters, Marquee Letters
Large Format Digital Printing, Banners
Imitation Metal Plaques
All types of interior signs

Worlds of Wow　　(817) 380-4215
2126 Hamilton Rd, Argyle, TX, 76226
Monument Signs and Custom 3D Signage - foam designed, hard-coated, painted and finished signs.
www.worldsofwow.com

Signs, Foreign

D'ziner Sign Co.　　(323) 467-4467
801 Seward Street, Los Angeles, CA 90038
9 languages, any material, aging
sales@dzinersign.com * www.dzinersign.com

E.C. Prop Rentals　　(818) 764-2008
Chinese, Spanish, European road signage

Universal Studios Property & Hardware Dept　　(818) 777-2784
Many signs available for different countries for rent.

Silk Screening

See: Embroidery, Screen Printing, Etc. Fabric Dyeing/Tie Dyeing/Painting/Aging*

Silverware, Silver Serving Pieces

See Also: Prop Houses Tableware/Flatware*

Badia Design, Inc.　　(818) 762-0130
5420 Vineland Ave, N. Hollywood, CA, 91601
info@badiadesign.com * www.badiadesign.com

The Hand Prop Room LP.　　(323) 931-1534
period-present, incredible collection

History For Hire, Inc.　　(818) 765-7767

LCW Props　　(818) 243-0707
Period - Present

Omega/Cinema Props　　(323) 466-8201

Pasadena Antique Warehouse　　(626) 404-2422
1609 East Washington Blvd., Pasadena, CA, 91104
Antique German, Spanish, English, and French .925 sterling silver serving and decorative pieces.
pasadenaantiquewarehouse@gmail.com * www.pasadenaantiquewarehouse.com

Prop Services West　　(818) 503-2790

Sony Pictures Studios-Prop House (Off Lot)　　(310) 244-5999
Assorted flatware, butter knife, dinner knife, salad fork, dessert fork, silver sets, silver flatware sets, soup spoons and more

Universal Studios Property & Hardware Dept　　(818) 777-2784
Large selection of silver and silverware for rent.

Single/Double Drop Trailers

See: Production Vehicles/Trailers

Sinks

Alley Cats Studio Rentals	**(818) 982-9178**
period ceramic pedestal styles, metal janitor sink, stainless steel, prison toilet sink combo, fountain sink	
E.C. Prop Rentals	**(818) 764-2008**
stainless lab counter/sink/castered cabinet units, utility sinks	
LCW Props	**(818) 243-0707**
Pedestal Sinks, Kitchen, Bathroom	
Modern Props	**(323) 934-3000**
modern, hi-tech, stainless steel	
Universal Studios Property & Hardware Dept	**(818) 777-2784**
Prop sinks for rent.	

Siren Lights

E.C. Prop Rentals	**(818) 764-2008**
110v red/amber/green/blue/clear with mounts, also some 12 VDC	
History For Hire, Inc.	**(818) 765-7767**
LCW Props	**(818) 243-0707**
Sirens, Bells, Police Bars, Revolving Flashing Lights	

Sisal

See: Carpet & Flooring

Skate Ramps

See: Ramps: Skateboard, BMX, Freestyle, etc.* Scenery/Set Construction

Skeletons

See: Bones, Skulls & Skeletons* Fossils

Ski Equipment

See Also: Prop Houses* Sporting Goods & Services

C. P. Valley	**(323) 466-8201**
ski equipment for rent	
Doc's Ski Haus	**(310) 828-3492**
3101 Santa Monica Blvd, Santa Monica, CA, 90404	
pro shop, also fly fishing	
The Hand Prop Room LP.	**(323) 931-1534**
History For Hire, Inc.	**(818) 765-7767**
vintage	
Jackson Shrub Supply, Inc.	**(818) 982-0100**
Ski lift gondola	
LCW Props	**(818) 243-0707**
Skis, Snow Shoes, Boots & Mountain Gear	
Universal Studios Property & Hardware Dept	**(818) 777-2784**
All kinds of ski equipment and ski props for rent.	

Ski Machines

See: Exercise & Fitness Equipment

Skulls & Skeletons

See: Bones, Skulls & Skeletons* Dinosaurs* Fossils* Taxidermy, Hides/Heads/Skeletons

Sky Lights (Rooftop)

See: Rooftop Dressing* Searchlights/Skytrackers, Architectural Lights

Slates/Clapboards

C. P. Two	**(323) 466-8201**
The Hand Prop Room LP.	**(323) 931-1534**
History For Hire, Inc.	**(818) 765-7767**
period	
Sobrante Film Accessories	**(817) 237-0137**
9700 Watercress Dr, Fort Worth, TX, 76135	
Universal Studios Property & Hardware Dept	**(818) 777-2784**
Prop slates and prop clapboards for rent.	

Sleds

The Hand Prop Room LP.	**(323) 931-1534**
period-present, toboggans to horse drawn	
History For Hire, Inc.	**(818) 765-7767**
vintage	
LCW Props	**(818) 243-0707**
Dog Sled, 1-4 Man Sleds, Period - Present	
Universal Studios Property & Hardware Dept	**(818) 777-2784**
Prop sleds/prop snow sleds for rent.	

Sleepwear - Pajamas, Nightgowns, Etc.

The Costume House	**(818) 508-9933**
pj's, nightgowns/baby dolls	
LCW Props	**(818) 243-0707**
Sony Pictures Studios-Wardrobe	**(310) 244-5995**
alterations, call (310) 244-7260	
Universal Studios Costume Dept	**(818) 777-2722**
Rental, mfg., & alterations	
Western Costume Co.	**(818) 760-0900**

Sleighs

See Also: Carriages, Horse Drawn

Bob Gail Special Events	**(310) 202-5200**
Bob Gail has an extensive list of themed props for movie sets, events, and tradeshows for rental in CA and Las Vegas.	
FROST	**(310) 704-8812**
Call for Appointment, 21515 Madrona Ave, Torrance, CA 90503	
Traditional full size Holiday Sleighs	
mdisplay@yahoo.com * www.frostchristmasprops.com	
Green Set, Inc.	**(818) 764-1231**
many Xmas/Santa, regular/oversize, w/reindeer	
The Hand Prop Room LP.	**(323) 931-1534**
Jackson Shrub Supply, Inc.	**(818) 982-0100**
Santa sleigh + more	
Universal Studios Property & Hardware Dept	**(818) 777-2784**
Snow sleighs, toboggans and Stanta sleighs for rent.	
Warner Bros. Studios Property Department	**(818) 954-2181**
Santa clause sleighs, wood sleighs	

Slipcovers

See Also: Upholstery Materials/Services

Larry St. John & Co.	**(310) 630-5828**
17021 S Broadway, Gardena, CA, 90248	
Custom, heavily discounted, locally made, quality sofa sectionals and slipcovers.	
info@larrystjohn.com * www. larrystjohn.com	

Slot Machines

See: Gambling Equipment

Smalls

See: Decorative Accessories* Prop Houses

Smoking Products

See Also: Marijuana Plants, Dispensary Dressing & Hydroponics

Badia Design, Inc.	**(818) 762-0130**
5420 Vineland Ave, N. Hollywood, CA, 91601	
info@badiadesign.com * www.badiadesign.com	
The Cigar Warehouse	**(818) 784-1391**
15141 Ventura Blvd, Sherman Oaks, CA, 91403	
large sel. cigars, cutters, pipes, tobacco, leather cases, humidors	
The Hand Prop Room LP.	**(323) 931-1534**
History For Hire, Inc.	**(818) 765-7767**
vintage cigars, cigar boxes, cigarettes, tobacco, etc.	
LCW Props	**(818) 243-0707**
full cigar shop, humidors	
RC Vintage, Inc.	**(818) 765-7107**
40s, 50s & 60s Ashtrays	
Sony Pictures Studios-Prop House (Off Lot)	**(310) 244-5999**
cigar cutters, cigarette boxes, cigarette holders, hookas, hookahs, ash trays, tobacco products & boxes, more	

Snow Blankets

See: Greens

Snow Shoes

C. P. Two	**(323) 466-8201**
History For Hire, Inc.	**(818) 765-7767**
period	

Snow, Artificial & Real

See Also: Ice & Ice Sculpture* Special Effects, Equipment & Supplies
Carving Ice & Big on Snow   (714) 224-1455
900 S Placentia Ave Ste B, Placentia, CA, 92870
You're the best at what you do & so are we. Carving Ice & Blowing Snow for
the TV & film industries for over 20 years.
info@carvingice.com * www.carvingice.com

714-224-1455

CONFETTI & FOG FX Special Effects Company   (786) 308-7063
2739 W 79 St Bay, #12, Hialeah, FL 33016
www.caffx.com
EFX- Event Special Effects   (626) 888-2239
125 Railroad Ave, Monrovia, CA, 91016
Snow Machines, Snow Blankets, Evaporative Snow, Real Snow
info@efxla.com * www.efxla.com

Green Set, Inc.   (818) 764-1231
snow props, including snowballs, icicles, glacier ice walls
Jackson Shrub Supply, Inc.   (818) 982-0100
snow blankets, plastic snowflakes

L. A. Party Works   (888) 527-2789
9712 Alpaca St, S El Monte, CA, 91733
Snow machines, confetti cannons, cryo and much more.
partyworks@aol.com * www.partyworksusa.com

LCW Props   (818) 243-0707
blowers and flake
Reliable Snow Service   (661) 269-2093
3932 Sourdough Rd, Acton, CA, 93510
We make snow at your location and offer ice delivery in Acton and Aqua
Dulce!
reliablesnow@earthlink.net * www.reliablesnowservice.com
Special Effects Unlimited, Inc.   (323) 466-3361
1005 N. Lillian Way, Hollywood, CA, 90038
buy it, or have us do the whole job (including cleanup)
www.specialeffectsunlimited.com

Snow-cone Machines

See: Vendor Carts & Concession Counters

Snowboards

See: Ski Equipment* Sporting Goods & Services

Snowmobiles

See: Sporting Goods & Services

Soccer Goals & Balls

See: Sporting Goods & Services

Societies

See: Guilds, Unions, Societies, Associations

Soda Fountain Dressing

AIR Designs   (818) 768-6639
Complete Dressing, Dishes to Signage, Counters, Equipment
C. P. Two   (323) 466-8201
Soda fountain signs and accessories, soda fountain dispensers, soda fountain
machines.
History For Hire, Inc.   (818) 765-7767
RC Vintage, Inc.   (818) 765-7107
40s, 50s & 60s Counters, Ice Cream Chairs, Freezers, Soda Jerks, Lemonade
dispensers, etc
Universal Studios Property & Hardware Dept   (818) 777-2784
Soda fountain dressing, soda dispensers, soda machines, soda fountain signs,
soda fountains and more for rent.

Soda Guns

See: Bars, Nightclubs, Barware & Dressing* Soda Fountain Dressing

Soldier Toys & Drums

See Also: Christmas
History For Hire, Inc. (818) 765-7767
Universal Studios Property & Hardware Dept (818) 777-2784
Prop toy soldiers, Christmas toy soldiers, toy soldier lawn ornament, Toy soldier nutcrackers and more for rent.

Sono Tubes

Linoleum City, Inc. (323) 469-0063
4849 Santa Monica Blvd, Hollywood, CA, 90029
Cardboard tubes. 6 foot sono tubes, 12 foot sono tubes.
sales@linocity.com * www.linoleumcity.com
Superior-Studio Specialties (323) 278-0100
2239 S Yates, Commerce, CA, 90040
3" up to 60" dia.

Sound Equipment

See: Audio Equipment* Lighting & Sound, Concert/Theatrical/DJ/VJ* Recording Studio (Prop)* Rock 'n' Roll Lighting & Sound

Sound Stages

See: Stages/Studios, Film/TV/Theatre/Events

South Seas Decorative Items

See: Light Fixtures, South Seas* Seashells* Tikis & Tropical Dressing

Souvenirs

See: Memorabilia & Novelties* Statue Of Liberty

Space Shuttle/Space Hardware

See Also: Space Suits* Spaceship Computer Panel
Action Sets and Props / WonderWorks, Inc. (818) 992-8811
Space shuttle & station, space suit, specialty props, miniatures, mechanical effects, cityscape, miniature buildings

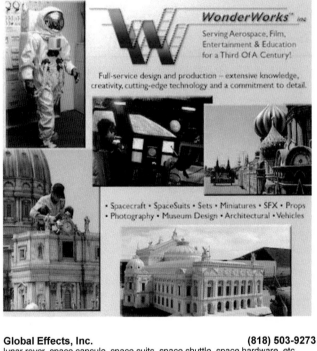

WonderWorks inc

Serving Aerospace, Film, Entertainment & Education for a Third Of A Century!

Full-service design and production – extensive knowledge, creativity, cutting-edge technology and a commitment to detail.

• Spacecraft • SpaceSuits • Sets • Miniatures • SFX • Props
• Photography • Museum Design • Architectural • Vehicles

Global Effects, Inc. (818) 503-9273
lunar rover, space capsule, space suits, space shuttle, space hardware, etc.
Kansas Cosmosphere & Space Center (800) 397-0330
1100 N Plum, Hutchinson, KS, 67501-1499
U.S. Space Program equipment
Modern Props (323) 934-3000
electronic racks

Space Suits

See Also: Space Shuttle/Space Hardware
Action Sets and Props / WonderWorks, Inc. (818) 992-8811
Space shuttle & station, space suit, specialty props, miniatures, mechanical effects, cityscape, miniature buildings
Global Effects, Inc. (818) 503-9273
the finest available, every type of U.S. space suit, NASA space suits, including accessories.

Spaceship Computer Panel

See Also: Control Panels/Boxes* Space Shuttle/Space Hardware
Action Sets and Props / WonderWorks, Inc. (818) 992-8811
Space shuttle & station, space suit, specialty props, miniatures, mechanical effects, cityscape, miniature buildings
Kansas Cosmosphere & Space Center (800) 397-0330
1100 N Plum, Hutchinson, KS, 67501-1499
U.S. Space Program equipment
LCW Props (818) 243-0707
Large Quantity, Wall Dressing, Futuristic, Blinking Eye Candy, etc.
Modern Props (323) 934-3000
futuristic/electronic, consoles, wall units, more

Spas & Jacuzzis

See Also: Salon & Spa Equipment
Lifestyle Pool & Spa (818) 997-3255
5830 Sepulveda Blvd, Van Nuys, CA, 91411
full showroom, all makes/models pools & spas in stock

Speakers

See: Audio Equipment* Lighting & Sound, Concert/Theatrical/DJ/VJ* Stereo Equipment

Special Effects, Electronic

See Also: Special Effects, Equipment & Supplies* Special Effects, Lighting & Lasers
Astro Audio Video Lighting, Inc. (818) 549-9915
6615 San Fernando Rd, Glendale, CA, 91201
Including lighting, lasers, fog machines, confetti machines, black lights, foam machines and bubble machines.
www.astroavl.com
EFX- Event Special Effects (626) 888-2239
125 Railroad Ave, Monrovia, CA, 91016
Snow- Confetti- Cryo- Bubbles- Fog- Foam- Fluid- Lighting- Fabrication
info@efxla.com * www.efxla.com
Flix FX Inc. (818) 765-3549
7327 Lankershim Blvd #4, N Hollywood, CA, 91605
Electronic & lighted props, design & fabrication
info@flixfx.com * www.flixfx.com
Gilderfluke & Company, Inc (818) 840-9484
205 S Flower St, Burbank, CA, 91502
cust. computerized animation show control systems & components
LCW Props (818) 243-0707
Custom Graphics Department. We Make Any Video Files Needed & Have A Huge Stock
Woody's Electrical Props (818) 503-1940
period to futuristic

Special Effects, Equipment & Supplies

See Also: Audio/Visual Film Equipment* Backings* Breakaways (Glass, Props, Scenery)* Bubble Machines* Confetti* Conveyor Equipment* Expendables* Fog Machines* Lighting & Sound, Concert/Theatrical/DJ/VJ* Lighting, LED, Fiber Optic & Specialty* Mechanical Effects* Motion Control* Prop Design & Manufacturing* Puppets, Marionettes, Automata, Animatronics* Pyrotechnics* Rigging, Equipment or Services* Robots* Scenery/Set Construction* Snow, Artificial & Real* Special Effects, Electronic* Special Effects, Lighting & Lasers* Special Effects, Make-up/Prosthetics* Stage Lighting, Film/Video/TV
Astro Audio Video Lighting, Inc. (818) 549-9915
6615 San Fernando Rd, Glendale, CA, 91201
Special effects equipment and special effects supplies; visual effects and theatrical special effects.
www.astroavl.com
Bill Ferrell Co. (818) 767-1900
10556 Keswick St, Sun Valley, CA, 91352
Motion FX turntables, winches, scissor lifts, conveyors, treadmills. Computer automation. Sets, props. Confetti effects.
www.billferrell.com

DISPLAY ADS AND LISTINGS FOR THIS CATEGORY CONTINUE ON THE FOLLOWING PAGE

CONFETTI & FOG FX Special Effects Company (786) 308-7063
2739 W 79 St Bay, #12, Hialeah, FL 33016
www.caffx.com
Castex Rentals (323) 462-1468
1044 N. Cole Ave, Hollywood, CA, 90038
effects fans, foggers, bubble machines, special effects, special fx
service@castexrentals.com * www.castexrentals.com
EFX- Event Special Effects (626) 888-2239
125 Railroad Ave, Monrovia, CA, 91016
Snow- Confetti- Cryo- Bubbles- Fog- Foam- Fluid- Lighting- Fabrication
info@efxla.com * www.efxla.com
Flix FX Inc. (818) 765-3549
7327 Lankershim Blvd #4, N Hollywood, CA, 91605
Foggers, fans, turntables, specialty equipment & rigs
info@flixfx.com * www.flixfx.com
J & M Special Effects, Inc. (718) 875-0140
524 Sackett St, Brooklyn, NY 11217
Formerly Jauchem & Meeh. breakaway glass, atmospheric, weapons, pyro,
show packages
info@jmfx.net * www.jmfx.net
Jet Effects (818) 764-5644
6910 Farmdale Ave, N Hollywood, CA, 91605
atmospheric & mechanical effects for film & TV
tito@jeteffects.net * www.jeteffects.net

Custom Mechanical Effects
Complete Fabrication Shop
Atmospheric & Pyro Effects
Specialty Rigging for Film & TV

L. A. Party Works (888) 527-2789
9712 Alpaca St, S El Monte, CA, 91733
Special effects equipment including fog machines, bubble machines, foam
machines, misting fans, confetti cannons & more.
partyworks@aol.com * www.partyworksusa.com
LCW Props (818) 243-0707
Custom Graphics Department. We Make Any Video Files Needed & Have A
Huge Stock
Mee Industries Inc. (626) 359-4550
16021 Adelante St, Irwindale, CA, 91702
Mfg. custom, turnkey large scale devices for pure water, ultra fine fog droplet
effects
NAC Effects & Prop Animation (805) 376-0206
1772-J E Avenida de los Arboles #396, Thousand Oaks, CA, 91362
Flying rigs, motion bases, misc. special effects, hydraulic pumps
Rando Productions, Inc (818) 982-4300
11939 Sherman Rd, N Hollywood, CA, 91605
turntables, lifts, rolling rooms, gimbals, hydraulics & custom
Reel EFX, Inc (818) 762-1710
5539 Riverton Ave, N Hollywood, CA, 91601
atmospheric, fire, wind, rain, etc. & cust. tabletop effect illusions
Reynolds Advanced Materials: Smooth-On (818) 358-6000
Distributor
10856 Vanowen St, N. Hollywood, CA, 91605
Hollywood's F/X source for Liquid Rubbers, Plastics, lifecasting, rubber and
plastic breakaway glass, and more.
LA@reynoldsam.com * www.moldmakingmaterials.com

Set Stuff (323) 993-9500
1105 N Sycamore Ave, Hollywood, CA, 90038
rent/operate fire/rain/smoke/wind, canopies, comm equip.
Special Effects Unlimited, Inc. (323) 466-3361
1005 N. Lillian Way, Hollywood, CA, 90038
A complete line of rental equipment & expendables, along with custom special
effects services.
www.specialeffectsunlimited.com
Technifex, Inc. (661) 294-3800
25261 Rye Canyon Rd, Valencia, CA, 91355
Design, mfg. mechanical, fluid, video & optical special effects, turnkey shows,
themed environments
Universal Studios Special Effects Equip. (818) 777-3333
wind, wave, rain, snow, fog, bubble, cobweb machines/supplies
Warner Bros. Studios Special Effects & Prop (818) 954-1365
Shop
4000 Warner Blvd, Burbank, CA, 91522
Consultation, Script Break-down, Equipment Rentals, Expendable Sales,
Picture Car Prep, Action Props
www.wbspecialeffects.com

Special Effects, Lasers

See: Lighting & Sound, Concert/Theatrical/DJ/VJ Lighting, LED,
Fiber Optic & Specialty* Special Effects, Lighting & Lasers*

Special Effects, Lighting & Lasers

See Also: Lighting & Sound, Concert/Theatrical/DJ/VJ Lighting, LED,
Fiber Optic & Specialty* Searchlights/Skytrackers, Architectural
Lights* Stage Lighting, Film/Video/TV*
Astro Audio Video Lighting, Inc. (818) 549-9915
6615 San Fernando Rd, Glendale, CA, 91201
Special effects lighting, special effects lasers; machines, production and
design.
www.astroavl.com
CONFETTI & FOG FX Special Effects Company (786) 308-7063
2739 W 79 St Bay, #12, Hialeah, FL 33016
www.caffx.com
Luminous Systems Corp (800) 321-3644
11961 Sherman Rd, N Hollywood, CA, 91605
see web site for dealers. mfg. lightning simulators
Universal Studios Special Effects Equip. (818) 777-3333

Special Effects, Make-up/Prosthetics

See Also: Animal Costumes & Walk Around Characters Blood*
Make-up & Hair, Supplies & Services* Tattoos (Temporary)
Body/Face Painting*
Amalgamated Dynamics, Inc. (818) 882-8638
20100 Plummer St, Chatsworth, CA, 91311
make-up, design & build prosthetics & creature effects
The Character Shop (805) 306-9441
4735 Industrial St #4B-G, Simi Valley, CA, 93063
Extraordinary Custom Animatronic Animals & Creatures, Puppets, Marionettes,
Replicas, Robots, Props, Special Makeup FX
lazzwaldo@mac.com * www.character-shop.com
Chiodo Bros Productions, Inc (818) 842-5656
511 5th St, Suite A, San Fernando, CA, 91340
animatronix, puppets, special effects for TV/film
CONFETTI & FOG FX Special Effects Company (786) 308-7063
2739 W 79 St Bay, #12, Hialeah, FL 33016
www.caffx.com
Creative Character Engineering (818) 901-0507
16110 Hart St, Van Nuys, CA, 91406
Dinair Airbrush Make-up & Institute (818) 780-4777
6215 Laurel Canyon Blvd, N. Hollywood, CA, 91606
Make-Up Designory (MUD) (818) 729-9420
129 S San Fernando Blvd, Burbank, CA, 91502
Los Angeles School of Make-Up, Inc.
Make-up Effects Laboratories (818) 982-1483
7110 Laurel Canyon Blvd Bldg E, N Hollywood, CA, 91605
prosthetic pieces
Masters FX, Inc. (818) 834-3000
10316 Norris Ave Unit C, Arleta, CA, 91331
demons, aliens, age, fat, gore, etc.
Premiere Products Inc. (800) 346-4774
10312 Norris Ave, Ste C, Pacoima, CA, 91331
make-up/prosthetic adhesives & removal solvents
Professional Visioncare Assoc. (818) 789-3311
14607 Ventura Blvd, Sherman Oaks, CA, 91043
special FX lenses for film/TV/theatre
Reel Creations, Inc. (818) 346-7335
7831 Alabama Ave Ste 21, Canoga Park, CA, 91304
reel blood, temp. tattoos, airbrush/body paint, prosthetic inks

Tech Works FX Studios (504) 722-1504
13405 Seymour Meyers Blvd. #5, Covington, LA, 70433
Specializes in Special Make Up FX, Creature Suit Design, Monsters, Costumes and Gore FX.
info@techworksstudios.com * www.techworksstudios.com

W. M. Creations, Inc. (800) 454-8339
5755 Tujunga Ave, N. Hollywood, CA, 91601
Makeup FX, latex effect
mm@wmmufx.com * www.wmcreationsinc.com

Special Events

See: Events, Decorations, Supplies & Services Events, Design/Planning/Production* Events, Entertainment*

Spinning Wheels

History For Hire, Inc. (818) 765-7767

Spittoons

AIR Designs (818) 768-6639
Bar Dressing, Brass

History For Hire, Inc. (818) 765-7767

LCW Props (818) 243-0707
Brass, Silver Plated

Universal Studios Property & Hardware Dept (818) 777-2784
Prop brass spitoons, antique spitoons, decorative spitoons and metal spitoons for rent.

Sporting Goods & Services

See Also: Archery Equipment, Training Baseball Pitching Machine* Basketball Court & Backboards* Bicycles & Bicycling Supplies* Bowling Equipment* Boxing, Wrestling, Mixed Martial Arts (MMA)* Camping Equipment* Exercise & Fitness Equipment* Fall Pads & Crash Pads* Fishing Equipment & Tackle* Gymnasium & Gymnastic Equipment* Nets* Prop Houses* Rigging, Equipment or Services* Ski Equipment* Snow Shoes* Surfboard, Wakeboard* Track & Field Equipment* Uniforms, Trades/Professional/Sports* Volleyball Setup*

Above It All Kites (360) 665-5483
312 Pacific Blvd S, Long Beach, WA, 98631
Kites, stunt kites, windsocks, also custom orders

Athletic Room (818) 764-9801
12750 Raymer St, N Hollywood, CA, 91605
Golf, Camping, Surf, Baseball, Soccer, Football, Basketball, Hockey, Yoga, Boxing, Water Sports, Variety of Sports Props
athleticroom@mac.com * www.athleticroomprops.net

Best Buy Figure Skating (714) 518-3240
300 W Lincoln Ave, Anaheim, CA, 92805
ice & roller skates, sticks, protective equip.

C. P. Two (323) 466-8201
Sports related items from gear and equipment to trophies and posters.

Dick's Sporting Goods (626) 351-1843
3359 E. Foothill Blvd, Pasadena, CA, 91107
multiple stores, sporting goods, esp. good sel. apparel

Escalade Sports (812) 467-1200
817 Maxwell Avenue, Evansville, IN 47711
Accudart darts, Stiga, Goalrilla, Harvard, Bear archery, Woodplay playsets, Atomic game table

Fold-A-Goal (800) 542-4625
4856 W. Jefferson Blvd, Los Angeles, CA, 90016
everything for soccer; goals, nets & balls, uniforms, and field lining equipment & service
www.fold-a-goal.com

The Hand Prop Room LP. (323) 931-1534
lrg sel, all sports

History For Hire, Inc. (818) 765-7767
Vintage baseball equipment, ice skates, roller skates, sports graphics, sport ticket fabrication & more!

I & I Sports Supply, Inc. (310) 715-6800
19751 S Figueroa St, Carson, CA, 90745
multiple stores; martial arts, boxing, paintball

Into The Wind (800) 541-0314
1408 Pearl St, Boulder, CO, 80302
Kites, windsocks, wind art

LCW Props (818) 243-0707
Balls, Equipment, Scoreboards, Memorabilia

Roger Dunn Golf Shop (818) 763-3622
5445 Lankershim Blvd, N Hollywood, CA, 91601
a wide array of golf products

Ski Net Sports (818) 505-1294
11378 Ventura Blvd, Studio City, CA, 91604
Closed on Wed. inline skates, hiking/walking boots/shoes, foldup go boards

Soccer Plus Sports Shop (800) 945-7291
1640 E Washington Blvd, Pasadena, CA, 91104
only soccer

The Soccer Store (818) 243-7790
520 S Brand, Glendale, CA, 91204
only soccer

Sony Pictures Studios-Prop House (Off Lot) (310) 244-5999
Cricket sticks, volleyballs, air hockey, badminton racket, baseball equipment, basketball equipment, bicycles, billiard equipment

Sport Chalet (310) 235-2847
11801 W Olympic Blvd, Los Angeles, CA, 90025
Website has store locator. full pro shop: tennis, golf, kayaks, canoes, skis

Stunt Wings/Adventure Sports Productions (818) 367-2430
12623 Gridley St, Sylmar, CA, 91342
hang gliding, paragliding, ultralight talent & equipment, cinematography, stunts

Universal Studios Property & Hardware Dept (818) 777-2784
Prop sports equipment and goods for rent.

Val-Surf (818) 769-6977
4810 Whitsett Ave, Valley Village, CA, 91607
skateboards, surfboards, snowboards, wakeboards

Warner Bros. Studios Property Department (818) 954-2181
Weight & exercise machines, assorted sports equipment, skis, bowling equipment, bikes, surf boards

Sports & Games Themed Events

See Also: Arcade Equipment, Games & Rides Events, Decorations, Supplies & Services* Events, Design/Planning/Production* Events, Entertainment* Scoreboards & Scoring Systems*

Bob Gail Special Events (310) 202-5200
Want to create your own arcade? We have the games for you! We have a prop for pretty much every sport!

L. A. Party Works (888) 527-2789
9712 Alpaca St, S El Monte, CA, 91733
Scoreboards, Bleachers, sports related games and more. Vancouver tel.
604-589-4101
partyworks@aol.com * www.partyworksusa.com

Sports Bar Dressing

AIR Designs **(818) 768-6639**
Unique Items, Pictures, Signs, Games, Memorabilia
Bob Gail Special Events **(310) 202-5200**
Want to create your own arcade? We have the games for you! We have a prop for pretty much every sport!
History For Hire, Inc. **(818) 765-7767**
Lots!
LCW Props **(818) 243-0707**
TV's, Kegs, Taps, Seating, Tables, Memorabilia
Lennie Marvin Enterprises, Inc. (Prop Heaven) **(818) 841-5882**
signs, memorabilia, counter, glassware, etc.
Universal Studios Property & Hardware Dept **(818) 777-2784**
Sports bar dressing, sports bar props and sports bar menus for rent.

Sports Fan Items, Memorabilia, Photographs

See Also: Collectibles Memorabilia & Novelties*
Athletic Room **(818) 764-9801**
12750 Raymer St, N Hollywood, CA, 91605
Framed Jerseys, Sports Art, Trophies, Tailgate Dressing, Fan Props, Vintage Memorabilia, Furniture, Banners, Beach.
athleticroom@mac.com * www.athleticroomprops.net
History For Hire, Inc. **(818) 765-7767**
Hollywood Studio Gallery **(323) 462-1116**
LCW Props **(818) 243-0707**
Balls, Equipment, Scoreboards, Memorabilia
Sony Pictures Studios-Prop House (Off Lot) **(310) 244-5999**
baseball card collections
Universal Studios Property & Hardware Dept **(818) 777-2784**
Many kinds of sports memorabilia for rent.

Sports Lockers

See: Lockers

Sports/Athletic Field Lining/Graphics

See: Sporting Goods & Services

Sportswear

See Also: Knickers Uniforms, Trades/Professional/Sports*
Dick's Sporting Goods **(626) 351-1843**
3359 E. Foothill Blvd, Pasadena, CA, 91107
multiple stores, sporting goods, esp. good sel. apparel
Fila U.S.A., Inc. **(212) 726-5937**
1411 Broadway 30th Flr, New York, NY, 10018
product placement
Sony Pictures Studios-Wardrobe **(310) 244-5995**
alterations, call (310) 244-7260
Team Leader **(877) 365-7555**
Call for Appt
Online uniform catalog. Will make custom pom pons.
www.teamleader.com
Universal Studios Costume Dept **(818) 777-2722**
Rental, mfg., & alterations
Warner Bros. Studios Costume Dept **(818) 954-1297**
Collection of period & contemporary costumes for rent categorized by era, decade and style

Spray Paint Booth

See: Paint & Painting Supplies

Sprinklers, Fire Protection

See: Plumbing Fixtures, Heating/Cooling Appliances

Spy Items

See: Surveillance Equipment

Squadroom

See: Police Equipment

Squawk Boxes

See: Military Props & Equipment

Stadium Seats

See: Audience Seating

Staff Shops

American Wood Column Corp. **(718) 782-3163**
913 Grand St, Brooklyn, NY, 11211-2785
catalog sales; large sel. of millwork, architectural/decorative small finials to tall columns, plain to ornate, custom t
The Decorators Supply Corporation **(773) 847-6300**
3610 South Morgan St, Chicago, IL, 60609
catalog sales; 15,000 cast plaster & wood carved ornaments for woodwork & furniture, also custom mantels, custom work
Sony Pictures Studios-Staff Shop **(310) 244-5541**
10202 W Washington Blvd, Culver City, CA, 90232
www.sonypicturesstudios.com
Universal Studios Staff Shop **(818) 777-2337**
Warner Bros. Studios Staff Shop **(818) 954-2269**
Manufacturer of exterior & interior details used for the creation of sets in all architectural styles & eras.

Stage Lighting Equipment

See: Lighting & Sound, Concert/Theatrical/DJ/VJ Stage Lighting, Film/Video/TV*

Stage Lighting, Film/Video/TV

See Also: Chase Lights Lighting & Sound, Concert/Theatrical/DJ/VJ* Lighting Control Boards* Special Effects, Lighting & Lasers*
Astro Audio Video Lighting, Inc. **(818) 549-9915**
6615 San Fernando Rd, Glendale, CA, 91201
wash, concert, followspot, intelligent, control, video, screen
www.astroavl.com
Blue Feather Lighting & Design **(818) 701-5404**
19630 Lanark St, Reseda, CA, 91335
Unilux stroboscopic lights to shoot things that pour, spritz or splash
Castex Rentals **(323) 462-1468**
1044 N. Cole Ave, Hollywood, CA, 90038
HMIs, Kino Flos, Fresnels, Source 4s, stage lighting
service@castexrentals.com * www.castexrentals.com
EFX- Event Special Effects **(626) 888-2239**
125 Railroad Ave, Monrovia, CA, 91016
Stage Lighting- LED Screens- Event Lighting
info@efxla.com * www.efxla.com
Filmmaker Production Services Company - Atlanta **(404) 815-5202**
219 Armour Drive NE, Atlanta, GA, 30324
Grip & rigging equip. & services, lighting & sound
http://www.filmmakerproductionservices.com
Filmmaker Production Services Company - Chicago **(678) 628-1997**
2558 W 16th Street Dock #4, Chicago, IL, 60608
Grip & rigging equip. & services, lighting & sound
http://www.filmmakerproductionservices.com
High End **(800) 890-8989**
2105 Gracy Farms Ln, Austin, Tx 78758
mfg. lighting equip., also office in NYC, TX, Europe
History For Hire, Inc. **(818) 765-7767**
vintage
Leonetti Co. **(818) 890-6000**
10601 Glenoaks Blvd, Pacoima, CA, 91331
Rent lighting & grip equip., truck packages, generators, & sell expendables
Luminous Systems Corp **(800) 321-3644**
11961 Sherman Rd, N Hollywood, CA, 91605
see web site for dealers. mfg. Softsun special purpose lighting
Mac Tech LED Lighting **(818) 777-1281**
3900 Lankershim Blvd, Universal City, CA, 91608
Uses 30-70% less power than equivalent conventional production lighting - Superior quality of light for stage & location
info@mactechled.com * www.mactechled.com
New Mexico Lighting & Grip Co. **(505) 227-2500**
5650 University Blvd SE Bldg 2, Albuquerque, NM, 85107
Grip & rigging equip. & services, lighting & sound
www.newmexicolightingandgrip.com
Pacific Northwest Theatre Associates **(800) 622-7850**
2414 SW Andover C100, Seattle, WA, 98106
catalog sales; theatrical supplies, make-up, expendables, rigging, drops, lighting, sound, effects
Radiance Lightworks, Inc. **(818) 879-1516**
4607 Lakeview Canyon Rd, Ste 500, Westlake Village, CA, 91361
full svc. lighting design for film/video, special events, architecture, themed environments & theatre systems
Tobins Lake Sales **(888) 525-3753**
3313 Yellowstone Dr, Ann Arbor, MI, 48105
installation too

Universal Studios Grip Dept (818) 777-2291
100 Universal City Plaza, Universal City, CA, 91608
Extensive inventory of quality grip equipment incl. digital screens, steel deck & more
universal.grip@nbcuni.com * www.filmmakersdestination.com

Universal Studios Set Lighting Dept (818) 777-2291
100 Universal City Plaza, Universal City, CA, 91608
Extensive inventory of quality stage & location lighting
universal.setlighting@nbcuni.com * www.filmmakersdestination.com

Stage Turntables

Bill Ferrell Co. (818) 767-1900
10556 Keswick St, Sun Valley, CA, 91352
Turntables 4"-40'; simple or computer-automated. Surrounds, guardrails, stairs, ramps, lifts, winches. Set construction.
www.billferrell.com

Flix FX Inc. (818) 765-3549
7327 Lankershim Blvd #4, N Hollywood, CA, 91605
3" (product) to 8' motorized tables, 5' glass top lazy susan
info@flixfx.com * www.flixfx.com

Stages, Portable & Steel Deck

See Also: Audience Seating Bleachers & Grandstand Seating*
Accurate Staging (310) 324-1040
1820 W. 135th Street, Gardena, CA, 90249
rolling risers, platforms

Astro Audio Video Lighting, Inc. (818) 549-9915
6615 San Fernando Rd, Glendale, CA, 91201
Temporary stages and portable stages custom in any size, height; stairs, rails, etc.
www.astroavl.com

Bill Ferrell Co. (818) 767-1900
10556 Keswick St, Sun Valley, CA, 91352
Steel Deck, Ferrellels, rounds, ramps, triangles, rollers, risers. Sets, props. Turntables, winches, lifts, conveyors.
www.billferrell.com

EFX- Event Special Effects (626) 888-2239
125 Railroad Ave, Monrovia, CA, 91016
Steel Deck- Stage- Drape- Carpet- Back Drop- Steps- Railing
info@efxla.com * www.efxla.com

L. A. Party Works (888) 527-2789
9712 Alpaca St, S El Monte, CA, 91733
Portable staging/temporary staging for rent
partyworks@aol.com * www.partyworksusa.com

Upstage Parallels (818) 247-1149
4000 Chevy Chase Dr, Los Angeles, CA, 90039
Steel Deck Platform Rental - steps and truss rental
www.upstagerentals.com

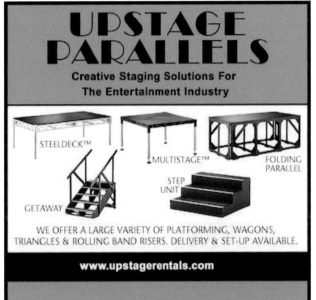

Stages, Road Tour Rehearsal

See: Locations, Insert Stages & Small Theatres Stages/Studios, Film/TV/Theatre/Events*

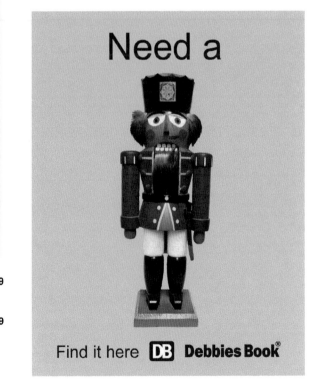

Stages/Studios, Film/TV/Theatre/Events

See Also: Locations, Insert Stages & Small Theatres

ABC 7 Broadcast Center (818) 560-7450
500 Circle Seven Dr, Glendale, CA, 91201
www.studioservices.go.com

Ahmanson Theater (213) 628-2772
135 N Grand, Los Angeles, CA, 90012
for admin office, see Dorothy Chandler Pavillion, Filming (213) 972-7334,
Rentals (213) 972-7478
www.centertheatregroup.org

Air Hollywood - Prop House & Standing Sets (818) 890-0444
Air Hollywood is the largest aviation-themed studio serving the motion picture
and television industry.

Albuquerque Studios (505) 227-2000
5650 University Blvd SE, Albuquerque, NM, 87106
www.abqstudios.com

Anaheim Convention Center (714) 765-8950
800 W Katella Ave, Anaheim, CA, 92802
www.anaheimconventioncenter.com

Anaheim Grove (714) 712-2700
2200 E Katella Ave, Anaheim, CA, 92806
event inquiries: (714) 712-2703
www.citynationalgroveofanaheim.com

Angel Stadium of Anaheim (714) 940-2000
2000 Gene Autry Way, Anaheim, CA, 92806
http://losangeles.angels.mlb.com/ana/ballpark/index.jsp

The Barker Hangar Santa Monica Air Center (310) 390-9071
3021 Airport Ave Ste 203, Santa Monica, CA, 90405
Large clearspan interior, high ceilings
www.barkerhangar.com

Ben Kitay Studios (323) 466-9015
1015 N Cahuenga Blvd, Hollywood, CA, 90038
www.benkitay.com

Bob Gail Special Events (310) 202-5200
The Bob Gail Production Studio is the newest addition to LA's production studio
scene.

The Burbank Studios (818) 840-3000
3000 W Alameda Ave, Burbank, CA, 91523
www.theburbankstudios.com

California Theatre of Performing Arts (909) 885-5152
562 W 4th St, San Bernardino, CA, 92402
www.californiatheatre.net

CBS Studio Center (818) 655-5000
4024 Radford Ave, Studio City, CA, 91604
Residential streets, central park, new york street, and subway car mock up and
subway station mock up.
www.cbssc.com

CBS Television City (323) 575-2676
7800 Beverly Blvd, Los Angeles, CA, 90036
www.cbstelevisioncity.com

Cerritos P.A.C. (562) 916-8510
12700 Center Court Dr, Cerritos, CA, 90703
www.cerritoscenter.com

Chandler Valley Center Studios (818) 424-4551
13927 Saticoy St, Van Nuys, CA, 91402
Commercials & music videos, TV/Movies
www.cvcstudios.us

The Culver Studios (310) 202-1234
9336 W Washington Blvd, Culver City, CA, 90232
www.theculverstudios.com

Delfino Studios (818) 361-2421
12501 Gladstone Ave, Sylmar, CA, 91342
www.delfinostudios.com

Dodger Stadium (323) 224-1507
1000 Elysian Park Ave, Los Angeles, CA, 90012
http://losangeles.dodgers.mlb.com

Dolby Theater (323) 308-6300
6801 Hollywood Blvd Ste 180 Admin, Hollywood, CA, 90028
www.dolbytheatre.com

Dorothy Chandler Pavilion (213) 972-7211
135 N Grand Ave, Los Angeles, CA, 90012
venue for Music Center, Opera, Master Chorale admin office for Ahmanson &
Mark Taper
www.musiccenter.org

El Capitan Theater (323) 467-7674
6838 Hollywood Blvd, Hollywood, CA, 90028
www.elcapitantheatre.com

Empire Studio (818) 840-1400
1845 Empire Ave, Burbank, CA, 91504
www.lbimedia.com

Fantastic Lane Studios (661) 505-8182
27567 Fantastic Lane, Castaic, CA, 91384
Full-service studio with 80 acre wilderness backlot, prod. & post-prod. facilities
www.fantasticlane.com

The Fonda Theater (323) 464-0808
6126 Hollywood Blvd, Hollywood, CA, 90028
www.fondatheatre.com

The Forum (310) 330-7300
3900 W Manchester Blvd, Inglewood, CA, 90305
www.thelaforum.com

Glendale Production Center (818) 550-6000
1239 S Glendale Ave, Glendale, CA, 91205
www.glendalestudios.com

GMT Studios (310) 649-3733
5751 Buckingham Pkwy, Culver City, CA, 90230
www.gmtstudios.com

Greek Theatre (213) 202-2621
2700 N Vermont Ave, Los Angeles, CA, 90027
www.lagreektheatre.com

Historic Hudson Studios (323) 461-1044
1106 N Hudson Ave, Hollywood, CA, 90038
Boutique photo studio: wifi, meeting area, full kitchen, diffused/black out
curtains, easy elevator & addl. equipment.
renee@rafotostudio.com * www.historichudsonstudios.com

historichudsonstudios.com   renee@rafotostudio.com
323.461.1044

Hollywood Bowl (323) 850-2000
2301 N Highland Ave, Los Angeles, CA, 90078
www.hollywoodbowl.com

Hollywood Center Studios (323) 860-0000
1040 N Las Palmas Ave, Los Angeles, CA, 90038
see floor plans, lighting/grip & tech dept on our website
www.hollywoodcenter.com

Hollywood Palladium (323) 962-7600
6215 Sunset Blvd, Hollywood, CA, 90028
www.thehollywoodpalladium.com

The Honda Center, AKA Arrowhead Pond (714) 704-2400
2695 E. Katella Ave, Anaheim, CA, 92806
www.hondacenter.com

Irvine Meadows Amphitheatre (949) 855-8095
8808 Irvine Center Dr, Irvine, CA, 92618
AKA Irvine Meadows
http://amphitheaterirvine.com/

John Anson Ford Theaters (323) 856-5793
2580 Cahuenga Blvd E, Los Angeles, CA, 90068
box office (323) 461-3673
www.fordtheatres.org

KCAL TV Studios (818) 655-2000
4200 Radford Ave, Studio City, CA, 91604
http://losangeles.cbslocal.com/station/cbs-kcal/

KCBS TV Studios (818) 655-2000
4200 Radford Ave, Studio City, CA, 91604
http://losangeles.cbslocal.com/station/cbs-kcal/

KCET TV Studios (747) 201-5000
2900 W Alameda Ave, Burbank, CA, 91505
contact@kcet.org * www.kcet.org

KLCS TV Studios (213) 241-4000
1061 W Temple St, Los Angeles, CA, 90012
http://klcs.org/

KMEX TV Studios (Univision) (310) 216-3434
5999 Center Drive, Los Angeles, CA, 90045
http://losangeles.univision.com

KTLA TV Studios (323) 460-5500
5800 Sunset Blvd, Los Angeles, CA, 90028
www.ktla.com

KTTV TV Fox 11 Studios (310) 584-2000
1999 S Bundy Dr, Los Angeles, CA, 90025
www.myfoxLA.com

The L. A. Lofts (323) 462-5880
6442 Santa Monica Blvd, Los Angeles, CA, 90038
www.thelalofts.com

Lacy Street Production Center (323) 222-8872
2630 Lacy St, Los Angeles, CA, 90031
standing sets, music videos, commercials
www.lacystreet.com

Long Beach Convention Center (562) 436-3636
300 E Ocean Blvd, Long Beach, CA, 90802
www.longbeachcc.com

Los Angeles Center Studios (213) 534-3000
1201 W 5th Street Ste T-110, Los Angeles, CA, 90017
www.lacenterstudios.com

Los Angeles Convention Center (213) 741-1151
1201 S Figueroa St, Los Angeles, CA, 90015
Event Services X5360
www.lacclink.com

Los Angeles Memorial Coliseum (213) 747-7111
3911 S Figueroa St, Los Angeles, CA, 90037
www.lacoliseum.com

Los Angeles Sports Arena (213) 747-7111
3939 S Figueroa St, Los Angeles, CA, 90037
www.lacoliseumlive.com

The Lot (323) 850-3180
1041 N Formosa Ave, W Hollywood, CA, 90046
http://www.thelotstudios.com/

Mack Sennett Studios (323) 660-8466
1215 Bates Ave, Los Angeles, CA, 90029
www.macksennettstudios.net

Mark Taper Forum (213) 628-2772
135 N Grand Ave, Los Angeles, CA, 90012
for admin office, see Dorothy Chandler Pavilion
www.centertheatregroup.org

Microsoft Theater (213) 763-6030
777 Chick Hearn Court, Los Angeles, CA, 90015
www.microsofttheater.com

Occidental Studios (213) 384-3331
201 N Occidental Blvd, Los Angeles, CA, 90026
12 locations, stages from 1,000 to 43,000 sq. ft., lighting, grip, offices, props, etc.
www.occidentalstudios.com

Panavision (818) 316-1000
6101 Variel Ave, Woodland Hills, CA, 91367
Cameras & film. Commercials, music videos, hair & make-up test, trailers
www.panavision.com

Pantages Theatre (323) 468-1700
6233 Hollywood Blvd, Hollywood, CA, 90028
www.hollywoodpantages.com

Pasadena Civic Auditorium (626) 793-2122
300 E Green St, Pasadena, CA, 91101
Also, Pasadena Convention Center.
www.thepasadenacivic.com

The Pasadena Playhouse (626) 792-8672
39 S El Molino Ave, Pasadena, CA, 91101
www.pasadenaplayhouse.org

The Production Group (323) 469-8111
1626 N Wilcox Ave Ste 281, Hollywood, CA, 90028
www.productiongroup.tv

Prospect Studios (323) 671-5000
4151 Prospect Ave, Los Angeles, CA, 90027
http://studioservices.go.com/prospectstudios/index.html

Quixote Studios (323) 851-5030
1011 N Fuller Ave, W Hollywood, CA, 90046
trucks and stages, greenrooms, production stages
www.quixotestudios.com

Raleigh Studios (323) 960-FILM
5300 Melrose Ave, Hollywood, CA, 90038
www.raleighstudios.com

Red Studios Hollywood (323) 463-0808
846 Cahuenga Blvd, Los Angeles, CA, 90038
http://www.redstudio.com/

Rose Bowl (626) 577-3100
1001 Rose Bowl Dr, Pasadena, CA, 91103
www.rosebowlstadium.com

Saban Theatre (323) 655-4900
8440 Wilshire Blvd, Beverly Hills, CA, 90211
www.sabantheatre.org

San Gabriel Mission Playhouse (626) 308-2865
320 S Mission Drive, San Gabriel, CA, 91776
Location, Sound Stage, Venue, Rehearsal Space, Theater, Spanish style, wurlitzer organ
swilkinson@missionplayhouse.org * www.missionplayhouse.org

San Manuel Amphitheater (909) 880-6500
2575 Glen Helen Pkwy, San Bernardino, CA, 92407
www.sanmanuelamphitheater.net

Santa Barbara Bowl (805) 962-7411
1122 N Milpas St, Santa Barbara, CA, 93103
www.sbbowl.com

Santa Clarita Studios (661) 294-2000
25135 Anza Dr, Santa Clarita, CA, 91355
www.santaclaritastudios.com

Santa Monica Civic Auditorium (310) 458-8551
1855 Main St, Santa Monica, CA, 90401
www.santamonicacivic.org

Segerstrom Center (714) 556-2121
600 Town Center Dr, Costa Mesa, CA, 92626
Five performing arts & event venues
www.scfta.org

Shrine Auditorium (213) 748-5116
665 W Jefferson Blvd, Los Angeles, CA, 90007
www.shrineauditorium.com

Sketch Paper Design (818) 442-0284
7771 Lemona Ave, Van Nuys, CA, 91405
White Cyc stage that can be painted depending on production's needs, stage for rent
info@sketchpaperdesign.com * www.sketchpaperdesign.com

Sony Pictures Studios (310) 244-6926
10202 W Washington Blvd, Culver City, CA, 90232
www.sonypicturesstudios.com

Stage 1001 (323) 876-1001
1001 N Poinsettia Pl, Los Angeles, CA, 90046
www.stage1001.com

Staples Center (213) 742-7100
1111 S Figueroa St, Los Angeles, CA, 90015
www.staplescenter.com

The Studios At Paramount (323) 956-5000
5555 Melrose, Hollywood, CA, 90038
Call (323) 956-8811 for booking stages.
www.thestudiosatparamount.com

Sunset Gower Studios (323) 467-1001
1438 North Gower Box 21, Hollywood, CA, 90028
Call (323) 315-9460 for new inquiries
www.sgsandsbs.com

Thunder Studios (310) 762-1360
20434 S Santa Fe Ave, Long Beach, CA, 90810
15 stages, hard cycs, fisher boxes/flats
www.thunderstudios.com

Twentieth Century Fox (310) 369-1000
10201 W Pico Blvd, Los Angeles, CA, 90035
www.foxstudios.com

Universal Studios Stages & Backlot (818) 777-3000
100 Universal City Plaza, Universal City, CA, 91608
universal.locations@nbcuni.com * www.filmmakersdestination.com

The Walt Disney Concert Hall (213) 972-7211
135 N Grand Ave, Los Angeles, CA, 90012
http://www.wdch.com/

The Walt Disney Studios (818) 560-7450
500 Buena Vista St, Burbank, CA, 91505
www.stu-ops.disney.com

Warner Bros. Studios (818) 954-6000
4000 Warner Blvd, Burbank, CA, 91522
For facilities, call (818) 954-3000
www.warnerbros.com

The Wiltern (213) 388-1400
3790 Wilshire Blvd, Los Angeles, CA, 90010
call (213) 380-5005 for box office
www.thewiltern.net

Stained Glass

See: Glass & Mirrors, Art/Finishing/Etching/Etc.

Stair Climbers

See: Exercise & Fitness Equipment

Stanchions & Rope

See Also: Audience Seating Crowd Control: Barricades, Turnstiles Etc.*

AIR Designs (818) 768-6639
Airport, Car Lot, Traffic Delineators, Bar & Club, Tape, & Rope

Air Hollywood - Prop House & Standing Sets (818) 890-0444
Aviation-themed props and set dressing. We have thousands of items available to dress airport terminals.

Astro Audio Video Lighting, Inc. (818) 549-9915
6615 San Fernando Rd, Glendale, CA, 91201
Stanchions and rope dividers for rent.
www.astroavl.com

Bob Gail Special Events (310) 202-5200
Bob Gail has a huge inventory of special events equipment perfect for any premier event!

C. P. Two (323) 466-8201
Stanchion ropes, stanchion signs, stanchion carts, stanchion tape, vinyl stanchions and retractable stanchions.

The Hand Prop Room LP. (323) 931-1534
bank, theatre, airport

History For Hire, Inc. (818) 765-7767

LISTINGS FOR THIS CATEGORY CONTINUE ON THE FOLLOWING PAGE

Lennie Marvin Enterprises, Inc. (Prop Heaven) (818) 841-5882
period to modern-bank, theatre, airport
RC Vintage, Inc. (818) 765-7107
rope, velvet rope & ribbon for stanchions
Sony Pictures Studios-Linens, Drapes, Rugs (310) 244-5999
5933 W Slauson Ave, Culver City, CA, 90230
Chrome stanchions and black ropes
www.sonypicturesstudios.com
Sony Pictures Studios-Prop House (Off Lot) (310) 244-5999
Black wire stanchions, brass stanchions, chrome stanchions, black retractable
stanchions, chrome retractable stanchions
Universal Studios Property & Hardware Dept (818) 777-2784
Prop stanchions and stanchion ropes for rent.

Stand-Ups

See: Audience Cutouts & Stand-Ups

Stationery

See: Art, Supplies & Stationery

Statuary

See Also: Mold Making Sculpture*
Antiquarian Traders (310) 247-3900
4851 S. Alameda Street, Los Angeles, CA 90048
Bronze sculptures and marble sculptures from 19th century and 20th century
antiques@antiquariantraders.com * www.antiquariantraders.com
C. P. Valley (323) 466-8201
Green Set, Inc. (818) 764-1231
fountains, waterfalls, garden statuary, Greek statuary
The Hand Prop Room LP. (323) 931-1534
bronze pcs, assorted styles
Jackson Shrub Supply, Inc. (818) 982-0100
garden statues, garden monuments, bird baths, giant Venus clam shell
LM Treasures (626) 252-7354
10557 Juniper Ave Unit A, Fontana, CA 92337
All our items are hand painted and crafted to provide each customer with their
own personally unique piece.
lmtreasures.ll@gmail.com * www.lifesizestatues.net
Ob-jects (818) 351-4200
Omega/Cinema Props (323) 466-8201
Sony Pictures Studios-Prop House (Off Lot) (310) 244-5999
abstract statuary, animal statuary, bust statuary, human statuary, bird baths,
carousel horse, columns, decorative statuary, more
Universal Studios Property & Hardware Dept (818) 777-2784
Many prop statues and statuettes for rent.
Used Church Items, Religious Rentals (239) 992-5737
216 Cumer Road, McDonald, PA, 15057
400 Religious Statues, Angels, Patron Saints, Jesus, Joseph, Mary, Crucifixes,
Stations of the Cross, Stands, Altars.
warehouse@religiousrentals.com * www.religiousrentals.com
Warner Bros. Studios Property Department (818) 954-2181

Statue Of Liberty

Bob Gail Special Events (310) 202-5200
Bring the streets of the "Big Apple" to life with our many New York Props!
Green Set, Inc. (818) 764-1231
7' tall, full figure
History For Hire, Inc. (818) 765-7767
desk-top size
Modern Props (323) 934-3000
6 ft.
RC Vintage, Inc. (818) 765-7107
multiples & various sizes
Universal Studios Property & Hardware Dept (818) 777-2784
Prop statue of liberty and fiberglass statue of liberty for rent.

Steam Cabinets

See: Exercise & Fitness Equipment Gymnasium & Gymnastic
Equipment*

Steam Punk

See Also: Carriages, Horse Drawn Eyewear, Glasses, Sunglasses,
3D* Fantasy Props, Costumes, or Decorations* Western Dressing*
Western Wear*
History For Hire, Inc. (818) 765-7767
Jadis (310) 396-3477
2701 Main St, Santa Monica, CA, 90405
Motorized gear units, control panels with vintage switches and gauges, Tesla
coils, Van de Graaff generators.
jadis1@gmail.com * www.jadisprops.com

LCW Props (818) 243-0707
Our Specialty. We Have A Large Selection Of Many Items. Rigged, Large &
Small. Check Us Out Online.
Lux Lounge EFR (888) 247-4411
106 1/2 Judge John Aiso St #318, Los Angeles, CA, 90012
Steampunk Furniture Collection, Steampunk Sofa, Steampunk Chairs,
Steampunk Banquete, Steampunk Chandelier
info@luxloungeefr.com * www.luxloungeefr.com
The Rational Past (310) 476-6277
By Appointment, West Los Angeles, CA
Authentic science, industrial, technical antiques & collectibles. Many
professions & eras represented. See web site.
info@therationalpast.com * www.therationalpast.com
Sword & Stone (818) 562-6548
Custom steam punk apparel and weapons fabrication.
Warner Bros. Studios Property Department (818) 954-2181
Steam punk, Victorian copper and brass rolling control panels, consoles with
gauges, levers and hand controls.

Steamer Trunks

The Hand Prop Room LP. (323) 931-1534
period-present, antique Louis Vuitton
History For Hire, Inc. (818) 765-7767
dozens
Universal Studios Property & Hardware Dept (818) 777-2784
Vintage steamer trunks, antique steamer trunks, wooden steamer trunks, old
steamer trunks and more for rent.

Steel Deck Platforms

See: Stages, Portable & Steel Deck

Steel Folding Gates & Roll-Up Doors

E.C. Prop Rentals (818) 764-2008
storefront scissor style
Lawrence Roll Up Doors (626) 869-0837
4525 Littlejohn St, Baldwin Park, CA, 91706
Sales, service, installation & mfg. of all types of doors, grills & gates,
commercial & industrial
McMaster-Carr (562) 692-5911
9630 Norwalk Blvd, Santa Fe Springs, CA, 90670
Sales - (562) 695-2323; entry security gates

Stemware

See: Crystal Stemware

Stencils

See: Art, Supplies & Stationery Graphics, Digital & Large Format
Printing* Signs*

Step & Repeats

See: Graphics, Digital & Large Format Printing Signs*

Stereo Equipment

See Also: Audio Equipment Radios*
Astro Audio Video Lighting, Inc. (818) 549-9915
6615 San Fernando Rd, Glendale, CA, 91201
Speakers, stereo equipment and stereo systems for rent.
www.astroavl.com
C. P. Two (323) 466-8201
Speakers, component stereos, portable stereos, stationary stereos. Antique to
modern.
The Hand Prop Room LP. (323) 931-1534
History For Hire, Inc. (818) 765-7767
period
Kitsch N Sync Props (323) 343-1190
Specializing in 70's and 80's props. Large collection of cameras, electronics,
phones, art, games, stereos, & much more.
LCW Props (818) 243-0707
DJ Equipment, Turntables, Speakers, Media, Recievers, Amplifiers
Modern Props (323) 934-3000
contemporary
Sony Pictures Studios-Prop House (Off Lot) (310) 244-5999
Universal Studios Property & Hardware Dept (818) 777-2784
Prop speakers, stereo equipment stereo systems for rent.

Stock Certificates

See: Certificates

Stone

See: Architectural Pieces & Artifacts* Columns* Concrete Block, Brick, Gravel, Sand, Rocks, Etc.* Sculpture* Tile, Marble, Granite, Etc.

Stone Restoration

See: Sanitation, Waste Disposal

Stools

See Also: Chairs

E.C. Prop Rentals	**(818) 764-2008**
industrial & stainless, also wood	
FormDecor, Inc.	**(310) 558-2582**
America's largest event rental supplier of 20th Century furniture and accessories for Modern and Mid-Century styles.	
LCW Props	**(818) 243-0707**
Garage, Lab, Medical, Office	
Lux Lounge EFR	**(888) 247-4411**
106 1/2 Judge John Aiso St #318, Los Angeles, CA, 90012	
Bar Stools & High Chairs for rent	
info@luxloungeefr.com * www.luxloungeefr.com	
Modern Props	**(323) 934-3000**
contemporary, large selection, multiples	
Prop Services West	**(818) 503-2790**
Rapport International Furniture	**(323) 930-1500**
435 N La Brea Ave, Los Angeles, CA, 90036	
Variety of contemporary stools perfect for kitchen or bar settings.	
rapport@rapportusa.com * www.rapportfurniture.com	
Sony Pictures Studios-Prop House (Off Lot)	**(310) 244-5999**
Bar stools, cafe stools, camp stools, counter stools, country stools, dinner stools, drafting stools, foot stool, more	
Taylor Creative Inc.	**(888) 245-4044**
At Taylor Creative Inc. we offer a large selection of seating options, from plush cubes to Lucite barstools.	
Universal Studios Property & Hardware Dept	**(818) 777-2784**
Many kinds of stools for rent for all kinds of spaces and occasions	
ZG04 DECOR	**(818) 853-8040**
Poofs, Ottomans, Stools, Barstools	

Stop Signs

See: Railroad Crossing Signal* Traffic/Road Signs, Lights, Safety Items

Storage

See: Archiving Media/Records Management* Hampers, Theatrical* Property Master Storage Rooms* Scenery/Set Storage* Set Boxes* Transportation, Trucking and/or Storage* Warehouse Dressing

Store Dressing

See: Bakery* Bookstores* Cash Registers* Counters* Credit Card Imprint Machine* Department Store* Display Cases, Racks & Fixtures (Store)* Drugstore/Apothecary* General Store* Graphics, Digital & Large Format Printing* Grocery Check-out Stands (Complete)* Hardware Store Dressing* Jewelry Store* Market Equipment/Fixtures* Record/Video Store* Sandwich Board Store Sign* Security Walk-Through & Baggage Alarms* Shoe Store* Steel Folding Gates & Roll-Up Doors* Store Shelf Units & Shelving* Surveillance Equipment* Video Rental/Sales Store* Video Store Dressing

Store Front Folding Gates

See: Steel Folding Gates & Roll-Up Doors

Store Front Rental Location

See: Locations, Insert Stages & Small Theatres* Scenery/Set Rentals

Store Shelf Units & Shelving

See Also: Candy Racks* Display Cases, Racks & Fixtures (Store)* Garment Racks

Acme Display Fixture & Packaging	**(888) 411-1870**
3829 S Broadway St., Los Angeles, CA 90037	
Complete store setups: garment racks, displays/display cases, counters, packaging, shelving, hangers, mannequins	
sales@acmedisplay.com * www.acmedisplay.com	
Alley Cats Studio Rentals	**(818) 982-9178**
dressed or empty/gondola shelving	
C. P. Valley	**(323) 466-8201**
E.C. Prop Rentals	**(818) 764-2008**
Industrial Shelving & Racks, Warehouse Shelving & Racks, Many Styles, Many Castered	
Faux Library Studio Props, Inc.	**(818) 765-0096**
Bookcases and book shelving units, library shelving	
LCW Props	**(818) 243-0707**
Call For An Updated Listing	
Modern Props	**(323) 934-3000**
contemporary/futuristic, multiples	
Outwater Plastics Industries	**(800) 248-2067**
4720 W Van Buren, Phoenix, AZ, 85043	
catalog sales; plastics. slatwall, gridwall, pegboard, hanging holders	
Universal Studios Property & Hardware Dept	**(818) 777-2784**
Store shelving units and store display shelves for rent.	

Stores, Retail

See: Barber Shop* Beauty Salon* Bookstores* Delicatessen Equipment* Department Store* Drugstore/Apothecary* General Store* Hardware Store Dressing* Jewelry Store* Record/Video Store* Shoe Store* Video Rental/Sales Store

Story Book Themed Parties

See: Costume Rental Houses* Costumes* Events, Decorations, Supplies & Services* Events, Design/Planning/Production* Fantasy Props, Costumes, or Decorations* Prop Houses

Storyboards, Illustrations

See: Art, Artists For Hire

Storyboards, Production Illustration

See: Art, Artists For Hire

Stoves

See Also: Restaurant Kitchens/Equip./Supplies

AIR Designs (818) 768-6639
Restaurant, Ranges, Ovens, Pizza

Angel Appliances (877) 262-6435
8545 Sepulveda Blvd, Sepulveda, CA, 91343
LP/natural gas/electric, customized, practical, classic-current
props@angelappliances.com * www.angelappliances.com/rentals.php

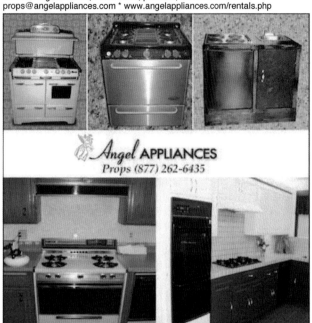

Angel APPLIANCES
Props (877) 262-6435

Antique Stove Heaven (323) 298-5581
5414 Western Ave, Los Angeles, CA, 90062
Antique, early 1900s - 1950s, sales, restorations, service

C. P. Two (323) 466-8201
stoves and botbelly stoves

History For Hire, Inc. (818) 765-7767
potbelly stoves only

LCW Props (818) 243-0707
Appliances Of All Kinds. Period - Present.

Modern Props (323) 934-3000
30s to present day

Ob-jects (818) 351-4200
industrial

RC Vintage, Inc. (818) 765-7107
40s, 50s & 60s Asst Colors Pink, Yellow, Green, and Boring White. Gas or electric

Sony Pictures Studios-Prop House (Off Lot) (310) 244-5999
stoves & potbellies too

Universal Studios Property & Hardware Dept (818) 777-2784
Stoves for rent from potbellies & period to modern stoves.

Warner Bros. Studios Property Department (818) 954-2181
Black Smith's Stove, camp stoves, kitchen stoves, restaurant stoves, cast iron stoves

Streaks 'N Tips

See: Expendables* Make-up & Hair, Supplies & Services

Street Dressing

See Also: Alarms* Alley Dressing* Antenna* Bag Lady Carts*
Billboards & Billboard Lights* Bus Shelter* Fences* Guard Shacks*
Kiosks* Lamp Posts & Street Lights* Mailboxes* Marquees* Parking
Meters & Sign Poles* Sandwich Board Store Sign* Signs* Steel
Folding Gates & Roll-Up Doors* Street Dressing, Exterior Signs*
Telephone Poles Prop* Traffic/Road Signs, Lights, Safety Items*
Vendor Carts & Concession Counters

AIR Designs (818) 768-6639
Mail Box, Parking Meters, Street Lamps, Street Signs, Trash Cans,
Newsstands, Coin-Ops, Construction

Alley Cats Studio Rentals (818) 982-9178
street signals/signs, manhole vents, period/modern hydrants, benches, street vendors, parking meters

C. P. Two (323) 466-8201
Street signs, road signs, commercial signs, construction signs and more.

C. P. Valley (323) 466-8201
Newspaper vending machines and more.

E.C. Prop Rentals (818) 764-2008
cobra head street lights, K-rails, signs/posts, trash cans, bus shelters/benches

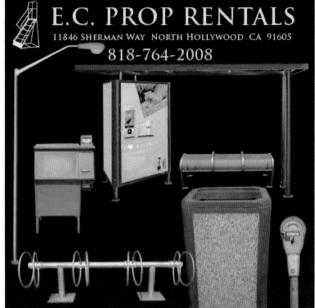

E.C. PROP RENTALS
11846 SHERMAN WAY NORTH HOLLYWOOD CA 91605
818-764-2008

The Hand Prop Room LP. (323) 931-1534
lrg sel.

History For Hire, Inc. (818) 765-7767

LCW Props (818) 243-0707
Trash bins, Roll-Off Containers, Recycling Bins, Yard Waste, Debris, Street Lights, Cross Arms, Stop Lights

Lennie Marvin Enterprises, Inc. (Prop Heaven) (818) 841-5882
signage,trash cans,benches,fireplugs,traffic lights,hydrants

Main Street Lighting (330) 723-4431
1080 Industrial Pkwy, Medina, OH, 44256
Nostalgic, ornamental-posts, fixtures, bollards, & brackets
tracyr@mainstreetlighting.com * www.mainstreetlighting.com

Omega/Cinema Props (323) 466-8201
Street lamps and more.

RC Vintage, Inc. (818) 765-7107
40s, 50s & 60s, signals, Period signals and Modern remote Control.

Universal Studios Property & Hardware Dept (818) 777-2784
All kinds of street dressing props for rent.

Street Dressing, European

C. P. Valley (323) 466-8201
European park benches, signs and more.

E.C. Prop Rentals (818) 764-2008
European road signage

Street Dressing, Exterior Signs

See Also: Billboards & Billboard Lights* Neon Lights & Signs

AIR Designs (818) 768-6639
Large Selection, Business, Location, Parking, Directional, Neon, Traffic, Construction, Store Front

Art, Signs & Graphics (818) 503-7997
6939 Farmdale Ave, N Hollywood, CA, 91605
props, banners, vinyl graphics, vehicle graphics, 3D router cut letters & logos
jessee@artsignsandgraphics.com * www.artsignsandgraphics.com

C. P. Two (323) 466-8201
Dangerous signs, radioactive signs, road construction signs, flammable signs, no parking signs and much more.

D'ziner Sign Co. (323) 467-4467
801 Seward Street, Los Angeles, CA 90038
illuminated & non-illuminated
sales@dzinersign.com * www.dzinersign.com

E.C. Prop Rentals (818) 764-2008
Parking Signs, Bus Stop Signs, Directional Signs, Speed Limit Signs, School Signs, Alley Signs, Sign Posts

LCW Props (818) 243-0707
Trash bins, Roll-Off Containers, Recycling Bins, Yard Waste, Debris, Street Lights, Cross Arms, Stop Lights

Sony Pictures Studios-Prop House (Off Lot)   (310) 244-5999
street lights, post lamps, barriades
Universal Studios Property & Hardware Dept   (818) 777-2784
Many exterior sign rentals for rent.
Warner Bros. Studios Property Department   (818) 954-2181
Street signs, Emergency signs, exit signs, neon signs, cardboard signs, caution
signs

Street Lights

See: Lamp Posts & Street Lights

Street Scene

See: Locations, Insert Stages & Small Theatres* Backlots/Standing
Sets

Street Vendor Carts

See: Catering* Flower Carts* Gypsy Wagon* Produce Carts*
Produce Stands* Taco Carts (Propmaster & Set)* Vendor Carts &
Concession Counters

Stretchers

A-1 Medical Integration   (818) 753-0319
Medical devices for Set Decoration & Property, from minor procedures to
detailed hospital units.
Alpha Companies - Spellman Desk Co.   (818) 504-9090
The #1 source for medical equipment in the industry.
The Hand Prop Room LP.   (323) 931-1534
period-present
History For Hire, Inc.   (818) 765-7767
Civil War to modern
Supply Sergeant   (323) 849-3744
503 N. Victory Blvd, Burbank, CA 91502
military stretchers, army stretchers, navy stretchers
david@jacksgt.com * www.supplysergeantshop.com

Strobe Lights

See: Bars, Nightclubs, Barware & Dressing* Light Fixtures* Lighting
& Sound, Concert/Theatrical/DJ/VJ

Studio Backlots

See: Locations, Insert Stages & Small Theatres

Studio Services

See: Wardrobe, Studio Services

Studio Tile Flooring

See Also: Carpet & Flooring
Linoleum City, Inc.   (323) 469-0063
4849 Santa Monica Blvd, Hollywood, CA, 90029
Studio tiles, stage floors, dance floors, solid color floors, solid color floors, shiny
floors.
sales@linocity.com * www.linoleumcity.com

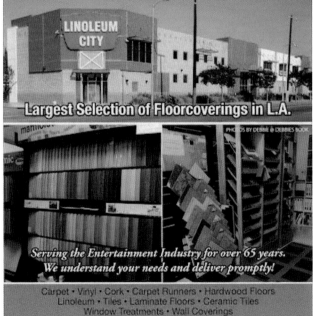

Studios

See: Stages/Studios, Film/TV/Theatre/Events

Stuffed Animals

See: Taxidermy, Hides/Heads/Skeletons* Toys & Games

Stunts

See Also: Aircraft, Charters & Aerial Services* Guilds, Unions,
Societies, Associations* Nautical/Marine Services & Charters*
Pyrotechnics* Rigging, Equipment or Services* Sporting Goods &
Services* Swords & Swordplay* Vehicle Preparation Services*
Vehicles
A1-STUNTWORLD inc   (310) 666-3004
Hollywood, CA 90028
stunt coordinators, stunt performers, master stunt riggers, stunt equipment
rental (large inventory), skydiver/parachute
www.stuntworldinc.com
CONFETTI & FOG FX Special Effects Company   (786) 308-7063
2739 W 79 St Bay, #12, Hialeah, FL 33016
www.caffx.com
L. A. Party Works   (888) 527-2789
9712 Alpaca St, S El Monte, CA, 91733
Free fall from up to 30' high on our 30ft square landing area. It's designed for
the general public and for all ages.
partyworks@aol.com * www.partyworksusa.com

Styrofoam

See Also: Foam
DeRouchey Foam   (888) 959-4852
13618 Vaughn Street, San Fernando, CA, 91340
We offer a full line of foam sculpting materials and services. Urethane, EPS,
HardCoat, Foam Adhesive. 24/7 Service.
dustin@derofoam.com * www.derofoam.com
Jackson Shrub Supply, Inc.   (818) 982-0100
garden styled foams, fluted column foam, foam blocks, foam rock clumps, foam
wailing wall, giant garden foam clam shell

Sublimation Dye Printing

See: Graphics, Digital & Large Format Printing

Suitcases

See: Luggage

Suits Of Armor

See: Armor, Chainmail, Suits of Armor

Sunglasses

See: Eyewear, Glasses, Sunglasses, 3D

Sunrise/Sunset Times

Old Farmer's Almanac   (603) 563-8111
P.O. Box 520, Dublin, NH, 03444
North America's oldest, continuously published periodical.
www.almanac.com
Sunrise/Sunset Times   (603) 563-8111
This U.S. Navy site gives access to Sunrise/Sunset/Twilight times in U.S. &
worldwide for 1000s of locations, past & fut
www.usno.navy.mil

Supermarket

See: Display Cases, Racks & Fixtures (Store)* Food, Artificial Food*
Grocery Check-out Stands (Complete)* Market Equipment/Fixtures*
Prop Products & Packages* Shopping Bags (Silent)* Shopping Carts*
Store Shelf Units & Shelving

Surface Protection

See: Floor, Ground & Surface Protection

Surfaces

See: Surfaces, Tabletop* Wall Coverings* Vacu-forms/Vacu-forming* Staff Shops* Scenery/Set Construction* Prop Reproduction & Fabrication* Plastics, Materials & Fabrication* Paneling, Veneers & Laminates* Paint & Painting Supplies* Moulding, Wood* Fiberglass Products/Fabrication* Fabrics

Surfaces, Tabletop

The Surface Library	**(323) 546-9314**

1106 N. Hudson Ave, 2nd Floor, Los Angeles, CA 90038
A curated prop house specializing in surfaces and table top props for food, product, and lifestyle shoots.
info@thesurfacelibrary.com * www.thesurfacelibrary.com

Surfboard, Wakeboard

See Also: Sporting Goods & Services* Wetsuits, Diving/Surfing

C. P. Two	**(323) 466-8201**

Wood surfboards and fiberglass surfboards in long board and short board sizes.

The Hand Prop Room LP.	**(323) 931-1534**

period-present, long boards

LCW Props	**(818) 243-0707**

Some Styles, Call For An Updated Listing

Lennie Marvin Enterprises, Inc. (Prop Heaven)	**(818) 841-5882**

60s to present, long boards & more

RC Vintage, Inc.	**(818) 765-7107**

surfboards; old long boards & modern

Warner Bros. Studios Property Department	**(818) 954-2181**

Surfboards, wakeboards

Surgery Equipment & Lighting

See: Hospital Equipment* Medical Equip/Furniture, Graphics/Supplies

Surplus Stores

See: Military Props & Equipment* Military Surplus/Combat Clothes, Field Gear

Surveillance Equipment

See Also: Binoculars, Scopes & Telescopes* Police Equipment* Security Devices or Services

Bolide Technology	**(909) 305-8889**

468 S. San Dimas Ave, San Dimas, CA, 91773
security, spying & surveillance equipment

E.C. Prop Rentals	**(818) 764-2008**

prop cameras, monitors, good multiples

Electronic City	**(818) 632-4494**

22287 Mulholland Highway #197, Calabasas, CA 91302
extensive variety of miniature components, consulting expertise

Gcom Consultants	**011 44 20 3355-4971**

42 Manchester St, London, England W1U7LW
High-tech security, surveillance, protection equip.

The Hand Prop Room LP.	**(323) 931-1534**
LCW Props	**(818) 243-0707**

Large Selection Of Cameras, Van Interiors, Electronics, Graphics, etc.

Modern Props	**(323) 934-3000**

cameras, monitors, briefcases, consoles

Surveying Equipment

LCW Props	**(818) 243-0707**

Surveyors Kits, Tripods

Swamp Coolers

Swamp Coolers

See: Rooftop Dressing

Swap Meets, Southern California

Canning Enterprises & Attractions	**(323) 560-7469**

4515 E. 59th Pl. Maywood, CA 90270
Promoter of many different flea markets, select events & swap meets in So. Cal. Call Mon-Fri 10AM-5PM

Long Beach Antique Market	**(323) 655-5703**

4901 E Conant Street, Long Beach, CA 90808
3rd Sunday of every month.
www.longbeachantiquemarket.com

Metropolitan Marketing	**(818) 884-6430**

6320 Canoga Ave, Suite 1630, Woodland Hills, CA, 91367
indoor swap meets & events

Pasadena City College Flea Market	**(626) 585-7906**

1570 E. Colorado Boulevard, Pasadena, CA 91106
1st Sunday of every month.
www.pasadena.edu/fleamarket

Rose Bowl Flea Market	**(323) 560-7469**

1001 Rose Bowl Dr., Pasadena, CA 91103
2nd Sunday of every month.
mlrshowbiz@aol.com * www.rgcshows.com/RoseBowl.aspx

San Bernardino Out Door Flea Market	**(323) 560-7469**

689 S E St., San Bernardino, CA 92408
Every Sunday.
www.rgcshows.com/SanBernardino.aspx

Topanga Vintage Market	**(310) 422-1844**

Victory Blvd. & Mason Ave., Pierce College, Woodland Hills, CA 91306
4th Sunday of every month.
info@topangavintagemarket.com * www.topangavintagemarket.com

Valley Indoor Swap Meet - Panorama City	**(818) 892-0183**

14650 Parthenia St., Panorama City, CA 91402
Every day except Tuesdays.
info@indoorswap.com *
www.indoorswap.com/index2.php?location=PanoramaCity

Valley Indoor Swap Meet - Pomona	**(909) 620-4792**

1600 East Holt Ave., Pomona, CA 91767
Every day except Tuesdays.
info@indoorswap.com * www.indoorswap.com/index2.php?location=Pomona

Ventura County Fairgrounds Flea Market	**(323) 560-7469**

10 W. Harbor Blvd., Ventura, CA 93001
Held 7 times a year, see website for details.
www.rgcshows.com/Ventura.aspx

Swat Team

See: Police Car, Police Motorcycle* Police Equipment

Swedish Stall Bars

See: Exercise & Fitness Equipment

Sweeping Compound

See: Expendables

Swim Wear

See: Bathing Suits, Swim & Beach Wear

Swimming Pools

See Also: Spas & Jacuzzis

Lifestyle Pool & Spa	**(818) 997-3255**

5830 Sepulveda Blvd, Van Nuys, CA, 91411
full showroom, all makes/models pools & spas in stock

Swings

See: Furniture, Outdoor/Patio* Playground Equipment

Switchboards

C. P. Valley	(323) 466-8201
History For Hire, Inc.	(818) 765-7767
some rigged, electrical walls	
LCW Props	(818) 243-0707
Period - Present, Lighting, Rigged, Security, Police, Head sets	
Universal Studios Property & Hardware Dept	(818) 777-2784

Telephone switchboard props with headphones and mics for rent. Vintage to contemporary.

Swords & Swordplay

See Also: Weapons

Academy of Theatrical Combat	(818) 364-8420
Call for appt, Burbank, CA, 91504	
on set choreographing/training for fencing, sword rental	
Costume Armour Inc.	(845) 534-9120
2 Mill Street, Building 1 Suite 101, Cornwall, NY 12518	
Medieval weapons	
The Hand Prop Room LP.	(323) 931-1534
period-present rubber, foam, military, medieval, ninja, cust.	
History For Hire, Inc.	(818) 765-7767
LCW Props	(818) 243-0707
Quanitities Of Swords, Period - Present	
Society of American Fight Directors	(818) 243-0707
1350 E Flamingo Rd #25, Las Vegas, NV, 89119	
contact regional rep. via their web site	
www.safd.org	
Sony Pictures Studios-Prop House (Off Lot)	(310) 244-5999
metal, rubber, leather & plastic	
Sword & Stone	(818) 562-6548
all nations & periods, steel, aluminum, custom made	
Universal Studios Property & Hardware Dept	(818) 777-2784

All kinds of prop swords from all time periods for rent.

T-shirts

See: Embroidery, Screen Printing, Etc. Fabric Dyeing/Tie Dyeing/Painting/Aging* Promotional Items & Materials* Wardrobe*

Tablecloths

See: Linens, Household

Tables

See Also: Cafe Tables/Chairs/Umbrellas Folding Chairs/Tables* Furniture, Outdoor/Patio* Furniture, Plexi/Lucite* Office Equipment & Dressing* Office Furniture* Prop Houses* Serving Tables*

Advanced Liquidators Office Furniture	(818) 763-3470

new, used, wide selection of office furniture, tables for any purpose in any size, design, model, and style.

AIR Designs	(818) 768-6639

Indoor, Outdoor, Restaurant, Diner, Fast Food, Bar, Coffee House, Auto

Badia Design, Inc.	(818) 762-0130

5420 Vineland Ave, N. Hollywood, CA, 91601
Badia Design Inc. imports many different types of Moroccan tables which include wood, wrought iron, metal and more.
info@badiadesign.com * www.badiadesign.com

Bridge Furniture & Props Los Angeles	(818) 433-7100

We carry modern & traditional furniture, lighting, accessories, cleared art,& rugs. Items are online for easy shopping.

BRIDGE LA
FURNITURE & PROPS

3210 Vanowen St.   BridgeProps.com
Burbank, CA 91505 | Tel: 818.433.7100

E.C. Prop Rentals	(818) 764-2008
office, utility, work tables, wood & metal	
LCW Props	(818) 243-0707
Folding, Restaurant / Bar, Plastic, Wood, Metal	
Lennie Marvin Enterprises, Inc. (Prop Heaven)	(818) 841-5882
variety of styles	
Lux Lounge EFR	(888) 247-4411
106 1/2 Judge John Aiso St #318, Los Angeles, CA, 90012	
Tables of Various Kinds in Multiples.	
info@luxloungeefr.com * www.luxloungeefr.com	
Modern Props	(323) 934-3000
conference tables, coffee tables, dining tables, end tables, cafe tables, consoles, drafting tables	
Modernica Props	(323) 664-2322
NEST Studio Rentals, Inc.	(818) 942-0339
dining, occasional	
Omega/Cinema Props	(323) 466-8201
Prop Services West	(818) 503-2790
Sony Pictures Studios-Prop House (Off Lot)	(310) 244-5999
Coffee, computer, sewing, serving, all kinds of tables	
Taylor Creative Inc.	(888) 245-4044
Universal Studios Property & Hardware Dept	(818) 777-2784
All kinds of tables for rent for all occasions and themes.	
Warner Bros. Studios Property Department	(818) 954-2181
Side tables & end tables, dining tables, console tables, buffet tables, cafe tables, work tables	
ZG04 DECOR	(818) 853-8040
Modern Tables, Contemporary Tables, Traditional Tables, Transitional Tables, Vintage Tables, Eclectic Tables	

Tableware/Flatware

See Also: Events, Decorations, Supplies & Services Fiesta Dinnerware* Kitchen Dressing* Pewter & Pewterware* Prop Houses* Silverware, Silver Serving Pieces*

Bargain Fair (Mid-City)	(323) 965-2227
4635 W Pico Blvd, Los Angeles, CA, 90019	
corner of Fairfax; dinnerware, glassware, silverware, cookware & more at unbelievable prices, open 7 days	
sheida@bargainfair.com * www.bargainfair.com	
History For Hire, Inc.	(818) 765-7767
restaurant, Old West	

LISTINGS FOR THIS CATEGORY CONTINUE ON THE FOLLOWING PAGE

LCW Props (818) 243-0707
Stainless Steel, Silver, Antique
Omega/Cinema Props (323) 466-8201
Prop Services West (818) 503-2790
Replacements, Ltd (800) 737-5223
1089 Knox Rd, McLeansville, NC, 27301
Enormous inventory of china, crystal, silverware, more than 300,000 patterns; matching, repairs, research
Universal Studios Property & Hardware Dept (818) 777-2784
All kinds of tableware and flatware for rent.
Warner Bros. Studios Property Department (818) 954-2181
Assorted patterns of flatware, silver flatware, serving flatware & utensils
ZG04 DECOR (818) 853-8040
Serving utensils, Dish-sets, Barware, Platters, Carafe, silverware, flatware

Tackle

See: Fishing Equipment & Tackle

Taco (Food) Carts

See: Vendor Carts & Concession Counters

Taco Carts (Propmaster & Set)

Backstage Studio Equipment (818) 504-6026
8052 Lankershim Blvd, N. Hollywood, CA, 91605
taco carts, magliners, set boxes, all kinds of carts & dollies

Tanker Desks

See: Office Furniture

Tanks

See Also: Aquariums & Tropical Fish* Barrels & Drums, Wood/Metal/Plastic* Factory/Industrial* Wine Kegs
E.C. Prop Rentals (818) 764-2008
large liq. storage, castered stainless nitrogen tanks, propane
LCW Props (818) 243-0707
Our Specialty. Large Selection Of Any Style Tanks. Industrial, Safety, Cryo, Nitrogen / Oxygen, Hi Vac, etc.

L.C.W PROPS
CRYOGENIC TANKS
NITROGEN & OXYGEN TANKS
6439 San Fernando Rd. Glendale, CA 91201
Phone: 818-243-0707 - www.lcwprops.com

Machinery & Equipment Co., Inc. (909) 599-3916
115 N Cataract Ave, San Dimas, CA, 91773
Over 3 acres of industrial processing equip., such as kettles, mixers, tanks, conveyors & other stainless machinery for
sherri@machineryandequipment.com * www.machineryandequipment.com

Tape

See: Expendables

Tape Recorders

C. P. Two (323) 466-8201
Various models, sizes, and types of tape recorders.
The Hand Prop Room LP. (323) 931-1534
period-present
History For Hire, Inc. (818) 765-7767
most eras
LCW Props (818) 243-0707
Period - Present, Data Racks, Reel To Reel

Tapestry Wall Hangings

Ob-jects (818) 351-4200
Omega/Cinema Props (323) 466-8201
Sony Pictures Studios-Prop House (Off Lot) (310) 244-5999
Wall decorations, dream catchers, fabric wall decorations, floral wall decorations, wall plaque, wicker wall decorations, more
Warner Bros. Drapery, Upholstery & Flooring (818) 954-1831
4000 Warner Blvd, Burbank, CA, 91522
Vintage; Modern
wbsfdrapery@warnerbros.com * www.wbdrapery.com
Warner Bros. Studios Property Department (818) 954-2181
Assorted wall hanging tapestries, see WBSF Drapery department
Y & B Bolour (310) 274-6719
321 S Robertson Blvd, Los Angeles, CA, 90048

Tarot Cards

See Also: Occult/Spiritual/Metaphysical
History For Hire, Inc. (818) 765-7767
Sony Pictures Studios-Prop House (Off Lot) (310) 244-5999

Tarps

See: Sewing Services, Industrial* Tarps, Covers, Custom Sewing

Tarps, Covers, Custom Sewing

See Also: Sewing Services, Industrial
AA Surplus Sales Co., Inc. (323) 526-3622
2940 E. Olympic Blvd, Los Angeles, CA, 90023
U.S. military camouflage nets, army cargo parachutes and personnel parachutes, desert OD tarps, etc.
surplusking@hotmail.com * www.aasurplus.com/
ProtecTarps, Inc. (818) 771-1211
11176 Penrose St, #10, Sun Valley, CA, 91352
Tarpaulins and custom covers. Onsite sewing fabrication, RF welding and custom fabrics. Fast turn-around.
www.protectarps.com

Tattoo & Body Piercing Equipment & Supplies

See Also: Goth/Punk/Bondage/Fetish/Erotica Etc.
The Hand Prop Room LP. (323) 931-1534
History For Hire, Inc. (818) 765-7767
period tattoo equip & flesh art
RC Vintage, Inc. (818) 765-7107
Tattoo Guns and Signs Swatches Chairs.
Sony Pictures Studios-Prop House (Off Lot) (310) 244-5999
photos & samples of tattoos

Tattoos (Temporary) Body/Face Painting

See Also: Make-up & Hair, Supplies & Services* Special Effects, Make-up/Prosthetics
Faux Tattoo Studio   **(323) 332-2882**
Temporary tattoos and body art for production, music videos and photo shoots using the latest of cutting edge technology.
info@fauxtattoostudios.com * www.fauxtattoostudios.com

Realistic Temporary Tattoos and Body Art 323-332-2882

FAUX TATTOO STUDIOS LOS ANGELES

L. A. Party Works   **(888) 527-2789**
9712 Alpaca St, S El Monte, CA, 91733
in Vancouver tel. 604-589-4101
partyworks@aol.com * www.partyworksusa.com
Reel Creations, Inc.   **(818) 346-7335**
7831 Alabama Ave Ste 21, Canoga Park, CA, 91304
innovator of the original temporary tattoo process, stock/custom
TATS   **(310) 686-1956**
Call for Appt
Mobile temp. airbrush tattoos, private parties, corp events, fundraisers, up to 5 artists.
Tinsley Transfers   **(818) 767-4277**
Web Based Business - Sun Valley, 91352
custom & in-stock SFX tattoos
www.tinsleytransfers.com

Tavern Dressing

See: Bars, Nightclubs, Barware & Dressing* Jukeboxes, Music/Dance Machines* Liquor Bottles* Paintings/Prints* Restaurant Furniture & Dressing

Taxidermy, Hides/Heads/Skeletons

See Also: Bones, Skulls & Skeletons* Fossils
Artkraft Taxidermy Rentals   **(818) 505-8425**
Taxidermied birds, fish, mammals, and much more from Africa, North America, and exotic locales.

MUSEUM QUALITY TAXIDERMIED ANIMALS - FROM ANTELOPES TO ZEBRAS
ESTABLISHED 1969 HOLLYWOOD, CA

C. P. Two   **(323) 466-8201**
Cow skulls, steer longhorns, deer heads, moose heads, coyote taxidermy, skunk taxidermy and more; Hunting lodge dressing.
Caravan West Productions   **(661) 268-8300**
35660 Jayhawker Rd, Aqua Dulce, CA, 91390
Deer heads, buffalo heads, cow heads, horse heads, coyote heads, bear heads, antlers, hides and skins, furs.
caravanwest@earthlink.net * www.caravanwest.com
Dapper Cadaver/Creatures & Cultures   **(818) 771-0818**
Fake lifelike & wounded animals. Butcher shop. Taxidermy, specimens, skeletons & rubber reptiles. Custom FX.
The Hand Prop Room LP.   **(323) 931-1534**
lrg sel.
History For Hire, Inc.   **(818) 765-7767**
animal hides, skulls, skeletons
Jonas Supply Company   **(800) 279-7985**
PO Box 480, Granite Quarry, NC 28072
catalog sales; taxidermy supplies & tools.
Lietzau Taxidermy   **(320) 877-7297**
320 N Saturn, Cosmos, MN, 56228
Catalog; reproduction craft & costuming supplies. Native American dressing.
LM Treasures   **(626) 252-7354**
10557 Juniper Ave Unit A, Fontana, CA 92337
We have animal heads ranging from life size tiger heads to moose heads, personally handcrafted to make each one unique.
lmtreasures.ll@gmail.com * www.lifesizestatues.net
Sony Pictures Studios-Prop House (Off Lot)   **(310) 244-5999**
Stuffed animals from birds to camels and everything in between. Animal traps
Universal Studios Property & Hardware Dept   **(818) 777-2784**
Many kinds of taxidermy of various animals for rent.

Tchotchkes

See: Children/Baby Accessories & Bedroom* Decorative Accessories* Miniatures/Models* Model Ships/Planes/Trains/Autos Etc.* Toys & Games

Tech Benches

LCW Props (818) 243-0707

6439 San Fernando Rd. Glendale, CA 91201
Phone: 818-243-0707 - www.lcwprops.com

Modern Props (323) 934-3000
RJR Props (404) 349-7600
Tech bench rentals; computers are our specialty so so we have a lot of tech bench dressing
Woody's Electrical Props (818) 503-1940

Teeter-Totter

See: Playground Equipment

Teeth

See: Dentist Equipment

Teeth & Braces

See: Special Effects, Make-up/Prosthetics

Telegrams (Prop)

The Earl Hays Press (818) 765-0700
services the Industry only. period, modern, US/foreign, originals
History For Hire, Inc. (818) 765-7767
custom
Sony Pictures Studios-Prop House (Off Lot) (310) 244-5999

Telephone Booths & Pay Telephones

AIR Designs (818) 768-6639
Period to Present, USA Phone Booths, Pedestal Phones
Air Hollywood - Prop House & Standing Sets (818) 890-0444
Aviation-themed props and set dressing. We have thousands of items available to dress airport terminals.
Alley Cats Studio Rentals (818) 982-9178
New York, L.A., various styles
C. P. Valley (323) 466-8201
Telephone booths from standing and walk in to British and wall mounted. Antique pay phones and modern.
E.C. Prop Rentals (818) 764-2008
pedestal-style booths, wall-mount payphones
The Hand Prop Room LP. (323) 931-1534
domestic, English
History For Hire, Inc. (818) 765-7767
LCW Props (818) 243-0707
Wood, Metal, Period - Present
Modern Props (323) 934-3000
contemporary/vintage, metallic pay phone sets, street pay phones, triple unit pay phones, airport phones, variety

RC Vintage, Inc. (818) 765-7107
large selection Oak, and Aluminum phone booths. 1930's - 1990's
Sony Pictures Studios-Prop House (Off Lot) (310) 244-5999
telephone booths, telephone signs, telephone oedestaks
Universal Studios Property & Hardware Dept (818) 777-2784
Many kinds of prop pay phones/phone booths for rent from different time periods and regions.

Telephone Directories

See: Telephones

Telephone Poles Prop

See Also: Electrical/Electronic Supplies & Services* Insulators
AIR Designs (818) 768-6639
12' wooden poles, call box poles
E.C. Prop Rentals (818) 764-2008
poles, crossbars, transformer cans, porc. insulators

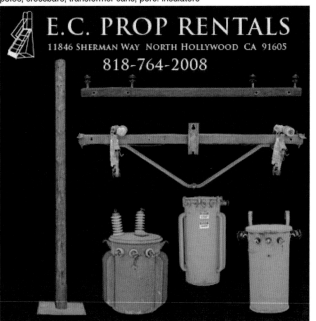

E.C. PROP RENTALS
11846 SHERMAN WAY NORTH HOLLYWOOD CA 91605
818-764-2008

Telephones

See Also: Intercoms* Switchboards* Telephone Booths & Pay Telephones* Telephones, Cellular
Advanced Liquidators Office Furniture (818) 763-3470
large sel. contemp. used desktop dressing
Airwaves Wireless (818) 501-8200
13400 Riverside Dr. # 103 Sherman Oaks, CA 91423
Cellular phones, cellphones, tablets, laptops, iPhones, iPads, dummy phones, walkies, Wi-Fi, satellite phones, macbooks
anita@airwaveswireless.com * www.airwaveswireless.com
Alley Cats Studio Rentals (818) 982-9178
dial, push-button, period, modern & cell phones
C. P. Valley (323) 466-8201
Office phones and desk phones antique to contemporary.
E.C. Prop Rentals (818) 764-2008
industrial, freeway, call box w/sign & pole/base unit
The Hand Prop Room LP. (323) 931-1534
period-present, lrg sel.
History For Hire, Inc. (818) 765-7767
big selection & colors, very good condition
Kitsch N Sync Props (323) 343-1190
Specializing in 70's and 80's props. Large collection of cameras, electronics, phones, art, games, stereos, & much more.
LCW Props (818) 243-0707
Large Selection Of Office Phones, Some Rigged / Working

Modern Props (323) 934-3000
contemporary/futuristic, large selection, many colors, themes, purposes, and time periods
Omega/Cinema Props (323) 466-8201
Residential phones from antique to modern.
Prop Services West (818) 503-2790
RC Vintage, Inc. (818) 765-7107
30s to 60s, period, modern, all colors
Sony Pictures Studios-Prop House (Off Lot) (310) 244-5999
cell phones, call boxes, grey command box, dialess phones, telephone intercom, military field phones, mobile telephone, more
Universal Studios Property & Hardware Dept (818) 777-2784
All kinds of phones with all kinds of functions from all kinds of periods for rent.

Telephones, Cellular

See Also: Telephone Booths & Pay Telephones Telephones* Walkie-Talkies*
Airwaves Wireless (818) 501-8200
13400 Riverside Dr. # 103 Sherman Oaks, CA 91423
Cellular phones, cellphones, tablets, laptops, iPhones, iPads, dummy phones, walkies, Wi-Fi, satellite phones, macbooks
anita@airwaveswireless.com * www.airwaveswireless.com

The Hand Prop Room LP. (323) 931-1534
rigged
LCW Props (818) 243-0707
Large Selection Of Older Model Cell Phones
Modern Props (323) 934-3000
contemporary/futuristic, hand flip

Teleprompting

Cue Tech Teleprompting (818) 487-2700
5527 Satsuma Ave, N. Hollywood, CA, 91601
Vision Prompt, Inc. (818) 223-8884
23958 Craftsman Rd, Calabasas, CA, 91302
Teleprompting services and equipment rental.

Telescopes

See: Binoculars, Scopes & Telescopes

Teletypes

History For Hire, Inc. (818) 765-7767
some practical

Television Antennas

See: Rooftop Dressing

Television Lighting

See: Stage Lighting, Film/Video/TV

Television Stations

See: Stages/Studios, Film/TV/Theatre/Events

Television Studio Dressing

See Also: Video Equipment
C. P. Valley (323) 466-8201
E.C. Prop Rentals (818) 764-2008
assorted parts/switches & dimmer boards
The Hand Prop Room LP. (323) 931-1534
History For Hire, Inc. (818) 765-7767
huge inventory, TV cameras all eras many practical, control room
LCW Props (818) 243-0707
AV Racks, Mics, Booms, Control Panels & Boards, Mixing, Cameras

Televisions

24Frame.com, Inc. (213) 745-2411
944 Venice Blvd, Los Angeles, CA, 90015
TV sets for sync playback
info@24frame.com * www.24frame.com
Astro Audio Video Lighting, Inc. (818) 549-9915
6615 San Fernando Rd, Glendale, CA, 91201
TVs 13" to 80" plasma TVs, LED TVs; video walls, projectors & projection screens in all sizes.
www.astroavl.com
C. P. Two (323) 466-8201
C. P. Valley (323) 466-8201
The Hand Prop Room LP. (323) 931-1534
History For Hire, Inc. (818) 765-7767
LCW Props (818) 243-0707
LCD, Plasma, Computer Monitors Large & Small. Also Fake TV's As Well
Modern Props (323) 934-3000
contemporary/futuristic
Old Time Replications (818) 786-2500
Call for appointment, Van Nuys, CA, 91411
old radio, TV knobs, escutcheons, pushbuttons, grills, handles, etc.
RC Vintage, Inc. (818) 765-7107
30s to 60s, floor models & portable
RJR Props (404) 349-7600
Prop televisions/prop TV's for rent; antique to modern; many different sizes.
Universal Studios Property & Hardware Dept (818) 777-2784
Many prop tvs/ prop television for rent.
Warner Bros. Studios Property Department (818) 954-2181
Big Screen Television, Console Television, Converter Boxes, Flat Panel Television, LCD televisions

Tennis Equipment

See: Prop Houses Sporting Goods & Services*

Tents

See: Canopies, Tents, Gazebos, Cabanas

Tepees

See: Native American

Text Books

See: Books, Real/Hollow & Faux Books School Supplies, Desks & Dressing*

Textilene

See: Fabrics Upholstery Materials/Services* Fabric Dyeing/Tie Dyeing/Painting/Aging*

Textiles

See: Fabrics

Theater Seating

See Also: Audience Seating

Alley Cats Studio Rentals (818) 982-9178
multiple seats, theater seats sections of 2 and 4, cinema chairs

C. P. Valley (323) 466-8201
Vintage theatre seating to vinyl theatre seating and upholstered theatre seating
& theatre seats

Lennie Marvin Enterprises, Inc. (Prop Heaven) (818) 841-5882
rows of seats

Sony Pictures Studios-Fixtures (310) 244-5996
5933 W Slauson Ave, Culver City, CA, 90230
period to present day, wooden auditorium chairs
www.sonypicturesstudios.com

Universal Studios Property & Hardware Dept (818) 777-2784
Theater seating for rent.

Theaters

See: Locations, Insert Stages & Small Theatres Stages/Studios,
Film/TV/Theatre/Events*

Theatrical Draperies, Hardware & Rigging

See Also: Backings Drapery & Curtains* Flameproofing* Rigging,
Equipment or Services*

American Silk Mills (305) 308-9411
2300 Chestnut Street 4th floor, Philadelphia, PA, 19103
United States manufacturer of the most exquisite textiles since 1896.
adriano.salucci@americansilk.com * www.sensuede.com

iWeiss Theatrical Solutions (888) 325-7192
815 Fairview Ave #10, Fairview, NJ 07022
draperies, curtain track, hanging hdw, fabric

Omega/Cinema Props (323) 466-8201

S & K Theatrical Draperies (818) 503-0596
7313 Varna Ave, N Hollywood, CA, 91605

Sapsis Rigging, Inc. (800) 727-7471
3883 Ridge Ave, Philadelphia, PA, 19132

ShopWildThings (928) 855-6075
2880 Sweetwater Ave, Lake Havasu City, AZ, 86406
Event Decor, Beaded Curtains, Chain Curtains, String Curtains & Columns,
Crystal Columns. Reliable service & delivery.
help@shopwildthings.com * www.shopwildthings.com

Sony Pictures Studios-Linens, Drapes, Rugs (310) 244-5999
5933 W Slauson Ave, Culver City, CA, 90230
large sel. of draperies/drapery
www.sonypicturesstudios.com

Triangle Scenery Drapery Co. (323) 662-8129
PO Box 29205, Los Angeles, CA 90029
Theatrical fabrics - fabrication - rigging
tcmill@aol.com * www.tridrape.com

Universal Studios Drapery Dept (818) 777-2761

Warner Bros. Drapery, Upholstery & Flooring (818) 954-1831
4000 Warner Blvd, Burbank, CA, 91522
Theatrical; Beaded; Rope tie backs; Vintage fringed; Velour, damask, velvet &
Mylar; Pipe & Base
wbsfdrapery@warnerbros.com * www.wbdrapery.com

Theatrical Make-up

See: Make-up & Hair, Supplies & Services Make-up Schools*

Themed Environment Construction

See Also: Architectural Pieces & Artifacts Audio/Visual Film
Equipment* Prop Design & Manufacturing* Scenery/Set
Construction* Special Effects, Electronic* Special Effects, Lighting &
Lasers* Stage Lighting, Film/Video/TV*

Barry Howard Ltd (805) 966-6622
420 E Carrillo St. Santa Barbara, CA 93101
museum & themed attraction design, planning, development

BRC Imagination Arts (818) 841-8084
2711 Winona Ave, Burbank, CA, 91504
design, plan, produce themed attractions, educational attractions, brand
experiences

BRPH Entertainment Design Studio (321) 254-7666
5700 N. Harbor City Blvd. Ste 400, Melbourne, FL, 32940
architectural, civil, structural, mechanical, electrical, program mgmnt, design &
build services to the Industry

Chicago Scenic Studios, Inc. (312) 274-9900
1315 N. North Branch St, Chicago, IL, 60642
Design and/or build spaces for museums, amusement parks, special &
corporate events, broadcast, retail

Cost of Wisconsin, Inc. (800) 221-7625
4201 Co Rd P, Jackson, WI, 53037
Themed facades, architectural panels, simulated trees, sculptures, rock &
water features, murals

Cuningham Group (310) 895-2200
8665 Hayden Place, Culver City, CA 90232
full range of design svcs; feasibility studies, planning, architecture, interior
design & construction svcs

David L. Manwarren Corp. (909) 989-5883
9146 East 9th Street, Rancho Cucamonga, CA, 91730
Design & build aquarium, zoo, and museum exhibits, international clientele

Designage, Inc. (407) 647-2950
311 Circle Dr, Maitland, FL, 32751
design, build themed environments for theme parks, resorts, entertainment
projects

Dillon Works! Inc. (425) 493-8309
11775 Harbour Reach Dr, Mukilteo, WA, 98275
interior/exterior dimensional and architectural elements, custom design &
fabrication

Duncan Design, Inc. (707) 636-2300
48 Barham Ave, Santa Rosa, CA, 95407
design/fabricate/install museum exhibits, retail displays, themed sets, props &
backings

KHS & S Contractors (714) 695-3670
5109 E La Palma Ave Ste A, Anaheim, CA, 92807
Interior & exterior finishes, rockwork/water features, large-scale projects

Morris Architects (407) 839-0414
622 E Washington St Ste 500, Orlando, FL, 32801
design & master planning services for themed public facilities

The Nassal Company (407) 648-0400
415 W Kaley St, Orlando, FL, 32806
Theming, exhibitory & rockwork fabrication, installation services provided
worldwide since 1984

Penwal Industries, Inc. (909) 466-1555
10611 Acacia St, Rancho Cucamonga, CA, 91730
Design, engineering, proj. mgmnt., & construction of exhibits, and retail spaces

R. D. Olson Construction (949) 474-2001
2955 Main Street, Third Floor, Irvine, CA, 92614
General construction for projects in entertainment, restaurant, retail &
hospitality industries, ask for Tim Cromwell

Reynolds Advanced Materials: Smooth-On (818) 358-6000
Distributor
10856 Vanowen St, N. Hollywood, CA, 91605
Hollywood's F/X source for Liquid Rubbers, Plastics & more. NEW Smooth-On
HABITAT Zoo Epoxy Putty and Fire Rated version.
LA@reynoldsam.com * www.moldmakingmaterials.com

Sparks Exhibits & Environments (562) 941-0101
3201A La Cienega Blvd, Los Angeles, CA, 90016
Design, construction, installation; extensive fabrication, special effects
capability, worldwide

ThemeWorks, Inc. (386) 454-7500
1210 S Main St, High Springs, FL, 32643
Design/build scenery, rockwork, architectural elements, sculpture, exhibits,
artificial animals

Utopia Entertainment, Inc. (818) 980-9940
12711 Ventura Blvd Ste 200, Studio City, CA, 91604
Full service, turnkey, design, fabrication, installation; permanent installations &
live shows

Warner Bros. Studios Construction Services (818) 954-7820
4000 Warner Blvd, Burbank, CA, 91522
Concept, Design, Fabrication of Interior & Exterior Standing Sets, Facades,
Exhibits, Road Shows
wbsfconstructionservices@warnerbros.com * www.wbsf.com

Themed Environments/Entertainment

See: Events, Decorations, Supplies & Services Events,
Design/Planning/Production* Events, Entertainment* Prop Design &
Manufacturing* Prop Houses* Scenery/Set Construction*

Thermometers, Wall

Alley Cats Studio Rentals (818) 982-9178
antique, modern

E.C. Prop Rentals (818) 764-2008
nice variety

LCW Props (818) 243-0707
Stainless Steel, Industrial, & Old Factory

Sony Pictures Studios-Prop House (Off Lot) (310) 244-5999

Thirties Theme Parties

See: Costume Rental Houses Costumes* Events, Backings &
Scenery* Events, Decorations, Supplies & Services* Events,
Design/Planning/Production* Historical Era Themed Events*
Wardrobe, Vintage*

Thrift Shops

See Also: Charities & Donations* Furniture, Used/Second Hand

American Way Thrift Store (818) 841-6013
3226 W. Magnolia Blvd, Burbank, CA, 91505

Carriage "Hope" Children's Charity (818) 509-9515
11311 Vanowen St, N. Hollywood, CA 91605
Thrift Store with 1000s of vintage, contemp. & antique household items,
clothing & collectibles; fine art, open 7 days.
hope@carriagehope.org * www.carriagehope.org

Goodwill Industries (818) 242-9399
1622 W. Glenoaks Blvd, Glendale, CA, 91202

Habitat for Humanity of Greater Los Angeles (424) 246-3637
8739 E Artesia Blvd, Bellflower, CA, 90706
Habitat's ReStores are home-improvement thrift stores, helping to fund our
mission. Free pick-up, tax-deductible.
www.ShopHabitat.org

Helping Hand Thrift Shop (323) 857-1191
1033 South Fairfax Ave, Los Angeles, CA 90019
We are a thrift store with a constantly changing inventory.
fairfaxhelpinghand@gmail.com * www.helpinghandthriftshop.com

La Providencia Guild for Childrens Hospital (818) 845-6606
3301 W Burbank Blvd, Burbank, CA, 91505
(open T, W, Th, Sat; 10-4) benefits Children's Hospital of L.A.

Out of the Closet Thrift Store (323) 664-4394
3160 Glendale Blvd, Glendale, CA, 90039

Thrones

FROST (310) 704-8812
Call for Appointment, 21515 Madrona Ave, Torrance, CA 90503
Oversized Santa thrones for all your santa set needs. Check our website for
styles available!
mdisplay@yahoo.com * www.frostchristmasprops.com

History For Hire, Inc. (818) 765-7767
Santa

Omega/Cinema Props (323) 466-8201

Sony Pictures Studios-Prop House (Off Lot) (310) 244-5999

Universal Studios Property & Hardware Dept (818) 777-2784
Many kinds of thrones from all kinds of periods.

Tiaras

See: Crowns & Tiaras

Ticker Tape & Machines

History For Hire, Inc. (818) 765-7767
Ticker tape machines

RC Vintage, Inc. (818) 765-7107
Early 1920's Type Glass dome

Ticket Booths

See Also: Carnival Dressing/Supplies

AIR Designs (818) 768-6639
Guard, Parking Lot, Toll Gate Arms, Ticket Dispensers

Alley Cats Studio Rentals (818) 982-9178
ornate deco

Amusement Svcs/Candyland Amusements (818) 266-4056
18653 Ventura Blvd Ste 235, Tarzana, CA, 91356
ticket vendors, Carnival entrance, Ticket carts, carnival booths, game booths,
stub booths, entry booths
www.candylandamusements.com

Bob Gail Special Events (310) 202-5200
Bob Gail has a huge inventory of special events equipment perfect for any
premier event!

C. P. Valley (323) 466-8201
Wooden ticket booths

Christiansen Amusements (800) 300-6114
Call for Appt
Carnival style for all events & productions
info@amusements.com * www.amusements.com

E.C. Prop Rentals (818) 764-2008
large castered units & small "shack" style

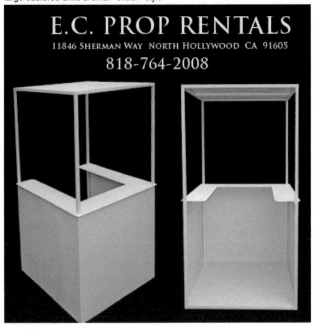

E.C. PROP RENTALS
11846 SHERMAN WAY NORTH HOLLYWOOD CA 91605
818-764-2008

LCW Props (818) 243-0707
Guard Shack, Ticket Machines

Tickets

See Also: Graphics, Digital & Large Format Printing* Prop Houses

The Earl Hays Press (818) 765-0700
services the Industry only. racing, sports, theatre more!

History For Hire, Inc. (818) 765-7767
stock items & custom

Sony Pictures Studios-Prop House (Off Lot) (310) 244-5999

Ties, Neckwear

See: Costumes* Uniforms, Trades/Professional/Sports* Wardrobe*
Wardrobe, Accessories

Tikis & Tropical Dressing

See Also: Carved Figures* Greens* Hawaiian Dressing* Jungle
Dressing* Light Fixtures, South Seas* Seashells

Benson's Tropical Sea Imports (714) 841-3399
7442 Vincent Cir, Huntington Beach, CA 92648
tiki/bird/fish carvings, masks, bamboo poles/fencing, thatching, tropical
decorations
sales@bensonsimport.com * www.bensonsimport.com

Bob Gail Special Events (310) 202-5200
Spend a night in paradise with our tropical props! Tiki Huts and Torches will do
the trick! Don%u2019t forget your ukulele

C. P. Two (323) 466-8201
Tropical dressing and tiki themed dressing.

Green Set, Inc. (818) 764-1231
facemasks, torches, figures, wide variety of tropical plants including many palm
tree styles real and faux

History For Hire, Inc. (818) 765-7767
Tikis, bamboo, tropical dressing/tropical decorations

Jackson Shrub Supply, Inc. (818) 982-0100
jungle vines, fantasy creations, Tiki heads, tropical decorations, tiki
decorations, tropical plants, tropical flowers

LCW Props (818) 243-0707
Tiki Torches, Bamboo

Lennie Marvin Enterprises, Inc. (Prop Heaven) (818) 841-5882
tikis, pictures, Hula Hoops, dolls, signage, nets, bars, chairs

Oceanic Arts (562) 698-6960
Carved wood Tikis & Fiberglass Tikis, Roof Thatching, Bamboo Poles,
Mattings, South Sea Lights, and more.

Omega/Cinema Props (323) 466-8201
Decorative tiki dressing, Polynesian dressing, and tropical dressing

Sony Pictures Studios-Prop House (Off Lot) (310) 244-5999
Tropical decorations and tropical rentals

Tile, Marble, Granite, Etc.

See Also: Bathroom Decorations* Carpet & Flooring

American Marble & Onyx (310) 649-1355
10321 S. La Cienega Blvd, Los Angeles, CA, 90045
only slab stone

Dal Tile (310) 559-8680
3633 Lenawee, Los Angeles, CA 90016

Emser International (323) 650-2010
8431 Santa Monica Blvd, W. Hollywood, CA, 90069

Firenze Ceramic Tile (818) 982-3961
7283 Bellaire Ave, Unit A, N. Hollywood, CA, 91605
tile

Global Stone (818) 767-8485
14533 Keswick St, Van Nuys, CA, 91405
tile & slab stone

Ground Floor (800) 540-3478
15812 Arminta St, Van Nuys, CA 91406
Steam cleaning & stone restoration. No sales, stone, tile, grout, metal and
glass restoration only.

Ideal Tile (212) 759-2339
405 East 51st Street, New York City, NY, 10022
web site has dealer locator. tile & pre-sized slab stone

Impression (310) 618-1299
22599 S Western Ave, Torrance, CA, 90501
limestone & terra cotta only

Intertile Marble & Granite (760) 773-1001
74-824 42nd Ave, Palm Desert, CA, 92260
tile, large slab stone

Marble/Unlimited, Inc. (818) 988-0100
14554 Keswick St, Van Nuys, CA, 91405
wholesale only; slab stone

Mission Tile West (626) 799-4595
853 Mission St, S Pasadena, CA, 91030

Mortarless Building Supply (323) 663-3291
2707 Fletcher Dr, Los Angeles, CA, 90039
vintage & replacement tile, Arts & Crafts tile

San Fernando Marble & Granite (818) 897-4033
9803 San Fernando Rd, Pacoima, CA, 91331
tile & slab stone

Simply Tiles (310) 373-7781
3968 Pacific Coast Hwy, Torrance, CA, 90505
tile & slab stone

Surfaces USA (818) 982-0069
11501 Hart St, N Hollywood, CA, 91605
tile & slab stone

Tile, Mile of Tile, Anaheim

Bedrosians-Tile-Marble (714) 778-8453
1235 S. State College Blvd, Anaheim, CA, 92806

California Wholesale Tile (714) 937-0591
1656 S. State College Blvd, Anaheim, CA, 92806
imported tile

Earthstone Quarries (714) 635-7666
1840 E. Ball Rd, Anaheim, CA, 92805
tile, slab stone

Marmol Export, U.S.A. (714) 939-0697
1550 S State College Blvd, Anaheim, CA, 92806
tile, slab stone

Orion Tile & Marble (714) 772-2300
1301 S State College Blvd, Anaheim, CA, 92806

Pacific Land Marble & Tile Corp. (714) 776-2424
1300 S State College Blvd, Anaheim, CA, 92806
tile, small precut slab stone

Porcelanosa (714) 772-3183
1301 S State College Blvd Ste E, Anaheim, CA, 92806
tile

SpecCeramics (714) 808-0134
851 Enterprise Way, Fullerton, CA, 92831
Summitville brand tile, thinbrick, tactile-tread

Stone Age Tile (714) 704-9293
1701 S State College Blvd, Anaheim, CA, 92806
tile, small & large stone slabs

Tile Expo (714) 635-0406
1360 S State College Blvd, Anaheim, CA, 92806
tile, pre-sized slab stone

Tinting

See: Make-up & Hair, Supplies & Services* Window Treatments

Tires

AIR Designs (818) 768-6639
Street Tires, Racing Tires, Tire Racks/Wheels, Displays, Period to Present &
Bling

Alley Cats Studio Rentals (818) 982-9178

C. P. Valley (323) 466-8201

E.C. Prop Rentals (818) 764-2008
lge inventory used tires & castered racks, auto, truck, tractor, tire racks

History For Hire, Inc. (818) 765-7767
period

LCW Props (818) 243-0707
Large & Small, With Or Without Rims

Tobacconist

See: Smoking Products

Toilets

See: Bathroom Fixtures* Production Vehicles/Trailers

Toilets, Portable Prop

See Also: Prop Houses

Alley Cats Studio Rentals (818) 982-9178
port-a-potties, jail cell toilets

Square Deal Plumbing Co., Inc. (323) 587-8291
2302 E Florence Ave, Huntington Park, CA, 90255

Tombstones

See: Cemetery Dressing

Tool Boxes & Tool Carts

See: Automotive/Garage Equip. & Parts

Tools

See Also: Expendables

AIR Designs (818) 768-6639
Large Selection of Automotive Dressing, Carpentry Dressing and Workshop
Dressing

C. P. Valley (323) 466-8201
Western tools, Indian tools, hand tools, shop tools, farm tools, metal tools,
prospecting tools. Antique to modern.

E.C. Prop Rentals (818) 764-2008
small-large, esp. power tools for shop/factory/industrial

Grainger (818) 253-7970
7565 N. Lockheed Dr, Burbank, CA, 91505
catalog sales; industrial supplies, tools, etc.

The Hand Prop Room LP. (323) 931-1534
period-present, rubber

History For Hire, Inc. (818) 765-7767
big selection

LCW Props (818) 243-0707
Construction, Industrial, Machine Shop, Garage, Medical, Dentistry

The Rational Past (310) 476-6277
By Appointment, West Los Angeles, CA
Authentic science, industrial, technical antiques & collectibles. Many
professions & eras represented. See web site.
info@therationalpast.com * www.therationalpast.com

Sony Pictures Studios-Prop House (Off Lot) (310) 244-5999
Home tools, office tools, garage tools, automobile tools, more

Top Hats

See: Headwear - Hats, Bonnets, Caps, Helmets Etc.

Topiary/Hedges, Artificial

See: Greens

Torture Equipment

Dapper Cadaver/Creatures & Cultures (818) 771-0818
Dungeon equipment, fake weapons & steel instruments. Electric chair,
guillotine, stocks, restraints & heads on spikes.

History For Hire, Inc. (818) 765-7767

LCW Props (818) 243-0707
Bed Of Nails, Iron Maiden, Water Boards, Guillotine, Shockers, Electric Chair

Sword & Stone (818) 562-6548
rack, iron maidens, flails, etc.

Universal Studios Property & Hardware Dept (818) 777-2784
Many torture props for rent.

Totem Poles

The Hand Prop Room LP.	**(323) 931-1534**
Native American Totems	
Universal Studios Property & Hardware Dept	**(818) 777-2784**
Totem poles and prop totem poles of various sizes for rent.	

Towing Services

See Also: Automotive/Garage Equip. & Parts* Transportation, Trucking and/or Storage* Vehicles

Gordy's Garage & Towing Service	**(626) 797-6591**
843 W Woodbury Rd, Altadena, CA 91001	
Larry's Towing Service	**(800) 281-4401**
1900 1st St, San Fernando, CA, 91340	

Toys & Games

See Also: Christmas* Dolls* Memorabilia & Novelties* Nodders* Prop Houses* School Supplies, Desks & Dressing* Soldier Toys & Drums

AIR Designs	**(818) 768-6639**
Pedal Cars, Skill Games, Rides	
B. Shackman & Co., Inc.	**(800) 221-7656**
9964 W. Miller Dr, Galesburg, MI, 49503	
mfr & importer; toys, novelties, paper dolls, decorations	
Benjamin Pollock's Toyshop	**+44 (0) 207 379**
44 The Market, Covent Garden, London, UK, WC2E - 8RF	**7866**
toy theatres & traditional European toys	
Cuddly Toys	**(323) 980-0572**
1833 N Eastern Ave, Los Angeles, CA, 90032	
All types of stuffed toys in a wide variety of sizes	
cuddlytoys@aol.com	
The Hand Prop Room LP.	**(323) 931-1534**
antique toys	
History For Hire, Inc.	**(818) 765-7767**
Hollywood Toys & Costumes	**(800) 554-3444**
6600 Hollywood Blvd, Hollywood, CA, 90028	
Modern Props	**(323) 934-3000**
contemporary, modern, small collection	
Ob-jects	**(818) 351-4200**
Omega/Cinema Props	**(323) 466-8201**
Prop Services West	**(818) 503-2790**
RC Vintage, Inc.	**(818) 765-7107**
rocking horses; lots of unusual, crazy little toys, board games, boardgames, children's bedroom smalls	
Sony Pictures Studios-Prop House (Off Lot)	**(310) 244-5999**
doll carriage, doll clothes, doll furniture, dollhouse, educational toys, educational kit, dollhouse furniture	
Stevenson Brothers	**011 44 20**
The Workshop, Ashford Road, Ashford TN26 3AP	**3382-0363**
Custom handcrafted rocking horses.	
sue@stevensonbros.com * www.stevensonbros.com	
Universal Studios Property & Hardware Dept	**(818) 777-2784**
Many toy props and game props for rent.	
Warner Bros. Studios Property Department	**(818) 954-2181**
Games, stuffed animals, board games, puzzles, dolls, rubber toys, new and used toys, sporting good toys	

Toys, Oversize

See: Oversized Props

Track & Field Equipment

See Also: Prop Houses* Sporting Goods & Services

OnTrack and Field, Inc.	**(800) 697-2999**
2901 Winona Ave, Burbank, CA, 91504	
Vintage collection, and complete line of track & field equipment and gear.	
sales@ontrackandfield.com * www.ontrackandfield.com	
VS Athletics	**(800) 676-7463**
1450 W 228th St Ste 8, Torrance, CA, 90501	

Traction Equipment

Trade Associations

See: Guilds, Unions, Societies, Associations

Trade Shows & Conventions

See Also: Audience Seating* Backings* Events, Decorations, Supplies & Services* Flags/Banners* Inflatables, Custom* Oversized Props* Prop Design & Manufacturing* Prop Houses* Rigging, Equipment or Services* Scenery/Set Construction* Scenery/Set Rentals* Signs* Stage Lighting, Film/Video/TV* Stages, Portable & Steel Deck* Stanchions & Rope* Transportation, Trucking and/or Storage

Astro Audio Video Lighting, Inc.	**(818) 549-9915**
6615 San Fernando Rd, Glendale, CA, 91201	
Video, screens, plasma, projectors, PA systems, podiums, pipe and drape, power distribution and lighting.	
www.astroavl.com	
EFX- Event Special Effects	**(626) 888-2239**
125 Railroad Ave, Monrovia, CA, 91016	
Custom Fabrication- CNC- Plasma Table- Pipe & Ring Benders- 3D Renderings	
info@efxla.com * www.efxla.com	
Taylor Creative Inc.	**(888) 245-4044**
We offer a number of rental items perfect for tradeshow booths and lounges as well as registration and amenities areas.	

Traffic Cones

See: Traffic/Road Signs, Lights, Safety Items

Traffic Management

See: Barricades* Crowd Control: Barricades, Turnstiles Etc.* Traffic/Road Signs, Lights, Safety Items

Traffic/Road Signs, Lights, Safety Items

See Also: Barricades* Parking Meters & Sign Poles* Railroad Crossing Signal

AIR Designs	**(818) 768-6639**
Practical Traffic Lights, Signage, Crosswalks, Call Box, Cones/Pylon Barricades & More	
Alley Cats Studio Rentals	**(818) 982-9178**
barricades, flashing lights/cones/arrows, stop signs on poles, men working, construction traffic lights, bus stop, street lights & more	
Art, Signs & Graphics	**(818) 503-7997**
6939 Farmdale Ave, N Hollywood, CA, 91605	
props, banners, vinyl graphics, vehicle graphics, 3D router cut letters & logos	
jessee@artsignsandgraphics.com * www.artsignsandgraphics.com	
C. P. Two	**(323) 466-8201**
Road signs, traffic signs, traffic lights, directional roads signs and more.	
Castex Rentals	**(323) 462-1468**
1044 N. Cole Ave, Hollywood, CA, 90038	
traffic signs, cones, barricades, vests, safety tape, no parking signs, highway tape	
service@castexrentals.com * www.castexrentals.com	
D'ziner Sign Co.	**(323) 467-4467**
801 Seward Street, Los Angeles, CA 90038	
domestic & foreign made to your specs	
sales@dzinersign.com * www.dzinersign.com	
E.C. Prop Rentals	**(818) 764-2008**
barricades, lanterns, delineators, signage, good inv./multiples	
The Hand Prop Room LP.	**(323) 931-1534**
signs, cones, road work barricades	
LCW Props	**(818) 243-0707**
Cones, Guard Rails, Traffic Signs, Deliniators, etc.	
Main Street Lighting	**(330) 723-4431**
1080 Industrial Pkwy, Medina, OH, 44256	
Nostalgic, ornamental-posts, fixtures, bollards, & brackets	
tracyr@mainstreetlighting.com * www.mainstreetlighting.com	
Modern Props	**(323) 934-3000**
wall-mounted traffic lights	
RC Vintage, Inc.	**(818) 765-7107**
Traffic lights, traffic signals	
Sony Pictures Studios-Prop House (Off Lot)	**(310) 244-5999**
lights & signs	
Statewide Traffic Safety & Sign	**(714) 468-1919**
13261 Garden Grove Blvd, Garden Grove, CA, 92840	
signage, barricades, equipment, traffic control personnel many credits	

**DISPLAY ADS AND LISTINGS FOR THIS CATEGORY
CONTINUE ON THE FOLLOWING PAGE**

Sterndahl Enterprises, Inc.   **(818) 834-8199**
11861 Branford St, Sun Valley, CA, 91352
traffic control equipment, signage, barricades, striping, trucks & bobcats
www.sterndahl.com

Traffic Control Equipment / K-rail / Signals
(Trucks/Cones / Arrow boards / Signs & more)
Certified Traffic Control Tech.
Striping / Marking & Removals / Bobcats
(Thermoplastic / Paint / Temporary Tape)

Warner Bros. Studios Property Department   **(818) 954-2181**
Safety Barricade, emergency signs, assorted road signs

Trailers

See: Production Vehicles/Trailers RV Vehicles & Travel Trailers,
Equip & Parts*

Trains

See Also: Bus Shelter Model Ships/Planes/Trains/Autos Etc.*
American Assn. of Private R.R. Car Owners   **(706) 326-6262**
PO Box 6037 Columbus, GA 31917
website lists private cars nationwide, contacts for usage
www.aaprco.com
California State Railroad Museum   **(916) 445-7387**
125 I Street, Sacramento, CA, 95814
Vintage trains & R.R. locations; Contact Paul Hammond, 2 sites, Old
Sacramento & Jamestown (in Sierra foothills)
Fillmore & Western Railway Co.   **(805) 524-2546**
351 Santa Clara St, Fillmore, CA, 93015
Dinner trains, excursion rides, special events, holiday theme trains
Grand Canyon Railway   **(800) 843-8724**
233 N. Grand Canyon Blvd, Williams, AZ, 86046
railroad/locations/excursions
Pacific Harbor Line, Inc.   **(310) 984-5773**
705 Henry Ford Ave, Wilmington, CA, 90744
Film location for scenes requiring RR tracks, equipment, and facilities
Pacific Southwest Railway Museum Assn.   **(619) 465-7776**
4695 Nebo Dr, La Mesa, CA, 91941
Museums at La Mesa, CA & Campo, CA
Travel Town Museum   **(323) 662-5874**
5200 W Zoo Drive, Los Angeles, CA, 90027
access to equip. & locations owned by the city
Verde Canyon Railroad   **(800) 582-7245**
300 N Broadway, Clarkdale, AZ, 86324

Tramp Art

See: Paintings/Prints

Trampolines

See: Gymnasium & Gymnastic Equipment

Transformers

See: Electrical/Electronic Supplies & Services

Transportation, Trucking and/or Storage

See Also: Limousine Service Property Master Storage Rooms*
Scenery/Set Storage* Vehicles* Towing Services*
BHC Crane LLC   **(310) 830-6450**
2190 W Willow St, Long Beach, CA, 90810
30-300 ton mobile crane & boomtruck rentals, trucking & storage at our 3 acre
facility along the 103 fwy, Long Beach, CA
www.bhccrane.com
Castex Rentals   **(323) 462-1468**
1044 N. Cole Ave, Hollywood, CA, 90038
truck shelves, racks, dollies, magliners, pads, ratchets, rope, dollies, magliner
carts, furniture pads, super shelves
service@castexrentals.com * www.castexrentals.com
Clark Transfer, Inc.   **(800) 488-7585**
800 A Paxton St, Harrisburg, PA, 17104
domestic/global, air/ocean, specialized equip.
Consolidated Scenic Services, Inc.   **(818) 409-3354**
4000 Chevy Chase Dr, Los Angeles, CA 90039
Production Trucks, Storage, Local 80 Grips, 399 teamster drivers, Strike
Services - Steel Deck Rentals
www.consolidatedscenicservices.com

Consolidated Scenic Services, Inc.
Production Transportation/Grip & Strike Services

Turn-key Grip, Production Drivers, Scenery transportation & storage

*Transportation & grip service solutions
for the entertainment industry*
www.consolidatedscenicservices.com

Gilbert Production Service   **(323) 871-0006**
Strike it, truck it, store it
Green Set, Inc.   **(818) 764-1231**
crane service & brush hauling also available (no storage)
Jackson Shrub Supply, Inc.   **(818) 982-0100**
Production Storage Group   **(818) 512-8472**
110 Topsail Mall, Marina Del Rey, CA, 90292
Also in West LA. Call before visiting us; band & production storage, musical
equip., cartage & trucking
Prop Transport Inc.   **(212) 594-2521**
552 W 43rd St, New York, NY, 10036
24X7 service; equip. transportation for Film & Theatrical productions
SAUGUS STATION STORAGE   **(661) 253-0944**
25655 Springbrook Ave Bld 24, Santa Clarita, CA, 91350
Secure storage for sets, props, vehicles & containers. Up to 35' clear. Low
rates-helpful staff. Studio/freeway close.
SaugusStation@gmail.com * www.saugusstationstorage.com

Scenic Expressions   **(818) 409-3354**
4000 Chevy Chase Dr, Los Angeles, CA, 90039
All Production needs - Double Drop, Single drop, A-frame trailers and
Construction wall trailers
mark@scenicexpressions.com * www.scenicexpressions.com

Silverado Coach Company, Inc.   **(818) 251-9700**
limousine production tranportation, LA, NYC, SF, Miami, Chicago, also picture cars

Studio Express   **(818) 352-9402**
10333 McVine Ave, Sunland, CA, 91040
studio trucking & storage

Universal Studios Transportation   **(818) 777-2966**
100 Universal City Plaza, Universal City, CA, 91608
range of vehicles available, SUVs to tractor trailers, no trucking or storage
universal.transpo@nbcuni.com * www.filmmakersdestination.com

Western Studio Service, Inc.   **(818) 842-9272**
4561 Colorado Blvd, Los Angeles, CA, 90039
We have the largest fleet of custom trailers to transport scenery of all sizes and heights. All trailers for rent too!
www.westernstudioservice.com

Trash

See: Salvage, Rubble, Clutter & Trash (Prop) Sanitation, Waste Disposal*

Trash Cans & Waste Baskets

AIR Designs   **(818) 768-6639**
Fast Food, Wire Gas Station, Park, Bus, Street, New York Style

Alley Cats Studio Rentals   **(818) 982-9178**
galvanized, plastic, wire, flare-top, residential

C. P. Valley   **(323) 466-8201**
Many kinds of trash cans from outdoor trash cans to indoor.

E.C. Prop Rentals   **(818) 764-2008**
interior/exterior, many styles, good multiples

FormDecor, Inc.   **(310) 558-2582**
America's largest event rental supplier of 20th Century furniture and accessories for Modern and Mid-Century styles.

The Hand Prop Room LP.   **(323) 931-1534**

History For Hire, Inc.   **(818) 765-7767**

LCW Props   **(818) 243-0707**
Huge Selection Of Trash Bins, Recycling, Yard Waste, Roll-Off Containers, etc.

Lennie Marvin Enterprises, Inc. (Prop Heaven)   **(818) 841-5882**
wire mesh, galvanized, plastic, wood, stone, metal

Modern Props   **(323) 934-3000**
modern, indoor, outdoor, silver, metal, gold, business, home, alley, heavy duty, professional, trash compactors

Omega/Cinema Props   **(323) 466-8201**

RC Vintage, Inc.   **(818) 765-7107**
many shapes, sizes and colors

Sony Pictures Studios-Prop House (Off Lot)   **(310) 244-5999**
commercial trash cans, dumpsters, domestic trash cans, hospital trash cans, park trash cans, recycle bins, rubber maid bins

TR Trading Company   **(310) 329-9242**
15604 S Broadway, Gardena, CA, 90248
85,000 sq/ft of items, selection and inventory changes weekly. old, new, rubber, steel, assorted, plastic
sales@trtradingcompany.com * www.trtradingcompany.com

Universal Studios Property & Hardware Dept   **(818) 777-2784**
Trash cans/wastebaskets of all kinds for all scenarios for rent.

Travel (City/Country) Themed Events

See Also: Costume Rental Houses Costumes* Events, Decorations, Supplies & Services* Events, Design/Planning/Production* Greens* Nautical Dressing & Props*

Bob Gail Special Events   **(310) 202-5200**
Take a trip around the globe with our Travel Props! Our Globe Centerpieces are perfect for Around the World events!

Travel Posters

See: Posters, Art/Movie/Travel/Wanted Etc.

Travel Trailers

See: RV Vehicles & Travel Trailers, Equip & Parts

Treadmills

See: Conveyor Equipment Exercise & Fitness Equipment* Special Effects, Equipment & Supplies*

Treasure Chests

See: Pirate, Chests & Treasures

Trees

See: Greens

Trims, Fringe, Tassels, Beading Etc.

See Also: Costume/Wardrobe/Sewing Supplies* Fabrics* Theatrical Draperies, Hardware & Rigging* Upholstery Materials/Services

Cheep Trims (877) 289-8746
3957 S. Hill St. 2nd Floor Los Angeles, CA 90037

Palladia Passementerie (651) 488-1603
Web Based Business
High quality trims, from Europe & Asia, 100s in stock & custom, blending past with present, wholesale
www.palladiapassementerie.com

ShopWildThings (928) 855-6075
2880 Sweetwater Ave, Lake Havasu City, AZ, 86406
Event Decor, Beaded Curtains, Chain Curtains, String Curtains & Columns, Crystal Columns. Reliable service & delivery.
help@shopwildthings.com * www.shopwildthings.com

Trophies/Trophy Cases

AIR Designs (818) 768-6639
Automotive, Boat, Awards, Flags

C. P. Valley (323) 466-8201
Sports trophies, army trophies, sports awards, army awards and more.

Charisma Design Studio, Inc. (818) 252-6611
8414 San Fernando Road, Sun Valley, CA, 91352
glass, metal, marble awards, label etching to carving it out
info@charismadesign.com * www.charismadesign.com

E.C. Prop Rentals (818) 764-2008
trophies & trophy cases

Faux Library Studio Props, Inc. (818) 765-0096
large selection of trophies and awards, high school trophy case

The Hand Prop Room LP. (323) 931-1534

History For Hire, Inc. (818) 765-7767
trophies, ribbons

Hollywood Cinema Arts, Inc. (818) 504-7333
Over 4,600 trophies. You have to see it to believe it.

Hollywood Studio Gallery (323) 462-1116
new & character (no cases)

LCW Props (818) 243-0707
Misc. Trohpies Of All Styles, Large Wood Cases Multiple Styles

Omega/Cinema Props (323) 466-8201
Trophy cups, trophy plaques, trophy stands, sports trophies, display cabinets and more.

Prop Services West (818) 503-2790
trophies

RC Vintage, Inc. (818) 765-7107
Asst Trophie Nice Oak Trophy Case Full Size

Sony Pictures Studios-Prop House (Off Lot) (310) 244-5999
Medals, plaques, ribbons, taxidermy, trophies of many kinds, trophy parts. Only trophies

Universal Studios Property & Hardware Dept (818) 777-2784
Many kinds of trophies for all kinds of occasions and trophy display cases for rent.

Tropical Dressing

See: Aquariums & Tropical Fish* Tikis & Tropical Dressing

Truck Rentals

See: Vehicles

Trucking

See: Transportation, Trucking and/or Storage* Towing Services

Trunks

See Also: Steamer Trunks

Alley Cats Studio Rentals (818) 982-9178

History For Hire, Inc. (818) 765-7767
huge selection

LCW Props (818) 243-0707
Period - Present, Antique

Prop Services West (818) 503-2790

Sony Pictures Studios-Prop House (Off Lot) (310) 244-5999

Universal Studios Property & Hardware Dept (818) 777-2784
Prop storage trunks and travel trunks for rent.

Warner Bros. Studios Property Department (818) 954-2181
Army Trunks, Leather Trunks, rustic trunks, steamer trunks, western trunks, trunks on wheels, metal trunks

Truss

See Also: Lighting & Sound, Concert/Theatrical/DJ/VJ* Stage Lighting, Film/Video/TV

Astro Audio Video Lighting, Inc. (818) 549-9915
6615 San Fernando Rd, Glendale, CA, 91201
Everything truss; box trusses, circle trusses, truss tables, truss tool sets and truss bolts.
www.astroavl.com

EFX- Event Special Effects (626) 888-2239
125 Railroad Ave, Monrovia, CA, 91016
Trussing- Arch- Cubes- Structures- Stage- Stands, Mount
info@efxla.com * www.efxla.com

LCW Props (818) 243-0707
Square, Triangle, Aluminum, Steel, Quantities

Turbines

Alley Cats Studio Rentals (818) 982-9178
small to extra large including roof top turbines.

E.C. Prop Rentals (818) 764-2008
rooftop all sizes, exhaust

LCW Props (818) 243-0707
Jet, Aero, Large Quantities

Turnstiles

See: Crowd Control: Barricades, Turnstiles Etc.

Turntables

See: Mechanical Effects* Phonographs* Stage Turntables

Tuxedo

See: Formal Wear

TV/Film Production Facilities

See: Stages/Studios, Film/TV/Theatre/Events

Twenties Themed Parties

See: Costume Rental Houses* Events, Backings & Scenery* Events, Decorations, Supplies & Services* Events, Design/Planning/Production* Historical Era Themed Events* Prop Houses* Wardrobe, Vintage

Twentyfour Frame Video

See: Video 24fps / Sync System / D.D.I.

Typewriters

Anderson Business Technology (626) 793-2166
120 E. Colorado Blvd, Pasadena, CA, 91105
Repairs & Sales of copiers, fax, printers & other office equipment
Batchelor Business Machine (818) 222-2152
5169 Douglas Fir Rd Ste 6, Calabasas, CA, 91302
IBM compatible typewriters & supplies
C. P. Valley (323) 466-8201
The Hand Prop Room LP. (323) 931-1534
period-present
History For Hire, Inc. (818) 765-7767
many practical, multiples
International Printing Museum (714) 529-1832
315 Torrance Blvd, Carson, CA, 90745
antique printing/office equipment 1450-1980. old typewriters, printing machines
www.printmuseum.org
LCW Props (818) 243-0707
Electric, Manual, Mystery Writer's Typewriter
Universal Studios Property & Hardware Dept (818) 777-2784
Electric typewriters and manual typewriters from various time periods for rent.

UFOs

See: Aliens* Fantasy Props, Costumes, or Decorations* Futuristic Furniture, Props, Decorations

Ultraviolet Lights

See: Light Strings* Lighting & Sound, Concert/Theatrical/DJ/VJ* Lighting, LED, Fiber Optic & Specialty* Neon Lights & Signs* Ultraviolet Products

Ultraviolet Products

See Also: Lighting, LED, Fiber Optic & Specialty* Neon Lights & Signs
History For Hire, Inc. (818) 765-7767
Like, the 60s, can you dig it?
Shannon Luminous Materials, Inc. (800) 543-4485
304 A North Townsend St, Santa Ana, CA, 92703
fluorescent & phosphorescent materials, paints, dyes, black lights

Umbrellas, Hand & Parasols

See Also: Canes* Headwear - Hats, Bonnets, Caps, Helmets Etc.* Protective Apparel* Wardrobe, Accessories
The Costume House (818) 508-9933
1890s parasols & umbrellas, 1940s umbrellas
The Hand Prop Room LP. (323) 931-1534
period-present
History For Hire, Inc. (818) 765-7767
period to present umbrellas & parasols
Lace-Parasols (915) 594-0878
9333 Shaver Drive, El Paso, TX, 79925
Unique cotton Battenburg lace parasols in various styles, sizes and colors. Other lace accessories too.
LCW Props (818) 243-0707
Omega/Cinema Props (323) 466-8201
umbrellas
Prop Services West (818) 503-2790
umbrellas
Sony Pictures Studios-Prop House (Off Lot) (310) 244-5999
Paper umbrellas, parasols, rain umbrellas, sun umbrellas
Universal Studios Property & Hardware Dept (818) 777-2784
Many parasols & umbrellas for rent.

Umbrellas, Patio

See: Furniture, Outdoor/Patio* Garden/Patio

Underwater Filming

See: Nautical/Marine Services & Charters

Underwear & Lingerie, Bloomers, Corsets, Etc.

The Costume House (818) 508-9933
Victorian corsets, bloomers, slips, 1950s merry widows
Dark Garden Unique Corsetry (415) 431-7684
321 Linden St, San Francisco, CA, 94102
custom, made-to-order & ready-to-wear corsets
Universal Studios Costume Dept (818) 777-2722
Rental, mfg., & alterations
Warner Bros. Studios Costume Dept (818) 954-1297
Bras, Panties, Lace, Garters, Stockings, Nylons, Pantyhose, Slips, Tights, Negligees, Nightgowns

Uniforms, Military

See Also: Badges, Patches & Buttons* Civil War Era* Military Props & Equipment* Military Surplus/Combat Clothes, Field Gear* Wardrobe, Antique/Historical
AA Surplus Sales Co., Inc. (323) 526-3622
2940 E. Olympic Blvd, Los Angeles, CA, 90023
US Military clothing, combat boots and accessories in used and new condition
surplusking@hotmail.com * www.aasurplus.com/
American Costume Corp. (818) 764-2239
1750s to present for film & TV industries
Costume Rentals Corporation (818) 753-3700
motion picture supplier & special order items
International Costume, Inc. (310) 320-6392
military uniforms & accessories
Lost Battalions (916) 221-2828
P.O. Box 478 Folsom, CA, 95763
WW I German & WW II German/Allied
Motion Picture Costume Company (818) 557-1247
uniforms & civilian wardrobe, 1775 to present
OPFOR Solutions, Inc (747) 666-7367
8100 Remmet Ave Unit #6, Canoga Park, CA, 91304
Opfor Solutions, Inc. brings you ethnic/military apparel from countries such as - Afghanistan, Iraq, Libya & more.
moe@opforsolutions.com * www.opforsolutions.com
RDD U.S.A. Inc. (213) 742-0666
4638 E Washington Blvd., Commerce, CA 90040
complete line of G. I. military uniforms & clothing
www.rddusa.com
The Russian Store/G & J Imports (818) 999-1257
7657 Winnetka Ave Ste 203, Canoga Park, CA, 91306
Sony Pictures Studios-Wardrobe (310) 244-5995
alterations, call (310) 244-7260
Supply Sergeant (323) 849-3744
503 N. Victory Blvd, Burbank, CA 91502
Military clothing including army uniforms, military uniforms, navy uniforms
david@jacksgt.com * www.supplysergeantshop.com
Western Costume Co. (818) 760-0900
World War II Impressions (562) 946-6768
12025 E Florence Ave #402, Santa Fe Springs, CA, 90670
Reproductions - By Appt Only.

Uniforms, Trades/Professional/Sports

See Also: Badges, Patches & Buttons* Clerical, Judicial, Academic Gowns/Apparel* Clowns* Costumes, International/Ethnic* Fireman Uniforms, Hats & Equipment* Sportswear* Uniforms, Military
Becnel Uniform Co. (213) 623-4522
758 S. San Pedro, Los Angeles, CA, 90014
police, transportation, industrial - also accessories & shoes
The Costume House (818) 508-9933
maid's, lab coats, nurses, waitresses, airline (60s, 70s)
Costume Rentals Corporation (818) 753-3700
motion picture supplier & special order items
Frank Bee Uniforms (800) 372-6523
3439 E. Tremont Ave, Bronx, NY, 10465
school uniforms, grad caps & gowns, police & law enforcement, military & camo, scouts
Glamour Uniform Shop (323) 666-2122
4951 W. Sunset Blvd, Los Angeles, CA, 90027
nurses, restaurant, mechanics, maids uniforms. sizes 3-56
LCW Props (818) 243-0707
school uniforms, others
Motion Picture Costume Company (818) 557-1247
uniforms & civilian wardrobe, 1775 to present

LISTINGS FOR THIS CATEGORY CONTINUE ON THE FOLLOWING PAGE

National Spirit   (800) 527-4366
6745 Lenox Center Court Ste 300, Memphis, TN, 38115
warm/cold weather cheerleader outfits, megaphones, pom-pons etc.

Professional Uniforms   (818) 242-3404
1102 E Colorado St, Glendale, CA, 91205
Medical

RDD U.S.A. Inc.   (213) 742-0666
4638 E Washington Blvd., Commerce, CA 90040
complete line of law enforcement and security uniforms & accessories
www.rddusa.com

Sony Pictures Studios-Wardrobe   (310) 244-5995
alterations, call (310) 244-7260

Sports Studio   (310) 559-3999
1831 W 208th St, Torrance, CA, 90501
Antique & contemporary sports uniforms

Supply Sergeant   (323) 849-3744
503 N. Victory Blvd, Burbank, CA 91502
david@jacksgt.com * www.supplysergeantshop.com

Tarpy Tailors   (310) 645-4694
9100 S Sepulveda Blvd Ste 103, Los Angeles, CA, 90045
airline/corporate pilot, flight attendant, customer service

The Team Supplier   (818) 571-1485
17423 Rushing Dr, Granada Hills, CA, 91344
team outfitting & apparel, embroidery, silk screening, numbering & lettering

Uniforms By Park Coats, Inc.   (718) 499-1182
790 3rd Ave, Brooklyn, NY, 11232
police, fire, EMS, coats, pants, shirts, hats, outerwear

Western Costume Co.   (818) 760-0900

Unions

See: Guilds, Unions, Societies, Associations

Upholstery Materials/Services

See Also: Fabrics Furniture & Art, Repair & Restoration* Furniture, Custom-made/Reproduction* Hardware, Decorative* Rubber & Foam Rubber* Slipcovers*

American Silk Mills   (305) 308-9411
2300 Chestnut Street 4th floor, Philadelphia, PA, 19103
US textile manufacturer and one of the largest suppliers of upholstery materials
to the furniture industry.
adriano.salucci@americansilk.com * www.sensuede.com

Diamond Foam & Fabric Co.   (323) 931-8148
611 S La Brea Ave, Los Angeles, CA, 90036
decorative fabrics & foam for upholstery, drapery & slipcovers, custom sewing
on premises
www.diamondfoamandfabric.com

Fine Custom Upholstery   (310) 837-5541
8929 National Blvd, Los Angeles, CA, 90034
leather upholstering

Larry St. John & Co.   (310) 630-5828
17021 S Broadway, Gardena, CA, 90248
Custom, heavily discounted, locally made upholstery materials and upholstery
services.
info@larrystjohn.com * www.larrystjohn.com

Leather Corral Inc   (818) 764-7880
13052 Raymer St., North Hollywood, CA, 91605
Upholstery supplies extending from vinyls, poly foam, carpet, headliner, leather
all the way to sewing threads.
leathercorral@yahoo.com * www.leathercorral.com

Lux Lounge EFR   (888) 247-4411
106 1/2 Judge John Aiso St #318, Los Angeles, CA, 90012
Upholstery Materials and Custom Upholstery Services
info@luxloungeefr.com * www.luxloungeefr.com

Omega/Cinema Props   (323) 466-8201

Pasadena Antique Warehouse   (626) 404-2422
1609 East Washington Blvd., Pasadena, CA, 91104
Full service and repair upholstery services for couches and sofas.
pasadenaantiquewarehouse@gmail.com *
www.pasadenaantiquewarehouse.com

Streamline Custom Upholstery Inc.   (562) 531-9119
11920 Garfield Ave, South Gate, CA, 90280
Reupholstery of antique chairs, sofas, headboards beds, ottomans, benches
etc.
streamline562@yahoo.com

Universal Studios Drapery Dept   (818) 777-2761
manufacturing

Warner Bros. Drapery, Upholstery & Flooring   (818) 954-1831
4000 Warner Blvd, Burbank, CA, 91522
Custom Furniture Manufacturing; Re-upholstery; Repair; Slip Covers; Fabric,
Vinyl & Leather Sales
wbsfdrapery@warnerbros.com * www.wbdrapery.com

ZG04 DECOR   (818) 853-8040
Custom Upholstery- Design made to customer specifications

Urinals

See: Bathroom Fixtures Plumbing Fixtures, Heating/Cooling Appliances*

Urns

See Also: Pottery

Bob Gail Special Events   (310) 202-5200
Our Urn Props can be used for any event!

Eric's Architectural Salvage, Wells Antique Tile   (213) 413-6800
2110 W Sunset Blvd, Los Angeles, CA, 90026
We have the largest selection of antique pottery and tile in the world.
ericstiques@aol.com * www.ericsarchitecturalsalvage.com

The Hand Prop Room LP.   (323) 931-1534

Jackson Shrub Supply, Inc.   (818) 982-0100
classic urns & contemporary urns, bontoc gourd urns, planter urns

Prop Services West   (818) 503-2790

Sony Pictures Studios-Prop House (Off Lot)   (310) 244-5999
burial urns, decorative urns, jardiniere urns, pottery urns, wall mounted urns

Universal Studios Property & Hardware Dept   (818) 777-2784
Many urns and prop urns for rent.

Vacu-forms/Vacu-forming

See Also: Staff Shops

Flix FX Inc.   (818) 765-3549
7327 Lankershim Blvd #4, N Hollywood, CA, 91605
Full vacuum forming services. Sculpting through trimming. Up to 5' x 10' and
pre printed vacuum forming
info@flixfx.com * www.flixfx.com

Warner Bros. Design Studio Scenic Art & Sign Shop   (818) 954-1815
4000 Warner Blvd, Burbank, CA, 91522
Thermal Former machine can pull up to 6'0 x 10'0 in plastic! We are ready for
any of your large scale project needs!
wbsigns@warnerbros.com * www.wbsignandscenic.com

Warner Bros. Studios Staff Shop   (818) 954-2269
Manufacturer of exterior & interior details used for the creation of sets in all
architectural styles & eras.

Vacuum Cleaners

AIR Designs   (818) 768-6639
Shop, Vintage, Gas Station, Car Wash

C. P. Valley   (323) 466-8201

Omega/Cinema Props   (323) 466-8201
Vacuum cleaners for rent, many periods.

Valves

See: Factory/Industrial Plumbing Fixtures, Heating/Cooling Appliances*

Vapor Lights

See: Caged Vapor Proof Lights

Vehicle Preparation Services

See Also: Special Effects, Equipment & Supplies

L. A. Prep, Inc.   (562) 595-8886
2700 Signal Pkwy, Signal Hill, CA, 90755
Complete vehicle preparation services

Rainbow Industries   (818) 786-9030
6911 Valjean Ave, Van Nuys, CA, 91406
Comprehensive car preparation facilities

Shelly Ward Enterprises   (818) 255-5850
7255 Radford Ave, N Hollywood, CA, 91605
camera rigging, stunt construction, car prep, car fabrication

Vehicle Effects   (818) 355-2676
7606 Clybourn Ave, Sun Valley, CA, 91352
Custom picture car modification and fabrication

Vehicle Wraps

See: Graphics, Digital & Large Format Printing

Vehicles

See Also: Aircraft, Charters & Aerial Services*
Ambulance/Paramedic* Children/Baby Accessories & Bedroom* Jet
Skis* Limousine Service* Military Props & Equipment* Motorcycles*
Nautical/Marine Services & Charters* Police Car, Police Motorcycle*
Production Vehicles/Trailers* Ramps, Automobile* RV Vehicles &
Travel Trailers, Equip & Parts* Transportation, Trucking and/or
Storage* Window Treatments* Towing Services

1A Action Picture Cars   **(818) 767-2355**
11040 Olinda St, Sun Valley, CA, 91352
picture vehicles, classics, exotics, late models, contemporary cars, wrecked
and collision recreation
rent@actionpicturecars.com * www.actionpicturecars.com

Action Antique Period Picture Cars   **(562) 693-5641**
2684 Turnbull Canyon Rd, City of Industry, CA, 91745
antique and classic cars & trucks, parts & garage items

Action Sets and Props / WonderWorks, Inc.   **(818) 992-8811**
Space shuttle & station, space suit, specialty props, miniatures, mechanical
effects, cityscape, miniature buildings

Advanced Fire & Rescue Services   **(661) 299-4801**
16654 Soledad Canyon Rd, #186 Canyon Country, 91387
Fire trucks, antique & modern, rescue trucks, onsite personnel, prof.
firefighters, EMTs, jaws of life
Eng12capt@yahoo.com * www.advancedfire.com

Art, Models & Props, Inc.   **(951) 206-9156**
1725 Marengo Ave, Pasadena, CA, 91103
Custom design/fabr. See ad in "Prop Design & Manufacturing"
modelsandprops@msn.com * www.artmodeltech.com

Castle Antiques & Design   **(855) 765-5800**
11924 Vose St, N Hollywood, CA, 91605
Classic Cars for rent.
info@castleantiques.net * www.castleprophouse.com

Classic Auto Rental Services   **(818) 905-6267**
15445 Ventura Blvd., Ste 60, Sherman Oaks, CA 91403
Classic Cars, Vintage Cars, Muscle Cars, Exotic Cars, Trucks, Motor Homes,
Busses, Motorcycles, Service Vehicles & Props.
classicautorental@gmail.com * www.classicautorental.com

Cornwell & Sheridan Picture Vehicles   **(310) 217-9060**
15700 S Broadway, Gardena, CA, 90248
Convertibles, Coupes, Sedans, Limos, Motorcycles
www.old-cars.net

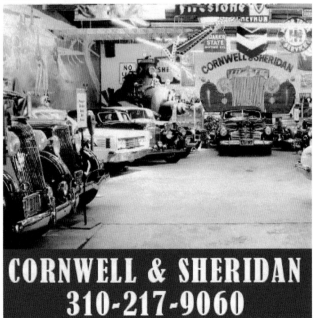

CORNWELL & SHERIDAN
310-217-9060

Fire In Motion   **(661) 510-5771**
27844 Ferguson Dr, Castaic, CA, 91384
Functional Pumpers, Ladder trucks, Ambulances, Suburban Battalion Chief and
Crown Vic.
jim@fireinmotion.net * www.fireinmotion.net

Galpin Motors Studio Rentals   **(323) 957-3333**
1763 N Ivar Ave, Hollywood, CA, 90028
Picture Vehicles. Period & contemporary. Specialize in new vehicles, all makes.
Prop/Set Dress Trucks & Wardrobe Cubes.
gsr@galpin.com * www.galpinstudiorentals.com

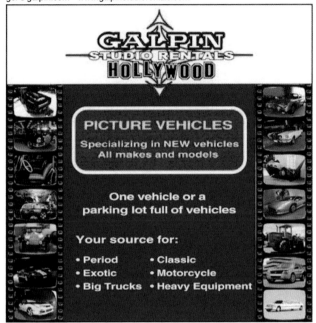

GALPIN STUDIO RENTALS HOLLYWOOD

PICTURE VEHICLES
Specializing in NEW vehicles
All makes and models

**One vehicle or a
parking lot full of vehicles**

Your source for:

• Period   • Classic
• Exotic   • Motorcycle
• Big Trucks   • Heavy Equipment

K4 Motorsports   **(818) 713-0552**
P.O. Box 8902, Calabasas, CA, 91372
Full NASCAR Racing Resources for Production, Features, T.V., and
Commercials; Race cars, haulers, pit equip., drivers.
www.k4motorsports.com

Michael Harper-Smith   **(818) 705-8655**
5375 Tampa Ave, Tarzana, CA, 91356
European picture vehicles, All owned by Michael.
mharperxke@aol.com * www.eurofilmcars.com

European Vehicles
British, German, Italian, French
From Common to Unusual

**DISPLAY ADS AND LISTINGS FOR THIS CATEGORY
CONTINUE ON THE FOLLOWING PAGE**

MovieMoto.com   **(626) 359-0016**
16015 Adelante St, Irwindale, CA, 91702
Rare, Odd, Classic, Exotic, Unknown MOTORCYCLE RENTALS. Specializing in Italian marks.
www.MovieMoto.com

Mr. Vintage Machine   **(213) 369-0281**
Call for Appointment, Los Angeles, CA 90027
Vintage vehicles, hot rods, custom classics, motorcycles, choppers, low riders, luxury & specialty cars
gabriel@mistervintagemachine.com * www.mistervintagemachine.com

Sterndahl Enterprises, Inc.   **(818) 834-8199**
11861 Branford St, Sun Valley, CA, 91352
traffic control equipment, signage, barricades, striping, trucks & bobcats
www.sterndahl.com

Studio Picture Vehicles, Inc   **(818) 765-1201**
7502 Wheatland Ave, Sun Valley, CA, 91352
police, ambulance
studiopicturevehicles@yahoo.com * www.studiopicturevehicles.com

Universal Studios Transportation   **(818) 777-2966**
100 Universal City Plaza, Universal City, CA, 91608
range of vehicles available, SUVs to tractor trailers
universal.transpo@nbcuni.com * www.filmmakersdestination.com

The Wood N' Carr   **(562) 498-8730**
2345 Walnut Ave, Signal Hill, CA, 90755
woodies from 30s-50s, restored old beach buggies

Vending Machines

AIR Designs   **(818) 768-6639**
Soda, Sandwich, Coffee, Ice Cream Dispensers/Ice Cream Machines, Popcorn, Candy, Snack

Alley Cats Studio Rentals   **(818) 982-9178**
candy, soda/beverage, snacks, cigarettes, subway/train ticket, gumball

C. P. Valley   **(323) 466-8201**
Candy vending machines, soda vending machines, cigarette vending machines, candy machines, and more. Antique to modern.

E.C. Prop Rentals   **(818) 764-2008**
newspaper, plastic & metal

History For Hire, Inc.   **(818) 765-7767**
vintage

Lennie Marvin Enterprises, Inc. (Prop Heaven)   **(818) 841-5882**
period-modern, gumballs, soda, snacks, tampons, condoms

RC Vintage, Inc.   **(818) 765-7107**
gumball, beverage to food. Modern Cola, and Snack Cleared art work

Sony Pictures Studios-Prop House (Off Lot)   **(310) 244-5999**
large selection, food, drink etc., candy vending machine, cigarette vending machine,

Vendor Carts & Concession Counters

See Also: Carnival Dressing/Supplies Circus Equipment/Dressing/Costumes* Events, Decorations, Supplies & Services* Produce Carts* Taco Carts (Propmaster & Set)* Vending Machines* Food, Food Stylists*

AIR Designs   **(818) 768-6639**
Concession Counters, Popcorn, Flower, Espresso, Hot Dog, Taco, Mall

Alley Cats Studio Rentals   **(818) 982-9178**
hot dog, coffee, candy, popcorn, churro, flower, mail, cell phone display

Amusement Svcs/Candyland Amusements   **(818) 266-4056**
18653 Ventura Blvd Ste 235, Tarzana, CA, 91356
Candy applies, shaved ice, snow cones, cotton candy, Harry's diner, many carts, booths, vendors, kiosks, counters and themed tables
www.candylandamusements.com

C. P. Valley   **(323) 466-8201**
Hot dog carts, snow cone carts, bicycle carts, popcorn carts, produce carts, wooden carts, steel carts, and more.

The Hand Prop Room LP.   **(323) 931-1534**
popcorn, hot dog, pretzel, cotton candy

History For Hire, Inc.   **(818) 765-7767**
plain & fancy

L. A. Party Works   **(888) 527-2789**
9712 Alpaca St, S El Monte, CA, 91733
Hot dog carts, popcorn carts, cotton candy carts, lemonade carts, bear making carts & more. Vancouver tel. 604-589-4101.
partyworks@aol.com * www.partyworksusa.com

LCW Props   **(818) 243-0707**
Multiple Styles

Lennie Marvin Enterprises, Inc. (Prop Heaven)   **(818) 841-5882**
hot dog, popcorn, coffee, chestnut, ice cream, floral, cot. cand

RC Vintage, Inc.   **(818) 765-7107**
Hot Dog Ice cream, popcorn, peanut, chestnut, cot. candy, 20s to present, mall carts

Sony Pictures Studios-Prop House (Off Lot)   **(310) 244-5999**

Universal Studios Property & Hardware Dept   **(818) 777-2784**
Prop vendor carts and prop concession counters/concession stands for rent.

Veneer

See: Paneling, Veneers & Laminates

Venetian & Vertical Blinds

See: Window Treatments

Ventriloquist Figures

See: Puppets, Marionettes, Automata, Animatronics

Victrolas/Gramophones

See Also: Phonographs
The Hand Prop Room LP.   **(323) 931-1534**
antique period, lrg sel.
History For Hire, Inc.   **(818) 765-7767**
RC Vintage, Inc.   **(818) 765-7107**
Large Brass Horn, maroon flower victrolas, wind up gramophones

Video 24fps / Sync System / D.D.I.

See Also: Video Camera Equipment & Services
24Frame.com, Inc.   **(213) 745-2411**
944 Venice Blvd, Los Angeles, CA, 90015
24Frame/24P sync playback of all video & computer
info@24frame.com * www.24frame.com

● Vintage, Contemporary &
High-Tech Televisions
or Computer Monitors

● 2D & 3D Interactive Computer
Graphics & Animations

● 24 Frame Playback for All
Video & Computer
Requirements

Let Us Sync You Up!

24frame.com, Inc.
944 Venice Boulevard
Los Angeles CA 90015

(213) 745-2411

Fax (213) 745-2410
info@24frame.com

Warner Bros. Studios Production Sound &   **(818) 954-2511**
Video
4000 Warner Blvd, Burbank, CA, 91522
A/V Equipment Rental, Design, Presentations, Install & Support; Visual Display
Creation; Communication
wbsfproductionsound@warnerbros.com * www.wbsoundandvideo.com

Video Camera Equipment & Services

See Also: Camera Equipment Radio/TV Station* Video 24fps / Sync
System / D.D.I.*
24Frame.com, Inc.   **(213) 745-2411**
944 Venice Blvd, Los Angeles, CA, 90015
televisions, monitors, decks, switchers, sync
info@24frame.com * www.24frame.com
Bexel   **(818) 565-4399**
2701 N. Ontario St, Burbank, CA, 91504
camera packages
CCI Digital   **(818) 562-6300**
2921 W. Alameda Ave, Burbank, CA, 91505
post production rentals & services
Innovision Optics   **(310) 453-4866**
1834 Broadway, Santa Monica, CA, 90404
camera motion control systems, special purpose lens systems
Runway   **(310) 636-2000**
1330 N Vine St, Hollywood, CA, 90028
camera packages
Sim Digital   **(323) 978-9000**
738 N Cahuenga, Hollywood, CA, 90038
camera packages

Sweetwater   **(818) 902-9500**
7635 Airport Business Park Way, Van Nuys, CA, 91406
video production truck package, video projection, flypacks
VER Video Equipment Rentals   **(800) 794-1407**
912 Ruberta Ave, Glendale, CA, 91201
Located nationwide, camera packages, hi-def, AV/audio
Westcoast Video Productions, Inc.   **(818) 785-8033**
14141 Covello St, Ste 9A, Van Nuys, CA, 91405
broadcast video remote facility, equip. & crew pkgs.
Wintech Video   **(818) 501-6565**
7625 Hayvenhurst Ste 22, Van Nuys, CA, 91406
equip., rentals, production crew & equip. pkgs.
World Wide Digital Services   **(818) 500-7559**
1819 Dana Unit E, Glendale, CA, 91201
camera & recording packages

Video Equipment

See Also: Audio/Visual Film Equipment Camera Equipment* Control
Boards* Editing Equipment & Services* Press Equipment*
24Frame.com, Inc.   **(213) 745-2411**
944 Venice Blvd, Los Angeles, CA, 90015
televisions, monitors, decks, switchers, sync
info@24frame.com * www.24frame.com
Astro Audio Video Lighting, Inc.   **(818) 549-9915**
6615 San Fernando Rd, Glendale, CA, 91201
High Def, projectors, recorders, players, screens, plasmas, LED video walls
www.astroavl.com
LCW Props   **(818) 243-0707**
Large Selection, Monitors, Security, LCD / Plasma, Video Projection, Video
Walls
Sony Pictures Studios-Prop House (Off Lot)   **(310) 244-5999**
televisions, tape recorders, tape players, AV VCR player, video cassette
recorders, AV Viewer, Video rewinder
Warner Bros. Studios Production Sound &   **(818) 954-2511**
Video
4000 Warner Blvd, Burbank, CA, 91522
All types of A/V Equipment Rental, Design, Presentations, Install & Support;
Visual Display Creation; Communication
wbsfproductionsound@warnerbros.com * www.wbsoundandvideo.com
Woody's Electrical Props   **(818) 503-1940**
Period to futuristic. Fantasy sets, military sets, industrial sets, air tower/mission
control.

Video Games

See Also: Arcade Equipment, Games & Rides
Arcade Amusements   **(866) 576-8878**
802 West Washington Ave Ste E, Escondido, CA, 92025-1644
Planning a Party? How about having some games there? How about 10? How
about 20? How about... Well, you get the idea.
phil@arcadeamusements.com * www.arcadeamusements.com
L. A. Party Works   **(888) 527-2789**
9712 Alpaca St, S El Monte, CA, 91733
in Vancouver tel. 604-589-14101. X-Box, PS3, & Wii, LaserTag, RockWall,
V.R.,Gyros
partyworks@aol.com * www.partyworksusa.com
Lennie Marvin Enterprises, Inc. (Prop Heaven)   **(818) 841-5882**
period to modern, arcade equip.
RC Vintage, Inc.   **(818) 765-7107**
vintage/modern, practical, 1970s-1990s Cleared Art Large Selection. Sit Down
Motorcycle and Race Car games

Video Rental/Sales Store

See Also: Cash Registers Counters* Credit Card Imprint Machine*
Steel Folding Gates & Roll-Up Doors* Store Shelf Units & Shelving*
Cinefile   **(310) 312-8836**
11280 Santa Monica Blvd, Los Angeles, CA, 90025
Euro-trash, Italian horror, big goofy monsters
Continental Shop   **(310) 453-8655**
1619 Wilshire Blvd, Santa Monica, CA, 90403
British films, TV series, specials
Eddie Brandt's Saturday Matinee   **(818) 506-4242**
5006 Vineland Ave, N. Hollywood, CA, 91601
Tues.-Fri. 1:00-6:00 pm Sat. 8:30am - 5:00 pm. vintage & hard to find video
Movies and More   **(310) 391-6206**
4036 Centinela Ave, W Los Angeles, CA, 90066
foreign, action, wrestling, comedy, horror, cult (2 locations)
Vidiots   **(310) 392-8508**
302 Pico Blvd, Santa Monica, CA, 90405
video, DVD; foreign, documentaries, indep. & mainstream titles, cult, gay &
lesbian, etc.

Video Store Dressing

See Also: Video Rental/Sales Store
AIR Designs (818) 768-6639
Wall Racks, Counters, Display Units, VCR Cases, CD's, Records, Signs
Alley Cats Studio Rentals (818) 982-9178
DVD store counters & racks, signs, DVDs, CDs, VHS Tapes, Cassette Tapes
C. P. Valley (323) 466-8201
Video rack, video cartridge stand, VHS boxes, VHS tapes and more.
LCW Props (818) 243-0707
Media, Shelving, Cases, POS System, Beta, VHS, DVD, CD, Video Games

Vintage Clothing

See: Jewelry, Costume* Jewelry, Fine/Reproduction* Wardrobe, Vintage

Vinyl

See: Clear Vinyl* Fabrics* Phonograph Records* Plastics, Materials & Fabrication

Vinyl Letters

See: Signs

Virtual Reality Games

See: Arcade Equipment, Games & Rides

Volleyball Setup

The Hand Prop Room LP. (323) 931-1534
Universal Studios Property & Hardware Dept (818) 777-2784
Volleyball set up for rent.

Voting

See Also: Game Show Electronics & Equipment
County of L.A. Registrar/Recorder (800) 815-2666
12400 Imperial Hwy, Norwalk, CA, 90650
Voting booth rentals
LCW Props (818) 243-0707
Voting Booths, Stanchions, Swags, Flags, Desks
Sony Pictures Studios-Prop House (Off Lot) (310) 244-5999
ballot boxes

Wagons

See Also: Gypsy Wagon* Horses, Horse Equipment, Livestock* Western Dressing
C. P. Valley (323) 466-8201
large wagon wheels, small wagon wheels; Hollywood's largest selection!
Caravan West Productions (661) 268-8300
35660 Jayhawker Rd, Aqua Dulce, CA, 91390
historically accurate Western wagons, buckboards, chuckwagons, Covered stagecoach
caravanwest@earthlink.net * www.caravanwest.com
Jackson Shrub Supply, Inc. (818) 982-0100
wagons & buggies
Movin' On Livestock (661) 252-8654
20527 Soledad St, Canyon Country, CA, 91351
livestock, many wagons & stagecoaches, jail wagon too
Sony Pictures Studios-Prop House (Off Lot) (310) 244-5999
Universal Studios Property & Hardware Dept (818) 777-2784
Western wagons, fancy wagons, beat up wagons, covered wagons and more for rent.

Waiting Room

See Also: Lobby Seating
Alpha Companies - Spellman Desk Co. (818) 504-9090
medical waiting room dressing, doctors office dressing, doctors office furniture

Wakeboard

See: Surfboard, Wakeboard

Walk Around Characters

See: Animal Costumes & Walk Around Characters* Prop Design & Manufacturing

Walkie-Talkies

See Also: Radios* Telephones* Telephones, Cellular
Airwaves Wireless (818) 501-8200
13400 Riverside Dr. # 103 Sherman Oaks, CA 91423
Cellular phones, cellphones, tablets, laptops, iPhones, iPads, dummy phones, walkies, Wi-Fi, satellite phones, macbooks
anita@airwaveswireless.com * www.airwaveswireless.com
Castex Rentals (323) 462-1468
1044 N. Cole Ave, Hollywood, CA, 90038
Motorola CP200, headsets, surveillance kits, walkie-talkies
service@castexrentals.com * www.castexrentals.com
E.C. Prop Rentals (818) 764-2008
police/security type w/charging stands/racks
The Hand Prop Room LP. (323) 931-1534
military, police, civilian, real & prop
History For Hire, Inc. (818) 765-7767
police, militiary, civilian
LCW Props (818) 243-0707
Military, Security, Personal, CB Radios, Home Base
Warner Bros. Studios Production Sound & Video (818) 954-2511
4000 Warner Blvd, Burbank, CA, 91522
A/V Equipment Rental, Design, Presentations, Install & Support; Visual Display Creation; Communication
wbsfproductionsound@warnerbros.com * www.wbsoundandvideo.com

Walking Sticks

See: Canes

Wall "O" Fects

See: Masks

Wall Coverings

See Also: Tapestry Wall Hangings
Adelphi (518) 284-9066
102 Main St, POB 135, Sharon Springs, NY, 13459
period wallpaper hand-made by wood blocks
American Silk Mills (305) 308-9411
2300 Chestnut Street 4th floor, Philadelphia, PA, 19103
United States manufacturer of the most exquisite textiles since 1896.
adriano.salucci@americansilk.com * www.sensuede.com
Bradbury & Bradbury Art Wallpapers (707) 746-1900
P.O. Box 155, Benicia, CA, 94510
Historic wallpapers from the Victorian, Arts & Crafts, Art Deco & Modern styles
Linoleum City, Inc. (323) 469-0063
4849 Santa Monica Blvd, Hollywood, CA, 90029
Decorative wall cork, bulletin board cork. No wallpaper.
sales@linocity.com * www.linoleumcity.com

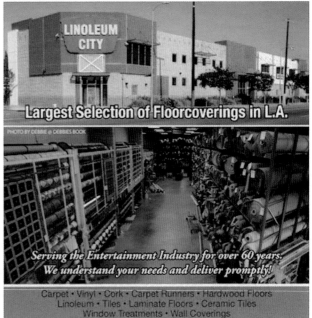

LINOLEUM CITY

Largest Selection of Floorcoverings in L.A.

PHOTO BY DEBBIE @ DEBBIES BOOK

Serving the Entertainment Industry for over 60 years.
We understand your needs and deliver promptly!

Carpet • Vinyl • Cork • Carpet Runners • Hardwood Floors
Linoleum • Tiles • Laminate Floors • Ceramic Tiles
Window Treatments • Wall Coverings

Oceanic Arts (562) 698-6960
Native Tropical Mattings woven from Palm Leaves, Banana Leaves, Bamboo.
17 Varieties. Lauhala in 5 sizes.
Outwater Plastics Industries (800) 248-2067
4720 W Van Buren, Phoenix, AZ, 85043
catalog sales; plastics. stamped steel, pressed tin, embossed vinyl
Prop Services West (818) 503-2790
Pulp Art Surfaces (818) 655-5804
4021 Radford Ave, Studio City, CA, 91604
Finished and unfinished wall skins
Secondhand Rose (212) 393-9002
230 5th Ave Ste #510, New York, NY, 10001
vintage wallpaper
Wallpaper City & Flooring (310) 393-9422
1758 Lincoln Blvd, Santa Monica, CA, 90404
especially vintage, American/European, also will fabricate
Worlds of Wow (817) 380-4215
2126 Hamilton Rd, Argyle, TX, 76226
Custom designed digital wall covering.
www.worldsofwow.com

Wall Hangings

See: Paintings/Prints* Photographs* Posters,
Art/Movie/Travel/Wanted Etc.* Tapestry Wall Hangings* Wall
Coverings

Wall Maps

See: Maps

Wallpaper

See: Wall Coverings

Wanted Posters

See: Police Equipment* Posters, Art/Movie/Travel/Wanted Etc.

Wardrobe

See Also: Costume Rental Houses* Costumes* Wardrobe,
Accessories* Wardrobe, Antique/Historical* Wardrobe, Construction
& Alterations* Wardrobe, Contemporary* Wardrobe,
International/Ethnic* Wardrobe, Vintage
Action Sets and Props / WonderWorks, Inc. (818) 992-8811
Space shuttle & station, space suit, specialty props, miniatures, mechanical
effects, cityscape, miniature buildings
Adele's of Hollywood (323) 663-2231
American Costume Corp. (818) 764-2239
1770s through 1970s for film & TV industries
The Costume House (818) 508-9933
1880s-1980s civilian, men/women/children
Costume Rentals Corporation (818) 753-3700
motion picture supplier & special order items
Des Kohan (323) 857-0200
671 Cloverdale, Los Angeles, CA, 90036
designer clothing, vintage jewelry & home accessories, celebrity stylists
available
Global Effects, Inc. (818) 503-9273
medieval replicas, science fiction, futuristic, space suits
Gohn Bros. (574) 825-2400
105 S. Main St, P.O. Box 1110, Middlebury, IN, 46540
Fabrics and needs of the Amish community
History For Hire, Inc. (818) 765-7767
full racks, rented as set dressing only
LCW Props (818) 243-0707
Call For An Updated Listing
The New Mart (213) 627-0671
127 E 9th St, Los Angeles, CA, 90015
wholesale trade, 90+ agents rep 100s of directional manufacturers; call for
tenant directory
OPFOR Solutions, Inc (747) 666-7367
8100 Remmet Ave Unit #6, Canoga Park, CA, 91304
Opfor Solutions, Inc. brings you ethnic/military apparel from countries such as -
Afghanistan, Iraq, Libya & more.
moe@opforsolutions.com * www.opforsolutions.com
RDD U.S.A. Inc. (213) 742-0666
4638 E Washington Blvd., Commerce, CA 90040
military jackets, rain & cold weather clothing, dress jackets
www.rddusa.com
Returner Rentals (818) 506-7695

ReVamp (213) 488-3387
818 South Broadway Ste 801, Los Angeles, CA, 90014
Vintage reproductions for men & women, focusing on 1910-1950
info@revampvintage.com * www.revampvintage.com
Roxy Deluxe (818) 487-7800
1860-1970 clothing accessories & jewelry
Sony Pictures Studios-Wardrobe (310) 244-5995
alterations, call (310) 244-7260
Syren (213) 989-0334
2809 1/2 W Sunset Blvd, Los Angeles, CA, 90026
M/W rubber clothing, variety of colors/styles
Universal Studios Costume Dept (818) 777-2722
Rental, mfg., & alterations
Used Church Items, Religious Rentals (239) 992-5737
216 Cumer Road, McDonald, PA, 15057
Catholic Church Priest Vestments, Religious Robe, Liturgical, Christian, Clergy
Apparel, Chasuble, Stole, Cope, Dalmatic
warehouse@religiousrentals.com * www.religiousrentals.com
The Way We Wore, Inc. Retail (323) 937-0878
334 S La Brea Ave, Los Angeles, CA, 90036
huge sel. of women's clothing: access. from 1910-1979. hard-to-find items like
bathing suits, stockings etc.
Western Costume Co. (818) 760-0900

Wardrobe Racks

See: Garment Racks

Wardrobe Supplies

See: Costume/Wardrobe/Sewing Supplies

Wardrobe, Accessories

See Also: Archery Equipment, Training* Armor, Chainmail, Suits of
Armor* Badges, Patches & Buttons* Bling* Crowns & Tiaras* Doctor's
Bags* Environmental (Cool/Heat) Suits* Eyewear, Glasses,
Sunglasses, 3D* Fabric Dyeing/Tie Dyeing/Painting/Aging* Feathers*
Firearms, Gunsmith, Firearm Choreography* Fireman Uniforms, Hats
& Equipment* Flameproofing* Fur, Artificial & Real* Headdresses*
Headwear - Hats, Bonnets, Caps, Helmets Etc.* Jewelry, Costume*
Jewelry, Fine/Reproduction* Keys & Locks* Knickers* Leather
(Clothing, Accessories, Materials)* Lunch Boxes* Pom Pons* Trims,
Fringe, Tassels, Beading Etc.* Umbrellas, Hand & Parasols*
Underwear & Lingerie, Bloomers, Corsets, Etc.* Weaponry,
Historical* Weaponry, Medieval* Weapons* Western Wear* Wigs*
Steam Punk
The Costume House (818) 508-9933
hats, purses, jewelry, shoes, vintage purses, vintage shoes, vintage ties,
vintage hats
Early Halloween (212) 691-2933
130 West 25th St, 11th Floor, New York, NY, 10001
Neckties, etc.; old stock never worn 1940-50
The Hand Prop Room LP. (323) 931-1534
period-present, jewelry, hair clips, hat pins
Helen Uffner Vintage Clothing LLC (718) 937-0220
authentic 1860s to 1970s M/W/children
History For Hire, Inc. (818) 765-7767
gloves, collars & cuffs, hair clips, etc.
Ob-jects (818) 351-4200
OPFOR Solutions, Inc (747) 666-7367
8100 Remmet Ave Unit #6, Canoga Park, CA, 91304
Opfor Solutions, Inc. brings you ethnic/military apparel from countries such as -
Afghanistan, Iraq, Libya & more.
moe@opforsolutions.com * www.opforsolutions.com
Screaming Mimi's (212) 677-6464
382 Lafayette St, New York, NY, 10003
vintage clothing for men & women 1940s - 1980s
Sony Pictures Studios-Prop House (Off Lot) (310) 244-5999
Universal Studios Costume Dept (818) 777-2722
Rental, mfg., & alterations
Western Costume Co. (818) 760-0900

Wardrobe, Antique/Historical

See Also: Native American

Amazon Drygoods   (812) 852-1780
3788 Wilson St, Osgood, IN 47037
catalog sales; 19 C. wardrobe/patterns, home access., books. clothing, access, footwear

American Costume Corp.   (818) 764-2239
1770s through 1970s for film & TV industry

Black Swan Designs   (760) 789-2299
17228 Voorhes Ln, Ramona, CA, 92065
men/women Dark Ages, Medieval & Renaissance; web sales ONLY via www.historicenterprises.com

Blockade Runner   (931) 389-6294
1027 Bell Buckle Wartrace Rd, Wartrace, TN, 37183
Antebellum, Southern US authentic uniforms & civilian wear, Civil War research center

The Costume House   (818) 508-9933
clothes, 1870s to 1980's & medieval & colonial costumes

Fall Creek Corporation   (765) 482-1861
PO Box 92, Whitestown, IN, 46075
Civil War era, military & civilian. leather clothing, civil war uniforms, shoes, accessories
ajfulks@fcsutler.com * www.fcsutler.com

Jas. Townsend & Son, Inc.   (574) 594-5852
133 N 1st St, P.O. Box 415, Pierceton, IN, 46562
catalog sales; American Colonial period inspired reprod. of wardrobe & household items, books/patterns of Colonial perio

Make Believe, Inc.   (310) 396-6785
We also sell masks, wigs, theatrical makeup & access. historical/biblical figures, Renaissance,18th-19th centuries

The Smoke & Fire Co.   (800) 766-5334
27 N River Rd, Waterville, OH, 43566
Supplies for Colonial re-enactors, patterns, clothes, books

Sword & Stone   (818) 562-6548
Medieval tiaras, crowns, sceptres, boots, shoes

Used Church Items, Religious Rentals   (239) 992-5737
216 Cumer Road, McDonald, PA, 15057
Church Robes, Catholic Priest Vestments, Pope, Bishop, Pastor, Deacon, Minister, Vicar, Clergy, Vintage Clothing, Mitre.
warehouse@religiousrentals.com * www.religiousrentals.com

Western Costume Co.   (818) 760-0900

Wardrobe, Construction & Alterations

See Also: Costume Rental Houses Costume/Wardrobe/Sewing Supplies* Costumes* Wardrobe* Wardrobe, Accessories*

The Costume House   (818) 508-9933
work room, will built to your design, wardrobe alterations on site, fitting rooms available

Costume Rentals Corporation   (818) 753-3700
motion picture supplier & special order items

JFF Uniforms-Costumes   (310) 320-1327
557 Van Ness Ave, Torrance, CA, 90501
Custom garments 1-10,000 pcs made from sketch or sample. Period, military, modern & more.

Milt & Edie's   (818) 846-4734
4021 W Alameda at Pass, Burbank, CA, 91505
Tailoring & Alterations available 24/7/365. Instant alterations available at no extra charge.
info@miltandedies.com * www.miltandedies.com

Universal Studios Costume Dept   (818) 777-2722
Rental, mfg., & alterations

Warner Bros. Studios Costume Dept   (818) 954-1297
Made-to-order mens tailoring & ladies dressmaking, expert alterations, Custom manufacturing, Repairs

Western Costume Co.   (818) 760-0900

Wardrobe, Contemporary

See Also: Costume Rental Houses

American Rag Cie   (323) 935-3154
150 S. La Brea, Los Angeles, CA, 90036
clothing, shoes, hats, accessories
www.amrag.com

California Market Center   (213) 630-3600
110 E. 9th St, Los Angeles, CA, 90079
1,000+ wholesale showrooms for registered buyers, see web site for directory, info desk (213) 630-3600
www.californiamarketcenter.com

Garment District Alliance   (212) 764-9600
209 W. 38th St, 2nd Floor, New York, NY, 10018
promotes garment district, our website lists resources/contacts. Assists with business Improvement.
www.fashioncenter.com

LCW Props   (818) 243-0707
Call For An Updated Listing

Los Angeles Fashion District   (213) 488-1153
319 E Olympic Blvd, Los Angeles, CA, 90015
website/directory lists shops by types

Ravishing Resale   (323) 655-8480
8127 W 3rd St, Los Angeles, CA, 90048
high quality & designer

Sony Pictures Studios-Wardrobe   (310) 244-5995
alterations, call (310) 244-7260

Warner Bros. Studios Costume Dept   (818) 954-1297
Collection of period & contemporary costumes for rent categorized by era, decade and style

Western Costume Co.   (818) 760-0900

Wardrobe, International/Ethnic

See Also: Costumes, International/Ethnic

Alberene Royal Mail   **(800) 843-9078**
catalog sales; books, clan tartans/prints/mugs, pub dressing

The Costume House   **(818) 508-9933**
Scottish, Japanese kimonos & obis

OPFOR Solutions, Inc   **(747) 666-7367**
8100 Remmet Ave Unit #6, Canoga Park, CA, 91304
Opfor Solutions, Inc. brings you ethnic/military apparel from countries such as - Afghanistan, Iraq, Libya & more.
moe@opforsolutions.com * www.opforsolutions.com

OPFOR SOLUTIONS INC.

INTERNATIONAL MILITARY COSTUMES · TRADITIONAL COSTUMES
PROPS · ATMOSPHERICS

MIDDLE EAST · SOUTH AFRICA · SOUTH AMERICA · ASIA

R.P. Blandford & Son, Ltd.   **(909) 483-1070**
8439 White Oak Ave. Ste 107, Rancho Cucamonga, CA, 91730
Scottish, clan tartans, accessories, bagpipes, etc.

The Tartan Patch   **(714) 841-1860**
Call for Appt
Ethnic Scottish/Irish apparel

Western Costume Co.   **(818) 760-0900**

Wm. Glen & Son   **(415) 989-5458**
360 Sutter St, San Francisco, CA, 94108
Retail sales; ethnic Scottish apparel for M/W/Children. Kilt wear and more for all tartans and clans.

Wardrobe, Studio Services

See Also: Expendables* Grip Equipment* Stages/Studios, Film/TV/Theatre/Events* Transportation, Trucking and/or Storage* Heavy Machinery, Equipment & Specialists

Alandales   **(310) 838-5100**
9715 Washington Blvd., Culver City, CA 90232
Men's apparel

American Rag Cie   **(323) 935-3154**
150 S. La Brea, Los Angeles, CA, 90036
Men's & women's vintage & designer clothing
www.amrag.com

Barney's New York - Beverly Hills   **(310) 777-5709**
9570 Wilshire Blvd., Beverly Hills, CA 90212
Men's & women's apparel, 4th floor

Barney's New York - New York   **(212) 833-2136**
660 Madison Ave., New York, NY 10021
Men's & women's apparel

Bloomingdale's - Beverly Center   **(310) 277-5555**
8500 Beverly Blvd., Los Angeles, CA 90048
Full line of apparel

Bloomingdale's - Fashion Square   **(818) 325-2301**
14060 Riverside Dr., Sherman Oaks, CA 91423
Full line of apparel

Bloomingdale's - New York City   **(212) 705-3673**
155 East 60th Street, Floor #3 on Bridge, New York, NY 10022
Full line of apparel

Carroll & Co.   **(310) 273-9060**
425 N. Canon Dr., Beverly Hills, CA 90210

Emporio Armani   **(310) 271-7790**
9533 Brighton Way, Beverly Hills, CA 90210

Ermenegildo Zegna   **(310) 247-8827**
337 N. Rodeo Dr., Beverly Hills, CA 90210
Men's apparel

Giorgio Armani   **(310) 271-5555**
436 N. Rodeo Dr., Beverly Hills, CA 90210
Men's & women's apparel

Hugo Boss   **(310) 859-2888**
414 N. Rodeo Dr., Beverly Hills, CA 90210
Ask for marketing contact. Studio services & product placement

Italian Fashion Group - di Stefano Suits   **(213) 622-7756**
1414 Santee St., Los Angeles, CA 90015
Ready made and custom men's wear; shirts, suits, tuxedos, contemporary & period wardrobe.

Macy's - Beverly Center   **(310) 854-6655**
8500 Beverly Blvd., Los Angeles, CA 90048
Women's, 7th Floor (310) 659-9660 - Men's, 1st Floor (310) 659-4752

Macy's - Fashion Square   **(818) 788-8350**
14000 Riverside Dr., Sherman Oaks, CA 91367
Full line of apparel

Neiman Marcus   **(310) 975-4336**
9700 Wilshire Blvd., Beverly Hills, CA 90212
Men's & women's apparel, also try (310) 550-5900 x4336

Nordstrom - Galleria at South Bay   **(310) 750-1459**
1835 Hawthorne Blvd., Redondo Beach, CA 90278
Full line of apparel

Nordstrom - Westfield Topanga   **(818) 592-4565**
21725 Victory Blvd., Canoga Park, CA 91303
Full line of apparel

Nordstrom - Westside Pavilion   **(310) 254-1670**
10830 W. Pico Blvd., Los Angeles, CA 90064
Full line of apparel

Polo/Ralph Lauren   **(310) 281-7200**
444 N. Rodeo Dr., Beverly Hills, CA 90210

Rochester Big & Tall   **(310) 274-9468**
9737 Wilshire Blvd., Beverly Hills, CA 90212
Men's apparel, specializing in big & tall sizes

Ron Herman   **(323) 653-3221**
8100 Melrose Ave, Los Angeles, CA 90046
Call to set up account first, extension 230

Saks Fifth Avenue - Beverly Hills   **(310) 271-6726**
9600 Wilshire Blvd., Beverly Hills, CA 90212
Full line of apparel

Saks Fifth Avenue - New York   **(212) 940-4324**
611 Fifth Avenue, New York, NY 10022
Full line of apparel

Sy Devore   **(818) 783-2700**
12930 Ventura Blvd., Studio City, CA 91604
Men's apparel

Wardrobe, Vintage

American Costume Corp.   **(818) 764-2239**
1770s through 1970s for film & TV industry

American Rag Cie   **(323) 935-3154**
150 S. La Brea, Los Angeles, CA, 90036
fashionable vintage men's & women's, 50s - 80s styles
www.amrag.com

Armani Wells   **(818) 985-5899**
12404 Ventura Blvd, Studio City, CA, 91604
Men's high fashion at 60% to 90% below retail; new & vintage

Buffalo Exchange   **(323) 938-8604**
131 N. La Brea Ave, Los Angeles, CA, 90036
chic apparel recycler, buy, sell, trade, also Sherman Oaks location (818) 783-3420

Catherine Nash's Closet   **(520) 620-6613**
1102 W. Huron St, Tucson, AZ, 85745
wholesale to Industry only: finest quality vintage clothing, 1860s-1970s

The Costume House   **(818) 508-9933**
genuine & original, 1870s to 1880s/Renaissance, childrens vintage clothing, womens vintage clothing

Decades   **(323) 655-0223**
8214 Melrose Ave, Los Angeles, CA, 90046
designer 60s-80s; Decadestwo has contemp. couture resale

Early Halloween   **(212) 691-2933**
130 West 25th St, 11th Floor, New York, NY, 10001
men/women/child 1900-1960

Helen Uffner Vintage Clothing LLC   **(718) 937-0220**
authentic 1850-1973 M/W/children apparel & accessories

International Costume, Inc.   **(310) 320-6392**
men's & women's, full line of vintage clothing

LISTINGS FOR THIS CATEGORY CONTINUE ON THE FOLLOWING PAGE

Jet Rag (323) 939-0528
825 N La Brea Ave, Hollywood, CA, 90038
Lily Et Cie (310) 724-5757
9044 Burton Way, Beverly Hills, CA, 90211
ladies designer vintage
Maxfield (310) 274-8800
8825 Melrose Ave, Los Angeles, CA, 90069
largest sel. of vintage Hermes items
Meow (562) 438-8990
2210 E 4th St, Long Beach, CA, 90814
original "never worn" 1940s-80 men/women/kid apparel/accessories
Ozzie Dots - Vintage Clothing & Costumes (323) 663-2867
4637 Hollywood Blvd, Los Angeles, CA, 90027
Victorian to 70s, full line of access, open 7 days
Palace Costume & Prop Co. (323) 651-5458
men, women, children 1850s-1980s
The Paper Bag Princess, Inc. (310) 385-9036
8818 W Olympic Blvd, Beverly Hills, CA, 90211
designer vintage, also construction/custom couture, red carpet design
Playclothes (818) 557-8447
3100 W Magnolia Blvd, Burbank, CA, 91505
men's, women's & children-1920s-1980s clothing & access.
Polkadots and Moonbeams (323) 651-1746
8367 W 3rd St, Los Angeles, CA, 90048
Turn of century to 70s, plus new stock from latest designers
Ragg Mopp Vintage (323) 666-0550
3816 W Sunset Blvd, Los Angeles, CA, 90026
very reasonable "vintage" prices
Ravishing Resale (323) 655-8480
8127 W 3rd St, Los Angeles, CA, 90048
ladies vintage
Repeat Performance (323) 938-0609
Web Based Business
whitneyr@artdimensionsonline.com * www.rpvintage.com
Resurrection (323) 651-5516
8006 Melrose Ave, Hollywood, CA, 90046
designer vintage
ReVamp (213) 488-3387
818 South Broadway Ste 801, Los Angeles, CA, 90014
Vintage reproductions for men & women, focusing on 1910-1950
info@revampvintage.com * www.revampvintage.com
Screaming Mimi's (212) 677-6464
382 Lafayette St, New York, NY, 10003
vintage clothing, accessories for men & women 1940s - 1980s
Squaresville (323) 669-8464
1800 N Vermont Ave, Los Angeles, CA, 90027
vintage clothing, low prices, clean/good merchandise, 30s to 80s,
buy/sell/trade
Una Mae's (323) 662-6137
1768 N Vermont, Los Angeles, CA, 90027
specializing in M/W vintage/new clothing, jewelry & gifts by local designers
Unique Vintage (818) 953-2877
2013 W Magnolia Ave, Burbank, CA, 91506
Vintage inspired clothing
Universal Studios Costume Dept (818) 777-2722
Rental, mfg., & alterations
Warner Bros. Studios Costume Dept (818) 954-1297
Collection of period & contemporary costumes for rent categorized by era,
decade and style.
Wasteland, Inc. (323) 653-3028
7428 Melrose Ave, Los Angeles, CA, 90046
Mon-Sat 11-8, Sun 11-7
Western Costume Co. (818) 760-0900

Warehouse Dressing

See Also: Barrels & Drums, Wood/Metal/Plastic Conveyor
Equipment* Grating, Grated Flooring, Catwalks* Lighting, Industrial*
Pallets*

Absolute Packaging (800) 567-9190
11940 Sherman Road, N. Hollywood, CA 91605
oakket jacks, pallet wrap machines, commercial shelving, warehouse racks,
tape machines, rollng ladders, hand carts
www.absolutepackagingsupply.com
AIR Designs (818) 768-6639
Shelving, Ladders, Dollies, Pallet Jacks, etc.
Alley Cats Studio Rentals (818) 982-9178
Barrels, pallets, crates, lighting
Basaw Manufacturing, Inc. (818) 765-6650
7300 Varna, N Hollywood, CA, 91605
Basaw builds crates to order, large inventory in stock. crates, boxes, railroad &
ship containers too
fredy@basaw.com * www.basaw.com
E.C. Prop Rentals (818) 764-2008
Drums, Crates, Shelving, Containers, Pallets/Jacks, Signage

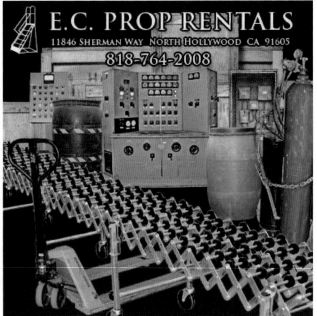

E.C. PROP RENTALS
11846 SHERMAN WAY NORTH HOLLYWOOD CA 91605
818-764-2008

History For Hire, Inc. (818) 765-7767
LCW Props (818) 243-0707
Pallets, Drums, Pallet Jacks, Forklifts, Rolling Ladders, Inventory Carts,
Shipping / Receiving, Marine/Dock
Modern Props (323) 934-3000
plastic shipping crates, lights, metro shelving, industrial dressing.
Omega/Cinema Props (323) 466-8201
Sony Pictures Studios-Prop House (Off Lot) (310) 244-5999

Wash Tubs

C. P. Valley (323) 466-8201
Caravan West Productions (661) 268-8300
35660 Jayhawker Rd, Aqua Dulce, CA, 91390
Old West, historically accurate & museum quality.
caravanwest@earthlink.net * www.caravanwest.com
History For Hire, Inc. (818) 765-7767

Washing Machines/Dryers

See Also: Laundry Carts
Angel Appliances   (877) 262-6435
8545 Sepulveda Blvd, Sepulveda, CA, 91343
customized, practical, heavy-duty, classic-current, coin-op machs
props@angelappliances.com * www.angelappliances.com/rentals.php

C. P. Two   (323) 466-8201
contemp./antique
LCW Props   (818) 243-0707
Stock Of Different Styles & Colors. Call For An Updated Listing.
Sony Pictures Studios-Prop House (Off Lot) (310) 244-5999
Universal Studios Property & Hardware Dept (818) 777-2784
Prop washing machines & prop dryers for rent.

Waste Baskets

See: Trash Cans & Waste Baskets

Watches & Pocket Watches

See Also: Clocks
The Costume House   (818) 508-9933
reproduction Victorian pocket watches
Feldmar Watch & Clock Center   (310) 274-8016
9000 W. Pico Blvd, Los Angeles, CA, 90035
Repairs
The Hand Prop Room LP.   (323) 931-1534
period-present, wristwatches, doubles, 18th-19th C. pocket
History For Hire, Inc.   (818) 765-7767
vintage watches, chains, fobs
LCW Props   (818) 243-0707
Silver, Gold, Modern, Timex, Antique, Fakes
Sony Pictures Studios-Prop House (Off Lot) (310) 244-5999
watches & pocket watches
Universal Studios Property & Hardware Dept (818) 777-2784
Prop watches, prop wristwatches & prop pocket watches for rent.
Warner Bros. Studios Property Department (818) 954-2181
Womens & mens watches, costume watches, high end watches, mens pocket
watches, Wrist watches

Water Coolers

AIR Designs   (818) 768-6639
Wall & Stand, Period & Present, Some Rigged
Alley Cats Studio Rentals   (818) 982-9178
E.C. Prop Rentals   (818) 764-2008
per/contemp, wall-mounted & free standing
History For Hire, Inc.   (818) 765-7767

LCW Props   (818) 243-0707
Large Selection
Sony Pictures Studios-Prop House (Off Lot) (310) 244-5999
Universal Studios Property & Hardware Dept (818) 777-2784
Office water coolers, ice chests and camping water containers for rent.

Water Fountains

See: Fountains, Drinking (Wall & Stand) Greens* Statuary*

Water Jet CNC Services

See Also: CNC Router & Laser Etching Services Prop Design &
Manufacturing*
Charisma Design Studio, Inc.   (818) 252-6611
8414 San Fernando Road, Sun Valley, CA, 91352
waterjet can cut through 8" thickness of almost any material. 0,005" accuracy,
smooth edging.
info@charismadesign.com * www.charismadesign.com

Water Sports/Water Craft

See: Boats & Water Sport Vehicles Ski Equipment* Sporting Goods
& Services* Surfboard, Wakeboard* Vehicles*

Waterfalls

See: Greens Mold Making* Statuary* Wedding Props*

Watering Cans

See: Garden/Patio

Waterproofing

See: Floor, Ground & Surface Protection

Weaponry, Historical

See Also: Archery Equipment, Training Armor, Chainmail, Suits of
Armor* Civil War Era*
Caravan West Productions   (661) 268-8300
35660 Jayhawker Rd, Aqua Dulce, CA, 91390
Old West, exact reprod. all types, plain & fancy, gunsmiths too
caravanwest@earthlink.net * www.caravanwest.com
The Hand Prop Room LP.   (323) 931-1534
great pcs; cust design & mfg
History For Hire, Inc.   (818) 765-7767
replica firearms, swords
Sword & Stone   (818) 562-6548
ancient, medieval to futuristic, swords, knives, armor

Weaponry, Medieval

See Also: Archery Equipment, Training* Armor, Chainmail, Suits of Armor

The Hand Prop Room LP.	(323) 931-1534
great pcs; cust design & mfg	
History For Hire, Inc.	(818) 765-7767
Sword & Stone	(818) 562-6548
poleaxes, knives, spears, swords, shields, crossbows	

Weapons

See Also: Armor, Chainmail, Suits of Armor* Firearms, Gunsmith, Firearm Choreography* Knives* Military Props & Equipment* Non-Guns & Non-Pyro Flashes* Police Equipment* Swords & Swordplay

Art, Models & Props, Inc.	(951) 206-9156

1725 Marengo Ave, Pasadena, CA, 91103
Custom design/fabr. Old World to Sci-Fi, Fantasy. See ad in "Prop Design & Manufacturing"
modelsandprops@msn.com * www.artmodeltech.com

CONFETTI & FOG FX Special Effects Company	(786) 308-7063

2739 W 79 St Bay, #12, Hialeah, FL 33016
www.caffx.com

Dapper Cadaver/Creatures & Cultures	(818) 771-0818

Foam, rubber and plastic fake weapons. Knives, axes, hammers, crowbars, baseball bats, etc.

Emerson Knives	(310) 539-5633

1234 254th St., Harbor City, CA 90710
Emerson Knives are the only choice of Elite Military and U.S. Covert Units. They are truly, "Famous In the Worst Places"
eknives@aol.com * www.emersonknives.com

Global Effects, Inc.	(818) 503-9273
prop swords, daggers, polearms, axes, crossbows	
The Hand Prop Room LP.	(323) 931-1534
great pcs; cust design & mfg	
History For Hire, Inc.	(818) 765-7767
J & M Special Effects, Inc.	(718) 875-0140

524 Sackett St, Brooklyn, NY 11217
Formerly Jauchem & Meeh. rifles & shotguns, handguns, trick weapons, accessories
info@jmfx.net * www.jmfx.net

LCW Props	(818) 243-0707

Futuristic Weapons, Guns, Knives, Swords, Martial Arts Weapons, Training Equipment, Prepper Supplies

Sony Pictures Studios-Prop House (Off Lot)	(310) 244-5999

Guns, gun accessories, blow guns, bow and arrows, clubs, crossbows, blades, maces, and more

Sword & Stone	(818) 562-6548

poleaxes, knives, spears, swords, retractable weapons. Experienced blacksmith. Man at Arms videos.

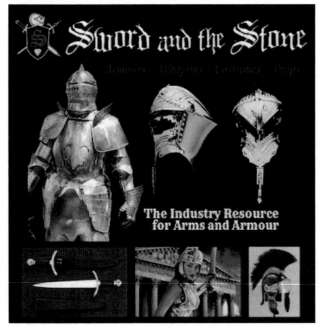

Weather Instruments

See: Lab Equipment* Nautical Dressing & Props* Science Equipment* Weather Vanes

Weather Vanes

See: Farm Equipment & Dressing* Rooftop Dressing

Wedding Attire

See Also: Formal Wear

The Costume House	(818) 508-9933
gowns, tails & tuxes, 1890s through 1980s, veils, shoes	
Dark Garden Unique Corsetry	(415) 431-7684

321 Linden St, San Francisco, CA, 94102
divine historical to fantasy custom made

David's Bridal	(818) 238-9001

2050 W. Empire Ave (Burbank Empire), Burbank, CA, 91504
Special occasion dresses, wedding consultant, alterations, also loc. in Northridge

Sony Pictures Studios-Wardrobe	(310) 244-5995
alterations, call (310) 244-7260	
Universal Studios Costume Dept	(818) 777-2722
Rental, mfg., & alterations	
Warner Bros. Studios Costume Dept	(818) 954-1297
Bride, Bridesmaids, Flower Girl, Tuxedos, Ring Bearer, Bridal Party, Dresses, Veils	
Western Costume Co.	(818) 760-0900

Wedding Cakes, Prop

See: Food, Artificial Food

Wedding Props

See Also: Balloons & Balloon Sculptures* Dance Floors* Events, Decorations, Supplies & Services* Florists/Floral Design* Wrapped Prop Gift Packages

Aah-Inspiring Balloons	(562) 494-7605

Call for an Appointment.
After 14 years in the TV and Film Industry, Aah-Inspiring Balloon Decor has been seen in over 200 TV shows and Films.
aahinspiring1@aol.com * www.aahinspiringballoons.com

Arc de Belle	(855) 332-3553

Call for Consultation
Unique brand of Wedding/Event Arches, Gazebos, Chuppah, Column & Canopy Rentals. Themed Photo Booths & Vintage Airstream
info@arcdebelle.com * www.arcdebelle.com

Bob Gail Special Events	(310) 202-5200

Bob Gail's skilled team of planners works with each client to design, and produce every affair with style and ease!

Flower Art	(323) 935-6800

5859 West 3rd Street, Los Angeles, CA, 90036
Full-service Wedding florals: From lavish soap opera weddings, to an Indian-inspired theme we helped create for New Girl
info@flowerartla.com * http://www.flowerartla.com

FormDecor, Inc.	(310) 558-2582

America's largest event rental supplier of 20th Century furniture and accessories for Modern and Mid-Century styles.

Lux Lounge EFR	(888) 247-4411

106 1/2 Judge John Aiso St #318, Los Angeles, CA, 90012
Wedding Props for Rental
info@luxloungeefr.com * www.luxloungeefr.com

Sandy Rose Floral, Inc	(818) 980-4371

6850 Vineland Ave Unit C, N Hollywood, CA, 91605
Bouquets, boutonnieres, corsages, pedestals, urns, centerpieces. 24 hr service
www.sandyrose.com

ShopWildThings	(928) 855-6075

2880 Sweetwater Ave, Lake Havasu City, AZ, 86406
Event Decor, Beaded Curtains, Chain Curtains, String Curtains & Columns, Crystal Columns. Reliable service & delivery.
help@shopwildthings.com * www.shopwildthings.com

Sony Pictures Studios-Prop House (Off Lot)	(310) 244-5999
Taylor Creative Inc.	(888) 245-4044

From tables & chairs for receptions to specialty sweetheart tables, our collection has rentals for every bride & budget.

Weightlifting Equipment

See Also: Exercise & Fitness Equipment
C. P. Valley (323) 466-8201
Curtis Gym Equipment (818) 897-2804
10275 Glenoaks Blvd, Ste #7, Pacoima, CA, 91331
Prop Rentals and Servicing. Fitness Machines, Gymnastics & Weightlifting.
Fake & Real Weights
curtisgymequipment@hotmail.com
The Hand Prop Room LP. (323) 931-1534
History For Hire, Inc. (818) 765-7767
strongman type barbells, dumbbells
Hollywood Gym Rentals (310) 663-6161
200 West Chevy Chase Drive Unit B, Glendale, CA 91204
Hollywood Gym Rentals specializes in short and long term rentals of fitness
equipment in the Los Angeles area.
chris@hollywoodgymrentals.com * www.hollywoodgymrentals.com

Welding Equipment/Stations

See Also: Blacksmith Shop/Foundry CNC Router & Laser Etching*
Services Metalworking, Welding & Structural*
AIR Designs (818) 768-6639
Acetylene Torches, MIG Carts, Masks, Gloves, Screens
Alley Cats Studio Rentals (818) 982-9178
tanks with gauges, hoses, push carts
E.C. Prop Rentals (818) 764-2008
fully dressed carts & elec units, masks/goggles/gloves/aprons

E.C. PROP RENTALS
11846 SHERMAN WAY NORTH HOLLYWOOD CA 91605
818-764-2008

History For Hire, Inc. (818) 765-7767
period welding tanks
LCW Props (818) 243-0707
Welding Carts, Electrical, Gas, Masks, Screens, Welding Salvage

Western Americana

The Earl Hays Press (818) 765-0700
services the Industry only. large research base, reproductions
History For Hire, Inc. (818) 765-7767
Lots!
Western Ways Studio Prop Rentals (661) 269-2296
Call for appt, Acton, CA, 93510
Western Props & Set Dressing, wagons, hand carts, luggage, directors chairs,
mannequins
www.wwprops.com

Western Dressing

See Also: Cactus, Live & Artificial Horse Saddles & Tack* Horses,*
Horse Equipment, Livestock Native American* Wagons* Wheels,*
Wooden
C. P. Two (323) 466-8201
C. P. Valley (323) 466-8201
western barrels, troughs, water pumps, cast iron stoves, western tools, western
lanterns
Caravan West Productions (661) 268-8300
35660 Jayhawker Rd, Aqua Dulce, CA, 91390
Western signage, Old West, cowboy, historically accurate, everything you
need
caravanwest@earthlink.net * www.caravanwest.com

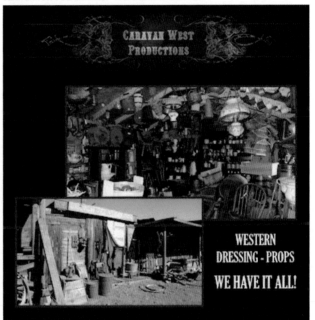

CARAVAN WEST PRODUCTIONS

WESTERN DRESSING - PROPS
WE HAVE IT ALL!

Dapper Cadaver/Creatures & Cultures (818) 771-0818
Animal props & steer skulls. Apothecary props. Rattlesnake props. Gallows, toe
pincher coffins & standing stocks.
FILM ART LA (323) 461-4900
Culver City Warehouse at Jefferson & Hauser. Call for address.
Large Inventory of cleared rentals 19th Century to Present. Western Art
Rentals and High rez Images
filmartla@gmail.com * www.artimagela.com
Green Set, Inc. (818) 764-1231
wagons, wagon wheels, F.G. horses, buffalos, straw bales, cows, carts,
western & rustic decorations
The Hand Prop Room LP. (323) 931-1534
saddles, gambling, saloon, cavalry equip, badges, etc.
History For Hire, Inc. (818) 765-7767
Lots, including: western advertising, period posters, American Indian, archery,
wooden barrels, western drums, blacksmiths tools
Hollywood Studio Gallery (323) 462-1116
prints & paintings of rodeos
Jackson Shrub Supply, Inc. (818) 982-0100
split rail fence, wagon wheels, cactus, hitching post, tumble weeds, carts,
wagons, tumbleweeds
Omega/Cinema Props (323) 466-8201
Sony Pictures Studios-Prop House (Off Lot) (310) 244-5999
Basin & pitchers, branding irons, western buckets, western barrels, horse gear,
indian items, lassos, animal pelt, more
Universal Studios Property & Hardware Dept (818) 777-2784
Western dressing and western props for rent.
Warner Bros. Studios Property Department (818) 954-2181
Horse Bits, leather saddles, stirrups, saw horses, western smalls,
stagecoaches, wagon wheels

Western Theme Events

See Also: Events, Decorations, Supplies & Services Events,
Design/Planning/Production*

Bob Gail Special Events   **(310) 202-5200**
Hoedowns, rodeos, and barbeques are among some of the Western themed
events you can throw with our many Western Props!

L. A. Party Works   **(888) 527-2789**
9712 Alpaca St, S El Monte, CA, 91733
in Vancouver tel. 604-589-4101. Western theme parties, mech. bull, card
sharks
partyworks@aol.com * www.partyworksusa.com

888-527-2789
partyworksusa.com

COMPLETE WESTERN THEME EVENTS AVAILABLE / MECHANICAL BULLS
PROPS / PHOTO OPS / GREEN SCREEN SYSTEMS / & MORE

PARTYWORKS
I N T E R A C T I V E

LM Treasures   **(626) 252-7354**
10557 Juniper Ave Unit A, Fontana, CA 92337
The place to find cowboys, indians, bulls, and all types of different western
theme statues perfect for any occasions.
lmtreasures.ll@gmail.com * www.lifesizestatues.net

Western Wear

See Also: Horse Saddles & Tack Native American* Wardrobe,
Accessories* Wardrobe, Antique/Historical* Western Dressing*
Western Theme Events*

Alfonso of Hollywood Leather Co.   **(818) 769-0362**
1512 W. Magnolia Blvd, Burbank, CA, 91506
Primarily fancy gunbelts/holsters, custom fitting/orders, we also do saddles!
www.alfonsosgunleather.com

Broken Horn Saddlery   **(626) 337-4088**
1022 Leorita St, Baldwin Park, CA, 91706
10-6 Wed.- Sat. 10-5 Sun. Closed Mon & Tues

Caravan West Productions   **(661) 268-8300**
35660 Jayhawker Rd, Aqua Dulce, CA, 91390
1800s-19002 cowboy western wear, cowboy chaps, pocket watches, belt
buckles, and more. Historically accurate, everything
caravanwest@earthlink.net * www.caravanwest.com

CARAVAN WEST PRODUCTIONS

WESTERN COSTUMES & WARDROBE

PERIOD WESTERN INDIAN CIVIL WAR MILITARY
WOMEN • MEN • CHILDREN
BOOTS SPURS SHOES VESTS CHAPS HOLSTERS
ACCESSORIES JEWELRY POCKET WATCHES
CARPET BAGS CONCHOS GAUNTLETS BADGES
SADDLES & TACK WEAPONS

Country General Store   **(800) 269-9836**
6279 Van Nuys Blvd, Van Nuys, CA, 91401
complete contemp. western & work outfitters

Falconhead   **(310) 471-7075**
Call for Custom Orders - El Paso TX & Cody WY
very special western wear/goods; custom belts, buckles, boots... If we don't
have it, we'll make it.

Warner Bros. Studios Costume Dept   **(818) 954-1297**
Frontier, Pioneer, Cowboy, Chaps, Boots, Bolo Ties, Flannel, Jeans, Hats,
Bandanas

Western Costume Co.   **(818) 760-0900**

Wetsuits, Diving/Surfing

Action/Watersports   **(310) 827-2233**
4144 Lincoln Blvd, Marina del Rey, CA, 90292
kayaks, kiteboards, scuba, water skis, surf boards, wake boards, paddle board

Body Glove   **(310) 374-3441**
504 N Broadway, Redondo Beach, CA, 90277
Ask for Scott, X200. regular/skin color

Dive and Surf   **(310) 372-8423**
504 N Broadway, Redondo Beach, CA, 90277
scuba diving & surfing equipment

Divers' Discount Supply   **(949) 221-9300**
1752 Langley Ave, Irvine, CA, 92614
scuba diving equipment

Scuba Haus   **(310) 828-2916**
2501 Wilshire Blvd, Santa Monica, CA, 90403
swimming equipment, scuba diving equipment, underwater cameras

Universal Studios Costume Dept   **(818) 777-2722**
Rental, mfg., & alterations

Wharf Dock Lights

See: Lamp Posts & Street Lights

Wheel of Fortune

See: Gambling Equipment

Wheelchairs

C. P. Valley   **(323) 466-8201**
Modern wheelchairs to antique wheelchairs and vintage wheelchairs.

The Hand Prop Room LP.   **(323) 931-1534**
period-present

History For Hire, Inc.   **(818) 765-7767**
all eras, big selection, FDR

LCW Props   **(818) 243-0707**
Electric, Manual

Sony Pictures Studios-Prop House (Off Lot)   **(310) 244-5999**

Wheels, Wooden

C. P. Valley	**(323) 466-8201**
Caravan West Productions	**(661) 268-8300**

35660 Jayhawker Rd, Aqua Dulce, CA, 91390
Old West, historically accurate & museum quality.
caravanwest@earthlink.net * www.caravanwest.com

History For Hire, Inc.	**(818) 765-7767**

Whiteboards (Dry Erase)

See: Office Equipment & Dressing School Supplies, Desks & Dressing*

Wi-Fi Boxes

Airwaves Wireless	**(818) 501-8200**

13400 Riverside Dr. # 103 Sherman Oaks, CA 91423
Cellular phones, cellphones, tablets, laptops, iPhones, iPads, dummy phones, walkies, Wi-Fi, satellite phones, macbooks
anita@airwaveswireless.com * www.airwaveswireless.com

Castex Rentals	**(323) 462-1468**

1044 N. Cole Ave, Hollywood, CA, 90038
Wi Fi Boxes, WiFi boxes
service@castexrentals.com * www.castexrentals.com

LCW Props	**(818) 243-0707**

Wifi Disconnects, Bridges, Routers, Switches, Antennas, Rackmount Wifi Equipment

Wicker

See: Furniture, Rattan & Wicker

Wigs

See Also: Clowns Make-up & Hair, Supplies & Services*

Charlie Wright, Ltd.	**(818) 347-4566**

18645 Hatteras St #121, Tarzana, CA 91356
custom only

The Costume House	**(818) 508-9933**

mens wigs, womens wigs, 18th century wigs, white wigs, brown wigs,fantasy wigs, colored wigs

Favian Wigs	**(818) 388-0853**

5819 Capistrano Ave, Woodland Hills, CA, 91367
By appt. only: custom made lace front wigs, huge sel. of lace front rentals, all human hair

THE Historical Hairdresser	**(760) 534-2664**

1895 Avenida Del Oro #6591, Oceanside, CA, 92056
Historical and Period wigs and hairpieces Fantasy, Victorian, Renaissance, 18th Century, Regency, Edwardian and more.
thehistoricalhairdresser@gmail.com * www.TheHistoricalHairdresser.com

Hollywood Wig	**(323) 466-6479**

6530 Hollywood Blvd, Hollywood, CA, 90028
real/synthetic, period-contemp, men/women

National Fiber Technology, LLC	**(978) 686-2964**

15 Union St, Lawrence, MA, 01840
catalog sales; hair & fur fabrics for wigs, headdresses, 'make-up' hair, & animal costumes, wigs custom made.

Wilshire Wigs & Accessories, Inc.	**(800) 927-0874**

5241 Craner Ave, N Hollywood, CA, 91601
real/synthetic, period-contemp, men/women

Wind Machines

See: Special Effects, Equipment & Supplies

Windmill

See Also: Farm Equipment & Dressing

American Windmills	**(530) 644-3008**

5981 Silver Ridge Rd, Placerville, CA, 95667
Vintage windmills & towers set up at your location. Last minute notice is our specialty.

Halsted & Hoggan, Inc.	**(800) 286-3303**

935 S Santa Fe Ave, Los Angeles, CA, 90021
small ones, for irrigation

Window Treatments

See Also: Awnings Drapery & Curtains* Flameproofing*

American Silk Mills	**(305) 308-9411**

2300 Chestnut Street 4th floor, Philadelphia, PA, 19103
United States manufacturer of the most exquisite textiles since 1896.
adriano.salucci@americansilk.com * www.sensuede.com

Linoleum City, Inc.	**(323) 469-0063**

4849 Santa Monica Blvd, Hollywood, CA, 90029
Custom window treatments. Blinds, shades, woven shades, natural shades, pleated shades, wood blinds, aluminum blinds.
sales@linocity.com * www.linoleumcity.com

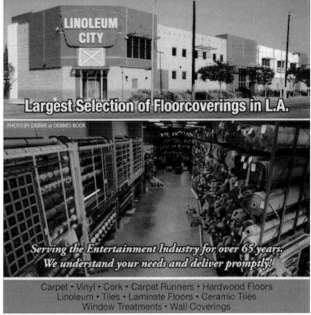

LINOLEUM CITY

Largest Selection of Floorcoverings in L.A.

PHOTO BY DEBBIE @ DEBBIES BOOK

*Serving the Entertainment Industry for over 65 years.
We understand your needs and deliver promptly!*

Carpet • Vinyl • Cork • Carpet Runners • Hardwood Floors
Linoleum • Tiles • Laminate Floors • Ceramic Tiles
Window Treatments • Wall Coverings

Omega/Cinema Props	**(323) 466-8201**

drapery dept

**DISPLAY ADS AND LISTINGS FOR THIS CATEGORY
CONTINUE ON THE FOLLOWING PAGE**

Strickland's Window Coverings   **(800) 279-0944**
2817 N. 23rd Street, Wilmington, NC 28401
Strickland's Window Coverings Set Services has been providing window coverings to the film industry for over 26 years.
laurasalo@stricklandswindowcoverings.com *
www.stricklandswindowcoverings.com

E.C. Prop Rentals   **(818) 764-2008**
59 Gallon Oak Casks, With Wood Storage Racks

Fast, *reliable* service specializing in the film industry for over *26 years*.

www.StricklandsWindowCoverings.com
LauraSalo@StricklandsWindowCoverings.com
910•762•0944 LOCAL 800•279•0944 TOLL FREE
910•762•1615 FAX

2817 N. 23rd Street, Wilmington, NC 28401

Evans Family Barrels   **(818) 523-8174**
7918 Fairchild Ave, Canoga Park, CA, 91306
59 gal oak wine barrels (casks or kegs) and 55 gal oak whiskey barrels and metal winery barrel racks (rental only)
evansbarrels@gmail.com * www.EvansFamilyBarrels.com

The Hand Prop Room LP.   **(323) 931-1534**

Wire

See: Electrical/Electronic Supplies & Services

Witchcraft

See: Crystal Balls Occult/Spiritual/Metaphysical* Tarot Cards*

Wood

See: Building Supply, Lumber, Hardware, Etc. Greens*

Wood Shop

See Also: Factory/Industrial Tools*

E.C. Prop Rentals   **(818) 764-2008**
Carpentry dressing including power & hand tools, tables, signage & more.

LCW Props   **(818) 243-0707**
Tools, Saws, Sanders, Presses, Planers, Dust Collector, Work Benches, Tech Benches & other Carpentry Dressing

Wood Turnings

See: Moulding, Wood

Woodworking

See: Doors Moulding, Wood* Staff Shops*

Workbenches

See: Benches Tools* Wood Shop*

Workrooms

See: Sewing Equipment & Workrooms

World Globe Maps

See: Globes, World Map

Worms

See: Fishing Equipment & Tackle

Universal Studios Drapery Dept   **(818) 777-2761**
Warner Bros. Drapery, Upholstery & Flooring   **(818) 954-1831**
4000 Warner Blvd, Burbank, CA, 91522
Puffs; Balloon Shades; Beaded Curtains; Drapes; Sheers; Swags; Sunbursts; Tiebacks; Shades & Blinds
wbsfdrapery@warnerbros.com * www.wbdrapery.com

Warner Bros. Studios Property Department   **(818) 954-2181**
Custom fabrication, See WBSF Drapery department

Windsocks

Aradyne Industries, Inc.   **(281) 934-1776**
4631 11th St. Brookshire, TX, 77423
3' to 12', classic styles, & frames, masts, accessories

E.C. Prop Rentals   **(818) 764-2008**
2 sizes with poles & bases

Windtek, Inc.   **(800) 468-7697**
Call to Order, Girard, PA, 16417
airport & industrial windsocks, also airport lights
www.bestwindsocks.com

Wine Kegs

See Also: Barrels & Drums, Wood/Metal/Plastic
AIR Designs   **(818) 768-6639**
Multiple Kegs, Winery Racks, Barrels, Racks

Wrap Parties

See: Events, Decorations, Supplies & Services* Events, Design/Planning/Production* Events, Entertainment

Wrap Party Gifts

See: Embroidery, Screen Printing, Etc.* Leather (Clothing, Accessories, Materials)

Wrapped Prop Gift Packages

See Also: Christmas* Gift Wrapping* Wedding Props

FROST **(310) 704-8812**
Call for Appointment, 21515 Madrona Ave, Torrance, CA 90503
Individual wrapped gifts, stacked wrapped gifts, prop gifts of all kinds.
mdisplay@yahoo.com * www.frostchristmasprops.com
Jackson Shrub Supply, Inc. **(818) 982-0100**
Gift presents, boxed gifts, assorted wrapped gifts

Wrought Iron Furniture & Decorations

See Also: Bedroom Furniture & Decorations* Furniture, Rustic* Metalworking, Decorative* Metalworking, Welding & Structural

Badia Design, Inc. **(818) 762-0130**
5420 Vineland Ave, N. Hollywood, CA, 91601
Our Moroccan Wrought Iron Furniture includes tables, chairs and stools for your indoor or outdoor decorating needs.
info@badiadesign.com * www.badiadesign.com
C. P. Two **(323) 466-8201**
C. P. Valley **(323) 466-8201**
Prop Services West **(818) 503-2790**
Susanne Hollis, Inc. **(626) 441-0346**
230 Pasadena Ave, South Pasadena, CA, 91030
20th - 17th century Antiques, Accessories, and Fine Art from around the world in our 19,000sqft. warehouse and showrooms
sales@susannehollis.com * www.susannehollis.com
Sword & Stone **(818) 562-6548**
Universal Studios Property & Hardware Dept **(818) 777-2784**
Many wrought iron pieces; furniture, dressing, and decorations for rent.
Used Church Items, Religious Rentals **(239) 992-5737**
216 Cumer Road, McDonald, PA, 15057
Wrought Iron Religious Furniture and Decorations. Kneelers, Baptismals, Censers, Candlesticks, Lights, Lamps, Stands.
warehouse@religiousrentals.com * www.religiousrentals.com
Warner Bros. Studios Metal Shop **(818) 954-1265**
4000 Warner Blvd, Burbank, CA, 91522
Custom metal fabrication creating anything from structural steel elements to intricate custom furniture
wbsfconstructionservices@warnerbros.com * www.wbmetalshop.com
Warner Bros. Studios Property Department **(818) 954-2181**
Wrought iron benches, barstools, andirons, tables, chairs, fireplace tools, patio chairs, beds, plant stands

X-ray Machine

See Also: Hospital Equipment* X-ray Viewer* X-rays

Air Hollywood - Prop House & Standing Sets **(818) 890-0444**
We have many Airport Security / TSA/ sets and props available including X-Ray Machines.
LCW Props **(818) 243-0707**
Light Boxes, Baggage Checker, Industrial, pallet X-Ray Machines
Modern Props **(323) 934-3000**
airport hangar, baggage & conveyor

X-ray Viewer

See Also: Hospital Equipment* X-ray Machine* X-rays

History For Hire, Inc. **(818) 765-7767**
LCW Props **(818) 243-0707**
Different Sizes Of Light Boxes, Medical, Dental
Universal Studios Property & Hardware Dept **(818) 777-2784**
X-ray lightboxes and x-ray viewers for rent.

X-rays

A-1 Medical Integration **(818) 753-0319**
Medical devices for Set Decoration & Property, from minor procedures to detailed hospital units.
Dapper Cadaver/Creatures & Cultures **(818) 771-0818**
Assorted human X-rays. Normal and broken bone x-rays.
History For Hire, Inc. **(818) 765-7767**
LCW Props **(818) 243-0707**
Large Selection, Medical, Dental, Assortment, Head, Foot, Bones

Xerox Machines

See: Copy Machines* Office Equipment & Dressing

Xylophone

See: Musical Instruments

Yurts

See: Canopies, Tents, Gazebos, Cabanas

Guilds, Unions, Societies, Associations

Academy of Motion Picture Arts & Sciences **(310) 247-3000**
8949 Wilshire Blvd, Beverly Hills, CA, 90211
www.oscars.org
Actors Equity Association (A.E.A) **(323) 978-8080**
5636 Tujunga Ave, North Hollywood, CA, 91601
www.actorsequity.org
AFTRA, American Fed. of TV & Radio Artists **(323) 954-1600**
5757 Wilshire Blvd, 7th Floor, Los Angeles, CA, 90036
www.sagaftra.org
Alliance of Spec. Effects & Pyro. Oper. **(818) 506-8173**
12522 Moorpark St Ste 100, Studio City, CA, 91604
www.asepo.org
American Assn. of Community Theatre **(817) 732-3177**
1300 Gendy St, Fort Worth, TX, 76107
www.aact.org
American Pyrotechnics Association **(301) 907-8181**
7910 Woodmont Ave Ste 1220, Bethesda, MD, 20814
Trade association for fireworks industry
www.americanpyro.com
American Rental Assn. (ARA) **(800) 334-2177**
1900 19th St, Moline, IL, 61265
www.ararental.org
AMPTP - Alliance of M.P. & TV Producers **(818) 995-3600**
15301 Ventura Blvd Bldg E, Sherman Oaks, CA, 91403
www.amptp.org
APA American Photographic Artists - LA **(323) 933-1631**
9190 West Olympic Blvd #212, Beverly Hills, CA, 90212
Volunteer organization, run by photographers for photographers, many member discounts throughout the industry
director@apa-la.com * http://apa-la.org/
Art Directors Guild **(818) 762-9995**
11969 Ventura Blvd 2nd Floor, Studio City, CA, 91604
Art Directors Guild & Scenic, Title & Graphic Artists, Set Designers, Model Makers, Illustrators, Matte/Digital Artists
www.adg.org
ASA Entertainment Group, LLC **(321) 722-9300**
201 N Riverside Dr Ste C, Indialantic, FL, 32903
ASA demo skating team can spice up an event
www.asaskate.com
ASID - American Society Of Interior Designers **(202) 546-3480**
718 7th St NW 4th Floor, Washington, DC, 20001
Has chapters throughout the entire U.S.
www.asid.org
ASID CA Los Angeles Chapter **(310) 659-4716**
8687 Melrose Bldg B245, W Hollywood, CA, 90069
asidoffice@asidla.org * http://asidla.org/
ASID NY New York Metro Chapter **(212) 641-0018**
555 Eighth Ave Ste 1902, New York, NY, 10018
info@asidnymetro.org * http://www.asidnymetro.org/
Assn. of Independent Commercial Producers **(323) 960-4763**
650 N. Bronson Ave, Ste 223b, Los Angeles, CA, 90004
7 offices in U.S., see web site for more info.
Contract Services Admin. Trust Fund **(818) 565-0550**
2800 Winona, Burbank, CA, 91504
www.csatf.org
Dance/USA **(202) 833-1717**
1111 16th Street NW Ste 300, Washington, DC, 20036
Provide professional development & networking opportunities that advance & support the art form of dance.
www.danceusa.org
Directors Guild of America (DGA) **(310) 289-2000**
7920 Sunset Blvd, Los Angeles, CA, 90046
www.dga.org
Dramatists Guild **(212) 398-9366**
1501 Broadway Ste 701, New York, NY, 10036
www.dramatistsguild.com
Exhibit Designers and Producers Assn. **(203) 899-8434**
10 Norden Pl, Norwalk, CT, 06855
Provides leadership, education & networking for advancement of its members & the exhibition industry.
www.edpa.com

LISTINGS FOR THIS CATEGORY CONTINUE ON THE FOLLOWING PAGE

Greater S.F. Bay Area Costumer's Guild   (203) 899-8434
P.O. Box 6392, Alameda, CA, 94501
good links to resources for patterns, research, historical & vintage wardrobe, & fashion shopping in garment districts
www.gbacg.org

IATSE General Office   (212) 730-1770
207 W 25th St 4th Fl, New York, NY, 10001
www.iatse-intl.org

IATSE West Coast Office   (818) 980-3499
10045 Riverside Dr, Toluca Lake, CA, 91602
www.iatse-intl.org

International Interior Design Association   (888) 799-4432
222 Merchandise Mart Ste 567, Chicago, IL, 60654
Regional chapters throughout U.S. & the world
www.iida.org

International Stunt Association   (818) 501-5225
4454 Van Nuys Blvd Ste 214, Sherman Oaks, CA, 91403
www.isastunts.com

The League of Resident Theatres   (212) 944-1501
1501 Broadway Ste 2401, New York, NY, 10036   x19
www.lort.org

Local # 1 Theatrical Stage Employees   (212) 333-2500
320 West 46th Street, New York, NY, 10036
IATSE #1, New York, Westchester/Putnam counties
www.iatselocalone.org

Local # 4 Theatrical Stage Employees   (718) 252-8777
2917 Glenwood Rd, Brooklyn, NY, 11210
IATSE #4, Brooklyn & Queens
www.iatselocal4.org

Local # 122 Theatrical & Stage, San Diego   (619) 640-0042
3737 Camino Del Rio South Ste 307, San Diego, CA, 92108
www.iatse122.org

Local # 161 Script Sup. & Continuity Coor.   (212) 977-9655
630 9th Ave Ste 1103, New York, NY, 10036
Script Sup., Continuity Coor., Prod. Office Coor., Accountants
www.local161.org

Local # B192 Amusement Area Employees   (818) 509-9192
5250 Lankershim Blvd Ste 600, N Hollywood, CA, 91601
www.b192iatse.org

Local # 399 Studio Transportation Drivers   (818) 985-7374
4747 Vineland Ave, N Hollywood, CA, 91602
Teamsters Local 399
www.ht399.org

Local # 44 Affil. Property Craftspersons   (818) 769-2500
12021 Riverside Dr, N Hollywood, CA, 91607
Local 44, IATSE, AFL, Property Masters, Set Decorators, Greens, Special Effects, Upholsterer-Draper, Sewing Persons, Pro
www.local44.com

Local # 442 Theatrical & Stage Employees   (805) 898-0442
PO Box 413, Santa Barbara, CA, 93102
Serving Santa Barbara, Ventura, San Luis Obispo Counties

Local # 480 Studio Mechanics   (505) 986-9512
1418 Cerrillos Rd, Santa Fe, NM, 87505
Film & TV technicians of New Mexico
www.iatselocal480.com

Local # 495 Film & TV, San Diego Area   (619) 275-0125
1717 Morena Blvd, San Diego, CA, 92110
Motion picture studio mechanics
www.ia495.org

Local # 504 Theatrical & Stage Employees   (714) 774-5004
671 S Manchester Ave, Anaheim, CA, 92802
Orange County & parts of Corona
www.iatselocal504.com

Local # 52 Studio Mechanics   (718) 906-9440
19-02 Steinway St, Astoria, NY, 11105
Allied Crafts, Electricians, Grips, Properties, Shop Crafts, Sound, Video; NY, NJ, CT, PA, DE
www.iatselocal52.org

Local # 53 NABET-CWA   (818) 846-0490
1918 W Burbank Blvd, Burbank, CA, 91506
www.nabet53.org

Local # 600 Int'l Cinematographers Guild   (323) 876-0160
7755 Sunset Blvd, Los Angeles, CA, 90046
Local 600, IATSE; also Publicist Guild
www.cameraguild.com

Local # 695 Int'l Sound/TV Eng./Video   (818) 985-9204
5439 Cahuenga Blvd, N Hollywood, CA, 91601
IATSE Prod. Sound/TV Engineering/Video Assistants, Tech. & Studio Projectionists
www.local695.com

Local # 700 Motion Picture Editors Guild   (323) 876-4770
7715 Sunset Blvd Suite #200, Hollywood, CA, 90046
www.editorsguild.com

Local # 705 Motion Picture Costumers   (818) 487-5655
4731 Laurel Canyon Blvd Ste 201, Valley Village, CA, 91607
Local 705, IATSE, MPTAA, AFL-CIO
www.motionpicturecostumers.org

Local # 706 Make-up Artists & Hair Stylists   (818) 295-3933
828 N Hollywood Way, Burbank, CA, 91505
Local 706, IATSE/MPMO of U.S. & Canada
www.local706.org

Local # 728 Studio Electrical Lighting Tech   (818) 954-0728
1001 W Magnolia Blvd, Burbank, CA, 91506
Local 728
www.iatse728.org

Local # 729 Motion Picture Set Painters   (818) 842-7729
1811 W Burbank Blvd, Burbank, CA, 91506
Local 729, IATSE, AFL-CIO
www.ialocal729.com

Local # 755 Sculpturers & Plasterers   (818) 379-9711
13245 Riverside Dr Ste 350, Sherman Oaks, CA, 91423
Local 755, OP & CMIA
www.local755.com

Local # 764 Theatrical Wardrobe Union   (212) 957-3500
545 W 45th Street, New York, NY, 10036
www.ia764.org

Local # 768 Theatrical Wardrobe Union   (818) 843-8768
1023 N Hollywood Way #203, Burbank, CA, 91505
(Live theatre only!) L.A., Long Beach, Pasadena, Santa Monica, Cerritos
www.wardrobe768.com

Local # 784 Theatrical Wardrobe   (415) 861-8379
1182 Market St Ste 213, San Francisco, CA, 94102
All costume crewing needs for Northern California
www.iatwu784.org

Local # 798 Make-up Artist, Hair Stylists   (212) 627-0660
70 West 36th St Suite 4A, New York, NY, 10018
www.local798.net

Local # 80 M.P. Studio Grips & Craft Svc.   (818) 526-0700
2520 W Olive Ave, Burbank, CA, 91505
Local 80, IATSE, AFL
www.iatselocal80.org

Local # 800 Art Directors Guild   (818) 762-9995
11969 Ventura Blvd 2nd Floor, Studio City, CA, 91604
Art Directors Guild & Scenic, Title & Graphic Artists,Set Design Model Makers, Illustrators & Matte Artists,Digital Arti
www.adg.org

Local # 829 United Scenic Artists, LA   (323) 965-0957
6363 Wilshire Blvd #400, Los Angeles, CA, 90048
IATSE Local 829 West Coast office
www.usa829.org

Local # 829 United Scenic Artists, NY   (212) 581-0300
29 W 38th Street 15th floor, New York, NY, 10018
IATSE Local USA 829
www.usa829.org

Local # 839 The Animation Guild   (818) 845-7500
1105 N Hollywood Way, Burbank, CA, 91505
www.animationguild.org

Local # 871 Script Supervisors   (818) 509-7871
4011 W Magnolia Blvd, Burbank, CA, 91505
Script Supervisors/Continuity, Coordinators, Accountants, & Allied Production Specialists Guild
www.ialocal871.org

Local # 884 Studio Teachers   (818) 559-9600
PO Box 461467, Los Angeles, CA, 90046
dispatch phone: (818) 559-9600. Studio Teachers/Welfare Workers
www.thestudioteachers.com

Local # 892 Costume Designers Guild   (818) 752-2400
11969 Ventura Blvd 1st floor, Studio City, CA, 91604
www.costumedesignersguild.com

Local # 33 Stage Technicians   (818) 841-9233
1720 W Magnolia Blvd, Burbank, CA, 91506
Local 33, IATSE, AFL
www.ia33.org

Motion Picture Assn. of America   (818) 995-6600
15301 Ventura Blvd Bldg E, Sherman Oaks, CA, 91403
Advocate for American motion picture, home video & TV industries
www.mpaa.org

OPERA America   (212) 796-8620
330 7th Ave 7th Floor, New York, NY, 10001
service & support opera companies

PLASA North America   (212) 244-1505
630 9th Ave Ste 609, New York, NY, 10036
Non-profit trade association concerned with entertainment technology
www.plasa.org

Producers Guild of America   (310) 358-9020
8530 Wilshire Blvd Ste 400, Beverly Hills, CA, 90211
www.producersguild.org

Screen Actors Guild (S.A.G.)   (323) 954-1600
5757 Wilshire Blvd 7th Floor, Los Angeles, CA, 90036
www.sagaftra.org

Set Decorators' Society of America (818) 255-2425
7100 Tujunga Ave Ste A, N Hollywood, CA, 91605
www.setdecorators.org

Society of American Fight Directors (818) 255-2425
1350 E Flamingo Rd #25, Las Vegas, NV, 89119 contact
regional rep. via their web site
www.safd.org

Stage Directors & Choreographers Society 321 (212) 391-1070
W 44th St Ste 804, New York, NY, 10036
www.sdcweb.org

Stuntmen's Assn. of Motion Pictures (818) 766-4334
5200 Lankershim Blvd Suite 190, N Hollywood, CA, 91601
www.stuntmen.com

Television Academy (818) 754-2800
5220 Lankershim Blvd, N Hollywood, CA, 91601
www.emmysfoundation.org

Themed Entertainment Association (818) 843-8497
150 E Olive Ave Ste 306, Burbank, CA, 91502
Alliance of themed entertainment companies
www.teaconnect.org

U. S. Institute for Theater Technology (800) 938-7488
315 S Crouse Ave Ste 200, Syracuse, NY, 13210
www.usitt.org

University Resident Theatre Assn (212) 221-1130
1560 Broadway Ste 1103, New York, NY, 10036
www.urta.com

Women In Film (323) 935-2211
6100 Wilshire Blvd Ste 710, Los Angeles, CA, 90048
www.wif.org

Writer's Guild of America (323) 951-4000
7000 W Third St, Los Angeles, CA, 90048
www.wga.org

Stages/Studios, Film/TV/Theatre/Events

See Also: Locations, Insert Stages & Small Theatres

ABC 7 Broadcast Center (818) 560-7450
500 Circle Seven Dr, Glendale, CA, 91201
www.studioservices.go.com

Ahmanson Theater (213) 628-2772
135 N Grand, Los Angeles, CA, 90012
for admin office, see Dorothy Chandler Pavillion, Filming (213) 972-7334,
Rentals (213) 972-7478
www.centertheatregroup.org

Air Hollywood - Prop House & Standing Sets (818) 890-0444
Air Hollywood is the largest aviation-themed studio serving the motion picture
and television industry.

Albuquerque Studios (505) 227-2000
5650 University Blvd SE, Albuquerque, NM, 87106
www.abqstudios.com

Anaheim Convention Center (714) 765-8950
800 W Katella Ave, Anaheim, CA, 92802
www.anaheimconventioncenter.com

Anaheim Grove (714) 712-2700
2200 E Katella Ave, Anaheim, CA, 92806
event inquiries: (714) 712-2703
www.citynationalgroveofanaheim.com

Angel Stadium of Anaheim (714) 940-2000
2000 Gene Autry Way, Anaheim, CA, 92806
http://losangeles.angels.mlb.com/ana/ballpark/index.jsp

The Barker Hangar Santa Monica Air Center (310) 390-9071
3021 Airport Ave Ste 203, Santa Monica, CA, 90405
Large clearspan interior, high ceilings
www.barkerhangar.com

Ben Kitay Studios (323) 466-9015
1015 N Cahuenga Blvd, Hollywood, CA, 90038
www.benkitay.com

Bob Gail Special Events (310) 202-5200
The Bob Gail Production Studio is the newest addition to LA's production studio
scene.

The Burbank Studios (818) 840-3000
3000 W Alameda Ave, Burbank, CA, 91523
www.theburbankstudios.com

California Theatre of Performing Arts (909) 885-5152
562 W 4th St, San Bernardino, CA, 92402
www.californiatheatre.net

CBS Studio Center (818) 655-5000
4024 Radford Ave, Studio City, CA, 91604
Residential streets, central park, new york street, and subway car mock up and
subway station mock up.
www.cbssc.com

CBS Television City (323) 575-2676
7800 Beverly Blvd, Los Angeles, CA, 90036
www.cbstelevisioncity.com

Cerritos P.A.C. (562) 916-8510
12700 Center Court Dr, Cerritos, CA, 90703
www.cerritoscenter.com

Chandler Valley Center Studios (818) 424-4551
13927 Saticoy St, Van Nuys, CA, 91402
Commercials & music videos, TV/Movies
www.cvcstudios.us

The Culver Studios (310) 202-1234
9336 W Washington Blvd, Culver City, CA, 90232
www.theculverstudios.com

Delfino Studios (818) 361-2421
12700 Gladstone Ave, Sylmar, CA, 91342
www.delfinostudios.com

Dodger Stadium (323) 224-1507
1000 Elysian Park Ave, Los Angeles, CA, 90012
http://losangeles.dodgers.mlb.com

Dolby Theater (323) 308-6300
6801 Hollywood Blvd Ste 180 Admin, Hollywood, CA, 90028
www.dolbytheatre.com

Dorothy Chandler Pavilion (213) 972-7211
135 N Grand Ave, Los Angeles, CA, 90012
venue for Music Center, Opera, Master Chorale admin office for Ahmanson &
Mark Taper
www.musiccenter.org

El Capitan Theater (323) 467-7674
6838 Hollywood Blvd, Hollywood, CA, 90028
www.elcapitantheatre.com

Empire Studio (818) 840-1400
1845 Empire Ave, Burbank, CA, 91504
www.lbimedia.com

Fantastic Lane Studios (661) 505-8182
27567 Fantastic Lane, Castaic, CA, 91384
Full-service studio with 80 acre wilderness backlot, prod. & post-prod. facilities
www.fantasticlane.com

The Fonda Theater (323) 464-0808
6126 Hollywood Blvd, Hollywood, CA, 90028
www.fondatheatre.com

The Forum (310) 330-7300
3900 W Manchester Blvd, Inglewood, CA, 90305
www.thelaforum.com

Glendale Production Center (818) 550-6000
1239 S Glendale Ave, Glendale, CA, 91205
www.glendalestudios.com

GMT Studios (310) 649-3733
5751 Buckingham Pkwy, Culver City, CA, 90230
www.gmtstudios.com

Greek Theatre (213) 202-2621
2700 N Vermont Ave, Los Angeles, CA, 90027
www.lagreektheatre.com

Historic Hudson Studios (323) 461-1044
1106 N Hudson Ave, Hollywood, CA, 90038
Boutique photo studio: wifi, meeting area, full kitchen, diffused/black out
curtains, easy elevator & addl. equipment.
renee@rafotostudio.com * www.historichudsonstudios.com

Hollywood Bowl (323) 850-2000
2301 N Highland Ave, Los Angeles, CA, 90078
www.hollywoodbowl.com

Hollywood Center Studios (323) 860-0000
1040 N Las Palmas Ave, Los Angeles, CA, 90038
see floor plans, lighting/grip & tech dept on our website
www.hollywoodcenter.com

Hollywood Palladium (323) 962-7600
6215 Sunset Blvd, Hollywood, CA, 90028
www.thehollywoodpalladium.com

The Honda Center, AKA Arrowhead Pond (714) 704-2400
2695 E. Katella Ave, Anaheim, CA, 92806
www.hondacenter.com

Irvine Meadows Amphitheatre (949) 855-8095
8808 Irvine Center Dr, Irvine, CA, 92618
AKA Irvine Meadows
http://amphitheaterirvine.com/

John Anson Ford Theaters (323) 856-5793
2580 Cahuenga Blvd E, Los Angeles, CA, 90068 box
office (323) 461-3673
www.fordtheatres.org

KCAL TV Studios (818) 655-2000
4200 Radford Ave, Studio City, CA, 91604
http://losangeles.cbslocal.com/station/cbs-kcal/

KCBS TV Studios (818) 655-2000
4200 Radford Ave, Studio City, CA, 91604
http://losangeles.cbslocal.com/station/cbs-kcal/

**LISTINGS FOR THIS CATEGORY CONTINUE ON THE
FOLLOWING PAGE**

KCET TV Studios (747) 201-5000
2900 W Alameda Ave, Burbank, CA, 91505
contact@kcet.org * www.kcet.org

KLCS TV Studios (213) 241-4000
1061 W Temple St, Los Angeles, CA, 90012
http://klcs.org/

KMEX TV Studios (Univision) (310) 216-3434
5999 Center Drive, Los Angeles, CA, 90045
http://losangeles.univision.com

KTLA TV Studios (323) 460-5500
5800 Sunset Blvd, Los Angeles, CA, 90028
www.ktla.com

KTTV TV Fox 11 Studios (310) 584-2000
1999 S Bundy Dr, Los Angeles, CA, 90025
www.myfoxLA.com

The L. A. Lofts (323) 462-5880
6442 Santa Monica Blvd, Los Angeles, CA, 90038
www.thelalofts.com

Lacy Street Production Center (323) 222-8872
2630 Lacy St, Los Angeles, CA, 90031
standing sets, music videos, commercials
www.lacystreet.com

Long Beach Convention Center (562) 436-3636
300 E Ocean Blvd, Long Beach, CA, 90802
www.longbeachcc.com

Los Angeles Center Studios (213) 534-3000
1201 W 5th Street Ste T-110, Los Angeles, CA, 90017
www.lacenterstudios.com

Los Angeles Convention Center (213) 741-1151
1201 S Figueroa St, Los Angeles, CA, 90015
Event Services X5360
www.lacclink.com

Los Angeles Memorial Coliseum (213) 747-7111
3911 S Figueroa St, Los Angeles, CA, 90037
www.lacoliseum.com

Los Angeles Sports Arena (213) 747-7111
3939 S Figueroa St, Los Angeles, CA, 90037
www.lacoliseumlive.com

The Lot (323) 850-3180
1041 N Formosa Ave, W Hollywood, CA, 90046
http://www.thelotstudios.com/

Mack Sennett Studios (323) 660-8466
1215 Bates Ave, Los Angeles, CA, 90029
www.macksennettstudios.net

Mark Taper Forum (213) 628-2772
135 N Grand Ave, Los Angeles, CA, 90012
for admin office, see Dorothy Chandler Pavilion
www.centertheatregroup.org

Microsoft Theater (213) 763-6030
777 Chick Hearn Court, Los Angeles, CA, 90015
www.microsofttheater.com

Occidental Studios (213) 384-3331
201 N Occidental Blvd, Los Angeles, CA, 90026
12 locations, stages from 1,000 to 43,000 sq. ft., lighting, grip, offices, props, etc.
www.occidentalstudios.com

Panavision (818) 316-1000
6101 Variel Ave, Woodland Hills, CA, 91367
Cameras & film. Commercials, music videos, hair & make-up test, trailers
www.panavision.com

Pantages Theatre (323) 468-1700
6233 Hollywood Blvd, Hollywood, CA, 90028
www.hollywoodpantages.com

Pasadena Civic Auditorium (626) 793-2122
300 E Green St, Pasadena, CA, 91101
Also, Pasadena Convention Center.
www.thepasadenacivic.com

The Pasadena Playhouse (626) 792-8672
39 S El Molino Ave, Pasadena, CA, 91101
www.pasadenaplayhouse.org

The Production Group (323) 469-8111
1626 N Wilcox Ave Ste 281, Hollywood, CA, 90028
www.productiongroup.tv

Prospect Studios (323) 671-5000
4151 Prospect Ave, Los Angeles, CA, 90027
http://studioservices.go.com/prospectstudios/index.html

Quixote Studios (323) 851-5030
1011 N Fuller Ave, W Hollywood, CA, 90046
trucks and stages, greenrooms, production stages
www.quixotestudios.com

Raleigh Studios (323) 960-FILM
5300 Melrose Ave, Hollywood, CA, 90038
www.raleighstudios.com

Red Studios Hollywood (323) 463-0808
846 Cahuenga Blvd, Los Angeles, CA, 90038
http://www.redstudio.com/

Rose Bowl (626) 577-3100
1001 Rose Bowl Dr, Pasadena, CA, 91103
www.rosebowlstadium.com

Saban Theatre (323) 655-4900
8440 Wilshire Blvd, Beverly Hills, CA, 90211
www.sabantheatre.org

San Gabriel Mission Playhouse (626) 308-2865
320 S Mission Drive, San Gabriel, CA, 91776
Location, Sound Stage, Venue, Rehearsal Space, Theater, Spanish style,
wurlitzer organ
swilkinson@missionplayhouse.org * www.missionplayhouse.org

San Manuel Amphitheater (909) 880-6500
2575 Glen Helen Pkwy, San Bernardino, CA, 92407
www.sanmanuelamphitheater.net

Santa Barbara Bowl (805) 962-7411
1122 N Milpas St, Santa Barbara, CA, 93103
www.sbbowl.com

Santa Clarita Studios (661) 294-2000
25135 Anza Dr, Santa Clarita, CA, 91355
www.santaclaritastudios.com

Santa Monica Civic Auditorium (310) 458-8551
1855 Main St, Santa Monica, CA, 90401
www.santamonicacivic.org

Segerstrom Center (714) 556-2121
600 Town Center Dr, Costa Mesa, CA, 92626
Five performing arts & event venues
www.scfta.org

Shrine Auditorium (213) 748-5116
665 W Jefferson Blvd, Los Angeles, CA, 90007
www.shrineauditorium.com

Sketch Paper Design (818) 442-0284
7771 Lemona Ave, Van Nuys, CA, 91405
White Cyc stage that can be painted depending on production's needs, stage
for rent
info@sketchpaperdesign.com * www.sketchpaperdesign.com

Sony Pictures Studios (310) 244-6926
10202 W Washington Blvd, Culver City, CA, 90232
www.sonypicturesstudios.com

Stage 1001 (323) 876-1001
1001 N Poinsettia Pl, Los Angeles, CA, 90046
www.stage1001.com

Staples Center (213) 742-7100
1111 S Figueroa St, Los Angeles, CA, 90015
www.staplescenter.com

The Studios At Paramount (323) 956-5000
5555 Melrose, Hollywood, CA, 90038
Call (323) 956-8811 for booking stages.
www.thestudiosatparamount.com

Sunset Gower Studios (323) 467-1001
1438 North Gower Box 21, Hollywood, CA, 90028
Call (323) 315-9460 for new inquiries
www.sgsandsbs.com

Thunder Studios (310) 762-1360
20434 S Santa Fe Ave, Long Beach, CA, 90810
15 stages, hard cycs, fisher boxes/flats
www.thunderstudios.com

Twentieth Century Fox (310) 369-1000
10201 W Pico Blvd, Los Angeles, CA, 90035
www.foxstudios.com

Universal Studios Stages & Backlot (818) 777-3000
100 Universal City Plaza, Universal City, CA, 91608
universal.locations@nbcuni.com * www.filmmakersdestination.com

The Walt Disney Concert Hall (213) 972-7211
135 N Grand Ave, Los Angeles, CA, 90012
http://www.wdch.com/

The Walt Disney Studios (818) 560-7450
500 Buena Vista St, Burbank, CA, 91505
www.stu-ops.disney.com

Warner Bros. Studios (818) 954-6000
4000 Warner Blvd, Burbank, CA, 91522
For facilities, call (818) 954-3000
www.warnerbros.com

The Wiltern (213) 388-1400
3790 Wilshire Blvd, Los Angeles, CA, 90010
call (213) 380-5005 for box office
www.thewiltern.net

Prop Houses

See Also: Prop & Set Design Supplies, Parts, Tools* Prop Design & Manufacturing* Prop Reproduction & Fabrication* Scenery/Set Construction

A-1 Medical Integration (818) 753-0319
7344 Laurel Canyon Blvd, North Hollywood, CA, 91605
Medical devices for Set Decoration & Property, from minor procedures to detailed hospital units.
a1medwarehouse@aol.com * www.a1props.com

Advanced Liquidators Office Furniture (818) 763-3470
11151 Vanowen St., N. Hollywood, CA, 91605
Specializes in new and used office furniture as well as studio rentals.
sales@advancedliquidators.com * www.advancedliquidators.com

Aero Mock-Ups (888) 662-5877
13126 Saticoy St, N Hollywood, CA, 91605
full service aviation prop house. Complete airplane interiors & airport dressing, model airplanes
info@aeromockups.com * www.aeromockups.com

AIR Designs (818) 768-6639
11900 Wicks St, Sun Valley, CA, 91352
Auto, Gas, Racing, Fast Food, Coffee, Diner, Cafeteria, Store, Street, Vendor Carts
info@airdesigns.net * www.airdesigns.net

Air Hollywood - Prop House & Standing Sets (818) 890-0444
13240 Weidner St, Los Angeles, CA, 91331
Aviation-themed props and set dressing. We have thousands of items available to dress Airport Terminals.
info@airhollywood.com * www.airhollywood.com

Alley Cats Studio Rentals (818) 982-9178
7101 Case Ave, N Hollywood, CA, 91605
alleycatsprops@gmail.com * www.alleycatsprops.com

Alpha Companies - Spellman Desk Co. (818) 504-9090
7990 San Fernando Rd, Sun Valley, CA, 91352
The #1 source for medical equipment in the industry.
rentals@alphaprops.com * www.alphaprops.com

Arenson Prop Center (917) 210-2562
396 Tenth Avenue, New York, NY, 10001
info@aof.com

Artkraft Taxidermy Rentals (818) 505-8425
10847 Vanowen St., N. Hollywood, CA 91605
Taxidermied animals of all kinds: birds, fish, mammals, and much more from Africa, North America, and exotic locales.
info@artkrafttaxidermy.com * www.artkrafttaxidermy.net

Bob Gail Special Events (310) 202-5200
3321 La Cienega Pl, Los Angeles, CA, 90016
Bob Gail has an extensive list of themed props for movie sets, events, and tradeshows for rental in CA and Las Vegas.
eSales@BobGail.com * www.bobgail.com

Bridge Furniture & Props Los Angeles (818) 433-7100
3210 Vanowen St, Burbank, CA, 91505
We carry modern & traditional furniture, lighting, accessories, cleared art,& rugs. Items are online for easy shopping.
la@bridgeprops.com * http://la.bridgeprops.com

C. P. Two (323) 466-8201
5755 Santa Monica Blvd, Los Angeles, CA, 90038
www.omegacinemaprops.com

C. P. Valley (323) 466-8201
7545 N. San Fernando Road, Burbank, CA, 91505
www.omegacinemaprops.com

Dapper Cadaver/Creatures & Cultures (818) 771-0818
7648 San Fernando Rd, Sun Valley, CA, 91352
Specializes in horror, science, medical, crime, oddity & Halloween props. Custom fabrication & FX. Rent & buy online.
info@dappercadaver.com * www.dappercadaver.com

The Earl Hays Press (818) 765-0700
10707 Sherman Way, Sun Valley, CA, 91352
services the Industry only
ehp@la.twcbc.com * www.theearlhayspress.com

E.C. Prop Rentals (818) 764-2008
11846 Sherman Way, N Hollywood, CA, 91605
Factory, Industrial, Loading Dock, Warehouse, Locker Room, Garage, Street/Alley, Shipping Yard
ecprops@aol.com * www.ecprops.com

Eccentric Trading Company Ltd. 011 44 20 8453-1125
Unit 2 Frogmore Estate, Acton Lane, London NW10 7NQ
www.eccentrictrading.com

Eclectic/Encore Props (212) 645-8880
47-51 33rd St, Long Island City, NY 11101
sbieler@eclecticprops.com * www.eclecticprops.com

The Farley Group 011 44 20 8749-9925
1-17 Brunel Rd, London, W3 7XR UK
props@farley.co.uk * www.farley.co.uk

Faux Library Studio Props, Inc. (818) 765-0096
7100 Case Avenue, N Hollywood, CA, 91605
large selection of hollow books, office furniture, desk dressing, decorative accessories and of course books
fauxlibrary@sbcglobal.net

FormDecor, Inc. (310) 558-2582
14371 Industry Circle, La Mirada, CA, 90638
America's largest event rental supplier of 20th Century furniture and accessories for Modern and Mid-Century styles.
info@formdecor.com * www.formdecor.com

Green Set, Inc. (818) 764-1231
11617 Dehougne St, N Hollywood, CA, 91605
www.greenset.com

The Hand Prop Room LP. (323) 931-1534
5700 Venice Blvd, Los Angeles, CA, 90019
Large Prop House for prop rentals, prop weapons, custom graphic design & custom graphic printing, expendables and more.
info@hpr.com * www.hpr.com

History For Hire, Inc. (818) 765-7767
7149 Fair Ave, N Hollywood, CA, 91605
info@historyforhire.com * www.historyforhire.com

Hollywood Cinema Arts, Inc. (818) 504-7333
8110 Webb Ave, N. Hollywood, CA, 91605
Hollywood Cinema Arts, "The Pro's Prop House."
hollywoodcinemaarts@gmail.com * www.hcarts.com

Hollywood Cinema Production Resources (310) 258-0123
9700 S. Sepulveda Blvd, Los Angeles, CA, 90045
props@hollywoodcpr.org * www.hollywoodcpr.org

Hollywood Studio Gallery (323) 462-1116
1035 Cahuenga Blvd, Hollywood, CA, 90038
hsginfo@hollywoodstudiogallery.com * www.hollywoodstudiogallery.com

Independent Studio Services, Inc (818) 951-5600
9545 Wentworth St, Sunland, CA, 91040
www.issprops.com

Jackson Shrub Supply, Inc. (818) 982-0100
11505 Vanowen St, N Hollywood, CA, 91605
Plant rentals, shrub rentals, tree rentals. Christmas decorations and Halloween decorations and more.
gary@jacksonshrub.com * www.jacksonshrub.com

Kitsch N Sync Props (323) 343-1190
5290 Valley Blvd Unit #1, Los Angeles, CA, 90032
Specializing in 70's and 80's props. Large collection of cameras, electronics, phones, art, games, stereos, & much more.
kitschnsyncprops@gmail.com * www.kitschnsyncprops.com

LCW Props (818) 243-0707
6439 San Fernando Rd, Glendale, CA, 91201
LCW Is Your 1-Stop Shop For Almost Anything. We Work With Any Budget.
props@lcwprops.com * www.lcwprops.com

Lennie Marvin Enterprises, Inc. (Prop Heaven) (818) 841-5882
3110 Winona Ave, Burbank, CA, 91504
catering to the entertainment industry
info@propheaven.com * www.propheaven.com

Modern Props (323) 934-3000
5500 W Jefferson Blvd, Los Angeles, CA, 90016
Modern Props, Contemporary Props, Futuristic Props, & Electronic Props
ken@modernprops.com * www.modernprops.com

Modernica Props (323) 664-2322
2805 Gilroy Street, Los Angeles, CA, 90039
huge inventory 50s-70s furniture & decor, multiples up to 500
www.modernicaprops.net

NEST Studio Rentals, Inc. (818) 942-0339
7007 Lankershim Blvd, N Hollywood, CA, 91605
contemporary furniture, rugs, lighting, art, drapery, smalls
sales@neststudiorentals.net * www.neststudiorentals.net

Ob-jects (818) 351-4200
10623 Keswick St, Sun Valley, CA, 91352
fred@ob-jects.com * www.ob-jects.com

Oceanic Arts (562) 698-6960
12414 Whittier Blvd, Whittier, CA, 90602-1017
We Rent and We Sell Hawaiian, Polynesian, Tropical, and Nautical Decor.
oceanicarts@earthlink.net * www.oceanicarts.net

Omega/Cinema Props (323) 466-8201
5857 Santa Monica Blvd, Los Angeles, CA, 90038
www.omegacinemaprops.com
  C. P. Two
  5755 Santa Monica Blvd, Los Angeles, CA, 90038
  C. P. Valley
  7545 N. San Fernando Road, Burbank, CA, 91505

Pinacoteca Picture Props (818) 764-2722
7120 Case Ave, N Hollywood, CA, 91605
Cleared art, linens, furniture & custom framing
sales@pinaprops.com * www.pinaprops.com

LISTINGS FOR THIS CATEGORY CONTINUE ON THE FOLLOWING PAGE

Premiere Props.   (818) 768-3800
11500 Sheldon St, Sun Valley, CA, 91352
Prop Mart, Inc.   (773) 772-7775
2343 W St Paul Ave, Chicago, IL, 60647
table top, mainly commercials; dishes, linens, flatware, more
Prop Services West   (818) 503-2790
7040 Laurel Canyon Blvd, North Hollywood, CA 91605
www.propserviceswest.com
Propabilities   (773) 278-2384
1517 N Elston, Chicago, IL, 60642
hand props, set dressing, furniture, smalls, park benches, photo surfaces
propNspoon / Props for Today   (212) 244-9600
32-00 Skillman Ave, 3rd Floor, Long Island City, NY, 11101
RC Vintage, Inc.   (818) 765-7107
7100 Tujunga Ave, N Hollywood, CA, 91605
specializing in 40s, 50s, 60s & 70s
rcvintage@aol.com * www.rcvintage.com
RJR Props   (404) 349-7600
5300 Westpark Drive SW, Ste B, Atlanta, CA 30336
RJR Props can provide working realistic Props for your feature film, show,
commercial, music video, or event.
rjrelectronics@aol.com * www.rjrprops.com
Seasons Textiles Ltd   011 44 20
9 Gorst Road, London NW10 6LA   8965-6161
enquiries@seasonstextiles.net * www.seasonstextiles.co.uk
Sony Pictures Studios
10202 W Washington Blvd, Los Angeles, CA, 90232
www.sonypicturesstudios.com
   Events   (310) 244-4456
   Staff Shop   (310) 244-5541
Sony Pictures Studios (Off Lot)
5933 W Slauson Ave, Culver City, CA, 90230
www.sonypicturesstudios.com
   Fixtures   (310) 244-5996
   Linens, Drapes, Rugs   (310) 244-5999
   Prop House   **(310) 244-5999**
   Wardrobe   (310) 244-5995
Sword & Stone   (818) 562-6548
723 N Victory Blvd, Burbank, CA, 91502
medieval & fantasy props
tony@swordandstone.com * www.swordandstone.com
Taylor Creative Inc.   (888) 245-4044
1220 West Walnut St, Los Angeles, CA, 90220
Set decorators look to Taylor Creative Inc. to furnish their film and television
shoots on both the East and West Coast.
info@taylorcreativeinc.com * www.taylorcreativeinc.com
Technical Props, Inc.   (818) 761-4993
6811 Farmdale Ave, North Hollywood, CA, 91605
www.techpropsinc.com
Trading Post Ltd.   011 44 20
1-3 Beresford Avenue, Wembley, Middlesex, HA0 1NU   8903-3727
info@tradingposthire.co.uk * www.tradingposthire.co.uk
Trevor Howsam Ltd   011 44 20
182 Acton Lane, Park Royal, London NW10 7NH   8838-6166
props@trevorhowsam.co.uk * www.retrowallpaper.co.uk

Universal Studios Departments
100 Universal City Plaza, Universal City, CA, 91608
www.filmmakersdestination.com
   Costume Dept.   (818) 777-2722
   Drapery Dept.   (818) 777-2761
   Graphic Design & Sign Shop   (818) 777-2350
   Grip Dept.   (818) 777-2291
   Property & Hardware Dept.   **(818) 777-2784**
   Set Lighting Dept.   (818) 777-2291
   Special Effects Equip.   (818) 777-3333
   Special Events   (818) 777-9466
   Staff Shop   (818) 777-2337
   Stages & Backlot   (818) 777-3000
   NBCUniversal StudioPost Editorial Facilities   (818) 777-5163
   Transportation   (818) 777-2966
   Filmmaker Production Svcs - Atlanta   (404) 815-5202
   Filmmaker Production Svcs - Chicago   (678) 628-1997
   Mac Tech LED Lighting   (818) 777-1281
   New Mexico Lighting & Grip   (505) 227-2500
Warner Bros. Studios Departments
4000 Warner Blvd, Burbank, CA, 91522
www.wbpropertydept.com
   Cabinet & Furniture Shop   (818) 954-1339
   Construction Services   (818) 954-7820
   Costume Dept.   (818) 954-1297
   Design Studio Scenic Art & Sign Shop   (818) 954-1815
   Drapery, Upholstery & Flooring   (818) 954-1831
   Grip Dept.   (818) 954-1590
   Hardware Rentals   (818) 954-1335
   Metal Shop   (818) 954-1265
   Mill Store   (818) 954-4444
   Paint Dept.   (818) 954-1817
   Photo Lab   (818) 954-7118
   Production Sound & Video   (818) 954-2511
   Property Dept.   **(818) 954-2181**
   Property Dept. - Atlanta   (404) 878-0002
   Special Efects & Prop Shop   (818) 954-1365
   Staff Shop   (818) 954-2269
   The Collection   (818) 954-2181
Woody's Electrical Props   (818) 503-1940
5323 Craner Ave., North Hollywood, CA 91601-3313
Period to futuristic. Electronic equipment. Custom built to specifications. Electrical
paneling
woody@woodysprops.com * www.woodysprops.com
Zap Props   (773) 376-2278
3611 S Loomis Pl, Chicago, IL, 60609
hand props, set dressing, street dressing, big & small
ZG04 DECOR   (818) 853-8040
12224 Montague Street, Sun Valley, CA, 91331
Rental & Sale
saul@zg04decor.com * www.zg04decor.com

Made in the USA
Charleston, SC
01 August 2016